OSI
A Model for Computer Communications Standards

Uyless Black

PRENTICE HALL, Englewood Cliffs, New Jersey 07632

Library of Congress Cataloging-in-Publication Data

Black, Uyless D.
OSI : a model for computer communications standards / Uyless
Black.
p. cm.
Includes index.
ISBN 0-13-637133-7
1. Computer networks—Standards. 2. Computer network protocols.
3. Computer network architectures. I. Title.
TK5105.5.B5656 1991
004.6′2—dc20   90-38674
CIP

Editorial/production supervision: Evalyn Schoppet
Cover design: Bruce Kenselaar
Interior Artwork: Asterisk Group
Manufacturing buyer: Laura Bolen

 ©1991 by Prentice-Hall, Inc.
A Division of Simon & Schuster
Englewood Cliffs, New Jersey 07632

Printed in the United States of America
10 9 8 7 6 5 4 3 2 1

ISBN 0-13-637133-7

Prentice-Hall International (UK) Limited, *London*
Prentice-Hall of Australia Pty. Limited, *Sydney*
Prentice-Hall Canada Inc., *Toronto*
Prentice-Hall Hispanoamericana, S.A., *Mexico*
Prentice-Hall of India Private Limited, *New Delhi*
Prentice-Hall of Japan, Inc., *Tokyo*
Simon & Schuster Asia Pte. Ltd., *Singapore*
Editora Prentice-Hall do Brasil, Ltda., *Rio de Janeiro*

To these educators, who made a difference to my family and me: Florence Anderson, Howard Howell, Benjamin Sacks, and Ralph Tasker, and my brothers, Ross Black and Tom Black.

Contents

Chapter 2.   OSI Suite Examples   47

Chapter 3.   The Physical Layer   65

Chapter 6.   The Network Layer, Internetworking   *203*

Chapter 7.   The Transport Layer   *239*

Chapter 9. The Presentation Layer   *329*

Chapter 10.   Architecture of the Application Layer   *361*

Chapter 11. The Application Layer Application Service Elements (ASEs)   *413*

Preface

The idea for this book originated during my writing an earlier book for Prentice Hall, titled *Data Networks: Concepts, Theory, and Practice*. This book was created for a college class dealing with data communications and networks. One of its three sections is organized around the Open Systems Interconnection Model (OSI).

During the review process of the *Data Networks* manuscript, some of the reviewers suggested that the section on OSI should be expanded. The expansion was not practical because the book had to maintain its theme. Nonetheless, the reviewers' comments aroused my interest about books dealing with OSI. After a rather brief investigation, I found that a few tutorial books on OSI existed. Some of these books did little more than copy the OSI standards explanations (almost verbatim). I had not noticed this gap on OSI information, because much of my day-to-day work as a consultant requires reading the OSI standards, and I had adapted the practice of studying the actual source OSI documents for information. Even with a background in hardware systems and software programming, I find these documents somewhat abstract. Notwithstanding, they are absolutely indispensable for designers and programmers. But the OSI documents are "instant sleeping pills" to many other people. They are intended to be succinct, non-tutorial descriptions of computer/communications protocols for people who need detailed information on a communications protocol. Therefore, they do not pretend to be "user friendly."

My goal in this book is to examine and explain the OSI Model in nonabstract terms. I have attempted to keep the book relatively free of communications theory and engineering jargon. (The reader can refer to the *Data Networks* book for discussions on theory and engineering concepts.) I hope this approach will aid the reader in gaining an understanding of the OSI Model and the confidence to delve into the OSI documents.

Not all the OSI standards are examined. I have attempted to include those that are the most widely used and of the most importance. However, I am sure some of the exclusions will be sought by some readers. If so, please let me know, and I will consider them for subsequent editions.

TECHNICAL NOTES FOR THE READER

The term *primitive* is used in earlier CCITT and ISO documents to describe the interactions between adjacent layers. The more recent documents use the term service definition. This book uses both terms.

The OSI specifications are undergoing rapid changes. In order to reflect these changes, some organizations use a prefix in front of a number to describe the status of an OSI standard. For example, a draft international standard may be labeled DIS, and the final international standard may be labeled IS. Due to these rapid changes, the practice in this book is to exclude the prefix and use the number alone. The reader should consult with the specific organization to ascertain the latest status of the standard and its prefix identifier.

A rose by any other name is still a rose. A standard by any other name is still a standard. Notwithstanding, some organizations do not use the term *standard*. The practice in this book is to use the terms *standard, recommended standard,* and *recommendation* interchangeably. Therefore, the book does not always use these terms in the same manner as the standards organizations use them. Explanations are provided in the book, where appropriate.

The image that is transmitted across a communications channel between computers and terminals is identified by several names: *message, packet, frame, protocol data unit, data unit,* or just *unit.* Older systems use the terms *block* or *record.* The OSI Model uses the term *protocol data unit* (PDU) to describe this image, and this book adheres to the OSI convention, although the terms data unit and unit sometimes are used to relieve the tedium associated with using long terms throughout a book. Where appropriate, the other terms are also applied.

The OSI Model includes a number of documentation tools to describe the actions between communicating entities. One such tool is the state table. While the state table is quite valuable to an engineer or a designer, its level of detail may be too much for the reader who wishes a general view of the OSI operation. Consequently, to satisfy both readers, the book is written in such a way that it is not necessary to study the sections dealing with the state tables unless you wish to know about the detailed operations of the protocol. Be aware that you should be prepared to spend more than just a passing moment if you decide to analyze the state table sections of the book. I have provided tutorial explanations to assist the reader through this material.

Do not rely solely on this text for the detailed specifications on OSI. There is no substitute for reading the actual CCITT and ISO documents.

ACKNOWLEDGMENTS

In previous books, I have expressed my thanks to the CCITT and the ISO for their permission to use portions of their documents. I wish to repeat these thanks. In addition, several of the engineers at the CCITT have been most helpful in answering my questions.

Some of my material for this book was developed in a series of lectures I conducted for AT&T, Bell Northern Research (BNR), and BellCore. Several people from these organizations provided their analysis of the subject matter and helped make my manuscript a better book. My special thanks to BNR's Kathy St. Marie and Rosemary Aguilar for their support in the scheduling of my lectures at BNR.

Evalyn Schoppet was my production editor for this book. This is our third collaboration. I hope it will not be our last. Her competence is evident throughout the project. Richard Lutzke at Asterisk Group is once again responsible for the superior artwork.

During the past few months, I had the good fortune to have the services of Jane Jessey, who has been working as my personal editor. She worked with Evalyn in the preparation of this manuscript. I know she must leave eventually for greener pastures and the profession of her training and choice, but I hope her stay is prolonged. I am indebted to Jane for her outstanding work, her patience, and her sense of humor.

On a personal note, my thanks and appreciation go to Susan McDermott, Steve and Ceil Malphrus, Ray and Sandy Massey, Jerry Semrod, Bob and Betty Taylor, and Gene and Dee White for their friendship. For my friends, and for my ski friends in particular, "To no broken bones!"

CHAPTER 1

Layered Protocols and Network Architectures

INTRODUCTION

This book describes the first successful worldwide attempt to develop a set of comprehensive standards for computer communications. These standards have been developed within the framework of the *Open Systems Interconnection* (OSI) architecture. In the last few years, OSI has become a pervasive model for defining how heterogeneous computer systems can communicate with each other. The intent of this book is to provide the reader with a reference guide and a tutorial on OSI. Before we examine the concepts of OSI, it is necessary to pause briefly to examine computer communications standards in general.

One of the most interesting aspects about computers is how they exchange information with each other. Remarkably, their communications are similar to the communications between humans, because, like humans, computers communicate with each other through symbols and agreed-upon conventions. The symbols, called *codes*, provide instructions to the machines to direct their activities and interactions, and are similar to the words in human languages. The conventions are rules on how to interpret the symbols, similar to the rules of grammar in our languages. The computer uses these codes and conventions to make decisions on how to process the user's data.

The goal of computer communications is to support the transfer of information between two machines, such as computers or terminals. For example, in Figure 1-1 we see a personal computer receiving a file from a remote computer, perhaps information on the stock market. In order for this seemingly simple process to occur, the computers and their communications facilities must perform many actions. The two machines must accept the file formats of each other (the form in which the data are to appear), and they must agree on the

1

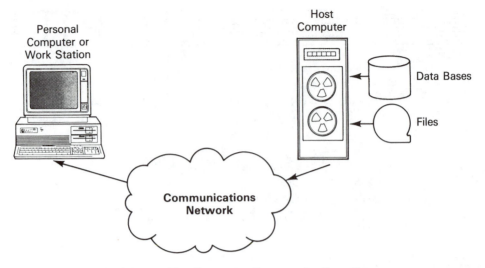

FIGURE 1-1. The Computer Communications Process

syntax of the data (text, numeric, the number of decimal points, etc.). If an intervening network is supporting the session between the machines, it must know about their communications characteristics (for example, on a typical telephone line, the dial-up procedures each machine uses to connect to the network). If the data are important, some means must be provided to ensure that both machines know that all data has been transferred without any problems. One can appreciate the importance of all these activities going well, as, for example, in the transfer funds from one bank account to another.

Computers do not perform these tasks easily due to their limited "intelligence." Yet computers usually communicate without ambiguity if: (a) they are instructed (programmed) correctly; (b) the communications signals between them are not distorted; and (c) the computers understand the intent and meaning of each other's symbols. This last requirement presents a formidable challenge, because it implies a high degree of understanding and cooperation between the machines. In effect, it implies that the computers communicate with a common set of symbols and, equally important, an unambiguous interpretation of those symbols. It implies the use of *standards*. Thus, a communications standard sets bounds on how computers communicate with each other.

Because a standard sets bounds, many people think the very idea of a standard is unattractive. After all, a standard means adherence to a convention, with the resulting loss of freedom and flexibility. Some critics of standards believe they fly in the face of the real world.

To illustrate, let's consider a convention in the real world of human communications: the dangling preposition. The statement "That is something I won't put up with" is far less awkward than the strictly correct "That is something up with which I will not put."

Other critics of standards believe their use discourages new technology,

Layered Protocols and Network Architectures

and that because they are developed by committees, the inevitable compromises found in committee decision-making result in a-less-than ideal solution.

While these contentions do have merit, their adherents most likely have not experienced the exciting adventure of attempting to interface the computer hardware and software developed and sold by different manufacturers. In the majority of instances, the systems do not communicate with each other. They usually require a lengthy and expensive modification, or the acquisition of a converter to "translate" their different proprietary protocols. All too often the end result of all this activity for a company is loss of income, loss of opportunity, and loss of productivity while their technicians spend hundreds of hours deciphering the details of the vendors' proprietary systems in order to make them compatible with the company's systems.

Standards not only ease the task of interfacing different computers, they also give the user more flexibility in equipment and software selection by allowing a choice of interfaces. In addition, the acceptance and use of a standard often leads to lower costs to consumers because the widely accepted standard can be mass-produced and perhaps implemented in very large scale integrated (VLSI) chips.

The Emergence of Standards

The Open Systems Interconnection (OSI) standards that are in use today owe their origin to two developments in the 1970s: (a) the emergence of layering and structured techniques in the design of complex networks and (b) the recognition of the need for compatible communications architectures between different manufacturers' protocols. We will address both of these important subjects in this section. Before we begin the analysis, however, some definitions are in order.

The term *architecture* is commonly used today to describe networks. Paraphrasing the dictionary definition, an architecture is a formation of a structure. A network architecture describes what things exist, how they operate, and what form they take. An architecture encompasses hardware, software, data link controls, standards, topologies, and protocols.

Like architecture, the term *protocol* is borrowed from other disciplines and professions. In basic terms, a protocol defines the conventions of how computers establish communications, exchange data, and terminate communications with each other.

The early computers that provided communications services were relatively simple. In a typical configuration, terminals were connected to a computer in which several software programs controlled the communications process by transmitting and receiving data over a telephone line. The line was usually attached to an interface unit within or connected to the computer. The unit provided signaling (how the symbols were coded) and synchronization (how the symbols appeared on the line).

These early systems used conventions based on the telegraph and telex applications, and transmitted messages with special codes, such as the so-called

Baudot five-digit code. Later, a seven-bit character code was developed for teletype machines. This code is known as ANSI code (for the American National Standards Institute Code), and is the basis for the ISO 646 standard.

These codes were often used and interpreted differently by the manufacturers of communications products. Some companies, such as IBM, introduced their own codes into their product line. One of these codes, EBCDIC, has also become a de facto industry standard.

These early activities led to compatibility problems between the different vendors' terminals and computers. If two machines were to communicate with each other, they had to use the same code set. If they did not have the same code, some form of conversion process had to take place in one or both of the computers or terminals. The problem was quite similar to two humans attempting to communicate with each other using different languages.

Moreover, the earlier networks not only used different codes such as Baudot, ASCII, and EBCDIC, but they often used several different proprietary protocols that had been added in a somewhat evolutionary and unplanned manner. (Many systems today still suffer from these deficiencies.) The protocols in the networks were often poorly and ambiguously defined. Consequently, it was not uncommon for a change in the network software at one site to adversely affect a seemingly unrelated component at another site. In many instances, the components in a network were simply incompatible.

During the 1970s, several large manufacturers realized that they could not afford to continue operating in an unorganized and ill-structured environment. Consequently, they began to develop a more coherent approach to their own products and embarked on efforts to build a structured framework (architecture) for their communications protocols. Continuing our comparison to human communications, it was similar to two people agreeing on a common language for conversing with each other.

The implementation of vendor-specific architectures alleviated the incompatibility problem of the products within the vendor's product line, but it did nothing to address the serious problem of incompatibility between the different vendors' computers, terminals, and other equipment. If anything, the development of vendor-specific systems made matters worse, because each manufacturer embarked upon a separate course in order to "build a better mousetrap."

One of the dominant proprietary data communications systems introduced during this time was Systems Network Architecture (SNA). It was developed by IBM to address the problem of hardware and software incompatibility within IBM's products. Due to IBM's leading position in the computer industry, SNA has become a "standard," and many products are now available to emulate or "hook into" IBM equipment. This approach was fine for IBM, but it did not set well with other vendors, who found they had to adhere to IBM's approach if they were to sell products to customers who owned IBM computers.

Moreover, because almost all computer and communications vendors had a "closed system," a customer was often forced to continue doing business with the original supplier or opt for the expensive and lengthy conversion to yet another vendor's proprietary hardware and software.

Before too long the end users began to question this environment. User groups sprouted up across countries. Their purpose was to provide input into a vendor's decisions about products and to exert more influence with the vendor than could be achieved by a single customer. The end user also began to question the necessity for vendor-specific closed systems. After all, other industries had a baseline set of standards (building codes for houses, standards for highway construction, etc.), why not the computer/communications industry as well?

At this time, several standards groups became active in these issues. The International Standards Organization (ISO) began work in 1979 on the Open Systems Interconnection Architecture, now known as OSI. The OSI model was published in 1984 to serve as a standard model for computer communications. Other organizations such as the American National Standards Institute (ANSI), the Consultative Committee of the International Telegraph and Telephone (CCITT), the Institute of Electrical and Electronic Engineers (IEEE), and the Electronic Industries Association (EIA), also began working on the development of standards. Many of these efforts have found their way into the OSI specifications that are examined in this book. (Appendix 1A at the end of this chapter provides a description of the standards organizations that are instrumental in the development of the OSI standards.)

The majority of the standards that have become part of the OSI suite of protocols are founded upon the concept of layered protocols and structured design techniques. No explanation of OSI can be fully understood unless this subject is also known, so let us take an excursion into the basic concepts of structured design and its use in layered protocols.

LAYERED PROTOCOLS

The software and hardware of the stations operating on data communications networks typically consist of a wide range of functions to support the communications activities. Without question, the network designer is faced with an enormous task in dealing with the number and complexity of these functions. To address these problems, many systems are designed by a well-ordered and structured "layering" of the functions. The term used today to describe the technique is layered protocols. The term is used so often it is almost a cliché, but it identifies some very worthy concepts. As we shall see in this section, a well-designed layered protocol system can provide:

- a logical decomposition of a complex system into smaller, more comprehensible parts (layers)
- standard (and limited) interfaces between the layered functions
- symmetry in functions performed at each layer in a system—each layer in a computer performs the same function(s) as its counterpart in other computers

- a means to predict and control any changes made to logic (software or microcode

Ideally, layered protocols that use common conventions permit different systems to communicate *openly* with each other without changing the logic of the communicating layers. Therefore, heretofore "closed" systems that were unable to communicate with each other should be able to communicate with relatively few changes to the software and hardware.

The name associated with open communications is, logically enough, Open Systems Interconnection (OSI). The layers of OSI serve as a foundation for many standards and products in the industry today and hence are used as the structure for this book.

Design Principles of Layered Systems

In this section we examine the principles behind the OSI reference model and compare them to some well-accepted concepts in system design. Many of these concepts have been in use in the software industry since the early 1970s, so we are not discussing any revolutionary concepts.

Binding, Coupling, and Atomic Actions. Layered functions owe their origin to several concepts generally called structured techniques. These ideas provide an impetus to design hardware or software systems that have clearly defined interfaces. The systems contain modules that perform one function or several closely related functions (sometimes called the cohesiveness of functions or the binding of related functions together). These techniques can also provide for loose coupling, wherein a change to a module in the system does not affect any other component that the changed module does not control. For computing resources to function efficiently and logically, they must adhere to the following atomic action principles.

- *An action is atomic if it is not aware of the existence of other active processes and other processes are not aware of process X, during the time that process X is performing the action.* That is, processes such as layers should operate independently from each other.
- *An action is atomic if the process performing the action does not communicate with other processes while the action is being performed.* This means the transactions between the process (layer) and other processes (layers) are quite restricted during periods when the layer is changing data or states.
- *An action is atomic if the process performing the action can detect no changes except those performed by itself and if it does not reveal its state changes until the action is complete.* In other words, a process should not be interrupted while it is running if the interruption will cause an alteration to the outcome of the process.

Layered Protocols and Network Architectures

To meet the principles of atomic actions, layered network protocols allow interaction between functionally paired layers in different locations without affecting other layers. This concept aids in distributing the functions to the layers. In the majority of layered protocols, the data unit, such as a message or packet, passed from one layer to another is usually not altered, although the data unit contents may be examined and used to append additional data (trailers/headers) to the existing unit.

The relationship of the layers is shown in Figure 1-2. Each layer contains entities that exchange data and provide functions (horizontal communications) with peer entities at other computers. For example, layer N in machine A communicates logically with layer N in machine B, and the N + 1 layers in the two machines follow the same procedure. Entities in adjacent layers in the same computer interact through the common upper and lower boundaries (vertical communications) by passing parameters to define the interactions.

Typically, each layer at a transmitting station (except the lowest in most systems) adds "header" information to data. The headers are used to establish peer-to-peer sessions across nodes, and some layer implementations use headers to invoke functions and services at the N + 1 or N − 1 adjacent layers. The important point to understand is that at the receiving site, the layer entities use

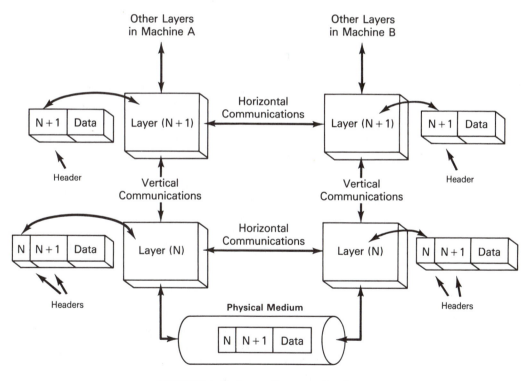

FIGURE 1-2. Layer Communications

the headers created by the peer entity at the transmitting site to implement actions.

Now that we have described the principles, advantages, and goals in layered protocol design, let us examine the ideas behind the layering concept as implemented in the OSI seven-layer model.

THE OSI MODEL

The Open Systems Interconnection (OSI) was developed by several standards organizations and is now a widely used layered functional model. It warrants serious study, because it is becoming a pervasive approach to implementing data communications systems.

The stated purpose of the model is to:
- Establish a common basis for standards development.
- Qualify products as open by their use of these standards.
- Provide a common reference for standards.

From the author's perspective, the model also:
- Provides standards for communications between systems.
- Removes any technical impediment to communication between systems.
- Removes concern with description of the internal operation of a single system.
- Defines the points of interconnection for the exchange of information between systems.
- Narrows the options in order to increase the ability to communicate without expensive conversions and translations between systems. This means different vendors' products can communicate more easily with each other.
- Provides a reasonable point of departure from the model in the event it does not meet all needs.

In summary, OSI is intended to diminish the effects of the vendor-specific mentality that has resulted in each vendor system operating with unique protocols. This approach has "closed" the end users to options of interconnecting and interfacing with other systems, and has necessitated the purchase of expensive and complex protocol converters to translate the different protocols.

The OSI Layers

The seven OSI layers are depicted in Figure 1-3. The lowest layer in the model is called the *physical layer*. The functions within the layer are responsible for activating, maintaining, and deactivating a physical circuit between the data terminal equipment (DTE) and the data circuit terminating equipment (DCE) and providing clocking signals. It is responsible for identifying the signals as binary ones and zeros. There are many standards published for the physical

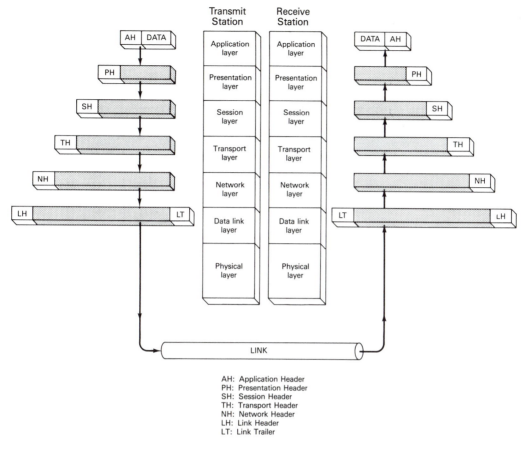

AH: Application Header
PH: Presentation Header
SH: Session Header
TH: Transport Header
NH: Network Header
LH: Link Header
LT: Link Trailer

FIGURE 1-3. The Open Systems Interconnection Model (OSI)

layer; for example, EIA-232, V.22 bis, and V.35 are physical level protocols. Physical level protocols are frequently called physical level interfaces. (Refer to Chapter 3.)

The *data link layer* is responsible for the transfer of data across the link. It delimits the flow of bits from the physical layer. It also provides for the identity of the bits in relation to their place in a data unit. It usually ensures that the data arrives safely at the receiving DTE. It often provides for flow control to ensure that the DTE does not become overburdened with too much data at any one time. One of its most important functions is to provide for the detection of transmission errors and provide mechanisms to recover from lost, duplicated, or erroneous data. (Refer to Chapter 4.)

The *network layer* specifies the interface of the user into a network, as well as the interface of two DTEs with each other through a network. It also defines network switching/routing and the communications between networks (internetworking). (Refer to Chapters 5 and 6.)

The *transport layer* provides the interface between the data communications network and the upper three layers (generally part of the user's system). It is the layer that gives the user options in obtaining certain levels of quality (and cost) from the network itself (i.e., the network layer). It is designed to keep the user isolated from some of the physical and functional aspects of the network. It also provides for the end-to-end accountability of data transfer across more than one link (it is the first layer to provide this important function). (Refer to Chapter 7.)

The *session layer* serves as a user interface into the transport layer. The layer provides for an organized means to exchange data between users, such as simultaneous transmission, alternate transmission, checkpoint procedures, and resynchronization of user data flow between user applications. The users can select the type of synchronization and control needed from the layer. (Refer to Chapter 8.)

The *presentation layer* is used to ensure that user applications can communicate with each other, even though they may use different representations for their protocol data units. The layer is concerned with preservation of the syntax of the data. For example, it can accept various data types (such as character, Boolean, integer, etc.) from the application layer and negotiate an acceptable syntax representation with its peer presentation layer. It also provides a means to describe data structures in a machine-independent way. It is used to code data from an internal format of a sending machine into a common transfer format, and then decode this format to a required representation at the receiving machine. (Refer to Chapter 9.)

The *application layer* is concerned with the support of the end-user application process. Unlike the presentation layer, this layer is concerned with the semantics of data. The layer contains service elements to support application processes such as job management, file transfers, electronic mail, and financial data exchanges. The layer also supports the virtual terminal and virtual file concepts. Directory services are obtained through this layer. (Refer to Chapters 10 and 11.)

THE OSI ARCHITECTURE

Figure 1-3 also depicts how the layers of a network communicate. The vast majority of networks use this approach, so the reader is encouraged to study this section carefully.

At a transmitting computer, user data is presented by a user application to the upper (application) layer. This layer adds its PCI (protocol control information, which the reader probably knows as a header) to the user data and often performs some type of support service to the user. It then passes its header and the user data to the next lower layer, which repeats the process.

Each layer adds a header (in many systems a header is not added at the physical layer). This concept is somewhat inaccurately called encapsulation, although the data from the upper layers have only headers added at one end.

The only layer that completely encapsulates the data is the data link layer, which adds both a header PCI and a trailer PCI.

The fully encapsulated data are transported across the communications circuit to a receiving station. Here the process is reversed: the data go from the lower layers to the upper layers, and the header created by the transmitting peer layer is used by the receiving peer layer to invoke a service function for (a) the transmitting site and/or (b) the upper layers of the receiving site. As the data goes up through the layers, the headers are stripped away after they have been used. This process is called decapsulation.

Insofar as possible, the internal operation of the layers are independent of each other. The idea is to reduce complexity and to allow changes to be made in one layer without affecting others. For example, a change to a routing algorithm in one layer should not affect the functions of say, sequencing, that are located in another layer in the architecture. Layered protocols also permit the partitioning of the design and development of the many network components.

Layered network protocols allow interaction between functionally paired layers in different locations. This concept aids in permitting the distribution of functions to remote sites. In the majority of layered protocols, the data unit passed from one layer to another is not altered. The data unit contents may be examined and used to append (i.e., encapsulate) additional PCIs (trailers/headers) to the existing unit.

Communications Between Layers

Figure 1-4 depicts a layer providing a service or a set of services to users A and B. The users communicate with the service provider through an address or identifier commonly known as the *service access point* (SAP). Through the use of four types of transactions, called *primitives* (Request, Indication, Response,

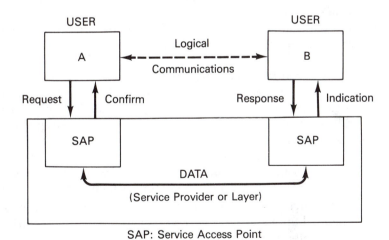

SAP: Service Access Point

FIGURE 1-4. The OSI Layer as a Service Provider

and Confirm), the service provider coordinates and manages the communications process between the users. (Some sessions do not require all primitives.)

- *Request*. Primitive by service user to invoke a function.
- *Indication*. Primitive by service provider to (a) invoke a function or (b) indicate a function has been invoked at a service access point (SAP).
- *Response*. Primitive by service user to complete a function previously invoked by an Indication at that SAP.
- *Confirm*. Primitive by service provider to complete a function previously invoked by a Request at that SAP.

A primitive is coded in software with a very specific format. For example, let us assume we wish to establish a connection to a network in order to access a computer in another city. Let us also assume the network communicates with us through primitives. We could request the connection with the following primitive:

N-CONNECT request (called address, calling address, quality-of-service parameters, user data).

This is a request primitive, or more precisely, a network layer (N) connect-request primitive. Notice the parameters associated with the connect request. The addresses are used to identify the called and calling parties. The quality-of-service (QOS) parameters can be translated into facilities. They inform the service provider about what type of services are to be invoked (expedited delivery, for example). It is possible that the primitive could contain many QOS parameters to invoke many facilities. The user data parameter contains the actual data to be sent to the called address.

The primitive is used by the layer to invoke the service entities and create any headers that will be used by the peer layer in the remote station. This point is quite important. The primitives are used by adjacent layers in the local site to create the headers used by peer layers at the remote site.

The Advantages of Abstract Primitives. One might question why the primitives are so abstract. Indeed, why are they not specific to a language, or at least to a convention, such as a subroutine call-by-value or a subroutine call-by-address? The abstract nature of the primitives makes good sense for the following reasons:

- They permit a common convention to be used between layers, without regard to specific vendor operating systems and specific languages.
- They give the vendor a choice as to how the primitives will be implemented on a specific machine. For example, the primitives are often implemented with a vendor's architecture-specific I/O calls.
- At the same time, if common languages and compilers are used among

vendors, the standard primitives ease the task of layer transportability between different vendor machines.

- The use of standard primitives encourages the use of common formats of the data units (packets, blocks, messages, frames, etc.). (The most common term used today is protocol data units [PDUs]). This point is critical for achieving open systems interconnection (OSI), since common PDUs are quite important in achieving compatibility between different architectures. Returning to our simple example of a common language among all people: The imposition of a common tongue "encourages" the individual to think in that tongue and use a common syntax. Common protocol data units are to machines what common linguistics are to humans.

The layer in Figure 1-4 is a service provider and may consist of several services. For example, one layer could provide a service for code conversion such as International Alphabet #5 (IA5) to/from EBCDIC. Each layer is considered a subsystem and may also be made up of entities. An entity is a specialized module within the layer. For example, a single layer could contain a data compression entity, an encryption entity, a multiplexing entity, and so on.

The entities within a layer are called peer entities. It is not necessary that all entities in a layer communicate with each other. Indeed, they may not be allowed to communicate. For example, they may not support the same subsets within the layers and therefore they would have no logical relationship to each other. In our example, a data compression entity would not be associated with an encryption entity.

A layer can also be divided into smaller logical substructures called sublayers. Entities can also exist within the sublayers.

The basic idea of layered protocols is for a lower layer to add a value to the services provided by the layers above it. Consequently, the top layer, which interfaces directly with an end-user application, is provided with the full range of services offered by all the lower layers. The actual services invoked are dictated by the upper layers to the lower layers, but it is the responsibility of the lower layers to perform the service. The upper layers are generally unaware of how the service is performed. As long as the service meets the requirements established by the upper layers, the detail of the service activities is transparent to the upper layer service user.

PRINCIPLES OF THE SEVEN-LAYER MODEL

The CCITT and ISO use several principles to determine the number and nature of the layers. These principles should be compared to the design principles explained in the previous section:

P1   For simplicity, keep the number of layers within a small limit.

P2   Create layer boundaries that minimize layer interactions and the description of services.

P3   Separate layers should exist in which functions are different from each other. Also, separate layers should exist that use different kinds of technology.

P4   Similarly, place similar functions in the same layer.

P5   Select layer boundaries that past experience shows have functioned successfully.

P6   As a complement to P4, localized functions should be established which allow a redesign with minimal effect to adjacent layers.

P7   Create boundaries that might permit the corresponding interface to be standardized.

P8   As a complement to P4, create a layer when the data must be handled differently.

P9   As a complement to P6, changes made in a layer should not affect other layers.

P10   Each layer has boundaries (interfaces) only to its upper and lower adjacent layers.

For the use of sublayers, similar principles apply:

P11   As a complement to P3, P4, P6, P8, P9, and P10, create further subgrouping if necessary.

P12   Create sublayers to allow interface with adjacent layers.

P13   Sublayers may be bypassed if the services are not needed.

A close examination of these principles reveals that they closely follow the design principles of structured techniques and atomic actions. Let us use some of these principles to evaluate the functional design scheme shown in Figure 1-5. The left side of the figure shows a structured design chart that meets several of the OSI design principles. The chart on the left side exhibits very "clean" interfaces between the modules, and adheres to principles 2, 10, and 12.

The chart on the right side of the figure violates some of the principles. For example, principle 2 is violated because several of the modules have multiple connections to other modules. Principles 10 and 12 are also violated because several of the modules are connected to nonadjacent modules.

Of course, it is impossible to determine from Figure 1-5 if this system meets all the principles of the OSI model. To verify conformance to all the principles, we would have to examine the software/firmware logic within each module.

Designations of the Layers

To expound on some ideas conveyed in Figures 1-2 and 1-3, a layer in the OSI model is identified generally as an (N)-layer. The layer above it (if one exists) is designated as the (N + 1)-layer. The layer below the (N)-layer (if one exists) is

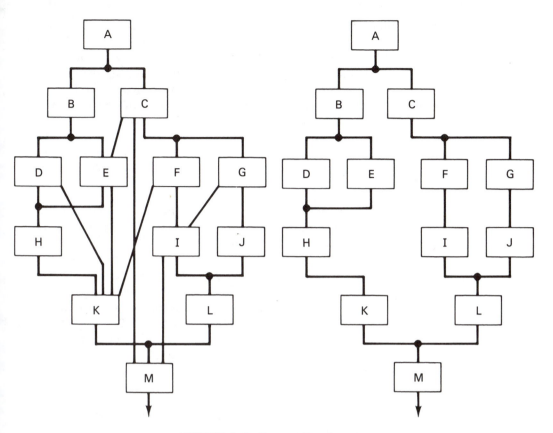

FIGURE 1-5. Connecting Layers

designated as the (N − 1)-layer. These designations are relative. For example, in Figure 1-3, if we were referring to the transport layer, we refer to it as the (N)-layer. The layer above it is the session layer, and is designated as the (N + 1)-layer. The layer below the transport layer is the network layer, and relative to the transport layer, it is designated as the (N − 1)-layer. As another example, if the presentation layer is the layer of interest, it is designated as the (N)-layer and the layers above and below it are (N + 1) and (N − 1), respectively.

The advantage of using relative designators is that it allows the model to describe the interactions of the layers without regard to a specific layer. In other words, all layers communicate with a common set of conventions.

Using Facilities to Tailor Services

Many services provided by an (N)-layer can be tailored. A user can select certain desired services from a layer by passing identifiers to the layer known as *facilities*. Through the use of (N)-facilities, the specific attributes of a service can be selected. If an (N)-entity cannot support a service requested by an (N + 1)-entity, it may call upon other (N)-entities to complete the service request.

Connection-endpoints

The entities within a layer can be connected on a many-to-one or a one-to-many basis. That is to say, entities may service more than one entity or use the services of more than one entity. These services are provided at the (N)-service access point (SAP) and called an (N)-*connection-endpoint*. In OSI, a connection is an association established by the (N)-layer between two or more (N + 1)-entities, usually for data transfer.

OSI DOCUMENTATION TOOLS

For most people, the review of an OSI document is not considered recreational reading (one pundit describes the process as akin to taking an instant sleeping pill). In fairness, the CCITT and ISO documents are not written to serve as tutorials for the edification of ordinary mortals, but are intended as technical references for engineers, designers, and programmers. Nonetheless, the specifications include a variety of very helpful documentation tools to depict and explain some rather complex subjects. With one exception, we examine these tools in this section. The last tool is reviewed in Chapter 9, Abstract Syntax Notation One (ASN.1). It is necessary to introduce these concepts at this point in order to examine the OSI architecture in more detail.

Time Sequence Diagrams

A very useful way to view the communications between a user layer and a service provider layer is with a time sequence diagram [see Figure 1-6(a)]. The sequence of events take place in the order of the relative positions of the arrows on the vertical lines; these lines are time lines. In between the time lines is the service provider, which could be any of the layers or an entity within a layer. The position of the arrows in this figure means that the Indication primitive can only be issued after the issuance of the Request primitive, and the Response primitive is issued after the Indication primitive.

The OSI model allows a considerable number of time sequence scenarios. For example, in Figure 1-6(b), the Confirm primitive could be returned without depending upon a Response primitive from the remote user. In this case, the local service provider provides the confirmation without regard to the actions of the remote user. Another example, in Figure 1-6(c), shows that the service provider issues an Indication primitive to both users without regard to the time of any previous primitives. This is noted with the tilde (~). We will expand these diagrams as we proceed through the examination of each of the layers.

State Transition Diagrams

Many of the protocols in the OSI Model are also explained with state transition diagrams. Figure 1-7 shows the use of such a diagram from the CCITT X.213 network layer procedures. Each ellipse depicts a "state" of the protocol. While

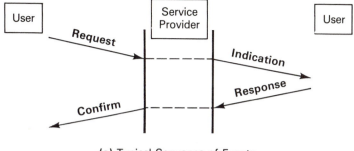

(a) Typical Sequence of Events

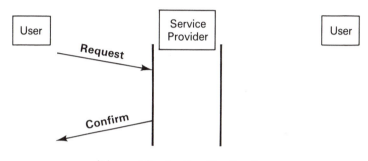

(b) Local Service Provider Confirms

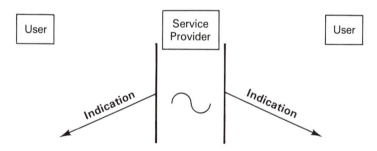

(c) Service Provider Issues Indications

FIGURE 1-6. Time Sequence Diagrams

in a particular state, the protocol entity can issue certain primitives and can receive and act upon certain primitives. Any other action is logically inconsistent with the intent of the protocol and violates the protocol convention. For example, if the entity is in the idle state, it cannot accept Data primitives. It can issue and receive Connect and Disconnect primitives, and then if it successfully sets up a connection and enters the data transfer ready state, it can send and receive data.

State transition diagrams impose a discipline upon the logic of the proto-

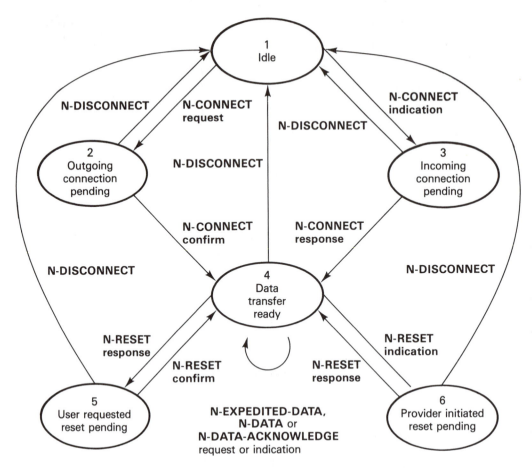

FIGURE 1–7. State Diagram for CCITT X.213 Procedures

col, and provide a means to verify the protocol's behavior. They also are quite useful tools for use in programming the protocol. We will use state diagrams throughout the book to describe the logic of several of the OSI standards.

Protocol Machines, State Tables, Event Lists, Predicates, and Action Tables

Several of the OSI documents describe a protocol with the use of state tables. These tables govern the sequence of events taken by the protocol "machine." To provide an example of a state table, consider the following information taken from an OSI applications layer protocol, the reliable transfer service element.

```
                STA0
    RT-OPreq    p1:
                RTORQ
```

These cryptic entries contain a wealth of information about the protocol. We will analyze them in the following material.

Assume two protocol machines are to communicate with each other. Both machines must be in an idle state before they can exchange primitives/protocol data units. Further assume that a state table in the OSI specification shows that a reliable transfer Open primitive is received by the protocol machine from a reliable transfer user. In the above example, this primitive is RT-OPreq and the idle state is STA0.

Since most of the OSI protocols contain many state tables, we first find a table entry with the Open primitive as a row entry. As the above example reveals, the primitive is shown to operate on the idle state as described in Table 1-1.

It is fair to say that the OSI specifications are not intended to be light reading. They are written to be concise and succinct descriptions of a protocol. However, if a person is really interested in knowing how the protocol works, these documentation tools are invaluable.

Example of the Use of a Primitive

At this point in the analysis of OSI it is fitting to pause and reflect on some of the abstract OSI concepts such as primitives and primitive parameters. It is certainly reasonable for the reader to wonder how such abstract ideas can be made meaningful in an actual operating environment. We attempt to bridge the abstractions of OSI to the real world with the example in Figure 1-8. This figure shows how an abstract primitive could be implemented with a FORTRAN subroutine call statement. The top part of the figure shows a primitive coded to request a network connection. It is coded as N-Connect.request, followed by the parameters called address, calling address, quality of service (QOS) requests, data.

The FORTRAN statement is CALL NWSETUP, followed by subroutine call arguments. These arguments are really nothing more than a mapping of the primitive parameters. The called address is coded as three fields: (1) DDCC is the destination country code; (2) DNWC is the destination network address; (3) DDTE is the destination end-user identification. The same scheme is used for the calling address, with the S prefix meaning the source address component.

The quality of service (QOS) parameters are coded as 1,,256. These values could stipulate the following: 1 = reverse charging requested; ,, = default to the standard packet window size; 256 = negotiate a packet size of 256 octets. The DATA argument in the call statement is a variable that identifies the user data stored in a memory location in the computer.

It should be obvious by now that the abstract primitives are implemented with real-world tools, such as language subroutine calls, function calls, examinations of the contents of registers, etc.

TABLE 1-1. Example of a State Table

Table Entry	Explanation of Entry
STA0	The identification of the state—in this example, state 0. A state description table can be examined to find out more about STA0. It stipulates that the protocol machine is idle and unassociated (not logically connected).
p1	This entry is a predicate, and belongs to yet another table, called the predicate table. A predicate is often used to provide supplemental information about the state. In this example, p1 states that the machine in this state can support a requested association (connection) from another machine.
RTORQ	This entry is a reliable transfer open request protocol data unit. It too is used as an entry in another table. This table is called an incoming event list. In this example, the table entry implies that the source of this protocol data unit is an initiating peer reliable transfer machine (in this example, the machine that received the Open primitive from the user), and states that it is received by the acceptor machine as user data within an associated Indication primitive. If necessary, a reader can then read about the purpose and contents of this protocol data unit in another section in the OSI manual. This entry in this table means the initiator machine must issue this data unit to the acceptor machine. Another part of the document states that it must be issued as a data parameter in an Open primitive to the next lower service provider entity.
[a1]	This entry is called specific actions. Once again, another table must be read to determine what the actions are. In this example, the a1 action states that the initiating machine is now identified by a Boolean condition of TRUE. This condition is used later to determine other actions. Specific action entries also define actions such as the setting of timers, the setting of values in the parameters in primitives, and so forth.
STA01	This entry describes the resultant state of the association. Looking up this descriptor in another table (the state descriptor table) reveals that the protocol machine is awaiting a confirm, reject, or abort protocol data unit from the peer machine.

COMPONENTS OF LAYERED COMMUNICATIONS

With the assumption that the reader is now convinced that the OSI abstract concepts can be related to the real world, we now delve into some of the more detailed aspects of the OSI architecture. In so doing, this section expands the discussion of layer communications.

Five components are involved in the layers' communications processes (see Figure 1-9). Their functions are:

Layered Protocols and Network Architectures

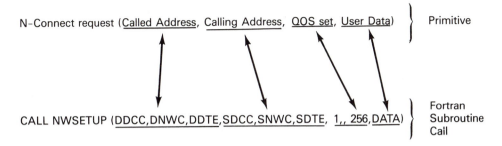

N-Connect request (<u>Called Address</u>, Calling Address, <u>QOS set</u>, User Data) } Primitive

CALL NWSETUP (<u>DDCC,DNWC,DDTE</u>,<u>SDCC,SNWC,SDTE</u>, 1,, 256,<u>DATA</u>) } Fortran Subroutine Call

FIGURE 1-8. Primitives and a Subroutine Call

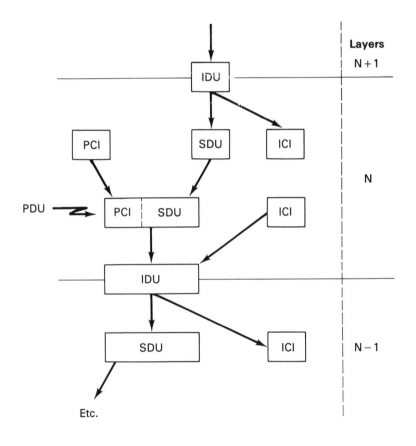

SDU	Service Data Unit
PCI	Protocol Control Information
PDU	Protocol Data Unit = PCI + SDU
IDU	Interface Data Unit = PDU + ICI
ICI	Interface Control Information

FIGURE 1-9. OSI Layer Components

- *SDU (service data unit)*. Consists of user data and control information created at the upper layers which is transferred transparently by layer (N + 1) to layer (N), and subsequently to (N − 1). The SDU identity is preserved from one end of an (N)-connection to the other.
- *PCI (protocol control information)*. Information exchanged by peer (the same) entities at different sites on the network to instruct an entity to perform a service function (that is, headers and trailers).
- *PDU (protocol data unit)*. The combination of the SDU and PCI.
- *ICI (interface control information)*. A temporary parameter or parameters passed between (N) and (N − 1) to invoke service functions between the two layers. The primitive typically performs this function.
- *IDU (interface data unit)*. The total unit of information transferred across the layer boundaries; it includes the PCI, SDU, and ICI. The IDU is transmitted across the service access point (SAP).

To assist the reader with these terms, consider the following:

- (N) to (N) remote entities use
    PCI for control
    User data (SDU)
    PDU combines the PCI and SDU
- (N + 1) to (N) adjacent entities use
    ICI for control
    User data (SDU)
    IDU combines the ICI and SDU

To summarize the OSI layering concepts, the following actions constitute a typical operation. Please use Figure 1-9 to follow this explanation. When the IDU from layer (N + 1) passes to layer (N), it becomes the SDU to that layer. In turn, the ICI is broken out in layer (N), performs its functions and is discarded. The SDU at layer (N) has a PCI added to it, as well as another ICI, to become the IDU to layer (N − 1). Thus, a full protocol data unit (PDU) is passed through each layer. The SDU has a PCI added to each layer. In effect, this is adding a header at each layer. The header is used by the peer layer entity at another node of the network to invoke a function. The peer entity at the other node receives the SDU that is created at the other peer entity. The process repeats itself through each layer.

OSI Type and Instance. OSI draws a distinction between two terms used in the model, type and instance. A type is a description of a class of objects; an instance of a type conforms to the description of that type. These abstract descriptors are really quite simple. A piece of software is a type of something; instances of that type are created each time the software is executed on a computer.

In OSI, the type of an (N)-entity is the specific set of (N)-layer functions it performs. An instance of that type is the invocation of the specific function(s). In other words, an (N)-entity instance refers to the actual occasion of communications to (N)-entities.

ELEMENTS OF OSI LAYERS

The OSI model defines the elements of a layer's operation (see Table 1-2). The reader is encouraged to study the contents of the table, because these elements are found in one form or another in several of the layers (but not in all the layers). The usefulness of several of the elements may escape the reader. Therefore, we now provide some additional information on several of them (the others are covered in later chapters).

TABLE 1-2. Elements of Layers

Protocol identifier. An identifier between communicating entities to select a protocol to be used in the logical connection.

Centralized/Decentralized multi-endpoint connection. The ability to associate data from one to many and/or many to one connection endpoint(s).

Multiplexing. An (N)-layer function that uses one (N−1)-connection to support multiple (N)-connections.

Demultiplexing. The reverse function of multiplexing.

Splitting. An (N)-layer function that uses more than one (N−1)-connection to support multiple (N)-connections.

Recombining. The reverse function of splitting.

Flow control. A function to control the flow of data between adjacent layers or within a layer.

Segmenting. An (N)-entity function that maps an (N) service data unit into multiple (N) protocol data units.

Reassembling. The reverse function of segmenting.

Blocking. An (N)-entity function that maps multiple (N)-service data units into one (N)-protocol data unit.

Deblocking. The reverse function of blocking.

Concatenation. An (N)-entity function that maps multiple (N)-protocol data units into one (N−1)-service data unit.

Separation. The reverse function of concatenation.

Sequencing. An (N)-layer function that preserves the order of data units submitted into it.

Acknowledgment. An (N)-layer function that a receiving (N)-entity uses to acknowledge a protocol data unit from a sending (N)-entity.

Reset. An (N)-layer function that returns correspondent (N)-entities to a state, with possible loss or duplication of data.

Notice the relationship between:

Dealing with connections:
- multiplexing and demultiplexing
- splitting and recombining

Dealing with data units (PDUs and SDUs):
- segmenting and reassembling
- blocking and deblocking
- concatenation and separation

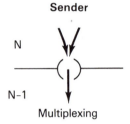 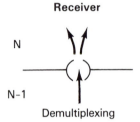

(a) Multiplexing and Demultiplexing

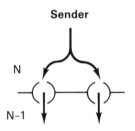 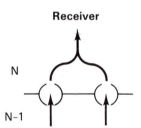

(b) Splitting and Recombining

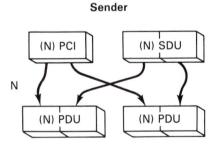 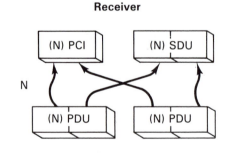

(c) Segmenting and Reassembling

FIGURE 1–10. OSI Management of Connections and Data Units

As suggested by this list, these services deal with (a) the connections between entities (via a service access point [SAP]) and (b) the data units exchanged between entities. A layer may or may not furnish all these functions.

The OSI Model describes procedures for multiplexing more than one user session (connection) into one lower level connection [see Figure 1-10(a)]. This is called multiplexing more than one (N + 1)-connection over an (N)-connection. This service can be useful (as an example) if an organization wishes to establish a connection to a network and maintain the connection throughout an operating period. After the connection is established, multiple users can be multiplexed onto the ongoing network connection, and each user does not have to go through the delay and expense of obtaining a connection to the network. As another example, this service is quite useful if a connection has the capacity

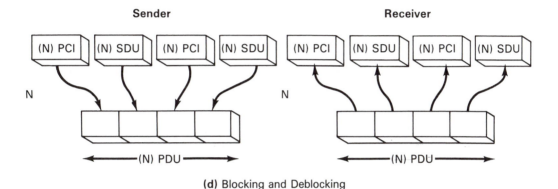

(d) Blocking and Deblocking

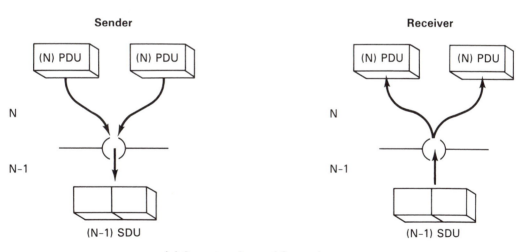

(e) Concatenation and Separation

Note: ( ) Denotes a Connection

FIGURE 1-10. (Continued)

(bandwidth) to support more than one individual (N + 1)-connection. As shown in Figure 1-10(a), the OSI model also defines a complementary demultiplexing service at the receiving site. The multiplexing/demultiplexing service is confined to the transport, network, and data link layers.

In contrast to the multiplexing/demultiplexing services, a user may wish to establish multiple connections to a network (or some other layer), so OSI defines the procedures for splitting one (N + 1)-connection into multiple lower (N)-connections [see Figure 1-10(b)]. This service is useful when a user wishes to increase throughput and/or increase resiliency with multiple connections. If this service is invoked, the model defines procedures for recombining the lower level connections into one connection at the receiving site. Splitting and recombining is also restricted to the transport, network, and data link layers.

It is possible to have multi-endpoint connections. For example, a broadcast network such as a satellite or local area network sends/receives data to/from one entity and from/to multiple entities. OSI permits this type of connection, and it can be represented as a multiple representation of N pair connections.

Data units (such as packets frames) in different layers and vendor products are not always the same size. The OSI Reference Model describes three methods for handling this problem. First, segmenting permits the mapping of a service data unit (SDU) into more than one protocol data unit (PDU) within the same layer. Figure 1-10(c) shows that the protocol control information (PCI) is appended to each protocol data unit. This PCI (header) is needed to preserve the identity of the unit, and to allow for reassembly at the receiving site.

Conversely, it may be desirable to block smaller service data units into one larger protocol data unit within the same layer [see Figure 1-10(d)]. For example, some packet networks place smaller user packets into a larger packet for transmission through a network. The PCI must contain sufficient information to allow deblocking at the receiving site.

Lastly, the process of concatenation is similar to blocking, except smaller protocol data units are placed into one larger service data unit [see Figure 1-10(e)]. This function assumes the (N)-PDUs are passed to an (N − 1)-SDU. In other words, concatenation occurs between two layers, whereas blocking occurs within a layer. Concatenation/separation is often implemented with the connection multiplexing/demultiplexing procedures.

OSI ADDRESSING

Earlier in this chapter, the concept of a service access point (SAP) was introduced. To review the SAP, the OSI Model states:

An (N + 1)-entity requests (N)-services via an (N)-service access point (SAP) which permits the (N + 1)-entity to interact with an (N)-entity.

As Figure 1-11(a) shows, an (N)-service access point [or (N)-address] can identify a one-to-one connection between an (N + 1)-entity and an (N)-entity

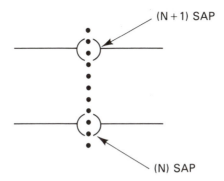

(a) One-to-One Relationship

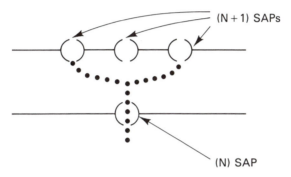

(b) Many-to-One Relationship

FIGURE 1-11. SAP Relationships

through a one-to-one relationship between the (N+1)-SAP and the (N)-SAP. It is also possible to use an (N)-connection endpoint identifier to identify the corresponding (N)-connection at an (N)-service access point.

Figure 1-11(b) shows a many-to-one relationship between (N)-addresses and (N−1)-addresses. OSI also permits this type of connection.

The following points summarize the most important properties of service access points:

- An (N+1)-entity may concurrently be attached to one or more (N)-service access points attached to the same or different (N)-entities.
- An (N)-entity may concurrently be attached to one or more (N+1)-entities through (N)-service access points.
- An (N)-service access point is attached to only one (N)-entity and to only one (N+1)-entity at a time.

An addendum to the ISO specification, IS 7489 (Part 3), provides other guidelines for addressing. First, a name identifies an entity and is classified into three types:

Title	Names a layer entity
Address	Names a service access point (SAP)
Identifier	Names something else

A title must be mapped through a directory into an address. The directories are located in the network and application layers to manage addresses and titles, respectively. The reader should be aware that additional translations may take place between the application and network layers, but a direct mapping between a title and an address is certainly permitted.

Network Level Addressing

The data communications industry uses the term "network address" to identify different things in the network. The OSI Model defines the network address in three contexts.

First, a network address identifies the interface to a public or private data network. The reader may recognize this address as the more common term DTE address. This definition of a network address does not pertain to an OSI service access point (SAP).

Second, a network address refers to the network service access point (NSAP). The N-CONNECT primitive uses the NSAP address in the called address, calling address, and responding address fields. As stated before, the SAP and primitives are conceptual and abstract. The OSI Model does not specify a particular method of representing an SAP.

Third, a network address refers to field(s) within the network protocol control information (PCI). CCITT refers to this context as an address signal.

Since the primitives are used between adjacent layers for exchanging data and control, they are generally used to form the DTE address(es) and/or the address in the PCI. Indeed, the DTE address(es) and the address in the PCIs could be the same.

The NSAP address is an abstract concept used by OSI to identify the network service. The NSAP appears in the called address, calling address, and responding address parameters of N-CONNECT primitives. (It also appears in the source address and destination address of another primitive called N-UNIT-DATA, discussed in later chapters). We will have more to say about network layer addressing in Chapter 5.

CONNECTIONLESS-MODE AND CONNECTION-ORIENTED COMMUNICATIONS

The connectionless-mode and connection-oriented services are both widely used types of OSI architecture (see Figure 1-12), and are discussed throughout this book. Their principal characteristics are:

Layered Protocols and Network Architectures

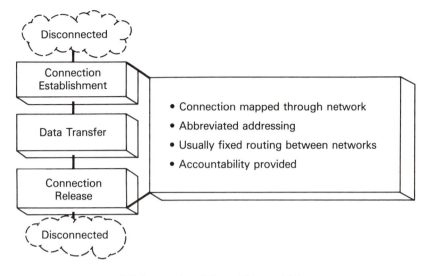

(a) Connection-Oriented Network(s)

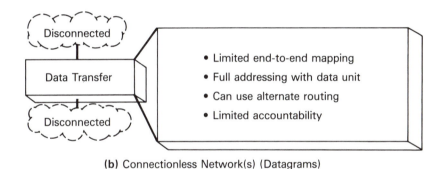

(b) Connectionless Network(s) (Datagrams)

FIGURE 1–12. Connecting into Networks

- *Connection-oriented operations.* Sets up a logical connection before the transfer of data. Usually, some type of relationship is maintained between the data units being transferred through the connection.
- *Connectionless-mode operations.* No logical connection is established. The data units are transmitted as independent units.

The connection-oriented service requires a three-way agreement between the two end users and the service provider. It also allows the communicating parties to negotiate certain options and quality of service (QOS) functions. During the connection establishment, all parties store information about each other, such as addresses and QOS features. Once data transfer begins, the protocol data units need not carry all this overhead protocol control information (PCI).

All that is needed is an abbreviated identifier to allow the parties to look up the full addresses and QOS features. A connection-oriented system can also perform sequencing, error control, and flow control of the traffic. Since the session can be negotiated, the communicating parties need not have prior knowledge of all the characteristics of each other. If a requested service cannot be provided, any of the parties can negotiate the service to a lower level or reject the connection request.

The connectionless type service manages user protocol data units (PDUs) as independent and separate entities. No relationship is maintained between successive data transfers and few records are kept of the ongoing user-to-user communications process through the network(s). The (N + 1)-entities must have a prior agreement on how to communicate, and the QOS features must be prearranged. The (N)-service provider is not aware of these arrangements. The term "datagram" network is also associated with a connectionless network.

By its very nature, connectionless service achieves (a) a high degree of user independence from specific protocols within a subnetwork, (b) considerable independence of the subnetworks from each other, and (c) a high degree of independence of the subnetworks(s) from the user-specific protocols.

A connectionless network is more robust than its connection-oriented counterpart, because each PDU is handled as an independent entity. Therefore, data units can take different routes to avoid failed nodes or congestion at a

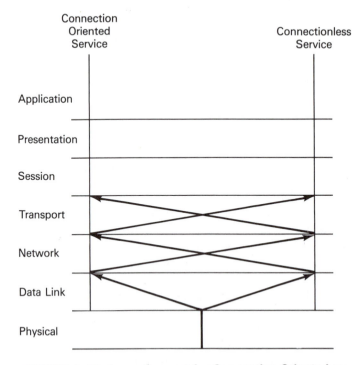

FIGURE 1-13. Layer Support for Connection-Oriented or Connectionless Services

point in the network(s). However, they do consume more overhead (in relation to headers versus user data) than their connection-oriented counterparts.

ISO 7489 was the original standard that defined a connection-oriented operation. It required that a connection be established at the immediate lower layer before data from the next higher layer could be exchanged. In recognition of the need for more flexibility, the ISO issued an addendum (ISO 7498/DAD1) to allow a connectionless operation.

It is intended that the data link, network, and transport layers support either connection-oriented or connectionless service. Later enhancements to the data link layer also permit the use of either mode. The possible conversions between the modes are illustrated in Figure 1-13. Notice that conversions are not allowed at the upper three layers.

Later chapters will examine these two modes of operation in more detail.

A PRAGMATIC ILLUSTRATION

The OSI concept may be more easily understood by an examination of Figure 1-14. The abstract concepts of SDUs and PCIs are replaced with the words

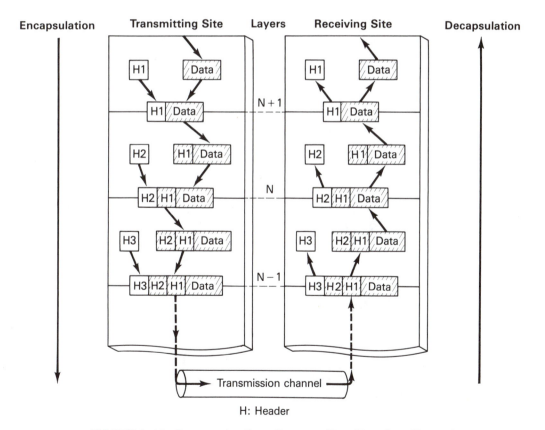

FIGURE 1-14. Communications Between Two Sites in a Network

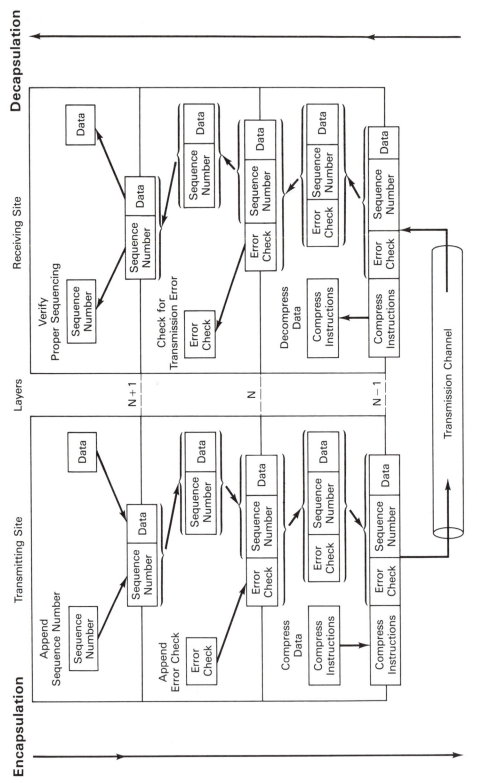

FIGURE 1-15. Invoking Support Functions with the PCI (Header)

"user data" and "headers." As each unit traverses through the layers, it has a header added to it (encapsulation). This becomes the user data unit to the subsequent lower layers. Finally, the full protocol data unit (PDU) is transferred to the communications path. It arrives at the receiving site, coming up through the layers in the reverse order as it went through them from the sending site. The headers added at the peer layers at the transmitting site are used to invoke symmetrical and complementary functions at the receiving site. After the functions are performed, the protocol data unit is passed up to the next layer. The header that was added by the peer entity at the transmitting site is stripped-off (decapsulated) by the peer entity at the receiving site.

On close observation, it can be seen that the header is instrumental in invoking the functions across the network to the peer layer. Again, let us take a more pragmatic approach to these concepts and see what some of these functions might be. Figure 1-14 is expanded in Figure 1-15.

Instructions have been placed in the headers to invoke functions in the peer entities at another node in the network. Three layers are involved. The layers will invoke one service entity from each layer. Layer $(N+1)$ invokes a service entity to provide a sequence check field at the transmitting site. The receiving site's $(N+1)$-layer checks for any sequence errors in the transmission by using the sequence check field as a comparison to a receive counter. The service entity in layer (N) adds an error-check field in the form of a header to be used at the receiving (N)-layer to ensure that data is arriving error-free. Last, an entity in $(N-1)$ compresses the code. At the receiving node, the header will be used to instruct the $(N-1)$-layer to convert (decompress) the code back to its original form (although this particular function could be performed without the use of headers).

COMPARISON OF SERVICE DEFINITIONS AND PROTOCOLS

Previous discussions in this chapter emphasized the importance of definitions to define the services between the adjacent upper and lower layers (vertical communications). We learned that the services are requested, confirmed, etc., with primitives. We also learned that the primitives are used within the layer to create the header (PCI) for the protocol data unit (PDU). The PDUs and their PCIs are used by a remote peer layer to invoke specific operations (horizontal communications).

Figure 1-16 shows the most widely used service definitions. The majority of these protocols are published by the ISO and the CCITT. In many instances, these different standards organizations' protocols are comparable. For example, the ISO 8348 and CCITT X.213 documents are almost identical. However, in other instances the ISO and CCITT specifications differ. The reader should be aware of these potential differences, and review both documents if necessary. Fortunately, the 1988 CCITT Blue Books contain explanations of where the two organizations differ and where they are "technically aligned" in regard to the OSI documents.

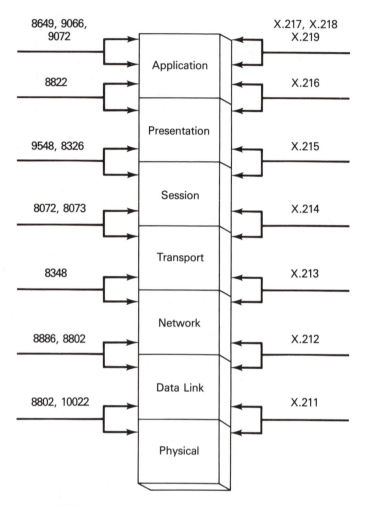

ISO   CCITT

8649, 9066,   X.217, X.218
   9072   X.219

                        Application

8822   X.216

                        Presentation

9548, 8326   X.215

                        Session

8072, 8073   X.214

                        Transport

8348   X.213

                        Network

8886, 8802   X.212

                        Data Link

8802, 10022   X.211

                        Physical

FIGURE 1-16. Prevalent Service Definitions

Figure 1-17 shows the principal ISO and CCITT protocols used within and between the peer layers. Please be aware that not all the inner-layer protocols are shown—they are too numerous to show in one picture.

It should be noted that the IEEE 802 service definitions and the ISO 8802 service definitions are identical. Also, these standards define both the service definitions and the protocol operations between the peer layer.

This book uses both the CCITT recommendations and ISO standards in discussing the OSI Model. They will be so identified in the respective sections and chapters. Appendix A at the back of this book provides a general description of the ISO standards. Appendix B provides a similar description of the

34   *Layered Protocols and Network Architectures*

ISO		CCITT
8649 CASE 8571 FTAM 8831 JTM 9040 VT 9804 CCR	Application	X.400 MHS X.229 ROSE X.228 RTSE X.227 ACSE
8824, 8825, 9576	Presentation	X.208 X.209 X.226
8327, 8824, 9548, 8825, 9576	Session	X.225
8602, 10025	Transport	X.224
8208, 4731, 9068, 8473, 8648, 10028, 8881, 8882, 9577	Network	X.25 X.75
3309, 4335, 7776, 7809, 8471, 8802, 8885	Data Link	LAPB LAPD LAPX LAPM
Many	Physical	Many

FIGURE 1–17. Prevalent Protocols

CCITT recommendations. Table 1-3 lists and compares the CCITT and ISO OSI "foundation" specifications: those that serve as the building blocks for OSI. These foundation service definitions and protocols are described in Chapters 1, 9, 10, and 11.

The ISO uses the following initials to indicate the services provided by the layers and protocols in the OSI Model:

- Ph: Physical layer service
- DL: Data link layer service
- N: Network layer service

TABLE 1-3.   OSI "Foundation" Service Definitions and Protocols

CCITT	ISO	Subject
X.200	7498	OSI Reference Model
X.210		OSI Service Definition Conventions
X.220		Use of X.200 Series in CCITT Applications
X.211	8802	Physical Layer Service Definitions
X.212	8886	Data Link Layer Service Definitions
X.213	8348	Network Layer Service Definition
X.223	8878	Use of X.25 for OSI Connection-Mode Service
	8473	Connectionless Network Service
X.208	8824	Abstract Syntax Notation
X.209	8825	Basic Encoding Rules
X.214	8072	Transport Service Definition
X.224	8073	Transport Protocol Specification
	8602	Connectionless Transport Service
X.215	8326	Session Service Definition
X.225	8327	Session Protocol Specification
X.216	8822	Presentation Service Definition
X.226	8823	Presentation Protocol Specification
X.217	8649	Association Control Service Definition
X.227	8650	Association Control Protocol Specification
X.218	9066/1	Reliable Transfer Service Definition
X.228	9066/2	Reliable Transfer Protocol Specification
X.219	9072/1	Remote Operations Service Definition
X.229	9072/2	Remote Operations Protocol Specification

- T: Transport layer service
- P: Presentation layer service
- S: Session layer service
- A: Application layer service and other application layer services:
    - F: FTAM service
    - J: JTM service
    - V: Virtual terminal service
    - C: CCR service
    - TP: Transaction processing service
    - M: OSI management service

CRITICISM OF THE OSI MODEL

This section describes some criticisms of the OSI model and includes some of the author's opinions on the subject.

The layers as currently specified by ISO and the CCITT require substantial computing resources to perform their functions, and it is fair to say they could be made more efficient. However, as more functions are provided to a user, more resources are required to provide those functions. Network services such as end-to-end reliability, fast response time, and high throughput do not happen with "vaporware." Software and hardware of sufficient power must be available to meet these requirements.

A close examination of the OSI architecture reveals: (a) some duplication of functions and redundancy of primitives between and across several of the layers, and (b) considerable overhead in the headers and trailers used in several of the layers, especially the upper ones.

Regarding point (a), the redundant negotiation of services between and across layers, it must be realized that a service performed at, say, layer 5 requires a request from an end user residing above layer 7. How is this service to be requested and invoked if not by relaying the "parameters" to the responsible layer? It would appear the only other alternative is to pre-map the requests and services. They would then be invoked without the use of primitives. It is certainly an alternative, and indeed it is used as an option in parts of the OSI Model.

However, this approach also degrades the flexibility of requesting services dynamically. A practical approach is to pre-map the users' profiles as default options and use the parameters in the primitives only to override the defaults. Several of the OSI entities provide this flexibility.

Regarding point (b), the number of octets needed to construct PCI (protocol control information) in the layer headers could be reduced. The use of fields to indicate multiple functions with Boolean bit comparisons would reduce the number of overhead bits.

However, these schemes require more complex software and additional machine processing cycles to encode and decode the fields. The slow-speed channels that currently support networks can certainly benefit from a fewer number of overhead octets, but the increased channel throughput must be weighed against increased processing time.

If OSI is altered and customized, it could lead to increased incompatibility. If it is not altered, it will continue to require substantial processing and transmission resources. The opponents of changes to OSI state that the forthcoming faster processors and faster transmission systems will be capable of supporting a fully layered OSI network very effectively.

From the author's perspective, some of the OSI layers can be improved, but there is no such thing as a "free lunch"—functionality requires resources. For example, after working with a variety of vendors' networks for several years, I have observed that their richness of functions do not come without cost.

Many OSI applications will perform better if their programmers and designers are more skillful in their work. Moreover, functions such as session control, segmentation, concatenation, end-to-end accountability, and resequencing cannot be implemented unless sufficient software and computing resources are available.

As a practical matter, many vendors and manufacturers simply choose to implement a specific part of the OSI layer or entity that they deem advantageous to their product.

By the very nature of a standard as wide-ranging as OSI, it must give a variety of options to accommodate a wide variety of needs. Some people believe these options make the OSI standards too general, so that they are less suited to specific needs. The author disagrees. The OSI standards are quite specific in most of the layers, as we learned by our analysis of the OSI documentation tools earlier in this chapter. Indeed, and ironically, some people believe the OSI Model does not give them enough leeway in using it. They fail to understand that a standard must be specific; otherwise, we would find ourselves using incompatible products from vendors who have interpreted the standards differently.

Another criticism revolves around the fact that some OSI documents are issued with certain entries described as "For Further Study." Critics state that it is impossible to develop a OSI-based system with such spotty documentation. Yet consider the alternative: If the OSI standards bodies delayed the publication of a standard until all issues were settled, the standard would be delayed for many months. The alternative is to settle as many issues as possible, then get the document to the public for actual use. Inevitably, the specification will require changes as it is tested in the real world, and the changes can be incorporated at the same time the "For Further Study" clauses are replaced with specific protocol specifications.

Finally, it has also been said by many people that a successful standard must be equally unfair to all who use it. This statement is true, because a standard very rarely can accommodate to all the specific needs of its users.

SUMMARY AND CONCLUSIONS

Even though standards impose some limitations on systems developers and designers, they appear to be the best answer to the problem of interconnecting diverse communications equipment and software. Taking the lead in the computer communications standards has been the Open Systems Interconnection (OSI) Model. The OSI Model is divided into seven layers to aid in the design of complex systems.

The OSI documentation tools are an important part of the standards. Time sequence diagrams and state transition diagrams are tools found in earlier OSI documents but are still used widely today. The newer documentation tools dealing with state tables, event lists, predicates, and action tables are found in all the recent OSI documents.

APPENDIX 1A. STANDARDS ORGANIZATIONS

The growing acceptance of common conventions and protocols is the result of the efforts of several standards organizations. An overview of these groups is provided here. Their addresses are given in Table 1A-4.

Standards are usually classified as voluntary, regulatory, or a combination of the two, which we will call regulated use of voluntary standards. Voluntary standards are not required to be used, but are used if a manufacturer considers it to be to its own interest to adhere to the standard. A regulatory standard is one that is usually required by a government agency, and must be used by certain groups. The third category is a growing area. It defines a set of voluntary standards that must be used to satisfy certain applications. For example, the U.S. Government Open Systems Interconnection Profile (GOSIP) suite fits this last category.

The work of the ISO and CCITT has begun to overlap as computer and communications technology merges. Fortunately, the two organizations cooperate with each other and, in many instances, promulgate identical standards.

The American National Standards Institute (ANSI)

The American National Standards Institute (ANSI) is a national clearing house and coordinating agency for standards implemented in the United States on a voluntary basis. ANSI is the U.S. voting member of the ISO, and also develops and coordinates standards in data communications for the OSI. It develops standards for encryption activities and office systems. ANSI tries to adopt the ISO standards, but their specifications may differ due to the unique aspects of the North American systems.

In 1960, ANSI formed X3, a committee to establish standards for data communications, programming languages, magnetic storage media, and the OSI Model. It parallels the work of the ISO technical committee (TC) 97. The X3 technical committees are summarized in Table 1A-1.

The Electronic Industries Association (EIA)

The Electronic Industries Association is a national trade association which has been active in the development of standards for many years. Its best known standard is EIA-232. The EIA publishes its own standards and also submits proposals to ANSI for accreditation.

The EIA work is hardware-oriented. The TR-30 Technical Committee, Data Transmission, is responsible for EIA-232 (first issued in 1962). TR-30 meets with ANSI X3S3 to ensure that work of the two groups is cohesive. TR-30 is responsible for the physical layer part of the OSI Reference Model; X3S3 deals with the data link and network layers.

TABLE 1A-1. ANSI Committees

Data communications (X3S3). The work of X3S3 parallels that of the EIA Technical Committee TR-30, Data Transmission. X3S3 is responsible for the lower four layers of the Reference Model. It has seven Task Groups, which are responsible for specific areas of work.

Open Systems Interconnection (OSI) (X3T5). X3T5 deals with the OSI reference model and the upper three layers of the architecture. X3T5 has three active Task Groups.

Office and Publication Systems (X3V1). X3V1 was formed in 1981. It supports work of ISO SC 18 and the telematic services defined by CCITT. Seven Task Groups have been formed.

ANSI T1. This committee was formed by the ECSA (Exchange Carriers Standards Association) which was established by ANSI to deal with the AT&T divestiture and the deregulated environment. The T1 committee deals with many issues and is best known for the work on ISDN.

ANSI Accredited Standards Committee (X12). X12 is responsible for developing standards for business-related electronic interchange systems such as purchase orders and invoices. X12 also defines formats for business transactions and its standards are in use in some segments of the industry.

The Corporation for Open Systems (COS)

In 1986, more than 50 major data processing and data communications suppliers formed a nonprofit venture titled the Corporation for Open Systems to provide a means to accelerate the use of multi-vendor products that operate under OSI, ISDN, and related international standards. One of its more important activities is the development of a consistent set of testing and certification methods.

The Standards Promotion and Application Group (SPAG)

SPAG is a European-based organization consisting of communications/mainframe vendors. It is concerned with the development and implementation of conformance testing products. SPAG has several conformance testing systems being used in Europe and is now coordinating its activities with COS and POSI.

The Japanese Promoting Conference for OSI (POSI)

The major Japanese computer vendors and the Nippon Telephone and Telegraph Corporation established POSI in 1985 to promote the OSI standards and the efforts of COS and SPAG. POSI is also involved in conformance testing through the Interoperability Technology Association for Information Products (INTAP).

The Australian National Protocol Support Center (NPSC)

The Australian government has been the focal point for the founding of NPSC. As with COS, SPAG, and POSI, this organization is promoting OSI and the development of conformance testing procedures in Australia.

The European Computer Manufacturers Association (ECMA)

The European Computer Manufacturers Association is dedicated to the development of standards applicable to computer and communications technology. It is not a trade organization, as the name might imply, but a standards and technical review group. It was formed in 1961 as a non-commercial organization to promulgate standards for data processing and communications systems. The ECMA works in close coordination with many of the ISO and the CCITT technical committees and study groups. Initially organized by Compagnie des Machines Bull, the IBM World Trade Europe Corporation, and International Computers and Tabulators Limited, it now includes all European computer manufacturers.

The Institute of Electrical and Electronic Engineers (IEEE)

The Institute of Electrical and Electronic Engineers has been involved in standards activities for many years. It is a well-known professional society with chapters located throughout the world, and is a member of ANSI. Its recent efforts in local area networks have received much attention. The IEEE activity addresses local area networks and many other standards as well.
The 802 structure is as follows:

- IEEE 802.1 Higher Layer Interface Standard (HILI)
- IEEE 802.2 Logical Link Control Standard (LLC)
- IEEE 802.3 Carrier Sense Multiple Access with Collision Detection (CSMA/CD)
- IEEE 802.4 Token Bus
- IEEE 802.5 Token Ring
- IEEE 802.6 Metropolitan Area Network (MAN)
- IEEE 802.7 Broadband Technical Advisory Group
- IEEE 802.8 Fiber-Optics Technical Advisory Group

The International Organization for Standardization (ISO)

The International Organization for Standardization (ISO) is a voluntary body. It consists of national standardization organizations from each member country, and many members are actually government standards bodies from member countries. The activities of ISO stem principally from the user committees and manufacturers, in contrast to the communications carriers that are represented in CCITT. The American National Standards Institute (ANSI) is the primary U.S. member organization of the ISO.

The development of an ISO standard is a time-consuming process because many countries and steps are involved. A brief summary of the process is provided here:

- A new proposal is assigned to a Technical Committee (TC) which produces a document containing the technical features of the specification. This document is called a working draft (WD).
- As a result of a technical review and editorial refinements on the WD, a modified document is prepared. At this time, the document becomes a draft proposal (DP).
- The TC and a Central Secretariat review the proposal and issue it as a draft international standard (DIS). At this juncture, the major comments and corrections have been taken into account, and the document is circulated for a member body vote.
- The DIS is reviewed and voted upon by members, and eventually published as an international standard (IS). At this point the document is considered to be technically and editorially correct. It is then published in French, English, and Russian.

Technical Committee 97 (TC97) deals with information technology. As such, its activities affect many of the products and systems that are used in the industry. Table 1A–2 summarizes the ISO Subcommittees (SC) and Working Groups (WG).

International Telegraph & Telephone Consultative Committee (CCITT)

The International Telegraph & Telephone Consultative Committee is a member of the International Telecommunications Union (ITU), a treaty organization formed in 1965. The ITU is now a specialized body within the United Nations. CCITT sponsors a number of recommendations dealing primarily with data communications networks, telephone switching standards, digital systems, and terminals. The State Department is the voting member of CCITT from the United States, although several levels of membership are permitted. For example, the recognized private operating agencies (RPOAs), such as the regional Bell Operating Companies, are allowed to participate at one level.

The CCITT's recommendations (standards) are very widely used. Its specifications are updated every four years and published in a series of books that take up considerable space on a book shelf. The four-year period books are identified by the color of their covers. The 1960 books were red; 1964, blue; 1968, white; 1972, green; 1976, orange; 1980, yellow; and, in 1984, once again red. The 1988 Blue books consume about four feet of shelf space and number about 16,000 pages! The CCITT Study Groups are summarized in Table 1A-3.

TABLE 1A-2. Subcommittees (SC) and Working Groups (WG)

SC 2: Character Sets and Information Coding

WG 1: Code extension techniques
WG 2: 2-bit graphic character set
WG 4: Coded character sets for text communication
WG 6: Additional control functions
WG 7: 8-bit coded character set
WG 8: Coded representation of pictures

SC 6: Telecommunications and Information Exchange between Systems

---

WG 1: Data Link Layer
WG 2: Network Layer
WG 3: Physical interface characteristics
WG 4: Transport Layer
WG 5: Architecture and coordination of layers 1–4

SC18: Text and Office Systems

WG 1: User requirements
WG 2: Symbols and terminology
WG 3: Text structure
WG 4: Procedures for text interchange
WG 5: Text preparation and presentation
WG 6: Text preparation and interchange equipment
WG 7: Keyboards for office machines and data processing equipment
WG 8: Text

SC20: Data Cryptographic Techniques

WG 1: Secret key algorithms and applications
WG 2: Public key cryptosystems and use
WG 3: Use of encryption techniques in communications

SC21: Information Retrieval, Transfer and Management of OSI

WG 1: OSI architecture
WG 2: Computer graphics
WG 3: Databases
WG 4: OSI management
WG 5: Specific application services and protocols
WG 6: Session, Presentation, Common Application Service Elements

---

TABLE 1A-3. CCITT Study Groups

Number	Name
I	Definition, operation, and quality of service aspects of telegraph, data transmission, and telematic services (facsimile, Teletext, Videotex, etc.)
II	Operation of telephone network and ISDN
III	General tariff principles, including accounting
IV	Transmission maintenance of international lines, circuits, and chains of circuits; maintenance of automatic and semi-automatic networks
V	Protection against dangers and disturbances of electromagnetic origin
VI	Outside plant
VII	Data communications networks
VIII	Terminal equipment for telematic services (facsimile, Teletext, Videotex, etc.)
IX	Telegraph networks and terminal equipment
X	Languages and methods for telecommunications applications
XI	ISDN and telephone network switching and signaling
XII	Transmission performance of telephone networks and terminals
XV	Transmission system
XVII	Data transmission over the telephone network, including modems.
XVIII	Digital networks, including ISDN

U.S. National Committee (to CCITT)

As mentioned earlier, in the United States the State Department is the principal member of CCITT, and a National Committee is the coordination group for U.S. participation in CCITT. Moreover, advisory committees coordinate contributions to CCITT Study Groups. These U.S. CCITT Study Groups prepare actions for CCITT consideration:

Study Group A	U.S. Government Regulatory Policies
Study Group B	Telegraph Operations
Study Group C	Worldwide Telephone Network
Study Group D	Data Transmissions

Several other government organizations have important roles in developing international standards. The National Communications System (NCS) is a consortium of federal agencies that have large telecommunications capabilities. The NCS works very closely with other organizations such as the EIA, ISO, and

Layered Protocols and Network Architectures

TABLE 1A-4. Standards Organizations

ANSI	American National Standards Institute 1430 Broadway, New York, NY 10018 Telephone: (212) 354-3300
EIA	Electronic Industries Association 2001 Eye Street, Washington DC 20006 Telephone: (202) 457-4966
FED-STD	General Services Administration Specification Distribution Branch Building 197, Washington Navy Yard Washington, DC 20407 Telephone: (202) 472-1082
FIPS	U.S. Department of Commerce National Technical Information Service 5285 Port Royal Road, Springfield, VA 22161 Telephone: (703) 487-4650
CCITT	*Outside USA:* General Secretariat International Telecommunications Union Place des Nations, 1121 Geneva 20, Switzerland Telephone: 41 22 995111 *In the USA:* United States Department of Commerce National Technical Information Service 5285 Port Royal Road, Springfield, VA 22161 Telephone: (703) 487-4650
ISO	*Outside USA:* International Organization for Standardization Central Secretariat 1 rue de Varembe, CH-1211, Geneva, Switzerland Telephone: 41 22 341240 *In the USA:* American National Standards Institute (address above)
ECMA	European Computer Manufacturers Association 114 rue du Rhone, CH-1204, Geneva, Switzerland Telephone: 41 22 353634
IEEE	Institute of Electronic and Electrical Engineers 345 East 47th Street, New York, NY 10017 Telephone: (212) 705-7900
NIST	National Institute of Standards and Technology Technology Building Gaithersburg, MD 20899 Telephone: (301) 921–2731
CBEMA	Computer & Business Equipment Manufacturer's Assn. 311 First Street NW, Suite 300 Washington, DC 20001 Telephone: (202) 737-8888

CCITT. One of its jobs is to develop federal input to the international standards organizations, and NCS is using the OSI architecture for its work. Indeed, the majority of government organizations are using OSI.

The National Institute of Standards and Technology (NIST)

The NIST is also very active in international standards committees. Currently, it is working on the upper layers of the OSI standard. It is also responsible for the Federal Information Processing Standards (FIPS). A large number of ANSI documents are incorporated into the FIPS standards.

NIST is also responsible for the publication of GOSIP (U.S. Government Open Systems Interconnection Profile), a specification that defines the specific protocols to be used by U.S. Government agencies. GOSIP is explained in Chapter 8.

CHAPTER 2

OSI Suite Examples

INTRODUCTION

This chapter examines several implementations of the seven OSI Reference Model layers (suites). The first part of the chapter covers five standards that use the OSI, CCITT, ISO, and IEEE standards:

> GOSIP (U.S. Government Open Systems Interconnection Profile)
> COSAC (Canadian Open Systems Application Criteria)
> MAP (Manufacturing Automation Protocol)
> TOPS (Technical Office Products System)

The second part of the chapter explains four examples of prevalent operating systems that use layered protocols and, to a certain extent, the OSI-related standards:

> DOD DDN (Department of Defense's Defense Data Network)
> SNA (Systems Network Architecture, from IBM)
> DECnet (from Digital Equipment Corp)
> AdvanceNet (from Hewlett-Packard Corp)

This chapter is meant as a reference guide and is not written as a tutorial. Before reading this chapter, the uninitiated reader may wish to refer to subsequent chapters that describe the OSI layers and protocols.

U.S. GOVERNMENT OPEN SYSTEMS INTERCONNECTION PROFILE (GOSIP)

The U.S. Government Open Systems Interconnection Profile (GOSIP) is likely to play a major role in the future of the data communications industry. GOSIP is based on a series of workshops conducted at the National Institute of Standards and Technology (NIST) and represents the final agreements on a set of OSI protocols for computer networking. Its importance lies in the fact that it is to be used by government agencies in the acquisition of products and services. GOSIP provides implementation specifications from standards issued by the ISO, CCITT, IEEE, ANSI, EIA, and others.

Before discussing GOSIP in more detail, a few definitions are in order. In the U.S. Government, the acquisition authority is a contracting officer, who has the authority to enter into, terminate, and administer a government contract. GOSIP describes several procedures that the acquisition authority will administer in the areas of conformance, inter-operability, and performance testing.

The conformance testing procedures are set up by the acquisition authority. Conformance testing will be done on the protocols required by GOSIP. At the present time, conformance tests are being developed by several organizations. Regardless of who develops the testing specifications (and regardless of the specifications of the layers), GOSIP stipulates that the acquisition authority is responsible for determining which of the systems will be required for certification.

The acquisition authority may also specify that a specific set of systems must adhere to test inter-operability. This could be in addition to, or in lieu of conformance testing. The NIST recognizes the vehicles suitable for inter-operability testing.

Interestingly, GOSIP does not specify any performance criteria for performance testing. However, the acquisition authority must determine acceptable performance testing parameters and administer them within the organization of the acquisition authority.

GOSIP Architecture

The U.S. Government OSI architecture as seen through GOSIP is summarized in this section. Many of these specifications/recommendations are discussed in the following chapters. Our immediate purpose is to provide a framework for GOSIP in order to understand the implication of the U.S. Government's efforts toward standardization.

To begin our examination of GOSIP, please examine Figure 2-1. A larger variety of network protocols exist at the lower levels. This implementation is necessary because different protocols are needed to handle different communications requirements, such as local and wide area networks. As OSI and GOSIP evolve, more protocols will be included in the upper levels. Presently, the major high-level protocols are X.400 and the FTAM recommendations. The following

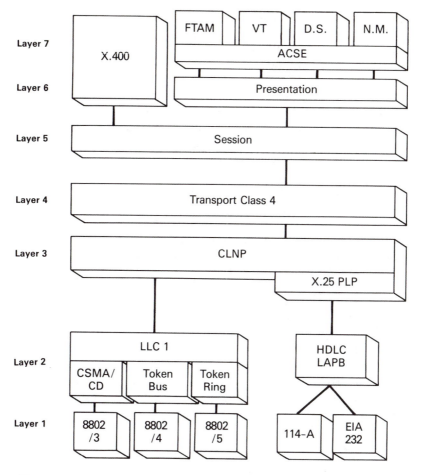

Note: Figure represents Red Book Architecture at the Application and Presentation Layers

FIGURE 2-1. GOSIP

section is based on the GOSIP specification. The specific references are provided in the chapters of this book that describe each specification. The reader is encouraged to contact the NBS for more detail on GOSIP.

GOSIP Layers

The physical layer is to be selected by the acquisition authority from the following protocols. In conjunction with the use of X.25 at the network layer, the choices are Interim MIL-STD-188-114 and EIA-232. In conjunction with the use of IEEE 802.2 Logical Link Control Type 1, the choices are IEEE 802.3 and IEEE 802.4.

The data link layer protocols are to be selected from the following specifications. High Level Data Link Control (HDLC) and its subset Link Access Procedure Balanced (LAPB) will be used in conjunction with X.25. The Logical Link Control (LLC) IEEE 802.2 protocol is to be used in conjunction with IEEE 802.3 or IEEE 802.4.

The network layer can use the ISO connectionless internetwork protocol (IP). The IP must be implemented for the internetworking of concatenated networks and single networks as well. ISO 8348 and ISO 8473 are selected for connectionless networks. X.25 is selected for connection-oriented networks.

The transport layer must use the transport specifications from the ISO and CCITT, in accordance with the workshop agreements. Transport class 4 (TP4) is the preferred protocol class. Transport class 0 (TP0) is to be used in conjunction (and as appropriate) with CCITT X.400.

The upper three layers use both CCITT and ISO recommendations. The session layer uses ISO IS 8326 and IS 8327 or CCITT X.215 and X.225. The presentation layer uses ISO DIS 8822, DIS 8823, DIS 8824, and DIS 8825. The application layer uses FTAM and the X.400 Message Handling Systems set of protocols.

CANADIAN OPEN SYSTEMS APPLICATION CRITERIA (COSAC)

On April 1, 1987, the Canadian federal government announced a policy of endorsing OSI as a federal information technology strategy in preference to any vendor-specific or installation-specific architecture. This policy, published as the Canadian Open Systems Application Criteria (COSAC), requires that federal government departments gradually migrate to systems based on the OSI standards. The COSAC suite is quite similar to the GOSIP suite. Its layers are summarized in Table 2-1.

TABLE 2-1. COSAC Standards

Layers	Standards
Networking Standards (Connection-oriented)	X.25 (1984, 1980), X.21, X.21 bis, 8878 using X.25 8880/2
Networking Standards (Connectionless)	8473, 8802/2, 8802/3, 8802/4, 8802/5
Transport Layer	8072, 8073 (Classes 0, 2, 4)
Session Layer	8326, 8327
Presentation Layer	8822, 8823
Application Layer	8571 FTAM, 8831/2 JTM, 9040/1 VT, X.400 MHS, 8649.50 CASE

MANUFACTURING AUTOMATION PROTOCOL (MAP)

The Manufacturing Automation Protocol (MAP) was established by General Motors Corporation in 1962 and later transferred to the Society of Manufacturing Engineers (SME). The intent of the specification is to provide for a common standard to achieve compatibility among communications devices that operate in manufacturing environments, for example, automobile assembly plants, petroleum manufacturing processes, and other factory floor devices.

In environments such as an automobile assembly plant, many vendors' products are connected to provide the communications services to the work stations on the floor. The MAP specification was designed to provide for a common reference for the different vendors' products so that they could interface without extensive protocol conversion facilities. By the end of the 1970s, GM found itself with over 20,000 programmable controllers, 2,000 robots, and 40,000 intelligent devices in its manufacturing operations. Approximately 15% of these devices could communicate outside their proprietary environment. Like many organizations, GM was spending an enormous amount of money on communications protocol converters.

General Motors developed the MAP specification in accordance with the Open Systems Interconnection (OSI) model. The MAP protocols correspond to the following OSI layers (see Figure 2-2):

Layer 7:   ISO CASE Kernel, Four ASEs: FTAM,
            Directory Service, Network Management, MMS

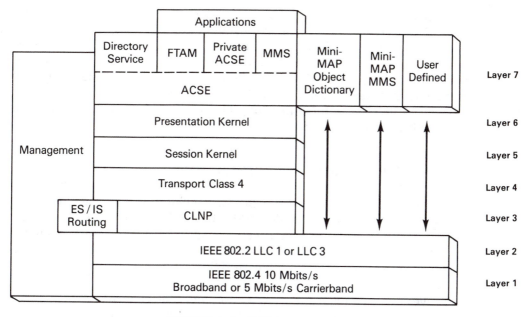

FIGURE 2–2. MAP Layers

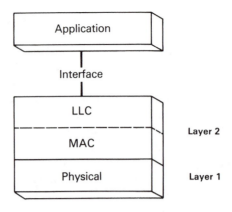

FIGURE 2-3. Mini-MAP

Layer 6:   ISO 8822, 8823, 8824, 8825
Layer 5:   ISO 8326, 8327, 8326/DAD2, 8327/DAD2
Layer 4:   ISO 8072 and 8073 Class 4
Layer 3:   ISO Connectionless Internet 8473 and others
Layer 2:   IEEE 802.2, various types and classes
Layer 1:   IEEE 802.4 Broadband (10 MBits/s) and Carrierband
           (5 MBits/s)

MiniMAP

Some applications may not need all the services of all the MAP layers. Other applications may be time-critical and cannot afford the delay incurred in executing the services in all the layers. If this is the case, the MiniMAP can be used. As depicted in Figure 2-3, MiniMAP uses layers 1 and 2 and an end-user application. While MiniMAP is certainly faster than the MAP, the application must interface directly with the data link layer. Moreover, the guarantee of the delivery of traffic is confined to a local channel only, and only one data unit can be outstanding at a time.

TECHNICAL AND OFFICE PRODUCTS SYSTEM (TOPS)

The Technical and Office Products System (TOPS) was developed by Boeing Computer Services and is now under SME. It is designed to be compatible with General Motors' MAP. However, even though the two systems are very similar, some differences exist at certain levels. The common protocols for the TOPS specifications are as follows (see Figure 2-4):

Layer 7:   ISO File Transfer, Access, and Management
           (FTAM) [ISO8571/1-4], ISO 8649/2, and 8650/2 for
           ACSE, ISO 9040, and 9041 for Virtual Terminal (VT),

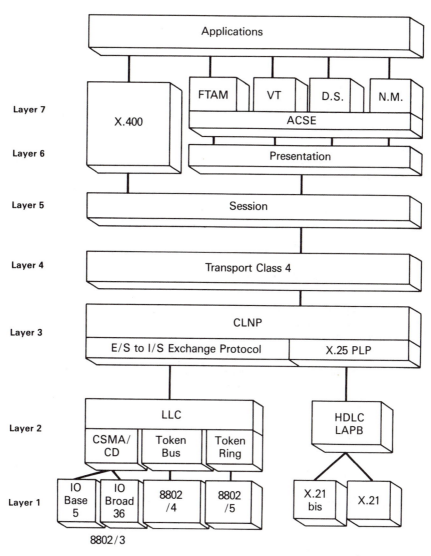

FIGURE 2-4. TOPS

ISO/DIS 9594/1 for Directory Services, ISO 7498/4 for Network Management

Layer 6:   Same as MAP

Layer 5:   Same as MAP

Layer 4:   Same as MAP

Layer 3:   Same as MAP plus ISO 8208

Layer 2:   IEEE 802.2 Logical Link Control and LAPB

Layer 1:   IEEE 802.3 CSMA/CD with baseband and broadband options

DEFENSE DATA NETWORK (DDN)

Introduction

In 1982 the Department of Defense (DOD) directed the establishment of the Defense Data Network (DDN), based on ARPANET technology. The ARPANET was designed under a 1969 Defense Advanced Research Projects Agency (DARPA) research and development program and was the pioneer of packet switching networks. Initially, ARPANET was designed as an experimental network to advance the embryonic computer resource sharing projects. It was also designed to provide communications between heterogeneous computers. As ARPANET evolved, it grew in functionality and complexity. In 1975, it was transferred to the Defense Communications Agency (DCA). Later, in 1983, the DDN was established based on the ARPANET technology.

DDN is a packet switching network grouped into two major functional areas: (1) the backbone network, which consists of the packet switches and the trunks between them, and (2) the access network, which consists of the user access lines connected to the backbone. Figure 2-5 illustrates the basic DDN layers and components.

Host systems can be connected to the packet switches using X.25 or the ARPANET 1822 interface specification. The host trunks can operate at 9.6 to 56 Kbits/s. Each host system can be directly connected to one or more packet switches by one or more links. The host systems may also connect directly or through a host front-end processor.

The terminals are connected directly to the network through a terminal access controller (TAC). Terminals also can be connected indirectly through the host. A TAC supports 63 terminals and a mini version of the TAC (the mini-TAC) supports 16 devices. The terminals are connected to the TACs or mini-TACs with direct lines or dial-up lines operating from 110 bits/s to 9600 bits/s. Each of the TACs is connected to a packet switch in the network via a link operating at 9.6 or 56 Kbits/s. The major layers and protocols of DDN are summarized in Table 2-2.

The DDN has been designed to provide survivability, security, and privacy. As a consequence, much of the equipment is configured with high-altitude electromagnetic pulse protection (HEMP) in the form of electromagnetic shielding, line isolation circuits, and surge-suppressing components. Some of the nodes are configured with uninterrupted power supply (UPS). Several of the nodes are also configured to operate with redundant equipment to prevent a single failure from isolating a node.

DDN is a dynamic routing network and adjusts itself to any damage without disrupting service to the surviving subscribers. Distributed routing allows the nodes to automatically route the data around damaged, congested, or destroyed links and switches. DDN also provides extensive monitoring of the system and enables a graceful degradation to route around damaged or congested areas.

DDN also provides secure traffic transmission, if needed, by using end-to-

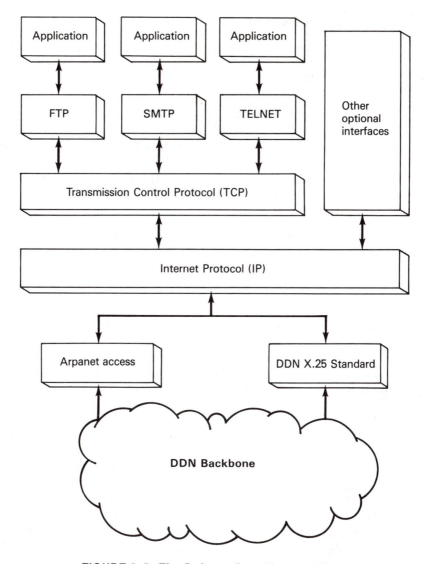

FIGURE 2-5. The Defense Data Network (DDN)

end encryption and other security measures. To provide this security, DDN is composed of two backbone networks, one classified and the other unclassified. The unclassified network uses encryption techniques based on the Bureau of Standards' Data Encryption Standard (DES). The classified network uses a higher level, military grade encryption and service.

As depicted in Table 2-2, the DDN users may use the DDN standard X.25 protocol (an adaptation of the CCITT specification), or the ARPANET (1822) interface protocol. Host computer systems must also use the TCP/IP protocol to communicate. Terminal users must use the TELNET to operate any DDN

TABLE 2-2. Layers and Protocols of DDN

- The DOD Standard Transmission Control Protocol/Internet Protocol (TCP/IP): used to permit the end-to-end flow control and accountability of data between two computer systems or between a computer system and a TAC.
- The standard X.25 protocol and the ARPANET (1822): network access protocols.
- The virtual terminal protocol TELNET: provides terminal access into the network using calling virtual terminal formats.
- The file transfer protocol (FTP): enables files to be transferred between computer systems.
- The simple mail transfer protocol (SMTP): provides the reliable transfer of electronic mail through the DDN.

terminal on the network. The TELNET protocol permits terminals to communicate not only directly with the host computers, but also indirectly with other computers. Each TAC provides specific device handlers to profile itself to specific terminal characteristics.

THE INTEGRATED SERVICES DIGITAL NETWORK (ISDN)

Presently, over 600 million telephone users can make a voice call practically anywhere in the world. Digital technology is extending this ubiquitous service to other forms of information. Ultimately, the Integrated Services Digital Network (ISDN) will provide this service for voice, data, text, graphics, music, and video.

In essence, ISDN is digital connectivity for the end user. At present, virtually every subscriber local loop is analog. This is acceptable for voice communications, but it is far too slow and unreliable for data communications. Data transmission now accounts for more than 10% of total network traffic and its use in North America is growing at a rate of 30% a year. ISDN is intended to extend digital technology over the subscriber loop to the end-user terminal by using common telephone wiring and a standard interface plug. Ideally, the numerous diverse interfaces will be reduced (or eliminated) with a limited set of common conventions.

ISDN has five major goals:

1. to provide a worldwide uniform digital network which supports a wide range of services and uses the same standards across different countries
2. to provide a uniform set of standards for digital transmission across and between networks
3. to provide a standard ISDN user interface, such that internal changes to a network are transparent to the end user
4. in conjunction with the third objective, to provide for end-user application independence—no consideration is made as to their characteristics in relation to the ISDN itself

5. as an adjunct to goals three and four, to provide portability of user DTEs and applications

ISDN Layers

The ISDN approach is to provide an end user with full support through the seven layers of the OSI Model (see Figure 2-6). In so doing, ISDN is divided into two kinds of services—the bearer services, responsible for providing support for the lower three levels of the seven-layer standard; and teleservices (for example, telephone, Teletex, Videotex, message handling) responsible for providing support through all seven layers of the model and generally making use of the underlying lower-level capabilities of bearer services. The services are referred to as low-layer and high-layer functions, respectively. The ISDN functions are allocated according to the layering principles of the OSI and CCITT standards. Various entities of the layers are used to provide full end-to-end capability. These layered capabilities may be supplied by Postal Telephone and Telegraph Administrations (PTTs), telephone companies, or other suppliers. Subsequent

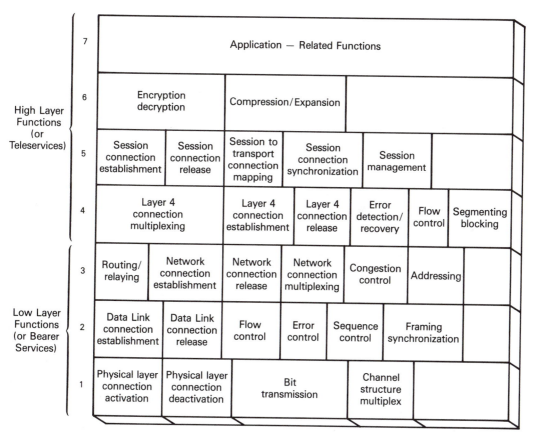

FIGURE 2-6. The ISDN Layers

chapters will explain the ISDN layers and their relationship to the OSI Reference Model.

SYSTEMS NETWORK ARCHITECTURE

IBM introduced Systems Network Architecture (SNA) in September 1973 as its major commitment to communications systems and networks. By 1977, 350 SNA sites existed. By year end 1978, the number had increased to 1250 and, by 1978 over 4000 installations had SNA. Today, over 20,000 licensed SNA sites are in operation. Even if the reader does not use SNA, it is a good idea to understand its basic features, since it is so pervasive in the industry.

SNA is a specification (of many, many documents) describing the architecture for a distributed data processing network. It defines the rules and protocols for the interaction of the components (computers, terminals, software) in the network. SNA uses many of the layering concepts found in the OSI Model, but most of its layers are not compatible with the prevalent CCITT, ISO, and IEEE standards. However, IBM has a wide array of protocol converters that allow a user to interface IBM equipment with OSI-based products.

SNA Services and Layers

SNA networks use the layering concept. To add confusion in these matters, various IBM documents use different terms to describe the upper layers. Moreover, some of the layers' boundaries are ill-defined. Figure 2-7 illustrates the SNA layers, as well as a comparison to the DECnet and Hewlett-Packard (HP) layers. (The DECnet and HP layers are examined next.) OSI is shown in Figure 2-8.

SNA Function Management. This layer provides a very wide range of services. It corresponds to the OSI application and presentation services. The layer provides for common formats between end users and for common device control characters between dissimilar devices. Presentation services provides compression and compaction facilities. The layer also provides for a common set of display screen formats between applications. (The application program need only transmit the name of the screen format.) This layer also performs sync-point processing and selected profiles for the user session. It is also responsible for providing network services.

Network services is divided into several categories. First, network operator services facilitates communication among network operators and Systems Services Control Points (SSCPs). Second, configuration services is responsible for activating/deactivating links, loading programs into SNA nodes, and maintaining tables within SSCP containing the name, address, and status of each link and Network Addressable Unit (NAU) in the domain in the network. Configuration services are invoked by a network operator using a SSCP-PU session.

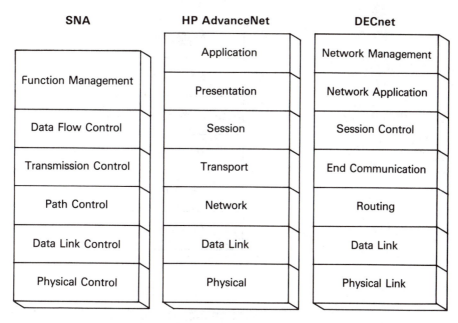

SNA	HP AdvanceNet	DECnet
Function Management	Application	Network Management
	Presentation	Network Application
Data Flow Control	Session	Session Control
Transmission Control	Transport	End Communication
Path Control	Network	Routing
Data Link Control	Data Link	Data Link
Physical Control	Physical	Physical Link

FIGURE 2-7. Comparison of Layered Protocols

Third, session services is responsible for conversion of the logical network names provided by Logical Units (LUs) into corresponding network addresses. This service is similar to the address mapping feature found in ISO's transport layer. Fourth, the maintenance and management services performs diagnostic tasks and error testing. Last, the application-to-application services provides for program-to-program communications support.

Data Flow Control Layer. This layer is roughly analogous to the OSI session layer and supports full-duplex dialogues between network-addressable units. It also supports sending a "chain" of data until it is complete. The chaining allows the layer to group unidirectional, related messages together and treat them as a whole. This is a useful feature when downline loading files or jobs to other sites in the network. The Data Flow Control Layer also provides for brackets. This permits grouping bidirectional, related messages together that move between two logical units, thus keeping messages related to one transaction logically together.

Messages transmitted through an SNA network are acknowledged by the LUs that receive them. Data Flow Control allows the receiving LU to provide a response for every message (definite response), a response only under error conditions (exception response), or no response at all (no response). This capability allows the network user to tailor the quality of service and data integrity in accordance with the individual applications requirement. This layer also manages the sequence numbers in the SNA protocol data unit.

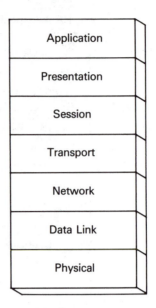

FIGURE 2–8. The OSI Layers

Transmission Control Layer. This layer is similar to the OSI transport layer and maintains the status of an active session, provides for sequencing of the data messages, and paces the flow of data into and out of user sessions. It also routes data to appropriate points within a network unit. Transmission Control provides session window management by session-level pacing, which allows the LUs to control the number of messages processed. This prevents the overrun of LUs that have limited processing and buffering capabilities. Transmission Control also provides headers (request/response header, or RH) to the message for the chaining, bracket, and pacing functions. Encryption and decryption can also be obtained in this layer.

Path Control Layer. The Path Control Layer has two primary responsibilities, routing and flow control. Routing through the SNA nodes is accomplished by Path Control examining network names in the message and determining the appropriate link (or perhaps a group of links) in order for the message to move its destination. The layer resolves addressing for both subareas and elements. Path Control also performs message segmenting, which is similar to the OSI segmenting functions discussed earlier. SNA allows different segment sizes for each link or group of links. In addition, Path Control also groups messages together. This is a useful function for reducing channel input/output interrupts and operations. Path Control provides for various classes of service such as fast response, secure routes, or more reliable connections. Three transmission priorities (high, medium, and low) are provided.

The layer also contains a flow-control mechanism, called virtual-route pacing, to limit the flow of data from a transmitting subarea node. SNA assigns

OSI Suite Examples

virtual routes to the two subareas involved in a session. The virtual route is assigned to an explicit route. The concept is similar to session-level pacing found in Transmission Control, but virtual-route pacing affects the flow of data in all sessions assigned to a virtual route between two subareas. Session-level pacing applies only to individual sessions.

Data Link Control and Physical Layers. These layers are equivalent to the two lower OSI layers. The data link layer is implemented with SDLC and the physical layer is available with RS-232-C, X.21, and other specifications.

DIGITAL NETWORK ARCHITECTURE (DECnet OR DNA)

DECnet is the major data communications network offering from the Digital Equipment Corporation. Developed as a distributed network, it supports a wide range of applications and programs. DECnet was designed to achieve the following goals:

- to create a common user interface across varied applications and implementations
- to provide resource-sharing capabilities to data, computers, and peripheral devices
- to support distributed computation, allowing cooperating programs to execute in different computers in a network
- to support a wide range of communication facilities, such a Ethernet and X.25
- to maintain a high level of availability, even in the event of node or link failure

DECnet Layers

DECnet is designed around the concept of layered protocols (see Figure 2-7). It consists of seven layers.

The *Physical Link Layer* is the lowest layer. It is quite similar to the layers of other networks in that it encompasses specifications such as RS232, X.21, and CCITT V.24/V.28.

The *Data Link Layer* is quite similar to the data link layer of other specifications. It controls the communications path between adjacent nodes. The data link layer ensures the error-free transmission of data across an otherwise error-laden link. Many of the data link layer's functions are implemented through Ethernet and Digital Data Communication Message Protocol (DDCMP). Interestingly, DEC includes its X.25 module in the data link layer.

The *Routing Layer* (previously called the transport layer) provides the routing functions between nodes. It also is responsible for network congestion control and determining the lapsed time of a packet within the network.

The *End Communication Layer* (which was previously called the Network Services Layer) is similar to the Transport Layer of the OSI Reference Model. It is responsible for the end-to-end error control, segmentation, reassembly, and data flow control.

The *Session Control Layer* is responsible for a logical communications between users. For example, it provides the mapping of node names to specific node addresses. It identifies end users and activates and deactivates sessions between users. It also validates sessions between users.

The *Network Application Layer* provides for higher level functions such as remote file access, data transfer, and interactive terminal usage. The Network Application Layer contains functions similar to the application and presentation layers of the OSI Reference Model. This layer provides for the data access protocol (DAP), discussed later, and also provides the gateway access protocols to SNA and X.25.

The *Network Management Layer* is used principally for the controlling and monitoring of the network operations. For example, it permits downline loading of resources, testing links, and setting and displaying the states of links and nodes.

Finally, the *User Layer* contains most of the user-supplied routines. It also contains some DECnet systems, such as the network control program. The User Layer has direct access to the Network Management, Network Application, and Session Control Layers. The Network Management Layer has direct access to all the other layers.

HEWLETT-PACKARD'S ADVANCENET

Hewlett-Packard (HP) was a proponent of OSI long before some of the other major manufacturers jumped on the OSI bandwagon. HP was a founding member of the Corporation for Open Systems (COS) and is an active member of the European-based Standards Promotion and Application Group (SPAG). Its employees chair a number of the IEEE and ECMA standards groups.

Moreover, unlike some other companies, HP has committed itself to a timed migration to the OSI standards. Interestingly, its intent is to have migrated from the TCP/IP protocols within the 1990–92 time period.

Hewlett-Packard's "OSI on a Board"

Hewlett-Packard has announced its support of several variations of the OSI suites. One of its primary endeavors is OSI Express. The HP OSI Express implements all seven of the OSI layers on one integrated board. It contains a 12.5 MHz Motorola 68020 processor, two HP VLSI chips, one Mbyte of dynamic RAM, 32 Kbytes of ROM, and an IEEE 802.4 broadband or baseband interface. The card can be connected directly to a host system, with the ROM used to download instructions from the host to the board. The RAM supports up to 100 connections of computers or other devices. The OSI Express stack is described in Table 2-3.

TABLE 2-3.   The Hewlett-Packard OSI Express Stack of Protocols

Layer Name and Number	Standard(s) Used
Application (7)	ISO 8650 CASE
Presentation (6)	ISO 8823 Kernel
Session (5)	ISO 8327 Basic Combined Subset (BAS)
Transport (4)	Transport Class 4
Network (3)	ISO 8473 CLNP, ISO 9542
Data Link (2)	IEEE 802.2, IEEE 802.4
Physical (1)	IEEE 802.4: 5 MBits/s for carrierband and 10 MBits/s for broadband

SUMMARY AND CONCLUSIONS

This chapter reviewed some of the major implementations of the OSI Model such as GOSIP, MAP, and TOP. Several approaches used by prominent vendors such as IBM, Digital Equipment Corporation, and Hewlett Packard were also examined. The chapter also provided a general view of one of the pioneers of layered network protocols, the Department of Defense Data Network (DDN). These standards and vendor implementations are paving the way for more ambitious undertakings in the OSI arena.

CHAPTER 3

The Physical Layer

INTRODUCTION

The standards groups, the computer industry, and vendors have developed many specifications defining the interfaces of DCEs, such as modems and digital service units (DSUs), with DTEs, such as terminals and computers. Acceptance of these specifications has made it possible to interface equipment from different vendors.

Our goal in this chapter is to gain an understanding of the concepts of physical level signaling and to review the prevalent recommended standards and vendor products. The reader is encouraged to obtain the specific document if more detail is needed on an interface. These documents are cited throughout the chapter.

Physical level protocols (or physical level interfaces) are so named because the DTE and DCE are physically connected by either wires and cables or by sky or ground wave signals through the atmosphere. Physical level interfaces perform several functions:

- provide data transfer across the interface between the DTE and DCE
- provide control signals between the devices
- provide clocking signals to synchronize data flow and regulate the bit rate
- provide for electrical ground
- provide the mechanical connectors (such as pins, sockets, and plugs)

The OSI Model views the physical level in abstract terms and does not stipulate the physical medium such as coaxial cable, twisted pair, optical fiber, etc. However, some of the specific standards that use the OSI concepts do indeed specify the medium. For example, the ISDN basic rate channel is four-wire twisted pair.

It should be noted that the OSI physical layer service data unit (SDU) is one bit and has no header or trailer control information, yet many physical level specialists consider that the physical level must use headers to properly control and synchronize the circuit. For example, the T1 and ISDN framing conventions are considered by some people to be a physical layer function.

Where the Physical Level Resides

It is sometimes assumed that a physical level interface encompasses only the interchange circuit(s) between the DTE and the DCE. While this view is correct for some products and standards, the physical level also includes the signaling between the two DCEs (see Figure 3-1).

The CCITT publishes the V-Series physical level protocols to include both the DTE-to-DCE interface and the DCE-to-DCE interfaces. Other standards, such as EIA-232, encompass only the DTE-to-DCE side of the interface. Even though EIA-232 does not specify the DCE-to-DCE exchange, many vendors use the relevant portion of the CCITT V-Series recommendations and/or the AT&T/Bell specifications to describe this part of the physical level interface. For example, this is a practice of the Hayes modem products. The CCITT I Series specifies a digital physical level interface.

Physical layer functions also include the tasks of signal coding, decoding, and modulation and demodulation. If these topics are not familiar, please refer

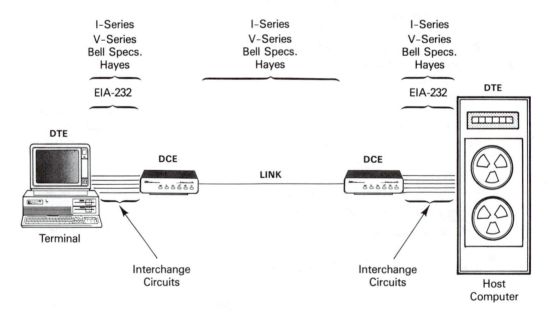

FIGURE 3-1. The Physical Layer Interfaces

to the tutorial in Appendix 3A at the end of this chapter, because this chapter is meant to be primarily a reference guide.

Physical Layer Primitives and State Diagrams

Like other layers of the OSI Model, the physical layer services can be obtained with primitives. The CCITT specifies these primitives in X.211. They are quite simple, and are concerned primarily with the physical activation and deactivation of the circuit and the transfer of data across the physical interface. The primitives are summarized in Table 3-1.

The physical layer primitives have not seen much use, in comparison to the primitives in the other layers, mainly because many physical layer interfaces and protocols were in place and embedded into the vendor's product line before these primitives were published.

The physical level can also be modeled with a state diagram, as shown in Figure 3-2. The states can be entered in various combinations to provide for full-duplex, half-duplex, or simplex operations.

CONTRIBUTORS TO PHYSICAL LAYER STANDARDS

The specifications for the operations of modems, digital service units, and other DCE type components with user devices (DTEs) are published by the CCITT, the Electronic Industries Association (EIA), the Institute of Electrical and Electronic Engineers (IEEE) and others. In addition, the International Standards Organization (ISO) publishes specifications on the mechanical connectors that connect DCEs with DTEs. In North America, the AT&T/Bell specifications have been accepted as de facto standards, and in the past few years the Hayes modem specifications have taken a large share of the market with the PC-based modem product line.

The OSI Model does not have much to say about the physical level. One reason is that many physical level protocols were in place before the Model was developed. The second reason is that ISO, the principal architect of OSI, has traditionally left this level to other standards groups, such as the CCITT

TABLE 3-1. Physical Layer Service Primitives

Phase	Primitive
Connection Activation	PH-Activate request
	PH-Activate indication
Data Transfer	PH-Data request
	PH-Data indication
Connection Deactivation	PH-Deactivate request
	PH-Deactivate indication

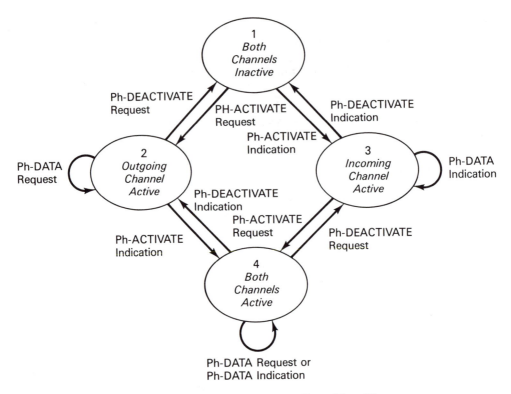

FIGURE 3-2. Physical Layer State Transition Diagram

and the IEEE. Nonetheless, we shall see that OSI conventions still apply to the physical level.

THE CCITT V-SERIES RECOMMENDATIONS AND EIA-232-D

The majority of data transmissions take place over the telephone line, or over lines that are engineered to the telephone line specifications. In recognition of this fact, the standards organizations have published many recommendations defining how these connections and communications are to be made. The CCITT V-Series recommendations are the most widely used physical level specifications in the world.

Table 3-2 summarizes the most widely used V-Series interfaces. A brief summary of Table 3-2 is provided for the reader in Box 3-1.

The ISO publishes many standards, some of which describe the mechanical connectors used by computers, terminals, modems, and other devices. Figure 3-3 shows the major ISO physical level connectors.

EIA-232-D is one of the most widely used physical interfaces in the world. It is sponsored by the Electronic Industries Association (EIA) and is most prev-

TABLE 3-2.   CCITT V-Series Interfaces

Series Number	Channel Line Speed	Separation	Modulation Rate	Carrier Frequency	Use of V.2	FDX or HDX	Synchronous or Asynchronous	Modulation Technique	Bits Encoded	Backward Channel	Switched Lines	Leased Lines	Use of V.25	Use of V.28	ISO Pin Connector	Equalization	Scrambler
V.21	300	FD	300	1080 & 1750	Yes	FDX	Either	FS	1:1	ND	Yes	0	Yes	Yes	2110	ND	ND
V.22	1200	FD	600	1200 & 2400	Yes	FDX	Either	PS	2:1	ND	Yes	PP 2W	Yes	Yes	2110	Fixed	Yes
V.22	600	FD	600	1200 & 2400	Yes	FDX	Either	PS	1:1	ND	Yes	PP 2W	Yes	Yes	2110	Fixed	Yes
V.22 bis	2400	FD	600	1200 & 2400	ND	FDX	Either	QAM	4:1	ND	Yes	PP 2W	Yes	Yes	2110	Either	Yes
V.22 bis	1200	FD	600	1200 & 2400	ND	FDX	Either	QAM	2:1	ND	Yes	PP 2W	Yes	Yes	2110	Either	Yes
V.23	600	NA	600	1300 & 1700	ND	HDX	Either	FM	NA	Yes	Yes	0	ND	Yes	2110	ND	ND
V.23	1200	NA	1200	1300 & 2100	ND	HDX	Either	FM	NA	Yes	Yes	0	ND	Yes	2110	ND	ND
V.26	2400	4-Wire	1200	1800	Yes	FDX	Synchronous	PS	2:1	Yes	No	PP MP 4W	ND	Yes	2110	ND	ND
V.26 bis	2400	NA	1200	1800	Yes	HDX	Synchronous	PS	2:1	Yes	Yes	No	Yes	Yes	2110	Fixed	ND
V.26 bis	1200	NA	1200	1800	Yes	HDX	Synchronous	PS	1:1	Yes	Yes	No	Yes	Yes	2110	Fixed	ND
V.26 ter	2400	EC	1200	1800	Yes	Either	Either	PS	2:1	ND	Yes	PP 2W	Yes	Yes	2110	Either	Yes
V.26 ter	1200	EC	1200	1800	Yes	Either	Either	PS	1:1	ND	Yes	PP 2W	Yes	Yes	2110	Either	Yes
V.27	4800	ND	1600	1800	Yes	Either	Synchronous	PS	3:1	Yes	No	Yes	ND	Yes	2110	Manual	Yes
V.27 bis	4800	4-Wire	1600	1800	Yes	Either	Synchronous	PS	3:1	Yes	No	2W 4W	ND	Yes	2110	Adaptive	Yes
V.27 bis	2400	4-Wire	1200	1800	Yes	Either	Synchronous	PS	2:1	Yes	No	2W 4W	ND	Yes	2110	Adaptive	Yes
V.27 ter	4800	None	1600	1800	Yes	HDX	Synchronous	PS	3:1	Yes	Yes	No	Yes	Yes	2110	Adaptive	Yes
V.27 ter	2400	None	1200	1800	Yes	HDX	Synchronous	PS	2:1	Yes	Yes	No	Yes	Yes	2110	Adaptive	Yes
V.29	9600	4-Wire	2400	1700	Yes	Either	Synchronous	QAM	4:1	ND	No	PP 4W	ND	Yes	2110	Adaptive	Yes
V.29	7200	4-Wire	2400	1700	Yes	Either	Synchronous	PS	3:1	ND	No	PP 4W	ND	Yes	2110	Adaptive	Yes
V.29	4800	4-Wire	2400	1700	Yes	Either	Synchronous	PS	2:1	ND	No	PP 4W	ND	Yes	2110	Adaptive	Yes
V.32	9600	EC	2400	1800	Yes	FDX	Synchronous	QAM	4:1	ND	Yes	PP 2W	Yes	Yes	2110	Adaptive	Yes
V.32	9600	EC	2400	1800	Yes	FDX	Synchronous	TCM	5:1	ND	Yes	PP 2W	Yes	Yes	2110	Adaptive	Yes
V.32	4800	EC	2400	1800	Yes	FDX	Synchronous	QAM	2:1	ND	Yes	PP 2W	Yes	Yes	2110	Adaptive	Yes
V.33	14000	4-Wire	2400	1800	Yes	FDX	Synchronous	TCM	7:1	ND	FS	PP FW	ND	ND	2110	Adaptive	Yes
V.35	48000	4-Wire	NA	100000	ND	FDX	Synchronous	AM-FM	NA	ND	No	Yes	ND	ND	ND	Adaptive	Yes

ND = Not Defined

NA = Not Applicable

BOX 3-1. Explanation of Table 3-2.

A V Series number may be entered into the table more than once. This means the recommended standard permits more than one option. The initials ND mean "not defined" in the specification. The initials NA mean "not applicable."

Entries	Explanation
Line Speed	Speed in bits per second (bit/s).
Channel Separation	If the recommended standard permits multiple channels, the method of deriving the channels is noted as: FD: Frequency Division 4-Wire: Each set of wires carries a channel EC: Echo Cancellation Note that the standard may also use a backward channel.
Modulation Rate	The rate of the signal change of the carrier on the channel; in baud.
Carrier Frequency	The frequency of the carrier or carriers used on the channel(s). The carrier(s) may be altered to yield different modulated frequencies. For example, the V.21 modem uses two mean frequencies of 1080 and 1750. Each carrier is then modulated with a frequency shift of $+100$ Hz for binary 1 and -100 Hz for binary 0.
Use of V.2	A CCITT specification, which establishes specified power ranges and levels.
Full Duplex or Half Duplex	FDX: Full Duplex HDX: Half Duplex
Synchronous or Asynchronous	"Either" means the specification will work with one or the other.
Modulation Technique	The description of the modulation technique where: FS: Frequency Shift PS: Phase Shift QAM: Quadrature Amplitude Modulation AM: Amplitude Modulation TCM: Trellis Coded Modulation
Bits Encoded	Describes the number of bits encoded per signal change (baud). For example, 2:1 means two bits encoded per baud.
Backward Channel	Describes an alternate channel used for transmission in a reverse direction, at a lower rate, usually 75 baud. Its absence does not imply that the modem is only HDX, because a FDX modem may not use a backward channel.
Switched Lines Leased Lines	Describes the use of conventional dial-up circuits. 0: Optional 2W: Two-wire PP: Point-to-point 4W: Four-wire MP: Multipoint
V.25	A CCITT specification which describes the procedures for automatic dial-and-answer. May also offer features on call and answer beyond that of V.25.
V.28	A CCITT specification which describes the electrical characteristics of unbalanced circuits.
ISO Pin Connector	Specifications from the International Standards Organization that describe the actual connector (dimensions, etc.) between the DTE and DCE.
Equalization	A technique to improve signal quality where: Fixed: Established when modem left the factory Adaptive: Changes and adjusts to received signal Either: Can be fixed or adaptive
Scrambler	A technique for altering the data stream to enhance the timing and synchronization between the two modems on the circuit.

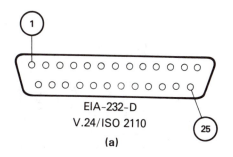

EIA–232–D

V.24/ISO 2110

(a)

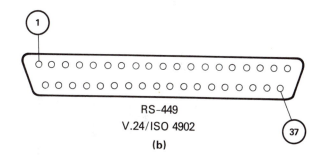

RS–449

V.24/ISO 4902

(b)

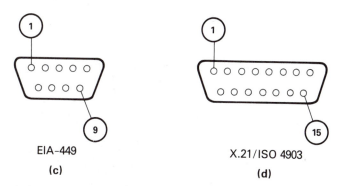

EIA–449

(c)

X.21/ISO 4903

(d)

FIGURE 3-3. ISO Connectors

alent in North America. It specifies 25 interchange circuits for DTE/DCE use. The circuits are actually 25 pin connections and sockets (see Figure 3-4). It is rare that all circuits are used; most devices utilize eight or fewer pins. Later discussions in this chapter will examine EIA-232-D in more detail.

Prevalent V-Series Interfaces and Modems

Several V-Series recommendations are widely used throughout the industry, and if you use a personal computer or a terminal with a telephone line to connect to another computer, it is quite likely you have used a V-Series modem. This section describes several prevalent V-Series interfaces.

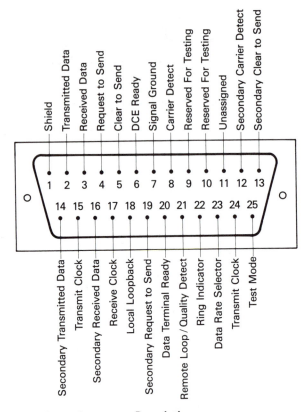

Pin	Circuit	Source	Description
1	AA	—	Shield
2	BA	DTE	Transmitted Data
3	BB	DCE	Received Data
4	CA	DTE	Request to Send
5	CB	DCE	Clear to Send
6	CC	DCE	DCE Ready
7	AB	—	Signal Ground
8	CF	DCE	Received Line Signal Detector
9	—	—	Reserved for Data Set Testing
10	—	—	Reserved for Data Set Testing
11	—	—	Unassigned
12	SCF	DCE	Secondary Received Line Signal Detector
13	SCB	DCE	Secondary Clear to Send
14	SBA	DTE	Secondary Transmitted Data
15	DB	DCE	Transmission Signal Element Timing
16	SBB	DCE	Secondary Received Data
17	DD	DCE	Receiver Signal Element Timing
18	LL	—	Local Loopback
19	SCA	DTE	Secondary Request to Send
20	CD	DTE	Data Terminal Ready
21	RL/CG	DCE	Remote Loopback / Signal Quality Detector
22	CE	DTE	Ring Indicator
23	CH	DTE	Data Signal Rate Selector
23	CI	DCE	Data Signal Rate Selector
24	DA	DTE	Transmit Signal Element Timing
25	TM	—	Test Mode

FIGURE 3-4. EIA-232-D (DTE Connector)

V.22 bis.   Many personal computers use V.22 bis for medium speed, dial-up systems. For example, the newer Hayes modems use V.22 bis as an option.

V.22 bis modems separate the channels by frequency division. Then each channel is quadrature amplitude modulated (QAM). A 600-baud signal carries 4 bits per baud (quadbits). Carrier frequencies are 1200 Hz for the low channel and 2400 Hz for the high channel. Both synchronous and start/stop transmissions are supported.

V.26 ter.   V.26 ter is considered by some to be a contender to V.22 bis. The modem operates with full-duplex (FDX) mode on switched and point-to-point leased circuits, and half-duplex (HDX) mode on switched and point-to-point leased circuits. Channel separation is done by echo cancellation, and differential phase-shift modulation is performed for each channel with synchronous line transmission at 1200 baud.

V.27.   V.27 is based on phase modulation. It is capable of operating in full-duplex (FDX) mode or half-duplex (HDX) mode and it uses differential eight-phase modulation with synchronous mode of operation. It can provide a backward (supervisory) channel at modulation rates up to 75 baud in each direction of transmission; the use of these channels is optional.

V.29.   V.29 is found in many North American and European products. The Bell V.29 modem is based on CCITT V.29. This modem operates in full-duplex (FDX) or half-duplex (HDX) mode using amplitude and phase modulation with synchronous transmission. It also provides for fallback data rates of 7200 and 4800 bits/s. The carrier frequency is 1700 Hz.

This recommendation uses a modulation rate of 2400 baud and provides for three types of bit encoding for the three available speeds. At 9600 bits/s, the bits are divided into groups of four (quadbits). The first bit is used to represent amplitude and the other three bits provide for 8 possible phase shifts.

At a fallback rate of 7200 bits/s, the same phase shifts are used, but the "amplitude bit" is not used. At a fallback rate of 4800 bits/s, the phase changes use 0°, 90°, 180°, and 270° shifts.

V.32.   These modems are relatively new to the industry and have created considerable interest because they can operate at rates up to 9600 bits/s at full-duplex on a dial-up, two-wire telephone network. This modem provides full-duplex mode of operation on switched and 2-wire point-to-point leased circuits. It provides channel separation by echo cancellation techniques. Quadrature amplitude modulation (QAM) is used for each channel, with synchronous line transmission at 2400 baud.

V.35.   Most people view V.35 as a 56 Kbits/s DCE. While this is the case in North America, the actual specification calls for the DCE to operate at 48 Kbits/s. The data signal is translated to the 60–108 KHz band as a sideband-suppressed carrier AM signal. The carrier frequency operates at 100 KHz. The interface cable is balanced twisted pair. In North America, the V.35 interface is typically used on a 56 KBits/s line.

THE CCITT V.24 AND V.28 RECOMMENDATION

The V-Series modems use V.24, as do standards such as EIA-232-D, although EIA-232-D uses different designations for the circuits. The V.24 100 series interchange circuits are listed in Table 3-3.

V.28 is applied to almost all interchange circuits operating below the limit of 20,000 bits/s. The recommendation provides specifications for other electrical interfaces as well. EIA-232-D uses this specification with some minor variations. On a general level, the signals must conform to the characteristics described below.

For data interchange circuits, the signal is in the binary 1 condition when the voltage on the interchange circuit measured at the interchange point is more negative than minus 3 volts. The signal is in the binary 0 condition when the voltage is more positive than plus 3 volts.

For control and timing interchange circuits, the circuit is considered ON when the voltage on the interchange circuit is more positive than plus 3 volts, and is considered OFF when the voltage is more negative than minus 3 volts.

EIA-232-D

The Electronic Industries Association (EIA) sponsors the EIA-232-D standard. It is used extensively in North America as well as other parts of the world, and the reader should become familiar with its characteristics. Table 3-4 describes the interchange circuits of EIA-232-D. These circuits are 25-pin connections and sockets (depicted in Figure 3-4). The terminal pins plug into the modem sockets. As stated earlier, rarely are all the circuits used; many modems utilize only 4 to 12 pins.

The EIA-232-D circuits perform one of four functions:

- data transfer across the interface
- control of signals across interface
- clocking signals to synchronize data flow and regulate the bit rate
- Electrical ground

The functional descriptions of the interchange circuits are summarized in Table 3-5. Each offering should be examined carefully, since many vendors do not use these circuits as specified by EIA-232-D.

EIA-232-D and the ISO/CCITT Standards

Many people are perplexed by the many initials and acronyms they read in their modem vendors' marketing material. Let us clear up some of these myster-

TABLE 3-3.   V.24 Interchange Circuits

Interchange Circuit Number	Interchange Circuit Name
102	Signal ground or common return
102a	DTE common return
102b	DCE common return
102c	Common return
103	Transmitted data
104	Received data
105	Request to send
106	Ready for sending
107	Data set ready
108/1	Connect data set to line
108/2	Data terminal ready
109	Data channel received line signal detector
110	Data signal quality detector
111	Data signal rate selector (DTE)
112	Data signal rate selector (DCE)
113	Transmitter signal element timing (DTE)
114	Transmitter signal element timing (DCE)
115	Receiver signal element timing (DCE)
116	Select standby
117	Standby indicator
118	Transmitted backward channel data
119	Received backward channel data
120	Transmit backward channel line signal
121	Backward channel ready
122	Backward channel received line signal detector
123	Backward channel signal quality detector
124	Select frequency groups
125	Calling indicator
126	Select transmit frequency
127	Select receive frequency
128	Receiver signal element timing (DTE)
129	Request to receive
130	Transmit backward tone
131	Received character timing
132	Return to nondata mode
133	Ready for receiving
134	Received data present
136	New signal
140	Loopback/maintenance test
141	Local loopback
142	Test indicator
191	Transmitted voice answer
192	Received voice answer

TABLE 3-4. EIA-232-D Interchange Circuits

Interchange Circuit	CCITT Equivalent	Description	End	Data From DCE	Data To DCE	Control From DCE	Control To DCE	Timing From DCE	Timing To DCE
AB	102	Signal ground/ common return	X						
BA	103	Transmitted data			X				
BB	104	Received data		X					
CA	105	Request to send					X		
CB	106	Clear to send				X			
CC	107	DCE ready				X			
CD	108.2	DTE ready					X		
CE	125	Ring indicator				X			
CF	109	Received line signal detector				X			
CG	110	Signal quality detector				X			
CH	111	Data signal rate selector (DTE)					X		
CI	112	Data signal rate selector (DCE)				X			
DA	113	Transmitter signal element timing (DTE)							X
DB	114	Transmitter signal element timing (DCE)						X	
DD	115	Receiver signal element timing (DCE)						X	
SBA	118	Secondary transmitted data			X				
SBB	119	Secondary received data	X						
SCA	120	Secondary request to send					X		
SCB	121	Secondary clear to send				X			
SCF	122	Secondary received line signal detector				X			
RL	140	Remote loopback					X		
LL	141	Local loopback					X		
TM	142	Test mode				X			

ies. They are really quite simple, once we understand the relationship of EIA-232-D and the ISO/CCITT standards.

The CCITT publishes the V.24 specification, from which the ISO connector arrangements and EIA-232-D pin assignments are derived. The ISO establishes the specification for the mechanical dimensions of the pins and connector, and EIA-232-D uses the ISO 2110 connector. EIA-232-D also uses two of the V-Series standards, V.24 and V.28.

At first glance, the EIA-232-D interface seems very confusing, but it simply uses the following CCITT/ISO recommendations:

Electrical: CCITT V.28
Functional: CCITT V.24

The Physical Layer

TABLE 3-5. EIA-232P-D Interchange Circuits

Circuit AB: Signal Ground or Common Return. This conductor establishes the common ground reference potential for all interchange.

Circuit BA: Transmitted Data. Signals are generated by the DTE and are transferred to the DCE.

Circuit BB: Received Data. Signals are generated by the receiving DCE to receiving DTE.

Circuit CA: Request to Send. Used to condition the local data communication equipment for data transmission and, on a half-duplex channel, to control the direction of data transmission of the local data communication equipment.

Circuit CB: Clear to Send. Signals generated by the DCE to indicate whether or not the DCE is ready to transmit data.

Circuit CC: DCE Ready. Signals used to indicate the status of the local DCE:

Circuit CD: Data Terminal Ready. Controls connecting the DCE to the communications channel. The ON condition prepares the data communication equipment to be connected to the communications channel.

Circuit CE: Ring Indicator. Indicates that a ringing signal is being received on the communications channel.

Circuit CF: Received Line Signal Detector. The ON condition is presented when the DCE is receiving a signal which meets its suitability criteria. These criteria are established by the data communications equipment manufacturer.

Circuit CG: Signal Quality Detector. Indicates whether or not there is a high probability of an error in the received data. An ON condition is maintained whenever there is no reason to believe that an error has occurred.

Circuit CH: Data Signal Rate Selector (DTE Source). Selects between the two data signaling rates in the case of dual rate synchronous DCEs, or the two ranges of data signaling rates in the case of dual range nonsynchronous DCEs.

Circuit CI: Data Signal Rate Selector (DCE Source). Selects between the two data signaling rates in the case of dual rate synchronous DCEs, or the two ranges of data signaling rates in the case of dual range nonsynchronous DCEs.

Circuit DA: Transmitter Signal Element Timing (DTE Source). Provides the transmitting signal converter with signal element timing information.

Circuit DB: Transmitter Signal Element Timing (DCE Source). Provides the DTE with signal element timing information.

Circuit DD: Receiver Signal Element Timing (DCE Source). Provides the DTE with received signal element timing information.

Circuit SBA: Secondary Transmitted Data. Equivalent to Circuit BA (Transmitted Data) except that it is used to transmit data via the secondary (i.e., reverse or backward) channel.

Circuit SBB: Secondary Received Data. Equivalent to Circuit BB (Received Data) except that it is used to receive data on the secondary (i.e., reverse or backward) channel.

Circuit SCA: Secondary Request to Send. Equivalent to Circuit CA (Request to Send) except that it requests the establishment of the secondary channel instead of requesting the establishment of the primary data channel.

Circuit SCB: Secondary Clear to Send. Equivalent to Circuit CB (Clear to Send) except that it indicates the availability of the secondary channel instead of indicating the availability of the primary channel.

Circuit SCF: Secondary Received Line Signal Detector. Equivalent to Circuit CF (Received Line Signal Detector) except that it indicates the proper reception of the secondary channel line signal instead of indicating the proper reception of a primary channel received-line signal.

Circuit LL: Local Loopback. Controls LL test condition in local DCE. The ON condition causes the DCE to transmit to the receiving signal converter at the same DCE.

Circuit RL: Remote Loopback. Controls RL test condition in remote DCE. The ON condition causes the local DCE to signal the test condition to the remote DCE.

Circuit TM: Test Mode. Indicates whether the local DCE is in a test condition.

Mechanical: ISO 2110
Procedural: CCITT V.24

Comparisons of RS-232-C and EIA-232-D

In January 1987, RS-232-C was renamed EIA-232-D. The D version brings the specification in line with CCITT V.24 and V.28 and ISO 2110. The revision also includes the addition of the local loopback, remote loopback, and test mode interchange circuits. Protective ground has been redefined and a shield has been added. Also, the term DCE is changed from data communications equipment (and data set) to data circuit-terminating equipment. The terms driver and termination are changed to generator and receiver, respectively. Table 3-6 compares RS-232-C and EIA-232-D.

TABLE 3-6.   Comparison of RS-232-C and EIA-232-D

| | RS-232-C | | | EIA-232-D | |
Pin	CCITT Number	EIA Name	Pin	CCITT Number	EIA Name
1	101	AA	1		
7	102	AB	7	102	AB
2	103	BA	2	103	BA
3	104	BB	3	104	BB
4	105	CA	4	105	CA
5	106	CB	5	106	CB
6	107	CC	6	107	CC
20	108.2	CD	20	108.2	CD
22	125	CE	22	125	CE
8	109	CF	8	109	CF
21	110	CG	21	140/110	RL/CG(1)
23	111/112	CH/CI	23	111/112	CH/CI(2)
24	113	DA	24	113	DA
15	114	DB	15	114	DB
17	115	DD	17	115	DD
14	118	SBA	14	118	SBA
16	119	SBB	16	119	SBB
19	120	SCA	19	120	SCA
13	121	SCB	13	121	SCB
12	122	SCF	12	122/112	SCF/CI(3)
			9	—	—
			10	—	—
			11	—	—
			18	141	LL
			25	142	TM

Notes: (1) CF no longer used
           (2) See Pin 12
           (3) If SCF not used then CI is on Pin 12

The Physical Layer

Examples of EIA-232-D Communications

Figures 3-5 and 3-6 are provided to illustrate the sequence of events at the EIA-232-D physical level interface for a full-duplex operation (Figure 3-5) and a half-duplex operation (Figure 3-6). The reader is encouraged to study these figures carefully, because gaining an understanding of their meaning will dispel much of the "mystery" about how physical level protocols actually operate.

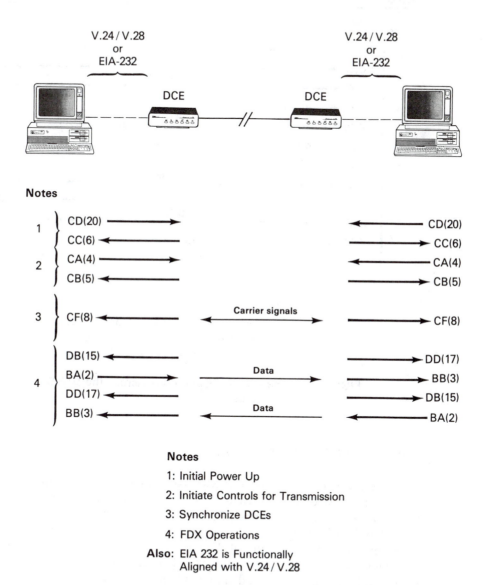

Notes

1: Initial Power Up

2: Initiate Controls for Transmission

3: Synchronize DCEs

4: FDX Operations

Also: EIA 232 is Functionally
Aligned with V.24 / V.28

FIGURE 3–5. Full-Duplex Operations Across the DTE/DCE Interface

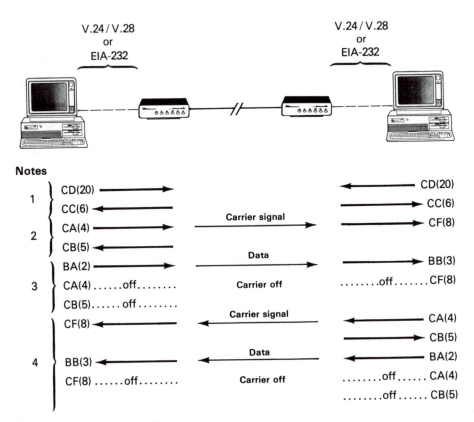

Notes

1: Initial Power Up
2: Initialize Controls and Synchronize DCEs
3: Send data, then turn off CA and CB
4: Repeat steps 1 & 2 in the other direction

FIGURE 3-6. Half-Duplex Operations Across the DTE/DCE Interface

EIA RS-449 (RS-422-A AND RS-423-A)

The EIA also sponsors RS-449. It was issued in 1975 to overcome some of the limitations of EIA-232. The EIA-232 standard has several electrical specifications that limit its effectiveness. For instance, EIA-232 is limited to 20 Kbits/s and a few hundred feet of space between the components. Actual distance depends on the size and quality of the circuits and is influenced by factors such as shielding and capacitance. EIA-232 also presents a noisy electrical signal which limits its data rate and distance. RS-449 provides 37 interchange circuits (see Table 3-7). It uses the ISO 4902 mechanical connector shown in Figure 3-3. In addition, the RS-449 specification establishes a bit rate up to two megabits/s.

The Physical Layer

TABLE 3-7. RS-449 Interchange Circuits

SG	Signal ground
SC	Send common
RC	Receive common
IS	Terminal in service
IC	Incoming call
TR	Terminal ready
DM	Data mode
SD	Send data
RD	Receive data
TT	Terminal timing
ST	Send timing
RT	Receive timing
RS	Request to send
CS	Clear to send
RR	Receiver ready
SQ	Signal quality
NS	New signal
SF	Select frequency
SR	Signaling rate selector
SI	Signaling rate indicator
SSD	Secondary send data
SRD	Secondary receive send
SRS	Secondary request to send
SCS	Secondary clear to send
SRR	Secondary receiver ready
LL	Local loopback
RL	Remote loopback
TM	Test mode
SS	Select standby
SB	Standby indicator

RS-449 uses two companion specifications, RS-422-A and RS-423-A. The electrical interface RS-422-A is a balanced electrical interface. RS-442-A is compatible with X.27. It is less noise sensitive and can transmit over a greater distance at a faster data rate than RS-423-A, which is a partially unbalanced electrical interface. The basic difference is that the balanced interface uses equipment that allows half the signal to be transmitted on each wire of the pair that is used. This is much less noise sensitive, because the receiver can use the noise on one wire to cancel the noise on the other. The unbalanced circuit provides for the transmission of the signal on one wire, with a common return for all wires, like EIA-232.

The RS-422-A specification provides a balanced configuration with differential signaling over both wires. RS-423-A uses a balanced differential receiver with a common return connected to signal ground only at the generator end. Both RS-422-A and RS-423-A specify a balanced differential receiver, even though they are different types of generators.

EIA-232 employs a single-end receiver with signal ground providing a common return. EIA-232 requires a very sharp rise time of the binary signal (less than 3% of the bit duration). As a consequence, considerable noise is created. RS-423-A allows the rise time to be 30% slower and is not as noisy.

To summarize the various recommended standards, some comparisons are provided in Table 3-8.

SUMMARY OF EIA DATA COMMUNICATIONS INTERFACES

Table 3-9 provides a brief summary of the prevalent EIA standards for data communications interfaces.

X-SERIES PHYSICAL LEVEL INTERFACES

A considerable number of systems operate at the physical level with the CCITT X-Series recommendations. These specifications are titled Data Communications Network Interfaces. The X-Series recommendations are found throughout the layers of the OSI Reference Model. This section explains the prevalent physical level recommendations.

The X.24 Recommendation

X.24 is analogous to V.24 for the V-Series in that it provides the descriptions of the interchange circuits used by the other X-Series interfaces. Table 3-10 shows how the interchange circuits are used and designates them as data, control, or timing circuits. Table 3-11 describes the functions of the X.24 interchange circuits.

The X.21 Recommendation

The X.21 recommendation is yet another interface standard that has received considerable attention in the industry. It is used in several European countries and in Japan, and has seen limited implementation in North America.

The X.24 T and R circuits transmit and receive data across the interface. The data is either user or control signals. Unlike EIA-232-D and the V Series, X.21 uses the T and R circuits for user data and control. The C circuits provide

The Physical Layer

TABLE 3-8. Comparisons of EIA-232-D, V.35, EIA RS-449 Interfaces

EIA-232-D/ CCITT V.24 25-Pin	CCITT V.35 37 or 15-Pin	EIA-449 37-Pin	EIA-232-D or EIA-449 9-Pin
1-Shield	1-Protective Ground	1-Shield	1-Shield
		37-Send Common	9-Send Common
2-Transmitted Data	2-Transmit Data	4-Send data (A)	
		22-Send Data (B)	
3-Received Data	3-Received Data	6-Receive Data (A)	
		24-Receive Data (B)	
4-Request to Send	4-Request-to-Send	7-Request to Send (A)	
		25-Request to Send (B)	
5-Clear to Send	5-Ready for Sending	9-Clear to Send (A)	
		27-Clear to Send (B)	
6-DCE Ready	6-Data Set Ready	11-Data Mode (A)	
		29-Data Mode (B)	
7-Signal Ground		19-Signal Ground	5-Signal Ground (C)
8-Signal Detect	8-Receive Line Signal Detect	13-Receiver Ready (A)	
		31-Receiver Ready (B)	
9-Reserved for Testing			
		20-Receive Common	6-Receive Common
10-Reserved for Testing		10-Local Loop (A)	
		14-Remote Loop (A)	
11-Unassigned		3-Spare	
		21-Spare	
12-Sec. Carrier Detect		32-Select Standby	2-Sec. Receiver Ready
13-Sec. Clear to Send			8-Sec. Clear to Send
14-Sec. Transmitted Data			3-Sec. Send Data
15-Transmit Clock (DCE Source)	15-TX Signal Element Timing	5-Send Timing (A) DCE Source	
		23-Send Timing (B) DCE Source	
16-Sec. Received Data			4-Sec. Received Data
17-Receive Clock	17-RX Signal Element Timing	8-Receive Timing (A)	
		26-Receive Timing (B)	
18-Local Loopback		18-Test Mode (A)	
		28-Term in Service (A)	
		34-New Signal	
19-Sec. Request to Send			7-Sec. Request to Send
20-Data Terminal Ready		12-Terminal Ready (A)	
		30-Terminal Ready (B)	
21-Signal Quality Detector/ Remote Loopback		33-Signal Quality (A)	
22-Ring Indicator		15-Incoming Call (A)	
23-Data Signal Rate Selector		2-Signaling Rate Indicator (A)	
		16-Signaling Rate Selector (A)	
24-Transmit Clock (DTE Source)		17-Terminal Timing (A)	
		35-Terminal Timing (B)	
25 Test Mode		36-Stand by Indicator	

TABLE 3-9. EIA Data Communications Interfaces

EIA-422-A	Electrical characteristics of balanced voltage digital interface circuits.
EIA-423-A	Electrical characteristics of unbalanced voltage digital interface circuits.
EIA-449 and EIA-449-1	General purpose 37-position and 9-position interface for data terminal equipment and data circuit-terminating equipment employing serial binary data interchange.
EIA-496	Interface between data circuit-terminating equipment (DCE) and the public switched telephone network (PSTN).
EIA-366-A	Interface between data terminal equipment and automatic calling equipment for data communication.
EIA-232-D	Interface between data terminal equipment and data circuit-terminating equipment employing serial binary data interchange.
EIA-491	Interface between a numerical control unit and peripheral equipment employing asynchronous data interchange over circuits having EIA-423-A characteristics.
EIA-334-A	Signal quality at interface between data processing terminal equipment and synchronous data communications equipment for serial data transmission.
EIA-339-A-1	Application of signal quality requirements to EIA-449.
EIA-485	Standard for electrical characteristics of generators and receivers for use in balanced digital multipoint systems.
EIA-363	Standard for specifying signal quality for transmitting and receiving data processing terminal equipment using serial data transmission at the interface with nonsynchronous data communications equipment.
EIA-410	Standard for the electrical characteristics of Class A closure interchange circuits.
EIA-404-A and EIA-404-1	Standard for start/stop signal quality for nonsynchronous data terminal equipment.
EIA-408	Interface between numerical control equipment and data terminal equipment employing parallel binary data interchange.

an off/on signal to the network and the I circuit provides the off/on to the DTE. These two circuits serve to activate and deactivate the DCE-DTE interface session. The S and B circuits provide for signals to synchronize the signals between the DTE and DCE. The G circuit acts as a signal ground or a common return.

X.21 is designed around the concepts of states and state diagrams. The X.21 states are shown in Table 3-12.

TABLE 3-10. X.24 Interchange Circuits

Interchange Circuit Designation	Interchange Circuit Name	DATA From DCE	DATA To DCE	CONTROL From DCE	CONTROL To DCE	TIMING From DCE	TIMING To DCE
G	Signal ground or common return						
Ga	DTE common return				X		
Gb	DCE common return			X			
T	Transmit		X		X		
R	Receive	X		X			
C	Control				X		
I	Indication			X			
S	Signal element timing					X	
B	Byte timing					X	
F	Frame start identification					X	
X	DTE signal element timing						X

TABLE 3-11. X.24 Interchange Circuits

Circuit G: Signal ground or common return.   Establishes the signal common reference potential for the interchange circuits.

Circuit Ga: DTE common return.   Connected to the DTE circuit common and used as the reference for the unbalanced X.26 type interchange circuit receivers within the DCE.

Circuit Gb: DCE common return.   Connected to the DCE circuit common and used as the reference for the unbalanced X.26 type interchange circuit receivers within the DTE.

Circuit T: Transmit.   Signals originated by the DTE are transferred on this circuit to the DCE.

Circuit R: Receive.   Signals sent by remote DTE are transferred on this circuit to the DTE.

Circuit C: Control.   This circuit controls the DCE for a particular signaling process.

Circuit I: Indication.   Indicates to the DTE the state of the call control process.

Circuit S: Signal element timing.   Provides the DTE with signal element timing information.

Circuit B: Byte timing.   Provides the DTE with 8-bit byte timing information.

Circuit F: Frame start identification.   Continuously provides the DTE with a multiplex frame start indication when connected to a multiplexed DTE/DCE interface.

Circuit X: DTE transmit signal element timing.   Provides signal element timing information for the transmit direction in cases where circuit S only provides signal element timing for the receive direction.

TABLE 3–12. X.21 States

State Number	State Name
1	Ready
2	Call request
3	Proceed to select
4	Selection signals
5	DTE waiting
6A	DCE waiting
6B	DCE waiting
7	DCE provided information (call progress signals)
8	Incoming call
9	Call accepted
10	DCE provided information (called DTE line identification)
10 bis	DCE provided information (calling DTE line identification)
11	Connection in progress
12	Ready for data
13	Data transfer
13S	Send data
13R	Receive data
14	DTE controlled not ready, DCE ready
15	Call collision
16	DTE clear request
17	DCE clear confirmation
18	DTE ready, DCE not ready
19	DCE clear indication
20	DTE clear confirmation
21	DCE ready
22	DTE uncontrolled not ready, DCE not ready
23	DTE controlled not ready, DCE not ready
24	DTE uncontrolled not ready, DCE not ready

Call establishment is accomplished by the DTE and DCE both signaling Ready (state 1). From this state, the DTE enters the Call Request state (state 2) which the DCE acknowledges by entering the Proceed to Select state (state 3). At the other end, the remote DCE signals its DTE by entering the Incoming Call state (state 8) and the DTE responds with Call Accepted state (state 9).

Hereafter, the components pass through several optional states. The DTE and DCE can wait for the calls (states 5, 6A, 6B). An additional state, Connection in Progress (state 11), is available to allow additional network delay. The DCEs now enter the Ready for Data state (state 12) and then data transfer begins (state 13). Figure 3-7 shows a state diagram for X.21 calls.

The X.21*bis* Recommendation

X.21bis is often used as the physical interface in an X.25 packet network. X.21 bis uses the V.24 circuits. It also has several options of how the ISO connectors

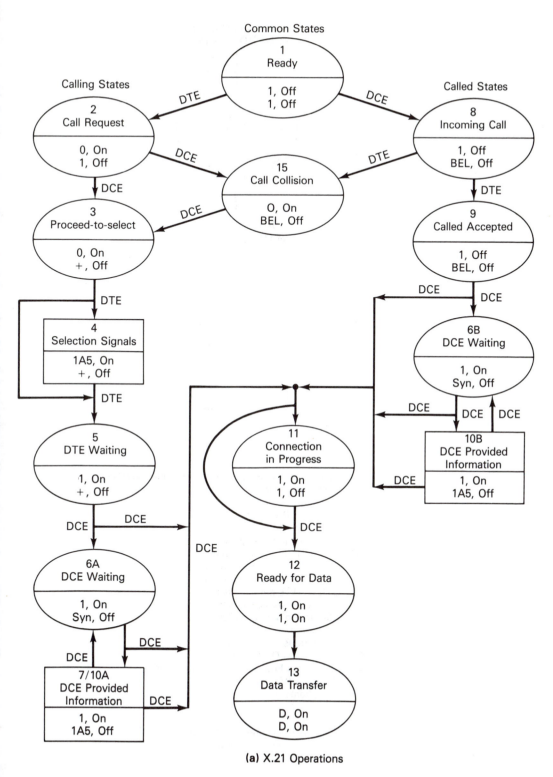

(a) X.21 Operations

FIGURE 3-7. X.21 Signaling

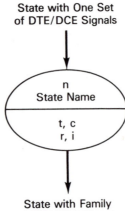

State with One Set
of DTE/DCE Signals

State with Family
of DTE/DCE Signals

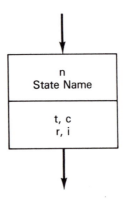

n: State Number (with State Name under Number)
t: Signal on T Circuit
c: Signal on C Circuit
r: Signal on R Circuit
i: Signal on I Circuit
T: Transmit Interchange Circuit
C: Control Interchange Circuit
R: Receive Interchange Circuit
I: Indication Interchange Circuit
D: DTE or DCE data signals
0 and 1: Steady binary conditions
01: Alternate binary 0 and binary 1
X: Any value
Off: Continuous Off (Binary 1)
On: Continuous On (Binary 0)
IA5: Characters From International Alphabet
Numbers (IA5)
+5: IA5 Character
BEL: IA5 Character
Syn: IA5 Character
Transition indicates whether DTE or DCE
is responsible for transmission

(b) Legend

FIGURE 3-7. (*Continued*).

and the other V and X interfaces are used. The electrical characteristics of the interchange circuits at both the DCE side and the DTE side of the interface may comply either with Recommendation V.28 using the 25-pin connector and ISO 2110, or with Recommendation X.26 using the 37-pin connector and ISO 4902. In North America, the V.28 convention is often used.

Other X-Series Interfaces

Several X-Series physical level interfaces are employed for the following functions:

X.20	Interface between DTE and DCE for start/stop transmission services on public data networks.
X.20bis	Used on public data networks with data terminal equipment (DTE) which is designed for interfacing to asynchronous duplex V-Series modems.
X.26	Electrical characteristics for unbalanced double-current interchange circuits for general use with integrated circuit equipment. Functionally equivalent to V.10.
V.27	Electrical characteristics for balanced double-current interchange circuits for general use with integrated circuit equipment. Functionally equivalent to V.11.

THE ISDN PHYSICAL LAYER

To begin the analysis of ISDN, consider the end-user ISDN terminal in Figure 3-8(a). This device (called a DTE in this book) is identified by the ISDN term TE1 (terminal equipment, type 1). The TE1 connects to the ISDN through a twisted-pair four-wire digital link. This link uses time division multiplexing (TDM) to provide three channels, designated as the B, B, and D channels (or 2B + D). The B channels operate at a speed of 64 Kbits/s; the D channel operates at 16 Kbits/s. The 2B + D is designated as the basic rate interface. ISDN also allows up to eight TE1s to share one 2B + D channel.

Figure 3-8(b) illustrates other ISDN options. In this scenario, the user DTE is called a TE2 device, which is the current equipment in use, such as IBM 3270 terminals, telex devices, etc. The TE2 connects to the terminal adapter (TA), which is a device that allows non-ISDN terminals to operate over ISDN lines. The user side of the TA typically uses a conventional physical level interface such as EIA-232 or the V-Series specification discussed earlier. It is packaged like an external modem or as a board that plugs into an expansion slot on the TE2 devices. The EIA or V-Series interface is called the R interface in ISDN terminology.

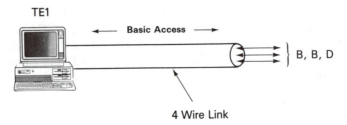

TE1: Terminal Equipment Type 1

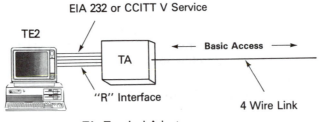

TA: Terminal Adapter
TE2: Terminal Equipment Type 2

FIGURE 3-8. ISDN Terminals

Basic Access and Primary Access

The TA and TE2 devices are connected through the basic access to either an ISDN NT1 or NT2 device (NT is network termination). Figure 3-9 shows several of the options. The NT1 is a customer premise device which connects the four-wire subscriber wiring to the conventional two-wire local loop. ISDN allows up to eight terminal devices to be addressed by NT1.

The NT1 is responsible for the physical layer functions (of OSI), such as signaling synchronization and timing. It provides a user with a standardized interface.

The NT2 is a more intelligent piece of customer premise equipment. It is typically found in a digital PBX, and contains the layer 2 and 3 protocol functions. The NT2 device is capable of performing concentration services. It multiplexes 23 B + D channels onto the line at a combined rate of 1.544 Mbits/s. This function is called the ISDN primary rate access.

The NT1 and NT2 devices may be combined into a single device called NT12. This device handles the physical, data link, and network layer functions.

In summary, the TE equipment is responsible for user communications and the NT equipment is responsible for network communications.

ISDN Reference Points and Interfaces

Figure 3-9 also shows other ISDN components. The reference points are logical interfaces between the functional groupings. The S reference point is the 2B + D

The Physical Layer

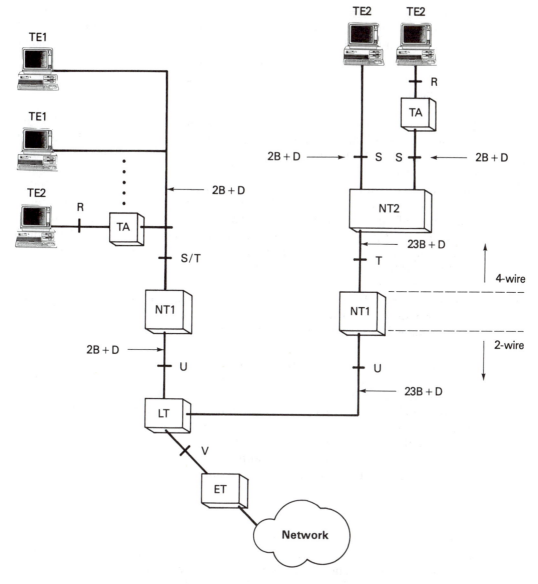

Note: S, T, U, R, V are the ISDN Reference Points.

FIGURE 3–9. ISDN Configurations

interface into the NT1 or NT2 device. The T interface is the reference point on the customer side of the NT1 device. It is the ISDN "plug-in-the-wall." It is the same as the S interface on the basic rate access lines. The U interface is the reference point for the two-wire side of the NT1 equipment. It separates a NT1 from the line termination (LT) equipment. The V reference point separates the line termination (LT) from the exchange termination (ET) equipment.

The S and T reference points support four-wire twisted pairs for a length of up to 3300 feet (1000 meters) or a point-to-point link of 500 feet (150 meters) on the multipoint configuration. The two-wire U reference point is operated at full duplex with channel splitting accomplished with echo cancellation.

ISDN Channels

The most common ISDN interface supports a bit rate of 144 Kbits/s. The rate includes two 64 Kbits/s B channels and one 16 Kbits/s D channel. In addition to these channels, ISDN provides for framing control and other overhead bits, which totals to a 192 Kbits/s bit rate. The 144 Kbits/s interfaces operate synchronously in the full-duplex mode over the same physical connector. The 144 Kbits/s signal provides time division multiplexed provisions for the two 64 Kbits/s channels and one 16 Kbits/s channel. The standard allows the B channels to be further multiplexed in the subchannels. For example, 8, 16, or 32 Kbits/s subchannels can be derived from the B channels. The two B channels can be combined or broken down as the user desires.

The B channels are intended to carry user information streams. They provide for several different kinds of applications support. For example, channel B can provide for voice at 64 Kbits/s; data transmission for packet-switch utilities at bit rates less than or equal to 64 Kbits/s; and broadband voice at 64 Kbits/s or less.

The D channel is intended to carry control and signaling information, although in certain cases ISDN allows for the D channel to support user data transmission as well. However, be aware that the B channel does not carry signaling information. ISDN describes signaling information as s-type, packet data as p-type, and telemetry as t-type. The D channel may carry all these types of information through statistical multiplexing. The ISDN includes other kinds of channels (the E channel and H channels) which are intended for channels at faster speeds and are derived from multiple B channels.

ISDN Local Loops

The ISDN uses the local loops currently in existence. Replacing the many millions of miles of unshielded copper wires comprising the local loop would entail astronomical costs. The voice signal is carried on the local loop over a frequency range from approximately 50 Hz to 4 KHz. The ISDN basic rate access operates at much higher frequencies, in the range of about 200 KHz.

Signal loss increases with higher frequencies. The high-frequency signal loss is quite significant for loops of medium to long distances. For example, a test by the Nynex regional telephone company revealed the following performances, on local loops using 26-gauge wire:

3700 feet:	Loss of 15 dB (decibels)
9000 feet:	Loss of 30 dB
18000 feet:	Loss of 40 to 50 dB

　　　　　　　　　　　　　　　　　　　　　　　　　　The Physical Layer

Since the majority of local loops are longer than 9000 feet, it is obvious that the high-frequency ISDN signals present problems. Moreover, the Nynex test demonstrated that noise and crosstalk creates significant distortion of ISDN frequencies.

The ANSI T1D1.3 working group has established a specification for local long basic access signaling that will ameliorate the problem. It is called 2 binary 1 quatenary (2B1Q). With 2B1Q, each signal change represents two binary bits. Consequently, a signaling rate of 80 KHz provides a D bit transfer rate of 160 Kbits/s. The lower frequencies provide better performance over the loops.

The Basic Rate Frames

The formats for the frames exchanged between the TE and the NT (reference points S and T) are shown in Figure 3-10. The formats vary in each direction of transfer, but are identical for point-to-point or multipoint configurations. The frames are 48 bits in length and are transmitted by the TE and NT every 250 microseconds. The first bit of the frame transmitted to the NT is delayed by two bit periods with respect to the first bit of the frame received from the NT.

The 250 microsecond frame provides 4000 frames a second (1 second/.000250 = 4000) and a transfer rate of 192 Kbits/s (4000 * 48 = 192,000). However, 12 bits in each frame is overhead, so the user data transfer rate is 144 Kbits/s (4000 * [48 − 12] = 144,000).

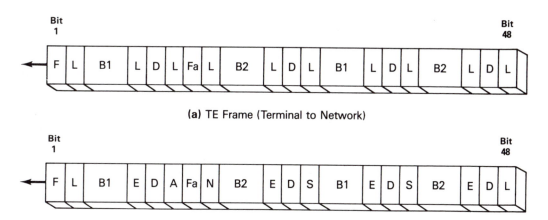

(a) TE Frame (Terminal to Network)

(b) NT Frame (Network to Terminal)

F: Framing Bit
L: DC Balancing Bit
B1: B1 Channel Bits
B2: B2 Channel Bits
D: D Channel Bits
Fa: Auxiliary Training Bit
E: Echo Bits

FIGURE 3-10. ISDN Basic Rate Frame Formats

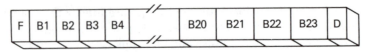

F = 001011 for Multiframes of 24 Frames in Length with the F Value in Every 4th Frame.

(a) 1.544 Mbits/s Frame Format

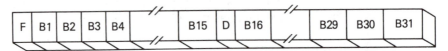

F = 0011011 in Positions 2 to 8 in Channel Time Slot 0 of Every Other Frame.

(b) 2.048 Mbits/s Frame Format

FIGURE 3-11. Primary Rate Frame Formats

The first two bits of the frame are the framing bit (F) and the DC balancing bit (L). These bits are used for frame synchronization. In addition, the L bit is used in the NT frame to electrically balance the frame and in the TE frame to electrically balance each B channel octet and each D channel bit. The auxiliary framing bit (F_a) and the N bit are also used in the frame alignment procedures. Bit A is used for TE activation and deactivation.

The Primary Rate Frames

The ISDN specification defines two formats for the primary rate frame. Figure 3-11(a) shows the format for the 1.544 Mbits/s frame used in North America and Japan. Figure 3-11(b) shows the 2.048 Mbits/s frame used in Europe.

SUMMARY AND CONCLUSIONS

The physical layer is so named because it is concerned with the physical connection of computing devices such as terminals, computers, and modems. Principal functions of the physical layer are the generation and reception of electrical, electromagnetic, or optical signals, and the descriptions of the wires and connectors between the computing machines.

The major physical level standards in the OSI Model are developed around the CCITT V-Series Recommendations, the EIA-232 specifications, and increasingly, the CCITT ISDN recommendations. The ISO restricts its participation at this level principally to the specifications dealing with physical connectors.

APPENDIX 3A. PHYSICAL LAYER CODING, DECODING, AND MODULATION

DIGITAL-TO-DIGITAL SIGNALING

Figure 3A-1 provides an illustration of several common digital coding schemes used in the industry. We will discuss each of them and describe their advantages and disadvantages. These signals exhibit one or several of the following four characteristics:

- *Unipolar or unbalanced code.* No signal below zero voltage or no signal above (i.e., algebraic sign does not change: 0 volts for 1, 3 volts for 0).
- *Polar or balanced code.* Signal is above and below zero voltage (opposite algebraic signs identify logic states: $+3$ volts and -3 volts).
- *Bipolar code.* The signal varies between three levels.
- *Alternate mark inversion (AMI) code.* Uses alternate polarity pulses to encode binary 1s.

Figure 3A-1(a) shows the non-return-to-zero code (NRZ). Notice the signal level remains stable throughout the bit cell. In this case, the signal level remains

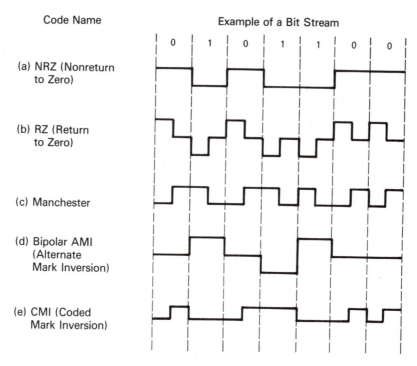

Code Name	Example of a Bit Stream
	0 1 0 1 1 0 0
(a) NRZ (Nonreturn to Zero)	
(b) RZ (Return to Zero)	
(c) Manchester	
(d) Bipolar AMI (Alternate Mark Inversion)	
(e) CMI (Coded Mark Inversion)	

FIGURE 3A-1. Digital Codes

low for a bit 1 and goes to a high voltage for a bit 0. (Opposite voltages are also used in many devices.) NRZ is a widely used data communications coding scheme because of its relative simplicity and low cost. The NRZ code also makes very efficient use of bandwidth, since it can represent a bit with each baud (signal change). However, it suffers from the lack of self-clocking capabilities, since a long series of continuous ones or zeros does not create a signal state transition on the channel. As a consequence, the receiver's clock could possibly drift from the incoming signal. The line sample would not occur at the right time, and the transmitter and the receiver might actually lose synchronization with each other. Balanced NRZ is widely used in communications because it requires simple encoding or decoding and it uses a channel's bandwidth very effectively.

Another disadvantage of NRZ is the presence of a direct current (dc) component. A long series of ones or zeros can create dc wander, which is a common source of errors. Moreover, most transmission links (telephone lines) do not pass dc signals, and many systems also use ac for coupling with transformers. The dc signal requires direct physical attachment.

Some NRZ systems use a technique called differential encoding. The signals are decoded by companding the polarity of adjacent signal elements. Absolute values are not used. An advantage to this approach is that it is more reliable to detect the signal elements in the presence of noise.

The return-to-zero code (RZ) usually entails the changing of the signal state at least once in every bit cell. This scheme is illustrated in Figure 3A-1(b). As a bipolar code, RZ codes provide a transition in every bit cell; therefore, they have very good synchronization characteristics. Moreover, the dc wander problem is eliminated with bipolar schemes since three levels are used to encode the data. The average voltage level is maintained at zero. The RZ code's primary disadvantage is that it requires two signal transitions for each bit. Consequently, an RZ code requires twice the baud of a conventional NRZ code. This type of code is found in some of the more sophisticated systems dealing with local area networks, lightwave technologies, and optical fibers.

Figure 3A-1(c) illustrates the Manchester code (or biphase code), a code found in many communications systems today. This code provides a signal state change in every bit cell. Consequently, it is a good clocking code and dc wander is nonexistent. The interface devices used to achieve this higher baud are more expensive than the NRZ interfaces. It should be also noted that biphase Manchester code does not have any means of monitoring the performance of the signal. It contains no bipolar violation capabilities, for example. Manchester code is commonly found in magnetic tape recording, optical fiber links, coaxial links, and local area networks.

Figure 3A-1(d) shows a code used by AT&T, the Bell Operating Companies, and other carriers. This was originally called the Bell System PCM Code. This signaling structure is an example of bipolar AMI (alternate mark inversion) where alternate polarity pulses are used to encode logic 1 (mark). This particular code presents some problems when a long series of zeros are contained in a transmission. The components in the system have no way to synchronize with zero bit cells because there are no changes in the state of the line.

The bipolar AMI scheme has an advantage in that it can detect polarity violations. For example, if the detection of two successive pulses indicates they are the same polarity, an error known as bipolar violation has occurred. In other words, no single bit error can occur without the notation of a bipolar violation. Many systems, such as the T1 carrier, were designed to monitor bipolar violations and to provide alarm measures in the event thresholds are exceeded. The T1 line repeaters maintain timing as long as no string greater than 15 zeros is allowed to occur.

Figure 3A-1(e) shows a variation of the AMI scheme called coded mark inversion (CMI). It is used on CCITT high-level multiplexers (139.264 Mbits/s). This code is a two-level NRZ. It uses the following coding rules:

- Binary 0 Always a positive transition at the midway point of the binary unit time interval (the bit cell).
- Binary 1 0 does not change state within a bit cell.
  Positive transition at the start of the bit cell if preceding level was high.
  Negative transition at start of bit cell if last binary 1 was encoded at low level.

CMI provides many signal transitions and, unlike other codes, no ambiguity exists in interpreting ones or zeros. However, because one-half of a 0 bit cell looks like a 1 bit cell, it does suffer in performance when compared to the bi-phase code.

THE BNZS CODES

Bipolar coding requires a minimum density of binary ones in the data stream to maintain timing at the repeaters. Even though a long string of zeros is precluded, a low density of pulses increases timing problems (called timing jitter). To solve this problem, most of the newer digital transmission systems perform some kind of substitution on the data by replacing strings of ones with special codes to increase pulse density. In fact, these systems replace N zeros with a special N length code that purposely produces bipolar violations. Hence, they are called Binary N Zero Substitution (BNZS) codes.

The B8ZS Code

A coding scheme used on several of the newer T-1 systems is known as Binary 8-Zeros Suppression, or B8ZS. The code is also specified for the T-1 (1.544 Mbits/s carrier by CCITT).

TABLE 3A-1. B8ZS Encoding Rules

Polarity of Preceding Pulse	Eight-Bit Substitution
−	000 − + 0 + −
+	000 + − 0 − +

B8ZS is another modified AMI code. Eight consecutive zeros are replaced with 000 + − 0 − + if the preceding pulse is +. If the preceding pulse is −, the substitution is 000 − + 0 + −. Table 3A-1 summarizes the B8ZS rules and Figure 3A-2 shows an example of the substitution logic.

The HDB3 Code

High-Density Bipolar Three (HDB3) replaces strings of four zeros with a substitution code. It does not allow more than three consecutive zeros—hence its name, HDB3. It substitutes four consecutive zeros for eight consecutive zeros. HDB3 adheres to the following rules (also see Table 3A-2):

- Ones alternate in polarity.
- Strings of four zeros are substituted.
- The first bit of the 4-bit code is coded as a 0 if the preceding 1 of the HDB3 signal has a polarity opposite to the polarity of the preceding violation and is not a violation by itself; otherwise, it is coded as a 1.

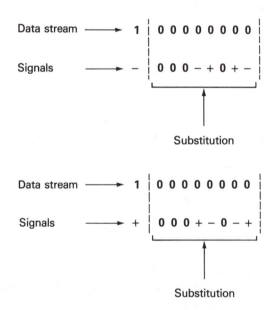

FIGURE 3A-2. The B8ZS Scheme

TABLE 3A-2. HDB3 Encoding Rules

	Number of 1 Pulses Since Last Substitution	
Polarity of Preceding Pulse	Odd	Even
−	000 −	+00+
+	000 +	−00 −

- The second and third bits are always coded as zeros.
- The last bit is coded as a 1, and the polarity must violate the AMI rule (therefore, successive substitutions produce successive violations).

ISDN Line Codes

The current CCITT ISDN specification uses pseudo-ternary coding with 100% pulse width. The ISDN pseudo-ternary code adheres to the following rules:

- Binary 1 is represented with no line signal.
- Binary 0 is represented with a positive or negative pulse.
- The first 0 following a framing balance bit is the same polarity as the balance bit.
- Subsequent 0s must alternate in polarity.
- A balance bit is 0 if the number of binary zeros following the previous balance bit is odd.
- A balance bit is a 1 if the number of binary zeros following the previous balance bit is even.

DIGITAL-TO-ANALOG SIGNALING

The physical level must accommodate to the prevalent analog circuits that are found in the vast majority of systems today. This section provides a brief discourse on the digital-to-analog signaling techniques.

Amplitude Modulation (AM)

AM modems alter the carrier signal amplitude in accordance with the modulating digital bit stream [see Figure 3A-3(a)]. The frequency and phase of the carrier are held constant and the amplitude is raised or lowered to represent a binary value of 0 or 1. In its simplest form, the carrier signal can be switched on or off to represent the binary state.

The use of AM for data communications has decreased because a multilevel scheme requires the use of several to many signal levels. As the number

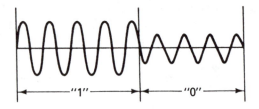

(a) Amplitude Modulation

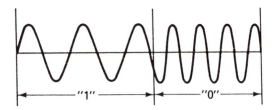

(b) Frequency Modulation

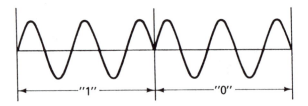

(c) Phase Modulation

FIGURE 3A-3. Modulation Techniques

of signal levels increase, the distance between them decreases. AM transmitters often "saturate" these narrow distances, and in some systems they must be used at less than maximum power to diminish the saturation problem.

Thus, AM modems must be designed: (a) with sufficiently long signaling intervals (low baud) to keep the signal on the channel long enough to withstand noise and to be detected at the receiver; and (b) with sufficient distances between the AM levels to allow accurate detection and to diminish saturation.

Frequency Modulation (FM)

Figure 3A-3(b) illustrates frequency modulation. This method changes the frequency of the carrier in accordance with the digital bit stream. The amplitude is held constant. In its simplest form, a binary 1 is represented by one frequency and a binary 0 by another frequency.

Several variations of FM modems are available. The most common FM

The Physical Layer

modem is the frequency shift key (FSK) modem using four frequencies within the 3-KHz telephone line bandwidth. The FSK modem transmits 1070 and 1270 Hz signals to represent a binary 0 (space) and binary 1 (mark), respectively. It receives 2025 and 2225 Hz signals as a binary 0 (space) and binary 1 (mark). This approach allows full-duplex transmission over a two-wire voice-grade telephone line.

FSK is used for low-speed modems (up to 1200 bits/s) because it is relatively inexpensive and simple. Many of the personal computers use FSK for communications over the telephone network. FSK is also used for radio transmission in the high-frequency ranges (3 to 30 MHz) and some local area networks (LANs) employ FSK on broadband coaxial cables. However, its use on voice-grade lines is decreasing as more manufacturers implement DCEs with phase modulation techniques. Moreover, phase modulation techniques are almost exclusively used today on high-speed digital radio systems.

Phase Modulation (PM)

The phase modulation method is also called phase shift key (PSK) [see Figure 3A-3(c)]. A common approach to PSK is to compare the phase of the current signal state to the previous signal state, which is known as differential PSK (DPSK). This technique uses bandwidth more efficiently than FSK because it puts more information into each signal, but it requires more elaborate equipment for signal generation and detection.

Phase shift key is used to provide multilevel modulation. The technique is called quadrature signal modulation. For example, a dibit modem (two bits per baud) typically encodes the binary data stream as follows:

$$11 = 45°$$
$$10 = 135°$$
$$01 = 225°$$
$$00 = 315°$$

CHAPTER 4

The Data Link Layer

INTRODUCTION

Data link controls (DLCs, also called line protocols) provide line services. They manage the flow of data across the communications path or link between computers and terminals. Their functions are limited to the individual link. That is to say, link control is responsible only for the traffic between adjacent nodes/ stations on a line. Once the data are transmitted to the adjacent node and an acknowledgment of the transmission is returned to the transmission site, the link control task is complete for that particular transmission.

The DLC provides the following functions:

- Synchronizing (logically, not physically) the sender and receiver through the use of flags/SYN characters.
- Controlling the flow of data to prevent the sender from sending too fast.
- Detecting and recovering from errors between two points on the link.
- Maintaining awareness of link conditions such as distinguishing between data and control and determining the identity of the communicating stations.

The data link layer rests above the physical layer in the OSI Model. Generally, the data link protocol is medium independent and relies on the physical layer to deal with the specific media (wire, radio, etc.) and physical signals (electrical current, laser, infrared, etc.).

The physical layer actions are dictated by the control functions of the data link layer. The physical layer provides services to the data link layer and the data link layer cannot function without the physical layer media-dependent interfaces. This separation allows link control protocols to be applied to different transmission media.

This chapter is written with the assumption that the reader has a basic understanding of data link protocols. Appendix 4A is provided at the end of this chapter as a tutorial on the subject.

THE SUBLAYERS OF THE DATA LINK LAYER

In its work with the IEEE 802 local area networks standards, the IEEE recognized the need to divide the data link layer into two sublayers in order to handle different link configurations. For example, the majority of wide area networks consist of many point-to-point links, and local area networks are built with multipoint broadcast channels. Obviously, these links have different access characteristics. The IEEE efforts have emphasized the need to keep the OSI and 802 specifications as compatible as possible. Consequently, the 802 committees split the data link layer into two sublayers: medium access control (MAC) and logical link control (LLC).

As illustrated in Figure 4-1, MAC encompasses the IEEE 802.3, 802.4, and 802.5 standards (and the recent FDDI [fiber optic] standard, which is patterned after 802.5 but with a considerable number of differences). The LLC is designated as 802.2. This sublayer was implemented to make the LLC sublayer inde-

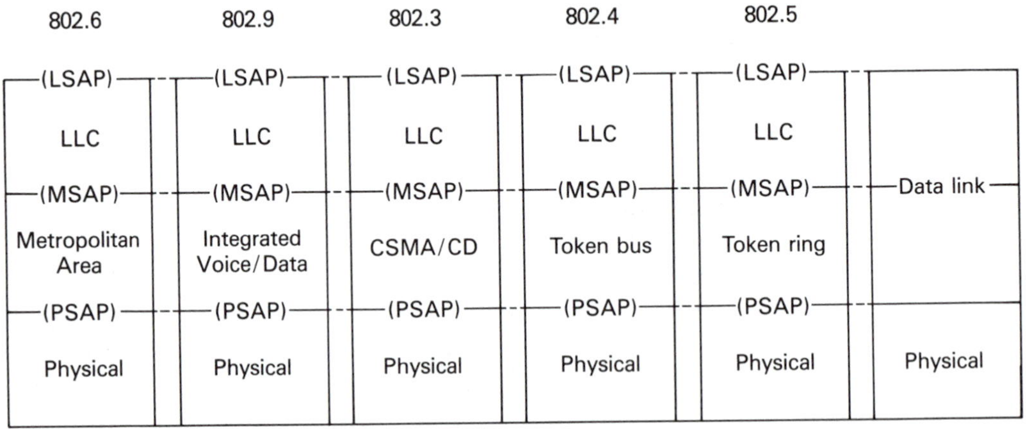

802.6	802.9	802.3	802.4	802.5	
(LSAP)	(LSAP)	(LSAP)	(LSAP)	(LSAP)	
LLC	LLC	LLC	LLC	LLC	
(MSAP)	(MSAP)	(MSAP)	(MSAP)	(MSAP)	Data link
Metropolitan Area	Integrated Voice/Data	CSMA/CD	Token bus	Token ring	
(PSAP)	(PSAP)	(PSAP)	(PSAP)	(PSAP)	
Physical	Physical	Physical	Physical	Physical	Physical

LLC: Logical Link Control
MAC: Medium Access Control
LSAP: LLC Service Access Point
MSAP: MAC Service Access Point
PSAP: Physical Access Point

FIGURE 4-1. The IEEE LAN Protocols

The Data Link Layer

pendent of a specific LAN access method. The LLC sublayer is also used to provide an interface into or out of the specific MAC protocol.

The MAC/LLC split provides several attractive features. First, it controls access to the shared local area channel among the autonomous user devices. Second, it provides for a decentralized (peer-to-peer) scheme that reduces the LAN's susceptibility to errors. Third, it provides a more compatible interface with wide area networks, since LLC is a subset of the HDLC superset. Fourth, LLC is independent of a specific access method (MAC is protocol-specific). This approach gives an 802 network a flexible interface with work stations and other networks. We return to these features later in this chapter when we examine the data link layer for LANs in more detail.

DATA LINK SERVICE DEFINITIONS AND PRIMITIVES

The ISO and CCITT have published a data link service definition. The ISO Standard is DIS 8886 and the CCITT Recommendation is X.212. As we have learned, layer services are defined by primitives, and these OSI specifications provide for both connection-oriented and connectionless services. These primitives are summarized in Table 4-1. They are independent of any specific protocol, such as HDLC (High Level Data Link Control).

To briefly summarize the functions of the link layer primitives, we assume a connection is to be established between two users. The connection setup begins with the user specifying a least-acceptable level of service in the quality of service parameters of a DL-CONNECT.request primitive. If the service provider cannot provide this level of service, it will send a DL-DISCONNECT.indication to the calling requester. The called user may also not accept the request, and could send back a DL-DISCONNECT.request. If all goes well, the DL-CONNECT.response and DL-CONNECT.indication primitives are returned by the user and provider respectively. Data can then be exchanged with the DL-DATA and DL-EXPEDITED-DATA primitives.

As depicted in Table 4-1, the specification also provides for connectionless-mode services with the DL-UNITDATA.request and DL-UNITDATA.indication primitives. This mode of operation does not require the establishment of a logical connection before the exchange of data takes place.

Quality of Service Parameters

The reader might expect that the quality of service parameters of the OSI Model are not sent down as far as the data link layer. However, several of the QOS parameters can be mapped all the way down to the data link layer.

The data link layer, as implemented by the CCITT X.212 recommendation, supports the following QOS parameters:

- Throughput
- Protection

TABLE 4-1.   Data Link Layer Service Primitives

Connection-Oriented

DL-CONNECT.request   (Called Address, Calling Address, Expedited Data Selection, Quality of Service Parameters)

DL-CONNECT.indication   (Called Address, Calling Address, Expedited Data Selection, Quality of Service Parameters

DL-CONNECT.response   (Responding Address, Expedited Data Selection, Quality of Service Parameters

DL-CONNECT.confirm   (Responding Address, Expedited Data Selection, Quality of Service Parameters)

DL-CONNECT.confirm   (Responding Address, Expedited Data Selection, Quality of Service Parameters)

DL-DISCONNECT.request   (Originator, Reason)

DL-DISCONNECT.indication   (Originator, Reason)

DL-DATA.request   (User-Data)

DL-DATA.indication   (User-Data)

DL-EXPEDITED-DATA.request   (User-Data)

DL-EXPEDITED-DATA.indication   (User-Data)

DL-RESET.request   (Originator, Reason)

DL-RESET.indication   (Originator, Reason)

DL-RESET.response

DL-RESET.confirm

DL-ERROR-REPORT.   indication (Reason)

Connectionless

DL-UNITDATA.request   (Source-address, Destination-address, Quality of Services, User Data)

DL-UNITDATA.indication   (Source-address, Destination-address, Quality of Services, User-Data)

- Priority
- Resilience
- Transit delay
- Residual error rate

Three QOS parameters can be negotiated during the data link control establishment. These are throughput, protection, and priority. The remainder of the QOS parameters are not allowed to be negotiated during the connection establishment on the link. They are defined and determined prior to link establishment.

Regardless of how the QOS is selected, it remains at the agreed-upon level during the lifetime of the connection. However, OSI does not guarantee that these original parameter values will be maintained. They could be degraded.

A brief explanation of each X.212 QOS parameter follows.

Throughput. Throughput is defined in this recommendation as the total number of link level bits successfully transferred through a data request or indication primitive divided by the input or output time for those sequence of bits. By successful transfer, it is meant that the bits are delivered to the intended receiver without any error and in the proper sequence.

X.212 defines throughput independently for each direction of transfer across the link. Typically, a throughput specification would have a desired value, called the target value, and a minimum accepted value, called the lowest level of quality of service.

Transit Delay. Transit delay is defined as the elapsed time between the issuance of the data request primitive and the corresponding data indication primitive. Elapsed time—that is to say, transit delay—is only calculated for those data units that are considered to be successfully transferred to the receiver. Like throughput, transit delay is specified independently for each direction of transmission across the link.

Residual Error Rate. The residual error rate is calculated as the ratio of the total number of lost, duplicate, or incorrect data units to the total number of data units transferred across the data link during some agreed-upon measuring period.

Resilience. This curious parameter defines the probability of a data link service provider initiating the release of the data link. In the terms of the primitives, this means the issuance of a DL-DISCONNECT indication primitive when there was no previous DL-DISCONNECT request primitive issued. Resilience can also be defined as the data link service provider-initiated reset.

Protection. Protection is defined as the extent to which the data link provider will attempt to prevent unauthorized monitoring of the link or manipulation of the data on the link. Protection is currently specified by a minimum and maximum protection option. Within this option X.212 provides a range of three other options: (1) no protection features, (2) protection against passive monitoring, and (3) protection against replay or modification. During the data link establishment, the data link service user is allowed to select a particular value within a range.

Priority. Priority is defined as the relative importance of the data link connection with regard to two components. The first component is the order in which a data link control session user would have its quality of service degraded if necessary. The second component is the order in which data link control would actually be released to recover resources if necessary. Priority is specified as a minimum and maximum value within a given range.

The reader should keep these quality of service parameters in mind as the service definitions of the other layers are examined. It will be quite evident that many of these parameters begin their journey down to this lower level from the upper layers. Indeed, some of the parameters can be mapped transparently through the layers and implemented at this layer (or at the upper layers above the data link layer.)

Rules for the Use of Service Definitions

X.212 provides very detailed rules for the use of primitives and their parameters. It is beyond the scope of this book to go into the rules for each of the primitives. The reader is encouraged to obtain the actual document for the specific rules.

HIGH-LEVEL DATA LINK CONTROL (HDLC)

A prerequisite to any discussion of the data link control sublayers is an understanding of the HDLC specification. It forms the basis for LLC, LAPB, LAPD, and many other standards and products.

HDLC is a line protocol specification published by the International Standards Organization (ISO) as ISO 3309 and ISO 4335 (and supporting documents 7809, 8471, 8885). It has achieved wide use throughout the world. The standard provides for many functions and covers a wide range of applications. It is frequently used as a foundation for other protocols which use specific options in the HDLC repertoire. For this reason, HDLC is covered in considerable detail in this chapter.

ADCCP is published as ANSI X3.66. With minor variations, it is identical to HDLC. ADCCP has been adopted by the U.S. National Institute for Standards and Technology (NIST) as FIPS PUB 71-1 and by the Federal Telecommunications Standards Committee at FED-STD-1003A. To keep matters simple, we only examine HDLC since its use is more widespread.

This section addresses the main functions of HDLC. It also covers some of the more important "subsets," such as SDLC, LAP, LAPB, LAPD, and LLC. The reader is encouraged to check with specific vendors for their actual implementation of HDLC. Most vendors have a version of HDLC available, although the protocol is often renamed by the vendor or designated by different initials.

HDLC Characteristics

HDLC provides for a number of link options to satisfy a wide variety of user requirements (see Figure 4-2). It supports both half-duplex and full-duplex transmission, point-to-point and multipoint configurations, as well as switched or nonswitched channels.

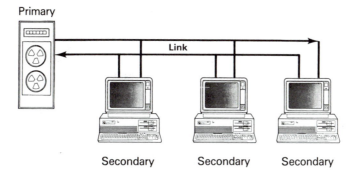

Unbalanced Mode or Normal Response Mode

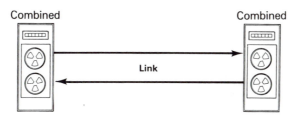

Balanced Mode or Asynchronous Balanced Mode

FIGURE 4-2. HDLC Link Configurations

An HDLC station is classified as one of three types:

- The *primary* station is in control of the data link. This station acts as a master and transmits *command* frames to the secondary stations on the channel. In turn, it receives *response* frames from those stations. If the link is multipoint, the primary station is responsible for maintaining a separate session with each station attached to the link.
- The *secondary* station acts as a slave to the primary station. It responds to the commands from the primary station in the form of responses. It maintains only one session, that being with the primary station, and has no responsibility for control on the link. Secondary stations cannot communicate directly with each other; they must first transfer their frames to the primary station.
- The *combined* station transmits both commands and responses and receives both commands and responses from another combined station. It maintains a session with the other combined station.

HDLC provides three methods to configure the channel for primary, secondary and combined station use:

- An *unbalanced* configuration provides for one primary station and one or more secondary stations to operate as point-to-point or multipoint, half duplex, full duplex, switched or nonswitched. The configuration is called unbalanced because the primary station is responsible for controlling each secondary station and for establishing and maintaining the link.
- The *symmetrical* configuration is used very little today. The configuration provides for two independent, point-to-point unbalanced station configurations. Each station has a primary and secondary status, and therefore each station is considered logically to be two stations: a primary and a secondary station. The primary station transmits commands to the secondary station at the other end of the channel and vice versa. Even though the stations have both primary and secondary capabilities, the actual commands and responses are multiplexed onto one physical channel.
- A *balanced* configuration consists of two combined stations connected point-to-point only, half duplex or full duplex, switched or nonswitched. The combined stations have equal status on the channel and may send unsolicited frames to each other. Each station has equal responsibility for link control. Typically, a station uses a command in order to solicit a response from the other station.. The other station can send its own command as well.

The terms "unbalanced" and "balanced" have nothing to do with the electrical characteristics of the circuit. In fact, data link controls should not be aware of the physical circuit attributes. The two terms are used in a completely different context at the physical and data link levels.

While the HDLC stations are transferring data, they communicate in one of the three modes of operation:

- *Normal response mode* (NRM) requires the secondary station to receive explicit permission from the primary station before transmitting. After receiving permission, the secondary station initiates a response transmission which may contain data. The transmission may consist of one or more frames while the channel is being used by the secondary station. After the last frame transmission, the secondary station must wait for explicit permission before it can transmit again.
- *Asynchronous response mode* (ARM) allows a secondary station to initiate transmission without receiving explicit permission from the primary station. The transmission may contain data frames, or control information reflecting status changes of the secondary station. ARM can decrease overhead because the secondary station does not need a poll sequence in order to send data. A secondary station operating in ARM can transmit only when it detects an idle channel state for a two-way alternate (half-duplex) data flow, or at any time for a two-way simultaneous (duplex) data flow. The primary station maintains responsibility for tasks such as error recovery, link setup, and link disconnections.

- *Asynchronous balanced mode* (ABM) uses combined stations. The combined station may initiate transmissions without receiving prior permission from the other combined station.

Normal response mode (NRM) is used frequently on multipoint lines. The primary station controls the link by issuing polls to the attached stations (usually terminals, personal computers, and cluster controllers). The asynchronous balanced mode (ABM) is a better choice on point-to-point links since it incurs no overhead and delay in polling. The asynchronous response mode (ARM) is used very little today.

The term "asynchronous" has nothing to do with the format of the data and the physical interface of the stations. It is used to indicate the stations need not receive a preliminary signal from another station before sending traffic. HDLC uses synchronous formats in its frames.

Frame Format

HDLC uses the term "frame" to indicate the independent entity of data (protocol data unit) transmitted across the link from one station to another. Figure 4-3 shows the frame format. The frame consists of four or five fields:

- Flag fields (F)   8 bits
- Address field (A)   8 or 16 bits
- Control field (C)   8 or 16 bits
- Information field (I)   variable length; not used in some frames
- Frame check sequence field (FCS)   16 or 32 bits

All frames must start and end with the flag (F) sequence fields. The stations attached to the data link are required to continuously monitor the link for the flag sequence. The flag sequence consists of the binary digits 01111110. Flags are continuously transmitted on the link between frames to keep the link in an active condition.

Other bit sequences are also used. At least seven but less than fifteen continuous ones (abort signal) indicates a problem on the link. Fifteen or more ones keep the channel in an idle condition. One use of the idle state is in support of a half-duplex session. A station can detect the idle pattern and reverse the direction of the transmission.

Once the receiving station detects a nonflag sequence, it is aware it has encountered the beginning of the frame, an abort condition, or an idle channel condition. Upon encountering the next flag sequence, the station recognizes it has found the full frame. In summary, the link recognizes the following bit sequences as:

01111110   = Flags
At least 7, but less than 15 1s   = Abort
15 or more 1s   = Idle

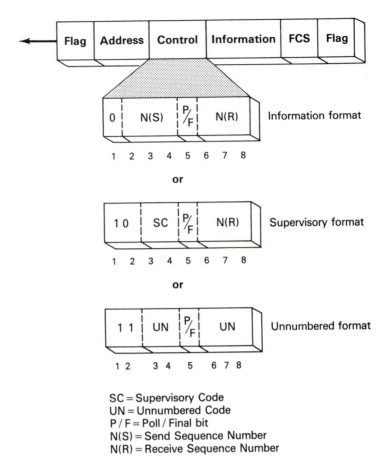

SC = Supervisory Code
UN = Unnumbered Code
P / F = Poll / Final bit
N(S) = Send Sequence Number
N(R) = Receive Sequence Number

FIGURE 4–3. HDLC Frame

The time between the actual transmission of the frames on the channel is called interframe time fill. This time fill is accomplished by transmitting continuous flags between the frames. The flags may be eight-bit multiples and they can combine the ending 0 of the preceding flag with the starting 0 of the next flag.

HDLC is a code-transparent protocol. It does not rely on a specific code (ASCII/IA5, EBCDIC, etc.) for the interpretation of line control. For example, bit position n within a line control octet has a specific meaning, regardless of the other bits in the octet. On occasion, a flag-like field, 01111110, may be inserted into the user data stream (I field) by the application process. More frequently, the bit patterns in the other fields appear "flag-like." To prevent "phony" flags from being inserted into the frame, the transmitter inserts a zero bit after it encounters five continuous ones anywhere between the opening and closing flag of the frame. Consequently, zero insertion applies to the address, control, information, and FCS fields. This technique is called bit stuffing. As the frame is stuffed, it is transmitted across the link to the receiver.

The procedure to recover the frame of the receiver is a bit more involved. The "framing" receiver logic can be summarized as follows: The receiver continuously monitors the bit stream. After it receives a zero bit with five continuous, successive one bits, it inspects the next bit. If it is a zero bit, it pulls this bit out; in other words, it unstuffs the bit. However, if the seventh bit is a one, the receiver inspects the eighth bit. If it is a zero, it recognizes that a flag sequence of 01111110 has been received. If it is a one, then it knows an abort or idle signal has been received and counts the number of succeeding one bits to take appropriate action.

In this manner, HDLC achieves code and data transparency. The protocol is not concerned about any particular bit code inside the data stream. Its main concern is to keep the flags unique.

Many systems use bit stuffing and the non-return-to-zero-inverted (NRZI) encoding technique to keep the receiver clock synchronized. With NRZI, binary ones do not cause a line transition, but binary zeros do cause a change. It might appear that a long sequence of ones could present synchronization problems since the receiver clock would not receive the line transitions necessary for the clock adjustment. However, bit stuffing ensures a 0 bit exists in the data stream at least every 5 bits. The receiver can use them for clock alignment.

The address (A) field identifies the primary or secondary station involved in the frame transmission or reception. A unique address is associated with each station. In an unbalanced configuration, the address field in both commands and responses contains the address of the secondary station. In balanced configurations, a command frame contains the destination station address and the response frame contains the sending station address.

The control (C) field contains the commands, responses and the sequence numbers used to maintain the data flow accountability of the link between the primary stations. The format and the contents of the control field vary, depending on the use of the HDLC frame. See Figure 4-3 for an illustration of the control field.

The Information (I) field contains the actual user data. The Information field only resides in the frame under the Information frame format. It is usually not found in the Supervisory or Unnumbered frame.

One option of HDLC allows the I field to be used with an Unnumbered Information (UI) frame. This is a very important feature of HDLC, because it provides a capability to use the Unnumbered frame to achieve a connectionless-mode operation at the link level. Several subsets of HDLC, such as LLC and LAPD, use the UI frame; if it does reside in these frames, it carries special link control information.

The frame check sequence (FCS) field is used to check for transmission errors between the two data link stations. The FCS field is created by a cyclic redundancy check. We summarize it here. The transmitting station performs Modulo 2 division (based on an established polynomial) on the A, C, and I fields plus leading zeros, and appends the remainder as the FCS field. In turn, the receiving station performs a division with the same polynomial on the A, C, I, and FCS fields. If the remainder equals a predetermined value, the chances are quite good the transmission occurred without any errors. If the comparisons do not match, it indicates a probable transmission error, in which case the receiving station sends a negative acknowledgment, requiring a retransmission of the frame.

The Control Field

Let us return to a more detailed discussion of the control field (C) because it determines how HDLC controls the communications process (see Figure 4-3). The control field defines the function of the frame and therefore invokes the logic to control the movement of the traffic between the receiving and sending stations. The field can be in one of three formats: Information, Supervisory, and Unnumbered transfer.

- The *information* format frame is used to transmit end-user data between the two devices. The Information frame may also acknowledge the receipt of data from a transmitting station. It also can perform certain other functions such as a poll command.
- The *Supervisory* format frame performs control functions such as the acknowledgment of frames, the request for the retransmission of frames, and the request for the temporary suspension of the transmission frames. The actual usage of the supervisory frame is dependent on the operational mode of the link (normal response mode, asynchronous balanced mode, asynchronous response mode).
- The *Unnumbered* format is also used for control purposes. The frame is used to perform link initialization, link disconnection, and other link control functions. The frame uses five bit positions, which allows for up to 32 commands and 32 responses. The particular type of command and response depends on the HDLC class of procedure.

The actual format of the HDLC frame determines how the control field is coded and used. The simplest format is the information transfer format. The N(S) (send sequence) number indicates the sequence number associated with a transmitted frame. The N(R) (receive sequence) number indicates the sequence number that is expected at the receiving site.

Piggybacking, Flow Control, and Accounting for Traffic

HDLC maintains accountability of the traffic and controls the flow of frames by the state variables and sequence numbers discussed in Appendix 4A. To briefly summarize: The traffic at both the transmitting and receiving sites is controlled by these state variables. The transmitting site maintains a send state variable [V(S)], which is the sequence number of the next frame to be transmitted. The receiving site maintains a receive state variable [V(R)], which contains the number that is expected to be in the sequence number of the next frame. The V(S) is incremented with each frame transmitted and placed in the send sequence field in the frame.

Upon receiving the frame, the receiving site checks the send sequence number with its V(R). If the cyclic redundancy check (CRC) passes and if V(R) = N(S), it increments V(R) by one, places the value in the sequence number field in a frame, and sends it to the original transmitting site to complete the accountability for the transmission.

If the V(R) does not match the sending sequence number in the frame (or the CRC does not pass), an error has occurred, in which case a reject or selective reject with a value in V(R) is sent to the original transmitting site. The V(R) value informs the transmitting DTE of the next frame that it is expected to send, i.e., the number of the frame to be retransmitted.

The Poll/Final Bit

The fifth bit position in the control field is called the P/F or poll/final bit. It is only recognized when set to 1 and is used by the primary and secondary stations to provide a dialogue with each other:

- The primary station uses the P bit = 1 to solicit a status response from a secondary station. The P bit signifies a poll.
- The secondary station responds to a P bit with data or a status frame, and with the F bit = 1. The F bit can also signify end of transmission from the secondary station under Normal Response Mode (NRM).

The P/F bit is called the P bit when used by the primary station and the F bit when used by the secondary station. Most versions of HDLC permit one P bit (awaiting a F bit response) to be outstanding at any time on the link. Consequently, a P set to 1 can be used as a checkpoint. That is, the P = 1 means, "Respond to me, because I want to know your status." Checkpoints are quite important in all forms of automation. It is the machine's technique to clear up ambiguity and perhaps discard copies of previously transmitted frames. Under some versions of HDLC, the device may not proceed further until the F bit frame is received, but other versions of HDLC (such as LAPB) do not require the F bit frame to interrupt the full-duplex operations.

How does a station know if a received frame with the fifth bit = 1 is an F or P bit? After all, it is in the same bit position in all frames. HDLC provides an elegantly simple solution: The fifth bit is a P bit and the frame is a command if the address field contains the address of the receiving station; it is an F bit and the frame is a response if the address is that of the transmitting station. This destination is quite important because a station may react quite differently to the two types of frames. For example, a command (address of receiver, P = 1) usually requires the station to send back specific types of frames.

A summary of the addressing rules follows:

- A station places its own address in the address field when it transmits a response.
- A station places the address of the receiving station in the address field when it transmits a command.

HDLC Commands and Responses

Table 4-2 shows the HDLC commands and responses. They are briefly summarized here.

The Receive Ready (RR) is used by the primary or secondary station to indicate that it is ready to receive an information frame and/or acknowledge previously received frames by using the N(R) field. The primary station may also use the Receive Ready command to poll a secondary station by setting the P bit to 1.

The Receive Not Ready (RNR) frame is used by the station to indicate a busy condition. This informs the transmitting station that the receiving station is unable to accept additional incoming data. The RNR frame may acknowledge previously transmitted frames by using the N(R) field. The busy condition can be cleared by sending the RR frame.

The Selective Reject (SREJ) is used by a station to request the retransmission of a single frame identified in the N(R) field. This field also performs inclusive acknowledgment: all information frames numbered up to N(R)-1 are acknowledged. Once the SREJ has been transmitted, subsequent frames are accepted and held for the retransmitted frame. The SREJ condition is cleared upon receipt of an I frame with a N(S) equal to V(R).

An SREJ frame must be transmitted for each erroneous frame; each frame is treated as a separate error. Only one SREJ frame can be outstanding at a time, since the N(R) field in the frame inclusively acknowledges all preceding frames, to send a second SREJ would contradict the first SREJ because all I frames with N(S) lower than N(R) of the second SREJ would be acknowledged.

The Reject (REJ) is used to request the retransmission of frames starting with the frame numbered in the N(R) field. Frames numbered N(R)-1 are all acknowledged. The REJ frame can be used to implement the Go-Back-N technique discussed in Appendix 4A.

The Unnumbered Information (UI) format allows for transmission of user data in an unnumbered (i.e., unsequenced) frame. The UI frame is actually a form of connectionless-mode link protocol in that the absence of the N(S) and N(R) fields preclude flow-controlling and acknowledging frames. The IEEE 802.2 logical link control (LLC) protocol uses this approach with its LLC type 1 version of HDLC.

The Request Initialization Mode (RIM) format is a request from a secondary station for initialization to a primary station. Once the secondary stations sends RIM it can monitor frames but can only respond to SIM, DISC, TEST, or XID.

TABLE 4-2. HDLC Control Field Format

Format	1	2	3	Control Field Bit Encoding		6	7	8	Commands	Responses
				4	5					
Information	0	–	N(S)	–	•	–	N(R)	–	I	I
Supervisory	1	0	0	0	•	–	N(R)	–	RR	RR
	1	0	0	1	•	–	N(R)	–	REJ	REJ
	1	0	1	0	•	–	N(R)	–	RNR	RNR
	1	0	1	1	•	–	N(R)	–	SREJ	SREJ
Unnumbered	1	1	0	0	•	0	0	0	UI	UI
	1	1	0	0	•	0	0	1	SNRM	
	1	1	0	0	•	0	1	0	DISC	RD
	1	1	0	0	•	1	0	0	UP	
	1	1	0	0	•	1	1	0		UA
	1	1	0	1	•	0	0	0	NR0	NR0
	1	1	0	1	•	0	0	1	NR1	NR1
	1	1	0	1	•	0	1	0	NR2	NR2
	1	1	0	1	•	0	1	1	NR3	NR3
	1	1	1	0	•	0	0	0	SIM	RIM
	1	1	1	0	•	0	0	1		FRMR
	1	1	1	1	•	0	0	0	SARM	DM
	1	1	1	1	•	0	0	1	RSET	
	1	1	1	1	•	0	1	0	SARME	
	1	1	1	1	•	0	1	1	SNRME	
	1	1	1	1	•	1	0	0	SABM	
	1	1	1	1	•	1	0	1	XID	XID
	1	1	1	1	•	1	1	0	SABME	
	1	1	0	0	•	1	1	1	TEST	TEST

LEGEND:

I	Information	NR0	Non-Reserved 0
RR	Receive Ready	NR1	Non-Reserved 1
REJ	Reject	NR2	Non-Reserved 2
RNR	Receive Not Ready	NR3	Non-Reserved 3
SREJ	Selective Reject	SIM	Set Initialization Mode
UI	Unnumbered Information	RIM	Request Initialization Mode
SNRM	Set Normal Response Mode	FRMR	Frame Reject
DISC	Disconnect	SARM	Set Async Response Mode
RD	Request Disconnect	SARME	Set ARM Extended Mode
UP	Unnumbered Poll	SNRM	Set Normal Response Mode
RSET	Reset	SNRME	Set NRM Extended Mode
XID	Exchange Identification	SABM	Set Async Balance Mode
DM	Disconnect Mode	SABME	Set ABM Extended Mode
•	The P/F Bit	TEST	Test

The Set Normal Response Mode (SNRM) places the secondary station in the Normal Response Mode (NRM). The NRM precludes the secondary station from sending any unsolicited frames. This means the primary station controls all frame flow on the line.

The Disconnect (DISC) places the secondary station in the disconnected mode. This command is valuable for switched lines; it provides a function similar to hanging up a telephone. UA is the expected response.

The Disconnect Mode (DM) is transmitted from a secondary station to indicate it is in the disconnect mode (not operational).

The Test (TEST) frame is included in the European Computer Manufacturers Association (ECMA) version of HDLC. It is used to solicit testing responses from the secondary station. HDLC does not stipulate how the TEST frames are to be used. An implementation can use the I field for diagnostic purposes, for example.

The Set Asynchronous Response Mode (SARM) allows a secondary station to transmit without a poll from the primary station. It places the secondary station in the information transfer state (IS) of ARM.

The Set Asynchronous Balanced Mode (SABM) sets the mode to ABM, in which stations are peers with each other. No polls are required to transmit since each station is a combined station.

The Set Normal Response Mode Extended (SNRME) sets SNRM with two octets in the control field. This is used for extended sequencing and permits the N(S) and N(R) to be seven bits in length, thus increasing the window to a range of 1–127.

The Set Asynchronous Balanced Mode Extended (SABME) sets SABM with two octets in the control field for extended sequencing.

The Unnumbered Poll (UP) polls a station without regard to sequencing or acknowledgment. Response is optional if poll bit is set to 0. It provides for one response opportunity.

The Reset (RESET) is used as follows: The transmitting station resets its N(S) and receiving station resets its N(R). The command is used for recovery. Previously unacknowledged frames remain unacknowledged.

HDLC Timers

The vendors vary in how they implement link level timers in a product. HDLC defines two timers, T1 and T2. Most implementations use T1 in some fashion. T2 is used, but not as frequently as T1. The timers are used in the following manner:

T1   A primary station issues a P bit and checks if a response is received to the P bit within a defined time. This function is controlled by the timer T1 and is called the "wait for F" time-out.

T2   A station in the ARM mode that issues I frames checks whether acknowledgments are received within a timer period. This function is controlled by timer T2 and is called "wait for N(R)" time-out.

Since ARM is not used much today, timer T1 is typically invoked to handle the T2 functions.

To examine T1 further, refer to Figure 4-4 which illustrates the state diagram for primary station time-out functions (with a normal response mode [NRM]). Table 4-3 explains the use of the timer for NRM (derived from ECMA documentation).

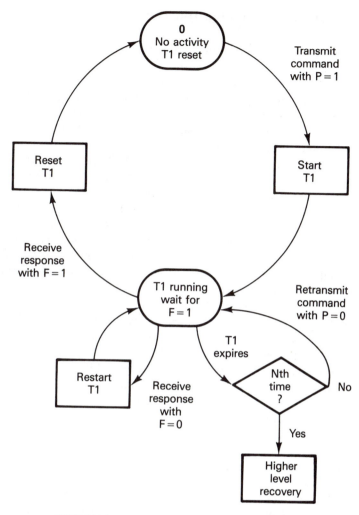

FIGURE 4-4. HDLC T1 Timer Operations

TABLE 4-3.   T1 Activity at Primary Station

Action	Reason
Start T1 from 0	When a command is sent with P = 1
Restart T1 from 0	When a response is received with F = 1
Reset T1 to 0	When a response is received with F = 1
Retransmit command with P = 1	T1 expires

Many other link protocols are derived from HDLC. The practice has proved to be quite beneficial to the industry because it has provided a "baseline" link control standard from which to operate. In some companies, their existing HDLC software has been copied and modified to produce HDLC variations and "subsets" for special applications. But be aware that while these link control systems are referred to as subsets, they sometimes include other capabilities not found in HDLC.

The major published subsets of HDLC are summarized in this section. The overall HDLC schema is shown in Figure 4-5. Two options are provided for unbalanced links (Normal Response Mode (UN) and Asynchronous Response Mode (UA)) and one for balanced (Asynchronous Balanced Mode [BA]).

In order to classify a protocol conveniently, the terms UN, UA, and BA are used to denote which subset of HDLC is used. In addition, most subsets use the functional extensions. For example, a protocol classified as UN 3,7 uses the unbalanced normal response mode option and the selective reject and extended address functional extensions.

From an examination of Figure 4-5, it is evident that HDLC provides a wide variety of options. Consequently, the full range of functions is not implemented as a single product. Rather, a vendor chooses the subset that best meets the need for the link protocol. The reader should be aware that using an HDLC product does not guarantee link compatibility with another vendor's HDLC product, because each may implement a different subset of HDLC. Furthermore, some vendors implement features not found in the HDLC standards. When in doubt, read the manuals!

LAP—Link Access Procedure

LAP (Link Access Procedure) is an earlier subset of HDLC. LAP is based on the HDLC Set Asynchronous Response Mode (SARM) command on an unbalanced configuration. It is classified UA 2,8 except it does not use the DM response. LAP is still used to support some X.25 network links.

To establish a LAP data link, the sending end (primary function) transmits a SARM in the control field to the receiving end (secondary function). Concurrent with the transmission of the SARM, the primary function will start a no-response timer (T1). When the secondary function receives the SARM correctly, it transmits an acknowledgment response (UA: unnumbered acknowledgment). Receipt of the UA by the primary function confirms the initiation of one direction of the link and resets the T1 timer. The receipt of the SARM in a given direction will be interpreted by the secondary function as a request to initiate the other direction of transmission, so the procedure may be repeated in the other direction at the discretion of the secondary function.

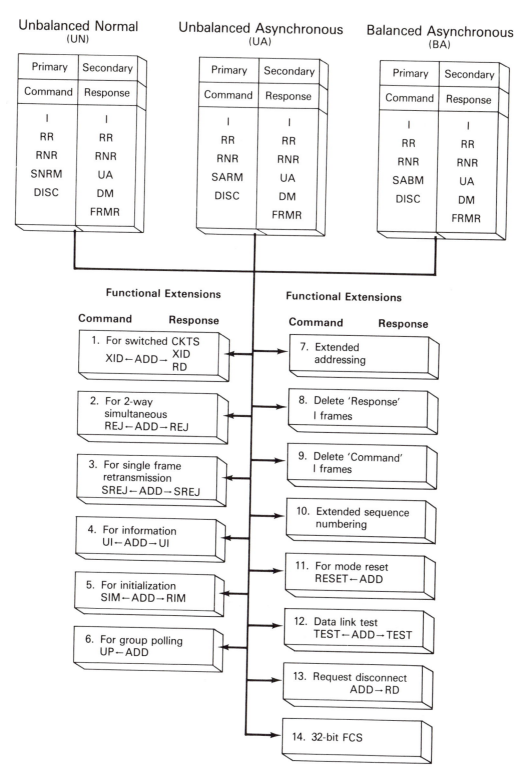

FIGURE 4-5. HDLC Options

LAPB—Link Access Procedure, Balanced

LAPB (Link Access Procedure, Balanced) is used by many private and public computer networks throughout the world. LAPB is classified as a BA 2,8 or BA 2,8,10 subset of HDLC. Option 2 provides for simultaneous rejection of frames in a two-way transmission mode.

Option 8 does not permit the transmitting of information in the response frames. This restriction presents no problem in asynchronous balanced mode, because the information can be transferred in command frames, and since both stations are combined stations, both can transmit commands. Moreover, with LAPB, the sending of a command frame with the P bit = 1 occurs when the station wants a "status" frame and not an information frame. Consequently, the responding station is not expected to return an I field.

LAPB is the link protocol layer for an X.25 network. It is used extensively worldwide and is found in many vendor's ports on a chip with the X.25 network level software. An extensive discussion on LAPB can be found in The X.25 Protocol by Uyless Black, published by the IEEE Computer Society.

LLC—Logical Link Control (IEEE 802.2)

LLC (Logical Link Control) is a standard sponsored by the IEEE 802 standards committee for local area networks (LANs). The standard permits the interfacing of a local area network to other local networks as well as to a wide area network. LLC uses a subclass of the HDLC superset. LLC is classified as BA 2,4.

LLC permits three types of implementations of HDLC: type 1, using the UI frame (Unacknowledged Connectionless Service); type 2, using the conventional I frame (Acknowledged Connection-oriented Service); and type 3, using AC frames (Acknowledged Connectionless Service).

LLC is intended to operate over a peer-to-peer multipoint channel using the UI or SABME frames. Therefore, each frame contains the address of both the sending and receiving station. The next section examines LLC in considerable detail.

LAPD—Link Access Procedure, D Channel

LAPD (Link Access Procedure, D Channel) is another subset of the HDLC structure, although it has extensions beyond HDLC. It is derived from LAPB. LAPD is used as a data link control for the integrated services digital network (ISDN).

ISDN provides LAPD to allow DTEs to communicate with each other across the ISDN D Channel. (Many users want LAPD for B channels as well.) It is specifically designed for the link across the ISDN user-network interface.

LAPD has a very similar frame format to HDLC and LAPB. Moreover, it provides for unnumbered, supervisory, and information transfer frames. LAPD also allows a Modulo 128 operation. The control octet to distinguish between the information format, supervisory format, or unnumbered format is identical to HDLC.

LAPD provides for two octets for the address field (see Figure 4-6). This is valuable for multiplexing multiple functions onto the D channel. Each ISDN basic access can support up to 8 stations. The address field is used to identify the specific terminal and service access point (SAP). The address field contains the address field extension bits, a command/response indication bit, a service access point identifier (SAPI), and a terminal end-point identifier (TEI). These entities are discussed in the following paragraphs.

The purpose of the address field extension is to provide more bits for an address. The presence of a 1 in the first bit of an address field octet signals that it is the final octet of the address field. Consequently, a two-octet address would have a field address extension value of 0 in the first octet and a 1 in the second octet. The address field extension bit allows the user of both the SAPI in the first octet and the TEI in the second octet, if desired.

The command/response (C/R) field bit identifies the frame as either a com-

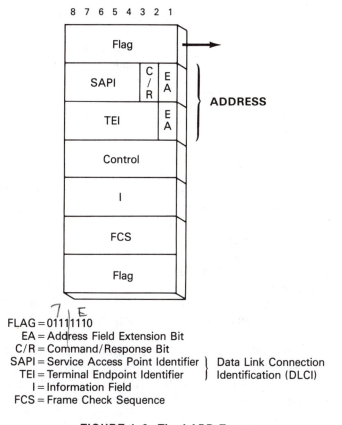

FLAG = 01111110
EA = Address Field Extension Bit
C/R = Command/Response Bit
SAPI = Service Access Point Identifier } Data Link Connection
TEI = Terminal Endpoint Identifier   } Identification (DLCI)
I = Information Field
FCS = Frame Check Sequence

FIGURE 4-6. The LAPD Frame

mand or a response. The user side sends commands with the C/R bit set to 0. It responds with the C/R bit set to 1. The network does the opposite—it sends commands with C/R set to 1 and responses with C/R set to 0.

The service access point identifier (SAPI) identifies the point where the data link layer services are provided to the layer above (that is, layer 3). (If the concept of the SAPI is vague, review Chapter 1.)

The terminal endpoint identifier (TEI) identifies a specific connection within the SAP. It can identify either a single terminal (TE) or multiple terminals. The TEI is assigned by a separate assignment procedure. Collectively, the TEI and SAPI are called the data link connection identifier (DLCI), which identifies each data link connection on the D channel. As stated earlier, the control field identifies the type of frame as well as the sequence numbers used to maintain windows and acknowledgments between the sending and receiving devices.

Presently, the SAPI values and TEI values are allocated as follows:

SAPI

Value	Related Entity
0	Call Control Procedures
16	Packet Procedures
32–47	Reserved for National Use
63	Management Procedures
Others	Reserved

TEI

Value	User Type
0–63	Non-Automatic Assignment
64–126	Automatic Assignment

Two commands and responses in LAPB do not exist in the HDLC schema. These are sequenced information 0 (SI0) and sequenced information 1 (SI1). The purpose of the SI0/SI1 commands is to transfer information using sequentially acknowledged frames. These frames contain information fields provided by layer 3. The information commands are verified by the means of the end (SI) field. The P bit is set to 1 for all SI0/SI1 commands. The SI0 and SI1 responses are used during single frame operation to acknowledge the receipt of SI0 and SI1 command frames and to report the loss of frames or any synchronization problems. LAPD does not allow information fields to be placed in the SI0 and SI1 response frames. Obviously, information fields are in the SI0 and SI1 command frames.

LAPD differs from LAPB in a number of ways. The most fundamental difference is that LAPB is intended for point-to-point operating (user DTE-to-Packet Exchange [DCE]). LAPD is designed for multiple access on the link. The other major differences are summarized as follows:

- LAPB and LAPD use different timers.
- The addressing structure differs, as explained earlier.

- LAPD implements the HDLC unnumbered information frame (UI).
- LAPB uses only the sequenced information frames.

LAPD Primitives. LAPD uses a number of primitives for its communications with the network layer, the physical layer and a management entity which resides outside both layers. The primitives are summarized in Table 4-4.

SDLC—SYNCHRONOUS DATA LINK CONTROL

SDLC (Synchronous Data Link Control) is IBM's widely used version of the HDLC superset. SDLC uses Unbalanced Normal Response Mode (NRM), which means the link is managed by one primary station. In addition, it uses several options of the superset. One of its classifications, for example, is UN 1,2,4,5,6,12, but it does use other subschemas.

SDLC is an effective protocol for multipoint links, since it uses the NRM. However, IBM is placing LLC into some of its products that are connected to

TABLE 4–4. LAPD Primitives

Primitive	Function
DL-ESTABLISH (level 2/3 boundary)	Issued on the establishment of frame operations
DL-RELEASE (level 2/3 boundary)	Issued on the termination of frame operations
DL-DATA (level 2/3 boundary)	Used to pass data between layers with acknowledgments
DL-UNIT-DATA (level 2/3 boundary)	Used to pass data with no acknowledgments
MDL-ASSIGN (level management/2 boundary)	Used to associate TEI value with a specified endpoint
MDL-REMOVE (level management/2 boundary)	Removes the MDL-ASSIGN
MDL-ERROR (level management/2 boundary)	Associated with an error that cannot be corrected by LAPD
MDL-UNIT-DATA (level management/2 boundary)	Used to pass data with no acknowledgments
PH-DATA (level 2/1 boundary)	Used to pass frames across layers
DH-ACTIVATE (level 2/1 boundary	Used to set up physical link
PH-DEACTIVATE (level 2/1 boundary)	Used to deactivate physical link

multipoint local area networks. A typical configuration is the IBM token ring, in which the token ring protocol resides at the MAC sublayer and LLC resides above it. LLC is used to manage the dialogue and flow control between the stations on the link.

EXAMPLES OF LINK OPERATIONS

Figures 4-7 through 4-10 are provided as examples of HDLC, LAPB, and SDLC link operations. Each figure is accompanied with a short explanation of the events taking place on the link. The reader should note that the figures are drawn with the frames occupying the link in non-varying time slots. This is usually not the case, but this approach keeps the illustrations relatively simple and the illustrations are conceptually accurate. The figures depict the following link configurations:

Figure 4-7	Link set up with SABM and half-duplex operations
Figure 4-8	A typical SDLC error recovery with an NRM link
Figure 4-9	An LAPB error recovery with an ABM link
Figure 4-10	An SDLC multipoint operation

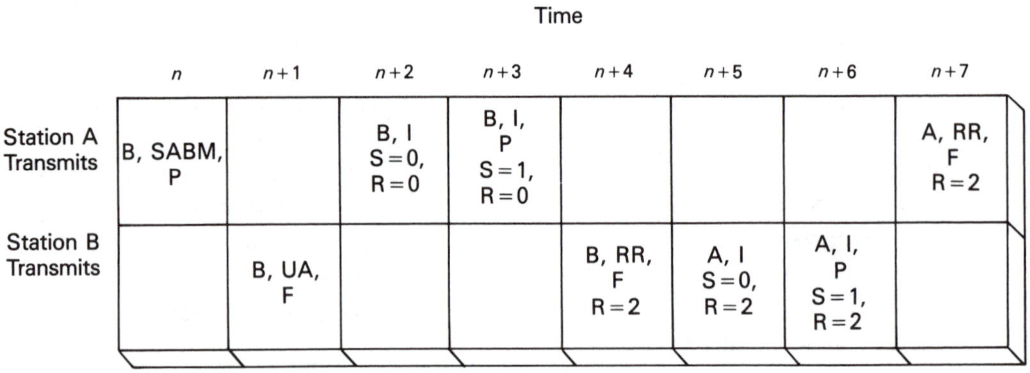

Time

	n	$n+1$	$n+2$	$n+3$	$n+4$	$n+5$	$n+6$	$n+7$
Station A Transmits	B, SABM, P		B, I S=0, R=0	B, I, P S=1, R=0				A, RR, F R=2
Station B Transmits		B, UA, F			B, RR, F R=2	A, I S=0, R=2	A, I, P S=1, R=2	

Legend (I means I field present):

n: Station A transmits *Set Asynchronous Balanced Mode* (SABM) command with P bit set.

$n+1$: Station B responds with an *Unnumbered Acknowledgment* (UA) response with F bit set.

$n+2, 3$: Station A sends information frames 0 and 1, sets P bit.

$n+4, 5, 6$: Station B acknowledges A's transmission by sending 2 in the receive sequence number field. Station B also transmits information frames 0 and 1, and sets P=1.

$n+7$: Station B acknowledges A's frames of 1 and 2 with N(R)=2 and responds to P=1 with F=1.

FIGURE 4-7. Asynchronous Balanced Mode with Half-Duplex Data Flow (using P/F for checkpointing)

The Data Link Layer

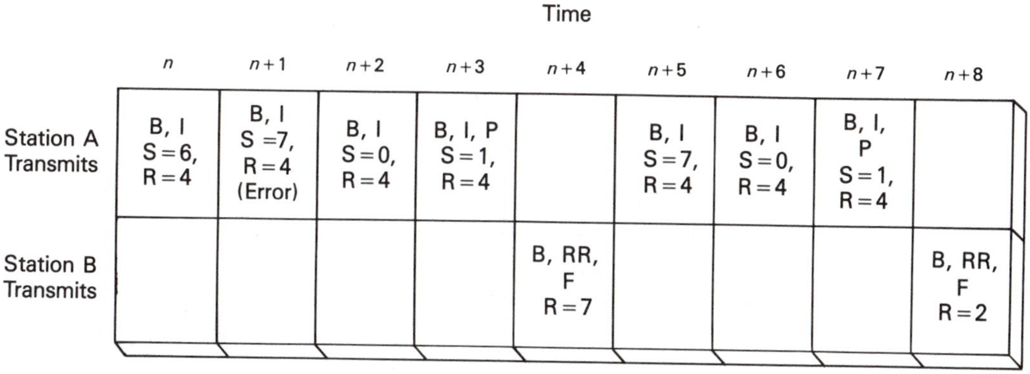

Figure Illustrates an Ongoing Session

Legend (I means I field present):

n, n+1, 2, 3: Station A sends information frames 6, 7, 0, and 1

n+4: Station B returns a *Receive Ready* (RR) with a send sequence number of 7 and a final bit. This means station B is expecting to receive frame 7 again (and all frames transmitted after 7).

n+5, 6, 7: Station A retransmits frames 7, 0, and 1 and sets the P bit for a checkpoint.

n+8: Station B acknowledges frames 7, 0, and 1 with a *Receive Ready* (RR) and a receive sequence number of 2, and sets the F bit.

FIGURE 4-8. An SDLC Error-Recovery Operation

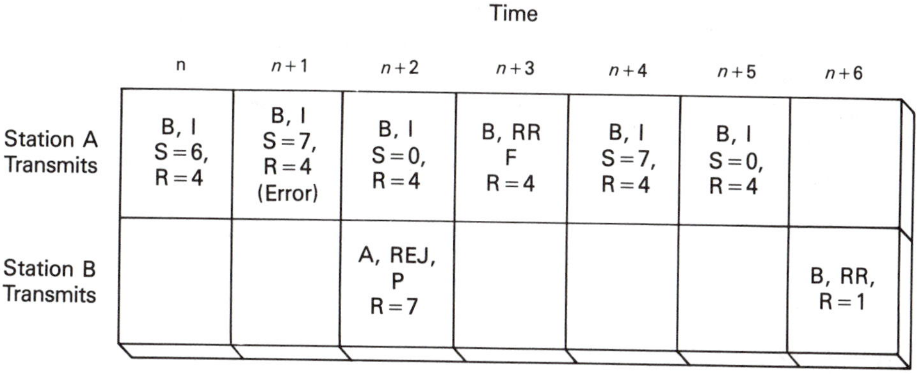

Figure Illustrates an Ongoing Session

Legend:

n, n+1, 2: Station A sends information frames 6, 7, and 0. Station B detects an error in frame 7, and immediately sends a *Reject* frame with a receive sequence number of 7. Notice the use of the address field and P bit to depict a command frame.

n+3, 4, 5: Station A returns an RR and retransmits the erroneous frames.

n+6: Station B acknowledges the retransmission.

FIGURE 4-9. An LAPB Error-Recovery Operation

Examples of Link Operations

Time

	n	n+1	n+2	n+3	n+4	n+5	n+6	n+7
Station A Transmits	C, RR, P, R=0	B, I, S=0, R=0	B, I, S=1, R=0		B, RR, P, R=0		C, RR, P, R=3	B, RR, P, R=2
Station B Transmits						B, I, S=0, R=2	B, I, F, S=1, R=2	
Station C Transmits		C, I, S=0, R=0	C, I, S=1, R=0	C, I, F, S=2, R=0				

Figure Illustrates an Ongoing Session

Legend (I means I field present):

n: Station A uses *Receive Ready* command to poll station C with poll bit set.

n+1, 2: Station A sends frames 0 and 1 to B, which station C responds to the previous poll and sends frames 0 and 1 to A on the other subchannel of the full-duplex circuit.

n+3: Station C sends information frame 2 and sets final bit.

n+4: Station A polls B for a checkpoint (confirmation).

n+5: Station B responds by acknowledging A's 0 and 1 frames with a receive sequence of 2. Station B also sends information frame 0.

n+6: Station A acknowledges C's frames 0, 1 and 2 with a *Receive Ready* (RR) and a receive sequence of 3. Station B sends frame 1, and sets F to 1 in response to the P bit in n+4.

n+7: Station A acknowledges B's frames 0 and 1 with a *Receive Ready* (RR) and a receive sequence of 2.

FIGURE 4–10. An SDLC Multipoint Operation

MULTILINK PROCEDURES (MLP)

In recent years, many manufacturers have developed link-level protocols to manage more than one link. The advantages are obvious. First, additional throughput can be achieved. Second, a faulty link can be replaced easily by a predefined back-up link.

In 1984, LAPB was amended to include provisions for multilink procedures (MLP), and the ISO published specifications for multilink operations in DIS 7478. The MLP resets above the single link procedures such as LAPB. Figure 4-11 shows the relationship.

Each single-link channel behaves just as we have learned in this chapter.

The Data Link Layer

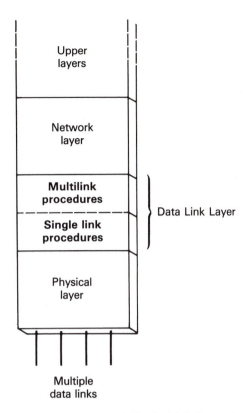

FIGURE 4-11. Multilink and Single Link Procedures

Basically, MLP adds one additional component, a sequence number for all the multilinks. This sequence number is used to manage the windows and flow control across all the links that are identified to the multilink. The multilink sequence number ranges from 0 to 4095 in order to accommodate many links operating at high data transfer rates.

The flow control, sequencing, and window management of MLP closely follow the concepts of individual single links. The main difference is MLP's management of the multiple physical links as if they were one logical link. MLP uses sequence numbers and state variables to accomplish multilink management:

MV(S)	Multilink send state variable
MN(S)	Multilink send sequence number
MV(T)	Multilink transmitted frame acknowledgment state variable
MV(R)	Multilink receive state variable
MW	Multilink window size
MX	Multilink receive window guard region
MV	Multilink system parameter

MV(S) identifies the sequence number of the next send sequence number [MN(S)] to be given to a SLP. It is incremented by 1 with each frame assignment.

MN(S) contains the value of the sequence number of the multilink frame. Note that it is not the same as the N(S) in the SLP control field. The two values perform independent functions. The N(S) sequences the frame on the single link and the MN(S), acting as a higher level sequence number, sequences the frame traversing the multiple links. The MN(S) is used at the receiver to resequence incoming frames that may have arrived out of order across the multiple links (due to SLP retransmission); and to check for duplicate frames (due to the transmitting MLP placing a copy of the frame on more than one SLP to increase the probability of delivery).

MV(T) is maintained at the transmitting station. It identifies the oldest multilink frame that has not yet been acknowledged from the remote station. Due to the existence of more than one link at the interface, it is possible that multilink frames with sequence numbers higher than MV(T) may have been acknowledged.

MV(R) is maintained at the receiving station to identify the next expected in-sequence frame to be delivered to the next layer (usually X.25, X.75, or a vendor's proprietary network layer). As previously stated, multilink frames with sequence numbers higher than MV(R) may have been received.

MW is the window of frames that the transmitting site can give to its SLPs and the receiving site can give to its next higher level. The MW window parameter is significant for both the transmit and receive sites. Its value is affected by factors such as propagation delay, frame lengths, the number of links, the SLP T1 timer, and N2 retry parameter. The multilink MW is defined as:

$$\text{Transmit MW} = \quad \text{MV(T) } \text{Æ } \text{M(V)T} + \text{MV-1 inclusive}$$
$$\text{Receive MW} = \quad \text{MV(R) } \text{Æ } \text{M(V)R} + \text{MV-1 inclusive}$$

MLP permits any received multilink frame whose MN(S) is within the window to be released to the upper level. Of course, the MN(S) must also equal the multilink receive state variable, MV(R).

The MX parameter identifies a range of multilink sequence numbers beginning at MV(R) + MW. The parameter permits the receiving station to accept multilink frames that are outside its receive window.

The MV is a parameter to denote the maximum number of sequentially numbered frames that the transmitting station can give to the SLPs beyond the value of MV(T), the oldest multilink frame awaiting an acknowledgment. The value is established at both sites on the link and is the same value for a given direction of transmission. Its purpose is to prevent overrunning the receiver's window guard region. Therefore, it is not allowed to exceed the maximum MN(S) value less the value of the window guard region.

These numbers and variables can be quite perplexing to the uninitiated, so let us develop a practical example of MLP operations. Figure 4-12 shows two stations (computers, switches, front-ends, etc.) connected with three physical links. Each link is controlled by a single link protocol, such as LAPB. The re-

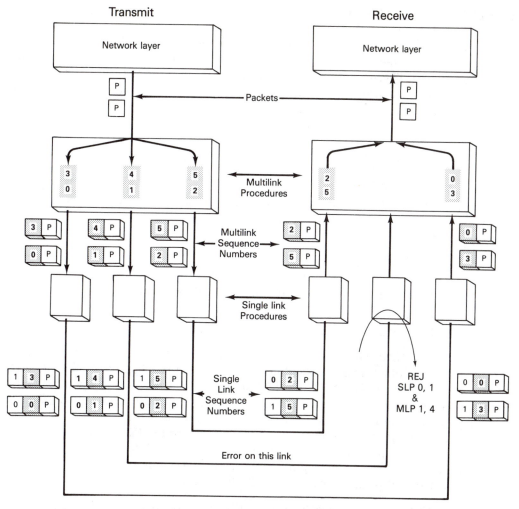

Note: Shaded Boxes Represent MLP Sequence Numbers

FIGURE 4-12. Multilink Operations on Three Single Links

ceiving single link protocols only deliver the protocol data units (PDUs, or frames) to the MLP sublayers when the FCS error-check passes and all edits on the control fields are satisfactory. Then, the MLP sublayer resequences the data before sending it to its next upper layer (usually the network layer).

In Figure 4-12 we assume link 2 experiences some problems (such as noise) and the transmitting SLP retransmits its SLP frames 0 and 1, which are MLP frames 1 and 4. In the meantime, SLP frames 2 and 3 have been delivered to MLP. However, it may hold these data units until it receives a frame with an MLP sequence of 1. Upon receipt of this unit, it passes MLP 1, then 2, then 3 to its next layer. In this example, it resequences the traffic from the single links.

LAN LINK LAYER STANDARDS

The majority of link layer standards are based on the work done by the IEEE 802 Committees, which publish several widely accepted LAN recommended standards. These standards are very important because they encourage the use of common approaches for LAN protocols and interfaces. As a consequence, chip manufacturers are more willing to spend money to develop relatively inexpensive hardware to sell to a large market. The IEEE LAN Committees are organized as follows:

IEEE 802.1	High Level Interface (and MAC Bridges) ✓
IEEE 802.2	Logical Link Control (LLC)
IEEE 802.3	Carrier Sense Multiple Access/Collision Detect (CSMA/CD)
IEEE 802.4	Token Bus
IEEE 802.5	Token Ring
IEEE 802.6	Metropolitan Area Networks
IEEE 802.7	Broadband Technical Advisory Group
IEEE 802.8	Fiber Optic Technical Advisory Group
IEEE 802.9	Integrated Data and Voice Networks

The IEEE standards are gaining wide acceptance. The European Computer Manufacturers Association (ECMA) voted to accept the 802.5 Token Ring as its standard. The NBS, the ISO, and ANSI have accepted these standards and, as we shall see, vendors and user groups are also using them. The ISO publishes these standards with four digits and uses the identifier of 8802 to identify them. For simplicity, in this book we use the IEEE 802 designation.

It was apparent to the 802 Committee that multiple systems were needed to satisfy different user requirements. Thus, the Committee adopted the CSMS/CD, Token Bus, and Token Ring with the following media:

CSMA/CD	Baseband (10 MBits/s); Broadband (10 MBits/s); Twisted Pair (1 MBit/s)
Token Bus	Broadband Coax (1, 5, 10 MBits/s); Carrierband (1, 5, 10 MBits/s)
Token Ring	Shielded Twisted Pair (1, 4 MBits/s)

In 1987, the IEEE made revisions to the 802 specifications. Several changes were made to bring them into conformance with the OSI Model. This chapter reflects these changes.

Relationship of the 802 Standards to the ISO/CCITT Model

The IEEE efforts have emphasized the need to keep the OSI and 802 specifications as compatible as possible. The 802 committees split the data link layer into two sublayers: medium access control (MAC) and logical link control (LLC).

As discussed earlier in this chapter and illustrated in Figure 4-1, MAC encompasses 802.3, 802.4, and 802.5. The LLC includes 802.2. This sublayer was implemented to make the LLC sublayer independent of a specific LAN access method. The LLC sublayer is also used to provide an interface into or out of the specific MAC protocol.

The MAC/LLC split provides several attractive features. First, it controls access to the shared channel among the autonomous user devices. Second, it provides for a decentralized (peer-to-peer) scheme that reduces the LAN's susceptibility to errors. Third, it provides a more compatible interface with wide area networks, since LLC is a subset of the HDLC superset. Fourth, LLC is independent of a specific access method while MAC is protocol-specific. This approach gives an 802 network a flexible interface with work stations and other networks.

Connection Options with LLC Types 1, 2, and 3

At the onset of the IEEE 802 work, it was recognized that a connection-oriented system would limit the scope and power of a local area network. Consequently, two connectionless models are now specified, unacknowledged connectionless model and acknowledged connectionless model.

Let us consider the reasons for this approach. First, many local applications do not need the data integrity provided by a connection-oriented network. For example, sensor equipment can afford to lose occasional data since the sensor readings typically occur quite frequently and the data loss does not adversely affect the information content. As an illustration, the forest service in Canada uses a connectionless system to collect data on lightning strikes. Since several thousand strikes can occur in a very short time span, the loss of a few observations does not bias the data. Also, inquiry-response systems, such as point-of-sale terminals, usually perform acknowledgment at the application level and do not need connection-oriented services at the lower levels. Packetized voice can tolerate some packet loss without affecting the quality of the voice reproduction.

Second, high-speed application processes cannot tolerate the overhead in establishing and disestablishing the connections. The problem is particularly severe in the local area network, with its high-speed channels and low error rates. Many LAN applications require fast setups with each other. Others require very fast communications between the DTEs.

An acknowledged connectionless (AC) service is useful for a number of reasons. Consider the operations of a LAN in a commercial bank. A data link protocol usually maintains state tables, sequence numbers, and windows for each station on the link. It might be impractical to provide this service for every station on the bank's local network, yet work stations like the bank's automated teller machines (ATMs) require they be polled for their transactions. The host computer must also be assured that all transactions are sent and received without errors. The data is too important to use a protocol that does not provide acknowledgments. Additionally, the bank's alarm system needs some type of acknowledgment to ensure the computer receives notice of security breaches in the bank. It is too time-consuming to establish a "connection" before sending the alarm data.

Classes of Service

The 802 LAN standards include four types of service for LLC users:

Type 1	Unacknowledged Connectionless Service
Type 2	Connection-oriented Service
Type 3	Acknowledged Connectionless Service
Type 4	All of the above services

All 802 networks must provide unacknowledged connectionless service (Type 1). Optionally, connection-oriented service can be provided (Type 2). Type 1 networks provide no ACKs, flow control, or error recovery. Type 2 networks provide connection management, ACKs, flow control, and error recovery. Type 3 networks provide no connection setup and disconnect, but they do provide for immediate acknowledgment of data units. Most Type 1 networks use a higher level protocol (i.e., transport layer) to provide connection management functions.

Logical Link Control (LLC)—IEEE 802.2

As we have learned, LLC is the top sublayer of the 802 data link layer. It is common to all MAC modules in 802. It is independent of the MAC access methodology and medium.

The LLC protocol data unit is shown in Figure 4-13. The LLC unit contains a destination service access point address (DSAP), source service access point address (SSAP), control field, and information field. The standard also provides for the address field to identify a specific ring on a token ring and a specific node on the ring. The control field is quite similar to the HDLC control field explained earlier in this chapter.

The HDLC-type commands and responses, established in the control field, depend on whether the LAN is Type 1, 2, or 3. The instruction sets allowed are

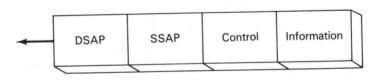

DSAP: Destination Service Access Point Address.
SSAP: Source Service Access Point Address.
Control Field: Uses HDLC Format (See Figure 4-3)

FIGURE 4-13. LLC Protocol Data Unit

TABLE 4-5. LLC Commands and Responses

	Commands	Responses
Type 1 *(UNACK CONLP)*	UI	
	XID	XID
	TEST	TEST
Type 2(I Format) *(CON ORIENTATED)*	I	I
(S Format)	RR	RR
	RNR	RNR
	REJ	REJ
(U Format)	SABME	UA, FRMR
	DISC	DM
Type 3 *(ACK CONLP)*	AC0	AC0
	AC1	AC1

shown in Table 4-5 (notice the UI frame for connectionless service and SABME for connection-oriented service). Since this material is covered in considerable detail earlier in this chapter, we need not repeat the explanation here.

802 Layer Interactions Through Primitives

The 802 LANs use primitives to specify services. The primitives are defined for both the LLC and MAC sublayers. On a general level, four generic primitives are defined:

Request — Passed from user to invoke a service.

Indication — Passed from the service layer to user to indicate an event which is significant to the user.

Response — Passed by user to acknowledge some procedure invoked by an indication primitive to the user

Confirm — Passed from the service layer to user to convey the results of previous service request(s).

The primitives are used in a variety of ways. Figure 4-14 illustrates the general time sequence diagrams for the LLC primitives. The examples in Figure 4-14 depict both the connection-oriented and connectionless service. The reader should note that the model provides for both locally confirmed service [Figure 4-14(b)] and provider-confirmed service [Figure 4-14(c)]. In neither case does 802 imply that the data unit is received safely by the remote user; it only states that the data unit is delivered for the user to retrieve.

Table 4-6 lists each of the 802 primitives used with LLC, and the following material describes them in more detail. The MAC primitives are also examined briefly.

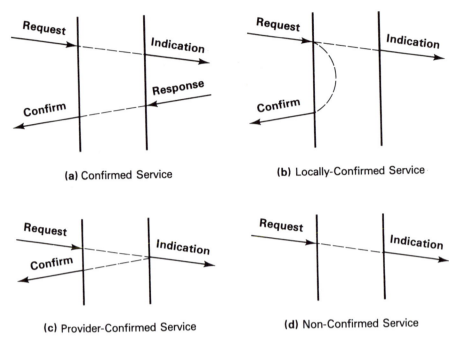

(a) Confirmed Service

(b) Locally-Confirmed Service

(c) Provider-Confirmed Service

(d) Non-Confirmed Service

FIGURE 4-14. LLC Time Sequence Diagrams

Network Layer/LLC Primitives

Connectionless Unacknowledged Data Transfer. Two primitives are used for connectionless data transfer:

- DL-UNITDATA.request (source-address, destination-address, data, priority)
- DL-UNITDATA.indication (source-address, destination-address, data, priority)

The request primitive is passed from the network layer to LLC to request a link service data unit (LSDU) be sent to a remote link service access point. The address parameters are equivalent to a combination of the LLC SAP and MAC addresses. The priority field is passed to MAC and implemented (except for 802.3, which has no priority mechanism). The indication primitive is passed from LLC to the network layer to indicate the arrival of a link service data unit from a remote entity. This relationship is depicted in Figure 4-14(d).

Setting up a Connection. Four primitives are used to establish a connection-oriented session [Figure 4-14 (a)]:

- DL-CONNECT.request (source-address, destination-address, priority)
- DL-CONNECT.indication (source-address, destination-address, priority).

TABLE 4-6.   LAN Primitives

LLC Primitives

Connectionless Data Transfer
  DL-UNITDATA.request
  DL-UNITDATA.indication

Connection-oriented Services
  DL-CONNECT.request
  DL-CONNECT.indication
  DL-CONNECT.response
  DL-CONNECT.confirm

  DL-DATA.request
  DL-DATA.indication

  DL-CONNECTION-FLOWCONTROL.request
  DL-CONNECTION-FLOWCONTROL.indication
  DL-RESET.request
  DL-RESET.indication
  DL-RESET.response
  DL-RESET.confirm

  DL-DISCONNECT.request
  DL-DISCONNECT.indication

MAC Primitives
  MA-UNITDATA.request
  MA-UNITDATA.indication
  MA-UNITDATA-STATUS.indication

- DL-CONNECT.response (source-address, destination-address, priority).
- DL-CONNECT.confirm (source-address, destination-address, priority).

Once these primitives have been exchanged, it is the responsibility of the LLC entities to manage the flow control of the data units.

Connection-oriented Data Transfer.   Two primitives are used for connection-oriented data transfer.

- DL-DATA.request (source-address, destination-address, data)
- DL-DATA.indication (source-address, destination-address, data)

Interestingly, no confirmation primitives are returned to the sender. Generally, the MAC sublayer will deliver the data error-free and the LLC ensures it is sent in the proper order. In the event of a problem, the protocol can issue disconnects or resets (discussed shortly).

Flow Control Procedures.   The network layer can control the amount of data it receives from LLC. Likewise, LLC can flow-control the network layer. Two primitives are used for flow control:

- DL-CONNECTION-FLOWCONTROL.request (source-address, destination-address, amount)
- DL-CONNECTION-FLOWCONTROL.indication (source-address, destination-address, amount)

The amount parameter specifies the amount of data the affected entity is allowed to pass. It can be set with each issuance of the request or indication primitive. If set to zero, data transfer is stopped.

Resetting an LLC Connection.   Four primitives are used to reset a connection:

- DL-RESET.request (source-address, destination-address)
- DL-RESET.indication (source-address, destination-address, reason)
- DL-RESET.response (source-address, destination-address)
- DL-RESET.confirm (source-address, destination-address)

A reset causes all unacknowledged data units to be discarded. LLC does not recover the lost data units, so a higher level protocol must assume this responsibility.

Disconnecting a Session.   Two primitives are used to disconnect the network/LLC session:

- DL-DISCONNECT.request (source-address, destination-address)
- DL-DISCONNECT.indication (source-address, destination-address, reason)

The reason parameter in the indication primitive states the reason for the disconnection. The disconnect can be initiated by either the LLC user or the LLC service provider. This action terminates the logical connection, and any outstanding data units are discarded.

Acknowledged Connectionless Data Transfer.   The acknowledged connectionless service was added with the 1987 revision to the IEEE 802 standards. It consists of two services:

DL-DATA-ACK	An acknowledged delivery service with no prior connection establishment
DL-REPLY	A poll and response service with no prior connection establishment

The DL-DATA-ACK service allows an LLC user to request an immediate acknowledgment to a transmission. A service-class parameter in the primitive stipulates if the MAC sublayer is to participate in the acknowledgment (802.4 supports this feature). A status parameter is used by the remote peer LLC entity to indicate whether or not the protocol data unit was received successfully. The scenario in Figure 4-14(b) is used for this service.

The DL-REPLY service is quite useful when a user wishes to solicit data from another user. The LLC entity can hold a data unit and pass it to any user that polls for the data, or a user can poll the remote user directly for the data. As examples, the DL-DATA-ACK service would be useful for an electronic mail box facility; the DL-REPLY service could be used to poll sensor devices on a factory floor.

LLC/MAC Primitives

The LLC and MAC sublayers use only three primitives to communicate with each other. The primitives operate as depicted in Figure 4-14(d).

- MA-UNITDATA.request (source-address, destination-address, data, priority, service-class)
- MA-UNITDATA.indication (destination-address, source-address, data, reception-status, priority, service-class)
- MA-UNITDATA-STATUS.indication (destination-address, source address, transmission status, provided-priority, provided-service-class)

The address parameters specify the MAC addresses. The reception-status parameter indicates the success of the transfer. An error would be reported to LLC, which might take remedial action. The transmission status parameter is also passed to LLC. Its value depends on the vendor's implementation.

Perhaps the most attractive feature of the LLC/MAC arrangement is that the MA-UNITDATA.request primitive is used to send any type of LLC data unit to any type of MAC network. In other words, the interface is portable across MAC protocols.

CSMA/CD and IEEE 802.3

The best-known scheme for controlling a local area network on a bus structure is carrier sense multiple access with collision detection (CSMA/CD). It is based on several concepts of the ALOHA protocol, which was originally designed for packet radio systems. The most widely used implementation of CSMA/CD is found in the Ethernet specification. Xerox Corporation was instrumental in providing the research for CSMA/CD and in developing the first baseband commercial product. The broadband network was developed by MITRE. In 1980, Xerox, the Intel Corporation, and Digital Equipment Corporation jointly published a specification for an Ethernet local network. This specification was later introduced to the IEEE 802 committees and, with several modifications, has found its way into the IEEE 802.3 standard. (Be aware that the Ethernet and 802.3 interfaces differ in some signaling and formatting conventions.)

CSMA/CD Ethernet is organized around the concept of layered protocols (see Figure 4-15). The user layer is serviced by the two CSMA/CD layers, the

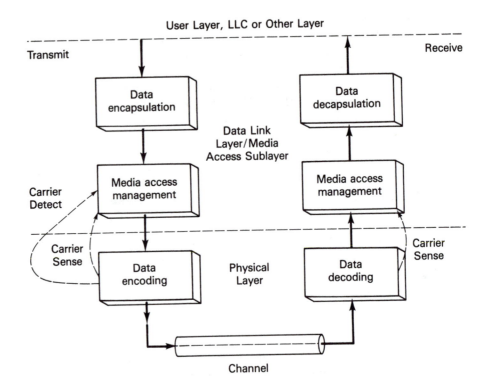

Note: The original Ethernet Channel Access sublayer is described as part of the Data Encoding and Data Decoding entities.

FIGURE 4-15. CSMA/CD Layers

data link layer and the physical layer. The bottom two layers each consist of two separate entities. The data link layer provides the actual logic to control the CSMA/CD network. It is medium independent and hence may be broadband or baseband. The 802 standard includes both broadband and baseband options.

The MAC sublayer consists of the following sublayers:

Transmit Data Encapsulation

- Accepts data from LLC
- Calculates the CRC value and places it in the FCS field

Transmit Media Access Management

- Presents a serial bit stream to the physical layer
- Defers transmission when a medium is busy
- Halts transmission when a collision is detected
- Reschedules a retransmission after a collision
- Inserts the PAD field for frames with a LLC length less than a minimum value
- Enforces a collision by sending a jam message

Receive Data Decapsulation

- Performs a CRC check
- Recognizes and accepts any frame whose DA field is an address of a station
- Presents data to LLC

Receive Media Access Management

- Receives a serial bit stream from the physical layer
- Discards frames that are less than the minimum length

The physical layer is medium dependent. It is responsible for such services as introducing the electrical signals onto the channel, providing the timing on the channel, and data encoding and decoding. Like the data link layer, the physical layer is composed of two major entities: the data encoding/decoding entity and the transmit/receive channel access (although the IEEE 802.3 standard combines these entities in its documents). The major functions of these entities are:

Data Encoding/Decoding

- Provides the signals to synchronize the stations on the channel (this sync signal is called the preamble)
- Encodes the binary data stream to a self-clocking Manchester code at the transmitting site and decodes the Manchester code back to binary code at the receiver.

Channel Access

- Introduces the physical signal onto the channel on the transmit side and receives the signal on the receive side of the interface
- Senses a carrier on the channel on both the transmit and the receive side (which indicates the channel is occupied)
- Detects a collision on the channel on the transmit side (indicating two signals have interfered with each other).

In a CSMA/CD network, each station has both a transmit and receive side to provide the incoming/outgoing flow of data. The transmit side is invoked when a user wishes to transmit data to another DTE on the network; conversely, the receive side is invoked when data is transmitted to the stations on the network.

The CSMA/CD Frame. The MAC level CSMA/CD frame is shown in Figure 4-16. The preamble is transmitted first to achieve medium stabilization and synchronization. The start frame delimiter follows the preamble and indicates the start of the frame. The address fields contain the addresses of the source and destination. The destination address can identify an individual station on the network or a group of stations. The length field indicates the length of the LLC data field. If the data field is less than a maximum length, the PAD field is

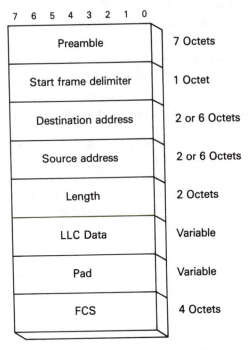

Bits

7 6 5 4 3 2 1 0

Preamble	7 Octets
Start frame delimiter	1 Octet
Destination address	2 or 6 Octets
Source address	2 or 6 Octets
Length	2 Octets
LLC Data	Variable
Pad	Variable
FCS	4 Octets

FIGURE 4-16. MAC CSMA/CD Frame

added to make up the difference. The FCS field contains the value of the CRC. The CRC is calculated on all fields except the preamble, SFD, and FCS. It is defined by the following polynomial:

$$G(x) = X^{32} + x^{26} + x^{23} + x^{22} + x^{16}$$
$$= x^{12} + x^{11} + x^{10} + x^{8} + x^{7} + x^{5} + x^{4} + x^{2} + x + 1$$

CSMA/CD Operations. This section is provided for the reader who wishes more detailed information on CSMA/CD. The transmit data encapsulation entity receives the user data and constructs the MAC frame. It also appends the frame check sequence field to the data and passes the frame to media access management, which buffers the frame until the channel is free. The channel is sensed as free when it sees a carrier sense signal turned off from the transmit channel access entity in the physical layer. After a brief delay, media access management passes the frame to the physical layer.

At the physical layer on the transmit side, data encoding transmits the synchronization signal (preamble). In addition, it encodes the binary data stream to a self-clocking Manchester code. The signal is then passed to transmit channel access, which introduces the signal onto the channel.

The Data Link Layer

The CSMA/CD (MAC) frame is transmitted to all stations connected to the channel. A receiving station senses the preamble, synchronizes itself onto the signal, and turns on the carrier sense signal. Then, receive channel access passes the signal up to data decoding. The data decoding entity translates the Manchester code back to a conventional binary data stream and passes the frame up to the media access management.

Like its counterpart on the transmit side, media access management buffers the frame until the carrier sense signal has been turned off from receive channel access. Media access management can now pass the data up to data decapsulation. Data decapsulation performs an error check on the data to determine if the transmission process created errors. If not, it checks the address field to determine if the frame is destined for its node. If it is, it passes it to the user layer with the destination-address (DA), source-address (SA), and, of course, the LLC data unit.

Since the CSMA/CD structure is a peer-to-peer network, all stations are vying for the use of the channel when they have data to transmit. The contention can result in the signals from various stations being introduced on the cable at approximately the same time. When this occurs, the signals collide and distort each other so that they cannot be received correctly by the stations.

A central aspect of collisions deals with the collision window. This term describes the length of time required for the signal to propagate through the channel and be detected by each station on the network. For example, let us assume that a network has a cable .6 mile (1 km) long. If stations are situated at the far end of the cable, the furthest station distance is about .6 mile. It takes approximately 4.2 microseconds for a signal to travel this distance. When station A is ready to transmit, it senses the cable to determine if a signal is on the circuit. If station B had previously transmitted its frame onto the channel, but it did not yet reach station A, then station A would falsely assume that the channel is idle and transmit its packet. In this situation, the two signals collide.

Under worst-case conditions for a baseband network, the amount of time to detect the collision (and acquire the channel) is twice the propagation delay, since the collided signal must propagate back to the transmitting stations. Propagation delay and collision detection is even longer for a broadband network that uses two cables for send and receive signals—under worst-case conditions, the time to detect the collision is four times the propagation delay.

Obviously, collision is undesirable, since it creates errors in the network. Moreover, if long frames are transmitted, the collision takes more time on the channel than with the use of short frames. CSMA/CD addresses this problem at the transmit media access management level by stopping the frame transmission immediately upon detecting a collision.

Another way to view collisions is through slot time, the time required for a frame to propagate through the entire channel and the delay in acquisition of the channel. An Ethernet 10 Mbits/s channel (baseband) has a propagation delay of 450 bit times. Ethernet requires a slot time to be larger than the sum of the propagation time (450 bits) and the maximum jam time (48 bits).

If the signal is sent to all parts of the channel without a collision, the station that transmitted the signal is said to have acquired or seized the channel. Once this occurs, collisions are avoided, since all stations have detected the signal and defer to it. However, in the event of the collision, the transmit channel access component notices the interference on the channel (in the form of voltage abnormalities for a baseband system) and turns on a special collision-detect signal to transmit media access management. (A broadband CSMA/CD requires other collision detection methods, such as bit comparisons on the send and receive cables.)

Transmit media access management performs two functions to manage the collision. First, it enforces the collision by transmitting a special bit sequence called the jam. The purpose of the jam is to ensure that the duration of the collision is long enough to be noticed by all the other transmitting stations that are involved in the collision. The CSMA/CD LAN requires that the jam be at least 32 but not more than 48 bits. This guarantees that the duration of the collision is sufficient to ensure its detection by all the transmitting stations on the network. Its limited length also ensures that the stations will not falsely interpret it as a valid frame. Any frame containing less than 64 bytes (octets) is presumed to be a fragment resulting from a collision and is discarded by any other receiving stations on the link.

Transmit media access management then performs the second function. After the jam is sent, it terminates the transmission and schedules the transmission for a later time, based on a random wait selection. The termination of frame transmission decreases the effect of a long frame collision manifesting itself on the channel for an extended time.

At the receiving station or stations, the bits resulting from the collision are decoded by the physical layer. The fragmented frames received from the collision are distinguished from valid frames by the receive media access management layer. It notices that the collision fragment is smaller than the shortest valid frame and discards the fragments. Consequently, the jam is used to ensure all transmitting stations notice the collision, and the fragmented frame is transmitted to ensure that any receiving stations ignore the transmission.

Both Ethernet and 802.3 use a 1-persistent technique to manage collisions and channel contention. However, this 1-persistent algorithm is applied to an integral multiple of a slot time (512 bits), and the scheduling of retransmission is performed by a controlled randomizing process called truncated binary exponential back-off. After 16 unsuccessful attempts, the station gives up.

Token Ring—IEEE 802.5

The token ring technique has been used for several years. The IEEE 802.5 standard is now implemented in a number of vendors' products. IBM uses a variation of 802.5 in its token ring network.

The IEEE 802.5 protocol uses the single token scheme discussed previously. The IEEE 802.5 standard provides for three possible formats for the token ring. These formats are depicted in Figure 4-17. The token format (Figure 4-17 [a]) consists of three bytes: the starting delimiter, the access control, and the

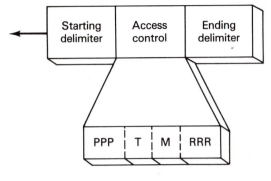

PPP: Priority Bits
T: Token Bit (0: Token, 1: Data)
M: Monitor Bit
RRR: Reservation Bits

(a) Token

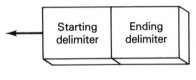

(b) Abort Token

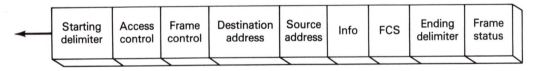

(c) Token and Data

FIGURE 4-17. Token Ring Frames

ending delimiter. The purpose of the two delimiters is to indicate the beginning and ending of the transmission. The access control contains eight bits. Three bits are used for a priority indicator, three bits are used for a reservation indicator, and one bit is the token bit. When the token bit is set to 0, it indicates that the transmission is a token. When it is set to 1, it indicates that a data unit is being transmitted. The last bit in the access control byte is the monitor bit. This provides for a designated station to monitor the ring for error control and back-up purposes. Figure 4-17(b) shows an abort token consisting only of the starting and ending delimiter. This transmission can be sent at any time to abort a previous transmission.

The information-transfer format is illustrated in Figure 4-17(c). In addition to the starting delimiter, access control, and ending delimiter, the standard provides for additional fields. The frame control field defines the type of frame (MAC or LLC data unit) and can be used to establish priorities between two LLC peer entities. The address fields identify the sending and receiving stations. The information field contains user data. The FCS field is used for error checking and the frame status field is used to indicate that the receiving station recognized its address and copied the data in the information field.

The token ring provides for priority access to the ring through the following parameters and logic values. These are stored, updated and checked at the ring interface units. It is suggested the reader review these items before reading the material that follows.

RRR	Reservation bits allow high-priority stations to request the use of the next token
PPP	Priority bits indicate the priority of the token and indicate which stations are allowed to use the ring
Rr	Storage register for the reservation value
Pr	Storage register for the priority value
Sr	Stack register to store old values of Pr
Sx	Stack register to store new values of token that was transmitted
Pm	Priority level of a frame queued and ready for transmission

The priority bits (PPP) and the reservation bits (RRR) reside in the token. They give access to the highest priority frame ready for transmission on the ring. These values are also stored in registers Pr and Rr. The current ring service priority is indicated by the priority bits (PPP) in the token circulating around the ring.

The priority mechanism operates to provide equal access to the ring for all stations within a specific level. The same station that raised the service priority level of the ring (the stacking station) returns the ring to the original service priority. This guarantees that lower priority stations will have an opportunity to use the ring in the event the higher priority stations are idle. The Sx and Sr stacks are used to perform this function.

When a station has a frame to transmit, it requests a priority token by changing the reservation bits (RRR) as the station receives and transmits the token. If the priority level (Pm) of the frame that is ready for transmission is greater than the RRR bits, the station increases the value of RRR to the value of Pm. If the value of RRR is equal to or greater than Pm, the reservation bits (RRR) are transmitted unchanged.

After a station has claimed the token, the station transmits frames until it has completed transmission or until the transmission of another frame could not be completed before a timer expires. The station then generates a new token for transmission on the ring.

If the station does not have additional frames to transmit, or if the station does not have a reservation request (contained in register Rr) which is greater

The Data Link Layer

than the present ring service priority (contained in register Pr), the token is transmitted with its priority at the present ring service priority and the reservation bits (RRR) at the greater of Rr or Pm. No further action is taken in this particular scenario.

On the other hand, if the station has a frame ready for transmission or a reservation request (Rr), either of which is greater than the present ring service priority, the token is generated with its priority at the greater of Pm or Rr and its reservation bits (RRR) as O. Since the station has raised the service priority level of the ring, the station becomes a stacking station and must store the value of the old ring service priority as Sr and the new ring service priority as Sx. These values are used later to lower the service priority of the ring when there are no frames ready to transmit on the ring whose priority is equal to or greater than the stacked Sx.

The stacking station claims every token that it receives that has a priority (PPP) equal to its highest stacked transmitted priority (Sx). The RRR bits of the token are examined in order to raise, maintain, or lower the service priority of the ring. The new token is transmitted with its PPP equal to the value of the reservation (RRR), but no lower than the value of the highest stacked received priority (Sr). Remember (Sr) was the original ring priority service level. This approach ensures that the highest priority gets access to the ring.

If the value of the new ring service priority (PPP equal to Rr) is greater than Sr, the RRR bits are transmitted as O, the old ring service priority contained in Sx is replaced with a new value Sx equal to Rr, and the station continues its role as a stacking station.

However, if the Rr value is equal to or less than the value of the highest stacked received priority (Sr), the new token is transmitted at a priority value of the Sr, both Sx and Sr are removed from the stack, and if no other values of Sx and Sr are stacked, the station discontinues its role as a stacking station. This technique allows the lower priority stations to use the ring once the high priority stations have completed their transmissions.

Token Bus—IEEE 802.4

The token bus approach recommended by the IEEE 802.4 committee is illustrated in Figure 4-18. This MAC sublayer consists of four major functions: the interface machine (IFM), the access control machine (ACM), the receive machine (RxM), and the transmit machine (TxM).

The ACM is the heart of the token bus system. It determines when to place a frame on the bus, and cooperates with the other stations' ACM to control access to the shared bus. It is also responsible for initialization and maintenance of the logical ring, including error detection and fault recovery. It also controls the admission of new stations.

The LLC frames are passed to the ACM by the interface machine (IFM). This component buffers the LLC sublayer requests. The IFM maps "quality of service" parameters from the LLC view to the MAC view and performs address checking on received LLC frames.

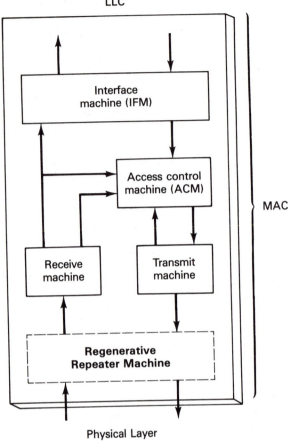

LLC

Interface
machine (IFM)

Access control
machine (ACM)

MAC

Receive
machine

Transmit
machine

Regenerative
Repeater Machine

Physical Layer

FIGURE 4-18. The IEEE 802.4 Token Bus

The TxM and RxM components have limited functions. The responsibility of the TxM is to transmit the frame to the physical layer. It accepts a frame from the ACM and builds a MAC protocol data unit (PDU) by prefacing the frame with the preamble and starting delimiter (SD). It also appends the FCS and the ending delimiter (ED). The RxM accepts data from the physical layer and identifies a full frame by detecting the SD and ED. It also checks the FCS field to validate an error-free transmission. If a received frame is an LLC type, it is passed from the RxM component to the IFM. The IFM indicates its arrival and then delivers it to the LLC sublayer. Once in the LLC sublayer, it goes through the necessary functions to service the end user application, or another layer provided by ISO or the High Level Interface (HILI) (IEEE 802.1).

The format of an 802.4 frame is identical to the token ring 802.5 frame except it has no access control (AC) field. Obviously, the AC is not needed, since this protocol does not use priority (PPP) and reservation (RRR) indicators.

The Data Link Layer

Token Bus Operations. A token determines the right of access to the bus. The station with the token has control over the network. The IEEE 802.4 determines the logical ring of the physical bus by the numeric value of the addresses. A MAC or LLC data unit provides the facility for the lowest address to hand the token to the highest address. Then, the token is passed from a predecessor station to its successor station.

The token (right to transmit) is passed from a station in descending numerical order of station address. When a station hears a token frame addressed to itself, it may transmit data frames. When a station has completed transmitting data frames, it passes the token to the next station in the logical ring. When a station has the token, it may temporarily delegate its right to transmit to another station by sending a request-with-response data frame.

After each station has completed transmitting any data frames it may have, the station passes the token to its successor by sending a token control frame.

After sending the token frame, the station listens for evidence that its successor has heard the token frame and is active. If the sender hears a valid frame following the token, it assumes that its successor has the token and is transmitting. If the token sender does not hear a valid frame following its token pass, it attempts to access the next station of the network and may implement measures to pass around the problem station by establishing a new successor. For more serious faults, attempts are made to re-establish the ring.

Stations are added to an 802.4 bus by an approach called response windows:

- While holding the token, a node issues a solicit-successor frame. The address in the frame is between it and the next successor station.
- The token holder waits one window time (slot time, equal to twice the end-to-end propagation delay).
- If no response occurs, the token is transferred to the successor node.
- If a response occurs, a requesting node sends a set-successor frame and token holder changes its successor node address. The requester receives the token, sets its addresses, and proceeds.
- If multiple responses occur, another protocol is invoked to resolve the contention.

A node can drop out of the transmission sequence. Upon receiving a token, it sends a set-successor frame to the predecessor, with orders to give the token hereafter to its successor.

Options exist in the 802.4 standard to include class of service, which would make the system priority-oriented. The class of service option permits stations access to the bus based on one of four types of data to transmit:

- Synchronous—class 6
- Asynchronous Urgent—class 4

- Asynchronous Normal—class 2
- Asynchronous Time-Available—class 0

A token-holding station is allowed to maintain bus control based on priority timers. The timers give more time to the higher classes of traffic.

SUMMARY AND CONCLUSIONS

The principal function of the data link layer is to detect errors that have occurred during the transmission of the data across a communications channel. The High Level Data Link Control (HDLC) protocol has become the most widely used data link layer standard in the world for wide-area networks. Its use in local networks is more limited, although one of its subsets, logical link control (LLC), is quite prevalent in ISO and IEEE-based LANs. Many implementations are derived from HDLC, notably LAPB and LAPD.

The upper layers assume that the data link layer provides link transmission integrity. However, some networks do not employ data link layer protocols between their switches and nodes. Rather, they rely upon an upper layer protocol residing in the transport layer or the application layer to perform negative and positive acknowledgments.

ADDENDIX 4A. A TUTORIAL ON DATA LINK CONTROLS

INTRODUCTION

This appendix provides a closer look at link level operations by highlighting the following interrelated topics (these procedures are not used by all link protocols but are pervasive enough to warrant our attention):

- Flow control of traffic between the computers
- Sequencing and accounting of traffic
- Actions to be taken in the event of error detection

The example in Figure 4A-1 illustrates several important points about data link (level 2) communications. It shows DTE A is to transmit data to DTE B. The transmission goes through an intermediate point, a computer located at C. The C station performs routing and switching functions since it also has lines to stations D and E, and thus fits the definition of data switching equipment (DSE).

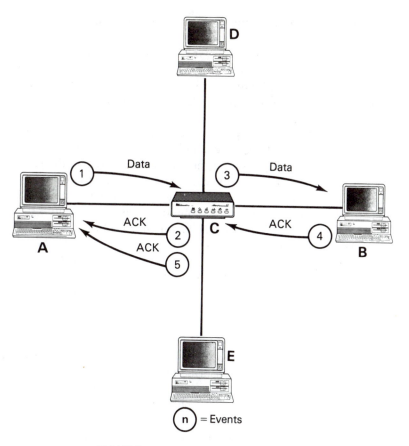

FIGURE 4A-1. Link Level Operations

The most common approach is to pass the data, like a baton in a relay race, from site to site until it finally reaches its destination. One important aspect of the process is in event 2, where station C sends an acknowledgment of the data it received to the transmitting station A. This acknowledgment means station C has checked for possible errors occurring during the transmission of the frame and, as best it can determine, the data has been received without corruption. It so indicates by transmitting an acceptance frame on the return path.

The data communications industry uses two terms to describe the event 2 response: ACK, denoting a positive acknowledgment, and NAK, representing a negative acknowledgment. A NAK usually occurs because the signal is distorted due to faulty conditions on the channel (lightning storm, etc.). The frame in event 2 to A will either be an ACK or a NAK. In the event of an error in the transmission, station A must receive a negative acknowledgment (NAK) so it can retransmit the data. It is also essential that the processes shown in events 1 and 2 are completed before event 3 occurs. If C immediately transmitted the data to B before performing the error check, B could possibly receive erroneous data.

If station A receives an ACK in event 2, it assumes the data has been received correctly at station B, and the communications system at site A can purge this data from its queue. (The application process often saves a copy on disk or tape for accounting, audit, or security reasons.)

Continuing the process in events 3 and 4, assume that an ACK is returned from B to C. The end user at A may assume through event 2 that the data arrived at C. A false sense of security could result, because event 2 only indicates that the data arrived safely in C. If the data is lost between the C and B sites, the A user assumes no problem exists. This scenario provides no provision for an end-to-end acknowledgment. If an end user wishes to have absolute assurance that the data arrived at the remote site, event 5 is required. Upon receiving event 4 at C, C sends another acceptance (ACK) to A.

As stated at the beginning of this chapter, the level 2 data link protocols do not provide end-to-end acknowledgment through multiple links. Some systems provide this service at level 3, the network layer. However, the OSI model intends end-to-end accountability to be provided by the transport layer (level 4).

Functions of Timers

Many link protocols use timers in conjunction with logic states to verify that an event occurs within a prescribed time. When a transmitting station sends a frame onto the channel, it starts a timer and enters a wait state. The value of the timer (usually called T1 [no relation to a digital T1 carrier]) is set to expire if the receiving station does not respond to the transmitted frame within the set period. Upon expiration of the timer, one to n retransmissions are attempted, each with the timer T1 reset, until a response is received or until the link protocol's maximum number of retries is met. In this case, recovery or problem resolution is attempted by the link level. If unsuccessful, recovery is performed by a higher level protocol or by manual intervention and troubleshooting efforts. (The retry parameter is usually designated as parameter N2.)

The T1 timer just described is designated as the acknowledgment timer. Its value depends on: (a) round trip propagation delay of the signal (usually a small value, except for very long and very high-speed circuits); (b) the processing time at the receiver (including queuing time of the frame); (c) the transmission time of the acknowledging frame; and (d) possible queue and processing time at the transmitter when it receives the acknowledgment frame.

The receiving station may use a parameter (T2) in conjunction with T1. Its value is set to ensure an acknowledgment frame is sent to the transmitting station before the T1 at the transmitter expires. This action precludes the transmitter from resending frames unnecessarily.

The number of timers varies, depending upon the type of protocol and the designer's approach to link management. Some other commonly used timers are:

- Poll timer (also called P bit timer): Defines the time interval during which a polling station (i.e., a station requesting a frame from another station) shall expect to receive a response.
- NAK timer (also called a reject or selective reject timer): Defines the time interval during which a rejecting station shall expect a reply to its reject frame.
- Link setup timer: Defines the time interval during which a transmitting station shall expect a reply to its link setup command frame.

The timing functions may be implemented by a number of individual timers, and the protocol designer/implementor is responsible for determining how the timers are set and restarted.

Automatic Request for Repeat (ARQ)

When a station transmits a frame, it places a send sequence number in a control field. The receiving station uses this number to determine if it has received all other preceding frames (with lower numbers). It also uses the number to determine its response. For example, after a station receives a frame with send sequence number of 3, it responds with an ACK with a receive sequence number of 4, which signifies it accepts all frames up to and including 3 and expects 4 to be the send sequence number of the next frame. The send sequence number is identified as N(S) and the receive sequence number is identified as N(R).

Continuous ARQ utilizes full-duplex (two-way simultaneous) transmission, which allows transmission in both directions between the communicating devices. This approach was developed in the 1970s, when better channel utilization became more important (for satellite links, fast-response packet networks). Because continuous ARQ has several advantages over a stop-and-wait, half-duplex system, its use has increased in the industry during the past several years.

Piggybacking. The newer line protocols permit the inclusion of the N(S) and N(R) field in the same frame. This technique, called piggybacking, allows the protocol to "piggyback" an ACK (the N(R) value) onto an information frame (sequenced by the N(S) value). As an example, assume a station sends a frame with N(R) = 5 and N(S) = 1. The N(R) = 5 means all frames up to a number 4 are acknowledged and the N(S) = 1 means Station B is sending a user information in this frame with a sequence of 1.

Flow Control with Sliding Windows. Continuous ARQ devices use the concept of transmit and receive windows to aid in link management operations. A window is established on each link to provide a reservation of resources at both stations. These resources may be the allocation of specific computer resources or the reservation of buffer space for the transmitting device. In most systems, the window provides both buffer space and sequencing rules. During the initiation of a link session (handshake) between the stations, a window is established. For example, if stations A and B are to communicate with each other, station A reserves a receive window for B and station B reserves a receive window for A. The windowing concept is necessary to full-duplex protocols because they entail a continuous flow of frames into the receiving site without the intermittent stop-and-wait acknowledgments. Consequently, the receiver must have a sufficient allocation of memory to handle the continuous incoming traffic. It can be seen that window size is a function of buffer space and the magnitude of the sequence numbers.

The windows at the transmitting and receiving site are controlled by state variables (which is another name for a counter). The transmitting site maintains a send state variable [V(S)]. It is the sequence number of the next frame to be transmitted. The receiving site maintains a receive state variable [V(S)] which contains the number that is expected to be in the sequence number of the next frame. The V(S) is incremented with each frame transmitted and placed in the send sequence field [N(S)] in the frame.

Upon receiving the frame, the receiving site checks for a transmission error. It also compares the send sequence number N(S) with its V(R). If the frame is acceptable, it increments V(R) by one, places it into a receive sequence number field [N(R)] in an acknowledgment (ACK) frame and sends it to the original transmitting site to complete the accountability for the transmission.

If an error is detected or if the V(R) does not match the send sequence number in the frame, a NAK (negative acknowledgment) with the receive sequence number field [N(R)] containing the value of V(R) is sent to the original transmitting site. This V(R) value informs the transmitting DTE of the next frame that it is expected to send. The transmitter must then reset its V(S) and retransmit the frame whose sequence matches the value of N(R).

A useful feature of the sliding window scheme is the ability of the receiving station to restrict the flow of data from the transmitting station by withholding the acknowledgment frames. This action prevents the transmitter from opening its windows and reusing its send sequence numbers' values until the same send sequence numbers have been acknowledged. A station can be completely "throttled" if it receives no ACKs from the receiver.

Many data link controls use the numbers of 0 through 7 for V(S), V(R), and the sequence numbers in the frame. Once the state variables are incremented through 7, the numbers are reused beginning with 0. Because the numbers are reused, the stations must not be allowed to send a frame with a sequence number that has not yet been acknowledged. For example, the protocol must wait for frame number 6 to be acknowledged before it uses a V(S) of 6 again. The use of 0 through 7 permits seven frames to be outstanding before the window is "closed." Even though numbers 0 through 7 give eight sequence numbers, the V(R) contains the value of the next expected frame, which limits the actual outstanding frames to 7.

We just learned that many systems use sequence numbers and state vari-

TABLE 4A-1.   Functions of State Variables and Sequence Numbers

Functions:
Flow control of frames (windows)
Detect lost frames
Detect out-of-sequence frames
Detect erroneous frames

Uses
N(S): Sequence number of transmitted frame
N(R): Sequence number of the acknowledged frame(s). Acknowledges all frames up to N(R)-1
V(S): Variable containing sequence number of next frame to be transmitted
V(R): Variable containing expected value of the sequence number N(S) in the next transmitting frame.

ables to manage the traffic on a link. As a brief review, please refer to Table 4A-1.

Other Considerations.   Three important goals of a line protocol are: (a) to obtain high throughput, (b) to achieve fast response time, and (c) to minimize the logic required at the transmitting/receiving sites to account for traffic (such as ACKs and NAKs). The transmit window is an integral tool in meeting these goals. One of the primary functions of the window is to ensure that by the time all the permissible frames have been transmitted, at least one frame has been acknowledged. In this manner, the window is kept open and the line is continuously active. The T1 and T2 timers discussed earlier are key to effective line utilization and window management.

One could argue that a very large window permits continuous transmissions regardless of the speed of the link and size of the frames, because the transmitter does not have to wait for acknowledgment from the receiver. While this is true, a larger window size also means that the transmitter must maintain a large queue to store those frames that have not been acknowledged by the receiver.

The goal of the continuous ARQ is to keep the windows open insofar as possible for all user sessions on the line. In so doing, the transmitting and receiving stations are more likely to experience fast response time. The continuous ARQ protocols also are designed to keep the expensive communications channel as busy as possible.

The concepts of continuous ARQ are relatively simple, yet it should be realized that with a large communications facility, the host computer or front-end processor is tasked with efficient transmission, data flow, and response time between itself and all the secondary sites attached to it. The primary host must maintain a window for every station and manage the traffic to and from each station on an individual basis.

CHAPTER 5

The Network Layer

INTRODUCTION

The data communications services described in Chapters 3 and 4 transfer data through only one communications link. This approach limits the options in situations where several users wish to communicate with each other across multiple channels. As an example, consider the telephone system. We do not have individual lines to every person with whom we have a telephone conversation. Obviously, that would be physically impossible—imagine the size of the telephone jack necessary to accommodate separate wires to our bank, the taxi company, etc. Consequently, both voice and data communications systems employ networks with switches or broadcast facilities to relay traffic between multiple users on a limited number of links.

These facilities are part of the network layer, and the OSI defines the procedures for establishing, managing, and terminating connections with networks in order to send protocol data units between the upper layers, typically the transport layer. The idea is to relieve the user from the details of the network operations, including routing and relaying within the network.

The network layer is responsible for providing transparent transfer of data (network service data units, or NSDUs) between the network service users. Ideally, the users do not know about the specific characteristics of the underlying services. For example, the network service users are unaware of the underlying network (referred to as a subnetwork or subnetworks). Indeed, if more than one subnetwork is involved in the end-to-end relay, the subnetworks might be dissimilar (heterogeneous).

The network service is responsible for providing routing and relaying functions between the two users. The network service is not concerned with

157

the format, syntax, semantics, or content of the data it transfers. Consequently, it is not concerned with the upper layers of the OSI model. This important concept is illustrated in Figure 5-1. The network is only concerned with the lower three layers of OSI. The data and layer headers (protocol control information, or PCI) that flow from the user's upper layers are merely NSDUs to the network.

The user provides the network with addresses and a desired quality of service (QOS) for the connection. The network is then responsible for relaying the NSDUs to the final destination. As with other layers, the network layer allows the network service user to request a variety of options in qualities of service. In addition, the network service requires addressing schemes that allow the network service users to refer to each other without ambiguity.

The network layer allows two network service users (DTEs) to exchange data with each other through one network connection or multiple network connections, and through one or multiple DCEs. The network service user may also be flow-controlled by the network service. This depends entirely on the type, quality, and speed of the underlying subnetworks. In some instances, the network service user may wish to transfer data with expedited protocol data units as well. The network services may also include: (a) specific acknowledgments of data; (b) release of the network connection (in which case the data may be destroyed); (c) resets; and (d) synchronization procedures.

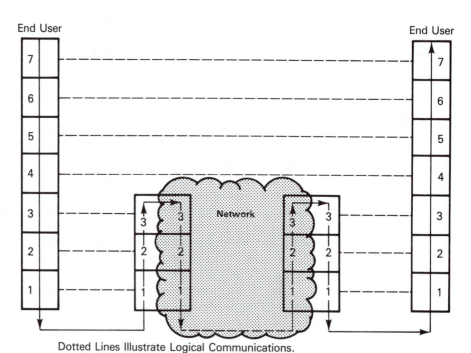

Dotted Lines Illustrate Logical Communications.
Shaded Area Illustrates the Internal Network and Its Probable Layers.

FIGURE 5-1. Network Layers

The Network Layer

THE DTE/DCE INTERFACE

The interface between the network and the user is commonly known as the DTE-DCE interface. The term DTE means data terminal equipment, and refers to the end-user machine or any process that contains the upper layers of the OSI Model. The term DCE means data circuit-terminating equipment and generally refers to the lower three layers within the network.

These terms can be quite confusing. After all, it is evident from Figure 5-1 that the lower three layers are found in both the DTE and the DCE. This configuration is necessary, because OSI stipulates that only peer layers can communicate. Therefore, both the DTE and the DCE must have these lower three layers in order to communicate. Indeed, the physical and data link layers at the two machines are likely mirror images of each other.

However, the network layer functions at the DTE and DCE are not the same (even though they must be compatible). As a simple example, the DCE is tasked with receiving connection requests from the DTE, not vice versa, so the responsibilities of the DTE and DCE network layers are different. Therefore, the network layers at the DTE and DCE are not identical, although many vendors load the same software in both the DTE and DCE and then execute the necessary routines to support either the DTE or DCE role.

The second source of confusion about the term DCE stems from its use to describe certain machines that support only the layer 1 physical level functions. Several standards groups and vendors use DCE to describe a modem, which is a physical layer device. Unfortunately, we are saddled with the term. In this chapter, DCE refers to the network interface between the network and the user DTE, containing the lower three layers of the OSI Model.

The reader should keep these thoughts in mind when reading the material on X.25, found later in this chapter.

DEFINING NETWORK SERVICES WITH X.213
OR DIS 8348

The interconnections between the transport and network layers is of special significance to an end-user because these layers represent the delineation between the network (lower three layers) and the user (upper four layers). The relationship of the layers is shown in Figure 5-2. In this section we learn how the layers communicate, using CCITT X.213 as the example. The ISO publishes a similar document designated as DIS 8348.

Network Connection Queue Model

One of the key aspects of the network service connections and service to the upper layers is the use of queue models. While this concept is somewhat abstract, it relates to some important features of the network and transport boundaries. Figure 5-3 illustrates the concept. Network service user A connects with

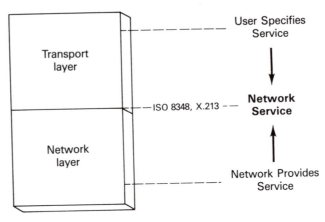

FIGURE 5-2. Network Layer Service Definitions

network service user B, each through a Network Service Access Point (NSAP). A has a queue to B and B has a queue to A. These two queues are used for flow control in each direction of transfer. Obviously, the ability of a user to add to its queue depends on the ability of the receiver to remove traffic from the queue. This concept is central to flow control and network congestion control. Many of the topics discussed in this chapter are based on the queue model concept.

During a network communications session, a pair of queues is maintained between NSAPs under the rules defined in Table 5-1. The addition of additional objects (such as packets) may or may not prevent the further additions of objects in the queue, based on whether the data is: (a) expedited; (b) an acknowledg-

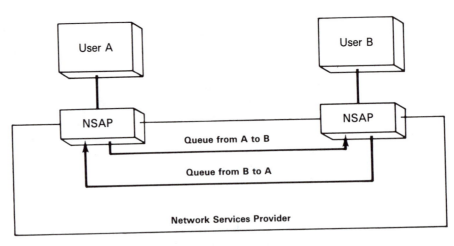

NSAP: Network Service Access Point

FIGURE 5-3. The Network Queue Model

The Network Layer

TABLE 5-1. Flow Control and Queues

May Prevent Further Addition of Object Y	The Addition Object X	Octets of Normal Data or End-of-NDSU	Expedited Data	Data Acknowledgment
Octets of Normal Data or End-of-NDSU		Yes	Yes	No
Expedited NDSU		No	Yes	No
Data Acknowledgment		No	No	No

ment; (c) end of a NSDU; or (d) octets of normal data. The network layer may change the queue relationships by altering the order of the objects in the queue. In other words, a network convention must exist to define how queues may be reordered. In addition, the network layer may delete objects in the queue (for example, resets could cause deletion of objects).

Since queues contain different objects, it is necessary to define their inter-relationships from two perspectives: (a) which objects are given precedence in the queue, and/or (b) which objects cause the destruction of preceding objects in the queue. Be aware that a network convention must exist to define how the queues may be reordered. The network layer describes these objects:

Connect
Octets of normal data
End-of-NSDU
Expedited NSDU
Data acknowledgment
Reset
Synchronization mark
Disconnect

Four of these objects can change the relationship of other objects in the queue.

- Expedited NSDU: Advances ahead of octets of normal data, end-of-NSDU and data acknowledgment.
- Data Acknowledgment: Advances ahead of octets of normal data, end-of-NSDU and, expedited NSDU (note that either data acknowledgment or expedited NSDU may take precedence over the other).
- Reset: Is destructive to octets of normal data, end-of-NSDU, expedited NSDU, data acknowledgement, synchronization mark.
- Disconnect: Is destructive to all other objects.

Network Service Primitives and State Diagrams

From the discussions in previous chapters, the reader should now have an idea of how the network services are invoked. As with all OSI layers, they are invoked with primitives. We return to this subject because it is fundamental to the concept of layered protocols. The primitives used by the network service are illustrated in Table 5-2. The parameters are also shown with the primitives. These primitives are used in various sequences to perform network establishment, network release, and, of course, data transfer. The parameters required in the primitives are described next.

The addresses in the parameters are all NSAP addresses. The called address identifies the receiving NSAP. The calling address parameter identifies the requesting address of the NSAP. The responding address identifies the address of the NSAP to which the actual network connection has been established.

The receipt confirmation selection parameter stipulates whether the network connection will use receipt confirmation. If this parameter is accepted by the local and remote network service users, then subsequent data primitives can request the confirmation of actual data through the use of the confirmation request parameter of the N-DATA request protocol data unit. The expedited data selection parameter stipulates the use of expedited data transfer during the actual network connection. Expedited data is used for higher priority traffic. The quality of service (QOS) parameters are invoked during session establishment. These parameters are explained later

Figure 5-4 summarizes the network primitives and the various ways that they can be used. A brief description is provided here to explain each possibility.

Figure 5-4(a) depicts a typical successful connection procedure where the two end users provide the necessary primitives for the network connection establishment. The network is responsible for relaying these primitives in the form of protocol data units to and from the two end users.

Figure 5-4(b) depicts a typical connection release occurring at the initiation of the network service user. It is possible for both network service users to initiate a connection release at approximately the same time. This situation is depicted in Figure 5-4(c).

Figure 5-4(d) illustrates the network provider initiating the release. The release is in the form of an N-DISCONNECT. indication primitive to both users.

Yet another possibility is shown in Figure 5-4(e), in which the network provider and the network service user initiate the release at approximately the same time.

Figure 5-4(f) shows a connection establishment attempt that is rejected by the end user. The rejection could occur because the user will not accept the quality of services requested in the N-CONNECT indication, or the user simply may not have the resources to support the session. In contrast, Figure 5-4(g) shows the rejection coming from the network, which could occur for the same reasons as a rejection from an end user.

TABLE 5-2. Network Service Primitives (X.213)

Primitive	Parameters
N-CONNECT request	(Called Address, Calling Address, Receipt Confirmation Selection, Expedited Data Selection, Quality of Service Parameter Set, NS User Data.)
N-CONNECT indication	(Called Address, Calling Address, Receipt Confirmation Selection, Expedited Data Selection, Quality of Service Parameter Set, NS User Data.)
N-CONNECT response	(Responding Address, Receipt Confirmation Selection, Expedited Data Selection, Quality of Service Parameter Set, NS User Data.)
N-CONNECT confirm	(Responding Address, Receipt Confirmation Selection, Expedited Data Selection, Quality of Service Parameter Set, NS User Data.)
N-DATA request	(NS User Data, Confirmation request.)
N-DATA indication	(NS User Data, Confirmation request.)
N-DATA ACKNOWLEDGE request	
N-DATA ACKNOWLEDGE indication	
N-EXPEDITED-DATA request	(NS User Data.)
N-EXPEDITED-DATA indication	(NS User Data.)
N-RESET request	(Reason.)
N-RESET indication	(Originator, Reason.)
N-RESET response	
N-RESET confirm	
N-DISCONNECT request	(Reason, NS User Data, Responding Address.)
N-DISCONNECT indication	(Originator, Reason, NS User Data, Responding Address.)

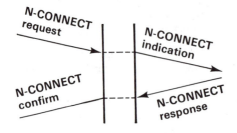

(a) Successful Connection Establishment

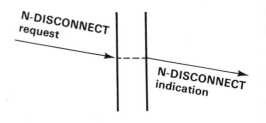

(b) NS User Initiated Connection Release

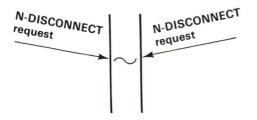

(c) Simultaneous NS User Initiated Connection Release

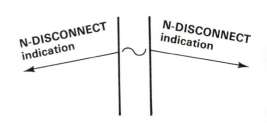

(d) NS Provider Initiated Connection Release

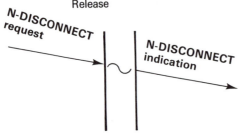

(e) Simultaneous NS User & NS Provider Initiated Connection Release

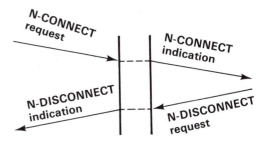

(f) NS User Rejection of an NC Establishment Attempt

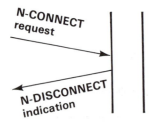

(g) NS Provider Rejection of an NC Establishment Attempt

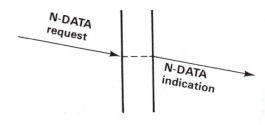

(h) Normal Data Transfer

FIGURE 5–4. Network Layer Primitive Operations

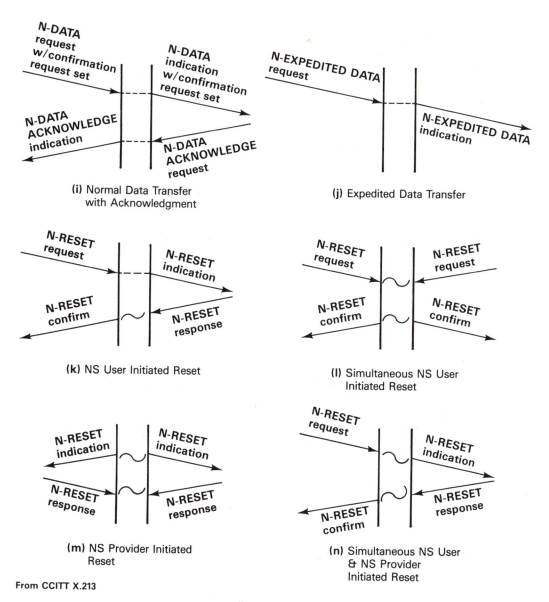

(i) Normal Data Transfer with Acknowledgment

(j) Expedited Data Transfer

(k) NS User Initiated Reset

(l) Simultaneous NS User Initiated Reset

(m) NS Provider Initiated Reset

(n) Simultaneous NS User & NS Provider Initiated Reset

From CCITT X.213

FIGURE 5–4. (Continued).

The next three figures show the options available for the transfer of data. Figure 5-4(h) depicts a normal data transfer between the two users. In this situation, the session is in a connectionless mode, because there is no acknowledgment of the traffic. Figure 5-4(i) shows the normal data transfer with acknowledgment back to the originator of the traffic. Figure 5-4(j) shows an expedited data transfer mode.

As stated earlier, the network connection can be released. Figure 5-4(k) shows a reset occurring from the network service user. Figure 5-4(l) shows the users both initiating a reset. Figure 5-4(m) shows the network issuing a reset. Figure 5-4(n) shows the release occurring simultaneously between the network service user and the network service provider.

The concepts illustrated in Figure 5-4 require considerable thought in their implementation. For example, the various possibilities of reset shown in Figures 5-4(k) through 5-4(n) require that the network provider and both end users be aware of the reset at the proper time and that all data units be recovered. These seemingly simple tasks offer many potential pitfalls to the unwary, so considerable material in this chapter and subsequent chapters is devoted to providing the reader with more detailed information on the actions shown in Figure 5-4.

To complete this description of the network services, Figure 5-5 shows the state diagram for the various primitive sequences of a network connection.

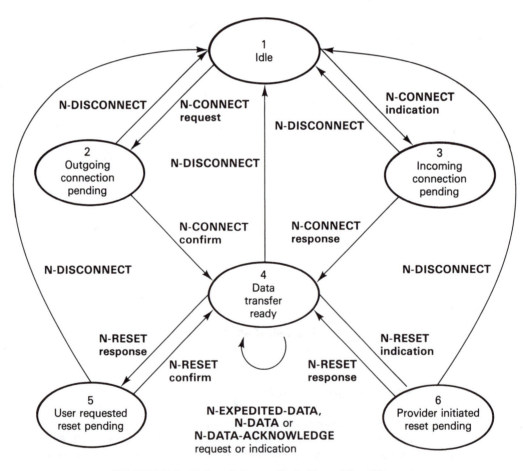

FIGURE 5-5. Network Layer State Transition Diagram

TABLE 5-3(a). QOS Performance Parameters

Phase of Connection	Performance Criteria	
	Speed	Accuracy/Reliability
NC Establishment	NC Establishment Delay	NC Establishment Failure Probability (includes mis-connection/refusal)
Data Transfer	Throughput Transit Delay	Residual Error Rate NC Resilience Transfer Failure Probability
NC Release	NC Release Delay	NC Release Failure Probability

Remember that the state diagram establishes the permissible primitives that can be issued from each state as well as the primitives that are allowed to be accepted by each state.

Quality of Service (QOS) Parameters for the Network Layer

Some of the layer service definitions in OSI networks have repeating functions. The quality of service (QOS) parameters introduced in Chapter 1 are such examples. We will see that the quality of service parameters for the transport layer are generally mapped directly to the complementary quality of service parameters for the network layer.

The performance aspects of the QOS parameters are depicted in Table 5-3. Most of the parameters deal with speed or reliability of the service. Table 5-3(a) shows the performance-oriented parameters, and Table 5-3(b) shows the non-performance-oriented parameters.

Functions of the QOS Parameters.   The QOS parameters depicted in Table 5-3 perform the following network services for the network connection between two endpoints. Once the connection is established, the network service users have the same knowledge of the QOS. This pertains to a connection through one network or multiple subnetworks. These QOS parameters are used by many networks today. They are also part of the ubiquitous X.25 protocol, and are called facilities in the X.25 documents (discussed later).

TABLE 5-3(b). QOS Nonperformance Parameters

NC Protection
NC Priority
Maximum Acceptable Cost

NC Establishment Delay is the maximum acceptable delay between the issuance of the N-CONNECT.request primitive and the associated N-CONNECT.confirm primitive. This delay also includes the delay encountered at the remote user. Simply stated, it places a time limit on how long a user will wait to get a connection.

NC Establishment Failure Probability is the ratio of total connection failures to total connection attempts. The failure could occur for a number of reasons, such as remote end refusal, expiration of an establishment delay timer, etc. It is a useful parameter for ascertaining the quality of the network service.

Throughput is measured for each direction of transfer through the network. Many private and public networks allow a user to "negotiate" throughput for each connection. Typically, the provision for a higher throughput rate will increase the cost to the user. Consequently, this QOS parameter allows a user to make cost/performance trade-offs for each network session. Given a sequence of an NSDUs with $n \geq 2$, throughput is defined as the smaller of:

1. the number of user data octets contained in the last N-1 NSDUs divided by the time between the first and last N-DATA requests in the sequence; and
2. the number of user data octets contained in the last N-1 NSDUs divided by the time between the first and last N-DATA indications in the sequence.

Transit Delay is the time between the N-DATA request and its associated N-DATA indication. The time includes only successfully transferred NSDUs. Many public networks provide this feature as an option. It is becoming increasingly important as users become more conscious of network performance and response time.

Residual Error Rate is the ratio of total number of incorrect, lost, or duplicate NSDUs to the total number of NSDUs transferred. It is defined as:

$$RER = [(n(e) + n(l) + N(x))]/N$$

Where: RER = residual error rate; n(e) = incorrect NSDUs; n(l) = lost NSDUs; N(x) = duplicate NSDUs; N = total NSDUs transferred. This QOS parameter is useful when a user wishes to obtain a quantitative evaluation of the network service reliability. The reader may keep this formula in mind as the other layers are described; it is repeated in other specifications to obtain consistency through the layers.

Transfer Failure Probability is the ratio of total transfer failures to total transfers. The ratio is calculated on an individual network connection. A failure is defined by an observed performance that is worse than the specified minimum level and is measured against three other QOS parameters: throughput, transit delay, and residual error rate.

Network Connection Resilience is defined as the probability of the network service provider (a) invoking a disconnect, and (b) invoking a reset. Both actions come as a result of network actions and not a user request (see Figure

5-4). This parameter is quite important in evaluating the quality of a network. Several public networks publish their performance data relating to connection resilience.

Network Connection Release Delay is the maximum acceptable delay between a user disconnect request and a receipt of a disconnect indication [see Figure 5-4(g)]; that is, when the user is able to initiate a new network connection request. This is an important consideration for users that need fast connections after "logging off" from a previous network session.

Network Connection Release Failure Probability is defined by probability that the user will not be able to initiate a new connection with a specified maximum release delay. It is the ratio of total network connection release failures to total release attempts.

Network Connection Protection is a qualitative QOS parameter to determine the extent to which the network service provider attempts unauthorized use of data. This parameter, if used by a public network, is not often revealed to a user.

Network Connection Priority is defined as (a) the order in which the connections have their QOS degraded; and (b) the order in which connections are broken. Typically, once a user obtains a network connection, it remains stable for the duration of the session.

Maximum Acceptable Cost, as its name implies, specifies the maximum acceptable cost to the user for a network connection. The costs are specified by the network in relative or absolute terms.

In summary, X.213 and ISO 8348 serve as a model for defining network interfaces and network services. The X.213 and ISO 8348 primitives, QOS parameters, and queue concepts are now used by a number of network vendors in their product lines.

NETWORK LAYER ADDRESSING

For purposes of continuity, the introductory material on network level addressing in Chapter 1 is summarized here in order to go into greater detail. Recall that a network address can take one of three forms.

- An address is the end-user interface to a network, referred to as a subnetwork address. An example is a user DTE address to an X.25 packet network.

- An address is the Network Service Access Point (NSAP). Examples are the called address, calling address, and responding address parameters in the network-level N-CONNECT primitive. Other examples are the source address and destination address in the connectionless-mode N-UNITDATA primitives.

- An address is the address code found in the network protocol control information (N-PCI). Typically, the NSAP address is mapped into the N-PCI address code in the protocol data unit. An example is an addressing convention, such as X.121 or E.164.

ISO 7498/PDAD 3 and X.213 (Annex A) describe a hierarchical structure for the NSAP address. Figure 5-6 shows the hierarchical concept of an inverted tree diagram. The term global network addressing domain refers to all NSAPs in the OSI environment. The domain can be divided further into subdomains, which are called network addressing domains.

These domains correspond to a specific type of network, such as an ISDN, a telephone network, an X.25 public network, etc. They can also correspond to networks within a geographical region, or to a specific organization, such as the International Telecommunications Union (ITU).

ISO 8348/DAD 2 (Draft Addendum 2) specifies the structure for the NSAP address (see Figure 5-7). It consists of four parts:

- *Initial Domain Part* (IDP): Contains the Authority Format Identifier (AFI) and the Initial Domain Identifier (IDI).
- *Authority Format Identifier* (AFI): Contains a two-digit value between 0 and 99. It is used to identify (a) the IDI format and (b) the syntax of the Domain Specific Part (DSP). Table 5-4 contains the AFI and DSP values.
- *Initial Domain Identifier* (IDI): Specifies the addressing domain and the network addressing authority. Table 5-5 contains a summary of the IDI formats and contents.
- *Domain Specific Part* (DSP): Contains the address determined by the network authority. It is an address below the second level of the addressing hierarchy. It can contain addresses of end-user systems on an individual subnetwork.

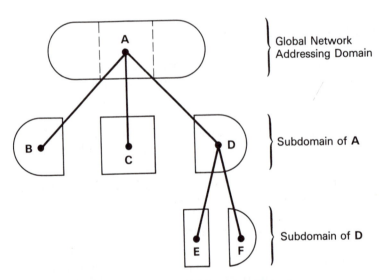

FIGURE 5-6. OSI Addressing Domains

The Network Layer

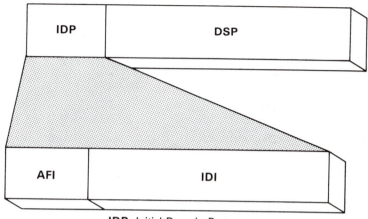

IDP: Initial Domain Part
AFI: Authority Format Identifier
IDI: Initial Domain Identifier
DSP: Domain Specific Part

(a) NSAP Address Structure

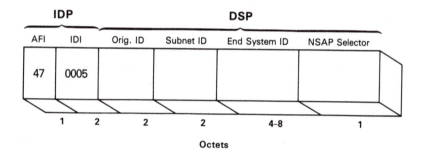

Octets

(b) U.S. Government NSAP Address Format

FIGURE 5-7. NSAP Address Structure

TABLE 5-4. Allocated AFI Values

IDI Format	DSP Syntax			
	Decimal	Binary	Character	National Character
X.121	36	37		
ISO DCC	38	39		
F.69	40	41		
E.163	42	43		
E.164	44	45		
ISO 6523	46	47		
Local	48	49	50	51

TABLE 5-5. IDI Formats

IDI Formats	DSP syntax	Binary DSP encoding (octets)	Decimal DSP encoding (digits)
X.121	Decimal	20	40
	Binary	17	39
ISO DCC	Decimal	20	40
	Binary	17	40
F.69	Decimal	20	40
	Binary	17	40
E.163	Decimal	20	40
	Binary	17	39
E.164	Decimal	20	40
	Binary	18	40
ISO 6523-ICD	Decimal	20	40
	Binary	16	39
Local	Decimal	20	40
	Binary	16	40
	Character	20	40
	Nat'l Character	15	37

The ISO 8348/DAD 2 scheme is not perfect and does not solve all addressing problems. However, it does provide a flexible and coherent framework for network addressing and will simplify future work in this important area.

NSAP Addresses for GOSIP

The U.S. Government GOSIP uses the ISO 8348/DAD 2 format for its addressing structure. Figure 5-7(a) shows this structure. The AFI value is 47. By consulting Table 5-4, the reader can infer that the DSP field is represented in binary, rather than decimal. The IDI value is 0005. It establishes that the address resolution authority (also called the network addressing authority) is the NIST. Code 5 is available for the entire U.S. Federal Government. The NIST has delegated its other code (a value of 6) to the U.S. Department of Defense.

The DSP field is divided into four subfields. The ORG ID value is assigned by NIST to identify a government organization, an agency or a bureau. The SUBNET ID is used by the organization to identify a subnetwork within the organization's subdomain. The END SYSTEM ID can be used in any way that the subnetwork administrator chooses. It could be a physical address (like an Ethernet physical hardware address) or a logical address. The NSAP SELECTOR subfield identifies a higher layer transport entity. A value of 1 in this field identifies the ISO Transport Protocol.

The NIST Special Publication provides the following example of the routing address:

47 00 05 00 32 12 34 53 18 44 27 01

where: 47 = the AFI; 00 05 = the IDI; 00 32 = organization's ID; 12 34 = the subnet ID; 53 18 44 27 = the end system ID (for example, a host computer); 01 = the NSAP selector value.

International Numbering Plan for Data Networks (X.121)

The CCITT publishes and administers the X.121 standard. It is used in almost all countries to identify the public data networks and, in some instances, private data networks. The X.121 plan is based on a four-digit data network identification code (DNIC), which is based on the format "DCCN," where DCC is a three-digit country code and N is the network digit to identify a specific network within a country.

The first digit of the DNIC must not be a 1, which is reserved for future use. Additionally, a first digit value of 8 indicates that the digits that follow are from the F.69 Telex numbering plan; a value of 9 or 0 indicates that the digits that follow are from the E.164 and E.163 ISDN numbering plans, respectively. The 0, 8, and 9 values are called escape codes. We will show some examples of escape codes in Chapter 6.

Some countries have more than ten networks. In this situation, multiple DCCs are assigned to the country. For example, the United States is assigned the DCC values of 310 through 316.

X.121 also defines a network terminal number (NTN). This value identifies the computer, terminal, etc., within the network and consists of a ten-digit identifier. Optionally, the NTN can be included as part of the terminal identifier. In this situation, the eleven-digit field is called a national number (NN).

X.25

X.25 is actually considerably older than the OSI Model. The CCITT issued the first draft of X.25 in 1974. It was revised in 1976, 1978, 1980, 1984, and last in 1988. Since 1974, the standard has been expanded to include many options, services, and facilities, and several of the newer OSI protocols and service definitions operate with X.25. X.25 is now the predominant interface standard for wide area packet networks.

The placement of X.25 in packet networks is widely misunderstood. X.25 is *not* a packet switching specification, but a packet network interface specification (see Figure 5-8). X.25 says nothing about the routing within the network. Hence, from the specification of X.25, the network is a "cloud." For example, the X.25 logic is not aware if the network uses adaptive or fixed directory routing. The reader may have heard of the term "network cloud." Its origin is derived from these concepts. The X.25 recommendation is examined in this chapter because it defines a network level interface.

X.25 defines the procedures for the exchange of data between a user device (DTE) and a network node (DCE). Its formal title is "Interface Between Data Terminal Equipment and Data Circuit Terminating Equipment for Terminals Operating in the Packet Node on Public Data Networks." In X.25, the DCE

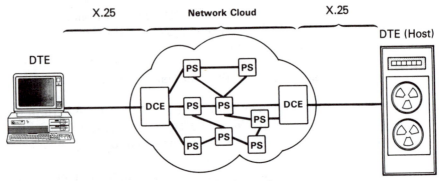

DTE: Data Terminal Equipment (User Equipment)
DCE: Data Circuit-Terminating Equipment (Network Node or Packet Exchange)
PS: Packet Switches Inside the Network

FIGURE 5-8. The X.25 Network Interface

is actually a packet exchange or a network node. We will use the term DCE to stay consistent with X.25.

X.25 establishes the procedures for two packet-mode DTEs to communicate with each other through a network. It defines the two DTEs' sessions with their respective DCEs. The idea of X.25 is to provide common procedures between a user station and a packet network (DCE) for establishing a session and exchanging data. The procedures include functions such as identifying the packets of specific user terminals or computers, acknowledging packets, rejecting packets, and providing for error recovery and flow control. X.25 also provides some useful quality of services features (QOS), such as the charging of a session to a DTE other than the transmitting DTE.

This section presents an overview of the X.25 standard. The book *The X.25 Protocol* by Uyless Black, published by the IEEE Computer Society, is devoted exclusively to X.25 and explains the protocol in more detail.

X.25 and the Physical Layer

The reader may wish to review Chapter 4 before reading this section. The X.25 DTE/DCE recommendation actually encompasses the third layer as well as the lower two layers or OSI. Figure 5-9 shows the relationships of the X.25 layers. The recommended physical layer (first layer) interface between the DTE and DCE is X.21.

Since few countries have implemented X.21, X.25 also provides a provision to use the EIA-232 or V.24/V.28 physical interface. In X.25, this physical level interface is called X.21 bis. In order to use X.21 bis, X.25 requires that specific V.24 control circuits be in the ON condition. Packets are then exchanged on the transmit and receive circuits. If these circuits are off, X.25 assumes the physical level is in an inactive state and any upper levels (such as

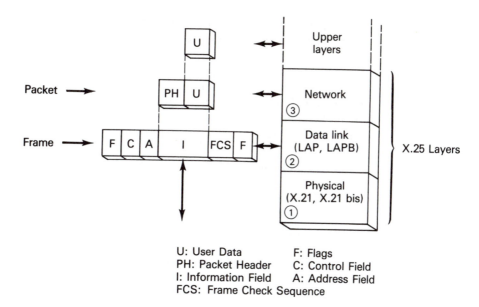

U: User Data   F: Flags
PH: Packet Header   C: Control Field
I: Information Field   A: Address Field
FCS: Frame Check Sequence

FIGURE 5-9. X.25 Layers and Protocol Data Units

data link and network) will not function. X.25 networks can operate with other physical layer standards (for example, RS-449 and V.35).

The physical level plays a very small role in the control of an X.25 network. In essence, it is an electrical path through which the packets are transported.

The principal EIA-232 or V.24 circuits required for X.25 are as follows (reference, timing, signal grounds, etc., are not shown):

	EIA-232	V.24
Send Data	BA	103
Receive Data	BB	104
Request to Send	CA	105
Clear to Send	CB	106
Data Set Ready	CC	107
Data Terminal Ready	CD	108.2
Carrier Detect	CF	109

X.25 and the Data Link Layer

X.25 assumes the data link layer (second level) to be LAPB. This line protocol is a subset of HDLC. It allows the use of LAP, but use of this older link protocol has fallen considerably. Some vendors also use other data link controls, such as Bisync (Binary Synchronous Control), for the link layer.

The X.25 packet is carried within the LAPB frame as the I (information) field. LAPB ensures that the X.25 packets are transmitted across the link from/ to the DTE/DCE, after which the frame fields are stripped and the packet is presented to network layer. The principal function of the link level is to deliver the packet error-free despite the error-prone nature of the communications link. In X.25, we must delineate between a packet and a frame. A packet is created at the network level and inserted into a frame which is created at the data link level, as shown in Figure 5-9.

Logical Channels and Virtual Circuits

X.25 uses logical channel numbers (LCNs) to identify the DTE connections to the network. As many as 4095 logical channels (i.e., user sessions) can be assigned to a physical channel, although not all numbers are actually assigned at one time due to performance considerations. In essence, the LCN serves as an identifier for each user's packet that is transmitted through the physical circuit to and from the network cloud.

Another aspect of X.25 that many people find confusing are the terms logical channel and virtual circuit. Figure 5-10 illustrates the principal difference. In essence, the logical channel has local significance, while the virtual channel has end-to-end significance.

X.25 explains quite specifically how logical channels are established, but allows the network administration considerable leeway in how the virtual circuit is created. However, the network administration must "map" the two logical channel connections together through the network so they can communicate with each other. How this is done is left to the network administration, but it must be done if X.25 is to be used as specified.

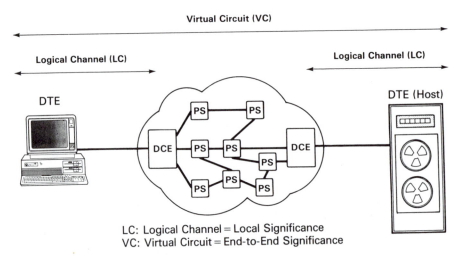

LC: Logical Channel = Local Significance
VC: Virtual Circuit = End-to-End Significance

FIGURE 5–10. X.25 Logical Channels and Virtual Circuits

X.25 Interface Options

We introduce X.25 in more detail by discussing the options for establishing sessions between DTEs and the packet network. The standard provides four mechanisms to establish and maintain communications (see Figure 5-11):

Permanent Virtual Circuit (PVC)

Virtual Call (VC)

Fast Select Call

Fast Select Call with Immediate Clear

Permanent Virtual Circuit (PVC). A permanent virtual circuit is somewhat analogous to a leased line in a telephone network: The transmitting DTE is assured of obtaining a connection to the receiving DTE through the packet network. X.25 requires that a permanent virtual circuit be established before the session begins. Consequently, an agreement must be reached by the two users and the network administration before a permanent virtual connection is allocated. Among other things, this includes the reservation of an LCN for the PVC user.

Thereafter, when a transmitting DTE sends a packet to the network, the logical channel number in the packet indicates that the requesting DTE has a permanent virtual circuit connection to the receiving DTE. Consequently, a connection will be made by the network and the receiving DTE without further arbitration and session negotiation. PVC requires no call setup or clearing procedures, and the logical channel is continually in a data transfer state.

Virtual Call (VC). A virtual call (also called a switched virtual call) resembles some of the procedures associated with telephone dial-up lines. The originating DTE issues a call request packet to the network with a logical channel number. The network routes the call request packet to the destination DTE. The destination DTE receives the call request packet as an incoming call packet from its network node with an LCN.

Logical channel numbering is done at each end of the network; the main requirement is to keep the specific DTE-to-DTE session identified at all times with the same LCNs. This is the responsibility of the network administration. Logical channels specifically identify the various X.25 sessions on each physical circuit at each end of the network. Inside the network, the intermediate packet-switching nodes may also perform their own LCN numbering, but X.25 does not require LCN identification within a network.

If the receiving DTE chooses to acknowledge and accept the call request, it transmits a call accepted packet. The network then transports this packet to the requesting DTE in the form of a call connected packet. The channel enters a data transfer state after the call establishment. To terminate the session, a clear request is sent by either DTE. It is received as a clear indication and confirmed at the clear confirm packet. Following is a summary of the connection establishment procedure:

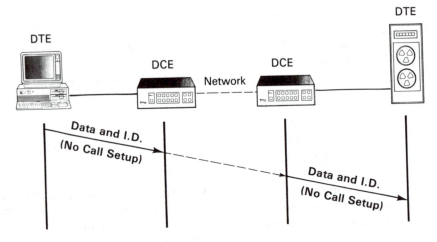

(a) X.25 Permanent Virtual Circuit (PVC)

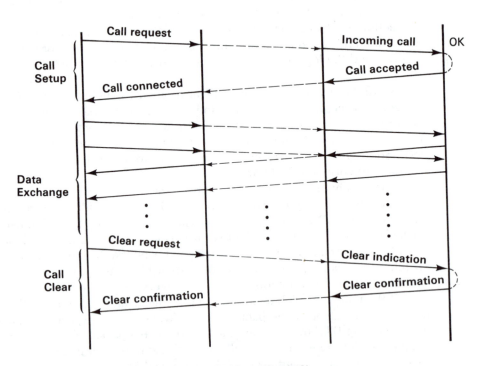

(b) X.25 Virtual Call (VC)

FIGURE 5-11. X.25 Interface Options

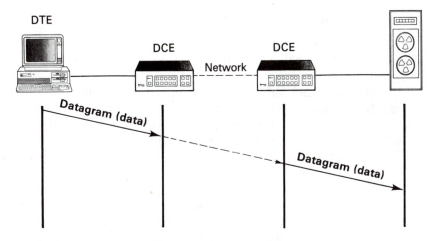

(c) Datagram (Not Supported in X.25)

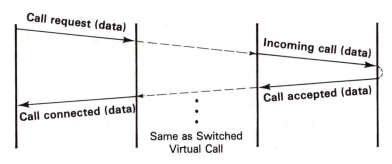

Same as Switched
Virtual Call

(d) X.25 Fast Select Call

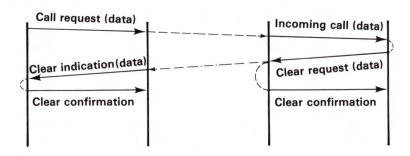

(e) X.25 Fast Select with Immediate Clear

FIGURE 5-11. X.25 Interface Options (Continued)

Packet	LCN Selected By
Call Request	Originating DTE
Incoming Call	Destination packet network node (DCE)
Call Accepted	Same LCN as in Incoming Call
Call Connected	Same LCN as in Call Request

Datagram Deleted.   The datagram facility is a form of connectionless service. No call setup and clear is required, nor is (network) error recovery stipulated. Datagram service was supported in earlier releases of the standard (1980), but it received little support from the commercial industry because of its lack of end-to-end integrity and security. Consequently, the 1984 release of X.25 standard does not contain the datagram option.

Fast Select.   The basic premise of the datagram—eliminating the overhead of the session establishment and disestablishment packets—makes good sense for certain applications, such as those with very few transactions or short sessions on the network. Consequently, the fast select facility was incorporated into the standard. The 1984 release of X.25 provides the fast select as an essential facility, which means that vendors or manufacturers implementing X.25 should implement fast select in order to be a certified X.25 network supplier. Most vendors have implemented fast select.

Fast select provides for two options. The first option is fast select call. A DTE can request this facility on a per-call basis to the network node (DCE) by means of an appropriate request in the header of a packet. The fast select facility allows the call request packet to contain user data of up to 128 bytes (octets). The called DTE is allowed to respond with a call accepted packet, which can also contain user data. The call request/incoming call packet indicates whether the remote DTE is to respond with clear request or a call accepted. If a call accepted is transmitted, the X.25 session continues with the normal data transferring and clearing procedures of a switched virtual call.

Fast Select with Immediate Clear.   Fast select also provides for a fourth call connection feature of the X.25 interface, the fast select with immediate clear. As with the other fast select option, a call request contains user data. This packet is transmitted through the network to the receiving DTE, which, upon acceptance, transmits a clear request (which also contains user data). The clear request is received at the origination site as a clear indication packet. This site returns a clear confirmation. The clear confirmation packet cannot contain user data. Thus, the forward packet sets up the network connection and the reverse packet ends the connection.

The idea of the fast selects (and the now-defunct datagram) is to provide support for user applications that have only one or two transactions, such as inquiry/response applications (point-of-sale transactions, credit checks, funds transfers). These applications cannot use a switched virtual call effectively because of the overhead and delay required in session establishment and disestablishment. Moreover, they cannot benefit from the use of a permanent virtual circuit because their occasional use would not warrant the permanent assignment of resources at the sites and the extra costs involved. Consequently, the fast selects have been incorporated into X.25 to meet the requirement for specialized uses of a network and to provide for more connection-oriented support than the datagram offered. Both DTEs must subscribe to fast select or the network will block the call within the DCE sending back a clear indication packet to the DTE.

Other Packet Types

In addition to the packets described in the previous discussion, the X.25 recommendation uses several other packet types (see Figure 5-12). The data packets are used to transport user data and/or control headers from the upper four layers of the OSI. All other packets are used for control by the DTE and DCE. In

Packet Type		Service	
From DCE to DTE	From DTE to DCE	VC	PVC
Call Set-up and Clearing			
Incoming call	Call request	X	
Call connected	Call accepted	X	
Clear indication	Clear request	X	
DCE clear confirmation	DTE clear confirmation	X	
Data and Interrupt			
DCE data	DTE data	X	X
DCE interrupt	DTE interrupt	X	X
DCE interrupt confirmation	DTE interrupt confirmation	X	X
Flow Control and Reset			
DCE RR	DTE RR	X	X
DCE RNR	DTE RNR	X	X
	DTE REJ	X	X
Reset indication	Reset request	X	X
DCE reset confirmation	DTE reset confirmation	X	X
Restart			
Restart indication	Restart request	X	X
DCE restart confirmation	DTE restart confirmation	X	X
Diagnostic			
Diagnostic		X	X
Registration			
Registration confirmation	Registration request	X	X

VC = Virtual Call   PVC = Permanent Virtual Circuit

FIGURE 5–12. X.25 Packets

most cases, the packets are associated with a procedure, which is controlled by timers. X.25 has very specific rules about the actions of these packets between the user device and the network.

The *interrupt* procedure allows a DTE to transmit one nonsequenced packet without affecting the normal flow control procedures established in X.25. The interrupt procedure is useful for situations where an application requires the transmittal of data for unusual conditions. For example, an extremely high-priority message could be transmitted as an interrupt packet to ensure the receiving DTE accepts the data. User data (32 octets) are permitted in an interrupt packet. The use of interrupts has no effect on regular data packets within the virtual call or permanent virtual circuit. The interrupt packet requires an interrupt confirmation before another interrupt packet can be sent on the logical channel. The confirmation must be returned by the remote DTE.

The *receive ready* (RR) and *receive not ready* (RNR) packets serve the important function of DTE (or DCE) initiated flow control. Both these packets provide a receive sequence number [P(R)] in the packet header to indicate the next packet sequence number expected from the transmitting DTE. The RR packet is used to tell the transmitting DTE to begin sending data packets and also uses the receive sequence number [P(R)] to acknowledge any packets that have been previously transmitted. The RR packet can be used to acknowledge packets received when there are no data packets to convey back to the transmitting station.

The RNR packet is used to request that the transmitting site stop sending packets and it also uses the receive sequence field [P(R)] to acknowledge any packets that have been previously received. The RNR is often issued when a computer or terminal experiences a temporary inability to receive traffic. Thus, both packet types provide flow control. It should be noted that an RNR issued for a specific DTE will likely cause the network to issue an RNR to the associated DTE on the other side of the cloud in order to prevent excess traffic from entering the network. Since the network packet switching nodes have a finite amount of buffering and queuing capability, an RNR often requires choking both sides of the DTE/DTE session.

These two packet types provide X.25 with an additional form of data flow control beyond the data link level support of the HDLC subset LAPB. The data link level does not flow control individual user devices (DTEs), but at the network layer X.25 uses RR and RNR with specific logical channel numbers to accomplish individual flow control on each session with the network. Thus, X.25 achieves a finer level of control than does LAPB.

The *reject* (REJ) packet specifically rejects the received packet. The DTE requests retransmission of packets beginning with the count in the receive sequence field [P(R)]. The DCE is not allowed to use the reject packet, and some networks do not use this packet at all.

The *reset* packets are used to reinitialize a switched virtual call or a permanent virtual circuit. The reset procedure removes in each direction between the two DTEs (for one logical channel session) all data and interrupt packets which may be in the network. Reset procedures may be necessary when problem conditions arise such as lost packets, duplicate packets, or packets that cannot be resequenced properly. Reset is used only during a data transfer state. A reset can be initiated by the DTE (reset request) or the network (reset indication).

The *restart* procedure and the supporting packets are used to initialize or reinitialize the packet level DTE/DCE interface. Up to 4095 logical channels on a physical link can be affected. The procedure clears all the virtual calls and resets all the permanent virtual circuits at the interface level. The restart might occur as a result of a severe problem, such as a crash in the network (for example, the network control center computer fails). All outstanding packets are lost and must be recovered by a higher level protocol. Due to the wide-scale effect of a restart, this packet type must be used judiciously.

The network may use a restart when reinitializing or starting up the system to ensure all sessions are reestablished. Upon a DTE sending a restart, the network must send a restart to each DTE that has a virtual circuit session with the DTE that issued the restart. Restart packets can also contain codes indicating the reason for the restart.

Packet loss is possible in an X.25 network. The clear, reset, and restart packets can cause undelivered packets to be discarded by the network. A situation such as this is not all that unusual. These control packets often arrive at the destination node before user data packets, because control packets are not subject to the delay inherent in flow control procedures that are used with user data packets. Consequently, higher level protocols (e.g., at the transport layer) are required to provide for the accounting for these lost packets.

The *clear* packet is used for a number of functions in an X.25 network, but primarily to clear a DTE-DTE session. One of its other uses is to indicate that a call request cannot be completed. If the remote DTE refuses the call (because of the lack of resources, for example), it issues a clear request to its network node. The packet is sent through the network to the originating network node and a clear indication is sent to the originating DTE. If the network cannot complete the call (for example, the remote network DCE node has no logical channel free or the network is congested), it must send a clear indication to the originating DTE. X.25 provides several codes to indicate the reason for the clear packet. A clear packet cannot be used on a permanent virtual circuit.

The *diagnostic* packet is used by X.25 networks to indicate certain error conditions that are not covered by other methods of indications, such as reset and restart. The diagnostic packet with LCN = 0 is issued only once (and only by the network) for a particular problem; no confirmation is required on the packet. X.25 defines 66 diagnostic codes to aid in determining network or DTE problems. These codes can also be used with other packets (clear, reset, restart).

Here are some examples of X.25 diagnostic codes:

- unidentifiable packet
- packet too long or too short
- unauthorized interrupt confirmation
- timers expired

- invalid address
- no logical channel available
- facility not provided
- unknown international address
- remote network problem
- temporary network routing problem

Finally, the *registration* packets are used to invoke or confirm the X.25 facilities. The 1984 addition allows the end user to request changes to facilities in an online mode, without the manual intervention and negotiation of the network vendor. A registration confirmation is returned to provide a status of the request.

Timers, Time-Outs, and Transition State Diagrams

Timers and state diagrams are used by X.25 to establish limits on how long it takes to get connections, clear channels, reset a session, etc. Without such timers, a user might wait indefinitely for an event if that event did not go to completion. Timers simply force X.25 to make decisions in the event of problems; hence, they facilitate error recovery. For example, consider the call setup state transition diagram in Figure 5-13 (simplified for this discussion). When a DTE issues a call request, the T20 time-limit parameter is started, and the logi-

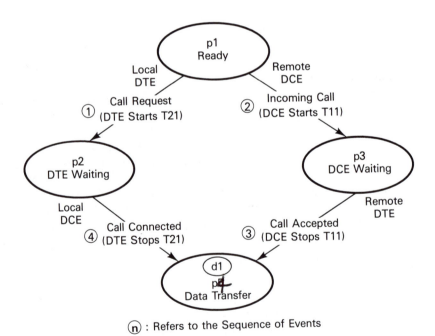

FIGURE 5-13. X.25 Timers and State Transitions

cal channel state moves from Ready (p1) to DTE Wait (p2). In the event of a delay or nonresponse from the network or the remote DTE, the timer expires. The DTE may then attempt another call request or ask for assistance from other support sources such as a network operator. At the remote side of the network, the DCE receives the call request and sends an incoming call packet to its DTE. It starts the T11 timer upon sending the incoming call packet.

X.25 provides five DTE time limits and four DCE time-outs. In all cases, if problems persist and the timers are reset and retried, eventually the channel must be considered out of order and network diagnostics and troubleshooting measures should be performed. These measures depend upon the vendor's specific implementation of X.25.

Packet Formats

The default user data field length in a data packet is 128 bytes or octets, but X.25 provides options for other lengths (see Figure 5-14). The following options are also available: 16, 32, 64, 256, 512, 1024, 2048, and 4096 octets. The latter two sizes were added in the 1984 revision. If the user data field in the packet exceeds the network-permitted maximum field, the receiving DTE will reset the virtual call by issuing a reset packet. Each logical channel can have a different packet size.

Every packet transferred across the DTE/DCE interface to the network must contain at least three octets (bytes). The three octets comprise the packet header. Other octets may also be used to make up the header. The first four bits of the first octet of the header contain the logical channel group number (introduced earlier and discussed in more detail shortly). The last four bits of the first octet contain the general format identifier (GFI). Bits 5 and 6 of the general format identifier are used to indicate the sequencing for the packet sessions. Two sequencing options are allowed in X.25. The first option is Modulo 8, which permits sequence numbers 0 through 7. Modulo 128, which permits sequence numbers ranging from 0 through 127, is also available. The seventh bit or Delivery-Option (D) bit of the general format identifier is used only with certain packets. (We discuss the D bit shortly.) The eighth bit is the Qualifier (Q) bit and is used only for special packets. The network does not "act upon" a packet with Q = 1, but passes it to the destination. During a call setup, this eighth bit is designated as the L bit and can be set to 1 to identify a long address. We discuss this feature shortly.

The second octet of the packet header contains the logical channel number (LCN). This 8-bit field combined with the logical channel group number provides the complete logical channel identification of 12 bits, which provides a total possibility of 4095 logical channels (256 × 16 less the 0 channel). The 0 LCN is reserved for control use (restart and diagnostic packets). Networks use these two fields in various ways. Some networks use the two together; others treat them as separate fields.

Logical channel numbers are used to identify the DTE to the packet node (DCE) and vice versa. The numbers may be assigned to: (a) permanent virtual

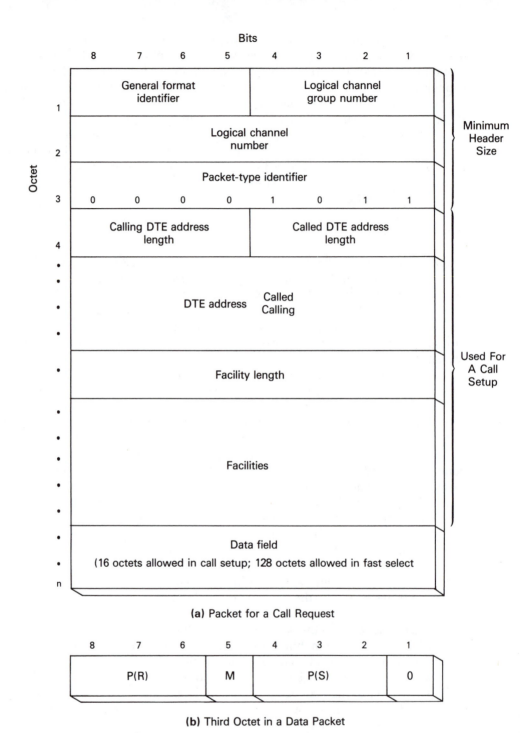

Bits

| 8 | 7 | 6 | 5 | 4 | 3 | 2 | 1 |

Octet

1 — General format identifier | Logical channel group number

2 — Logical channel number

3 — Packet-type identifier
| 0 | 0 | 0 | 0 | 1 | 0 | 1 | 1 |

4 — Calling DTE address length | Called DTE address length

DTE address — Called Calling

Facility length

Facilities

Data field
(16 octets allowed in call setup; 128 octets allowed in fast select

n

Minimum Header Size

Used For A Call Setup

(a) Packet for a Call Request

| 8 | 7 | 6 | 5 | 4 | 3 | 2 | 1 |

| P(R) | M | P(S) | 0 |

(b) Third Octet in a Data Packet

FIGURE 5-14. The X.25 Packet Format (example is a connection management packet)

The Network Layer

circuits; (b) one-way incoming calls; (c) two-way calls; and (d) one-way outgoing calls. The term "one-way" refers to the direction in which the call establishment occurs.

The assignment of LCNs is only pertinent to the DTE and its packet exchange DCE. At the other end of the network, the very same packet may contain a different LCN. Of course, the network must remember that the two different LCNs are the identifiers for the DTE-to-DTE communications.

The third octet of the X.25 packet header is the packet type identifier octet for nondata packets and sequencing octet for data packets. This field identifies the specific nondata packet types.

Additional fields may exist inside the X.25 packet. For call establishment packets, the DTE addresses and address lengths are included. The address fields can be in the fourth through nineteenth octet (maximum length) of the call request packet. The address fields are needed during a call establishment in order for the network to know the calling and called DTEs. Once the call is established, the logical channel numbers are used to identify the DTE-to-DTE session. Some networks do not require the calling address field.

The 1988 release of X.25 stipulates that the first part of the address fields can identify the following:

- International, national, or network numbers
- The following addresses: E.164, E.163, X.121, F.69, or others selected by the organization

The facility fields may also be used in the event the DTEs wish to use the facility options contained in the X.25 standard. The facilities are X.25's method of providing OSI-type quality of service functions for the end users. For example, an X.213 or ISO DIS 8348 service request (see Tables 5-2 and 5-3) for a minimum transit delay through the network is mapped into the transit delay field in the X.25 packet. The X.25 facilities are explained in Appendix 5B.

Finally, user data may exist in the call management packets. The maximum limit in the call request packet for user data is 16 octets. This field is useful for entries such as passwords and accounting information for the receiving DTE. This field is also used by X.25 for additional protocol identification. For instance, a PAD uses this field to identify itself as a PAD when it is calling a host DTE. In this context, this field is not an ordinary user data field. For the fast select option, 128 octets of user data are allowed.

The packet header is modified to facilitate the movement of user data through the network. The third octet of the header, normally reserved for the packet type identifier, is broken into four separate fields for user data packets:

Bits	Description or Value
1	0
2–4	Packet send sequence: P(S)
5	More data bit (the M bit)
6–8	Packet receive sequence: P(R)

The functions of these fields are as follows: The first bit of 0 identifies the packet as a data packet. Three bits are assigned to a send sequence number [P(S)]. One bit is assigned to an M bit function (more about this later). The three remaining bits are assigned to a receiving sequence number [P(R)].

Sequencing at the Packet Level

Note that sequence numbers exist at both the network level and the data link level (HDLC/LAPB). The sending and receiving numbers are used to coordinate and acknowledge packet transmissions between the DTE and DCE. As the packet travels through the network from node to node, the sequence numbers may be altered as the packet traverses the network switching nodes. Nonetheless, the receiving DTE or DCE must know which packet receiving sequence number to send back to the transmitting device to properly acknowledge the specific packet. X.25 is similar to the features found in the second ISO level, data link control; the use of P(R) and P(S) at the network level require the P(R) to be one greater than the P(S) in the data packet.

Remember that both HDLC/LAPB and X.25 provide (R) and (S) sequencing independently of each other. However, the difference between the link and network sequencing is significant. The link level sequence numbers are used to account for all users' traffic on the communications link and to manage flow control on the link. The network level sequence numbers can be used to manage the traffic of each DTE (or anything that has a logical channel number).

The D, M, Q, and A Bits

The D Bit. The D bit facility was added to the 1980 version of X.25. It is used to provide for one of two capabilities. First, when the bit is set to 0, the P(R) value indicates that acknowledgment of receipt of the data packets is done by the network. The second alternative is used when D is set to 1: the P(R) field is used to provide for an end-to-end acknowledgment of the packet, i.e., from one DTE to the other DTE.

The end-to-end acknowledgment does confirm that the packets did indeed arrive at the remote DTE. However, the delay in obtaining end-to-end acknowledgment translates into a greater number of outstanding packets and the requirement for larger window sizes.

Be aware that some networks do not allow the user to specify end-to-end confirmation.

The M Bit. The M (more data) bit of the general format identifier identifies a related sequence of packets traversing through the network. This capability aids the network and DTEs in preserving the identification of blocks of data when the network divides these blocks into smaller packets. For example, a block of data relating to a data base needs to be presented to the receiving DTE in the proper sequence. The capability is quite important when networks are internetworking each other, a topic discussed in the next chapter.

The Q Bit. This bit is optional and may be used to distinguish between user data and control information. One of the PAD standards, X.29, uses the Q bit. It is noted with bit 8 of the general format identifier with data packets.

The A Bit. This capability was added to the 1988 document. It is used to identify a short address (A = 0) or a long address (A = 1). The short address is the conventional X.25 addressing plan. The long address has been added to use the ISDN-related E.164 numbering plan. It is noted with bit 8 of the general format identifier during a call setup.

X.25 Quality of Service (QOS) Facilities

The 1988 release of X.25 contains a number of quality of service features called facilities. Some of these features are not required for a vendor to be "X.25 certified," yet they provide some very useful functions to end users and some are considered essential to a network. The facilities are requested by specific entries in the call request packet. However, most networks require the user to identify the requested facilities at subscription time. They are then invoked by coding values in the facilities field of a call request packet. Some facilities can be dynamically allocated. A summary of the X.25 facilities is provided in Appendix 5A.

X.223: Providing the X.25 Packet Layer Procedures from the X.213 Service Definitions

The 1988 Blue Books include X.223, which describes the mapping between X.25 and the primitives of X.213. X.223 provides the rules for the mapping of the connection-mode primitives and the X.25 packet elements. In its simplest form, it describes how the primitives are used to create the various packet types and how the parameters and the primitives are used to create the fields within the packets.

The use of X.223 for call establishment is shown in Table 5-6. This shows the X.213 connection primitives and their mapped counterparts in the X.25 packet procedures. In addition, the table also shows the X.213 primitive parameters and how they are mapped to the fields in X.25 connection management packets. The X.213 quality of service parameters are mapped into X.25 packet level procedures, principally through the use of X.25 facilities. Table 5-6 also shows the mapping relationship of the QOS subparameters and how they relate to the X.25 packets and the X.25 facilities.

The X.25 data packets are created from the X.213 data primitives. These are the N-DATA request primitive and the N-DATA indication primitive. These primitives carry two parameters which are mapped into fields of the X.25

TABLE 5-6. X.213 Connection Management Primitives and X.25 Call Management Packets

X.213 Primitives	X.25 Packets
N-CONNECT request	Call Request
N-CONNECT indication	Incoming Call
N-CONNECT response	Call Accepted
N-CONNECT confirm	Call Connected
N-DISCONNECT request	Clear Request
N-DISCONNECT indication	Clear Indication, Restart Indication, or Clear Request
N-DATA request	Data
N-DATA indication	Data
N-EXPEDITED DATA request	Interrupt
N-EXPEDITED DATA indication	Interrupt
N-RESET request	Reset Request
N-RESET indication	Reset Indication, Reset Request
N-RESET response	
N-RESET confirm	

Primitive Parameters	Fields in the Packets
Called Address	Called DTE address field or Called address extension facility
Calling Address	Calling DTE address field or Calling DTE address extension facility
Responding Address	Called DTE address field or Called DTE address extension facility
Receipt Confirmation Selection	General format identifier (GFI)
Expedited Data Selection	Expedited data negotiation facility
QOS Parameters	These X.25 facilities: Throughput class negotiation Minimum throughput class negotiation Transit delay selection and indication End-to-end transit delay
Originator and Reason	Cause code and diagnostic code
NS-User Data	User data field in a Fast Select packet
NS-User Data	User data field in a data packet
Confirmation Request	D bit with the P(S)

packet. First, the NS-user-data parameter is used to create the X.25 user data field and perhaps the M bit. Second, the X.213 confirmation request primitive is mapped into the X.25 D bit and the P(S) field.

As might be expected, the X.25 Interrupt packet is created from the X.213 expedited data request primitives, and the X.213 reset primitives are mapped into the X.25 reset packets. Finally, the disconnect primitives are mapped into the X.25 clear packets, which are also shown in the table.

The Network Layer

THE OSI CONNECTIONLESS-MODE NETWORK SERVICE (ISO 8348)

The ISO has published a standard for connectionless-mode network service, ISO 8348 DAD1. As the reader may now expect, only data-type primitives are used with this service. No connection management or acknowledgment primitives are invoked. The two primitives used are:

- N-UNITDATA.request (source-address, destination-address, quality-of-service, NS-user data)
- N-UNITDATA.indication (source-address, destination-address, quality-of-service, NS-user-data)

As with all connectionless operations, no logical connection between the users exists, and any quality of service (QOS) functions must be known before the data is exchanged. Therefore, the QOS values must be within the capabilities of the service provider. If the service provider cannot meet the stated QOS, it must attempt (ideally) to provide services to the closest approximation of the QOS requirements. Realistically, the service provider attempts to deliver the data unit in any manner it can.

The quality of service parameters for the ISO connectionless-mode service are as follows:

- *Transit delay.* Time expected between the issuance of the N-UNITDATA. request and the receipt of the associated N-UNITDATA.indication.
- *Unauthorized access.* Stipulates how much protection is needed. Four levels are defined.
- *Cost determinants.* Stipulates the cost of the service to convey the data unit. Two levels are defined.
- *Residual error probability.* Defines the acceptable probability of a data unit being lost, incorrectly delivered, or duplicated.
- *Priority.* Indicates how important the data units are in regard to (a) discarding the units in the event of problems, and (b) degrading the quality of service, if necessary.

THE ISDN NETWORK LAYER

The ISDN layer 3 specification (CCITT recommendations I.450 and I.451) uses many OSI concepts. It encompasses circuit switch connections, packet switch connections, and user-to-user connections. I.450 and I.451 specify the procedures to establish, manage, and clear a network connection at the ISDN user-network interface (see Figure 5-15).

Table 5-7 is provided to give the reader a better understanding of the ISDN session procedures, as well as information transfer and disestablishment proce-

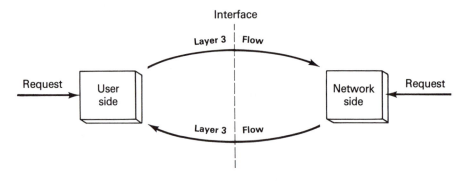

FIGURE 5-15. The ISDN Interface

dures for circuit-mode connections. The more widely used messages are summarized below. (Be aware that some carriers have not implemented all of the messages.)

The SETUP message is sent by the user or the network to indicate a call establishment. The message contains several parameters to define the circuit connection, and it must contain these three parameters:

- *Protocol discriminator*: Distinguishes between user-network call control messages and others, such as other layer 3 protocols (X.25, for example).

TABLE 5-7.   ISDN Layer 3 Messages

Call Establishment Messages	*Call Disestablishment Messages*
ALERTing	DETach
CALL PROCeeding	DETach ACKnowledge
CONNect	DISConnect
CONNect ACKnowledge	RELease
SETUP	RELease COMplete
SETUP ACKnowledge	
Call Information Phase Messages	*Miscellaneous Messages*
RESume	CANCel
RESume ACKnowledge	CANCel ACKnowledge
RESume REJect	CANCel REJect
SUSPend	CONgestion CONtrol
SUSPend ACKnowledge	FACility
SUSPend REJect	FACility ACKnowledge
USER INFOrmation	FACility REJect
	INFOrmation
	REGister
	REGister ACKnowledge
	REGister REJect
	STATUS

- *Call reference:* Identifies the ISDN call at the local user-network interface. It does not have end-to-end significance.
- *Message type:* Identifies the message function; that is to say, the types shown in Table 5-7.

As options, other parameters include the specific ISDN channel identification, originating and destination address, an address for a redirected call, the designation for a transit network, etc.

The SETUP ACKnowledge message is sent by the user or the network to indicate the call establishment has been initiated. The parameters for the SETUP ACK message are similar to the SETUP message.

The CALL PROCeeding message is sent by the network or the user to indicate the call is being processed. The message also indicates the network has all the information it needs to process the call.

The CONNect message and the CONNect ACKnowledge messages are exchanged between the network and the network user to indicate the call is accepted between either the network or the user. These messages contain parameters to identify the session and the facilities and services associated with the connection.

To clear a call, the user or the network can send a RELease or DISConnect message. Typically, the RELease COMplete is returned, but the network may maintain the call reference for later use, in which case, the network sends a DETach message to the user.

A call may be temporarily suspended. The SUSPend message is used to create this action. The network can respond to this message with either a SUSPend ACKnowledge or a SUSPend REJect.

During an ongoing ISDN connection, the user or network may issue CONgestion CONtrol messages to flow-control USER INFOrmation messages. The message simply indicates whether the receiver is ready or not ready to accept messages.

The USER INFOrmation message is sent by the user or the network to transmit information to a (another) user.

If a call is suspended, the RESume message is sent by the user to request the resumption of the call. This message can invoke a RESume ACKnowledge or a RESume REJect.

The STATUS message is sent by the user or the network to report on the conditions of the call.

The ISDN supports numerous facilities (see Table 5-8). They are managed with the following messages.

REGister	Initiates the registration of a
REGister ACKnowledge	facility (as well as confirmation
REGister REJect	or rejection)
FACility	Initiates access to a network
FACility ACKnowledge	facility (as well as

TABLE 5-8. ISDN Layer 3 Facilities

Delivery of origin address barred
Connected address required
Supply charging information after end of call
Reverse charging requested
Connect outgoing calls when free
Reverse charging acceptance (allowed)
Call redirection/diversion notification
Call completion after busy request
Call completion after busy indication
Origination address required on outgoing calls
Origination address desired on incoming calls
Destination address required on incoming calls
Connect incoming calls when free (waiting allowed)
X.25 extended packet sequence numbering (Modulo 128)
X.25 flow control parameter negotiation allowed
X.25 throughput class negotiation allowed
X.25 packet retransmission allowed
X.25 fast select (outgoing) allowed
X.25 fast select acceptance allowed
X.25 multilink procedure
X.25 Local charging prevention
X.25 extended frame sequence numbering

FACility REJect	confirmation or rejection)
CANcel	Indicates a request to
CANcel ACKnowledge	discontinue a facility (as well
CANcel REJect	as confirmation or rejection)

Most of these facilities are self-explanatory; others are explained in the X.25 part of this chapter. It is evident that the connections of ISDN and X.25 have been given much thought by the standards groups.

Network Layer Message Format

The ISDN network layer protocol uses messages to communicate. The format for these messages is shown in Figure 5-16. The message consists of the following fields (these fields were explained with the SETUP message):

- Protocol discriminator (required)
- Call reference (required)
- Message type (required)
- Mandatory information elements (as required)
- Additional information elements (when required)

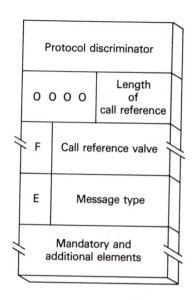

F: Origination side sets to 0
Destination side sets to 1
E: Set to 0 (Extension Bit)

FIGURE 5-16. The ISDN Message Format

TABLE 5-9. Other ISDN Information Elements

Procedure	Function
Locking Shift	Indicates a new active code set; allows a shift between international, national, network and user-specific information elements.
Bearer Capability	Indicates the ISDN is to provide a bearer service.
Call Identity	Identifies the suspended call.
Call State	Describes the current status of a call, such as received, active, suspend request, facility request.
Cause	Describes reason for generating certain diagnostic messages.
Channel Identification	Identifies a channel or subchannel within the interface controlled by ISDN signaling procedures (B1, B2, H0, H1, Basic, Primary, etc.)
Key Pad	Used to provide compatibility checking (e.g., ASCII character capability).
Transit Network Selection	Identifies a requested transit network between the communicating users.
User-User Information	ISDN user information; passed transparently by ISDN to users.

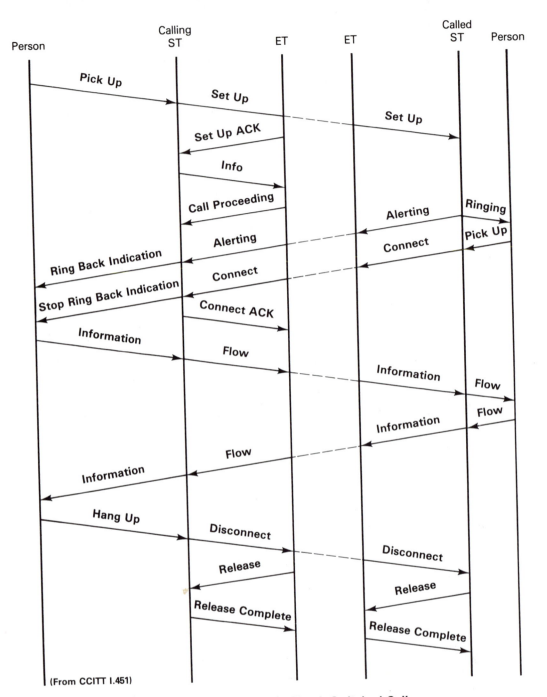

FIGURE 5-17. An ISDN Circuit Switched Call

(From CCITT I.451)

The ISDN also allows other message formats to accommodate equipment needs and different information elements. This feature provides considerable flexibility in choosing other options and ISDN services. Selected "other" ISDN network layer information elements are listed in Table 5-9.

Example of an ISDN Call

Figure 5-17 illustrates a typical procedure for a simple circuit switched call. Note the use of the ISDN messages that are listed in Table 5-7.

SUMMARY AND CONCLUSIONS

The OSI network layer defines the user-to-network interface operations for circuit-switched and packet-switched networks. The best-known standard residing in this layer is the X.25 interface protocol. It is the most widely used connection-oriented network layer standard in the world. Although OSI connectionless network protocols, such as ISO 8473, will become a dominant force in the industry, they usually are tasked with internetworking functions, and therefore are discussed in the next chapter. The ISDN network layer is gaining in use as countries migrate to digital interfaces. With publication of the Blue Book, the CCITT has published several specifications for the internetworking of X.25 and ISDN.

APPENDIX 5A. THE X.25 FACILITIES

The X.25 facilities are one of the most widely used parts of this protocol. At the same time, they sometimes lead to incompatible interfaces between different vendors' products because the vendors do not always support the same facilities. The X.25 user should check the use of facilities very carefully to ensure compatibility across product lines.

On-Line Facility Registration. This permits the DTE at any time to request facilities or to obtain the parameters (values) of the facilities, as understood by the DCE. The DTE/DCE dialogue takes place with the registration packets, and the packets indicate whether the facility value can be negotiated. This facility is new, but has great potential. For example, the ability to dynamically modify facilities during a session with a network gives a user considerable flexibility.

Extended Packet Numbering. This facility provides sequence numbering using Modulo 128. In its absence, sequencing is done with Modulo 8 (sequence numbers 1 to 7). This 1984 addition was deemed important in order to contend with the long propagation problems of satellite channels and radio transmission for ships at sea.

D Bit Modification. This facility is intended for use by DTEs developed prior to the introduction of the 1980 D bit procedure. It allows the DTEs to operate with end-to-end acknowledgment. (The D bit was explained earlier in the chapter.)

Packet Retransmission. A DTE may request retransmission of one to several data packets from the DCE. The DTE specifies the logical channel number and a value of $P(R)$ in a reject packet. The DCE must then retransmit all packets from $P(R)$ to the next packet it is to transmit for the first time. This facility is similar to the Go-Back-N technique used by the line protocols at the data link level (LAPB's Reject).

Incoming Calls Barred. Outgoing Calls Barred. These two facilities prevent incoming calls from being presented to the DTE or prevent the DCE from accepting outgoing calls from the DTE. Consequently, a DTE subscribing to Incoming Calls Barred can initiate calls but cannot accept them. A DTE subscribing to Outgoing Calls Barred can receive calls but cannot initiate them.

One-Way Logical Channel Outgoing. One-Way Logical Channel Incoming. These two facilities restrict a logical channel to originating calls only or receiving calls only. These facilities provide more specific control than the Calls Barred facilities, because they operate on a specific channel or channels. Hence, the subscribing DTE can control each logical channel. These facilities are useful in controlling and reserving resources for important incoming and outgoing calls.

Nonstandard Default Packet Sizes. This provides for the selection of default packet sizes that are supported by the network. Registration packets can be used to negotiate the packet sizes.

Nonstandard Default Window Sizes. This facility allows the window sizes for $P(R)$ and $P(S)$ to be expanded beyond the default size of 2 for all calls.

Default Throughput Classes Assignment. This facility provides for the selection of one of the following throughput rates (in bits/s): 75, 150, 300, 600, 1200, 2400, 4800, 9600, 19200, 48000. Throughput describes the maximum amount of data that can be sent through the network when the network is operating at saturation. Factors that influence this are line speeds, window sizes, and the number of active sessions in the network. Other values can be negotiated.

Flow Control Parameter Negotiation. This facility allows the window and packet sizes to be negotiated on a per-call basis. In many X.25 networks, the DTE suggests packet sizes and window sizes during the call setup. The called DTE (if it subscribes to these facilities) may reply with a counterproposal. If it does not, it is assumed that the call setup parameters are acceptable. The network DCE may control the window and packet sizes itself. It might modify the parameters from the sending DTE and present different ones to the receiving DTE. Some networks require that the negotiated flow control parameters be the same for each direction of transmission.

Throughput Class Negotiation. This allows the throughput rates to be negotiated on a per-call basis. A throughput greater than a DTE's default values is not allowed. The allowable rates that can be negotiated are: 75, 150, 300, 600, 1200, 2400, 4800, 9600, 19200, 48000 bits/s.

Closed User Groups (CUG). A set of facilities allow users to form groups of DTEs from which access is restricted. The CUG facility provides a level of security/privacy in an "open" public network. Some people call this feature a virtual private network. The facility has several options:

- *Incoming Calls Barred Within a CUG.* A DTE may initiate calls to other members of the CUG but cannot receive calls from them.
- *Outgoing Calls Barred Within a CUG.* A DTE may receive calls from other members of the CUG but cannot initiate calls to them.
- *CUG With Incoming Access.* A DTE will receive calls from DTEs belonging to the network, and from DTEs which are members of other CUGs with outgoing access.
- *CUG With Outgoing Access.* A DTE may initiate calls to DTEs belonging to the network, and to DTEs which are members of other CUGs with incoming access.

The calling DTE specifies the requested CUG by encoding the call request packet. It arrives at the called DTE as an incoming call. If the DTE has not subscribed to the CUG facility, or if the calling DTE is not a member of the called DTE's CUG, the call will be rejected by the network.

Bilateral Closed User Groups. This facility is similar to CUG, but allows access restrictions between pairs of DTEs.

Fast Select. Fast Select Acceptance. These two facilities were discussed earlier.

Reverse Charging. Reverse Charging Acceptance. These facilities allow the packet network charges to accrue to a receiving DTE. It can be used with virtual calls and fast selects. The facility is like calling collect on a telephone.

Local Charging Prevention. This facility authorizes the DCE to prevent the establishment of calls for which the subscribing DTE must pay. For example, a DTE may not be allowed to send a reverse charge to another DTE that has subscribed to reverse charging acceptance.

Network User Identification. This facility enables the transmitting DTE to provide billing, security, or management information on a per-call basis to the DCE. If invalid, the call is barred.

Charging Information. This facility requires the DCE to provide the DTE information about the packet session relating to the charges.

RPOA Selection. This allows a calling DTE to specify one or more recognized private operating agencies (RPOAs) to handle the packet session. The RPOA is a packet network carrier.

Hunt Group. This facility distributes incoming calls across a designated grouping of DTE/DCE interfaces. This 1984 addition gives users the ability to select multiple ports on a front-end processor or computer, or select different front-end processes or computers at a user site. The facility is quite valuable for organizations with large computing facilities that need flexibility in directing jobs to various, different resources. It is similar in concept to the familiar port selector found in most installations.

Call Redirection. This facility redirects packet calls when the DTE is out of order, busy, or has requested a call redirection. This facility is also part of the 1984 addition. It allows a call to be rerouted to a back-up DTE, which provides the very valuable function of keeping problems and failures isolated from the end user. The call redirection could also permit calls to be redirected to different parts of a country due to time zone considerations.

Called Line Address Modified Notification. In the event a call is redirected, this facility informs the calling DTE why the called address in a call connected or clear indication packet is different from the DTE's call request packet.

Call Redirection Notification. In the event a call is redirected, this facility so informs the alternate DTE and also gives the reason why and the address of the DTE that was originally called.

Transit Delay Selection and Indication. This facility permits a DTE to select a transit delay time through the packet network. This feature can be quite valuable to an end user by giving the user some control over response time in the network.

A Bit Facility. This facility permits the use of the long address format. It was added to the 1988 standard to permit the use of ISDN E.164 addresses.

Facilities on Permanent Virtual Circuits (PVCs). Since PVCs do not have call setup packets, facilities cannot be invoked on a per-call basis. Furthermore, some networks do not provide facilities for permanent virtual circuits. X.25

recommends the following facilities be made available for PVCs, but networks vary in how PVCs and facilities are supported:

- nonstandard packet size
- extended packet sequence numbering
- nonstandard default window size
- default throughput class assignment
- packet retransmission

CHAPTER 6

The Network Layer, Internetworking

INTRODUCTION

In the last few years, the OSI Model has been enhanced to include protocols and service definitions for connecting networks together. The term to describe this feature is *internetworking* (or interworking). Prior to the publication of the OSI internetworking standards, the Internet Protocol (IP) had been implemented in many systems throughout the world. Indeed, it is one of the most prevalent network level protocols in existence.

The ISO 8473 standard is meant as a replacement for IP. Notwithstanding, due to the prevalence of IP and because of its similarity to 8473, IP is included in this chapter, but be aware that it is not an OSI standard.

This chapter explains several of the prevalent internetworking standards used in the industry. The following standards/products are covered:

- Connectionless-mode Network Service (ISO 8473)
- The Internet Protocol (IP)
- X.75 Internetworking
- Internetworking X.25 and IEEE 802 LANs (ISO 8881, ISO 8208)
- Internetworking ISDNs and X.25 (X.30, X.31)
- Internetworking circuit switched systems with packet networks and an ISDN (X.80, X.81, X.82)
- CCITT X.300 interworking specifications

Problems with Internetworking

Data communications networks were developed to allow users to share computer and information resources, as well as a common communications system. As organizations brought the computer into almost every facet of business, it became obvious that a single network, while very useful, is inadequate to meet the burgeoning information needs of businesses and individuals. For example, a user of one network often needs to access computers and data bases that "belong" to another network. It is prohibitively complex and expensive to merge all resources into one network, not to mention the political and organizational problems of merging the disparate organizations' vital information resources.

As shown in Figure 6-1, an alternative is to interconnect the networks to obtain the required resources. Hereafter, a network is also called a *subnetwork*. The subnetwork forms an autonomous whole. It consists of a relatively homogeneous collection of equipment, physical media, and software which is used to support the user community. Some examples of subnetworks are privately owned networks, public networks (TELENET, Tymnet, Datapac), and local area networks.

Several difficult issues and problems arise in providing internetworking services:

- The subnetworks may use different sizes and formats for protocol data units (PDUs). If different sizes are supported, the subnetworks must provide for the segmentation and reassembly of the data units. In so doing, the identity of the data units must not be lost. The varying sizes of the data units do not eliminate the requirement to maintain a sequence number relationship on an end-to-end basis.
- The timers, time-outs, and retry values often differ between subnetworks. For example, assume network A sets a wait-for-acknowledgment timer when a data unit is sent into the "cloud." The timer is used to ensure that an end-to-end acknowledgment occurs within a specified period. Assume the data unit is passed from network A to network B, but this network does not have an end-to-end timer. Thus, we have a dilemma: should network A return the acknowledgment to the user upon passing the data unit to network B and assume the second network will indeed deliver the data unit? A false sense of security would result, since the data unit may not arrive at the end destination.
- The subnetworks may provide different types, levels, and qualities of service (QOS). For example, one network may support reverse charging and another may not allow the feature. Internetworking usually requires the QOS to be supported to the lowest common denominator—not a very attractive alternative for the user of the high-QOS network.
- The subnetworks may use different addressing conventions. For example, one may use logical names, and another may use physical node names. In

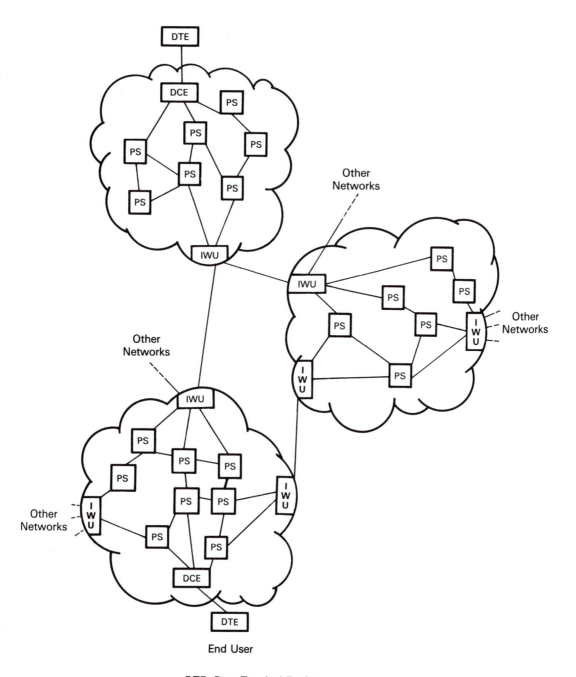

FIGURE 6-1. Internetworking Topologies

DTE: Data Terminal Equipment
DCE: Data Circuit-Terminating Equipment
IWU: Internetworking Unit
PS: Packet Switch

such a case, address resolution and mapping would differ between the two subnetworks. Indeed, most networks use network-specific addresses. For example, an SNA address simply does not equate to a DECnet address.

- The subnetworks may exhibit different levels of performance. For example, one subnetwork may be slower and exhibit more delay and less throughput than another network.
- The subnetworks may employ different routing methods. For example, one may use a fixed routing directory and another may use an adaptive routing directory. In the former case, the network logic for resequencing is sparse. In the latter case, resequencing logic is extensive.
- The subnetworks may require different types of user interfaces. For example, a subnetwork may employ a connection-oriented, user-to-subnetwork interface and another may use a connectionless, datagram protocol. The interface type influences error recovery and flow control.
- The subnetworks may require different levels of security. For example, one network may require encryption and another may only support clear-text transmissions.
- Troubleshooting, diagnostics, and network maintenance (a) may differ between the subnetworks, and (b) may not be used across more than one network. A problem created in one subnetwork may affect another subnetwork, yet the affected network may have no control in the error analysis and correction.
- The question of charging/billing is yet another problem. Which subnetwork(s) reap the revenue? How are costs allocated?

Clearly, the internetworking task is not simple, and it requires considerable analysis and forethought before it is implemented. Yet the task is not insurmountable. As we shall see, the vendors and standards organizations have developed and implemented many effective internetworking techniques.

Dividing the Network Layer

In its DIS 8648 specification, ISO divides the network layer into three functional groups to describe the internal organization of the layer (see Figure 6-2). This division provides a convenient method to identify internetworking operations. Several vendors are now using this convention in their commercial offerings.

At the top of the network layer is the *subnetwork independent convergence protocol* (SNICP), which provides the relay and routing services for internetworking. This sublayer contains the internetwork protocols to effect data transfer between networks. The SNICP use is based on a minimal service from the subnetwork, and is intended to be used over a variety of different kinds of networks. In this chapter, the IP is examined as an example of the SNICP.

The middle level is the *subnetwork dependent convergence protocol* (SNDCP). It requires a particular type of subnetwork below it and operates

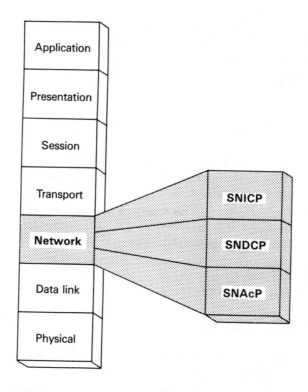

SNICP: Subnetwork Independence Convergence Protocol
SNDCP: Subnetwork Dependence Convergence Protocol
SNAcP: Subnetwork Access Protocol

FIGURE 6-2. The Network Layer Sublayers

based on the characteristics of the subnetwork. SNDCP may be used to bring the interconnecting subnetworks up to a level needed for the interconnection. The interconnecting networks (subnetworks) may not provide a needed service, so SNDCP provides a "mapping" of the required service, or it may operate an explicit protocol to provide the convergence. At its most basic level, SNICP serves as a network protocol converter.

The ISO publishes DIS 8878 as an SNDCP. It is used to support a 1980 X.25 network that does not have all the features of a 1984 X.25 network. It adds information to the 1980 packet in order to obtain the added services of the 1984 version.

The lowest sublayer is the *subnetwork access protocol* (SNAcP), which contains the services relevant to each of the interconnecting networks. For example, SNA, the X.25 network interface, and CSMA/CD are SNAcPs. The SNAcP provides the data transfer between the DTE and the DCE. It also manages the connections and receives the quality of service requests from the end user.

Following are several other ideas about these internetworking concepts.

- The SNDCP may perform some or all of the functions of the SNAcP. For example, the network service provisions may be completely absent and SNDCP would then assume these functions.
- It may be possible for two subnetworks to transmit using the same form of protocol data unit. This situation is possible when the same subnetwork independent convergence protocol is used in both subnetworks; or if the subnetwork access protocol provides identical or similar services; or if all the layers of the subnetworks are the same.
- Since a subnetwork service is satisfied with an SNAcP, and an SNICP only provides a minimal service, it follows that an SNDCP will not be used if an SNICP is present.
- The subnetwork access protocol may not exist in the network layer. For example, local area networks (LANs) may not use the subnetwork access protocol in the network layer.
- It is possible that the SNAcP and SNDCP could be absent from the network layer. In this situation, the network service functions can be performed by the SNICP using the data link layer.

Dividing the Data Link Layer

The reader should not confuse the network sublayers with the data link sublayers. Several vendors and standards also subdivide the data link layer into two sublayers. The approach, depicted in Figure 6-3, is published by the IEEE as part of the IEEE 802 LAN specifications. The MAC (media access control) sublayer is protocol-specific to a LAN, such as Ethernet. The LLC (logical link control) serves as an interface to an upper layer protocol, typically the network layer, and isolates the network layer from the specific actions of the MAC sublayer. Some local area networks use LLC to perform network and transport layer functions by the implementation of sequence numbers, flow control, ACKs, and NAKs. In this manner, the lower layers of the LAN are not concerned with these functions. These concepts are explained in more detail in Chapter 4.

CONNECTIONLESS-MODE NETWORK SERVICE DEFINITIONS (ISO 8348/DAD1)

The ISO 8348 standard describes the service definitions for a connectionless-mode service. As the reader might expect, only two primitives are used for the service:

- N-UNITDATA.request (source address, destination address, quality of service, NS user data)
- N-UNITDATA.indication (source address, destination address, quality of service, NS user data)

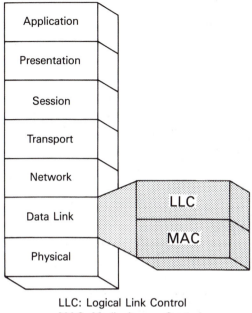

LLC: Logical Link Control
MAC: Media Access Control

FIGURE 6-3. Dividing the Data Link Layer

The address fields are internet addresses that uniquely identify the source and destination entities. The quality of service field can contain the following five parameters: (1) transit delay, (2) residual error probability, (3) protection from unauthorized access, (4) cost determinants, and (5) priority. The user data field is simply the user data.

CONNECTIONLESS-MODE NETWORK SERVICE (ISO 8473)

The connectionless-mode network service, introduced in Chapter 1, is examined in more detail in this section of the book. The reader may recall that this network type manages user protocol data units (PDUs) as independent and separate entities. No relationship is maintained between successive data transfers and few records are kept of the ongoing user-to-user communications process through the network(s).

This mode of service does not require a connection to be established before the exchange of data. Consequently, the service user and the service provider must have an understanding and agreement as to what levels of service are to be provided. The quality of service parameters in the primitives and the protocol data units should reflect this agreement. It is possible that a network cannot provide the agreed-upon service. For example, the network might be congested, so the transit delay request cannot be met. Ordinarily, the network will still attempt to deliver the data unit to the end user.

Our discussion on connectionless-mode networks will focus on the ISO 8473, which is also called the connectionless network protocol (CLNP). The standard is based on the widely used Internet Protocol (IP) and will eventually replace IP.

It will be evident that accommodating to different user data field sizes is a major concern. Since networks may use different sizes for user data, the protocol must ensure processing logic and resources are available to support the differences. These protocol resources are often wasted because most packet data networks use 128 or 256 user data octets in each packet. However, applications such as packetized voice and image processing require different packet sizes, so it is best that a protocol support these differences. Moreover, as internetworking increases, it is quite probable that the use of multiple packet sizes will also increase.

ISO 8473 has been designed to operate within the DTEs attached to public and private networks. As will be seen, the protocol does not involve itself with the particular characteristics of the underlying subnetworks. The basic idea is to demand little in the way of services from the subnetworks except to transport the protocol data unit. This concept is in conformance with the OSI connectionless model.

The protocol communicates by exchanging internetwork protocol data units (IPDUs) in a connectionless (datagram) fashion. Each IPDU is treated independently and does not depend on the state of the network for any particular establishment connection time (since no connection exists in a connectionless network). Generally, routing decisions are made independently by each forwarding internetworking node. It is also possible for the source user to determine the routing by placing the routing information in the IPDU source routing field.

The ISO 8473 connectionless-mode network service is provided by two ISO 8348 primitives, N-UNITDATA.request and N-UNITDATA.indication (see Figure 6-4). These two primitives are quite similar to the primitives used by the IP (Internet Protocol), discussed next. The reader should note that the protocol uses no connection and clear primitives, which is a rather obvious indication of its connectionless attributes. The two primitives each contain four parameters: NS-source-address, NS-destination-address, NS-quality-of-service, and NS-user-data. All parameters are explained shortly.

Layer Interaction

Figure 6-5 illustrates the actual use of several terms and concepts of connectionless operations. It also shows how the primitive parameters are placed into the fields of the protocol data units, which is the key concept of the OSI Model and layered protocols.

The connectionless network protocol (CLNP) receives the N-UNITDATA.request from the transport layer. The parameters with the request are

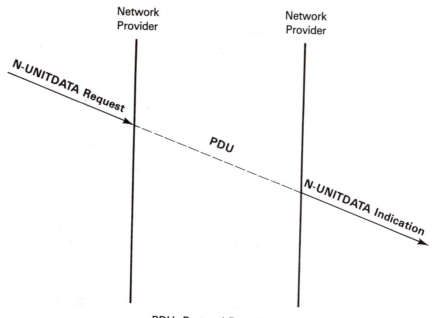

PDU: Protocol Data Unit

FIGURE 6-4. The Connectionless Service Definitions and Protocol Data Units

used to construct a protocol data unit (PDU). The address parameters contain the source and destination NSAP address parameters.

The underlying service to support ISO 8473 is also defined by two primitives: SN-UNITDATA.request and SN-UNITDATA.indication. The parameters are the same as above: SN-source-address, SN-destination-address, SN-quality-of-service, and SN-user-data. The primitives are used by the ISO 8473 machine to interface with an actual network (SNAcP), an intervening layer (SNDCP), or an actual data link protocol.

When the appropriate subnetwork has been selected, the SN-UNIT-DATA.request is issued by the CLNP to the local SNDCP. It then maps the request parameters to a DL-UNITDATA.request, which is used by ISO 8802 (IEEE 802.2 Type 1; known as LLC or Logical Link Control, discussed in Chapter 4). It must then invoke a procedure to create an HDLC/LLC unnumbered information (UI) frame. The SN-destination-address and SN-source-address of the NSDU are mapped into the source (SSAP) and destination (DSAP) of the LLC frame. The SN-user-data is placed into the I (information) field of the frame. The LLC frame is then given to the MAC sublayer with the DL-UNITDATA.request.

The receiving node reverses the process just described. Its LLC receives an MA-UNITDATA.indication and passes the protocol data unit (frame) to the SNDCP. It decapsulates the UI frame and derives the addresses and user data. It then maps these addresses onto the SN-destination-address and SN-source-

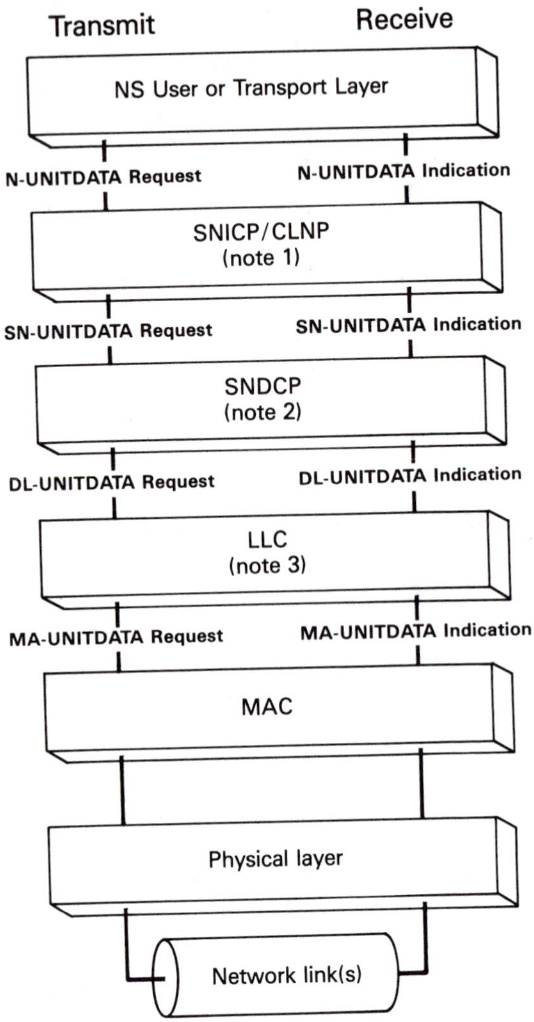
Transmit
Receive
NS User or Transport Layer
N-UNITDATA Request
N-UNITDATA Indication
SNICP/CLNP
(note 1)
SN-UNITDATA Request
SN-UNITDATA Indication
SNDCP
(note 2)
DL-UNITDATA Request
DL-UNITDATA Indication
LLC
(note 3)
MA-UNITDATA Request
MA-UNITDATA Indication
MAC
Physical layer
Network link(s)

Note 1: Chooses Subnetwork
Note 2: May Not Be Used
Note 3: SNAP Could Be Evoked Here

FIGURE 6-5. Connectionless-Mode Network

address parameters of the SN-UNITDATA.indication primitives. It also maps the I field onto the SN-user-data parameter of the SN-UNITDATA.indication.

The destination SNDCP then receives the data unit and notifies the receiving CLNP via a SN-UNITDATA.indication. The NSAP address in the PDU is then checked to determine if it corresponds to any of the NSAP addresses serviced by the receiving CLNP. If so, the PDU is decomposed and an N-UNITDATA.indication is passed to the NS user.

If the protocol data unit has not yet reached its destination, routing and forwarding functions are executed for internetwork transfer. The data is transferred transparently between the subnetworks.

The ISO 8473 Protocol Data Unit

The fields of the protocol data unit (see Figure 6-6) provide the functions described in Table 6-1. The reader should review these functions since they are used to explain the internetworking session.

Quality of Service (QOS) Functions

An underlying subnetwork may provide several quality of service (QOS) functions. The services are negotiated when the primitives are exchanged between layers. Of course, the primitive parameters must be based on *a priori* knowledge of the availability of the services within the subnetwork. It does little good to

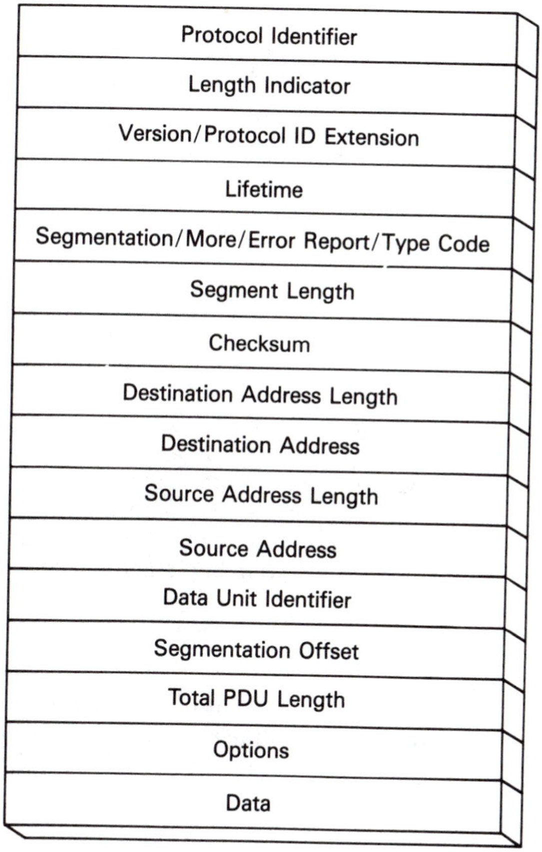

Protocol Identifier
Length Indicator
Version/Protocol ID Extension
Lifetime
Segmentation/More/Error Report/Type Code
Segment Length
Checksum
Destination Address Length
Destination Address
Source Address Length
Source Address
Data Unit Identifier
Segmentation Offset
Total PDU Length
Options
Data

FIGURE 6-6. The ISO 8473 Protocol Data Unit (PDU)

TABLE 6-1.   Functions of the Fields in the 8473 Data Protocol Data Unit

Network layer protocol identifier: This field identifies the protocol as ISO 8473.

Length indicator: This field describes the length of the header. **Version/protocol identifier extension:** This identifies the version of ISO 8473.

Lifetime: This field represents the lifetime of the PDU. It is coded in units of 500 milliseconds. **Segmentation permitted:** This bit indicates if segmentation is permitted. The originator of the PDU determines this value and it cannot be changed by any other entity.

More segments: This bit indicates if more user data is forthcoming. It is used when segmentation takes place. When the bit equals 0, it indicates that the last octet of the data in this PDU is the last octet of the user data stream (the network data service unit [NSDU]).

Error report: This bit is set to 1 to indicate that an error report is to be generated back to the originator if a data PDU is discarded. **Type code:** These five bits describe the PDU as a data PDU or an error PDU.

PDU segment length: This field specifies the entire length of the PDU (header and data). If no segmentation occurs, the value of this field is identical to the value of the total length field.

Checksum: The checksum is calculated on the entire PDU header. A value of 0 in this field indicates that the header is to be ignored. A PDU is discarded if the checksum fails.

Address length and addresses: Since the source and destination addresses are variable in length, the length fields are used to describe their length. The actual addresses are Network Service Access Points (NSAPs). **Data unit identifier:** This field identifies an initial PDU in order to correctly reassemble a segmented data unit.

Segmentation offset: If the original PDU is segmented, this field specifies the relative position of this segment in relation to the initial PDU. **PDU total length:** This field contains the entire length of the original PDU, which includes both the header and data. It is not changed for the lifetime of the PDU.

Option part: Optional parameters are placed in this part of the PDU. The source routing addresses are placed here as are the records of the path the PDU takes through the subnetworks to the destination. This field also can be coded to show quality of service parameters, priorities, buffer congestion indication, padding characters, and designation of security levels (specific security procedures are left to service implementation).

Data: This field contains the user data.

---

ask for a quality of service feature if it is known that the subnetwork does not provide it. Be aware that the values of QOS apply to both ends of the network session, even though the session may span several subnetworks that offer different services.

   Use of ISO 8348.   For quality of service choices, ISO 8473 uses the following QOS functions described in ISO 8348:

- *Transit delay.* Establishment of the elapsed time between a data request and the corresponding data indication. This QOS applies only to successful PDU transfers. The delay is specified by a desired value up to the maximum acceptable value. All values assume a PDU of 128 octets. User-initiated flow control is not measured in these values.
- *Residual error rate.* The ratio of total incorrect, lost, or duplicated PDUs to total PDUs transferred:

$$RER = \frac{N(e) + N(1) - N(x)}{N}$$

where: RER = residual error rate; N(e) = PDUs in error; N(1) = lost PDUs; N(x) = duplicate PDUs; N = PDUs.

- *Cost determinants.* A parameter to define the maximum acceptable cost for a network connection. It may be stated in relative or absolute terms. Final actions on this parameter are left to the specific network provider.
- *Priority.* Used to determine preferential service in the subnetwork. Outgoing transmission queues and buffers are managed based on the priority values contained in the PDU header options field.
- *Protection against unauthorized access.* Used to direct a subnetwork to prevent unauthorized access to user data.

Protocol Functions

ISO 8473 includes several optional or required protocol functions. Each function provides a specialized service to the network user. In a sense, the ISO 8473 protocol functions are similar to quality of service (QOS) features, except they are performed as an integral part of the protocol.

A connectionless protocol is sometimes viewed as having no support functions at all. However, as this material demonstrates, the 8473 network provides a wide variety of options for the user. The reader who is familiar with IP will see how similar the two protocols are.

The *PDU composition function* establishes the rules for construction of the protocol data unit. It establishes a procedure for creating the addresses and other data unit identifiers. The function provides the procedures for building the fields of the PDU.

The *PDU decomposition function* establishes the rules for interpreting the protocol control information (PCI) from the PDU and for mapping to the N-UNITDATA.indication (with the parameters for the primitive as well).

The *header format analysis function* determines if the full ISO 8473 protocol is to be employed or if the specific subset is to be used. It also provides the rules for the use of an inactive subset of the protocol.

The *PDU lifetime control function* is used to manage the lifetime of the PDU in the system. It determines whether a PDU shall be discarded because its lifetime has expired. We discuss this procedure in more detail later.

The *route PDU function* is used to determine the specific network entity that is to receive a protocol data unit if it is forwarded. It determines the underlying service that is to be used to reach the specific network entity. Furthermore, if segmentation is performed, this function determines where the segments will be sent (that is, to which underlying service).

The *forward PDU function* is responsible for issuing the SN-UNIT-DATA.request primitive to supply the subnetwork or the SNDCP with the addresses for routing. In other words, it identifies the next system that is to receive the PDU.

The *segmentation function* describes the procedures for segmenting a protocol data unit if it is larger than the maximum size supported by an underlying service. It also describes the use of the segmentation fields in the actual PDU.

The *reassembly function* provides complementary guidance on the rules for reassembling the segmented PDUs into the full PDU. It describes procedures for reassembly times and reassembly lifetimes in the system.

The *discard PDU function* is responsible for freeing resources which have been reserved when various situations have been encountered. For example, the protocol procedure has been violated, local congestion prevents delivery, a checksum is inconsistent, etc.

The *error reporting function* describes the procedures for creating the error report portion of the protocol data unit. This function is described in more detail shortly.

The *PDU header error detection function* is used to check the contents of the entire PDU header with a checksum. It can be used to verify the header at each point where the PDU header is processed. It protects against the corruption of the PDU header through the entire system.

The *padding function* simply provides space in the PDU header for the reservation of any other support function that may be invoked.

The *security function* is used to provide for certain protection services in the system. For example, data authentication and confidentiality of the data can be invoked. It is left up to the specific network provider to interpret how the security functions are actually used.

The *source routing function* can be invoked to allow the originator to specify the path for a specific protocol data unit. This function provides the rules for creating the addresses to designate the route of the PDU. These addresses are placed in the contents of the PDU itself.

The *record route function* is used to record the paths that are actually taken by the PDU as it traverses through the subnetworks to the final destination. More detail is provided on this important function shortly.

The *quality of service and maintenance function* is used to assist the subnetworks to make routing decisions where certain quality of service functions are to be invoked. It is used to attempt to provide a consistent level of service through the subnetworks (where possible). Obviously, if the subnetworks cannot provide the required quality of services, then the services cannot be met.

The *priority function* allows a PDU with a higher priority value to be treated preferentially over lower priority PDUs. The specific network entity is free to implement this function in the specific manner it chooses.

The *congestion notification function* is used to allow the network service users to take appropriate action when congestion is experienced. The congestion function provides a flag in the quality of service parameter in the PDU header. The flag can be set to 1 by any underlying system processing the PDU to indicate that it is actually experiencing congestion. How the congestion is handled is dependent upon the specific subnetworks and is considered a local matter.

Traffic Management Between Subnetworks

This section provides an illustration of how a connectionless-mode internetwork protocol transfers data between subnetworks. While different vendors use various techniques for the provision of connectionless service, many use the concepts described herein.

When the protocol receives the NS-source-address and NS-destination-address parameters in the N-UNITDATA.request primitive from an upper layer, it uses them to build a source address and destination address in the header of the PDU. The source address and NS-quality-of-service parameters are used to determine which optional functions are to be selected for the network user. At this time, a data unit identifier is assigned to uniquely identify this request from other requests. This identifier must remain unique for the lifetime of the initial PDU and any segmented PDUs in the network(s). Subsequent and/or derived PDUs are considered to correspond to the initial PDU if they have the same source address, destination address, and data unit identifier. At first glance, this rule may appear to be connection-oriented, but it applies only to PDUs created as a result of segmentation.

The protocol data unit is then forwarded through the subnetwork(s). Each node examines the destination address to determine if the PDU has reached its destination. If the destination address equals the NSAP (network service access point) served by the network entity, it has reached its destination. Otherwise, it must be forwarded to the next node.

When the PDU reaches its destination, the receiver removes the PCI (protocol control information) from the PDU. It also uses the addresses in the header to generate the NS-source-address and NS-destination-address parameters of the UNITDATA.indication primitive. It preserves the data field of the PDU until all segments (if any) have been received. The options part of the PDU header is used to invoke any quality of service parameters at the receiving end.

Unlike connection-oriented networks, an ISO 8473 connectionless-mode network has more flexibility in terminating service to a user. For example, if a new network connection request is received with a higher priority than an ongoing data transfer, the network may release the lower priority transfer. Moreover, users may also have priorities established for the data transfers. The network connections (NCs) with a higher priority will have their requests serviced first and the remaining resources of the network are used to attempt to satisfy the lower priority network connections.

User data is given a specific "lifetime" in the network(s). This mechanism is useful for several reasons. First, it prevents lost or misdirected data from accumulating and consuming network resources. Second, it gives the transmitting entity some control over the disposition of aged data units. Third, it greatly simplifies congestion control, flow control, and accountability logic in the network(s). (It should be emphasized that discarded data units can be recovered by the transport layer.)

The lifetime field in the PDU header is set by the originating network entity. The value also applies to any segmented PDUs and is copied into the header of these data units. The value contains, at any time, the remaining lifetime of the PDU. It is decremented by each network entity that processes it. The value is represented in units of 500 milliseconds and is decremented by one unit by each entity. In the event delays exceed 500 milliseconds, the value is decremented by more than one unit.

If the lifetime value reaches zero before it reaches its destination, it is discarded. If the error report bit is on, an error report data unit is generated to inform the originator of the lost data. This feature may be considered by some to be a connection-oriented service. Whatever its name, it is obviously very useful if end-to-end accountability is needed.

In addition to discarding aged data units, the network may also discard data for other reasons:

- The checksum reveals an error (if checksum is used).
- A PDU is received which contains an unsupported function such as a QOS.
- A local congestion occurs at the receiver.
- A header cannot be interpreted accurately.
- A PDU cannot be segmented and it is too large for the underlying network to handle.
- The destination address is not reachable or a path route is not acceptable to the network serving the PDU.

The protocol data unit is transferred on a node-to-node basis. The selection of the next system in the route may be influenced by the quality of service parameters and other optional parameters. For example, the next hop could be chosen because it supports the QOS requests.

Internetwork Routing. The routing technique in ISO 8473 is called *source routing*. The route is determined by the originator of the PDU by placing a list of the intermediate routes in the options part of the PDU header. The route indicators are called titles. The relaying is accomplished by each network entity routing the PDU to the next title in the list. The indicator is updated by each relay point to identify the next stage of the route.

The protocol provides two types of routing: complete source routing and partial source routing. Complete source routing requires that the specified route be used in the exact order as in the route list. If this route cannot be taken, the PDU must be discarded with the option of returning an error report to the originator. Partial source routing allows a system to route to intermediate systems that are not specified in the list.

Another routing option, called the record route function, requires that the intermediate systems add their title to a record route list in the options field of the header. The list is built as the PDU is forwarded to its destination. This list can be used for troubleshooting internetwork or subnetwork problems. It can also be used as a tool for efficiency analysis, audit trails, or simply as a "directory" for a returning PDU.

If this option is invoked, either complete route recording or partial route recording is used. With the former, all intermediate systems are recorded and PDU reassembly is performed only if all derived PDUs took the same route. Otherwise, the PDU is discarded. The partial route recording also requires the full list but does not require that the derived PDUs visit the same intermediate systems.

Segmentation and Reassembly. Several fields in the PDU header are used to evoke and manage segmentation and reassembly. These functions may be necessary if the size of a PDU (or a derived PDU) is greater than the maximum data size supported by the subnetwork that is to transmit the data. A segmented (derived) PDU must maintain its unique identity. Therefore, all header identifiers must be placed in the segmented PDU.

A reassembly timer is invoked at the receiving system to indicate an amount of time that must pass before any outstanding segments will be considered lost. If the timer "times out," all segments are discarded and an error report may be generated.

It can be seen that connectionless networks as described by ISO 8473 present the user and network managers with many options, but at the cost of increased complexity. However, the complexity may be warranted by the additional functionality and flexibility that these systems offer.

THE INTERNET PROTOCOL (IP)

The Internet Protocol (IP) is an internetworking protocol developed by the Department of Defense. The name is derived from the idea that an interconnected set of networks is an internet. The system was implemented as part of the DARPA internetwork protocol project, and is widely used throughout the world. It is designated as MIL-STD-1777 in the Department of Defense standards.

IP is an example of a connectionless service. It permits the exchange of traffic between two stations without any prior call setup. (However, these two stations do share a common connection-oriented transport protocol.)

IP is quite similar to the ISO 8473 specification explained in the previous section of the book. Many of the ISO 8473 concepts were derived from IP. The reader who opened this part of the book directly to learn about IP should turn back and first read the material on ISO 8473.

The data sent by the station is encapsulated into an IP datagram. The IP header identifies the network and host address of the receiving user. The IP datagram and header is further encapsulated into the specific protocol of the transit network. After the transit network has delivered the traffic to an IP gateway, its control information is stripped away. The gateway then uses the datagram header to determine where to route the traffic. It may then encapsulate the datagram header and user data into the headers and trailers of another network. Eventually, the datagram arrives at the final destination, where it is delivered to the receiving station.

The interface of IP with the network layer is quite simple, because IP is designed to operate with several diverse kinds of networks. Because of this requirement, the IP network interface performs relatively few functions.

IP Routing

The IP gateway must make routing decisions. For example, if the destination station resides in another network, the IP gateway must decide how to route to the other network. Indeed, if multiple hops are involved in the communications process, then each gateway must be traversed and the gateway must make decisions about routing the traffic. However, in order to keep the gateway computers simple (many are small minicomputers), the gateway's routing decisions are based on a destination network address and not the address of the host computer.

Figure 6-7 shows that network A may choose gateway 1 or gateway 2 to reach other networks. If the destination station is directly attached to the network serviced by the gateway, it is called directly connected. If the station is on an adjacent network to the gateway, it is referred to as a neighbor gateway. If more than one gateway is required to reach the final destination, it is called a multiple hop session.

Each station and gateway maintains a routing table that contains the next gateway to the final destination network. These tables may be static or dynamic, although both approaches provide alternate routes in the event of problems at a gateway.

The IP uses the source routing, route recording, fragmentation, and reassembly functions explained with ISO 8473. It also uses a datagram lifetime feature as well as an error report in the event data units are discarded.

Since the IP is a connectionless protocol, it is possible that the datagrams could be lost between the two end user's stations. For example, the IP gateway generally enforces a maximum queue length size, and if this queue length is violated the buffers will overflow. In this situation, the additional datagrams

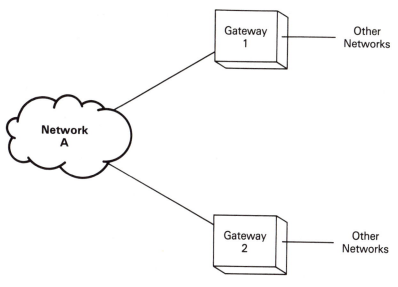

FIGURE 6-7. IP Gateways

are discarded in the network. For this reason, the higher level transport layer is essential.

Each IP gateway performs the following tasks:

1. Makes a routing decision on each datagram.
2. Performs an error check.
3. Checks the time-to-live parameter.
4. Performs fragmentation, if necessary.
5. Reconstructs parts of the IP header that change at each gateway, such as checksum, fragmentation, and time-to-live fields.

Routing Tables. IP controls routing through the use of routing tables stored at each station and each gateway. The table enables a gateway to determine the next network or gateway to which a protocol data unit is to be sent. In the event a gateway fails, the neighbors of the gateway issue a time-out and send status reports to other gateways and stations. This status traffic identifies the problem IP gateway and allows gateways and stations to change their routing tables to reflect the change.

Since many networks may be involved in the communications between two user stations, it is likely that different packet sizes will exist in the end-to-end process. To accommodate this requirement, IP permits datagrams to be fragmented through the system. The fragmented data units are each provided with an identifier to uniquely identify them with the other associated packets. In addition, a length indicator (LI) is placed in the protocol data unit to identify the relative position in the original datagram.

The Internet Protocol (IP)

IP Primitives. IP uses two primitives to communicate with the end user. The transmitting user utilizes the SEND primitive to request the services of the network. In turn, IP uses the DELIVER primitive to notify the destination user of the arrival of data. The use of the primitives is shown in Figure 6-8. The sending site uses the SEND primitive to instruct IP to construct a datagram to send to the receiving site. TCP usually performs this action at the sending site. The datagram is transferred through the network(s) to the receiving host machine. The data is then delivered to the user or to the TCP with the DELIVER primitive. Also notice in Figure 6-8 that the datagram can traverse through adjacent gateways (unusual, but possible), without traversing through an intervening network.

The parameters used in the primitives are:

- *Source address:* The network and host address of the sending host machine. The IP can select the source address if the sending host has more than one address.
- *Destination address:* The network and host address of the receiving machine.
- *Protocol:* Identifies the receiving protocol.

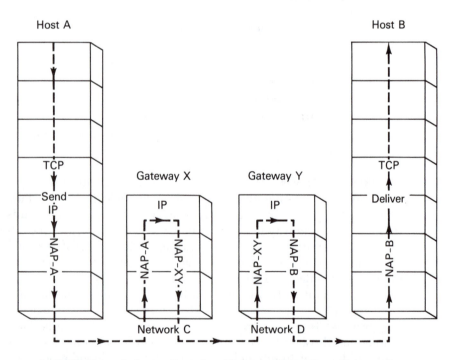

NAP: Network Access Procedure (Between Networks or Gateways)

FIGURE 6-8. IP Primitives and Layer Relationships

The Network Layer, Internetworking

- *Type of service indicators:* Identify the type of service requested for the datagram. Four indicators can be coded in the primitive:

  Precedence: Indicates relative importance of datagram (flash, immediate, priority, routine, etc.)

  Reliability: Indicates importance of delivery (normal, high)

  Delay: Indicates priority of prompt delivery (normal, low)

  Throughput: Indicates importance of throughput (normal, high)

- *Identifier:* An identifier for this datagram. When used with the addresses and the protocol parameter, it uniquely identifies this data unit. It is used for error reporting and reassembly.

- *Fragment indicator:* Used to inform IP if it can fragment (segment) the data units.

- *Time to live:* Stipulates the maximum lifetime of the datagram. It is established in one-second increments or number of hops.

- *Data Length:* Indicates the length of data in datagram.

- *Option Data:* Identifies certain options requested by the datagram user. Five parameters can be coded:

  Security labeling: Provides for classification of the datagram, as well as handling restrictions and interested user communities.

  Source routing: Identifies the gateways that can or cannot be used.

  Route recording: Identifies the gateways visited.

  Stream identification: Identifies that stream transmission will be used, and identifies resources to handle the stream service. Stream service permits 8-bit bytes to be sent at any time.

  Timestamping: Allows time stamps to be placed in the datagram as it traverses through the gateways.

- *Data:* The user data.

It should prove instructive to compare the IP protocol data unit (Figure 6-9) with the ISO 8473 protocol data unit (Figure 6-6). Again we see many similarities between the two protocols. A description of the IP datagram is provided in Table 6-2.

Each host in the internet is assigned a 32-bit address. The address fields can be coded in different formats to permit flexibility in the length of the network and local addresses. These address formats are illustrated in Figure 6-10. Typically, each adddress is divided into a network ID (netid) and a host ID (hostid). The addresses are classified by the format of the address field and the structure is governed by how many hosts and networks need to be identified. In fact, the internet address is actually an address of a host connection to a network because the address includes both a network address and a host address.

ICMP (Internet Control Message Protocol)

IP contains a module called the internet control message protocol (ICMP). The responsibility of ICMP is to provide status messages and diagnostics to IP re-

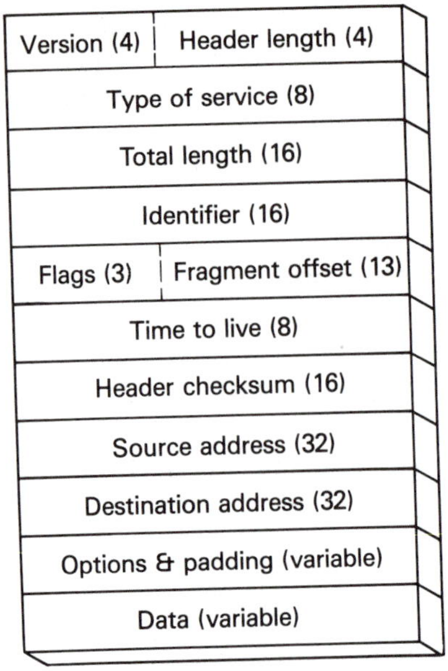

```
┌─────────────────────────────────────┐
│  Version (4) │  Header length (4)    │
├─────────────────────────────────────┤
│         Type of service (8)          │
├─────────────────────────────────────┤
│          Total length (16)           │
├─────────────────────────────────────┤
│           Identifier (16)            │
├─────────────────────────────────────┤
│  Flags (3)  │ Fragment offset (13)   │
├─────────────────────────────────────┤
│          Time to live (8)            │
├─────────────────────────────────────┤
│        Header checksum (16)          │
├─────────────────────────────────────┤
│        Source address (32)           │
├─────────────────────────────────────┤
│      Destination address (32)        │
├─────────────────────────────────────┤
│    Options & padding (variable)      │
├─────────────────────────────────────┤
│          Data (variable)             │
└─────────────────────────────────────┘
```

(n) = Number of bits

FIGURE 6-9. The Internet Protocol Data Unit (IP Datagram)

garding certain activities in the network. The ICMP notifies the IP when datagrams cannot be delivered, when gateways direct traffic on shorter routes, or when the gateway might not have sufficient buffering capacity to forward protocol data units. The ICMP will also notify a host if a destination is unreachable. ICMP is also responsible for managing or creating a time-exceeded message in the event that the lifetime of the datagram expires. ICMP also performs certain editing functions in the event the IP datagram header is in error.

In order to ascertain if two stations can communicate, ICMP also supports the echo and echo reply messages. An echo message recipient must return an echo reply message. The two protocol data units are used to determine if the two destinations can be reached from each other.

ICMP also supports time stamping and time stamp reply messages. These data units provide a means for examining and calculating the delay characteristics of the network. The sender of the data unit can place a time stamp in the message, or the receiver can append its time stamp and transmit this back to the originator of the traffic. ICMP also provides for source/quench messages, which allow either a user station or a gateway to stop transmitting traffic or reduce the rate in which the traffic is transmitted. The source/quench message contains the header of the datagram which created the problem.

The contents of the ICMP are shown in Figure 6-11. The type field specifies the type of ICMP message. The code field is used to identify parameters in the message. If this field is not long enough, the parameters field is also used. The information field provides additional information about the ICMP

The Network Layer, Internetworking

TABLE 6-2.   The IP Protocol Data Unit

The **version field** identifies the version of IP. The **internet header length** specifies the length of the IP header. The **type of service** field stipulates four functions similar to ISO 8473: transit delay, throughput, priority and reliability. The **total length** field specifies the total length of the TP datagram, including the header.

The **identifier** is used with the address fields to uniquely identify the data unit. It serves the same function as the ISO 8473 data unit identifier.

The **flags** are used to indicate (a) more data is forthcoming for a fragmented data unit or (b) fragmentation is prohibited. The **fragmentation offset** describes where the datagram belongs within the original protocol data unit.

The **time to live** field is identical to the function of the ISO 8473 lifetime field, except it is measured in number of gateway hops.

The **protocol** field is used to identify a next-level protocol that is to receive the user data at the final destination. This field serves the same functions as the NSAPs in ISO 8473. The **header checksum** is used to perform an error check on the header.

The **source and destination address** fields identify the networks and the specific hosts within the network. The address field lengths are 32 bits but can be used in combinations for variable addressing.

The **option** field is used to request the five additional service options for the IP user. It is similar to the option part field of ISO 8473. The **padding** field is used to give the header a 32-bit alignment.

The **user data** field contains user data. The user data field and the header cannot exceed 65,535 octets.

---

message. The checksum field performs an error check on the entire ICMP message.

In summary, ICMP uses these types of messages to perform the following major functions (not all-inclusive):

- Time exceeded on datagram lifetime
- Parameter unintelligible
- Destination unreachable (for a variety of reasons)
- Source quench for flow control
- Echo and echo reply
- Redirect for routing management
- Time stamping and time stamp reply

X.75 INTERWORKING

X.25 is designed for users to communicate with each other through one network. However, two users operating on two separate X.25 networks may need

Class a

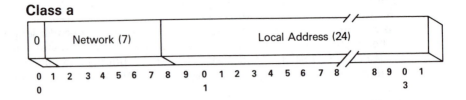

```
0 | Network (7) | Local Address (24)
```

0 1 2 3 4 5 6 7 8 9 0 1 2 3 4 5 6 7 8   8 9 0 1
0   1   3

Class b

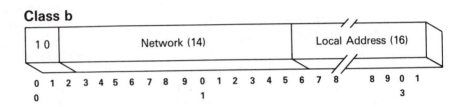

```
1 0 | Network (14) | Local Address (16)
```

0 1 2 3 4 5 6 7 8 9 0 1 2 3 4 5 6 7 8   8 9 0 1
0   1   3

Class c

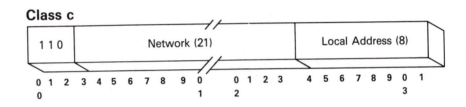

```
1 1 0 | Network (21) | Local Address (8)
```

0 1 2 3 4 5 6 7 8 9 0   0 1 2 3   4 5 6 7 8 9 0 1
0   1   2   3

Extended Addressing Class

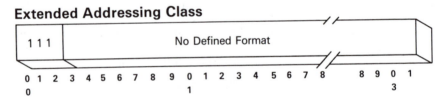

```
1 1 1 | No Defined Format
```

0 1 2 3 4 5 6 7 8 9 0 1 2 3 4 5 6 7 8   8 9 0 1
0   1   3

FIGURE 6-10. IP Address Formats

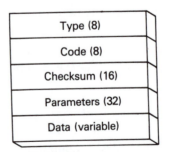

| Type (8) |
| Code (8) |
| Checksum (16) |
| Parameters (32) |
| Data (variable) |

FIGURE 6-11. The Internet Control Message Protocol Data Unit

to establish communications to share resources and exchange data. X.75 is designed to meet this need. It is also used to connect packet exchanges within a network. The standard has been in development for almost ten years; it was published by the CCITT as a provisional recommendation in 1978, amended in 1980, and again in 1984.

The objective of X.75 is to allow internetworking. It provides a gateway for a user to communicate through multiple networks with another user. As mentioned before, it is also used to connect exchanges within a network. The standard works best when user stations, networks, and packet exchanges to use X.25 packets, because X.75 uses the X.25 packet headers that are created at the user/subnetwork interface. However, the end user of an X.25 connection never sees X.75.

X.75 is quite similar to X.25. It has many of its features, such as permanent virtual circuits, virtual call circuits, logical channel groups, logical channels, and several of the control packets. The architecture is divided into physical, link, and packet levels, with X.75 sitting above X.25 in the network layer.

X.75 defines the operation of international packet switched services. It describes how two terminals are connected logically by an international link while each terminal is operating within its own packet mode data network. X.75 uses a slightly different term for the network interface. In the description of X.25, we used the term data circuit terminating equipment (DCE) to describe an X.25 packet exchange. The X.75 terminology defines this device as a signaling terminal (STE), even though it may be the same machine as the X.25 device.

Like X.25, the physical level can be implemented with appropriate V-Series recommendations (such as V.35). X.75 requires the signaling to be performed at 64 Kbits/s. (An optional rate is 48 Kbits/s.) Of course, many vendors use other link speeds (56 Kbits/s, 1.544 Mbits/s, etc.). The second level of X.75 uses the HDLC subset LAPB. X.75 does not support LAP.

X.75 and Multilink Procedures (MLP)

The X.75 link level frequently uses the multilink procedure (MLP). This procedure provides for the use of multiple links between STEs. MLP establishes the rules for frame transmission and frame resequencing for delivery to and from the multiple links. Multilink operations allow the use of parallel communications channels between STEs in such a manner that they appear as one channel with a greater capacity. The multilink operation provides for more reliability and throughput than can be achieved on a single channel.

Multilink procedures (MLP) exist at the upper part of the data link level. The X.25 network layer perceives it is connected to a single link and the LAPB single links operate as if they were connected directly to the network layer. MLP is responsible for flow control between layers 2 and 3, as well as resequencing the data units for delivery to the network layer. The network layer operates with a perceived higher bandwidth in the data link layer. MLP is described in more detail in Chapter 4.

X.75 Packet Types

X.75 does not use the variety of packet types that are found in X.25, primarily because the STE-to-STE communications have no relationship to the "other side of the cloud." In X.75, there is no other side, since the communications are only between two STEs and not two sets of DCEs/DTEs. The X.75 protocol uses the following packet types:

Call Setup and Clearing

Call Request
Call Connected
Clear Request
Clear Confirmation

Data and Interrupt

Data
Interrupt
Interrupt Confirmation

Flow Control and Reset

Receive Ready
Receive Not Ready
Reset
Reset Confirmation

Restart

Restart
Restart Confirmation

The X.75 packet format is almost identical to the X.25 format. The address fields are specifically defined as international data numbers (X.121). The logical channels only have significance for the STE/STE interface.

The similarities and differences between X.25 and X.75 can be seen by examining Figure 6-12. The DTE in network A is initiating a call to a DTE in network C. The call setup packet and logical channel relationships are depicted for each phase of the connection establishment. It is instructive to note that the X.75 interface does not use the incoming call and call accepted packets since X.75 is structured only for communications between two gateways and not (as in X.25) between two DTEs and two DCEs.

X.75 Utilities

The X.75 packet carries an additional field called network utilities (see Figure 6-13). Its purpose is to provide for network administrative functions and signaling. In many situations, a request in the X.25 user packet facility field invokes the use of an X.75 network utility. The X.25 facilities that do not require any STE action remain in the facilities field, and are relayed transparently through

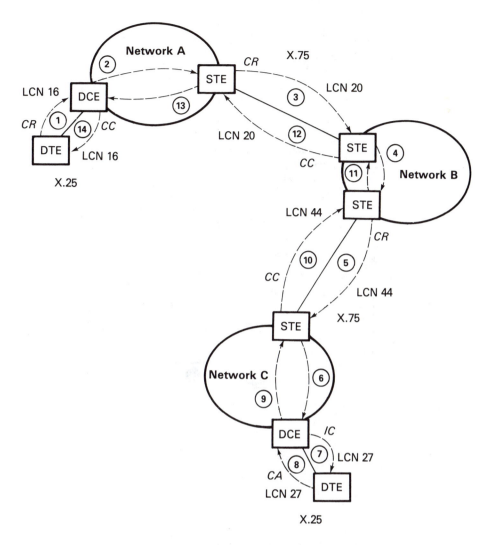

FIGURE 6–12. **Internetworking X.25 Networks with X.75.**
(Connection Establishment)

n = Sequence of Events

CR: Call Request
CC: Call Connected
IC: Incoming Call
CA: Call Accepted
LCN: Logical Channel Number

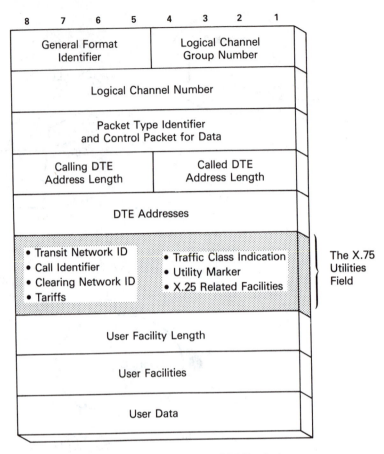

FIGURE 6-13. The X.75 Packet

the STE. Other user facilities which require STE action are mapped into the X.75 utilities field. These utilities are described in this section.

- *Transit network identification.* Contains the first four digits of the international data number of the transit network controlling a portion of the virtual circuit. If more than one transit network is involved in the call. This identification is also present in the call connected packet.
- *Call identifier.* An identifying name established by the originating network for each virtual circuit. When used in conjunction with the DTE address, it uniquely identifies the call.
- *Throughput class indication.* Indicates the throughput classes applying to the call.
- *Window size indication.* Identifies the negotiated window size between the STEs

- *Packet size indication.* Identifies the negotiated packet size between the STEs.
- *Fast select indication.* Indicates that a fast select is requested for the call.
- *Closed user group indication.* Used to enable the establishment of calls between DTEs that are members of an international closed user group. X.75 also supports closed user group with outgoing access indication.
- *Reverse charging indication.* Allows reverse charging of calls to be established across the networks.
- *Called line address modified notification.* Due to hunt groups and call redirections, this utility identifies the specific reason for the called address to be different from the address in the call request packet.
- *Clearing network identification code.* Provides additional information on the origin of the clear request packet.
- *Traffic class indication.* Identifies service information, such as terminal, facsimile, etc. This utility has not yet been fully defined.
- *Transit delay indication.* Identifies the transit delay on the virtual circuit. It has not been fully defined.
- *Utility marker.* Used to separate X.75 utilities from non-X.75 utilities. Its use is subject to bilateral agreements between networks.
- *Tariffs.* Could be used for billing purposes, but it is not yet defined.

THE X.300 INTERWORKING STANDARDS

The CCITT publishes a series of standards pertaining to the internetworking of various types of networks. They encompass several documents numbered X.300 through X.370, generally called the X.300 Interworking Standards. You may have noticed that we have used the word, *interworking*. The CCITT uses this word in place of internetworking.

This section examines the most important aspects of the X.300 standards. The reader should review the abbreviations in Table 6-3 before reading this material. It will also prove beneficial to review the X.213 protocol in Chapter 5. Other abbreviations used in this section have been defined in previous chapters.

Perhaps one of the most useful features of X.300 is its explanation of how the X-Series Recommendations fit into interworking. Figure 6-14 is a simplified view of the X.300/X-Series framework. The standards are divided into three categories:

1. Aspects of interworking pertinent to different cases
2. Aspects of interworking pertinent to each case
3. Aspects of internetwork signaling interfaces

This book examined the signaling interface standards in previous sections and chapters. Our task here is to examine the X.300 specifications.

TABLE 6-3.   Abbreviations Used in X.300

CCSN	Common Channel Signaling Network (SS No.7)
CSPDN	Circuit Switched Public Data Network
CTD	Cumulative Transit Delay
IDSE	International Data Switching Exchange
IWF	Interworking Function
MATD	Maximum Acceptable Transit Delay
NDSE	National Data Switching Exchange
PDN	Public Data Network
PLMN	Public Land Mobile Network
PSPDN	Packet Switched Public Data Network
PSTN	Public Switched Telephone Network
TDI	Transit Delay Indication
TDS	Transit Delay Selection
TDSAI	Transit Delay Selection and Indication
TOA	Type of Address
TTD	Target Transit Delay

Categories of Interworking

The X.300 transmission capability between two networks is divided into two categories (see Figure 6-15):

- *Call Control Mapping.* Call control information used for switching in one subnetwork (including addressing) is mapped into call control information in the other subnetwork [see Figure 6-15(a)].
- *Port Access.* Call control information is used by one network to select the interworking point. Then, a convergence protocol is used at this network and the call control information is mapped into call control information in the other subnetwork. Another possibility is the establishment of a "hot line" and then a connection is established [see Figure 6-15(b)].

In addition to these two categories, X.300 also defines subnetworks in relation to Recommendation X.213 (discussed in Chapter 5). Several tables are used to (a) identify subnetwork types, (b) establish the need for call control mapping or port access, (c) stipulate the requirement for a convergence protocol, (d) show resulting subnetworks from interconnecting two subnetworks, and (e) define the different subnetwork types used to provide an OSI connection-mode network service (connectionless services are not defined in X.300).

This information is provided as shown in Tables 6-4 through 6-7. Table 6-4 identifies four subnetwork types based on the X.213 connection establishment, data transfer, and connection release phases. Table 6-5 illustrates the resulting subnetwork type when two subnetworks are interconnected. Table 6-6 defines whether the subnetwork interconnecting requires call control mapping or port access. Finally, Table 6-7 stipulates if a convergence protocol is required by the four network types for the X.213 phases.

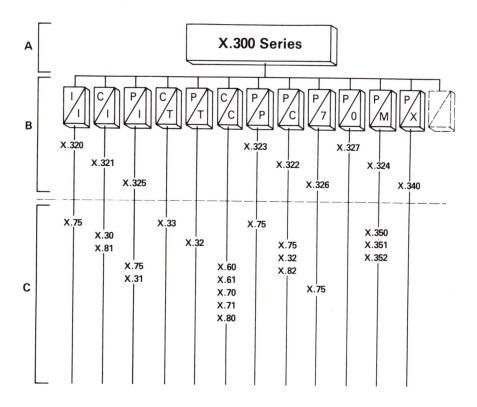

LEGEND:
A: ARRANGEMENTS GENERIC TO DIFFERENT CASES
B: ARRANGEMENTS FOR EACH CASE
C: INTERWORK SIGNALLING INTERFACES

ABBREVIATIONS:
C: CIRCUIT SWITCHED DATA NETWORK
I: ISDN
M: MOBILE NETWORK
O: PRIVATELY OWNED NETWORK
P: PACKET SWITCHED DATA NETWORK
T: TELEPHONE NETWORK
X: TELEX NETWORK
7: SIGNALLING SYSTEM NO. 7

FIGURE 6–14. The X.300 Framework

Transfer of Addressing Information

One of the more important parts of the X.300 recommendations is contained in X.301: rules for the transfer of addressing information. We learned about the various addressing schemes in Chapter 5. X.301 defines how X.121 and E.164 addresses are used between two networks.

Figure 6-16 shows the X.301 structure for the address form when the IWF

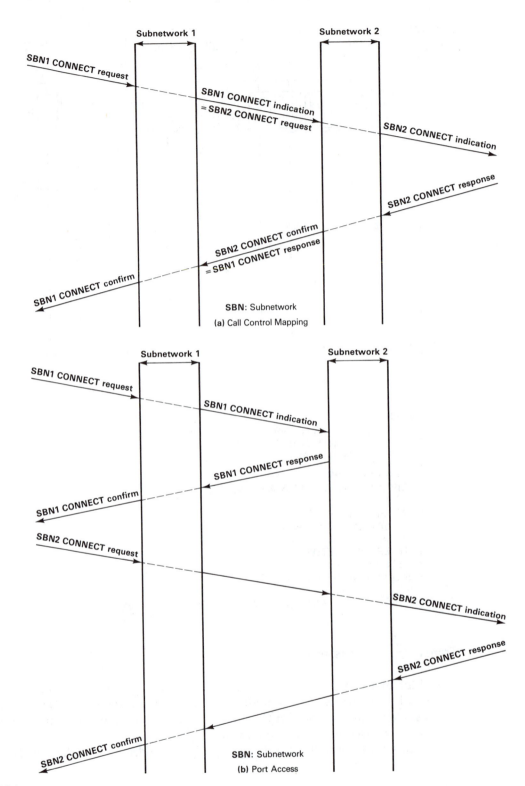

SBN: Subnetwork

(a) Call Control Mapping

SBN: Subnetwork

(b) Port Access

FIGURE 6-15. Call Control Mapping and Port Access

TABLE 6-4. Subnetwork Types

Subnetwork Type / Phase of the Call	Connection Establishment	Data Transfer Phase	Connection Release Phase
I	M	M	M
II	M	P	M
III	S	P	S

Legend:

M   All mandatory elements required for the provision of the OSI Network Service are signaled through the subnetwork by means of its signaling capability.

P   The functionality of the subnetwork corresponds to that of a physical connection.

S   A subset of all mandatory elements required for the provision of the OSI Network Service are signaled through the subnetwork by means of its signaling capability.

TABLE 6-5. Resulting Network from Interconnecting Two Networks

	I	II	III	IV
I	I / I	I / IV	I / IV	I / IV
II	I / IV	II / II	II / III	IV
III	I / IV	II / III	III / III	IV
IV	I / IV	IV	IV	IV

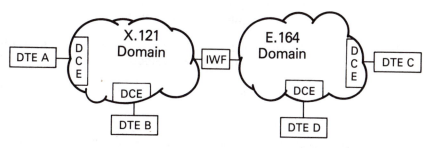

FIGURE 6-16. X.301 Addressing Rules

TABLE 6-6. Categories of Interworking from Interconnecting Two Networks

Subnetwork Type	I	II	III	IV
I	Internetworking by call control mapping	Internetworking by call control mapping or by port access	Internetworking by call control mapping or by port access	Internetworking by call control mapping or by port access
II	Internetworking by call control mapping or port access	Internetworking by call control mapping	Internetworking by call control mapping or by port access	Internetworking by call control mapping or by port access
III	Internetworking by call control mapping or by port access	Internetworking by call control mapping or by port access	Internetworking by call control mapping	Internetworking by call control mapping or by port access
IV	Internetworking by call control mapping or by port access	Internetworking by call control mapping or by port access	Internetworking by call control mapping or by port access	Internetworking by call control mapping

TABLE 6-7. Providing OSI Connection-Mode Network Service with Different Subnetwork Types

Phase of the OSI-NS Call Connection	Connection Establishment Phase	Data Transfer Phase	Connection Release Phase
Subnetwork Type			
I	No Convergence Protocol Required	No Convergence Protocol Required	No Convergence Protocol Required
II	No Convergence Protocol Required	Convergence Protocol Required	No Convergence Protocol Required
III	Convergence Protocol Required	Convergence Protocol Required	Convergence Protocol Required
IV	Convergence Protocol Required*	Convergence Protocol Required	Convergence Protocol Required

*If this subnetwork does not provide all the mandatory elements of the OSI Network Service in this phase.

The Network Layer, Internetworking

is interworking an X.121 address-based network and an E.164 address-based network. Table 6-8 depicts the permissible address forms for the call establishment phase. The prefixes P1 through P6 are not passed over the IWF, and their form and use is an internal network matter. The escape digits E1 and E2 indicate that the succeeding address is a different numbering plan. The prefixes may or may not precede the escape digit.

It is also permissible to use another field to indicate the type of address present. This element in the protocol is called the Number Plan Indicator /Type of Address (NPI/TOA). The form of this field depends upon the specific network access protocol employed.

SUMMARY AND CONCLUSIONS

The OSI internetworking protocols have emerged only in the last few years. Many of their features are borrowed from the Internet Protocol (IP). The publi-

TABLE 6-8. Call Establishment Phase Address Forms

Direction	Form of Address	Extent of Validity
A to B	NTN	Network
A to B	P1 + NTN	Network
A to B	DNIC + NTN	Internetwork
A to B	P2 + DNIC + NTN	Internetwork
A to B	NTN + [NPI/TOA]	Network
A to B	DNIC + NTN + [NPI/TOA]	Internetwork
C to D	SN	Network
C to D	P3 + SN	Network
C to D	CC + (NDC) + SN	Internetwork
C to D	P4 + CC + (NDC) + SN	Internetwork
C to D	SN + [NPI/TOA]	Network
C to D	CC + (NDC) + SN + [NPI/TOA]	Internetwork
A to C	E1 + CC + (NDC) + SN	Internetwork escape to E.164/E/163
A to C	P5 + E1 + CC + (NDC) + SN	Internetwork escape to E.164/E/163
A to C	CC + (NDC) + SN + [NPI/TOA]	Internetwork
C to A	E2 + DNIC + NTN	Internetwork escape to X.121
C to A	P6 + E2 + DNIC + NTN	Internetwork escape to X.121
C to A	DNIC + NTN + [NPI/TOA]	Internetwork

cation of the X.300 Recommendations by the CCITT has added an important piece to the internetworking puzzle. ISO 8473 [also known as connectionless network protocol (CLNP)] is assuming an increasing role in manufacturers' products and eventually (but not soon) will supersede IP. X.75 remains a dominant protocol at the internetworking layer, principally for interconnecting public data networks that use the X.25 protocol.

CHAPTER 7

The Transport Layer

INTRODUCTION

In previous chapters we emphasized that not all lower layer protocols recover from corrupted data. Examples are some local area network protocols and HDLC's unnumbered information (UI) frame option. We also emphasized that various network layer (level 3) protocols do not recover from certain problems. Our examples in Chapter 5 with X.25 and the clear, restart, and reset packet types showed how data packets may be discarded. Moreover, some networks are inherently unreliable. For example, connectionless networks, several types of mobile radio networks, and packet radio networks do not guarantee delivery of traffic. In addition, some networks are simply designed to discard packets that are outdated or have exceeded the number of permissible transit hops within and/or between networks (the Internet Protocol [IP], for example).

Certain user applications require absolute assurance that all protocol data units have been delivered safely to the destination. Furthermore, the transmitting user may need to know the traffic has been delivered without problems. The mechanisms to achieve these important services reside at the transport layer. Perhaps the best approach is to think of the transport layer as a security blanket. It attempts to take care of the data, regardless of the goings-on in the underlying networks.

As we shall see, the transport layer performs many other functions. One of its principal jobs is to shield the upper layers from the details of the lower layers' operations. Indeed, the user may be completely unaware of the physical network(s) that are supporting the user's activities, because the transport layer is providing the transparent interface between the user and the network(s). Ideally, the transport layer relieves the upper layers of concern about how to obtain a needed level of network service.

The transport layer is designed to reside outside a network. From the context of OSI, it resides above the OSI communications layers, as shown in Figure 7-1. This approach permits two transport layer entities to use different types of networks and to recover from problems that occur within the networks.

It should also be noted that some applications do not need a transport layer (or, for that matter, any of the upper layers). Some machines and applications do quite well with just the physical and data link layers.

As a final point to the introduction of the transport layer, the OSI transport layer may lose data during a transport layer disconnection. This is not a deficiency on the part of the design of OSI. Rather, it reflects the OSI philosophy that, unlike other transport layer protocols, such as TCP, the next upper layer is responsible for a *graceful close*. That is, the session layer is responsible for making certain that all data are secured before allowing a supporting transport layer session to end. This point is explained further in this chapter and in Chapter 8.

SUPPORT FOR NETWORK USERS

The job of the transport layer may be quite complex. It must be able to satisfy a wide range of applications requirements, and, equally important, it must accommodate to a wide array of network characteristics. Some of the networks may be connection-oriented and some may be connectionless; some may be reliable and some may be unreliable.

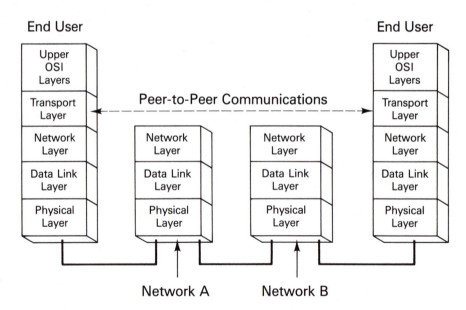

FIGURE 7-1. The Transport Layer and the OSI Layers

Thus, the transport is faced with matching the QOS needed by the applications with the QOS capabilities of the network(s). In many instances, the transport layer can do nothing but choose a network or networks that have the available levels of service. In other instances, it can take actions to achieve the desired level of service.

It should also be emphasized that the transport layer does not have to be all things to all users. It can be designed and built to support limited needs. It can be tailored to the individual applications and supporting networks, if necessary.

DEALING WITH NETWORK PROBLEMS

Networks can experience a wide variety of problems. This section provides examples of how the transport layer deals with these major problems:

- Establishing and terminating a network session
- Detecting duplicate, lost, and mis-sequenced data
- Controlling the flow of data

Establishing and Terminating a Transport Session

Transport protocols such as the ISO/CCITT connection-oriented standard establish a session (logical association) between two transport layer entities. This means the two transport entities maintain an awareness of each other's activities in order to support transport of a user's data transfer through a network or networks.

In order to establish a connection through a network (or networks), a connection request protocol data unit is conveyed to the remote user. This user returns a connection confirm to the requester, and the transport session is now in operation and ready to transfer data. A number of problems can occur in this seemingly simple process. Figure 7-2 shows one example. The connection for this transport layer association was terminated previously. A late-arriving, duplicate connection request unit for this specific connection is accepted by the receiver as a valid and new connection request. (The duplicate connection request could be the result of the retransmission of connection request units.) The receiver returns a connection confirm in response to the defunct connection request. When a new and valid connection request is received, it is discarded, and the receiver either ignores the request or sends a disconnect signal back to the originator to terminate the session. In either case, the receiver is not aware of the erroneous connection request. The result is that the subsequent data units are now associated with the wrong connection.

Other connection management problems can be cited. For example, what happens if the connection confirm is lost or arrives late at the requestor? What happens if the disconnect unit is late?

Clearly, measures must be taken to provide a reliable connection manage-

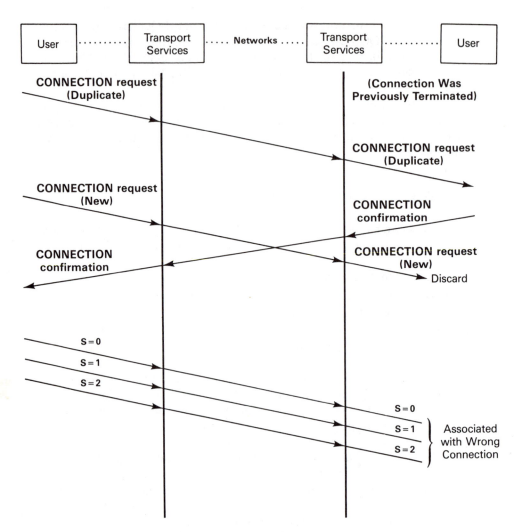

FIGURE 7-2. Connection Establishment

ment procedure. The answer to these problems is really quite simple: use a sequence number and an identifier in the connection request and connection confirm units to explicitly acknowledge a request and connection. These identifiers must be unique and contain the same values across both directions of the transport connection setup. Furthermore, the identifiers and sequence numbers must not be reused within a time in which they could be misinterpreted as belonging to a disconnected session. In our example, the duplicate connection request would have been detected and discarded by the receiver checking the unique identifiers.

The use of explicit acknowledgments and sequence numbers is known as a three-way handshake. The use of identifiers that cannot be reused and thus

The Transport Layer

lose their unique identity is referred to as frozen reference numbers. Later discussions on the CCITT and ISO standards will show examples of connection management procedures.

Detecting Duplicate, Lost, and Mis-sequenced Data

Connectionless networks, such as IP and CLNP, typically throw away packets that have exceeded the time-to-live value, and from the perspective of the network the packets are lost and not recovered. Additionally, networks that use adaptive routing schemes may present the packets in mis-sequenced order at the receiving end-user site. The transport layer is tasked with detecting and correcting these problems.

Figure 7-3 depicts an example of the problem. For the sake of simplicity, this example assumes a send window of 5 and a sequence number range of 0 to 6. The data unit with a send sequence number (S) = 1 is delayed in the

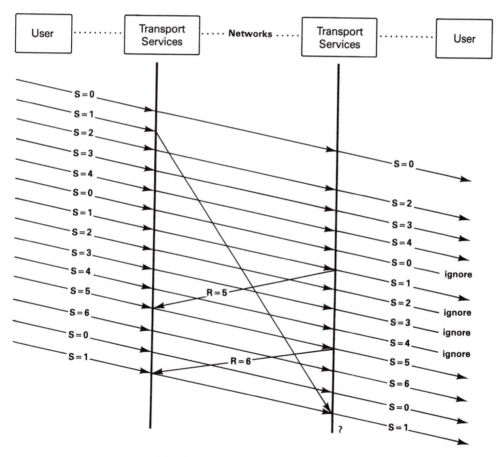

FIGURE 7-3. Detecting Duplicate Units

network(s). Also, before the receiver has an opportunity to acknowledge the data units with a receive sequence number (R), the transmitter exhausts its window of 5 (because data units 0 to 4 are still unacknowledged) and retransmits the data. These events could occur because the transmitter's wait-for-acknowledgment timer is set at too small a value, or the receiver is not responding fast enough due to congestion or some other problem.

Whatever the reason for the time-out, data units 0, 2, 3, and 4 are detected as duplicates and ignored. The receiver accepts data unit 1 and sends back an acknowledgment of R = 5 to inclusively acknowledge units 0 through 4. The R = 5 also states that it is expecting a data unit with S = 5 next.

As ill luck would have it, the late-arriving data unit with S = 1 finally arrives and is erroneously detected as valid. It is actually a duplicate that is not detected at the receiver. As the figure illustrates, the sequence numbers have been reused, so S = 1 appears to be correct.

What is the solution to the problem? Easily enough, it is to use a wide range of sequence numbers. If the value of S = 1 is not reused for an extended time, the late-arriving data unit will be detected as a duplicate. This approach is similar to the use of frozen references for identifying session names. In this situation we employ frozen sequence numbers.

While all these possibilities will improve matters, they require each machine to keep a lot of history about past events. This is an expensive approach, and if a machine fails the history is lost. Yet another solution is to establish a time-to-live value that ensures the delayed unit is discarded before it reaches the receiver. However, this action could create additional problems if the networks become congested and experience delay. As a consequence, the data units would be discarded and would have to be retransmitted, creating still more traffic. It is certainly possible that all this nonproductive activity could seriously degrade response time and throughput.

It should be evident that the transport layer designers must give careful consideration to windows, sequence numbers, timers, and time-to-live values.

Controlling the Flow of Data

Network congestion can be controlled with conventional schemes, such as withholding the issuance of the acknowledgment data units (the receive or R values). However, the R values are also used for acknowledgment. It is preferable to decouple flow control and acknowledgment, because the two functions provide different (if complementary) services.

Flow control is rather complex at the transport layer because: (a) multiple entities are involved (users, networks, gateways, etc.); and (b) the delay in all these entities introduces more queues and a wider range of delay times. Figure 7-4 illustrates some of the problems.

First, the user, transport, and network queues are affected by any flow control mechanisms in place across the peer entities (peer-entity control). For example, a user application will control the flow of records in a file transfer

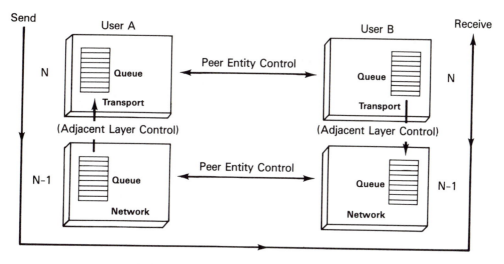

FIGURE 7-4. Flow Control and Queues

from a remote peer application. Second, the service provider (the N-1 layer) will control the flow of protocol data units from the service user (the N layer) at the local and remote sites (adjacent layer control). Third, the first two relationships affect each other. For example, if a user application stops the flow of data into it from the transport layer, it is possible that the transport layer will then flow-control its adjacent network layer, which in turn will flow-control its remote network peer layer, and so forth.

The transport layer manages flow control with a concept called credits (C). The credit is a field carried in the transport protocol data unit (TPDU), separately from the S and R fields. Its value ($R = n$) informs the other transport entity that it has the option of sending n TPDUs, without regard to any flow control or window restrictions. This approach decouples flow control from acknowledgment. It allows the credit allocation to change at any time, at the discretion of either transport entity.

Figure 7-5 shows how credit allocation operates. The remote entity sends a TPDU with $S = 4$ and $C = 7$. This means: (a) it acknowledges units 0 through 4; (b) it is expecting 5 next; (c) it is giving the local transport entity the option of sending seven more TPDUs.

The credit concept is an optimistic approach, because the entity that issues the credit is stating that it will be able to accommodate to whatever its sets as the C value. If it cannot, it must discard the excess data units. Therefore the credits must be established with some forethought.

It should also be noted that it is possible for the credit TPDUs to be delayed and arrive out of order. For example, the first transmitted data unit could have $C = 5$, and the next unit reduces the credit with $C = 1$. However, the $C = 1$ arrives first. When the delayed data unit with $C = 5$ arrives, it appears the

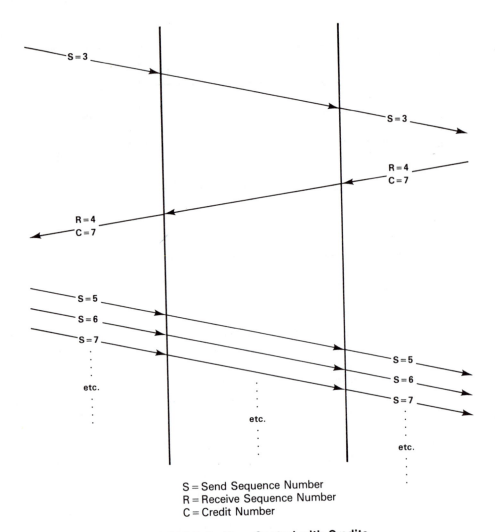

S = Send Sequence Number
R = Receive Sequence Number
C = Credit Number

FIGURE 7-5. Flow Control with Credits

credit has been increased, when the opposite action was intended. The solution is to use sequence numbers on the credit TPDUs. In this manner, the receiving transport entity can make rational decisions about the credit values.

With this background information, we can now examine the prevalent OSI transport layer standards.

THE CCITT AND ISO TRANSPORT LAYERS

After some five years of work, the CCITT and ISO approved the transport layer in 1984, and it is now implemented in many vendor products. Other organizations such as the NIST and ANSI have made contributions to the specification.

The Transport Layer

The importance of the OSI protocol lies in the fact that it is the end user's first opportunity to choose how an underlying network serves the user. One of its primary purposes is to provide consistent, end-to-end service for the user (and upper layers). It shields the user from the details of the lower levels and the types of networks used at these levels.

The CCITT transport layer functions (protocol specifications) are described in X.224. In addition, X.214 describes the interactions of the transport level and the session level (service definitions). For purposes of continuity and simplicity, our discussions incorporate these two recommendations. The ISO publishes similar specifications in ISO 8072 and ISO 8073.

The reader should be aware that the OSI transport layer is fairly complex. To lend structure to the analysis, we analyze the transport layer service definitions and the protocol specifications by an examination of these topics in the following order:

- Types of networks (at the OSI layer three)
- Classes of transport layer protocols
- Quality of service options at the transport layer
- Transport layer service definitions and primitives
- Relationship of transport layer to its upper and lower layers
- Managing connections and data transfer
- Transport protocol data units
  Coding
  Functions
- Elements of procedure
- An analysis of transport layer class 4

Types of Networks

The transport layer requires the user to specify a quality of service (QOS) to be provided by the underlying network(s). Consequently, the transport layer must know the *types* of services offered by the network(s) below it. Upon receiving the user's request for a network connection and a quality of service associated with the connection, the transport layer selects a class of protocol to match the user's quality of service parameters in relation to the supporting network(s). Even though a variety of networks exist (connection-oriented, connectionless, etc.), the transport layer ensures a consistent level of service is provided to the end user.

The QOS parameters are passed by the transport user to the transport layer, which uses them to pass parameters to the network layer to invoke the requested services. It is certainly conceivable that the underlying network or the remote user cannot or will not accept the QOS values. If this is the case, the services can be negotiated down to a lower quality level or the connection request can be rejected.

The quality of network services rests on the types of networks available to the end user and the transport layer. Three types of networks are defined by the CCITT and ISO recommendations:

- A type A network provides acceptable residual error rates and acceptable rates of signaled failures (acceptable quality). Packets are assumed not to be lost. The transport layer need not provide recovery or resequencing services. In other words, it is an ideal network.
- A type B network provides for acceptable residual error rates, but an unacceptable rate for signaled failures (unacceptable signaled errors). The transport layer must be able to recover from errors.
- A type C network connection provides a residual error rate not acceptable to the user (unreliable) or an unacceptable method of signaling failures. The transport layer must recover from failures and resequence packets. A type C network could include some local area networks, mobile networks, and datagram networks.

In describing the types of networks, an error is defined as a duplicated, incorrect, or lost protocol data unit. A signaled failure is one in which the network cannot recover and so notifies the transport layer. A residual error rate is the ratio of incorrect, lost, or duplicated data units to the total number of data units transferred.

The idea in defining network types is to recognize that different qualities of networks exist, yet provide the user with a consistent level of service regardless of network type. For example, a type C network could be one in which the transmissions take place in a connectionless mode. On the other hand, a type B network would likely be one using X.25 functions and capabilities and occasionally issuing network resets.

The existence of a type A network means the transport layer has an easy job. However, most of the complexity of this layer stems from the fact that many networks exhibit the characteristics of type B or type C networks.

The layer also gives the user options to obtain network services at a minimum cost on a per-connection basis.

FUNCTIONS ASSOCIATED WITH CLASSES
OF PROTOCOL AND QUALITY OF SERVICE

In the remainder of this chapter, the reader should remember that the transport layer supports a user with two types of services. One set of services is based on the *class of protocol* which is requested by the requesting user (the requestor), and negotiated with the responding user (the responder) and the transport entity. The second set of services revolves around a number of *quality of service* parameters that are passed by the service user to the transport layer. The following discussions clarify and expand these very important components of the transport layer. We begin with an examination of the classes of protocol available in the layer. Then, in the following section, the discussion on primitives and service definitions explains the use of the quality of service parameters.

Classes of Protocol

As stated earlier, the transport layer is responsible for selecting an appropriate protocol to support the quality of service (QOS) parameters established by the user. Since the transport layer knows the characteristics of a network (types A, B, or C) the layer can choose five classes of protocol procedures to support the QOS request from the user. The protocol classes are:

Class 0: Simple class
Class 1: Basic error recovery class
Class 2: Multiplexing class
Class 3: Error recovery class
Class 4: Error detection and recovery class

Class 0 protocol provides for a very simple transport connection establishment to support a type A network. Class 0 provides for connection-oriented support, during both the network connection and release phases. It does not provide for any support or user transfer data during connection establishment. This protocol can detect and signal protocol errors, but cannot recover from errors. If the network layer signals an error to the transport layer, the transport layer releases the connection to its network layer. In so doing, the end user is informed about the disconnection. The CCITT developed this class for its Teletex standard (CCITT T.70).

The class 1 protocol is associated with networks such as an X.25 packet network. In contrast to class 0, the TPDUs are numbered. The class 1 protocol provides for the segmenting of data, if necessary, and retention of all data and acknowledgments. It allows resynchronization of the session in the event of an X.25 reset or restart packet. The protocol also supports expedited data transfer. It responds to disconnect requests and responds to protocol errors. It is also responsible for resynchronization and performing reassignments in the event of a network failure (i.e., an X.25 reset packet).

It is possible to transmit user data in a class 1 connection request. Also, each data unit is sequenced to aid in ACKs/NAKs and error recovery. The ACKs release the copies of the data units at the transmitting sites. Class 1 also provides for either user acknowledgment or network receipt acknowledgment.

The class 2 protocol is an enhancement to class 0 that allows the multiplexing of several transport connections into a single network session, a concept introduced in Chapter 1. It also provides for explicit flow control to prevent congestion from occurring at the end-user sites. Class 2 provides no error detection nor recovery. If a reset or clear data unit is detected, this protocol disconnects the session and so informs the user. The class 2 protocol is designed to be used over very reliable type A networks. The flow control provided in this protocol uses the concept of credit allocation (discussed shortly). User data can be transmitted in the connection request data unit.

The class 3 protocol provides for the services included in the class 2 structure. It also provides recovery from a network failure without requiring the notification of the user. The user data are retained until the receiving transport layer sends back a positive acknowledgment of the data.

This class has a very useful mechanism to retransmit data. The packets in transit through a network are given a maximum "lifetime." All data requiring a response are timed through the network(s). If the timer expires before an acknowledgment is received, retransmission or other recovery procedures can be invoked. The class 3 protocol assumes a type B network service.

The class 4 protocol includes the flow control functions of classes 2 and 3 and assumes that practically anything can go wrong in the network. Like class 3, expedited data is allowed and the ACKs are sequenced. This protocol allows for "frozen" references (a reference is a connection identifier). Upon a connection release, the corresponding reference cannot be reused, since the network layer might still be processing late-arriving data associated with the references. The class 4 protocol is designed to work with type C networks.

In summary, the protocol classes and the associated network types are:

Class	Network Type
0	A
1	B
2	A
3	B
4	C

When two transport entities begin a transport connection establishment, the initiating entity must send the responding entity a connect request transport protocol data unit (TPDU) that contains, among other values, a value to signify the *preferred* protocol class and a number of *alternative* protocol classes to be used during the connection. The responder must then select one of these classes and so indicate in a connect confirm TPDU. The transport layer protocol establishes rules on the permissible combinations allowed for the preferred and alternative classes. Table 7-1 lists these rules.

At first glance, it might seem a good idea to use relatively simple, connectionless data link and network layers and place all the complexity and support functions into the one transport layer. In this manner, reliable service is in the hands of the user (assuming the transport layer is in the user's machine). However, we often do not have the liberty of choosing the nature of the lower layers' operating characteristics, so providing options for different transport protocol classes is a solid approach.

TABLE 7-1. Preferred and Permissible Alternative Classes

Preferred Class	Alternative Class				
	0	1	2	3	4
0	NV	NV	NV	NV	NV
1	1,0	1,0	NV	NV	NV
2	2,0	NV	2	NV	NV
3	3,2,0	3,2,1,0	3,2	3,2	NV
4	4,2,0	4,2,1,0	4,2	4,3,2	4,2

Notes:

1) NV = Not Valid

2) Multiple numbers mean more than one choice is permitted

Transport Layer Identifiers

The transport layer uses two types of identifiers to unambiguously identify the connection between the transport entities. The called and calling transport service access points (TSAPs) are addresses that can be used, but are optional. Their values and structure are not defined by the OSI model. It is possible that an underlying network address could define the transport address, in which case the TSAPs can be omitted. In any event, a transport layer address must definitely be mapped into—and be consistent with—a supporting network layer address.

The second type of identifiers are the source and destination references, abbreviated as SRC-REF and DST-REF, respectively. These values are required. They are defined to be 16 bits in length, which permits a range of values from 0 to 65536 (2^{16}). The assignment of these values is not defined by OSI. An organization that implements this protocol must devise a scheme to allocate and administer the reference numbers.

Quality of Service Options at the Transport Layer

The transport layer quality of service parameters (See Table 7-2) are created at the application layer and passed down to the transport layer. Insofar as possible, the parameters are intended to allow the user to define a level of service that is independent of the characteristics of the underlying network(s).

The transport layer designer can take certain actions at the transport layer to provide the user with the requested service. However, in other instances, the transport layer must rely on the network layer to fulfill the QOS requirements. Even if the transport layer cannot take any active measures to provide the service, the designer can certainly code the transport software to enable this layer to choose an appropriate network or an appropriate ongoing network connection to meet the user needs.

TABLE 7-2. Transport Layer Quality of Service Parameters

Parameter Name	Parameter Function
TC Establishment Delay	The maximum acceptable delay between a connect request and its corresponding connect confirm
TC Establishment Failure Probability	The ratio of connection establishment attempts to the total number attempted
Throughput	A sequence of at least two successfully transferred TSDUs, measured in the context of the time of the issuance of T-DATA requests
Transit Delay	Elapsed time between the issuance of a T-DATA request and a corresponding T-DATA indication
Residual Error Rate	During a measurement period, the ratio of total incorrect, lost, or duplicate TSDUs to total transferred TSDUs
Transfer Failure Probability	During a measurement period, the ratio of total transfer failures to total transfers
TC Release Delay	Maximum acceptable delay between a T-DISCONNECT request and the successful release of the peer transport service user
TC Release Failure Probability	Ratio of total release request failures to release requests
TC Protection	Extent the transport provider attempts to prevent unauthorized monitoring or manipulation of user information
TC Priority	Relative importance of connection in regard to degrading the QOS or breaking the connection
TC Resilience	Probability of a transport layer provider-initiated release

Therefore, the transport layer may attempt to meet the QOS requirements in a number of ways:

1. Take specific actions that are transparent to the network layer.
2. Choose from a number of networks a network that can meet the requirements.
3. Choose from one network with a number of ongoing network connections an ongoing network connection that meets the requirements.

The Transport Layer

4. Refuse the request because it cannot be satisfied.

5. Attempt to negotiate the user to a lower level of QOS.

TRANSPORT LAYER SERVICE DEFINITIONS AND PRIMITIVES

As the reader might expect, the transport layer service definition uses primitives to specify what services are to be provided through the network(s). The parameters associated with each primitive action provide the specific actions and events to be provided by the network. During the connection establishment phase, the characteristics of the connection are negotiated between the end users and the transport layer. The primitives and the parameters of the primitives are used to support the negotiation. It is possible that a connection will not be made if the network or an end user cannot provide the requested quality of service. Moreover, the requested services may be negotiated down to a lower level. Table 7-3 lists the transport layer primitives and parameters.

After the parameters are accepted between the two negotiating parties, data transfer is provided at the local site from the transport layer through the network layer, data link layer, physical layer, and finally through the channel. At the remote site, the data passes up through the physical layer, data link layer, network layer, and the transport layer to the user or another upper layer.

A brief explanation of the primitive parameters is in order. The called, calling, and responding addresses must be TSAPs. They are defined as follows:

- Called Address: Address of requested TSAP
- Calling Address: Address of requesting TSAP
- Responding Address: Identical to the called address TSAP

The quality of service parameters contain the values used to negotiate and use the services described in Table 7-2. As might be expected, the expedited data option is used to request for expedited data delivery during the transport connection. The reason parameter will be described in section titled "Connection Release."

The protocol places strict rules on how the primitives are used. The permissible transport layer services sequences are shown in Table 7-4, the primitive flow diagram in Figure 7-6, and the state diagram in Figure 7-7.

RELATIONSHIP OF TRANSPORT LAYER TO THE OSI NETWORK LAYER

The transport layer uses the QOS parameters depicted in Table 7-2 to communicate and negotiate with the underlying network layer. Indeed, many of the parameters passed to the transport layer are passed to the network layer. As evidence of this fact, please review the information in Tables 5-2 and 5-3 in Chapter 5.

TABLE 7-3. Transport Layer Primitives and Parameters

Phase	Primitive	Parameters
TC establishment	T-CONNECT	Called address, calling address, request expedited data option, quality of service, TS user data
	T-CONNECT indication	Called address, calling address, expedited data option, quality of service, TS user data
	T-CONNECT response	Quality of service, responding address, expedited data option, TS user data
	T-CONNECT confirm	Quality of service, responding address, expedited data option, TS user data
Data transfer	T-DATA request	TS user data
	T-DATA indication	TS user data
	T-EXPEDITED-DATA request	TS user data
	T-EXPEDITED-DATA indication	TS user data
TC release	T-DISCONNECT request	TS user data
	T-DISCONNECT indication	Disconnect reason, TS user data

The transport layer assumes the services described in X.213 are provided by the network layer. The conventions for the interaction of the network and transport layer are defined in the transport layer X.224 protocol specification. Table 7-5 summarizes these conventions. In all cases, the nature of how these primitives and parameters are exchanged is a local matter, not subject to OSI rules.

RELATIONSHIP OF TRANSPORT LAYER TO THE OSI UPPER LAYERS

The transport layer interacts with the upper layers with the transport layer primitives that are listed in Table 7-3. X.224 further stipulates that information

TABLE 7-4. Transport Layer Primitive Sequences

An initial primitive:

May be followed by:

	T-CONNECT request	T-CONNECT confirm	T-CONNECT indication	T-CONNECT response	T-CONNECT request	T-CONNECT indication	T-EXPEDITED-DATA request	T-EXPEDITED-DATA indicator	T-DISCONNECT request	T-DISCONNECT indication
T-CONNECT request	NP	NP	NP	NP	NP	NP	NP	NP	NP	NP
T-CONNECT confirm	+	NP	NP	NP	NP	NP	NP	NP	NP	NP
T-CONNECT indication	NP	NP	NP	NP	NP	NP	NP	NP	NP	NP
T-CONNECT response	NP	NP	+	NP	NP	NP	NP	NP	NP	NP
T-CONNECT request	NP	+	NP	+	+	+	+	+	NP	NP
T-CONNECT indication	NP	+	NP	+	+	+	+	+	NP	NP
T-EXPEDITED-DATA request	NP	+	NP	+	+	+	+	+	NP	NP
T-EXPEDITED-DATA indication	NP	+	NP	+	+	+	+	+	NP	NP
T-DISCONNECT request	+	+	+	+	+	+	+	+	NP	NP
T-DISCONNECT indication	+	+	+	+	+	+	+	+	NP	NP

+: Possible

NP: Not Possible

is transferred between the transport layer and the transport layer user in accordance with the conventions listed in Table 7-6.

MANAGING CONNECTIONS AND DATA TRANSFER

Connection Establishment

The transport layer functions can be divided into two categories: connection management (establishment and release) and data transfer. The connection establishment phase begins when the T-CONNECT request primitive is passed from the upper layer (the session layer, for example) to the transport layer. The primitive contains the parameters used to create a transport connection request (CR) protocol data unit (TPDU). As we shall see later, these parameters are mapped into certain fields of the TPDU for use at the destination transport entity. The parameters and TPDU fields are described in other sections of this chapter.

The typical sequence is shown in Figure 7-6. At this point in our analysis of OSI, the reader should be able to substitute these general sequences with the specific primitives found in Table 7-6.

During the connection establishment phase, the transport layer matches the transport user's requested QOS with the services offered by the network

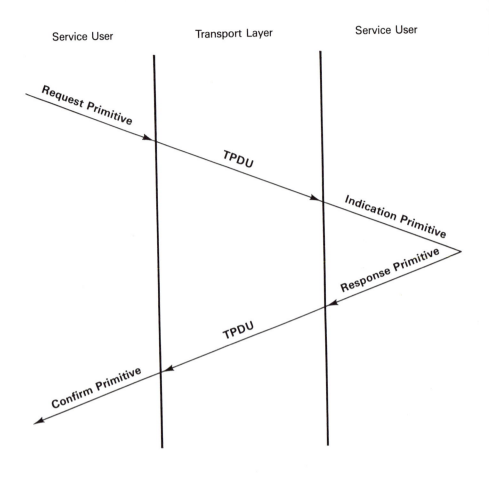

TPDU = Transport Protocol Data Unit

FIGURE 7-6. Transport Layer Primitives and Protocol Data Units

layer. At a general level, the following functions are provided by the transport layer:

- Selection of network service to match the user requirements, taking into account the costs to provide such service.
- Deciding to multiplex the connection with other connections onto a single network connection.
- Establishing the size of the transport protocol data unit (TPDU).
- Selection of functions that will be used during the data transfer phase.
- Mapping transport addresses onto network addresses.
- Providing a means to distinguish between different transport sessions.

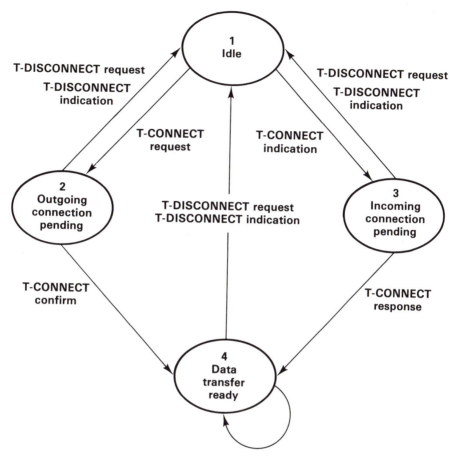

FIGURE 7-7. Transport Services State Transition Diagram
[CCITT X.214]

Connection Release

The transport connection release follows a similar pattern (see Figure 7-8), except additional disconnection scenarios are allowed. A typical disconnect occurs when one transport entity issues a T-DISCONNECT request. This is mapped to a T-DISCONNECT indication at the receiving transport entity [Figure 7-8(a)]. Another possibility is the issuance of the T-DISCONNECT request at both ends of the transport connection [Figure 7-8(b)]. This release is not coordinated and neither end knows the other end is issuing the disconnect. This absence of a time and dependency relationship is noted by the symbol ~. Another possibility is the release initiated by the transport services provider [Figure 7-8(c)]. Finally, Figure 7-8(d) shows the release initiated simultaneously by the transport services user and the transport services provider.

TABLE 7-5. Transport Layer Use of Network Layer Services

Primitives Exchanged between Transport and Network Layers	Parameters in the Primitives	Notes
N-CONNECT request	Called Address	1
N-CONNECT indication	Calling Address	1
	Receipt Confirmation Selection	2
	Expedited Data Selection	2
	QOS Parameters	1
	User Data	3
N-CONNECT response	Responding Address	1
N-CONNECT confirmation	Receipt Confirmation Selection	4
	Expedited Data Selection	4
	QOS Parameters	1
	User Data	5
N-DATA request	User Data	1
N-DATA indication	Confirmation Request	4
N-DATA ACKNOWLEDGE request		2
N-DATA ACKNOWLEDGE indication		2
N-EXPEDITED DATA request	User Data	2
N-EXPEDITED DATA indication	User Data	2
N-RESET request	Reason	5
N-RESET indication	Originator	5
N-RESET response	Reason	1
N-RESET confirmation		1
N-DISCONNECT request	Reason	
	User Data Responding Address	5
N-DISCONECT indication	Originator	5
	Reason	
	User Data	
	Responding Address	

Notes:

1. Transport layer assumes service and parameter are provided by network.

2. Transport layer assumes service and parameter are provided and can be invoked as an option (assuming a parameter is present).

3. Transport layer does not use this primitive parameter.

4. Transport layer assumes service is provided by network and parameter is used as an option by the transport layer.

5. Transport layer assumes service is provided by the network and the parameter is not used by the transport layer.

The Transport Layer

TABLE 7-6. Upper Layer Use of Transport Layer Services

Primitives Exchanged Between Transport Layer and Upper Layer	Parameters in the Primitives
T-CONNECT request T-CONNECT indication	Called Address Calling Address Expedited Data Option QOS Values User Data
T-CONNECT response T-CONNECT confirm	Responding Address QOS Values Expedited Data Option User Data
T-DATA request T-DATA indication T-EXPEDITED DATA request T-EXPEDITED DATA indication T-DISCONNECT request T-DISCONNECT indication	User Data User Data User Data User Data User Data Disconnect Reason User Data

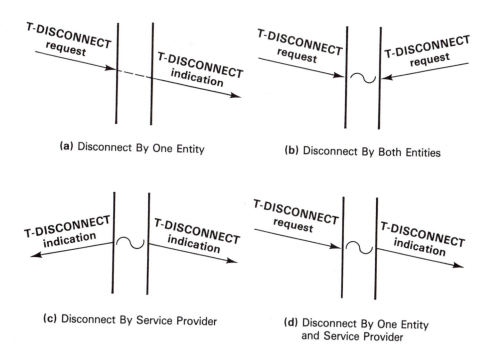

(a) Disconnect By One Entity

(b) Disconnect By Both Entities

(c) Disconnect By Service Provider

(d) Disconnect By One Entity and Service Provider

FIGURE 7-8. Possible Transport Level Disconnects

These disconnections can occur for a variety of reasons: the data cannot be delivered, the user decides to terminate the communications dialogue, one of the entities has exhausted the required resources to support the process, the quality of service is at an unacceptable level, etc. Although no reason must be given for the disconnection, a "reason" parameter is available in the T-DISCONNECT indication primitive to convey the problem and reason for the disconnection. This information is mapped into the reason field of the disconnect request (DR) TPDU and transmitted to the receiving transport entity. The reason parameter can convey the following information (more details on the reason parameter are provided in the next section):

- QOS is below a minimum level.
- Lack of resources at the local or remote transport provider.
- Transport provider malfunctions (known as misbehavior in OSI).
- Called transport user unknown or unavailable.
- Reason is unknown.

It should be emphasized that a transport layer connection release may cause the loss of data units that are in transit when the release is invoked. Notice that the transport service does not provide any disconnect confirm primitives. Notice from Figure 7-8 that the transport entities do not exchange any disconnect confirm primitives.

In the United States, the National Bureau of Standards specifies a "graceful close" in its version of the transport layer. With this approach, both transport service users must issue a close (disconnect) request primitive before the connection will be released. Therefore, all outstanding data can be delivered before the connection is released.

The OSI Model places the responsibility for a graceful close at the next upper layer, the session layer.

Data Transfer

During the data transfer phase, the transport layer may support eleven major functions. The functions are selected during the connection establishment phase. A brief summary of each function follows.

- *Data Transmission:* The transmission of TPDUs between the users.
- *Multiplexing/Demultiplexing:* Sharing a single network connection between two or more transport users.
- *Error Detection:* Detecting the loss, duplication, or corruption of TPDUs.
- *Error Recovery:* Recovering from detected errors.
- *Concatenation/Separation:* Combining several TPDUs into a single network layer NSDU.
- *Segmenting and Reassembling:* Splitting a single TSDU into multiple TPDUs.

- *Splitting and Recombining:* Using more than one network connection.
- *Flow Control:* Controlling the flow of TPDUs between two users.
- *Identification:* Providing a means to identify two users of a transport connection.
- *Expedited Data Transmission:* Bypassing normal flow control measures.
- *Delimiting the TSDU:* Determining the beginning and ending of the TSDU.

The data transfer takes place with the T-DATA request and T-DATA indication primitives. In addition, the transport layer can utilize expedited data transfer with the use of the T-EXPEDITED-DATA request and T-EXPEDITED-DATA indication primitives, in which case 1 to 16 octets of user data can be exchanged.

Certain options (protocol classes) in the transport layer permit the transport entities to acknowledge the successful receipt of TPDUs between each other. This capability is provided with the acknowledge (AK) protocol data unit. The AK can be implemented to provide an ACK with each unit of data. Using this option, a data unit is given to the transport layer as a T-DATA request primitive. Another choice is for the transport user to present user data with one T-DATA request primitive and the remote transport layer to issue a T-DATA indication primitive after receiving a complete data unit. These two choices are diagrammed in Figure 7-9.

Later discussions in this chapter provide more information on the data transfer phase.

TRANSPORT LAYER PROTOCOL DATA UNITS (TPDUs)

The transport layer is viewed by some people as one of the more difficult OSI layers to grasp. This is certainly a reasonable view because: (a) the layer provides for five major classes of protocol, some of which are fairly complex; (b) each protocol has different rules; and (c) each protocol class usually requires the transport protocol data units to be formatted and coded slightly differently.

This section describes the coding and the functions of these data units. Insofar as possible, we will attempt to stay at a level that provides the reader with sufficient depth to grasp the concepts of the material, but not at a level that discusses each and every rule of the five classes. However, in some instances it is necessary to examine the bit structure of the data units in order to understand how they operate.

Coding of the Protocol Data Units

The transport layer protocol uses several transport protocol data units to perform its functions (see Figure 7-10). All TPDUs have a similar structure, which consist of four parts:

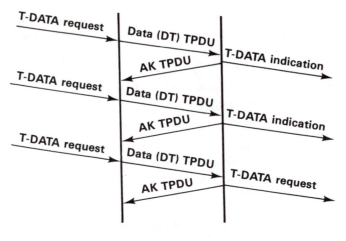

(a) Single TPDU Message

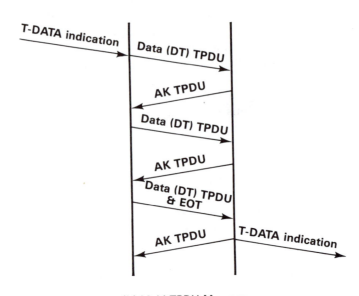

(b) Multi TPDU Message

FIGURE 7-9. Acknowledgment Options (with Class 4)

Length Indicator (LI): Length of header in octets
Fixed Part of Header: Control fields
Variable Part of Header: Control fields (if present)
Data Field: User data (if present)

The values in the fixed part contain frequently used parameters. The values in the variable part contain less frequently used parameters. These parame-

The Transport Layer

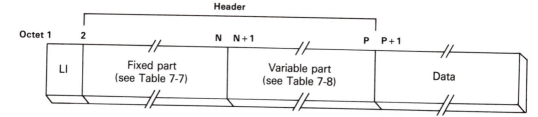

FIGURE 7–10. General Format of Transport Layer PDU

ters are listed in Tables 7-7 and 7-8. It is suggested the reader review these two tables, but not be too concerned about some of the details and footnotes, because they are used later in the chapter to explain features of the protocol.

The variable part of the data unit contains one or more of less frequently used parameters. Each parameter in this part must be coded as follows:

Octet $n + 1$: Parameter code
Octet $n + 2$: Parameter length (n)
Octet $n + 3 + n$: Parameter value

TABLE 7–7. Parameters for Fixed Part of the TPDU

Parameter Description	Parameter Length in Octets	Notes
Length Indicator	1	1
TPDU Code	1/2	
Credit (CDT)	1/2	
Destination Reference (DST-REF)	2	
Source Reference (SRC-REF)	2	
Class, Options	1	2
Reason	1	3
EOT	1 bit	4
TPDU-NR	(See Note 5)	5
ED-TPDU-NR	(See Note 5)	5
YR-TU-NR	(See Note 5)	5
YR-EDTU-NR	(See Note 5)	5
Reject Cause	1	6

Notes:

1. Length of both headers, excluding the LI. Maximum value is 254.

2. See Table 7–9 for explanation.

3. See Table 7–13 for explanation.

4. Set to 1 to indicate the end of a TSDU that is segmented into TPDUs. Uses one of the TPDU-NR and ED-TPDU-NR fields.

5. Seven bits in octet 5, plus all of octets 6, 7, and 8 for extended formats.

6. See Table 7–14 for explanation.

Transport Layer Protocol Data Units (TPDUs)

TABLE 7-8. Parameters for Variable Part of the TPDU

Parameter Description	Parameter Length in Octets	Notes
Identification of Calling TSAP	Variable	1
Identification of Called TSAP	Variable	1
Maximum TPDU Size	1	2
Version Number		
Protection	Variable	3
Checksum	2	4
Additional Options	1	7
Alternative Protocol Classes(es)	Variable	5
Acknowledge Time	2	4
Throughput	12 or 24	5
Residual Error Rate	3	5
Priority	2	5
Transit Delay	8	5
Reassignment Time	2	6
Subsequence Number	2	8
Flow Control Information	8	9
Invalid TPDU	Variable	10

Notes:
  1. If a TSAP ID is in a request, it may also be returned in the confirmation.

  2. Default is 128 octets; sizes range from 128–192 octets.

  3. User defined.

  4. Used only if Class 4 is the preferred class.

  5. Not used for Class 0.

  6. Not used for Classes 0, 2 or 4.

  7. See Table 7-6 for an explanation.

  8. Sequence the AK TPDUs to ensure they are processed sequentially.

  9. Contains copy of values of last received AK TPDUs YR-TU-NR, CDT, and Subsequence number.

  10. Contains the bit pattern of rejected TPDU header.

In this manner, the variable part is designed to be quite flexible in how it is coded. Of course, the CCITT and ISO documents provide very specific rules on how to use the parameters for each of the classes (0–4) of protocols. The variable part is shown in Table 7-8.

The class, options octet is coded to identify the class of protocol and several other features. Its format is shown in Table 7-9.

FUNCTIONS OF THE PROTOCOL DATA UNITS

Of course, the purpose of the transport layer is to support the transfer of end-user data between two end users. From the previous discussion, it is rather obvious that the transport layer makes extensive use of control headers to fulfill

TABLE 7-9. The Connection Request (CR) Class, Options Octet

		Bits		
8	7	6	5	Meaning
0	0	0	0	Class 0
0	0	0	1	Class 1
0	0	1	0	Class 2
0	0	1	1	Class 3
0	1	0	0	Class 4

Protocol Class Field

Bit	Value	Meaning
4	0	None
3	0	None
2	0	Normal formats for all classes
2	1	Extended formats in Classes 2, 3, 4
1	0	Explicit flow control in Class 2
1	1	No explicit flow control in Class 2

Options Field

this purpose. As in the other OSI layers, the user data is transferred between end users within a protocol data unit.

The data fields in the transport protocol data unit (TPDU) contain all the headers (protocol control information or PCIs) that have been added from higher layers and, of course, end-user data if appropriate. As explained earlier, the control fields are used to: (a) negotiate the level of service between the initiator and responder during a connection establishment; (b) manage the ongoing data transfer; and (c) provide the termination of the connection.

The specific kind of TPDU is identified by the type code in bits 8 through 5 of the second octet of the header. Table 7-10 explains the type code and the length of the user data field, if it is permitted.

Using the TPDUs to Invoke Operations

The remainder of this section describes the major functions of the transport layer protocol data units. As before, our goal is to provide a sufficient level of detail to understand the substance of the protocol, but leave the specific rules (which are many) to the reader who chooses to study the source document. Remember that the general format of the TPDUs is shown in Figure 7-10, and the reader may wish to refer back to this figure during this discussion.

Connection Request (CR) and Connection Confirm (CC) TPDU. The connection request (CR) and connection confirm (CC) TPDUs are used to establish a connection between two transport entities (see Figure 7-11). The second octet

TABLE 7-10. Transport Layer Protocol Data Units (TPDUs)

TPDU Type	Amount of Data Allowed	Notes
CR Connection Request	≤ 32 octets	1
CC Connection Confirm	≤ 32 octets	1
DR Disconnect Request	≤ 64 octets	1,2
DC Disconnect Confirm	None	
DT Data Transfer	As negotiated	3
ED Expedited Data	≤ 16 octets	
AK Acknowledgment	None	4
EA Expedited Acknowledgment	None	5
RJ Reject	None	
ER Error	None	
GR Graceful Close	None	6

Notes:

1. No user data permitted in Class 0; optional in other classes.

2. Successful transfer of data is not guaranteed by transport protocol.

3. Less 3 octets in Classes 0 and 1; less 5 octets (normal header) or 8 octets (extended header) in other classes.

4. Not permitted under following conditions: class 0; class 1 when network receipt confirmation is used; and class 2 when no explicit flow control option is used.

5. Not permitted in class 1 or class 2 when the no explicit flow control option is used.

6. Not defined by CCITT; defined by NBS.

contains the type code, which identifies the type of data unit, and the initial credit allocation code (CDT). We explain its use in the analysis of the class 4 option.

The destination-reference (DST-REF) octets are not used for a connection request and are set to all zeros; they are used with subsequent TPDUs.

The source-reference (SRC-REF) octets are used by the originator of the connection request to identify the originator. The DST-REF and SRC-REF are values that identify the two communicating entities during data transfer. For a connection setup, the TSAPs are also placed in the variable part of the CR header. The sending and receiving transport entities can map these addresses to the DST-REF and SRC-REF addresses. Thereafter, the TSAP addresses are not needed. Both transport entities use the values in the DST-REF and SRC-REF fields.

The reference fields are also needed for the transport classes 2, 3, and 4, because of the possibility of multiplexing multiple transport connections onto one network connection.

The class, options octet performs two functions: (a) it defines the preferred transport protocol class (0 through 4), and (b) it defines options within the protocol class to obtain either a 1-octet or 4-octet TPDU sequence number and to enable or disable explicit flow control for class 2. Earlier discussions explained the coding structure for this octet.

The Transport Layer

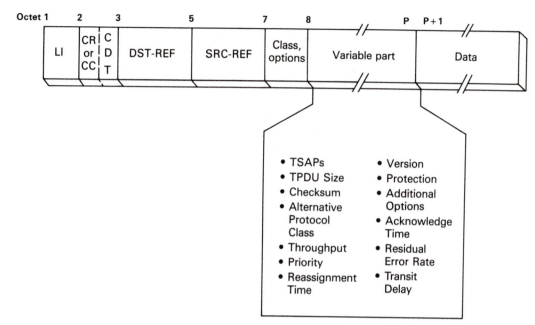

Note: DST–REF set to all zeros for the CR TPDU

**FIGURE 7-11. The Connection Request and Connection Confirm
TPDUs**

The protocol class and options can be negotiated between the two transport entities, but they can never be negotiated up. They must remain as coded or negotiated down. The option bits to establish formats, sequencing, and flow control are discussed later.

As discussed earlier, the variable part of the header contains the less frequently used parameters. The quality of service (QOS) parameters in the variable part are derived from the QOS parameters provided in the T-CONNECT request primitive. In turn, these parameters are used to create the N-CONNECT request primitive for the lower network layer. This concept is emphasized once again to ensure that the reader understands that a primitive is used to create the PCIs (headers) in the layer's protocol data unit (PDU).

A Closer Look at the Variable Parameters. Let us pause to examine the parameters in Table 7-8 and Figure 7-11. They reveal much about the services of the transport layer.

The *transport service access points* (TSAPs) contain the identifiers of the calling and called TSAPs. They are mapped into these fields during call establishment. These standards do not dictate the values of the TSAP, nor do they become involved in how the numbers are assigned. Some systems reserve TSAPs for specific purposes and others create new TSAPs to support each con nection. Others use directories and set up TSAP identifiers based on a general identifier and map the general IDs to TSAP addresses.

The *TDPU size* parameter is coded in powers of 2 to identify the maximum size of the TPDU (including the header). The values range from 128 to 8192 (0000 0111: $2^7 = 128$ to 0000 1101: $2^{13} = 8192$). X.224 allows the following maximum sizes:

- 8192 octets (not allowed in Class 0)
- 4096 octets (not allowed in Class 0)
- 2048 octets
- 1024 octets
- 512 octets
- 256 octets
- 128 octets

A *version number* is used to identify the version or release number of the protocol.

The *protection parameter* is user-defined and the standards have nothing to say about how it is used.

The *checksum* parameter was discussed earlier. Remember it is used only in class 4 and is mandatory for all CR TDPUs and all TPDUs in which a checksum option has been selected.

The *additional options* parameter is best explained by showing how it is coded (see Table 7-11). This parameter stipulates the use of network expedited data transfer, receipt confirmation, use of a checksum, and use of transport expedited data transfer.

The *alternative protocol class(es)* parameter permits the identification and negotiation of another protocol class.

The *alternative protocol parameter* is used to negotiate an alternative protocol class. As we learned earlier, Table 7-1 lists the rules for the use of alternative classes.

The *acknowledge time* parameter is used to provide guidance to the receiving transport entity. It indicates a maximum time which can elapse from the

TABLE 7-11.   The Additional Options Code in the Variable Part of TPDU

Bit	Value	Meaning
4	1	Use of network expedited in Class 1
4	0	No use of network expedited in Class 1
3	1	Use of receipt confirmation in Class 1
3	0	Use of explicit AK in Class 1
2	1	Checksum used in Class 4
2	0	Checksum not used in Class 4
1	1	Use of expedited data transfer
1	0	No use of expedited data transfer

The Transport Layer

time the transport entity receives the TPDU from the network layer to the time it transmits an acknowledgment. It is not a negotiable parameter. It conveys the maximum values for the acknowledgment timer, which is explained later.

The *throughput* parameter is coded in octets per second (usually passed down from a user-initiated primitive). It allows throughput to be negotiated as maximum and/or average. Maximum throughput is coded in the first 12 octets; average throughput uses the next 12 octets (its use is optional). The parameter is also best explained by showing how it is coded (see Table 7-12). These parameters are negotiated and may be reduced by the called entity. They cannot be negotiated up.

The *residual error rate* parameter defines the loss of transport data units that are not reported. The three octet field is defined as follows: (1) target value; (2) minimum acceptable value; and, (3) length of TPDU. Octets 1 and 2 are expressed as a power of 10; octet 3 is expressed as a power of 2.

The *priority* parameter is not defined concisely. It refers to the order in which the connections are to have their QOS degraded, if necessary, or the order in which communications will be broken, if necessary. The use of the parameter depends upon how a network administration chooses to apply it.

The *transit delay* parameter (see Table 7-12) describes the negotiated delay between the two entities. Values are expressed in milliseconds and are based on a transport service data unit (TSDU) of 128 octets.

The *reassignment time* parameter is used in protocol classes 1 and 3 to begin recovery after the network layer has signaled a failure (i.e., a disconnect). It stipulates low long to keep trying a recovery after a network reset (N-RESET).

The CC TPDU uses the same format as the CR TPDU except the DST-REF field is filled in by the remote entity.

Disconnect Request (DR) and Disconnect Confirm (DC) TPDU. The formats for the DR and DC TPDU are shown in Figure 7-12. Please note that their contents vary slightly. The fields previously explained are not explained again.

TABLE 7-12. Throughput and Transit Delay Parameters in Variable Part of the TPDU

Throughput 1st 12 Octets Maximum Throughput	Transit Delay 2nd 12 Octets Average Throughput	Meaning 8 Octets	
First 3 octets	Fifth 3 octets	First 2 octets	Target value calling-to-called
Second 3 octets	Sixth 3 octets	Second 2 octets	Minimum acceptable calling-to-called
Third 3 octets	Seventh 3 octets	Third 2 octets	Target value, called-to-calling
Fourth 3 octets	Eighth 3 octets	Fourth 2 octets	Minimum acceptable called-to-calling

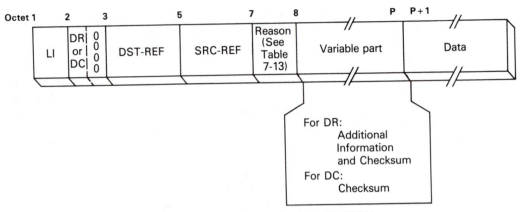

Octet 1   2   3   5   7   8   P   P+1

| LI | DR or DC | 0 0 0 0 | DST-REF | SRC-REF | Reason (See Table 7-13) | Variable part | Data |

For DR:
    Additional
    Information
    and Checksum
For DC:
    Checksum

Note: 1) SRC-REF field coded only in DR TPDU
      2) Reason field coded only in DR TPDU
      3) Data field coded only in DR TPDU

FIGURE 7–12. The Disconnect Request and Disconnect Confirm TPDUs

The reason for the disconnections are given in the reason field. Table 7-13 describes the coded values in the reason field. The reason field is coded only in the DR TPDU and not in the DC TPDU.

The variable part of the DR TPDU may contain the additional information field. It is used to hold any type of user data (perhaps diagnostic information)

TABLE 7–13.   Reasons for Transport Disconnection

Reason	Notes
Normal disconnect initiated by session entity	1,4
Remote congestion at transport entity during CC	1,4
Failed connection negotiation	1,3
Duplicate source reference for same NSAP pairs	1,4
References are mismatched	1,4
Protocol error	1,4
Reference overflow	1,4
Network refused connection request	1,4
Header or parameter length invalid	1,4
No reason specified	2,4
Congestion at TSAP	2,4
TSAP and session entity not attached	2,3
Unknown address	2,3

Notes:
1. Used for Classes 1 to 4
2. Used for all classes
3. Reported to TS user as persistent
4. Reported to TS user as transient

The Transport Layer

and its delivery is not guaranteed by the transport layer. Class 0 cannot carry this field. The checksum parameter can be carried in the variable part if the checksum is used.

Data (DT) TPDU. Several data (DT) TPDUs are used in the transport layer. The format of the TPDU depends on the following factors:

- Normal format for classes 0 and 1
- Normal format for classes 2, 3, and 4
- Extended format for classes 2, 3, and 4
- Normal format for expedited TPDUs for classes 1, 2, 3, and 4
- Extended format for expedited TPDUs for classes 2, 3, and 4

Figure 7-13 illustrates the formats for these TPDUs. As can be seen, all are variations on the same theme, but the reader should realize that several variations do exist. We now discuss the fields in Figure 7-13 as they pertain to each format.

The EOT bit (bit 8 in octet 5) is set to 1 to indicate the current DT TPDU is the last data unit of a sequence, i.e., the end of a complete TSDU.

The TPDU send sequence number (TPDU-NR) is used to sequence each data unit. It uses octet 5 for the normal format and octets 5 through 8 for the extended format (less the EOT bit).

The TPDU-NR is used only for flow control in class 2 because the network layer performs resequencing. In the class 4, it is also used to reorder DT TPDUs and to detect lost or duplicate TPDUs. The number is incremented by one with each transmission of a data unit. These services are explained shortly.

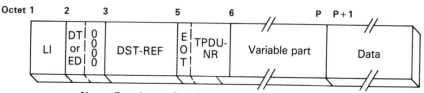

Note: For classes 0 and 1, the variable part is not used.

(a) Data TPDU

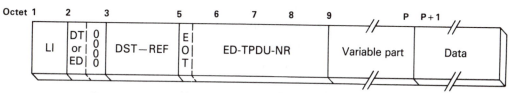

Note: Several variations of these formats are used.

(b) Extended Data TPDU

FIGURE 7-13. The Data TPDUs

The variable part of the DT TPDU contains only the checksum parameter, if relevant. The user data field contains the user data (a TSDU) and is restricted to the negotiated size. It is no greater than 16 octets for an expedited (ED) TPDU.

Data Acknowledgment and Expedited Data

Acknowledgment (EA) TPDU. The acknowledgment data units (see Figure 7-14) are used to acknowledge data TPDUs. They are not used with class 0, nor are they used with class 2 if the "no explicit flow control" option is used or with class 1 if the "network receipt confirmation" option is selected.

Two fields in the variable part of these data units were described earlier

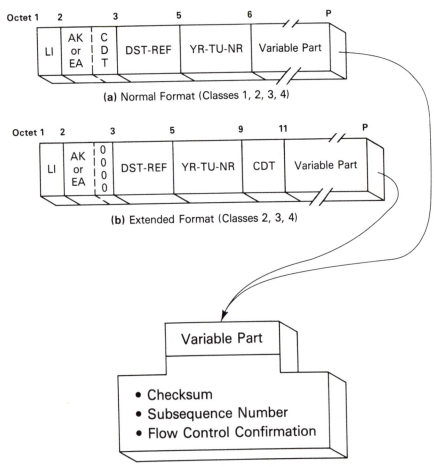

(a) Normal Format (Classes 1, 2, 3, 4)

(b) Extended Format (Classes 2, 3, 4)

Variable Part
- Checksum
- Subsequence Number
- Flow Control Confirmation

Note: The Expedited Acknowledgements do not use the CDT field and only place a Checksum in the Variable Part.

FIGURE 7-14. The Acknowledgment TPDUs

in the chapter but warrant a brief iteration. The subsequence number can be used to ensure that the AK data units are processed in the proper order. It is simply a sequence number on an acknowledgment unit. The flow control confirmation field contains a copy of the values received in the last AK TPDU received. It allows the sender of the AK TPDU to be aware of the conditions of the receiver. The field contains the YR-TU-NR, subsequence, and CDT parameters.

The expedited data AKs (normal and extended) use the same format, except they do not use the CDT and the variable part only contains a checksum.

Reject(RJ) TPDU. This data unit (see Figure 7-15) cannot be used with classes 0, 2, and 4. The value in the YR-TR-NR parameter stipulates the number of the next expected TPDU. In other words, the transport entity that receives ths data unit must begin the retransmission of the TPDU, commencing with the number in the YR-TR-NR. The reject contains no variable part.

Error (ER) TPDU. Finally, the ER TPDU is used to signal an error (see Figure 7-16). It contains a reject cause parameter that must be coded in accordance with the entries in Table 7-14. The variable part may contain a code that indicates that the TPDU is invalid and a succeeding field that mirrors the bit pattern of the rejected TPDU header. It can also contain a checksum.

ELEMENTS OF PROCEDURE

By this time in our analysis of the OSI transport layer, the reader may think that we have exhausted the subject matter. However, we have yet to discuss the elements of procedure that were introduced earlier in the chapter. This subject is important, because the elements of procedure and protocol classes form the foundation of the OSI transport layer. So without further ado, let us begin the analysis.

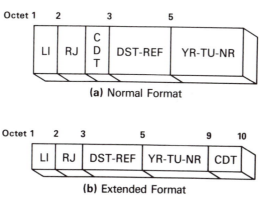

(a) Normal Format

(b) Extended Format

FIGURE 7-15. The Reject TPDU

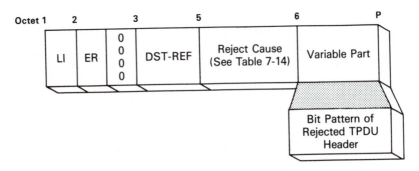

Octet 1   2   3   5   6   P

| LI | ER | 0 0 0 0 | DST-REF | Reject Cause (See Table 7-14) | Variable Part |

Bit Pattern of
Rejected TPDU
Header

FIGURE 7-16. The Error TPDU

Table 7-15 provides a list of the transport layer elements of procedure within each class. Notice that these elements of procedure are invoked based on the protocol class. Class 0 provides relatively few elements, but class 4 provides many because it is used with unreliable and/or connectionless networks. For example, retransmissions, resequencing, and checksums are used with the class 4 protocol. The reader is cautioned that the elements within different classes may not be identical, and the CCITT or ISO documents should be read to understand the specific differences. Many of these procedures are self-explanatory, but the following material provides a description of each element of procedure.

Assignment to Network Connection. The procedure assigns transport connections to network connections. It also releases an assignment. It uses the N-CONNECT and N-DISCONNECT primitives. An originator may assign the transport connection to an existing or a new network connection. If it is an existing network connection, the assignment cannot override any classes or elements of procedure that currently exist. If classes 1 or 3 are used, an existing transport connection can be reassigned after a network connection failure.

If the underlying network connection fails, the transport layer may reassign a transport connection to another network connection, as long as the connection joins the same NSAPs.

If the transport entity is splitting the connection, it may assign a transport connection to any network connection that joins the same NSAPs.

TABLE 7-14.   The Reject Cause Parameter

Permissible Entries
Reason not specified
Invalid parameter code
Invalid TPDU type
Invalid parameter type

TABLE 7-15. Elements of Procedure

Protocol Function	Variant	Protocol Class 0	1	2	3	4
Assignment to network connection		X	X	X	X	X
TPDU transfer		X	X	X	X	X
DT TPDU length and segmenting		X	X	X	X	X
Concatenation and separation			X	X	X	X
Connection establishment		X	X	X	X	X
Connection refusal		X	X	X	X	X
Normal release	Implicit	X				
	Explicit		X	X	X	X
Error Release		X	X			
DT TPDU numbering	Normal		X	X	X	X
	Extended			0	0	0
Expedited data transfer	Normal		X	X	X	X
	Expedited		0			
Association of TPDUS with TC		X	X	X	X	X
Reassignment after failure			X		X	
Retention until acknowledgment of TPDUS	Confirmation		0			
	Receipt AK		X		X	X
Resynchronization			X		X	
Multiplexing and demultiplexing				X	X	X
Explicit flow control	With			X	X	X
	Without	X	X	0		
Checksum	Use of					X
	Non-use of	X	X	X	X	0
Frozen references			X		X	X
Retransmission on time-out						X
Resequencing						X
Inactivity control						X
Treatment of protocol errors		X	X	X	X	X
Splitting and recombining						X

TPDU = Transport Protocol Data Unit   0 = Optional

This element of procedure contains a number of other conventions on how to assign a transport connection to a network connection.

TPDU Transfer. This procedure allows a TPDU to be conveyed in the data field of the network service primitives on established network connections. While such a statement might appear obvious, a well-written specification does not allow the designer to assume a procedure is to be used; rather, it explicitly explains the procedure. This procedure also allows a class 1 connection to use network layer expedited primitives; otherwise, the other classes use the ordinary network layer data primitives.

Segmenting and Reassembling. This procedure is used to map transport service data units (TSDUs) onto transport protocol data units (TPDUs). The procedure makes use of the DT TPDU and the end-of-TSDU parameter (explained later) to indicate if subsequent DT TPDUs exist in the sequence.

Concatenation and Separation. This procedure allows the transport entity to concatenate multiple TPDUs into one NSDU. The concatenated TPDUs may be from the same or different transport connections.

Connection Establishment. This procedure defines how a transport connection is established. (The procedure was described in general terms earlier in this chapter.) During the connection establishment, the transport entities choose a reference (a 16-bit field) to identify the specific transport connection. Also, the calling and called transport service access point (TSAPs) are exchanged, as are the following parameters (if relevant for the protocol class): initial credit, acknowledgment time, checksum parameter, and security parameter. During the connection establishment, the following services, procedures, and protocol classes can be negotiated:

- Protocol class (0–4)
- Transport protocol data unit (TPDU) size
- Normal or extended format
- Use of checksum
- These QOS parameters: throughput, transit delay, priority, residual error rate
- Non-use of explicit flow control (class 2)
- Network receipt confirmation
- Network expedited (for class 1)
- Expedited data transfer

This element of procedure also provides the rules for negotiating the preferred and alternative protocol classes (see Table 7-1).

Connection Refusal. This procedure is invoked when the transport entity refuses a connection request that was initiated with a CR TPDU. The refuser sends either a DR TPDU or an ER TPDU. These data units contain the reason (in the DR TPDU) or reject cause (in the ER TPDU). The source reference field (SRC-REF) is set to zero to indicate the reference is unassigned.

Normal Release. This procedure describes the protocol for disconnecting the network sessions. The normal release procedure provides two variants for the release, the implicit variant and the explicit variant. Using the implicit variant (only for class 0), the transport entity can request the release by the network. The release occurs when either entity receives an N-DISCONNECT indication.

The explicit variant occurs using the DR and DC TPDUs. This procedure provides for the possibility that either transport entity may issue a disconnect request. As another possibility, one may have issued a disconnect and one may have issued a connect. The explicit variant provides for various scenarios to ensure the two entities have terminated the session and both sides are aware that the connection has been released. It provides for more control across the two entities than is given with the implicit variant.

Error Release. This procedure is used for classes 0 and 2 in the event the transport layer receives one of two primitives from the network layer: N-DISCONNECT indication or N-RESET indication. When the transport entity receives either of these primitives from the network layer, it considers the network connection released and must inform the upper levels, i.e, the transport service users. All other classes invoke error recovery procedures.

Association of TPDUs with Transport Connection. The purpose of this procedure is to associate a received NSDU as TPDU(s). The procedure uses the N-DATA indication and N-EXPEDITED DATA indication network service primitives. This detailed procedure stipulates how the received primitives are handled. Generally, with ongoing data flow between the layers, the received TPDU is associated with the ongoing transport connection that is identified by the DST-REF parameter in the data unit. However, if the DST-REF parameter identifies other connections, if the data unit is corrupted, or if the data unit cannot be interpreted, then the procedure defines the methods by which the disconnection is implemented or how to handle the unusual conditions. The protocol associated with this procedure varies, depending on which class is being used for the connection.

Data TPDU Numbering. The numbering procedure requires each protocol data unit to have sequence numbers associated with it. These sequence values can be a normal format sequence (2^7) or an extended sequencing (2^{31}). These sequence numbers are used to maintain flow control sequencing between the two transport entities.

Expedited Data Transfer. The expedited data procedures are negotiated during connection establishment. Once established, this allows the user to create either an N-DATA primitive or an N-EXPEDITED DATA primitive. It defines how the receiver acknowledges the primitive with an expedited acknowledgment. This procedure restricts one expedited data unit at a time, i.e, only one of these units can be outstanding for each direction in each transport connection.

Reassignment After Failure. This procedure is used in protocol classes 1 and 3 and defines how recovery is made after receiving a disconnect indication primitive from the network layer. Generally, the transport connection is reassigned to another network connection and any lost TPDUs are retransmitted. The actual actions invoked are dependent on the transport connection waiting for reassignments or resynchronization, and are based on the current state of two: the TTR (time to try resynchronization/reassignment timer and the TWR (the time to wait for resynchronization/reassignment timer). Depending on the state of the timers, the transport entity will either release the connection and freeze the reference or take some remedial actions.

The TTR timer is used by the initiator of action. This procedure stipulates that its value will not exceed 2 minutes, less the total maximum disconnect propagation delay and the maximum transit delay of the network connections. The value of this timer can be negotiated during connection establishment. The TWR timer is managed by the receiver. Its parameter can also be negotiated in the connection request. The TWR value shall be greater than the TTR timer plus the maximum disconnection propagation delay plus the maximum transit delay through the network(s).

Retention Until Acknowledgment of TPDUs. This procedure describes the methods to retain data units (in classes 2, 3, and 4) to enable the recovery of TPDUs that may be lost. The procedure defines which types of protocol data units are to be retained and when they may be released. The following TPDUs must be retained for possible retransmission: CR, CC, DR, DT, ED. Table 7-16 summarizes the rules for this procedure.

Resynchronization. This procedure is used in classes 1 and 3 to recover from a reset or a reassignment after failure. The class 4 protocol uses a different technique for its recovery. The procedure defines three methods for resynchronization: active resynchronization, passive resynchronization, and data resynchronization. The rules for invoking one of these procedures depend on whether (a) the transport entity is the responder, or (b) the transport entity elects to reassign after failure. If the entity is a responder, passive synchronization occurs. If it has elected not to reassign, no synchronization occurs; otherwise, active synchronization occurs.

Multiplexing and Demultiplexing. This procedure allows several transport connections to simultaneously share one network connection. The TPDUs

TABLE 7-16. TPDUs: Retention Until Acknowledgment

Retained TPDU	Retained TPDU Until Acknowledged By
CR	CC, DR, ER
DR	DC, DR
CC(1)	N-DATA ACKNOWLEDGE indication, RJ, DT, ED, EA
CC(2)	RJ, DT, AK, ED, EA
DT(1)	N-DATA ACKNOWLEDGE indication, from a N-DATA request
DT(2)	AK or RJ: if YR-TU-NR $>$ TPDU-NR in DT
ED	EA: YR-EDTU-NR $=$ ED-TPDU-NR in ED TPDU

(1) Confirmation of Receipt
(2) AK

belonging to different transport connections can be transferred in the same N-DATA primitive. The multiplexing operation uses the concatenation procedure and the demultiplexing operation uses the association of TPDUs with transport connections procedure.

Explicit Flow Control. This procedure is invoked to regulate the flow of the DT TPDUs between transport entities. This flow control acts independently from the flow control of the other layers. For example, the receive ready (RR)/receive not ready (RNR) flow control at the network layer (e.g., X.25) and data link layer (e.g., HDLC/SDLC) are fully independent flow control procedures. The flow control procedures vary with each protocol class. In a section of this chapter, this procedure is highlighted with a discussion of the class 4 protocol.

Checksum. This procedure was explained earlier. It is used only in the class 4 protocol if the users so agree during the connection establishment. It is always used with the CR TPDU.

Frozen References. In earlier discussions, the use of DST-REF (destination reference) and SRC-DEF (source reference) were explained. To briefly reiterate, these fields in the TPDU identify the two communicating transport entities. This procedure prevents a reference identifier from being reused. It is needed because a retransmission or out-of-sequence TPDU may arrive at the receiving entity after a connection release. The actions of this procedure depend upon the specific protocol class. For class 4, the reference must remain frozen for a time greater than L (maximum time between a TPDU transmission and its expected acknowledgment).

Retransmission upon Time-out. This procedure is used only with protocol class 4 and is used to deal with lost TPDUs.

Resequencing. This procedure is used only with protocol class 4 and is used to resequence mis-ordered TPDUs.

Inactivity Control. This procedure is used only with protocol class 4 and is used to handle an unsignaled termination of a network connection.

Treatment of Protocol Errors. Upon receiving an erroneous TPDU, a transport entity takes one of the following actions (which one depends on the protocol classes used):

Transmit an ER TPDU
Reset network connection
Close network connection
Invoke protocol class-specific release procedures
Ignore the TPDU used on protocol-class

Splitting and Recombining. This procedure is used only in class 4. It is invoked to increase throughput or provide more resilience to network failure. It makes use of multiple network connections and utilizes the assignment to network connections and resequencing procedures.

CLASS 4 (TP4): A CLOSER LOOK

TP4 (transport protocol class 4) has received considerable attention and is now used in many systems. As noted earlier, it provides mechanisms for detecting and recovering from errors that might occur at the lower levels. It assumes that the underlying network may lose, duplicate, or mis-sequence data units. It provides similar services to that of the Transmission Control Protocol (TCP, discussed earlier), but the OSI protocol is much richer in function.

The TP4 Timers

As with other protocols that are responsible for these kinds of functions, TP4 uses end-to-end acknowledgment in combination with several timers, retry parameters, and timer parameters. They are summarized in Table 7-17 and described in more detail in this section.

Local Retransmission Timer (T1). One of the primary reliability tools used by TP4 is the local retransmission timer, T1. It is quite similar to the link level T1 described in Chapter 4, but in this case, T1 encompasses all point-to-point delays and processing times through the end-to-end transport connection. It is used to determine the appropriate time for the transport entity to retransmit a protocol data unit. (See the element of procedure discussed earlier titled "Retention Until Acknowledgment of TPDUs.") The value of T1 is bound on the time the transport entity will wait for an acknowledgment from the other transport entity. The T1 is defined as:

$$T1 = X + E_{LR} + A_R + E_{RL}$$

where X = the local time required to process the TPDU; E_{LR} = expected maximum transit delay from the local to remote entity; A_R = processing time required at the remote entity to acknowledge the TPDU; and, E_{RL} = expected maximum transit delay from remote to local entity.

The values of E_{LR} and E_{RL} depend on the performance of the network or networks that support the transport connection. The speeds and delay of each component must be considered. For example, the propagation delay is a much more significant factor for a wide area network than for a local area network, and a session traversing several subnetworks requires a larger T1 value than a connection involving only one network.

The values contributing to T1 are depicted in Figure 7-17. In addition an

TABLE 7-17. Class 4 Timer Parameters

Symbol	Use
A_L	Time lapse between receipt of TPDU by local transport entity and re-transmission of acknowledgment.
A_R	Time lapse between receipt of TPDU by remote transport entity and transmission of acknowledgment.
E_{LR}	Maximum delay of NDSUs from local to remote transport entity.
E_{RL}	Maximum delay of NDSUs from remote to local transport entity.
I	Time lapse between last received TPDU and the initiation of a release by a transport entity.
L	Maximum time lapse between transmission of any TPDU and the receipt of any acknowledgment related to it.
M_{LR}	Maximum time between the local transmission of an NDSU and receipt of any copy of it at the remote transport entity.
M_{RL}	Maximum time between the remote transmission of an NDSU and receipt of any copy of it at the local transport entity.
N	Maximum number of retransmission attempts of a TPDU that requires acknowledgment.
R	Maximum time a transport entity will attempt retransmission of a TPDU that requires acknowledgment.
T1	Maximum wait time for acknowledgment before a transport entity will attempt retransmission of a TPDU that requires acknowledgment.
W	Maximum time period a transport entity must wait before retransmitting update window information.
X	Time to process local TPDU.

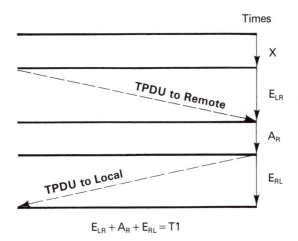

$$E_{LR} + A_R + E_{RL} = T1$$

FIGURE 7-17. Values Pertaining to T1

N parameter is used as the bound for the number of retries for a TPDU that requires an acknowledgment.

If T1 expires, the transport protocol data unit is retransmitted and T1 is restarted. After the retry value of N is reached, the release procedure is executed and the transport service user is informed.

The T1 can be maintained for each TPDU or it can be associated with each transport connection. In the latter case, the transport entity starts T1 upon sending a TPDU requiring acknowledgment, restarts T1 upon receiving an acknowledgment of any one of the TPDUs that are outstanding, and stops T1 upon receiving an ACK of the last outstanding data unit. The use of T1 must take into consideration the throughput implications. Obviously, an ACK of every data unit will affect throughput.

Retransmission can be accomplished in one of two methods: (1) retransmitting only the first DT TPDU, or (2) retransmitting all TPDUs waiting for acknowledgment (to the upper window edge).

The Persistence Timer (R). The local transport entity must be able to control how long it will continue to retransmit a TPDU that has not been acknowledged. This time is based on a persistence timer. It is related to the time that elapses between retransmissions (which is defined by T1) and the maximum number of retries (which is established by the parameter N). It may not be less than $T1 \times (N-1) + x$, where x is a quantity to allow for other internal delays (a fudge factor).

Time Bound on References and Sequence Numbers (L). TP4 must have some means of calculating the maximum length of time a TPDU might be expected to remain in the network(s). As we learned earlier, the source/destination references and the sequence numbers must not be reused if a chance exists that a TPDU that is using these values is still in the system. This situation can certainly occur with networks that use adaptive routing schemes and in internetworking situations in which the transit delay is highly variable.

To handle this situation, TP4 implements a reference value called L. It represents the bound for the maximum time between the transmission and/or retransmission of a TPDU and the receipt of any acknowledgment relating to it. It also represents the time during which a sequence number or reference number cannot be reused. As depicted in Figure 7-18, the bound on references and sequence numbers (i.e., L) is:

$$L = R + M_{LR} + A_R + M_{RL}$$

where R = the time required to retransmit the maximum number of TPDUs [where $R = T1 \times (N-1)$]; M_{LR} = maximum time between transmission and receipt of NSDUs in the underlying network from the local to remote entity; A_R = remote acknowledgment time; and, M_{RL} = maximum time between transmission and receipt of NSDUs in the underlying network between the remote and the local entity.

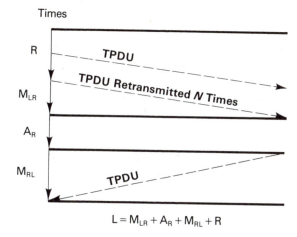

$$L = M_{LR} + A_R + M_{RL} + R$$

FIGURE 7-18. Values Pertaining to R and L

Timers for Data Transfer. Another timer used for flow control is the window timer (W). It is the bound for the maximum time the transport entity will wait before retransmitting a protocol data unit that updates the windows.

TP4 also uses an inactivity timer (I) to protect against a break in a network connection. Its value is several times the window timer (W), and is reset any time a TPDU from the remote entity is received. The window timer (W) is similar to a receive ready (RR) at the lower levels in that it ensures some units (AK TPDUs) flow between the transport entities in the absence of data units. The use of the inactivity and window timers is defined as:

$$I = 2 \times N \times max \; (T1 \; or \; W)$$

TP4 recommends that after N transmissions of a DT TPDU, the transport entity wait a period of time before entering the release phase. This time lapse provides for the possibility of receiving an ACK before the release is made. The recommended wait is $T1 + W + M_{R2}$. For TPDUs other than DT TPDUs, the recommended wait period is $T1 + M_{RL}$.

Managing the Flow of Data

TP4 provides powerful mechanisms to ensure that transport protocol data units (TPDUs) arrive safely at the receiving transport entity and that the sending transport entity is properly notified.

TP4 is somewhat unique among the protocols discussed in this book with its method of flow control. It uses the credit (CDT) field for the receiver to indicate to the transmitter how many data units it is willing to receive. This credit allocation scheme can be reduced or expanded as necessary. The initial credit is provided by the connection request and connection confirm TPDU and carried in the CDT fields. [The reader may recall that other layers (data link and network) control flow with one or a combination of three methods: (1) pre-established agreements, (2) negotiated window sizes, and (3) receive ready (RR) and receive not ready (RNR) frames/packets.]

TP4 uses a sliding window concept similar to the data link and network layers (see Figure 7-19). The acknowledgment TPDU contains the value of the next expected data unit (in the YR-TU-NR field) and the number of data units that can be sent (in the CDT field). A transport entity which receives an AK TPDU (an acknowledgment) uses the sum of the values in the YR-TU-NR and the CDT fields to determine the new upper window edge. The class 4 protocol also uses the YR-TU-NR to implicitly and inclusively acknowledge the correct receipt of all lower numbered data TPDUs.

Connection Establishment

A TP4 connection establishment must follow the connection establishment and connection refusal elements of procedure as well as these additional procedures:

1. A successful connection requires a three-way handshake. The sender of a CR TPDU must respond to the incoming CC TPDU by sending a ST, ED, DR, or AK protocol data unit. This rule is quite important for two reasons. First, if the sender of the CR goes down and does not transmit the AK, the entity that issues the CC might wait indefinitely for the next protocol data unit. However, with a three-way handshake, if the remote entity can time out and retransmit the CC, eventually its N value can be exhausted and it will know the connection did not take effect. Second, we learned earlier in this chapter that duplicate CR TPDUs can be entered into the network(s).

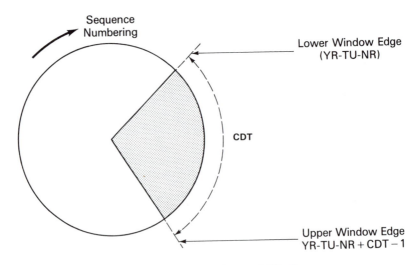

FIGURE 7-19. Credits and Windows

The Transport Layer

Therefore, the remote transport entity could possibly send a second CC TPDU after the associated connection has been released. However, through the use of frozen references and the third handshake, the local entity can be programmed to reply with a disconnect request (DR) TPDU.

2. The retransmission procedures (previously explained) must be used during connection establishment.

3. A CC TPDU using a frozen reference requires a response of DR TPDU.

4. If a duplicate CR TPDU is received, a CC TPDU is transmitted. If the three-way handshake has been completed, the CR TPDU is to be ignored.

Error Detection

One option in the class 4 protocol is the use of a checksum for error detection. The option is valuable if the link layer does not perform this function or if the link level does not signal its detection of an error. It is always used in a connection request protocol data unit and all other data units if the communicating parties so indicate. The checksum uses integer arithmetic and is not as effective in detecting errors as the cyclic redundancy check (CRC) explained in Chapter 4. However, it is more efficient and is designed to be executed in software. The CCITT checksum is summarized here.

$$\sum_{i=1}^{L} a_i = 0 \text{ (Modulo 255)}$$

$$\sum_{i=1}^{L} {}_i a_i = 0 \text{ (Modulo 255)}$$

where i = position of an octet within the TPDU; a_i = value of octet in position i; L = length of TPDU in octets.

TRANSMISSION CONTROL PROTOCOL (TCP)

Another widely used transport layer protocol is the Transmission Control Protocol (TCP). It was developed under the sponsorship of the U.S. Department of Defense for use in ARPANET but is used throughout the industry. It is found in several commercial networks as well as in networks in research centers and universities. It has many similarities to the CCITT transport protocol, and a large number of its features were incorporated into TP4. TCP is given general coverage in this book because it is not an OSI standard.

The goals of TCP are quite similar to TP4. Its job is to deliver and receive data across network boundaries. It recovers from damaged, duplicated, or missequenced data units. The TCP fits into the transport layer and rests below the upper layer protocols (designated as ULP) and above the Internet Protocol (IP) below, which resides in the network layer.

TCP Ports and Sockets

A *port* is an identifier of a host computer activity. This activity could be an application program, a security monitor, a data base management system, etc. A host machine can support multiple ports, and each port has its own unique port number within the host. A *socket* is formed from a concatenation of the port address and an internet address. The socket is a unique identifier throughout internet.

If an application in a host machine is to establish a connection with a process in a remote machine, it must request the connection by furnishing a source and destination socket in its request.

Connection Management

TCP works in a fashion quite similar to TP4 in that it requires a three-way handshake. One principal difference is the manner in which a connection is opened by the ULP. Two forms of connection establishment are permitted. The *passive open* mode allows the ULP to tell the TCP to wait for the arrival of connection requests for the specified port from the remote system. This type of protocol could be used to accommodate data base accesses from remote users. Passive opens can be implemented by one of two procedures:

- *Fully Specified.* A specific socket is identified from which a connection will be accepted.
- *Unspecified.* A connection will be accepted from any user.

The second form of connection establishment is the *active* mode. In this situation the ULP designates specifically another remote socket through which a connection is to be established. A connection is allowed if the remote socket has a matching passive open, or if both sockets have issued matching active opens. In either case, the connection is established at an agreed level of precedence and security.

The connection can be terminated with a *Close* or an *Abort*. The close is the normal procedure. It informs the remote user that all data transfer is complete. The close procedure also entails the use of the push function. The close procedure follows a sequence of events to ensure all data is delivered between the users:

- A Close is issued by the user to the TCP, which sends all data and a close protocol data unit to the remote TCP. During this period, the local user must continue to accept data.
- The remote TCP passes all data along with a close primitive to its user.

The remote user has the option of sending any outstanding data and a close primitive to its TCP.

- The remote TCP then sends back to the local TCP any data and its close protocol data unit. The local TCP passes this data (if any exists) to its user, and then signals its user with a terminate primitive. It also sends a termination protocol data unit to the remote TCP.
- Finally, the remote TCP issues a terminate primitive to its user.

A connection can also be terminated with an abort. This occurs by either the user or TCP issuing an abort primitive. Pending or outstanding data may be lost, because the user accepts no more data.

Data Transfer

Both TCP and TP4 provide for sequencing during the data transfer. As we learned earlier, TP4 sequences transport protocol data units. TCP uses a different scheme providing sequence numbers of the data octets within a block of data. In this manner, each data octet is numbered sequentially.

TCP accepts data from the upper layer protocols in a stream-oriented fashion. There is no specific block structure such as the CCITT transport service data unit (TSDU). However, the sending user actually sends data to TCP in blocks. The distinction lies in how a *push* function is implemented. The data are sent from the upper layer protocol (ULP) and transmitted to the network level, as appropriate, depending on the buffer management techniques at the TCP level. The push function is available to force the TCP to send data immediately. TCP sends the data associated with the push flag plus any other data that resides in the buffer. If the push function is not active, TCP may hold the data for assembly into more efficient segments. This function is used in a complementary fashion as the remote TCP.

TCP has a feature similar to the TP4 expedited data structure. Its term is the urgent data service. This service requires the receiving ULP to pay special attention to the traffic designated as urgent data and process it quickly.

TCP Primitives

TCP also works with the primitive concept, and we have made references to some of these primitives in previous discussions. Some of the primitives are similar to TP4, as Table 7-18 illustrates. Two types of primitives are implemented with TCP. The service request primitives are used from the ULP to the TCP and the service response primitives are used from the TCP to the ULP. Table 7-18 also lists the parameters associated with each primitive.

The principal differences between TP4 and TCP are summarized in Table 7-19.

TABLE 7-18. TCP Primitives

Service Request Primitives (ULP to TCP)	
Primitive	Parameters
UNSPECIFIED-PASSIVE-OPEN	Source port, ULP time-out (1), time-out action (1), precedence (1), security (1)
FULL-PASSIVE-OPEN	Source port, destination port, destination address, ULP time-out (1), time-out action (1), precedence (1), security (1)
ACTIVE-OPEN	Source and destination ports, destination address, ULP time-out (1), ULP time-out action (1), precedence (1), security (1)
ACTIVE-OPEN-WITH DATA	Source and destination ports, destination address, ULP time-out (1), ULP time-out action (1), precedence (1), security (1), data, data length, push flag, urgent flag (1)
SEND	Local connecting name, data, data length, push flag, urgent flag, ULP time-out (1), ULP time-out action (1)
ALLOCATE	Local connection name, data length
CLOSE	Local connection name
ABORT	Local connection name
STATUS	Local connection name

Service Response Primitives (TCP to ULP)	
Primitive	Parameters
OPEN-ID	Local connection name, source port, destination port, destination address
OPEN-FAILURE	Local connection name
OPEN-SUCCESS	Local connection name
DELIVER	Local connection name, data, data length, urgent flag
CLOSING	Local connection name
TERMINATE	Local connection name, description
STATUS RESPONSE	Local connection name, source port and address, destination port and address, connection state, receive and send window, amount waiting ack and receipt, urgent mode, time-out, time-out action
ERROR	Local connection name, error description

Note: (1) means parameters are optional.

TABLE 7-19. Principal Differences Between TP4 and TCP

TP Class 4 (TP-4)	Transmission Control Protocol (TCP)
Data placed in specific units and transmitted as discrete service data units (SDUs)	Data flow on an ongoing stream oriented basis.
Expedited data dequeued and may arrive before data sent earlier (on same session).	Expedited data remains in queue.
Uses OSI Service Access Point (SA) addressing concept.	Uses IP 32-bit address and a TCP port number.

CONNECTIONLESS TRANSPORT LAYER SERVICES

The ISO has also issued standards on connectionless transport services and protocols in relation to the underlying network layer. Four operations are defined:

- Connectionless service at the transport and network layers [DIS 8602]
- Connectionless service at transport layer and connection-oriented service at network layer [DIS 8602]
- Connection-oriented service at the transport and network layers [ISO 8073]
- Connection-oriented transport service and connectionless network service [ISO 8073 PDAD 2]

ISO 8072/DAD 1 defines the primitives for the connectionless transport service. They are identical to those used for the connectionless network service: T-UNITDATA.request and T-UNITDATA.indication. Each primitive carries four parameters, which are explained earlier in this and other chapters:

- Source address
- Destination address
- Quality of service
- TS user data

Figure 7-20 shows the only protocol data unit used by this protocol. It is called the UNITDATA (UD) TPDU. The source and destination addresses are passed from the user and translated into NSAPs, and also used as source and destination TSAPs, and thus are placed into the TPDU.

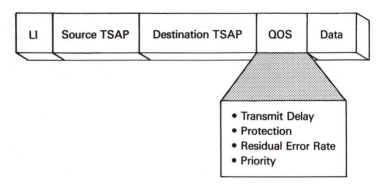

FIGURE 7-20. The Connectionless-Mode TPDU

SUMMARY AND CONCLUSIONS

The transport layer is the first layer in the OSI protocol stack, responsible for end-to-end data integrity across different machines and/or networks. However, it does not recover from its own disconnects, in which case data could be lost. The prevailing transport protocol in the industry is transmission control protocol (TCP). This standard is not part of OSI. The OSI transport layer standards are based on the ISO/CCITT specifications. They are organized around five classes to permit a user and network administrator a wide variety of options in obtaining services. Transport protocol class 4 is aligned somewhat with the TCP protocol, although it is richer in function. Eventually, but not any time soon, transport protocol class 4 will replace TCP.

The Transport Layer

CHAPTER 8

The Session Layer

INTRODUCTION

To gain an insight into the functions of this layer, let us assume you must design a system that manages the interactions between applications programs. For example, an application program must communicate and exchange information (such as files or an inquiry/response transaction) with other applications. This example assumes that the transfer of data is to take place between a host computer and a number of remote computers.

What would you consider to be the design issues? How would you coordinate the activities of each user application with the host application? Would you allow each application to send a file or transaction at any time? Should you provide periodic checkpoints to allow the applications to "back up" and recover from processing problems? Would you permit the applications to issue "Reads" and "Writes" at any time (full duplex), or would they have to restrict their input/output executions to an alternate two-way process (half duplex)? How do you pass control to the applications in a half-duplex exchange? Is it even necessary?

We could go on with more of these questions, but the point should be clear that designing a system to control the sessions between applications is a challenging task. Fortunately, several procedures have stood the test of time and are now available in vendors' products or in the standards organizations' specifications. These procedures and products are generally referred to as the session layer.

The session layer is so named because it manages the user application-to-application sessions. Most session layer systems provide the following services:

- Coordinating the exchange of data between applications by logically connecting and releasing sessions (also called dialogues) between the applications.
- Providing sychronization points (called checkpoints in some vendors' literature) to structure the exchange of data.
- Imposing a structure on the user application interactions.
- If necessary, providing a convention for users to take turns in exchanging data.
- Using a synchronization point to ensure all data units have been received by the applications before a session releases (a "graceful close").

Support from the Transport Layer

The session layer rests above the lower four layers of OSI and obtains a variety of support services from these layers. At a minimum, the session layer assumes it has a connection-oriented service from the transport layer. Typically, a session layer connection is mapped directly onto a transport layer connection. As shown in Figure 8-1(a), the session layer operates a session connection as a one-to-one relationship with the underlying transport layer connection. This approach is attractive because the session layer can avail itself of the transport layer flow control services.

It is also possible for multiple sessions to share one transport connection [see Figure 8-1(b)]. For example, a short session between two computers to verify a credit card sale need not terminate the transport connection, as it will likely be needed again a short time later to support another credit card transaction. It makes more sense to use an ongoing transport connection, since it obviates the overhead of continually reestablishing the connection.

It should not be inferred that we are multiplexing multiple sessions onto the transport connection. Rather, we are using the transport layer connection sequentially. Multiplexing at this layer is left for further study, and in any event, it should be approached carefully. For example, multiplexing a file transfer job with a short credit card job might delay the latter job, because the file transfer entails using the transport connection for an extended period with the possible requirement for different quality of service parameters (transit time, throughput, etc.).

It is also conceivable that one session could span multiple transport connections [see Figure 8-1(c)]. While this possibility is remote, it could happen if a long-running job between machines stays active when lower layers fail or are brought down for maintenance reasons. This scenario is certainly plausible if the transport layer is running on a different machine than the layers above it (for example, the transport layer could be operating in a front-end processor and the upper layers could be operating in the host).

To re-emphasize an important rule, a transport connection should support only one session connection. This is because different session connections may

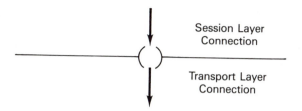

Session Layer
Connection

Transport Layer
Connection

(a) A One-to-One Relationship

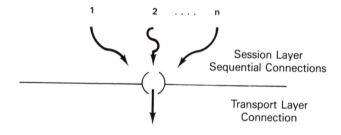

1   2 . . . . n

Session Layer
Sequential Connections

Transport Layer
Connection

(b) An *n*-to-One Relationship

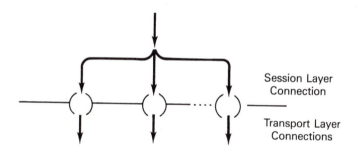

Session Layer
Connection

Transport Layer
Connections

(c) One-to-*n* Relationship

FIGURE 8-1. Transport and Session Layer Relationships

require different quality of service operations. Moreover, this rule assures the session layer that it has more control over the transport layer's operations.

A transport layer connection must be available before session data units can be exchanged. When the session users terminate their connection, the supporting transport connection has the option of also terminating or remaining active. If the transport connection is maintained, it can then support another session layer connection *if* it can support the session layer's requested quality of service operations.

It is quite important to understand that the session layer differs signifi-cantly from the transport layer in the way it releases a connection. The trans-port layer performs an abrupt release, which can cause the loss of any data in transit. In contrast, the session layer can be structured to perform an orderly release (a graceful close) so that all session service data units (SSDUs) can be delivered before the session is terminated.

Yet another aspect of the session layer should be emphasized. This layer permits the exchange of data to occur on a full-duplex or a half-duplex basis. Some applications need to operate on a half-duplex basis. For example, in an inquiry/response application, the inquiry is sent to a computer and the applica-tion waits for the reply before any other actions take place. The terms half du-plex and full duplex at this layer have nothing to do with the manner in which data are actually exchanged on the communications channel, but are used to describe how the dialogue between the two applications is managed.

The lower levels of a network generally assume they must execute rather elaborate mechanisms to provide reliable service to the upper layers. In con-trast, the session layer assumes it is receiving reliable data units from the net-work, so it uses few error-control procedures.

One last comparison of the transport and session layers is in order. The transport layer issues and receives two kinds of data units, regular and expe-dited. The session layer supports these data units and also the typed and capa-bility data units. These data units are covered later in this chapter.

Table 8-1 lists the transport layer primitives that are used by the session layer.

MAJOR SESSION SERVICES

CCITT X.215 and X.225 define the service definitions and protocol specifica-tions, respectively, for the exchange of data between session service (SS) layer users. The principal parts of X.215 describe how the users establish a session

TABLE 8-1. Session Layer Use of Transport Layer Primitives

Transport Layer Primitive	Parameters
T-CONNECT request/indication	Called Address, Calling Address, Expedited Data Option, QOS, TS User-Data
T-CONNECT response/confirm	QOS, Responding Address, Expedited Data Option, TS User-Data
T-DATA request/indication	TS-User-Data
T-EXPEDITED-DATA request/indication	TS-User-Data
T-DISCONNECT request	TS-User-Data
T-DISCONNECT indication	Disconnect Reason, TS-User-Data

through the session layer, exchange and account for data through synchroniza-tion points, use tokens to negotiate several types of dialogues, and release the session. X.225 describes the functions and protocol data units of the session layer. The ISO publishes comparable standards as DIS 8326 and DIS 8327.

Tokens

A key aspect to session level activities is the *token*. A token gives a user the exclusive right to use a service and is dynamically assigned to one user at a time to permit the use of certain services. For example, a user can issue the Please token to another user to request the transfer of one or more tokens (that is to say, the use of a service or services). The relinquishing user may respond by passing back a Give token. If tokens are not available when the session is established between the session users, they remain unavailable for the session.

Tokens are used to support dialogue management and full-duplex and half-duplex connections. They are used to determine which type of token function is being requested and/or granted.

Tokens are not used for all session service functions but are invoked for four specific functions:

- Data exchange procedures
- Releasing certain user dialogues
- Supporting synchronization functions
- Supporting an activity across more than one synchronization function

Synchronization Services

Synchronization (sync) points are another important part of the session layer. They are used to coordinate the exchange of data between session service users. Synchronization services are like checkpoint/restarts in a file transfer or trans-action transfer operation. They allow the users to (a) define and isolate points in an ongoing data exchange, and (b) if necessary, back up to a point for recovery purposes.

The session services do not actually save the session service data units (SSDUs) and do not perform the recovery operations. These activities are the responsibility of the application layer or the end-user application. The session layer merely decrements a number back to the sync point and the user must apply it to determine where to begin recovery procedures.

One might question why synchronization services are even needed. After all, the transport layer is responsible for delivering the data units safely to the session layer. However, consider the following scenario. The transport layer has passed the protocol data units for a data base update successfully to the upper layers, and the data are queued into a buffer. Unfortunately, the data base update file is loaded erroneously by an operator, and some of the data units are applied incorrectly. Obviously, the transport layer performed its job, and it cannot be faulted for the operator error and deficient software at the upper layers. In this example, the applications can use synchronization values (sequential numbers appended to each data unit) to reset the session activity back to a previous point and continue from there.

We now examine synchronization points in more detail. After defining some key terms, we show a real-life example of how sync points can be used.

Two types of synchronization points are available, minor and major. As Figure 8-2 illustrates, the sync points are used in conjunction with the following dialogue units and activities:

- *Major sync point.* Structures the exchange of data into a series of dialogue units. Each major sync point must be confirmed and the user is limited to specific services until a confirmation is received. The sending user can send no more data until the receiving user acknowledges a major synchronization point. A major sync point allows related units of work to be clustered together.

- *Dialogue unit.* An atomic action in which all communications within it are separated from any previous or succeeding communications. A major sync point delineates the beginning and ending of a dialogue unit.

- *Minor sync point.* Structures the exchange of data within a dialogue unit. This is more flexible than a major sync point. For example, each sync point may or may not be confirmed, and it is possible to resynchronize to any minor sync point within the dialogue unit. A confirmation confirms all previous minor sync points.

- *Activity.* Consists of one or more dialogue units. An activity is a logical set of related tasks; for example, the transfer of a file with related records. A useful feature of the dialogue unit is that it can be interrupted and later resumed. Each activity is completely independent of any other activity.

The OSI Model does not specify what types of applications are to be managed with synchronization points and dialogue units. As examples, a file trans-

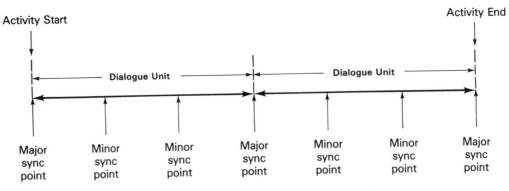

FIGURE 8-2. Session Layer Operations

The Session Layer

fer system could be managed with each complete file considered as a dialogue unit and delineated with major sync points, or an inquiry/response could be managed with each individual transaction delineated with a major sync point.

Resynchronization. A resynchronization allows the session service users to reestablish a logical sequence of operations, typically following a major sync point. It purges any undelivered data and sets a synchronization point number to a new value.

Resynchronization can be initiated by either user to provide one of three options: (a) the *set* option is invoked by the user to set the synchronization point serial number to any value the user chooses; (b) the *abandon* option sets the number to an unused value; (c) the *reset* option sets the synchronization point serial number to a used value. The value must be greater than a number which identifies the last major synchronization point. The reset is the most commonly used option of the three.

Activity Rules. The session layer restricts a session connection to one activity at a time, but several consecutive activities can be invoked during the session connection. An activity can perform resynchronization because it can span more than one session connection. It can be interrupted and reinvoked during another session connection.

The use of activities infers a *quarantine* service capability. This term describes the process of accumulating SSDUs and releasing them only upon permission from the user. This service is not mentioned in the CCITT documents, because it was realized that the activity management functions could be used to do quarantining. However, the ISO 7498 document does specify quarantine service.

QUALITY OF SERVICE PARAMETERS AT THE SESSION LEVEL

Like the lower layers of OSI, the session layer defines a number of quality of service (QOS) parameters that are negotiated between the service user and the service provider. These QOS parameters are listed and described in Table 8-2. Previous chapters in this book explain most of these parameters more thoroughly, and the reader can refer to them by examining the material titled "Quality of Service" in the table of contents.

SESSION LAYER PRIMITIVES

As you probably realize, all the layer services are provided by the use of primitives passed from the presentation and application layers. We have just described the most commonly used primitives used at the transport layer. The primitives for the session layer are listed in Table 8-3.

TABLE 8-2. Quality of Service Parameters for Session Services Layer

Service Performance Parameters

Connection establishment delay	Maximum acceptable delay between the connect request and connect confirm primitives.
Connection establishment failure probability	Ratio of total connection failures to connection attempts.
Throughput	Number of data octets transmitted between SS-users within a specified time.
Transit delay	Delay between completion of request primitive and corresponding indication primitive.
Residual error rate	Ratio of total incorrect, lost, or duplicate data units to total units transmitted.
Transfer failure probability	Ratio of transfer failures to total transfers during a specific period.
Session connection release delay	Maximum acceptable delay between abort request and its corresponding release.
Session connection release failure probability	Ratio of total abort requests resulting in session failure to total abort requests.
Session connection resilience	Probability of a non-orderly release of a session connection.

Other Session Service Characteristics

Session connection protection	Extent of effort to prevent unauthorized monitoring or manipulation of data.
Session connection priority	Extent of importance of session.
Extended control	Options to use resyncs, aborts, activity interrupts, activity discards due to problems (Note 1).
Optimized dialogue transfer	Option of concatenating certain service requests (SSDUs) and sending them as one unit (Note 1).

Note 1: These parameters are not passed to the transport layer. All others are.

The reader may wonder why the data exchange primitives provide no confirmation services. First, the session layer uses the transport layer, which can be structured to provide for the guarantee and confirmation of delivery. Second, the use of token rights for sending data keeps both users informed about the passing of data. Third, a sync point primitive can be issued if a confirmation is needed.

The Session Layer

TABLE 8-3. Session Layer Primitives

Primitive	Parameters
S-CONNECT request	identifier, calling SSAP, called SSAP, quality of service, requirements, serial number, token, data
S-CONNECT indication	identifier, calling SSAP, called SSAP, quality of service, requirements, serial number, token, data
S-CONNECT response	identifier, responding address, result, quality of service, requirements, serial number, token, data, result
S-CONNECT confirm	identifier, responding address, result, quality of service, requirements, serial number, token, data, result
S-DATA request	data
S-DATA indication	data
S-EXPEDITED-DATA request	data
S-EXPEDITED-DATA indication	data
S-TYPED-DATA request	data
S-TYPED-DATA indication	data
S-CAPABILITY-DATA request	data
S-CAPABILITY-DATA indication	data
S-TOKEN-GIVE request	tokens, data
S-TOKEN-GIVE indication	tokens, data
S-TOKEN-PLEASE request	tokens, data
S-TOKEN-PLEASE indication	tokens, data
S-CONTROL-GIVE request	data
S-CONTROL-GIVE indication	data
S-SYNC-MINOR request	type, serial number, data
S-SYNC-MINOR indication	type, serial number, data
S-SYNC-MINOR response	serial number, data
S-SYNC-MINOR confirm	serial number, data
S-SYNC-MAJOR request	serial number, data
S-SYNC-MAJOR indication	serial number, data
S-SYNC-MAJOR response	data
S-SYNC-MAJOR confirm	data
S-RESYNCHRONIZE request	type, serial number, tokens, data
S-RESYNCHRONIZE indication	type, serial number, tokens, data
S-RESYNCHRONIZE response	serial number, tokens, data

(continued)

TABLE 8-3.   (Continued)

Primitive	Parameters
S-RESYNCHRONIZE confirm	serial number, tokens, data
P-EXCEPTION-REPORT indication	reason
U-EXCEPTION-REPORT request	reason, data
U-EXCEPTION-REPORT indication	reason, data
S-ACTIVITY-START request	activity ID,data
S-ACTIVITY-START indication	activity ID,data
S-ACTIVITY-RESUME request	activity ID, old activity ID, serial number, old SC ID, data
S-ACTIVITY-RESUME indication	activity ID, old activity ID, serial number, old SC ID, data
S-ACTIVITY-INTERRUPT request	reason
S-ACTIVITY-INTERRUPT indication	reason
S-ACTIVITY-INTERRUPT response	data
S-ACTIVITY-INTERRUPT confirm	data
S-ACTIVITY-DISCARD request	reason, data
S-ACTIVITY-DISCARD indication	reason, data
S-ACTIVITY-DISCARD response	data
S-ACTIVITY-DISCARD confirm	data
S-ACTIVITY-END request	serial number, data
S-ACTIVITY-END indication	serial number, data
S-ACTIVITY-END response	data
S-ACTIVITY-END confirm	data
S-RELEASE request	data
S-RELEASE indication	data
S-RELEASE response	result, data
S-RELEASE confirm	result, data
U-ABORT request	data
U-ABORT indication	data
P-ABORT indication	reason

It is important to note that, with two exceptions, the quality of service parameters (QOS) are passed directly to the transport layer. The reader should compare the session layer QOS parameters with the transport layer QOS parameters described in Chapter 7.

Some of the parameters have been explained in previous discussions. Those that have not been covered are:

- *Connection Identifier:* Unique identifiers for the session connection which are unknown to the session users. They consist of a calling reference, a called reference, a common reference, and an additional reference.
- *Requirements:* The functional units which are to be requested for the session. Functional units are a convenient way to group the session layer services (see Tables 8-4 and 8-5 and the subsequent discussion on functional units).
- *Serial number:* The proposed initial synchronization number.
- *Token:* The initial side for the assignment of tokens. For each available token, this value can be: (1) the requestor side (that is, the initiator of the connection) gets the token(s); (2) the acceptor side (that is, the acceptor of the connection) gets the token(s); (3) the acceptor chooses the side for the initial assignment of token(s); (4) unavailable, so either side can use the tokens at any time.
- *Result:* The indication of success or failure of a connect attempt, and the reason if the result is a reject.
- *Reason:* The reason for use of several of the primitives.

HOW THE SESSION SERVICES COULD BE USED

The previous section introduced the major concepts of the session layer. This section shows how these concepts can be placed into operation. Let us assume an organization in Washington, D.C., must receive data each day from its twelve districts located throughout the country. (This example is an actual operation common in both, government and private enterprise.) The nature of the data is such that a district must successfully complete its transfer before another district can begin its transmission.

The central computing facility and the districts use session layer services to structure the file transfers as follows: The central site considers the twelve file transfers as one session level activity. Due to the nature of the activity service, the central site can interrupt the file transfer service (to perform maintenance in the evening, service higher priority jobs, etc.) and later resume the service without any loss of synchronization.

Within the activity are twelve dialogue units that begin and end with major synchronization points. The central site establishes and coordinates the sync point numbers to segregate the files from each district into a dialogue unit. This approach assures the districts and the central site that a file has been received and accepted from each district before another file is transmitted.

Within each dialogue, the specific district and central site use minor synchronization points to obtain flexible back-up and recovery options. Since each file transfer is quite time consuming, it makes sense to use the minor sync points during the transfer to prevent the retransmission of large amounts of data.

We see that this operation uses many of the features of the session layer.

It should also be obvious to the reader that the session layer services can be quite valuable to the end user. With this thought in mind, we now begin a more detailed analysis of the session layer protocols.

FUNCTIONAL UNITS

The *functional unit* concept is a key aspect of the session layer. It is used to define and group related services offered by the layer. Presently, the session layer provides twelve functional unit services. Table 8-4 describes these units and Table 8-5 lists the actual services associated with each unit. We examine these services in the following sections of this chapter.

SESSION SERVICE PHASES

The session service layer is divided into three phases, and primitives are used to manage them:

1. Session connection establishment phase
2. Data transfer phase
   Token management
   Synchronization management
   Resynchronization management
   Activity Management
   Exception reporting
3. Session connection release phase.

Session Connection Establishment Phase

This phase establishes a connection between two session service (SS) users. During the phase, the tokens and parameters to be used are negotiated between the SS-users. This phase performs the following functions:

- Mapping session layer addresses onto transport layer addresses
- Selecting transport layer QOS
- Negotiating session layer parameters
- Transferring session service access points (SSAPs)
- Distinguishing between session connections
- Transferring a small amount of user data

Figure 8-3 depicts the sequence of primitive exchanges to effect the session establishment. (A later section in this chapter is devoted to a more thor-

TABLE 8-4. Session Services Functional Units

Kernel	Provides five non-negotiable services.
Half-duplex	Alternate two-way transmission of data between SS-users. Data sent by owner of data token.
Duplex	Simultaneous two-way transmission of data between SS-users.
Typed data	Transfer of data with no token restrictions.
Exceptions	Reporting of exceptional situations by either SS-user or SS-provider.
Negotiated release	Releasing a session through orderly (normal) measures or by passing tokens.
Minor synchronize	Invoking a minor sync point.
Major synchronize	Invoking a major sync point.
Resynchronize	Reestablish communications and reset connection.
Expedited data	Transferring data that is free from token and flow control restrictions.
Activity management	Providing several functions (see write-up) within an activity.
Capability data exchange	Exchanging a limited amount of data while not operating within an activity.

TABLE 8-5. Session Layer Functional Units and Associated Services

Functional Unit	Associated Services
Kernel	Session connection, Normal data transfer, Orderly release, U-abort, P-abort
Half-duplex	Give tokens, Please tokens
Duplex	No additional service
Typed data	Typed data transfer
Exceptions	Provider exception reporting, user exception reporting
Negotiated release	Orderly release, Give tokens, Please tokens
Minor synchronize	Minor sync point, Give tokens, Please tokens
Major synchronize	Major sync point, Give tokens, Please tokens
Resynchronize	Resynchronize
Expedited data	Expedited data transfer
Activity management	Activity start, Activity resume, Activity interrupt, Activity discard, Activity end, Give tokens, Please tokens, Give control
Capability data exchange	Capability data exchange

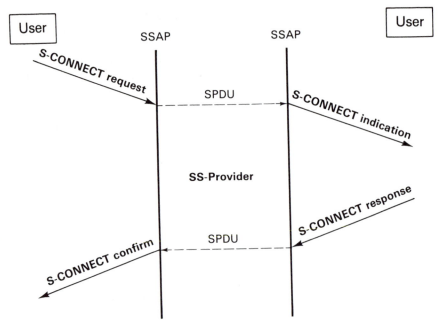

FIGURE 8-3. Session Layer Primitives and Protocol Data Units (Connection Management)

ough review of all the primitives.) The primitives carry the negotiable parameters needed to support the connection. Presently, nine parameters are used, although not all of them are required in each primitive. A brief description of these primitive parameters follows. Tables 8-3, 8-4, and 8-5 are provided to assist the reader in understanding the session layer operations. It is recommended you study their contents as you read this section.

> Session connection identifier
> Calling SSAP address
> Called SSAP address
> Result
> Quality of service
> Session requirements
> Initial synchronization point serial number
> Initial assignment of token
> SS-user data

The session connection identifier calling SSAP address, and called SSAP address are used to identify the SS-users and the SSAPs. They consist of the calling and called references, a common reference, and additional reference information, if necessary.

The result parameter provides information about the acceptance or rejection of the connection establishment request. The reasons for the rejection may also be provided (such as SS-provider busy, called SS-user is unavailable, unknown SSAP, etc.).

The quality of service (QOS) parameters (described earlier) define the services the SS-provider is to provide to the SS-users. Once the connection is negotiated and accepted, the communicating SS-users know the characteristics of their session with each other. The QOS parameters are either negotiated during the connection establishment or set up on an ongoing basis. If a user has different session QOS profiles with a variety of other users, it is possible to request the QOS based on the individual user-to-user session.

Several of the QOS parameters are used in other layers and others are unique to the session layer. Since they are directly supported by the transport layer, the transport layer must agree to their use. The initial synchronization point number is the proposed initial sync value (0 to 999999). This value is used for the major sync, minor sync, and resync functional units. The initial assignment of tokens contains the SS-user sides to which the tokens are initially assigned. The SS-user data is a parameter containing user data. It ranges from 1 to 512 octets.

As with the lower layers of OSI, the service provider and the other service user can reject the connection request with an appropriate primitive.

Data Transfer Phase

The data transfer phase is used to transfer data between two SS-users. The operations in this phase can be conveniently categorized by six major services. In this section, we examine each of them.

- Data Transfer Services
- Token Services
- Synchronization Services
- Resynchronization Service
- Activity Services
- Exception (error) Reporting Services

For the *Data Transfer Service*, session data units (see Figure 8-4) can be transferred in one of four ways. The first two ways are the normal or expedited rate. The latter option is free from any token control and flow control restrictions, but the SSDU is restricted to 14 octets of user data.

In the third method, data units can be transferred as typed data transfers. This option is subject to the same flow control restrictions as the normal rate but is not subject to token restrictions. This feature can be used in any manner the user chooses. It is often invoked to transfer "out-of-band" control information. Typed data can carry unlimited amounts of data and is not acknowledged.

Why would one wish to use the typed data option? As an example, let us

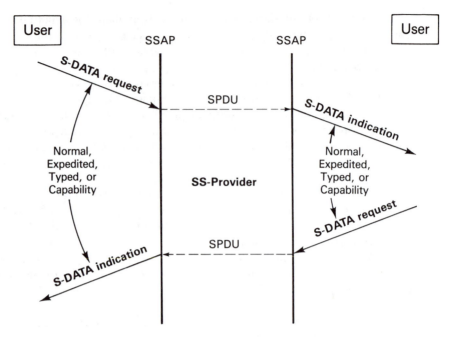

FIGURE 8-4. Session Layer Data Transfer

assume layer 7 needs to perform an error recovery operation. With typed data it can do so without considering the location of the data token. Indeed, the location of the data token should have nothing to do with error recovery at another layer.

The fourth data transfer option is the capability data exchange service. It allows SS-users to exchange data outside an established activity (no activity is in progress). In the file transfer example, this service might be invoked between the districts and the central site in order to exchange control information. Capability data is acknowledged.

With the *Token Service*, a user has the exclusive right to use certain services of the SS-provider. Four tokens are used to invoke these services:

- *Data Token.* Manages a half-duplex connection in which the users take turns passing the token to each other to send data.
- *Release Token.* Releases a connection.
- *Sync-Minor Token.* Manages the setting of minor synchronization points.
- *Sync-Major Token.* Manages the setting of major synchronization points.

The use of tokens must be negotiated during the connection establishment phase. A token is always in one of the following states.

The Session Layer

- *Available.* Assigned to a user who then has exclusive rights to a service.
- *Not Available.* Neither user has a right to the service but the token services are defined as:

    Inherently available. Used for data transfer and release tokens.

    Not available. Used for synchronization and activities.

Figure 8-5 provides an example of a typical connection between two users. Notice the use of the typed data exchange and tokens to govern the half-duplex dialogue. The figure shows how the Please token service is used to request the

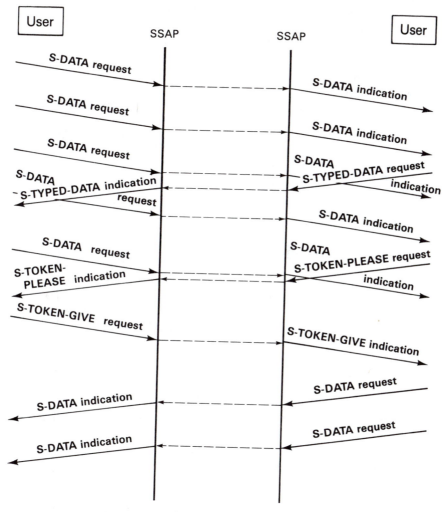

FIGURE 8–5. Tokens and Typed Data Service Definitions (SPDUs not shown)

transfer of one or more tokens. The Give token surrenders the token(s). A third option called the Give Control service (not shown in Figure 8-5) allows an SS-user to surrender all available tokens to the other SS-user.

The *Synchronization and Resynchronization Services* are used for managing the ongoing activities and for error recovery. As we learned earlier, the major synchronization point service can be used to completely separate the data flow before and after a major synchronization point. After the SS-user issues the S-SYNC-MAJOR request, it may not initiate any other normal activities until the S-SYNC-MAJOR confirm is received. The SS-user may issue other "special" requests such as giving tokens, aborts, activity interrupts, etc. Likewise, the SS-user receiving the S-SYNC-MAJOR indication is restricted from initiating any syncs, activity interrupts, or releases until it issues a S-SYNC-MAJOR response. This convention allows the SS-users to have a period of no data flow in which to determine whether the communications flow is correct and continuous.

Figure 8-6 illustrates the use of a major sync point. User A begins the operation by issuing a S-SYNC-MAJOR request. At this time, A cannot send any data units until the request is confirmed. Upon receiving the S-SYNC-

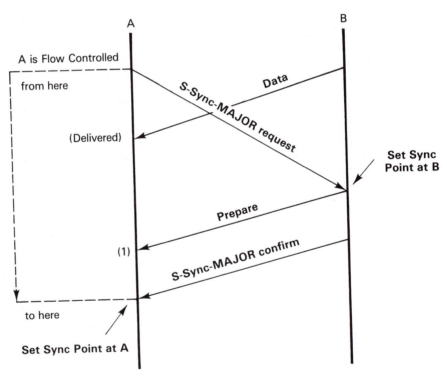

Note 1: Deliver any PDUS that were issued by B before the Prepare and hold any that were issued after the Prepare.

FIGURE 8-6. Synchronization Operations

MAJOR indication, user B's sync point is set. It then issues a Prepare SPDU by utilizing the transport layer expedited flow option. This unit is coded to alert the receiver to expect a sync point confirm or the initialization of resynchronization services. In this example, we assume it is coded to alert user A to expect a sync point confirm.

Upon receiving the Prepare signal, A knows to hold any new data units that are issued after the issuance of the Prepare data unit and to accept any late arriving data units that were issued before the issuance of the Prepare data unit. Next, B issues an S-SYNC-MAJOR response which, when received at A as an S-SYNC-MAJOR confirm, sets the sync point at A. Notice that both A and B now have sync points consistent with each other.

In addition to the major and minor synchronization point services, the resynchronize service is available to the SS-users. It is typically invoked following an error or disagreement between the SS-users. Its use sets the sync point number to an agreed value and the session to an agreed state. This service purges all undelivered data.

The process for resynchronization allows for three options (see Figure 8-7):

Abandon. Resynchronize the session connection to a new sync point number greater than or equal to the next sync point number. Do not recover; abort the current dialogue, but do not abort the connection.

Restart. Return to an agreed sync point, as long as it is greater than the last confirmed major sync point.

Set. Set the sync point number to any value. Do not recover; abort the current dialogue, but do not abort the connection.

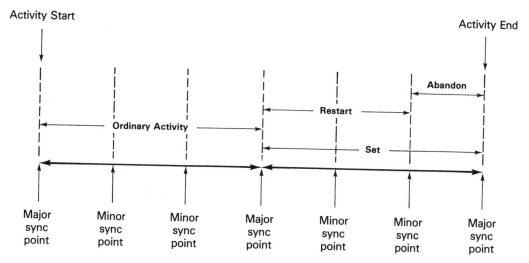

FIGURE 8-7. Synchronization Options

The procedures for synchronization are rather complex and detailed. The reader who wishes more information on the subject may refer to Appendix 8A.

The session services layer provides two general-purpose Error Reporting Services: P-exception and U-exception. The SS-provider uses the P-exception reporting service to notify the SS-users of any situations not covered by the other services. The P-exception forbids the users to initiate any other service until the error is cleared. They may do so by taking one of four actions: (1) resynchronization, (2) an abort, (3) an activity interrupt or discard, or (4) giving the data token. With the P-exception services, the SS-provider discards all outstanding data units.

The U-exception service is invoked by the SS-user to report an error condition. This service uses similar procedures as its SS-provider counterpart, the P-exception service. Up to 512 octets of data can be placed into the primitive and protocol data unit to explain the problem. The contents are user-specific.

The *Activity Service* is used to manage activities. The overall service is comprised of five major functions which are summarized in Table 8-6.

The interrupt and discard activity services recommend the SS-user that initiates the request to provide a reason for the invocation of the service. A reason parameter is associated with the request primitive. Its value may be set to indicate: (a) SS-user may not be handling data properly, (b) local SS-user error, (c) sequence error, (d) demand data token, (e) unrecoverable procedure error, (f) and a nonspecific error.

The initiation and conclusion of an activity for one user could conflict with a sync point request from another user. To prevent confusion, the standards require a user to hold the synchronization tokens and the data token before invoking an activity or a sync point. Of course, if one user wants to do something relating to an activity and the other user wants to perform a minor sync point, both users could possibly enter into a loop of incessantly sending the S-TOKEN-PLEASE to each other. One solution is to allow only a primary user (for example, the host computer) to invoke activities and give up tokens. This approach reduces flexibility but provides a clear level of responsibility to the session layer users.

TABLE 8-6. Session Layer Activity Services

Activity Start Service	Starts a new activity. Sync point value is set to 1. Only used when no activity is in progress.
Activity Interrupt Service	Terminates the current activity. Work is not lost and may be resumed later.
Activity Resume Service	Resumes a previously interrupted activity.
Activity Discard Service	Terminates the current activity. Previous work is canceled.
Activity End Service	Ends an activity and sets a major synchronization point.

Session Connection Release Phase

The session connection release phase is achieved in one of three ways: (a) orderly release; (b) U-abort; (c) P-abort (see Figure 8-8). The orderly release service allows the session connection to be released cooperatively between the two SS-users with complete accounting of all data. This means that, unlike the lower layers of OSI, the session layer can ensure that all in-transit data are delivered and accepted by the service users before the connection is released.

The release is subject to the token rules that are listed in Table 8-7 (discussed in more detail in the next section of this chapter).

The S-RELEASE response and S-RELEASE confirm primitives must contain a result parameter indicating whether the release is accepted.

The U-abort and P-abort services are used by the SS-users and SS-provider,

TABLE 8-7. Session Layer Token Rules

Protocol Data Units	Type of Token			
	DATA	SYNC-MINOR	MAJOR/ACTIVITY	RELEASE
Finish	2	2	2	2
Not Finished	no	no	no	no
Data (Half-duplex)	1	no	no	no
Data (Full-duplex)	3	no	no	no
Capability	2	2	1	no
Give Token				
Data	1	no	no	no
Sync-minor	no	1	no	no
Major/Activity	no	no	1	no
Release	no	no	no	1
Please Token				
Data	0	no	no	no
Sync-minor	no	0	no	no
Major/Activity	no	no	0	no
Release	no	no	no	0
Give Tokens Confirm	2	2	1	2
Minor Sync	2	1	no	no
Major Sync	2	2	1	no
Exception Report	0	no	no	no
Exception Data	0	no	no	no
Activity Start	2	2	1	no
Activity Resume	2	2	1	no
Activity Interrupt	no	no	1	no
Activity Discard	no	no	1	no
Activity Discard	2	2	1	no

0: token available and not assigned to user who initiated service

1: token available and assigned to user who initiated service

2: token not available or token assigned to user who initiated service

3: token not available

No: No restriction

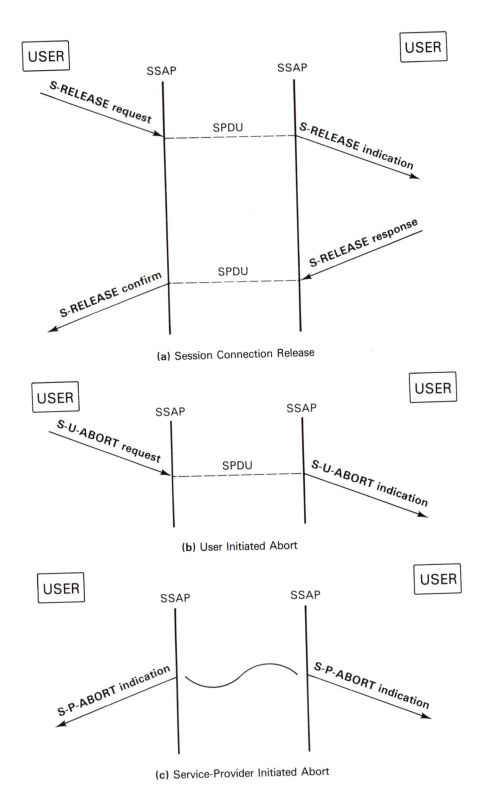

(a) Session Connection Release

(b) User Initiated Abort

(c) Service-Provider Initiated Abort

FIGURE 8-8. Session Termination Options

respectively. Both services permit the session connection to be released immediately with the loss of all undelivered data. The S-P-ABORT indication primitive must contain a reason primitive to indicate the reason for the abort.

Figure 8-9 depicts the release scenarios. Upon receiving a Finish protocol data unit from the requesting user, the responding user can issue:

1. a Not Finished SPDU, because other activity is to take place.
2. a Disconnect SPDU, which accepts the finish request and states the transport connection is to remain active (Idle, Transport Connection).
3. a Disconnect SPDU, which accepts the finish request and states the transport connection is to be disconnected (Idle only).

RULES FOR THE USE OF TOKENS

Certain tokens are associated with functional units and a session protocol machine (SPM) is allowed to send the following session protocol data units as part of a functional unit:

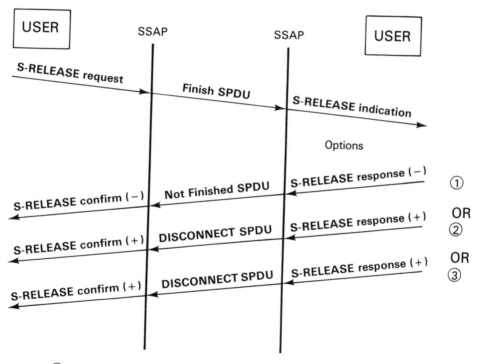

① : Refuse release, remain in data transfer state
② : Accept release, keep transport connection open
③ : Accept release, release transport connection

FIGURE 8-9. Release Scenarios

Functional Unit	Token
Negotiated release	Release token
Half-duplex	Data token
Minor synchronize	Synchronize-minor token
Major synchronize	Major/activity token
Activity management	Major/activity token

As listed in Table 8-3, three sets of primitives are used to manage tokens: (a) the S-TOKEN-PLEASE primitives, used to request a user to give up one or more tokens; (b) the S-TOKEN-GIVE, which passes listed tokens to a user; (c) the S-CONTROL-GIVE, which passes all tokens to a user.

A session protocol machine (SPM) can only send session protocol data units (SPDUs) in conformance with the rules stated in Table 8-7.

SESSION LAYER PROTOCOL DATA UNITS (SPDUs)

The session layer uses several protocol data units (PDUs) (see Figure 8-10). Three categories of PDUs exist (summarized in Table 8-8.)

- *Category O.* Mapped one-to-one onto a TSDU or concatenated with one or more Category 2 SPDUs
- *Category 1.* Always mapped one-to-one onto a TSDU
- *Category 2.* Never mapped one-to-one onto a TSDU

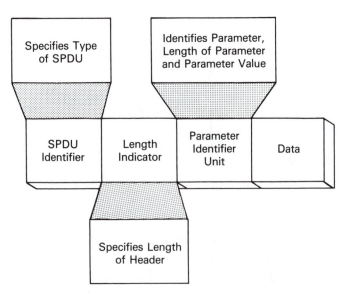

FIGURE 8-10. The Session Layer Protocol Data Unit (SPDU)

TABLE 8-8. Session Layer Protocol Data Units (SPDUs)

Category 0	Category 1	Category 2
Give Tokens	Connect	Data Transfer
Please Tokens	Accept	
		Minor Sync Point
	Refuse	Minor Sync ACK
	Finish	
	Disconnect	Major Sync Point
	Not Finished	Major Sync ACK
	Abort	
	Abort Accept	Resynchronize
		Resynchronize ACK
	Give Token Confirm	
	Give Token ACK	Activity Start
		Activity Resume
	Expedited	Activity Discard
	Prepare	Activity Discard ACK
	Typed Data	Activity Interrupt
		Activity Interrupt ACK
		Activity End
		Activity End ACK
		Capability Data
		Capability Data ACK
		Exception Report
		Exception Data

A summary of the functions of the SPDUs is provided in Table 8-9. The reader should notice the similarity between the SPDU and primitive functions. This is certainly logical, since the parameters of the primitives become the parameters of the SPDUs.

The structure of the PDU is shown in Figure 8-10. Be aware that a different PDU structure is used for each of the SDUs, but all are variations of the structure in the figure.

The SI (service identifier) field identifies the type of SPDU (connect, data token, etc.). The LI (length indicator) field represents the length of the parameter field. The parameter identification unit (PI) field contains the values used between the SS-provider to support the session layer service. Many parameters are used, some of which are explained in Table 8-10. The data (if present) are placed in the user data field.

The Prepare, Abort, Abort Accept, and Expedited Data SPDUs are sent with the T-EXPEDITED-DATA primitives if the transport layer supports expedited service. Otherwise, the Prepare SPDU cannot be used, and the Abort, Abort Accept, and Expedited Data SPDUs are transferred with the normal T-DATA primitives.

TABLE 8-9. Session Service Protocol Data Units' Functions

SPDU	Parameters	Function
Connect	Connection ID, protocol options, version number, serial number, token setting, maximum TSDU size, requirements, calling SSAP, called SSAP, user data	Initiate session connection
Accept	Same as CONNECT parameters	Establish session connection
Refuse	Connection ID, transport disconnect, requirements, version number, reason	Reject connection request
Finish	Transport disconnect, user data	Initiate orderly release
Disconnect	User data	Acknowledge orderly release
Not Finished	User data	Reject orderly release
Abort	Transport disconnect, protocol error code, user data	Abnormal connection release
Abort Accept	—	Acknowledge abort
Data Transfer	Enclosure item, user data	Transfer normal data
Expedited	User data	Transfer expedited data
Typed Data	Enclosure item, user data	Transfer typed data
Capability Data	User data	Transfer capability data
Capability Data Ack	User data	Acknowledge capability data
Give Tokens	Tokens	Transfer tokens
Please Tokens	Tokens, user data	Request token assignment
Give Token Confirm	—	Transfer all tokens
Give Tokens ACK	—	Acknowledge all tokens
Give Token Confirm	—	Transfer all tokens
Give Tokens ACK	—	Acknowledge all tokens
Minor Sync Point	Confirm required flag, serial number, user data	Define minor sync point
Minor Sync ACK	Serial number, user data	Acknowledge minor sync point
Major Sync Point	End of activity flag, serial number, user data	Define major sync point
Major Sync ACK	Serial number, user data	Acknowledge major sync point
Resynchronize	Token settings, resync type, serial number, user data	Resynchronize
Resynchronize ACK	Token settings, serial number, user data	Acknowledge resynchronize
Prepare	Type	Notify type SPDU is coming (Note 1)
Exception Report	SPDU bit pattern	Protocol error detected
Exception Data	Reason, user data	Put protocol in error state
Activity Start	Activity ID, user data	Signal beginning of activity
Activity Resume	Connection ID, old activity ID, new activity ID, user data	Signal resumption of activity
Activity Interrupt	Reason	Interrupt activity
Activity Interrupt ACK	—	Acknowledge interrupt
Activity Discard	Reason	Cancel activity
Activity Discard ACK	—	Acknowledge cancellation
Activity End	Serial number, user data	Signal activity end
Activity End ACK	Serial number, user data	Acknowledge activity end

Note 1: Used only with transport layer expedited data flow to alert receiver to be ready for some other action.

The Session Layer

TABLE 8-10.   Major Parameters of the SPDU

References and SSAPs	Identifies SS-users and SSAPs
Protocol Options	Indicates if concatenated SPDUs are to be used
TSDU Maximum Size	Used to negotiate the maximum TSDU size
Initial Serial Number	Value of serial number for use in sync point processing
Token Setting	Indicates initial position of tokens (release, activity, sync minor, etc.)
Session User Requirements	Identifies the functional units to be used with session
Reason Code	Identifies reason for a disconnect, abort, etc.
Transport Disconnect	Indicates if transport connection is to be kept
Enclosure Item	Identifies if data unit is the beginning, middle, or end of a segmented SSDU
Token Item	Indicates which tokens are being given by the sending-SS-user
Sync Type	Indicates if confirmation is required for a sync point SPDU
Prepare Type	Used to alert recipients to prepare for a sync or a resync

RELATIONSHIP OF SESSION LAYER SERVICES, PRIMITIVES AND SPDUs

As with the other layers of the OSI, the session layer primitives are used to create the session layer protocol data units (SPDUs). These primitives and SPDUs are used to control the services provided to the session layer users. Table 8-11 lists all the session services and their associated primitives and SPDUs.

SESSION LAYER SUBSETS

It may have occurred to the reader that the invocation of all the session layer services would likely be unnecessary for all applications. For example, our data transfers between Washington, D.C., and the districts certainly did not need all these services. In recognition of this fact, both the CCITT and the ISO divide the functional units and associated services into subsets, described in Figure 8-11. Table 8-12 and Table 8-13. The subsets are:

> *Basic Combined Subset(BCS).* Adds half-duplex and duplex functional units.

TABLE 8-11. Primitives and SPDUs

Service	Primitives	Associated SPDUs
Session Connection	S-CONNECT request	Connect
	S-CONNECT indication	Connect
	S-CONNECT (accept) response	Accept
	S-CONNECT (accept) confirm	Accept
	S-CONNECT (reject) response	Refuse
	S-CONNECT (reject) confirm	Refuse
Normal Data Transfer	S-DATA request	Data Transfer
	S-DATA indication	Data Transfer
Expedited Data Transfer	S-EXPEDITED-DATA request	Expedited Data
	S-EXPEDITED-DATA indication	Expedited Data
Typed Data Transfer	S-TYPED-DATA request	Typed Data
	S-TYPED-DATA indication	Typed Data
Capability Data Exchange	S-CAPABILITY-DATA request	Capability Data
	S-CAPABILITY-DATA indication	Capability Data
	S-CAPABILITY-DATA response	Capability Data ACK
	S-CAPABILITY-DATA confirm	Capability Data ACK
Give Tokens	S-TOKEN-GIVE request	Give Tokens
	S-TOKEN-GIVE indication	Give Tokens
Please Tokens	S-TOKEN-PLEASE request	Please Tokens
	S-TOKEN-PLEASE indication	Please Tokens
Give Control	S-CONTROL-GIVE request	Give Tokens Confirm
	S-CONTROL-GIVE indication	Give Tokens Confirm
Synchronization Point	S-SYNC-MINOR request	Minor Sync Point
	S-SYNC-MINOR indication	Minor Sync Point
	S-SYNC-MINOR response	Minor Sync ACK
	S-SYNC-MINOR confirm	Minor Sync ACK
Synchronization Point	S-SYNC-MAJOR request	Major Sync Point
	S-SYNC-MAJOR indication	Major Sync Point
	S-SYNC-MAJOR response	Major Sync ACK
	S-SYNC-MAJOR confirm	Major Sync ACK
Synchronize	S-RESYNCHRONIZE request	Resynchronize
	S-RESYNCHRONIZE indication	Resynchronize
	S-RESYNCHRONIZE response	Resynchronize ACK
	S-RESYNCHRONIZE confirm	Resynchronize ACK
Exception Report	S-P-EXCEPTION-REPORT Indication	Exception Report
Exception Reporting	S-U-EXCEPTION-REPORT request	Exception Data
	S-U-EXCEPTION-REPORT indication	Exception Data
Activity Start	S-ACTIVITY-START request	Activity Start
	S-ACTIVITY-START indication	Activity Start

The Session Layer

TABLE 8-11.   (Continued)

Service	Primitives	Associated SPDUs
Activity Resume	S-ACTIVITY-RESUME request	Activity Resume
	S-ACTIVITY-RESUME indication	Activity Resume
Activity Interrupt	S-ACTIVITY-INTERRUPT request	Activity Interrupt
	S-ACTIVITY-INTERRUPT indication	Activity Interrupt
	S-ACTIVITY-INTERRUPT response	Activity Interrupt ACK
	S-ACTIVITY-INTERRUPT confirm	Activity Interrupt ACK
Activity Discard	S-ACTIVITY-DISCARD request	Activity Discard
	S-ACTIVITY-DISCARD indication	Activity Discard
	S-ACTIVITY-DISCARD response	Activity Discard ACK
	S-ACTIVITY DISCARD confirm	Activity Discard ACK
Activity End	S-ACTIVITY-END request	Activity End
	S-ACTIVITY-END indication	Activity End
	S-ACTIVITY END response	Activity End ACK
	S-ACTIVITY END confirm	Activity End ACK
Orderly Release	S-RELEASE request	Finish
	S-RELEASE indication	Finish
	S-RELEASE (accept) response	Disconnect
	S-RELEASE (accept) confirm	Disconnect
	S-RELEASE (reject) response	Not Finished
	S-RELEASE (reject) confirm	Not Finished
U-Abort	S-U-ABORT request	Abort
	S-U-ABORT indication	Abort
P-Abort	S-P-ABORT indication	Abort

Basic Synchronized Subset(BSS). Adds the functional units needed for synchronization activities. This subset is used in many applications.

Basic Activity Subset (BAS). Uses most of the functional units.

AN EXAMPLE OF SESSION LAYER OPERATIONS

Since the session layer is the layer tasked with providing a graceful close of communications and operations between two applications, it seems appropriate to highlight this function. Figure 8-12 and Tables 8-14 and 8-15 are used to show how the session layer achieves a graceful close. This explanation is derived from the ISO and CCITT session layer documents and serves also to explain to the reader the OSI state diagrams, protocol machines, state tables, event

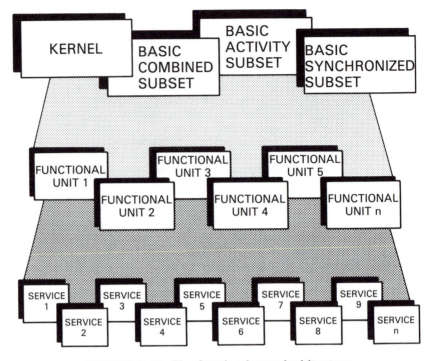

FIGURE 8-11. The Session Layer Architecture

TABLE 8-12. Session Layer Subsets and Functional Units

Functional Unit	Basic Combined Subset (BCS)	Basic Synchronized Subset (BSS)	Basic Activity Subset (BAS)
Kernel	X	X	X
Half Duplex	X	X	X
Duplex	X	X	
Typed Data		X	X
Exceptions			X
Negotiated Release		X	
Minor Synchronize		X	X
Major Synchronize		X	
Resynchronize		X	
Expedited Data			
Activity Management			X
Capability Data Exchange			X

TABLE 8-13. Session Layer Subsets and Services

Service	Kernel	Basic Combined Subset (BCS)	Basic Synchronized Subset (BSS)	Basic Activity Subset (BAS)
Session Connection	X	X	X	X
Normal Data Transfer	X	X	X	X*
Orderly Release	X	X	X	X
U-Abort	X	X	X	X
P-Abort	X	X	X	X
Give Tokens		X	X	X
Please Tokens		X	X	X
Expedited Data Transfer				
Typed Data Transfer			X	X
Capability Data Exchange				X
Minor Synchronization Point			X	X
Major Synchronization Point			X	
Resynchronize			X	
Provider Exception Reporting				X
User Exception Reporting				X
Activity Start				X
Activity Resume				X
Activity Interrupt				X
Activity Discard				X
Activity End				X
Give Control				X

*Half duplex

lists, predicates, and action tables that are used. (These topics are introduced in Chapter 1.)

Table 8-14 shows the relevant extractions from the session layer state tables dealing with a session layer disconnection. The reader should examine this table during the analysis that follows.

Our explanation assumes the users have previously agreed to a negotiated release and the token settings have been established to permit a release.

The SS-user asks the sending session protocol machine (SPM) to release the connection by sending it the S-RELEASE request primitive. The SPM accepts the primitive, constructs the Finish SPDU (FN-nr), and sends it to the transport layer through the T-DATA request primitive.

These events are modeled as State Table #1 in Table 8-14. The predicates p63 and p64 are shorthand notations that stipulate the rules for the token settings and the setting of several variables. All these settings determine the exact nature of the release. The entry FN-nr means the Finish SPDU is issued with a code stating that the transport connection is not to be reused. The specific ac-

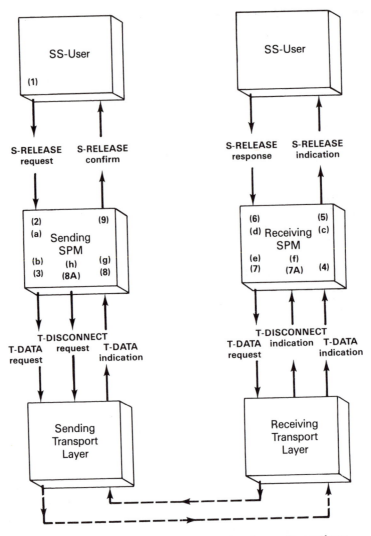

FIGURE 8–12. Example of Session Layer Operations

tions entry, [8], signifies that the variable Vtrr is set to true, which is used to govern how the transport connection will be handled. The last entry, STA03, explains that the SPM now enters state 3: await a Disconnect SPDU (DN).

The receiving SPM accepts the Finish SPDU and forwards any user data that was contained in the data unit to its SS-user through the S-RELEASE indication primitive. These actions are modeled as State Table #2 in Table 8-14. The p68 predicate describes the token and variable settings. The state table also shows that the S-RELEASE indication is sent to the SS-user, the [8] action is

The Session Layer

TABLE 8-14. Relevant State Table Entries for a Session Layer Disconnect

	State Table #1	
Event	S-Release request	**State** STA713 (Data Transfer) p63& ∧p64 FN-nr [8] STA03

	State Table #2	
Event	FN-nr	**State** STA713 (Data Transfer) p68 S-RELEASE indication [8] STA09

	State Table #3	
Event	S-Release response+	**State** STA09 (Await S-RELEASE response) p66 DN [4] STA16

	State Table #4	
Event	DN	**State** STA16 (Await T-DISCONNECT. indication) [3] STA01

	State Table #5	
Event	TDISind	**State** STA03 (Await Disconnect PDU) p66 S-RELEASE confirm T-DISCONNECT request STA01

TABLE 8-15.   Example of Session Layer Operations

Actions and Explanations

1. Issued if tokens are not available or tokens are assigned to SS-user who initiated the primitive.

2. Form Finish SPDU (FN-nr) from parameters in the S-RELEASE request primitive.

3. Send Finish SPDU in a T-DATA request primitive to transport layer and wait for a Disconnect, Connect, or Not Finished SPDU.

4. Receive a Finish SPDU from the transport layer.

5. Pass any user data to SS-user through the S-RELEASE indication primitive and await a response.

6. Receive the S-RELEASE response primitive and examine the "Result" field.

7. Send Disconnect SPDU in a T-DATA request primitive.

7A. Receive a T-DISCONNECT indication primitive.

8. Receive the Disconnect SPDU (DN) in a T-DATA indication primitive.

8A. Issue T-DISCONNECT indication primitive to transport layer

9. Send an S-RELEASE confirm to the SS-user and also send a T-DISCONNECT request to the transport layer.

Explanation of States

a. Accepted if in STA713: Data transfer state.

b. Enter STA03: Wait for Disconnect SPDU.

c. Enter STA09: Wait for S-RELEASE response.

d. Accepted in if STA09.

e. Enter STA16: Wait for T-DISCONNECT indication.

f. Enter STA01: Idle, no transport connection.

g. Accepted if in STA03.

h. Enter STA01: Idle, no transport connection.

---

invoked to control the transport connection, and the SPM enters STA09: await an S-RELEASE response primitive from the SS-user.

Upon receiving an S-RELEASE response primitive from the user with an "affirmative" coded in the result parameter (agreeing to the disconnect), the SPM forms the Disconnect SPDU (DN) and sends it to the transport layer with the T-DATA request. These operations are modeled in State Table #3 in Table 8-14, which shows the SPM setting timer TIM (the specific action [4]), and entering STA16 after completing these actions: wait for T-DISCONNECT indication from the transport layer; do not issue T-DISCONNECT request.

State Table #4 models the remote side in STA16. It receives the T-DISCON-NECT indication, performs specific action [3]: turn off TIM. It enters STA01: idle, no transport connection. Thus, the remote side is disconnected.

The sending SPM receives the Disconnect SPDU from the transport entity and notifies its user of the results with the S-RELEASE confirm. It sends a T-DISCONNECT request to the transport layer and enters STA01: idle, no transport connection. Thus, the local side is disconnected. These actions are modeled in State Table #5 in Table 8-14. Notice that the local side did not wait for a T-DISCONNECT indication. It went immediately to STA01.

Assuming the tokens and variable settings were established properly, the session layer has provided its users with a graceful close.

SUMMARY AND CONCLUSIONS

The session layer is the first layer in the OSI protocol suite to provide for a graceful close. Disconnects issued at lower layers will not take place until the session layer has secured all data units being transferred between the user applications. The session layer is very rich in function, and is somewhat complex. Fortunately, through the use of functional units and subsets, a user or engineer can tailor the OSI session layer to the needs of a specific application or network.

Most major manufacturers have developed their own proprietary session layer protocols. However, with the emergence of required protocol stacks, such as GOSIP and COSAC, is is likely the OSI session layer (at least the kernel) will be adapted in more commercial products.

APPENDIX 8A. AN EXAMINATION OF THE SYNCHRONIZATION PROCEDURES

This appendix is an extension of the last section in this chapter, which explained some of the more detailed operations of the session layer in regard to a disconnection operation. In this Appendix, we concentrate on the synchronization services.

Certain primitives contain the sync point serial number discussed in the main body of the text in Chapter 8. It is used to identify a synchronization point. The numbers are assigned by the SS-provider and range from 0 to 999998.

The services are provided by the SS-provider through the use of four sync variables: V(M), V(A), V(R), and Vsc. V(M) is the value of the next sync point serial number to be used. V(A) is the value of the lowest serial number to which a sync point confirm is expected. If V(A) = V(M), no confirmation is expected. V(R) is the value of the serial number to which the resync and restart is permitted. The Vsc variable determines if the SS-user has the right to issue minor sync point responses.

If Vsc = true, the SS-provider can issue a minor sync point response and V(A) = V(M). If Vsc = false, the SS-user cannot issue sync point responses.

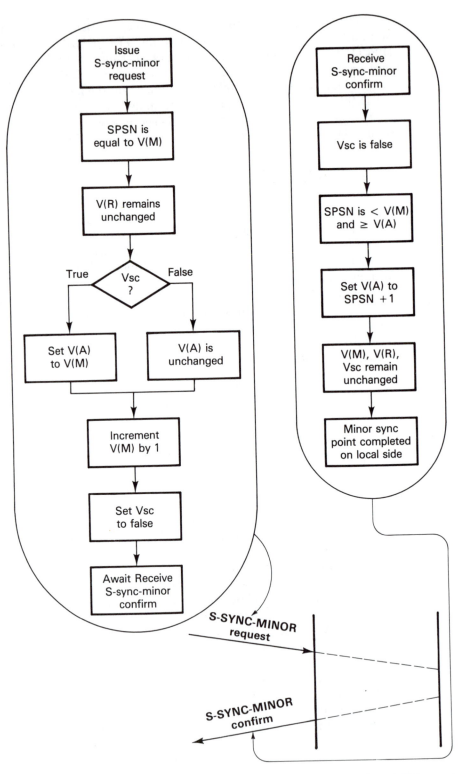

FIGURE 8A–1a. The Minor Sync Point Operations on the Local Side

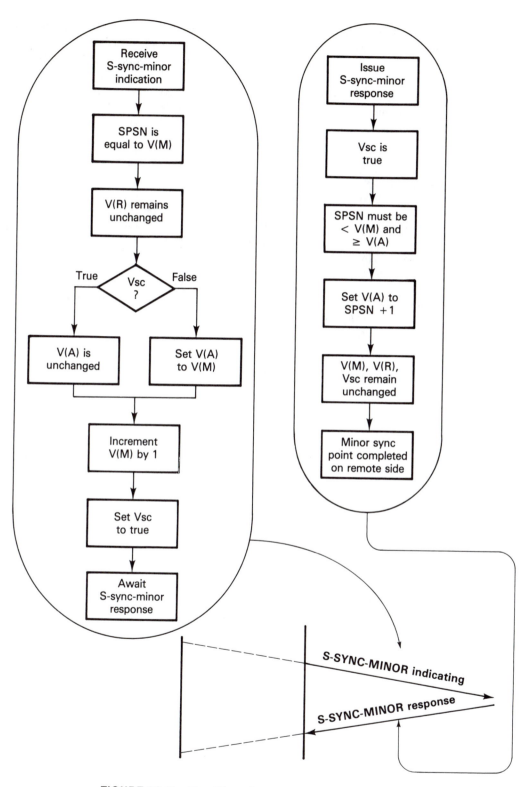

FIGURE 8A-1b. The Minor Sync Point Operations on the Remote Side.

The following paragraphs are excerpted from CCITT X.215. They describe the rules for a minor synchronization point. These rules are drawn as a flow chart in Figure 8A-1. Please study these rules and compare them to the figure.

When an S-SYNC-MINOR request is issued, the associated synchronization point serial number, which is indicated to the SS-user, is equal to V(M). V(R) remains unchanged. V(A) is set to V(M) if Vsc is true, otherwise, V(A) remains unchanged. V(M) is then incremented by one and Vsc is set to false.

When an S-SYNC-MINOR indication is received, the associated synchronization point serial number, which is indicated to the SS-user, is equal to V(M). V(R) remains unchanged. V(A) is set to V(M) if Vsc is false, otherwise it remains unchanged. V(M) is then incremented by one and Vsc is set to true.

When an S-SYNC-MINOR response is issued, Vsc is true and the associated synchronization point serial number, which is supplied by the SS-user, must be less than V(M) and equal to or greater than V(A). V(A) is set to the serial number plus one. V(M), V(R), and Vsc remain unchanged.

When an S-SYNC-MINOR confirm is received, Vsc is false and the associated synchronization point serial number, which is indicated to the SS-user, is less than V(M) and equal to or greater than V(A). V(A) is set to the serial number plus one. V(M), V(R), and Vsc remain unchanged.

CHAPTER 9

The Presentation Layer

INTRODUCTION

After using all the elaborate protocols provided by the lower levels, users may still be unable to communicate with each other. Several reasons can be cited for this problem, one of which is the different data codes, syntax, and formats that are used in different computers and user applications. To gain an appreciation of the problem, consider the following communications process between two end-user programs.

User A transmits a protocol data unit (PDU) to user B using ASCII/IA5 code for alphabetic symbols and double precision floating-point notation for the numeric symbols. We assume user B expects EBCDIC code for the alphabetic symbols and single precision floating-point notation for the numeric symbols. Obviously, the process must use conversion routines to translate between the different symbol representations.

The conversion process is simplified considerably if both users agree to a common convention for both applications—all ASCII and all double precision, for example. However, this agreement does not ensure that the same protocol data units (PDUs) can be used by both users, because they may be coded in different formats. For example, the PDU from user A could have field x placed before field y. If user B expects field y to precede field x, the wrong fields will be used by the user applications in their computations.

This situation has happened so many times in the industry that its incidence is incalculable. In some instances, the result has had dire consequences, such as errors in million-dollar transactions. It is not without good cause that many applications, such as funds transfer, airline reservations, and point-of-sale systems, contain hundreds of lines of code that perform edit checks on the data fields to detect errors and/or the "reasonableness" of the values in the data fields.

In addition, computer and communications vendors have implemented different methods for the structure of the bits within a character. Some systems transmit the low-order bits first and others transmit the high-order bits first. One may think that the solution to the low-order/high-order problem is rather straightforward: just change the positions with a conversion program. It is not so simple. For example, the conversion of binary fields must be done differently than Boolean fields, which in turn must be done differently than text fields. Moreover, the conversion program must know which type of field it is processing in order to perform the conversion correctly.

To complicate matters further, vendors use different schemes to represent symbols inside their computers. Some use one's complement arithmetic and others use two's complement.

Therefore, describing the order of the data fields, the bits within the data fields, and the structure and syntax of the protocol data units is quite important. In software terms, the users adapt the same "data description" notations to represent the structure of the data.

In some computer systems, hundreds of different data structures are used daily. For example, a commercial bank needs different data structures to support check processing, loan payments, credit card transactions, etc., and each of these applications typically needs scores of different data structures. Indeed, one of the most important jobs of the data administrator in an organization is the management of the company's data structures, and the job may require several full-time positions. In these organizations the data structures are stored, named, and cataloged in an automated library. These systems are sometimes called *meta-data* facilities because they contain data about data. Perhaps a more useful description of these systems is that they contain information about data and data structures.

Typically, an application uses these facilities when transmitting protocol data units (PDUs) by passing to them the PDU and the name of the data structure. The sending facility can then fetch the information from the library and use it to encode the protocol data unit for transmission to the lower layers of OSI. The receiving facility can use the cataloged name (which is encoded into the first part of the transmission) to determine how to decode and perhaps convert the PDU. It would make certain the data values are decoded into the proper fields (for example, the value for accounts receivable is so identified and not confused with the value for accounts payable). It would perform any necessary conversions (for example, converting one's complement to two's complement notation).

Presentation Layer Functions

The presentation layer performs the services of data structure description and representation described in the previous section. It is not concerned with knowing the meaning or semantics of the data, but is concerned with preserving the meaning and semantics of the data. Indeed, the layer would probably be more aptly named the Description/Representation layer.

This layer accepts various data types and negotiates/converts the representation. It is concerned with (a) the syntax of the data of the sending application, (b) the syntax of the data of the receiving application, and (c) the data syntax used between the presentation entities that support the sending and receiving applications.

The latter service is called a *transfer syntax*. It is negotiated between the presentation entities. Each entity chooses a syntax that is best for it to use between it and the user's syntax, and then attempts to negotiate the use of this syntax with the other presentation layer entity. Therefore, the two presentation entities must agree on a transfer syntax before data can be exchanged. Moreover, it may be necessary for the presentation layer to transform the data in order for the two users to communicate.

We are not really discussing anything revolutionary about these services. Many organizations have been using common transfer syntax and formatting conventions for years. However, each organization has used its own unique method to describe syntax and offer translations between different types of structures.

These data structures are usually created and stored in a corporate "Data Dictionary," and used as if they are a community-wide resource. Indeed they are, because their creation is quite time consuming, and programmers often forget where the numerous data structures are located or even if they exist. Usually, the important job of creating data structures and acting as their "custodian" has been given to the organization's data administration entity.

The OSI approach is to develop a standardized and limited set of syntax conventions to ease the task of describing data structures and data transfer operations between different machines and user applications. In this chapter, the prevalent ISO and CCITT presentation level protocols are examined.

ASN.1 (ABSTRACT SYNTAX NOTATION 1)

The ISO and CCITT have developed a presentation and transfer syntax to be used by application layer protocols. One widely used specification is ISO 8824. It is titled Abstract Syntax Notation One (ASN.1). In addition, ISO 8825 (the Basic Encoding Rules (BER)) provides a set of rules to develop an unambiguous bit-level description of data. That is to say, it specifies the representation of the data. In summary, ASN.1 describes an abstract syntax for data types and values and BER describes the actual representation of the data. ASN.1 is not an abstract syntax, but a language for describing abstract syntaxes. Some people use the term ASN.1 to include abstract syntax and basic encoding rules. However, the two are different from each other.

The CCITT specifies X.208 and X.209 for the presentation level. X.208 specifies the ASN.1 language and X.209 specifies the basic encoding rules for ASN.1. In the 1988 Blue Books, the X.208 specification was aligned with ISO

8824 plus ISO 8824, Addendum 1 (except 8824 does not define some conventions on describing encrypted structures). X.209 is aligned with ISO 8825 plus ISO 8825, Addendum 1. This chapter uses X.208 and X.209 to describe the OSI ANS.1 and basic encoding rules, and X.216 and X.226 to describe the presentation layer service definitions and protocol specifications.

ASN.1 has been used exclusively for the OSI upper layers, but it need not be restricted to these layers. Indeed, some of the examples in this chapter show ASN.1 with the network layer. Notwithstanding, OSI now requires that all data exchanges between the application and presentation layers must be described in abstract syntax.

If the reader chooses to study this chapter, it is essential that the coding examples be studied carefully. They are illustrations of the use of abstract syntax notation. Once you have analyzed a couple of the examples (assuming you understand them), the subject matter becomes fairly simple. We should also note that not all aspects of ASN.1 are described in this chapter; it is too varied and detailed to cover in so small a space. As suggested in previous chapters, the reader should refer to the ISO or CCITT document for the complete description of ASN.1.

PRESENTATION LAYER NOTATION

OSI Description Conventions

Each piece of information exchanged between users has a *type* and a *value*. The type is a class of information, such as integer, Boolean, octet, etc. A type can be used to describe a collection or group of values. For example, the type integer describes all values that are whole (non-decimal) numbers. The term data type is a synonym for type.

The value is an instance of the type, such as a number or a piece of alphabetic text. For example, if we describe "P of type integer," and "P: = 9," it means this instance of P has a value of 9. In an X.25 packet header, for example, the fields can be defined as of the integer or bit string type. In order for machines to know how to interpret data, they must first know the type of the data (values) to be processed. Therefore, the concept of type is very important to the presentation layer services.

ASN.1 defines three kinds of types:

- *Built-in.* Commonly used types in which a standard notation is provided
- *Character string.* Types containing elements from a known character set
- *Useful.* Types for representing dates and time and some other miscellaneous types

Built-in Types. X.208 defines several "built-in" types which are summarized in Table 9-1.

Another important feature of these standards is the use of *tags*. To distin-

TABLE 9-1. Built-in Types

Type	Function
Boolean	Identifies logical data (true or false conditions).
Integer	Identifies signed whole numbers (cardinal numbers).
Bit String	Identifies binary data (ordered sequence of 1s and 0s).
Octet String	Identifies text or data that can be described as a sequence of octets (bytes).
Null	A simple type consisting of a single value. Could be valueless placeholder in which there are several alternatives but none of them apply. A null field with no value does not have to be transmitted.
Sequence	A structured type, defined by referencing an ordered list of various types.
Sequence of	A structured type, defined by referencing a single type. Each value in the type is an ordered list (if a list exists). It can be used as a method of building arrays of a single type.
Set	A structured type, similar to the Sequence type except that Set is defined by referencing an unordered list of types. Allows data to be sent in any order.
Set of	A structured type, similar to the Sequence type except that Set of is defined by referencing a single type. Each value in the type is an unordered list (if a list exits).
Choice	Models a data type chosen from a collection of alternative types. Allows a data structure to hold more than one type.
Selection	Models a variable whose type is that of some alternatives of a previously defined Choice.
Tagged	Models a new type from an existing type but with a different identifer.
Any	Models data whose type is unrestricted. It can be used with any valid type.
Object Identifier	A distinguishable value associated with an object, or a group of objects, like a library of rules, syntaxes, etc.
Character String	Models strings of characters for some defined character set.
Enumerated	A simple type; its values are given distinct identifiers as part of the type notation.
Real	Models real values (for example: $M \times B^e$, where M = the mantissa, B = the base, and e = the exponent).
Encrypted	A type whose value is a result of encrypting another type.

guish the different types, a structure of values (for example, a data base record) or a simple element (for example, a field within the data base record) can have a tag attached that identifies the type. For example, a tag for a funds transfer record could be PRIVATE 22. This is used to identify the record and inform the receiver about the nature of its contents. As we shall see, tags can be put to very clever uses. ASN.1 provides a tag for every type.

ASN.1 defines four classes of *types*: Each tag is identified by its class and its number (as in our example PRIVATE 22). The type classes are defined as:

- *Universal*. Application-independent types.
- *Application-wide*. Types that are specific to an application and used in other standards (X.400 MHS, FTAM, etc.).
- *Context-specific*. Types that are specific to an application but are limited to a set within an application.
- *Private-use*. Reserved for private use and not defined in these standards. Used by other agencies.

Several tags are used for the universal assignment. Remember, the tag is used to identify a class. The tag has two parts, a class identifier and a number. Table 9-2 depicts the universal class tag assignments.

ASN.1 Case-Sensitive Rules and Format Rules

It is quite important to know that ASN.1 is a case-sensitive language. Uppercase and lowercase letters in names convey a meaning. The rules are:

- All type names begin with an uppercase letter.
- All module names (explained shortly) begin with an uppercase letter.
- Names of built-in types are all uppercase letters.
- All other identifiers begin with a lowercase letter.

Comments can be entered to explain the ASN.1 notations. Comments are preceded and followed by two hyphens (--).

ASN.1 is a free-format language. The programmer can terminate the code anywhere on a line, because it is merely interpreted as a blank (with the exception of comments).

Rules and Conventions

These OSI standards describe information with a series of replacement rules called *productions*. A production is a notation in which allowed sequences are associated with a name. The replacement rules allow any instance of information to be represented. Three classes of symbols appear in a production:

TABLE 9-2. Universal Class Tag Assignments

UNIVERSAL 1	BOOLEAN
UNIVERSAL 2	INTEGER
UNIVERSAL 3	BITSTRING
UNIVERSAL 4	OCTETSTRING
UNIVERSAL 5	NULL
UNIVERSAL 6	OBJECT IDENTIFIER
UNIVERSAL 7	Object Descriptor
UNIVERSAL 8	EXTERNAL
UNIVERSAL 9	REAL
UNIVERSAL 10	ENUMERATED
UNIVERSAL 11	ENCRYPTED
UNIVERSAL 12-15	Reserved for future use
UNIVERSAL 16	SEQUENCE and SEQUENCE OF
UNIVERSAL 17	SET and SET OF
UNIVERSAL 18	NumericString
UNIVERSAL 19	PrintableString
UNIVERSAL 20	TeletexString
UNIVERSAL 21	VideotexString
UNIVERSAL 22	IA5String
UNIVERSAL 23	UTCTime
UNIVERSAL 24	GeneralizedTime
UNIVERSAL 25	GraphicString
UNIVERSAL 26	VisibleString
UNIVERSAL 27	GeneralString
UNIVERSAL 28	CharacterString
UNIVERSAL 29+	Reserved for additions.

- *Terminals.* A symbol that actually appears in the information.
- *Non-terminal:* A symbol that can represent a series of symbols or several series of symbols.
- *Operator:* A symbol that assigns a value to a non-terminal or distinguishes between alternative symbol(s) values for a non-terminal.

Presently, two operators are used in productions. The equivalence operator is coded as ":: =." It assigns a value to a non-terminal. The alternative operator is "|." It distinguishes between several alternative symbols. For example, the ASN.1 coding of Boolean symbols are:

Boolean Type :: = BOOLEAN
Boolean Value :: = TRUE|FALSE

The other conventions used are described in Table 9-3 and should be studied before preceding further.

TABLE 9-3. X.208 Conventions

String	A sequence of zero or more characters.
Identifier	A sequence of one or more characters, capital letters, small letters, decimal digits, and hyphens.
Number	A non-negative integer expressed as a decimal value or a hexadecimal value. In the latter case, the number is followed by an H. (For clarification, binary values may be subscripted with $_2$ and hex numbers with $_{16}$). Both notations are used in this chapter.
Empty	A null or empty string of symbols.
Reserved words	Not used by user; noted with upper case letters.
Comments	Embedded in the notation and preceded and terminated by two hyphens.

ASN.1 Notation Symbols

The pair of angle brackets (< >) is a notation as a placeholder for an actual item such as type name, module name, a type definition, or a module body.

The following notation describes the rules for representing a *module* (which is one of several ASN.1 forms we will examine in this chapter).

    < module name > DEFINITIONS :: = BEGIN
        < module body >
    END

The module name identifies the module. It is an ASN.1 identifier. The "DEFINITIONS" indicate the module is defined as the ASN.1 definitions that are placed between the "BEGIN" and "END" words. In other words, a module contains other ASN.1 definitions.

Within the modules are definitions of types. They have the following form:

    <type name> :: = <type definition>

This notation is an example of a *simple type*. It is so-named because it directly specifies the set of its values. The type name is the identifier of the type. The type definition describes the class and several other attributes explained shortly.

The next example shows how four type definitions are coded within a module:

    < module name > DEFINITIONS :: = BEGIN
        < type name > :: = < type definition >
        < type name > :: = < type definition >
        < type name > :: = < type definition >
        < type name > :: = < type definition >
    END

This example is called a *structured type*. It contains a reference to one or more other types. The types within the structured type are called *component types*.

EXAMPLES OF ASN.1 NOTATIONS

Example One

The best way to explain these concepts is through examples. We will show how an X.25 call request packet header can be described with these standards. The placeholders are replaced with names and actual type definitions to describe the entries of an X.25 call request packet header (see Figure 9-1):

```
X25header DEFINITIONS :: = BEGIN
      Channelgroup :: = INTEGER
      Gfi :: = BITSTRING
      Channelnumber :: = INTEGER
      Packettype :: = INTEGER
END
```

As you can see, the fields in the header are named and typed as integer or bit string with the ASN.1 built-in types "INTEGER" OR "BITSTRING." Since the names of the module and the names of the X.25 packet fields are a module name or type names, they begin with an uppercase letter.

This definition is quite straightforward, but it needs some more refinement. As indicated in Figure 9-1, the general format identifier (GFI) field consists of "subfields." Bits 5 and 6 are used to indicate Modulo 8 or 128 numbering; bit 7 is used for the D (delivery confirmation) bit operation; and bit 8 is the A (extended length of the address) bit.

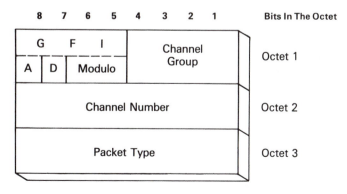

FIGURE 9-1. A Conventional Depiction of a Protocol Data Unit (An X.25 Packet Header)

For most applications it is necessary to further define the GFI field. ASN.1 provides several methods for this description. One option entails changing the module definition as follows:

```
X25header DEFINITIONS :: = BEGIN
    Channelgroup :: = INTEGER
    Gfi :: = SEQUENCE{
        Modulo :: = BIT STRING {first (0), last(1)}
        Dbit :: = INTEGER
        ABIT :: = INTEGER}
    Channelnumber :: = INTEGER
    Packettype :: = INTEGER
    UserData :: = OCTETSTRING
        --User data field is limited to 16 octets--
        --Unless the Fast Select option is used--
    END
```

The GFI field is now defined as an ordered sequence of a series of the same or different types. The sequence is bounded by the symbols "{" and "}." The notation for the "modulo" explains that the bit string is of fixed length, consisting of two bits. The new entries begin with a lowercase letter, coded for readability; no ASN.1 significance.

An additional line of code has been added as "UserData" :: = "OCTET-STRING." This code defines a user data field as containing octet values (since X.25 requires even octet alignment). The comments explain the limitation on the use of this field.

Several other options are available to decrease the amount of coding in our example. However, the example has been kept as simple as possible in order to give the reader the courage to read further and learn about some of the more detailed and complex aspects of the presentation layer protocols.

Example Two

Our second example is quite simple but illustrates several important aspects of ASN.1. Part of the notation in example one: "UserData :: = OCTETSTRING" is now coded as "UserData :: = [PRIVATE 2] IMPLICIT OCTETSTRING." This definition assigns a new tag to the built-in type of "OCTETSTRING." It causes the original type to be replaced with the tag whose class is private and whose number is 2. (We might wish to code the user data element as private because it is used in a company-specific protocol).

In the actual transfer syntax between two computers, the "OCTET-STRING" tag would be omitted. This feature is a very useful option of ASN.1, because the transmitted protocol data unit (the X.25 packet) would not have to carry both the new and old tag, but just the new tag. Consequently, fewer bits are transmitted. The section on encoding provides an example of how the implicit feature is used in the transfer syntax.

Example Three

The third example of ASN.1 notation illustrates other features of the language. The example is a protocol data unit used with the reliable transfer service element (RTSE, discussed in Chapter 10).

```
RTORQapdu :: = SET {
checkpointSize      [0] IMPLICIT INTEGER DEFAULT 1,
windowSize          [1] IMPLICIT INTEGER DEFAULT 3,
dialogueMode        [2] IMPLICIT  INTEGER  {monologue(0),twa(1)}
                    DEFAULT monologue,
connectionDATARQ [3] ConnectionData,
applicationProtocol [4] IMPLICIT INTEGER OPTIONAL }
```

This example shows how the type "SET" is used. This type is defined to be a series of other types, bounded by the { and } brackets. The order of the elements in the "SET" does not matter; any of the elements can precede each other when they are encoded. A "SET" is useful to define a known number of elements whose order is not important.

ASN.1 allows fields to be defined as "DEFAULT." This reserved word is followed by the value to be used as a default value if a value is not furnished. In this example, the default value for "windowSize" is "3."

This coding shows another example of "IMPLICIT." This notation indicates the coding rule to be used when the APDU is encoded. It causes the original tag to be omitted. For example, "checkpointSize [0] IMPLICIT INTEGER DEFAULT 1," means "INTEGER" will not be coded in the transfer syntax. However in this example there is no explicit class name (like "[PRIVATE 2]" in example two). If it had such a name, it would appear in front of the number in the brackets. If no class name is specified with a tag, it defaults to *context specific*. In this example, the tags "[0]" through "[4]" are associated with the elements of the set.

The mnemonic for the values must begin with a lowercase letter ("checkpointSize," "applicationProtocol"). To enhance the readability of the identifiers, lowercase letters are inserted for each new, meaningful, user-friendly word embedded in the identifier.

BASIC ENCODING RULES

X.209 and ISO 8825 describe the encoding rules for the values of types, in contrast to X.208 and ISO 8824, which are concerned with the abstract structure of the information. These basic encoding conventions provide the rules for the transfer syntax conventions.

The rules require that each type be described by a standard representation. This representation is called a *data element* (or just element). It consists of three components: type, length, and value (TLV), which appear in the following order:

Type   Length   Value

The type is also called the identifier. It distinguishes one type from another and specifies how the contents are interpreted. The length specifies the length of the value or contents. The value (contents) contains the actual information of the element. These components are explained shortly.

The transfer data element is illustrated in Figure 9-2. It can consist of a single TLV or a series of data elements, described as multiple TLVs. The element consists of an integral number (n) of octets, written with the most significant bit (MSB), 8, on the left and the least significant bit (LSB), 1, on the right:

XXXXXXXX
8 7 6 5 4 3 2 1

The single-octet identifier is coded as depicted in Figure 9-3(a). Bits 8 and 7 identify the four type classes by the following bit assignments:

Universal   00
Application-wide   01
Context-specific   10
Private-use   11

Bit 6 identifies the forms of the data element. Two forms are possible. A *primitive* element (bit 6 = 0) has no further internal structure of data elements. A *constructor* element (bit 6 = 1) is recursively defined in that it contains a series of data elements. The remaining five bits (5 through 1) contain the tag's number. For example, the field may distinguish Boolean from integer information. If the system requires more than five bits, bits 5 through 1 of the first octet are coded as 11111_2 and bit 8 of the subsequent octets are coded with a 1 to indicate more octets follow and a 0 to indicate the last octet. Figure 9-3 (b) illustrates the use of multi-octet identifiers.

The length (L) specifies the length of the contents. It may take one of three

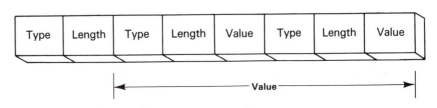

FIGURE 9-2. Transfer Data Element

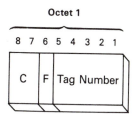

Octet 1

8 7 6 5 4 3 2 1

| C | F | Tag Number |

(a) Single-octet identifier

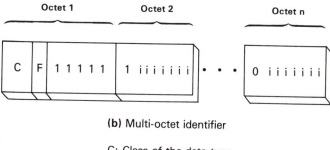

Octet 1 **Octet 2** **Octet n**

| C | F | 1 1 1 1 1 | 1 i i i i i i i | • • • | 0 i i i i i i i |

(b) Multi-octet identifier

C: Class of the data type
F: Form of the element

FIGURE 9-3. Structure of the Identifier

forms: short, long, or indefinite. The short form is one octet long and is used when L is less than 128. Bit 8 is always 0 and bits 7 through 1 indicate the length of the contents. For example, a contents field of 21 octets is described by the L field as 00010110_2.

The long form is used for a longer contents field: greater than or equal to 128 and less than 2^{1008} octets. With the long form, bit 8 is coded as 1 and the remaining seven bits of the octet indicate the number of octets that follow which contain the length value. The indefinite form can be used when the element is a constructor. It has the value of 1000000_2 or 80_{16}. For the indefinite form, a special end-of-contents (EOC) element terminates the contents. The representation of EOC is 00000000_{16}.

The contents (value) is the substance of the element, i.e., the actual information. It is described in multiples of eight bits and is of variable length. The contents are interpreted based on the coding of the identifier (type) field. Therefore, the contents are interpreted as bit strings, octet strings, etc.

EXAMPLES OF BASIC ENCODING RULES AND TRANSFER SYNTAX

This section provides several simple examples of the basic encoding rules and how they translate to the transfer syntax. The examples are not exhaustive; the reader should study the specific OSI document if more detailed information is needed.

The "Boolean built-in type" represents a logical quality of either true (1) or false (0). Its tag is universal class, number 1. The notations are:

BooleanType   :: = BOOLEAN
BooleanValue   :: = TRUE|FALSE

The identifier is coded as a 1 to note a Boolean type. FALSE is coded as all 0s. TRUE is coded with any bit combination. An example of the X.209 transfer syntax of the Boolean built-in type to describe a false condition for "employed" is:

Identifier	Length	Contents
00000001_2	00000001_2	00000000_2

The "Integer Type" represents an integer value, which can be positive, zero, or negative. The description can be followed by values and reference names assigned to them. The reference names begin with lowercase letters. The contents is the value of the integer coded as a two's complement binary number. The notations are:

IntegerType :: = INTEGER|INTEGER{NamedNumberList}
IntegerValue :: = number|number|identifier
NamedNumberList :: = NamedNumber|Named NumberList,
                          NamedNumber
NamedNumber   :: = identifier (number)

The identifier is coded as a 2 to note an Integer type. An example of the Integer built-in type to describe a value of 1 is:

Identifier	Length	Contents
00000010_2	00000001_2	00000001_2

An example of a list coded with the "INTEGER{red(0), green(1), yellow(2)}" to designate yellow is:

Identifier	Length	Contents
00000010_2	00000001_2	00000010_2

The "Bit String" represents an ordered set of zero or more bits. The identifier code is 3 to denote integer. The notation for the bit string is a series of binary or hexadecimal digits enclosed in apostrophes and followed by a "B" for binary or an "H" for hexadecimal. The notations are:

Bit StringType :: = BIT STRING|BIT STRING{NamedNumberList}
Bit StringValue :: = 'string' B|'string' H|{identifierList}
NamedNumberList :: = NamedNumber|NamedNumberList,
                 NamedNumber
NamedNumber :: = identifier(number)
IdentifierList :: = identifier|IdentifierList, identifier

If the binary form is primitive, the code is preceded by a binary number in the first octet that encodes the number of unused bits in the contents.
    As an illustration of a bit string, the value 'OC634521B' H is designated as:

Identifier	Length	Contents
00000011_2	00000110_2	$040C634521B0_{16}$

The value of 04 in the left-most part of the contents field stipulates that four bits of the field are not used. The 0 in the right-most position represents the binary string of 0000_2 which is coded to give a full octet alignment of six full octets. Notice the value —0C634521B' is only five and one-half octets in length.
    The "Octet String" type represents a set of zero or more octets. The notation can take the form of binary (B) or hexadecimal (H). If any bits are unspecified in the last octet, they are assumed to be zero. The notations are:

Octet String Type :: = OCTET STRING
OctetString Value :: = 'string' B|'string' H|"string"

Let us use the Octet String type to examine both a primitive and a constructor (with the indefinite form). For example, an octet string of '63E14C7832' H is coded as a primitive and constructor. Notice that the subscript 16 is omitted from the contents field. This is the normal practice.

Primitive Identifier	Length	Contents		
04_{16}	05_{16}	63E14C7832		
Constructor: Identifier	Length	Contents		
24_{16}	80_{16}	63E14C7832		
		Octet String	Length	Contents
		04_{16}	03_{16}	63E14C
		Octet String	Length	Contents
		04_{16}	02_{16}	7832
		Identifier	Length	
		00_{16}	00_{16}	

We examine the constructor coding further. First, the identifier for a constructor is a 1 in bit position 6. Thus, the coding for the identifier is 00101000_2 or 24_{16}. Second, the length field for a constructor of indefinite form is 10000000_2 or 80_{16}. Last, the EOC (end of contents) element terminates the contents.

The "Null" represents a valueless placeholder. The ID value is 5. The notations are:

NullType   :: = NULL
NullValue   :: = NULL

The "Sequence" represents an ordered set of zero or more values. Its identifier value is 16. These values are called the elements of the Sequence. The notation for the Sequence has three forms, each with different rules (constraints):

- Elements are variable in number, but of one type.
- Elements are fixed in number and possibly of several types.
- Elements are of multiple types and are optional.

The notations are:

SequenceType   :: = SEQUENCE|SEQUENCE OF Type|SEQUENCE
                      {ElementTypes}
SequenceValue   :: = {ElementValues}
ElementTypes   :: = OptionalTypeList|empty
OptionalTypeList :: = OptionalType|OptionalTypeList, OptionalType
OptionalType   :: = NamedType|NamedType OPTIONAL|NamedType
                      DEFAULT Value|Components OF
NamedType   :: = identifier Type|Type
ElementValues   :: = NamedValueList|empty
NamedValueList   :: = NamedValue|NamedValueList, Named Value
NamedValue   :: = identifier Value|Value

The construct "COMPONENTS OF" can be used to form inclusive equivalencies between elements. For those readers who write software, it is quite similar to a FORTRAN EQUIVALENCE. For example, the sequence of:

I :: = SEQUENCE {A, B, C, D}
J :: = SEQUENCE {E, F, G, COMPONENTS OF I}

is the same as:

J :: = SEQUENCE {E, F, G, A, B, C, D}

An example of the Sequence is illustrated with the IA5 string of "TOO STRUCTURED":

Sequence	Length	Contents		
30_{16}	11_{16}			
		IA5 String	Length	Contents
		16_{16}	03_{16}	$544F4F_{16}$
		IA5 String	Length	Contents
		16_{16}	$0A_{16}$	$53545255435455524544_{16}$

Again, let us examine this notation more closely. The sequence code is 30_{16} or 00110000_2. This code translates to bit 6 = 1 to identify a constructor and bits 5 through 1 = 10000_2 to identify a 16 for the sequence identifier. The values in the contents field are simply the hex equivalents of the ASCII/IA5 code.

The "Set" represents an ordered set of zero or more values. The values of the Set are called its members. The member of a Set may be variable in number but of one type, or a Set may have members that are fixed in number and of distinct types.

The notations for a Set are:

SetType	:: = SET|SET OF Type|SET MemberTypes
SetValue	:: = |MemberValues|
MemberTypes	:: = OptionalTypeList|empty
OptionalTypeList	:: = OptionalType|OptionalTypeList, OptionalType
OptionalType	:: = NamedType|NamedType OPTIONAL| NamedType DEFAULT Value|ComponentsOF
NamedType	:: = identifier Type|Type
MemberValues	:: = NamedValueList|empty
NamedValueList	:: = NamedValue|NamedValueList, NamedValue
NamedValue	:: = identifier Value|Value

The "Tagged" represents a value that already exists and has already been tagged for identification. The type of value being tagged can be either explicit or implicit representation. The notations are as follows:

TaggedType	:: = TAG IMPLICIT Type|Tag Type
TaggedValue	:: = Value
Tag	:: = [Class number]
Class	:: = UNIVERSAL|APPLICATION|PRIVATE|empty

Finally, the "Choice" represents a value whose type is selected (chosen) from a set of alternatives. The notations for Choice are:

ChoiceType	$::=$ CHOICE {AlternativeTypeList}
ChoiceValue	$::=$ identifierValue|Value
AlternativeTypeList	$::=$ NamedType|AlternativeTypeList, NamedType
NamedType	$::=$ identifier Type | Type

Defined Types

The OSI standards also describe several defined types. A defined type is one specified with a standard notation:

1. The IA5 String type is formally defined as shown below. The characters allowed and their graphical depictions and seven-bit numeric codes are those specified for the International Reference Version of IA5 by Recommendation T.50. Each octet contains a single code. Bit 8 of each octet is zero, and bits 7 through 1 correspond to b_7 through b_1 of the code (using the T.50 bit numbering convention).

2. A Numeric String represents an ordered set of zero or more characters that collectively encode numeric information in textual form. It models data entered from such devices as telephone handsets.

3. A Printable String represents an ordered set of zero or more characters chosen from a subset of the printable characters. It models data entered from devices with a limited character repertoire (for example, Telex terminals).

4. A T.61 String represents an ordered set of zero or more characters and representation commands chosen from the set defined by Recommendation T.61. It models textual data suitable for processing by Teletex terminals.

5. A Videotex String represents an ordered set of zero or more alphabetic characters, pictorial characters, pictorial drawing commands, display attribute commands, etc., chosen from the set defined by the Data Syntaxes of Recommendation T.101 or the options from Recommendation T.100. It models textual and graphical data suitable for processing by Videotex terminals.

6. A Generalized Time represents a calendar date and time of day to various precisions, as provided for by ISO 2014 and ISO 4031. The time of day can be specified as local time only, UTC time only (see Recommendation B.11), or as both local and UTC time.

7. The UTC Time type is a particular form of Generalized Time which is defined for use in international applications where the local time only is not adequate, and where the flexibility to use all of the possible forms of ISO 3307 and ISO 2014 is not required. The UTC Time type permits the time of day to be specified to a precision of one minute or one second.

The notations for the defined types are shown in Table 9-4.

TABLE 9–4. Defined Types

(1) IA5String	:: =	[UNIVERSAL 22] IMPLICIT OCTET STRING
(2) NumericString	:: =	[UNIVERSAL 18] IMPLICIT IA5STRING
(3) PrintableString	:: =	[UNIVERSAL 19] IMPLICIT IA5STRING
(4) T.61String	:: =	[UNIVERSAL 20] IMPLICIT OCTET STRING
(5) VideotexString	:: =	[UNIVERSAL 21] IMPLICIT OCTET STRING
(6) GeneralizedTime	:: =	[UNIVERSAL 24] IMPLICIT IA5STRING
(7) UTCTime	:: =	[UNIVERSAL 23] IMPLICIT GeneralizedTime

PRESENTATION LAYER SUPPORT FOR REGISTRATIONS AND TEMPLATES

The OSI Use of the Registration Hierarchy

The ISO and CCITT have developed jointly a scheme for naming and uniquely identifying objects, such as standards, member bodies, organizations, protocols—anything that needs an unambiguous identifier. The scheme is a hierarchical tree structure wherein the lower leaves on the tree are subordinate to the leaves above, except, of course, for the root. The upper branches identify the authorities as CCITT (0), ISO (1) or an object that is sponsored by both organizations (2).

The example in Figure 9-4 shows the approach used by the ISO. The ISO uses four arcs below the root to identify standards, registration authorities, member-bodies, and organizations. Below these four arcs are other subordinate definitions that are chosen to identify further some type of object.

Use of Templates in OSI

In an effort to simplify (and make less rigorous) some shorthand notations for macros, protocol data units, etc., the concept of templates was devised. The

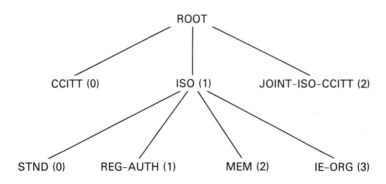

FIGURE 9–4. Example of Registration Hierarchy

```
<template-label>                    TEMPLATE NAME
            ELEMENT NAME1           [<element-definition>]
            ELEMENT NAME2           [<element-definition>]

                    •                       •
                    •                       •
                    •                       •

            ELEMENT NAMEn           [<element-definition>]
        REGISTERED AS <OBJECT-IDENTIFIER>
```

FIGURE 9-5. The Template Structure

coding scheme for a template is shown in Figure 9-5. Templates can be translated into ASN.1 macro notations and they serve a very useful function with the *object identifier* (see the bottom of the template in Figure 9-5). It is used with the registration authority hierarchy (see Figure 9-4) to identify the organization responsible for the registration of the object.

The coding scheme is quite similar to conventional ASN.1 coding, but uses slightly different rules.

Brackets delimit parts of the template that may or may not be present. Strings reside inside the brackets. If the closing bracket is followed by an asterisk, the contents within the brackets may appear more than one time. The template type governs whether the parts within the brackets may be omitted.

The placement values (< >) identify strings within them that must be replaced each time the template is used. Again, the meaning of the replacement and the structure depend on what is inside the brackets.

Uppercase notations identify key words. Key words are required each time the template is used. The exception to this rule is if the key words are enclosed in brackets.

The labels for templates must be unique within the OSI network management standard or, for that matter, any other standard in which they are used. As noted in our example, the last coding line of the template has a reserved word "REGISTERED AS" followed by "OBJECT IDENTIFIER." This is the line used to register the template of the standard organization. As an example, the <OBJECT IDENTIFIER> could be replaced by: {iso standard(0) ips-osi-mips(9596) cmip(2) version(1) expanded(2) invokePDU(12) create(8)}

By referring to the leftmost branch of the tree in Figure 9-4, we identify the object as a standard (0). Thereafter, the lower branches (not shown in Figure 9-4) further identify the object as belonging to the 9596 standard, as well as version 1 of CMIP. Continuing the analysis, the object is an expanded standard and is identified as an INVOKE protocol data unit, which is used to create an object.

The hierarchical classification scheme, used in conjunction with the templates, provides a very valuable tool for management of the OSI resources.

PRESENTATION CONTEXTS

During a presentation connection, the presentation service could be dealing with different presentation contexts. A presentation context defines the abstract syntax notation and the transfer syntax. It allows the users to describe the data structures that are needed to support an application.

It is conceivable that two users might need to alter their notation and syntax during a session. For example, one user might transfer a different format for a protocol data unit. The presentation layer allows the users to negotiate the presentation context. They can accept, refuse, or offer alternative contexts. Once the context is established, the users can change the contexts during an application session.

The presentation layer supports this type of dynamic presentation dialogue with two types of contexts:

- *Defined context set:* (DCS). The context set has been agreed upon by the service provider and the two users.
- *Default Context:* The presentation context set is always known to the presentation provider and is used if the defined context set is empty.

PRESENTATION LAYER FUNCTIONAL UNITS

Like the session layer, the presentation layer services are grouped and identified by functional units. With three exceptions (listed below), they are quite similar to the session layer functional units described in Chapter 8. They are included as part of the presentation layer in order to allow the user to request the session services during connection setup. The three presentation layer functional units are:

- *Kernel:* This functional unit is always present, and acts as a null if the user applications both use the same data representation. The kernel is also used if the applications have different data representations, and if negotiation occurs at connection establishment.
- *Context Management:* This functional unit allows the defined context set to be changed during a connection.
- *Context Restoration:* This functional unit allows a session layer synchronization to occur and still maintain a known defined context set. It works in conjunction with the session layer Abandon, Restart, and Set operations in the following manner:

    Abandon: The current dialogue is abandoned, but the context set remains the same.

    Restart: Since a restart moves a dialogue back to a synchronization point, the context set is also moved back to the value it was at the sync point.

Set: If the set synchronization number is for some other synchronization point, the defined context set is moved to that point. If it is within the range of the abandon or restart, it takes the actions cited above for these operations. Otherwise, it is set to the value negotiated at connection setup.

PRESENTATION LAYER FACILITIES

The presentation layer is made up of five facilities. The facilities are categorized by the primitives they use and the services they invoke. The functions of the facilities are as follows (we will show how they are invoked with the primitives in the next section):

- *Connection establishment:* This facility allows one presentation service user to establish a connection with another presentation service user. It also establishes a session layer connection, which is directly related to this presentation connection. During the execution of this facility, the user can establish values for the following session attributes: (a) the presentation functional units, (b) the initial defined context set (DCS), (c) the definition of the default context, and (d) the session-connection characteristics.
- *Connection termination:* This facility releases the presentation connection. It also makes use of the session layer operations to release the supporting session layer.
- *Context management:* This facility provides for the adding and deleting of presentation contexts to the DCS.
- *Information transfer:* This facility allows the users to exchange information with each other. Data can be exchanged with token control or without token control and can be typed data, capability data, or expedited data, if the corresponding session functional units are selected. Expedited data is passed with the default context, just in case it overtakes a signal that had asked for an alteration to the context. With this approach, the expedited data context will not be in disagreement.
- *Dialogue control:* Finally, this facility provides token management, synchronization, resynchronization, exception reporting, and activity management, if the corresponding session layer functional units are selected.

PRESENTATION LAYER PRIMITIVES

The presentation layer primitives are exchanged between the PS-user and the PS-provider. This interaction takes place at the two presentation layer service access points (PSAPs). Table 9-5 summarizes the primitives.

The Presentation Layer

PRESENTATION LAYER PROTOCOL DATA UNITS

ISO 8823 and CCITT X.226 define the formats of the presentation layer protocol data units, as well as the procedures (such as states) for the transfer of data and control units. The protocol data units are defined with Abstract Syntax Notation One (ASN.1). For purposes of brevity and simplicity, the ASN.1 notations are not shown (we use some ASN.1 examples in the application layer chapters). Rather, Table 9-6 lists the data units and their associated parameters. An explanation of these parameters follows.

The mode selector is used to indicate the mode of operation of the presentation layer. It is coded as either normal or the X.410 1984. Its use is to delineate between the 1984 or 1988 version of the X.400 protocol. The set for X.400 1984 version fields is used for the X.410 mode only.

The protocol version identifies the version that the presentation protocol machine (PPM) supports.

Two presentation layer identification parameters are mapped directly into two session layer parameters. The calling presentation selector is the calling presentation address parameter of the P-CONNECT request and indication primitives. The calling session address is the calling session address part of the calling presentation address parameter of the P-CONNECT request and indication primitives. The next two calling and called addresses follow the same conventions as the addresses just discussed.

The presentation context definition list contains one or more items. Each item contains:

- A presentation context identifier
- An abstract syntax name
- A transfer syntax list

The transfer syntax list identifies the transfer syntaxes that the initiating PPM can support. If a default context is used, the default context name contains an abstract syntax name and a transfer syntax name.

The quality of service parameter identifies the quality of service parameters passed from the application layer to the session layer. Their use is completely identical with the session layer service definitions (see Chapter 8).

The presentation requirements parameter is used to select optional functional units of the presentation service.

The session requirements parameter is identical with the session requirements parameter of the session layer service definitions (see Chapter 8).

The Initial synchronization point serial number, the initial assignment of tokens, and the session connection identifier provide the PS user with the parameters used at the session layer.

TABLE 9-5. Presentation Service Primitives and Parameters

Connection Establishment Facility	
P-CONNECT request	(calling PSAP, called PSAP, mode, context definition list, default context name, quality of service, presentation requirements, session requirements, serial number, tokens, session connection identifier, data)
P-CONNECT indication	(calling PSAP, called PSAP, mode, context definition list, context definition result list, default context name, default context result, quality of service, presentation requirements, session requirements, serial number, token, session connection identifier, data)
P-CONNECT response	(responding PSAP, mode, context definition result list, default context result, quality of service, presentation requirements, session requirements, serial number, tokens, session identifier, result, data)
P-CONNECT confirm	(responding PSAP, mode, context definition result list, default context result, quality of service, presentation requirements, session requirements, serial number, tokens, session identifier, result, data)

Connection Termination Facility	
P-RELEASE request	(data)
P-RELEASE indication	(data)
P-RELEASE response	(result, data)
P-RELEASE confirm	(result, data)
P-U-ABORT request	(data)
P-U-ABORT indication	
P-P-ABORT indication	(data)

Context Management Facility	
P-ALTER-CONTEXT request	(context addition list, context deletion list, data)
P-ALTER-CONTEXT indication	(context addition list, context deletion list, context addition result list, data)
P-ALTER-CONTEXT response	(context addition result list, context deletion result list, data)
P-ALTER-CONTEXT confirm	(context addition result list, context deletion result list, data)

Information Transfer Facility	
P-TYPED-DATA request	(data)
P-TYPED-DATA indication	(data)
P-DATA request	(data)
P-DATA indication	(data)
P-EXPEDITED-DATA request	(data)
P-EXPEDITED-DATA indication	(data)
P-CAPABILITY-DATA request	(data)
P-CAPABILITY-DATA indication	(data)

The Presentation Layer

TABLE 9-5. (Continued)

	Dialogue Control Facility
P-TOKEN-GIVE request	(tokens)
P-TOKEN-GIVE indication	(tokens)
P-TOKEN-PLEASE request	(tokens, data)
P-TOKEN-PLEASE indication	(token, data)
P-CONTROL-GIVE request	
P-CONTROL-GIVE indication	
P-SYNC-MINOR request	(type, serial number, data)
P-SYNC-MINOR indication	(type, serial number, data)
P-SYNC-MINOR response	(serial number, data)
P-SYNC-MINOR confirm	(serial number, data)
P-SYNC-MAJOR request	(serial number, data)
P-SYNC-MAJOR indication	(serial number, data)
P-SYNC-MAJOR response	(data)
P-SYNC-MAJOR confirm	(data)
P-RESYNCHRONIZE request	(type, serial number, tokens, data)
P-RESYNCHRONIZE indication	(type, serial number, tokens, context identifier list, data)
P-RESYNCHRONIZE response	(serial number, tokens, data)
P-RESYNCHRONIZE confirm	(serial number, tokens, context identifier list, data)
P-U-EXCEPTION-RE- PORT request	(reason, data)
P-U-EXCEPTION-RE- PORT indication	(reason, data)
P-P-EXCEPTION-RE- PORT indication	(reason)
P-ACTIVITY-START request	(activity ID, data)
P-ACTIVITY-START indication	(activity ID, data)
P-ACTIVITY-RESUME request	(activity ID, old activity ID, serial number, old SC ID, data)
P-ACTIVITY-RESUME indication	(activity ID, old activity ID, serial number, old SC ID, data)
P-ACTIVITY-END request	(serial number, data)
P-ACTIVITY-END indication	(serial number, data)
P-ACTIVITY-END response	(data)
P-ACTIVITY-END confirm	(data)
P-ACTIVITY-INTERRUPT request	(reason)
P-ACTIVITY-INTER- RUPT indication	(reason)
P-ACTIVITY-INTER- RUPT response	
P-ACTIVITY-INTERRUPT confirm	
P-ACTIVITY-DISCARD request	(reason)
P-ACTIVITY-DISCARD indication	(reason)
P-ACTIVITY-DISCARD response	
P-ACTIVITY-DISCARD confirm	

Presentation Layer Protocol Data Units

TABLE 9-6. Presentation Protocol Data Units and Parameters

PPDU	Parameters
Connect (CP)	Mode selector, Set for X.400 1894 version, Protocol version, Calling presentation selector, Calling session address, Called presentation selector, Called session address, Presentation context definition list, Default context name, Quality of service, Presentation requirements, User session requirements, Revised session requirements, Initial synchronization point serial number, Initial assignment of tokens, Session connection identifier, User data
Connect Accept (CPA)	Mode selector, Set for X.400 1894 version, Protocol version, Responding presentation selector, Responding session address, Called presentation selector, Called session address, Presentation context definition result list, Quality of service, Presentation requirements, User session requirements, Revised session requirements, Initial synchronization point serial number, Initial assignment of tokens, Session connection identifier, User data
Connect Reject (CPR)	Protocol version, Responding presentation selector, Responding session address, Presentation context definition result list, Default Context Result, Quality of service, User session requirements, Session connection identifier, Provider reason, User data
Abnormal Release User (ARU)	Presentation context identifier list, User data
Abnormal Release Provider (ARP)	Provider reason, Event Identifier
Data (TD)	User data
Typed Data (TTD)	User data
Expedited Data (TE)	User data
Capability Data (TC)	User data
Capability Data ACK (TCC)	User data
Alter Context (AC)	Presentation context addition list, Presentation context deletion list, User data
Alter Context ACK (ACA)	Presentation context addition result list, Presentation context deletion result list, User data
Resynchronize (RS)	Resynchronize type, Synchronization point serial number, Tokens, Presentation context identifier list, User data
Resynchronize ACK (RSA)	Resynchronization point serial number, Tokens, Presentation context identifier list, User data

The Presentation Layer

RELATIONSHIP OF PRESENTATION LAYER
TO SESSION LAYER

As the reader might expect, the presentation and session layers are tightly coupled. For example, a number of presentation layer protocol data unit parameters are mapped directly into the session layer primitive parameters. Table 9-7 shows this mapping relationship.

In addition, the following coupling relationships exist between the presentation and session layers:

- A normal release of the presentation connection occurs concurrently with the normal release of the session connection. Therefore, all the P-RELEASE primitives are mapped directly onto the corresponding S-RELEASE primitives.

- Since token services are provided by the session layer, all P-TOKEN-GIVE, P-TOKEN-PLEASE, and P-CONTROL primitives are mapped directly onto the corresponding S-TOKEN-GIVE, S-TOKEN-PLEASE, and S-CONTROL primitives.

- Since synchronization services are provided by the session layer, all P-SYNC primitives are mapped directly onto the corresponding S-SYNC primitives.

- Since exception reporting services are provided by the session layer, all P-P-EXCEPTION and P-U-EXCEPTION primitives are mapped directly onto the corresponding S-P-EXCEPTION and S-U-EXCEPTION primitives.

- Since activity services are provided by the session layer, all P-ACTIVITY primitives are mapped directly onto the corresponding S-ACTIVITY primitives.

EXAMPLE OF PRESENTATION LAYER OPERATIONS

This section provides an example of the use of X.216/X.226 to support the establishment of a presentation layer connection between two presentation protocol machines (PPMs). We will be using state tables, event lists, predicates, and action tables as documentation tools to aid in the analysis. You may wish to review the explanation of these tools. Refer to Chapter 1, "OSI Documentation Tools."

The material in Table 9-8 is an excerpt from the connection establishment state table for the presentation layer. It is described in the subsequent material in the section.

The following sequence of events occurs as noted by the numbers and letters in Figure 9-4 and Table 9-9. The numbers describe the specific actions of the protocol; the letters explain the related states and state transitions. Keep in mind that the actions and the states are interrelated; they are separated here only to simplify our analysis. Notice the relationship of these events to the ac-

TABLE 9-7.   Mapping of Presentation PDUs onto the Session Service

CP, CPA, and CPR PPDU Parameters	S-CONNECT Primitive Parameters
Mode selector	SS-user data
Protocol version	SS-user data
Calling presentation selector	SS-user data
Calling session address	Calling SSAP address
Called presentation selector	SS-user data
Called session address	Called SSAP address
Presentation context definition list	SS-user data
Default context name	SS-user data
Quality of service	Quality of service
Presentation requirements	SS-user data
User session requirements	SS-user data
Revised session requirements	Session requirements
Initial sync point number	Initial sync point number
Initial assignment of tokens	Initial assignment of tokens
Session connection identifier	Session connection identifier
User data	SS-user data
Responding presentation selector	SS-user data
Responding session address	Responding SSAP address
Presentation context definition result list	SS-user data
Default context result	SS-user data
Session requirements	Session requirements
Provider reason	SS-user data

ARU and ARP PPDU Parameters	S-U-ABORT Primitive Parameters
Presentation context identifier list	SS-user data
User data	SS-user data
Provider reason	SS-user data
Event identifier	SS-user data

AC and ACA PPDU Parameters	S-TYPED-DATA Primitive Parameters
Presentation context addition list	SS-user data
Presentation context deletion list	SS-user data
User data	SS-user data
Presentation context addition result list	SS-user data
Presentation context deletion result list	SS-user data

RS and RSA PPDU Parameters	S-RESYNCHRONIZE Primitive Parameters
Resynchronize type	Resynchronize type
Synchronization point serial number	Synchronization point serial number
Tokens	Tokens
Presentation context identifier list	SS-user data

TABLE 9-7.   (Continued)

TD PPDU Parameter	S-DATA request Primitive Parameter
User data	SS-user data
TE PPDU Parameter	S-EXPEDITED-DATA request Primitive Parameter
User data	SS-user data
TC PPDU Parameter	S-CAPABILITY-DATA request Primitive Parameter
User data	SS-user data
TCC PPDU Parameter	S-CAPABILITY-DATA response Primitive Parameter
User data	SS-user data

TABLE 9-8.   Presentation Layer Connection Establishment State Table

	STAI0 (Idle)	STAI1 (Await CPA)	STAI2 (Await P-CONrspt)
P-CONreq	p02 & p03 [04] [05] [02] [20] CP STAI1		
CP	p01 & p02 & p03 & p22 [01] [02] [20] P-CONind STAI2 ˆp01 OR ˆp02 OR ˆp22 [01] CPR STAI0		
P-CONrsp+			p04 [06] [12] CPA STAt0
CPA		p04 [03] [12] P-CONcnf+ STAt0	

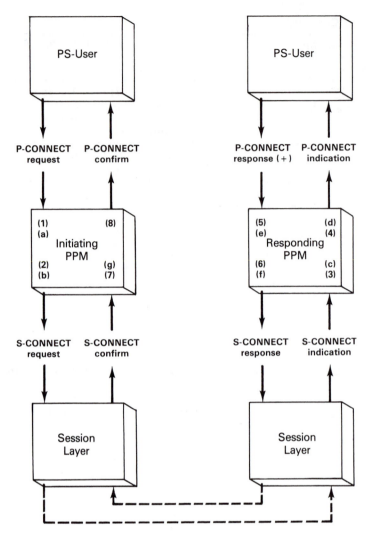

FIGURE 9-6. Establishing a Presentation Context

tions in the state table (Table 9-8). It is recommended you study the state table as you follow the explanation of the session layer connection establishment.

The operation begins when the PS-user sends a P-CONNECT request primitive to the initiating PPM. It uses the parameters in this primitive to invoke the actions described in the state table and constructs the CP PPDU. An important aspect of the presentation layer connection establishment is the negotiation of the transfer syntax between the two entities. Therefore, the PC user must provide the name of the abstract syntax for which a transfer syntax is required. The goal of the interchange of the PDUs between the two session PPMs is to achieve a successful negotiation of the named abstract syntax with a compatible transfer syntax, thus achieving a presentation context. You will notice from

TABLE 9-9. Establishing a Presentation Layer Connection

1. Receive P-CONNECT request primitive from the PS-user.
   Using the excerpted state table (see Table 9–8, column labeled STAI0 and row labeled P-CONreq):

   p02 If present, the named default context can be supported

   p03 Each presentation data value is from a presentation context of the DCS or from the default context if the DCS is empty

   [04] Propose at least one transfer context for each presentation context.

   [05] Propose a transfer context for the default context if one is named in the P-CONNECT request primitive

   [02] Set cr to false (which means there has been no collision of release requests

   Set r1 to false (which means the release phase has not started)

   [20] Set dep to false (which means the activity end is not pending)

2. Entry of CP (non-bold letters) in state table means: Create a CP PPDU, place it into the S-CONNECT request primitive and send to the session layer

   STAI1 Enter state I1

3. Receive CP PPDU from the session layer through the S-CONNECT indication primitive
   Using the excerpted state table (see Table 9–8, column labeled STAI0 and row labeled CP):

   p01 The presentation connection is acceptable to the PPM

   p02 If present, the named default context can be supported

   p03 Each presentation data value is from a presentation context of the DCS or from the default context if the DCS is empty

   p22 For each presentation data value, an instance of encoding is chosen by the PPM

   [01] Mark proposed presentation context which provider cannot support as "provider-rejection"

   [02] Set cr to false (which means there has been no collision of release requests

   Set r1 to false (which means the release phase has not started)

   [20] Set dep to false (which means the activity end is not pending)

4. Entry of P-CONind in state table means: Send P-CONNECT indication to PS-user

   STAI2 Enter state I2

   Note: The remainder of this state table entry is not executed in this operation

5. Receive a P-CONNECT response from PS-user (assuming a positive response)
   Using the excerpted state table (see Table 9–8, column labeled STAI2 and row labeled P-CONrsp+):

   p04 Each presentation data value is from presentation contexts of the DCS being accepted or from the default context if DCS is empty

   [06] Select one transfer syntax for each presentation context agreed for definition and include the agreed presentation contexts in the DCS

   [12] Record FU(f) for f in the fu-dom according to the presentation requirements in the CPA PDDU   *(continued)*

TABLE 9-9. (Continued)

6. Entry of CPA in the state table means: Send CPA PPDU in the S-SESSION response primitive to the session layer

   STAI0 Enter State t0: Connected-data transfer

7. Receive CPA PPDU in the S-SESSION confirm primitive
   Using the excerpted state table (see Table 9-8, column labeled: STAI1 and row labeled P-CONrsp+):

   p04 Each presentation data value is from presentation contexts of the DCS being accepted or from the default context if DCS is empty

   [03] Record abstract and transfer syntaxes for the presentation contexts of the agreed DCS and the default context

   [12] Record FU(f) for f in the fu-dom according to the presentation requirements in the CPA PDDU

8. Entry of P-CONcnf+ in state table means: Send P-CONNECT confirm to the PS-user

   STAt0: Enter State t0

Explanation of States:

a. A P-CONNECT request primitive is accepted if PPM is in STAI0: Idle, no connection
b. Enter STAI1: Await CPA PPDU
c. An S-CONNECT indication primitive is accepted if the PPM is in STAI0: Idle, no connection
d. Enter STAI2: Await P-CONNECT response
e. Only accepted if in STAI2
f. Enter STAt0: Connected-data transfer
g. Only accepted if in STAI1
h. Enter STAt0: Connected-data transfer

h. Enter STAt0

Table 9-7 that the parameters in the PPDUs reflect this process.

If the reader carefully studies Figure 9-4 and Tables 9-8 and 9-9, the operations of the protocol will be quite evident.

SUMMARY AND CONCLUSIONS

The presentation layer is relatively new to the OSI Model. Its principal function is syntax negotiation and resolution. The presentation layer is based on Abstract Syntax Notation 1 (ASN.1) as well as a transfer syntax protocol. All upper layer OSI protocols are now defined with the ASN.1 notation and templates. This includes not only protocol data units, but operation macros as well. While ASN.1 and the OSI transfer syntax are new to the industry, their use is increasing as ASN.1/C compilers come into the marketplace.

CHAPTER 10

Architecture of the Application Layer

INTRODUCTION

It is quite possible to devote an entire book to the application layer. Its functions are quite broad and encompass protocols for office document systems, electronic mail, file transfer, and terminal control. Due to the complexity and scope of the application layer, we examine it in two chapters. This chapter is devoted to an examination of the architecture of the layer, with emphasis on:

- Relationships of the application, presentation, and session layers
- Application Service Element (ASE)
- Common Application Service Element (CASE)
- Association Control Service Element (ACSE)
- Reliable Transfer Service Element (RTSE)
- Remote Operations Service Element (ROSE)
- Commitment, Concurrency, and Recovery (CCR)

Our objectives for the next chapter are to examine and understand the following major application layer protocol standards:

- Message Handling Systems (The X.400 Recommendations)
- The Virtual Terminal (VT) (The ISO 9040/9041 Standards)
- File Transfer, Access, and Management (FTAM) (The ISO 8571 Standards)
- Job Transfer and Manipulation (JTM) (The ISO 8831/8832 Standards)

It is important for the reader to understand that the application layer is not intended to include the end-user application. That is, the user application does not reside within the application layer. Some people consider the name "application layer" to be a misnomer, but it is aptly named because it provides *direct* services to the user application with features such as electronic mail, data base management, and file transfer operations. As is explained in the next section, the user application rests on top of the application layer.

RELATIONSHIPS BETWEEN THE APPLICATION, PRESENTATION, AND SESSION LAYERS

The boundaries between the application, presentation, and session layers are different from those in the lower layers. The layers are not completely independent from each other and, in certain cases, they perform complementary actions. The other difference pertains to the presentation layer. In several instances it is a "pass-through" layer between the application layer and the underlying session and transport layers.

Some of the pass-through dialogue between the application and session layers do not use any services of the presentation layer. Hence, these services are directly mapped between the application and session layers. For example, the P-TOKEN-PLEASE and S-TOKEN-PLEASE are not used by the presentation layer, and it is not affected by the passing of these parameters through its entities. This concept is shown in Figure 10-1. An applications service request is passed to the application layer through an application primitive. Several of the parameters in this primitive are used at the application layer and several others are passed directly to the presentation layer primitive. This process is also repeated at the next layer boundary with the session primitive. It can be seen that the application layer actually creates parameters for use at the lower layers.

The upper three layers are more tightly coupled together than are the lower four layers. This approach allows for the simultaneous negotiation and establishment of the connections for the session, presentation, and applications layers. After all, if the presentation layer were established, but the supporting session layer connection failed, nothing would be accomplished but a useless exchange of control primitives and control protocol data units.

Since the application layer is the highest layer in the OSI Model, it does not provide a service to a higher OSI layer. Consequently, the concept of an application service access point (SAP) does not exist. The interface between the actual end-user application and the application layer is not defined in OSI, and the SAP is relevant to the presentation entity and the lower layers.

OVERVIEW OF KEY TERMS

Before proceeding further with the explanation of the application layer, let us define a few terms. These definitions are explained later in relation to the lay-

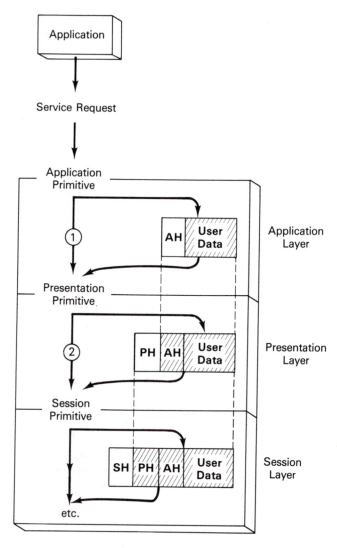

AH: Application layer header.
PH: Presentation layer header.
SH: Session layer header.

① : Parameters for presentation and lower layers.
② : Parameters for session and lower layers.

FIGURE 10-1. Relationships of the Upper Three Layers

ers. Be aware that the ISO provides these definitions in its 7498 and 9545 standards. Please refer to Figures 10-2 and 10-3 for a visual depiction of these terms.

- *Real Open System:* A system that complies with OSI in its communications with other real open systems.
- *Application Process (AP):* A component within a real open system. It is an abstract representation of the elements of the open system which performs processing for a particular application.
- *Application Entity (AE):* Represents the AP within OSI. Provides a set of OSI communications capabilities for the AP.
- *Applications Service Element (ASE):* Part of an applications entity that provides a defined OSI capability for a specific purpose. Permits the interworking of AEs of the same kind with the use of application protocol data units (APDUs).
- *Common Application Service Element (CASE):* An ASE that provides services generally useful to a wide variety of applications. (This term is falling into disuse.)
- *Specific Application Service Element (SASE):* An ASE that provides services to a limited number of applications (perhaps only one).
- *User Element (UE):* Part of an Application Entity. It is specific to the application, and it represents the AP to the AE. It is concerned with the actual OSI services.

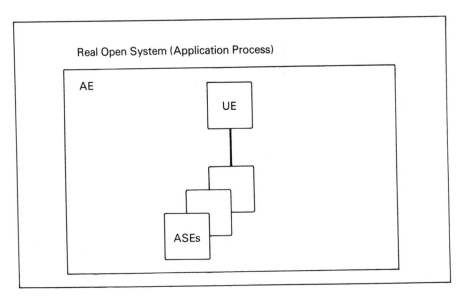

Note: ASEs consist of CASEs or SASEs

FIGURE 10-2. Application Layer Architecture

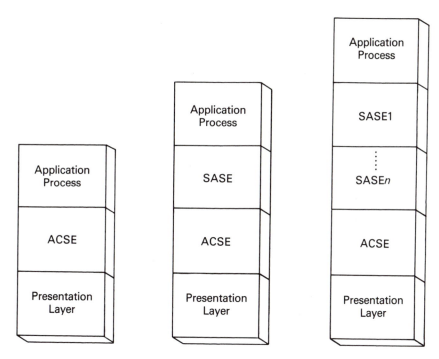

FIGURE 10-3. Possible Sublayers Between the Applications Process and the Presentation Layer

The idea of the ASE is to provide a defined set of services that are needed by a number of applications. In a sense, the ASE is like a common software subroutine that has been written to satisfy a community of users. The advantage of such an approach is that applications programmers or other ASE programmers need not write their own duplicate subroutine, but merely invoke the services of the ASE. (ISO 9545 does not make use of the term CASE, and only uses the term ASE.)

An application entity (AE) consists of one user element and one or more application service elements (ASEs), and operates through a single PSAP address with the presentation layer. In turn, the PSAP is mapped directly onto a SSAP.

It is quite possible that an end-user application could use more than one application-level protocol in a single session. As a consequence, the supporting application entity to the application process can contain (a) the single user element (UE), (b) a CASE kernel, and (c) multiple SASEs. This means that application service elements can be used in a variety of combinations to support the user application process. As we shall see, several of our subjects in Chapter 11 (VT, FTAM, JTM) are actually SASEs.

Figure 10-3 shows several possible sublayering structures for the application layer. This sublayering does not imply any hierarchy, because the ASEs are peers within the application entity. Nonetheless, as a general rule, an Association Control Service Element (ACSE) is invoked by the ASEs, and the ISO 9545 standard states that an ACSE provides a single means for the establishment and termination of all application associations.

It is also possible for an ASE to invoke another ASE. For example, a terminal could use the virtual terminal (VT) SASE to invoke the services of another SASE. The OSI model imposes no rules on how these systems are implemented in software. Indeed, they may be written as one module of code, although a prudent designer would not take such an approach.

The OSI service definitions and protocols within the Model impose strict rules on how the services are invoked from the other services and which features are used within each service. These rules are explained in this chapter and in Chapter 11.

Figure 10-4(a) shows the actual relationship of these services as defined in CCITT X.220. The vertical lines connecting the boxes indicate that the services may or may not invoke the other services. The uppermost entity in the application layer is the X.400 Message Handling Systems (MHS) protocol. It can invoke the Remote Operations Service Element (ROSE), the Reliable Transfer Service Element (RTSE), or the Association Control Service Element (ACSE). Notice these service elements can also invoke certain other service elements and/or the presentation layer. These points are explained further in this chapter.

Figure 10-4(b) shows several application layer relationships specified in the ISO standards. This figure does not exist in any one standard but was constructed from a number of documents. The lines connecting the boxes show several (but not all) invocation relationships. The ASEs in this figure are described in this chapter and in Chapter 11.

Application Associations and Application Contexts

The ACSE supports the establishment, maintenance, and termination of *application associations*. An application association is a detailed description of a cooperative relationship between two application entities through the use of presentation services within a defined *application context*. An application context is the set of service elements and supporting information used on the application association. Essentially, it is a set of rules for communicating in a given application association and the application entities' invocations (their actions).

In a sense, the application association and application context are like a "cataloged procedure" found in the IBM large-scale computer environment, because, like a cataloged procedure of Job Control Language (JCL), they identify all the programs, files, data bases, directories, and supporting system software needed for the user application to execute properly.

The application context must include a set of ASEs and may also include:

- Description of the relationships and dependencies of the ASEs
- Description of the optional features that may be invoked by the ASEs
- Description of the logical structure of information to be exchanged between the cooperating entities

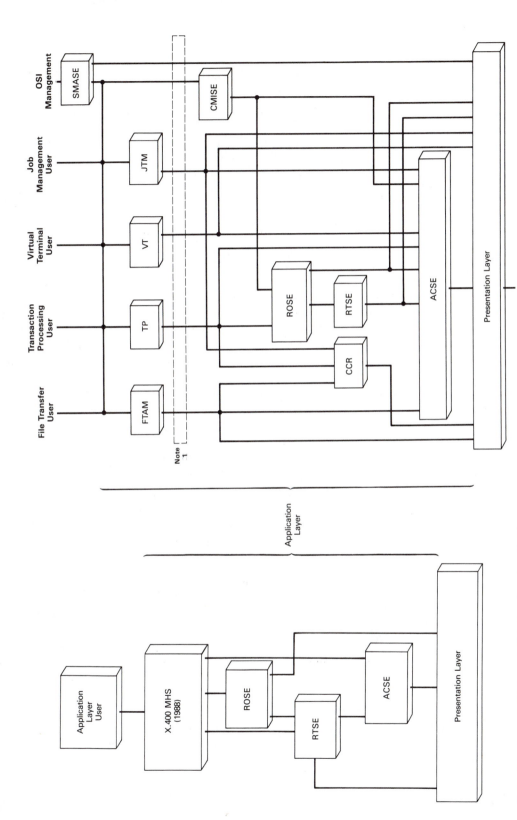

Note 1: Each of the standards may also invoke other SASEs at the junction of the dashed box. These SASEs are described in the relevant standards.

FIGURE 10-4. CCITT and ISO Application Sublayers

- Description of the interleaving of service requests and protocol data units (PDUs)
- Description of the rules for mapping the application entity's PCI (header) onto the presentation layer or another ASE
- Description of any additional rules or any modification or deletion of rules

The final point about the general architecture of the application layer is that the end user is still tasked with developing an interface that can communicate with the service elements in the application entity. The interface can be a system furnished by a vendor, or it can be developed by an organization's system personnel. Indeed, nothing precludes this interface from using the service definitions of the ACSE and the ASEs.

Our approach in the following three sections is to examine the ACSE, RTSE, and ROSE standards and recommendations. The following approach is used in these sections: First an overview of each is provided. Second, the primitives used with the services are examined. Third, the protocol data units are examined. Fourth, the relationships (if any) between the ACSEs and the presentation and session layers are shown. Fifth, the protocol machines and state tables of ACSE, RTSE, and ROSE are analyzed. Sixth, examples of key operations of each are provided.

ASSOCIATION CONTROL SERVICE ELEMENT (ACSE)

The association control service element provides several very basic and important functions to applications entities. It provides services needed between applications processes that are independent of any application-specific needs. In other words, it supports the use of common services.

The ISO and CCITT publish the following standards and recommendations for ACSE:

- Service Definitions: CCITT X.217; ISO 8649
- Protocol Specifications: CCITT X.227; ISO 8650

ACSE's main task is to support the associations between applications. In so doing, it performs four services:

- A-ASSOCIATE
- A-RELEASE
- A-ABORT
- A-P-ABORT

The A-ASSOCIATE service sets up the application association between the applications by the ASE procedures that are identified by an *application context name*. It is responsible for performing the following services:

1. Supporting application entity titles (optional)
2. Supporting the application context name (required)
3. Providing the presentation context (optional)
4. Providing a result of the operation (required)

As might be expected, the A-RELEASE service provides an orderly release of the association of the two applications. It can use the session layer orderly release to ensure both applications agree to the release. Otherwise, the association continues.

The A-ABORT and A-P-ABORT services cause the termination of the application, presentation, and session connections. The A-ABORT is initiated by the user or the association control service; the A-P-ABORT service is initiated by the presentation layer.

It is instructive to note that the ACSE is not involved with the transfer of user data between the application and presentation layers. This task is left to other ASEs, described later in this chapter.

On reviewing the functions of the services of ACSE, it might appear that this service element performs limited services. This supposition is correct, but upon further examination of ACSE it will become evident that its services are absolutely essential.

To illustrate this point, let us assume that two applications are executing (reading, writing, performing computations, etc.) and have not established an applications association (relationship) with each other. Further assume that an application sends data erroneously to the other application (because of problems in the code or in the way it is loaded by the operator, etc.). ACSE will not allow the data to be transferred, but will require that an association be established between the applications before the data transfer can take place. It also "knows" how to refuse release requests from applications, just in case they were issued regarding two applications that had no association between them.

To take the example further, let us assume that two applications have established an association with each other through the use of the ACSE services. ASE would perform monitoring services during the association connection by allowing releases to be performed under certain conditions, and also by allowing aborts under certain conditions. On the other hand, it would not allow the issuance of primitives and protocol data units to establish a redundant session (since a session already exists).

Finally, let us assume that the two applications have issued the necessary primitives to begin the release of the association. During this time, ACSE would not allow the transmission of any data between any two users. It would not accept any further releases (in the event that the systems were malfunctioning and issuing redundant releases). However, it would accept aborts from either application or an underlying service provider.

This brief example should illustrate that while the ACSE services are limited, they are essential for the proper coordination of transfer between applications. Indeed, the number of lines of code in an application would have to be increased substantially if it had to perform these rather mundane but important support functions.

A few more general points are pertinent to ACSE. Every application association is named by an ASN.1 Object Identifier. Also, the association control identifies with an ASN.1 Object Identifier the abstract syntaxes of the application protocol data units that an association can carry as a result of its use by the ASEs.

It is emphasized once again that these services are needed by many applications and are considered to be application-independent. Therefore, they are defined as a general service element.

The service user is not required to use all the features of the ACSE. For example, an electronic message service such as the X.400 message handling system (MHS) may choose to use the A-ASSOCIATE and A-RELEASE services and rely on a service element such as ROSE to make use of the A-ABORT and A-P-ABORT services. How all this fits together is determined by the people who actually establish the application context.

ACSE Primitives

Table 10-1 shows the association control primitives and their parameters. As the reader might expect, many of the parameters are passed to either the presentation layer or the session layer or to other service elements within the application (see Figure 10-4).

The relationship to the presentation layer is quite close, as the following coupling suggests: (a) A-ASSOCIATE and P-CONNECT; (b) A-RELEASE and P-RELEASE; (c) A-ABORT and P-U-ABORT; (d) A-P-ABORT and P-P ABORT. X.227 states that these services are directly related.

A brief description of the ACSE parameters follows. The mode parameter specifies if the ACSE services will operate with the normal or the X.410 1984

TABLE 10-1. Association Control Primitives

Parameter Name	Req	Ind	Rsp	Cnf
A-ASSOCIATE parameters				
Mode	U	M(=)		
Application Context Name*	M	M(=)	M	M(=)
Calling AP Title*	U	C(=)		
Calling AE Qualifier*	U	C(=)		
Calling AP Invocation-identifier*	U	C(=)		
Calling AE Invocation-identifier*	U	C(=)		
Called AP Title*	U	C(=)		
Called AE Qualifier*	U	C(=)		
Called AP Invocation-identifier*	U	C(=)		
Called AE Invocation-identifier*	U	C(=)		
Responding AP Title*			U	C(=)
Responding AE Qualifier*			U	C(=)

TABLE 10-1. *(continued)*

Parameter Name	Req	Ind	Rsp	Cnf
A-ASSOCIATE parameters				
Responding AP Invocation-Identifier*			U	C(=)
Responding AE Invocation-identifier*			U	C(=)
User Information	U	C(=)	U	C(=)
Result			M	M(=)
Result Source			M	
Diagnostic*			U	C(=)
Calling Presentation Address (1)	P	P		
Called Presentation Address (1)	P	P		
Responding Presentation Address (1)			P	P
Presentation Context Definition List (1)*	P	P		
Presentation Context Definition Result list (1)*		P	P	P
Default Presentation Context Name (1)*	P	P		
Default Presentation Context Result (1)*			P	P
Quality of Service (1)	P	P	P	P
Presentation Requirements (1)*	P	P	P	P
Session Requirements (1)	P	P	P	P
Initial Synchronization Point Serial Number (1)	P	P	P	P
Initial Assignment of Tokens (1)	P	P	P	P
Session-connection identifier (1)	P	P	P	P
A-RELEASE parameters				
Reason*	U	C(=)	U	C(=)
User Information*	U	C(=)	U	C(=)
Result			M	M(=)
A-ABORT parameters				
Abort Source*		M		
User Information	U	C(=)		
A-P-ABORT parameter				
Provider Reason	P			

Legend:
C Conditional
M Mandatory
P Subject to conditions in X.216
U User option
* Not used in X.410–1984 mode
= Sematically equal to the value to the left of this value
(1) Not used by the ACSE. Mapped directly through ACSE to the presentation layer during association establishment

mode. Table 10-1 shows the parameters that are applicable to either mode. It can be seen that the 1988 release has added a number of services to ACSE.

The application context name parameter contains the application context that is requested by the ACSE requestor. The responder may return the same name or may choose to return a different name, which provides a form of negotiation. In either case, the returned name is to be used for the association session. If the requestor does not accept a new application context name, it can issue the A-ABORT request primitive.

Logically enough, the A-ASSOCIATE primitives cause the start of an association by the ASE procedures identified by the application context name (which is not specified by the standard, but is application-specific).

The parameters listed in Table 10-1 from calling AP Title through responding AE Invocation-identifier are used to unambiguously identify the calling, called (intended acceptor), and responding (actual acceptor) of the A-ASSOCIATE service. As suggested in the table, the AP, AE, and Invocation-identifier are all provided in the appropriate primitives. The called, calling, and responding application entity titles are used to identify the application entities. While they are listed as parameters in the primitives, they are to be coded as ASN.1 type EXTERNAL.

The User Information parameter is optional and may contain user information or control information for initialization with other ASEs in the application context. Its use depends upon the application context within the primitive.

The Result and Result Source parameters indicate whether the A-ASSOCIATE service is accepted or rejected and the source of this information. The result can be: (a) accepted, (b) permanently rejected, or (c) temporarily rejected. The Result Source can be (a) the ACSE service-user acceptor, (b) the ACSE service provider, (c) the presentation service provider.

The Diagnostic parameter is used in case the service is rejected, or if more information is desired about the service. A rejection will occur if the application context name is not supported or if the AP and AE values are not recognized.

The parameters listed in Table 10-1 from Calling Presentation Address to Default Presentation Context Result are used to identify the associated presentation layer entities and the presentation context. The reader can refer to Chapter 9 for further information on these parameters.

The Quality of Service parameter is defined in Chapter 8. To reiterate briefly, it deals with factors such as delay, throughput, accuracy, priority, reliability, and protection. As the reader might expect, ACSE relies on the lower layers to obtain these services. Indeed, the QOS values are mapped directly to the session layer, which in turn passes them to the transport layer.

The Presentation Requirements and Session Requirements are used if the requestor wishes to select optional functional units of the presentation and session services. The parameters are explained in Chapters 8 and 9.

The next three parameters in Table 10-1—Initial Synchronization Point Serial Number, Initial Assignment of Tokens, Session-Connection Identifier— are passed to the session layer. Their functions are explained in Chapter 9.

The Reason parameter is used with the A-RELEASE service definition. The request primitive can convey one of the following units of information: (a) normal, (b) urgent, (c) user defined. The parameter in a response primitive is used by the recipient of the request to convey its reaction in one of three ways: (a) normal (the release occurs); (b) not finished (if a session layer negotiated release functional unit was not selected for this association, this is a handy method to inform the release requestor that the entity has additional information to send or receive); (c) user defined.

To summarize, the Reason parameter in these primitives is allowed to contain the following information:

- Request and indication primitives: normal, urgent, or undefined
- Response and confirm primitives: normal, not finished, or undefined

The Result parameter in the A-RELEASE service is used to indicate if the association release is acceptable. The value of the parameter can be affirmative or negative.

The A-ABORT Abort Source parameter identifies the source of the abort, which is either the ACSE service user or the ACSE service provider.

The A-P-ABORT Provider Reason parameter contains a value to identify the reason the presentation layer aborted the connection.

ACSE PROTOCOL DATA UNITS

ACSE uses five protocol data units (PDUs) to perform its operations. They are:

1. AARQ: A-ASSOCIATE request/indication
2. AARE: A-ASSOCIATE response/confirm
3. RLRQ: A-RELEASE request/indication
4. RLRE: A-RELEASE response/confirm
5. ABRT: A-ABORT request/indication

The protocol data units are largely self-descriptive. The AARQ and AARE are used to establish an application association. The RLRQ and RLRE protocol data units are used to release the association. The ABRT is used to abort the association. We will see an example of their actual use shortly.

The remainder of this section provides examples of the ACSE PDUs, and an explanation of the fields in the PDUs. All permissible PDUs are not shown here, but we include a sampling to give the reader an idea of how the ISO and CCITT uses ASN.1 to describe the structure of the data units. As always, the reader should read the actual standard for a complete description.

The first ASN.1 notation shows the choices available for the protocol data units by the use of ASN.1 CHOICE:

```
ACSE-apdu  ::  =CHOICE
{ aarq AARQ-apdu,
```

aare AARE-apdu,

rlrq RLRQ-apdu,

rlre RLRE-apdu,

abrt ABRT-apdu

}

The next ASN.1 notation describes the AARQ protocol data unit and the contents of the unit. The contents are derived from the parameters in the primitives, which are explained in Table 10-1. Notice the use of the IMPLICIT feature of ASN.1 (described in Chapter 9).

```
AARQ-apdu :: = [APPLICATION 0 ] IMPLICIT SEQUENCE
{ protocol-version              [0] IMPLICIT BIT STRING
{ version (0) }
DEFAULT version1,
application-context-name        [1] Application-context-name,
called-AP-title                 [2] AP-title
OPTIONAL,
called-AE-qualifier             [3] AE-qualifier
OPTIONAL,
called-AP-invocation-id         [4] AP-invocation-id
OPTIONAL,
called-AE-invocation-id         [5] AE-invocation-id
OPTIONAL,
calling-AP-title                [6] AP-title
OPTIONAL,
calling-AE-qualifier            [7] AE-qualifier
OPTIONAL,
calling-AP-invocation-id        [8] AP-invocation-id
OPTIONAL,
calling-AE-invocation-id        [9] AE-invocation-id
OPTIONAL,
implementation-information      [29] IMPLICIT Implementation-data
OPTIONAL,
user-information                [30] IMPLICIT Association-information
OPTIONAL
}
```

Relationship of ACSE to Other ASEs and Layers

Mapping ACSE to the Presentation Layer. The mapping of the ACSE to the presentation services is based either on the use of the 1984-X.410 mode or the 1988 normal mode. This section explains the normal mode. Be aware that the ACSE services assume (at least) the use of the presentation kernel. It requires access to the P-CONNECT, P-RELEASE, P-U-ABORT, and P-P-ABORT services.

As mentioned earlier, the ACSE and presentation layer primitives have a one-to-one correspondence with each other, and the ACSE protocol data units are exchanged through these primitives. The association protocol control information (APCI, also called the association header) and the user information are conveyed in the User Information parameter of these primitives. The APCI and the user information must be expressed using the abstract syntax within the standard (some examples were provided in the previous section). This abstract syntax is included as values of the Presentation Context Definition parameters in the A-ASSOCIATE request and response primitives. See Table 10-1 for a review of these parameters.

The minimum mapping of the ACSE and presentation primitives and their relationship to ACSE APDUs is shown in Table 10-2. The ACSE services require these presentation services. Optionally, other presentation services may be used.

Mapping ACSE to the Session Layer. The A-ASSOCIATE service requestor and acceptor determine the functional units that are to be used for the session services with the Session Requirements parameter.

ACSE Protocol Machines and State Tables

For the reader who skipped previous material and is not unfamiliar with this topic, there is a section on protocol machines and state tables in Chapter 1 which should be reviewed before reading this section.

The ACSE protocol is defined by three protocol machines:

- *Association Control Protocol Machine* (ACPM): This is the protocol machine (logic) for the ACSE.

- *Requesting Association Control Protocol Machine:* This is the protocol machine that is a requestor for a particular service.

TABLE 10-2.   Mapping of ACSE and the Presentation Layer

ACSE Primitive	APDU *	Presentation Primitive
A-ASSOCIATE request/indication	AARQ	P-CONNECT request/indication
A-ASSOCIATE response/confirm	AARE	P-CONNECT response/confirm
A-RELEASE request/indication	RLRQ	P-RELEASE request/indication
A-RELEASE response/confirm	RLRE	P-RELEASE response/confirm
A-ABORT request/indication	ABRT	P-U-ABORT request/indication
A-P-ABORT indication	—	P-P-ABORT indication

* ACSE APDUs are not used in the X.410–1984 mode.

- *Accepting Association Control Protocol Machine:* This is the machine that is the acceptor for a particular service.

ACSE sets strict rules on the actions that can be taken on the ACPM. These actions are defined in a state table in Annex A of X.227. As with all state tables and protocol machines, X.227 stipulates the permissible primitives and/or primitives that can enter a state, the permissible protocol data units and/or primitives that emanate from a state, and the resulting state after the machine has issued the protocol data unit.

An Example of ACSE Operations

The ACSE defines eight states that govern the association connection and release. To keep matters relatively simple, the following list shows the relevant state for the association connection establishment at the sending, requesting ACPM only (Figure 10-5). We will examine the contents of this state table in this section of this chapter.

STA0
Idle: unassociated

A-ASCreq   p1
AARQ
STA1

This example of ACSE operations concentrates on the actions involved in the establishment of an association between two applications, since this service is the principal aspect of the standard.

The sequence of events occurs during the association establishment as noted by the numbers and letters in Figure 10-5 and Table 10-3. The numbers describe the specific actions of the protocol. The letters explain the related states and state transitions. Keep in mind that the actions and the states are interrelated and are separated here only to simplify our analysis. Notice the relationship of these events to the actions in the state table listed above.

Association Establishment.   Figure 10-5 illustrates how ACSE supports a service user and also how it interacts with the presentation layer. The figure shows the operations for the establishment of an applications association. Remember that the users may be an end user or a service element such as RTSE. Figure 10-5 uses the more general terms requestor and acceptor to identify the users.

The operations begin when the ACPM receives an A-ASSOCIATE request primitive (A-ASCreq; see state table above) from the ACSE service user. The ACPM can only accept this request if it is in state 0 (idle and unassociated). The predicate p1 in the state table means the ACPM can support the requested connection. The ACPM constructs an AARQ APDU from the parameters of

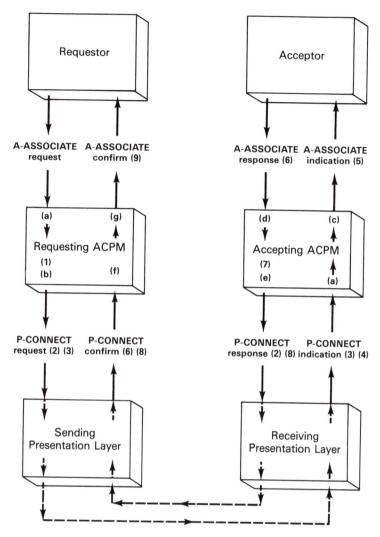

FIGURE 10-5. Establishing an Association

this primitive and, optionally, other information. It then issues a P-CONNECT request primitive to the presentation layer. The AARQ protocol data unit is carried in the user data parameter of the P-CONNECT primitive. After sending this primitive, the requesting ACPM enters into state 1 (awaiting an AARE APDU or abort units). This action completes the above state table. Be aware that subsequent actions are governed by state tables, but for the sake of simplicity are not shown in this example.

The presentation layer relays the AARQ through its layer to the lower layers of OSI.

Eventually, the receiving ACPM receives the AARQ data unit through a

TABLE 10-3. Establishing an Association

Explanation of Actions

1. Form AARQ APDU from parameters in A-ASSOCIATE request primitive.
2. Carries parameters to next service provider (presentation layer).
3. Carries AARQ APDU in the user data field of the primitive.
4. Carries parameters to next service user (ACSE).
5. Parameters derived from AARQ APDU and the P-CONNECT indication primitive.
6. Result primitive specifies if association is accepted or rejected.
7. Form AARE APDU from parameters in A-ASSOCIATE response primitive.
8. Carries AARE APDU in user data parameter of primitive.
9. Parameters derived from AARE APDU and P-CONNECT confirm primitive.

Explanation of States

a. A-ASSOCIATE request accepted if ACPM is in state 0 (STA0): idle and unassociated.
b. After sending AARQ APDU in the primitive, enter state 1 (STA 1): awaiting AARE APDU.
c. After sending AARQ APDU in the primitive, enter state 2 (STA 2): awaiting A-ASSOCIATE response.
d. Accepted if in STA 2 and receives an A-ASSOCIATE response, or the ACSE abort primitives.
e. After sending AARE SPDU in the primitive, enter state 5 (STA 5): associated.
f. Accepted if in STA 1 and receives an AARE APDU or the ACSE abort primitives.
g. After sending primitive, enter state 5 (STA 5): associated.

P-CONNECT indication primitive from the presentation layer. It accepts this primitive only if it is in state 0. The ACPM examines the fields in the AARQ data unit to determine if the unit is acceptable. If it is not acceptable, an association is not established. This means that an A-ASSOCIATE indication primitive will not be issued to the recipient ACSE service user.

If the AARQ is acceptable to the receiving ACPM, it issues an A-ASSOCIATE indication primitive to its service user (the acceptor). The parameters in this primitive are derived from the fields in the AARQ protocol data unit and the parameters in the P-CONNECT indication primitive. After the accepting ACPM sends this primitive to the user acceptor, it enters into state 2 (awaiting A-ASSOCIATE response).

We assume the accepting ACPM receives an A-ASSOCIATE response primitive from its upper layer service user acceptor. Since it is in state 2, it will not accept any other type of primitive (except aborts). This primitive contains the Result parameter, which signifies whether the receiving user has rejected or accepted the association. The ACPM then forms an AARE protocol data unit using the parameters in the A-ASSOCIATE response primitive. It sends a P-CONNECT response primitive to the presentation layer with the AARE protocol data unit carried in the data parameter. It then enters into state 5 (associated).

The presentation layer receives the AARE protocol data unit and relays the unit down to the lower OSI layers.

The requesting ACPM receives a P-CONNECT confirm primitive. Since it is in state 1, it only accepts an AARE or abort protocol data units. The P-CONNECT primitive contains information to identify three possible situations:

- An association is established.
- The accepting service user rejects the association.
- The presentation service rejects the association.

Assuming the association is accepted, the P-CONNECT confirm primitive Result parameter signifies acceptance and the User Information parameter contains the AARE APDU. The originating ACPM then issues an A-ASSOCIATE confirm primitive to the service requestor which contains parameters derived from the AARE ADPU and the P-CONNECT confirm primitive. The requesting ACPM now enters into state 5. The association is established.

Data Transfer. Hereafter, the mapping functions that were performed during the association establishment are used to support the ongoing communications between the applications. The ACSE is no longer involved in the data transfer between the users. Indeed, as we shall see when we examine the RTSE and ROSE, the data transfer primitives and data transfer control primitives flow directly between the user RTSE, ROSE, and the presentation layer.

Association Release. The release operation follows a similar scenario. The A-RELEASE service must accompany the underlying P-RELEASE service. A responder responds to an A-RELEASE indication primitive by setting the result field in an A-RELEASE response primitive. If the session layer negotiated release functional unit was selected for this association, the acceptor is permitted to respond negatively and keep the association open.

RELIABLE TRANSFER SERVICE ELEMENT (RTSE)

In recent years, the CCITT and the ISO have recognized the need to define an application service element to support the reliable transfer of application protocol data units (APDUs) between applications, and to ensure that the sender is notified as to whether the delivery is successful or unsuccessful. Obviously, these services are often applicable to more than one application. Therefore, they have been defined as a common service element called the reliable transfer service element (RTSE).

The RTSE supports other important functions. It recovers from communication and end-system failures. It supports the negotiation and use of size parameters for protocol data units, the segmenting of the units into smaller units, and the establishment of checkpoints to verify the delivery of segmented or unsegmented units to the receiving RTSE.

The ISO and CCITT publish the following standards and recommendations for RTSE:

- Service Definitions: ISO 9066-1; CCITT X.218
- Protocol Specifications: ISO 9066-2; CCITT X.208

RTSE provides seven services. A brief explanation of each of these services follows:

- RT-OPEN
- RT-TRANSFER
- RT-TURN-PLEASE
- RT-TURN-GIVE
- RT-P-ABORT
- RT-U-ABORT
- RT-CLOSE.

An association is established between two RTSEs with the RT-OPEN service. During this operation, several functions to be used during the association are negotiated (or refused) between the RTSEs:

- *Checkpoint size:* This value establishes the maximum amount of data that can be sent between minor synchronization points, or alternately, the stipulation that checkpoints will not be used.
- *Window size:* This value is used to place a limit on the maximum number of minor synchronization points that can be outstanding before the transfer of data is halted.
- *Dialogue-mode:* This value defines if the communication between the RTSEs is to be two-way alternate or monologue.
- *Initial turn:* Agreement on which RTSE is given the initial right to send data.

After the association is established, the RT-TRANSFER service is invoked to transfer an application protocol data unit (APDU). During this operation, RTSE is used to send data, initiate checkpoints, verify the safe delivery between the RTSEs, take turns exchanging data, and recover from nondelivered or misdelivered data units.

As the reader might expect, the RT-TURN-PLEASE and the RT-TURN-GIVE services enable the peer RTSE-user to request or relinquish the turn. The user cannot transfer an APDU if it does not have the turn. Moreover, the RTSE-user must also have the turn in order to release an application-association.

The RT-P-ABORT service is issued by the RTSE-provider to indicate it cannot maintain the application-association. This provider is responsible for taking the following actions to ensure the integrity of the APDU transfer: (a) If it is the APDU sender, it must first issue a negative confirm in an RT-TRANSFER confirm primitive for the nondelivered APDU, (b) if it is the APDU receiver, it must delete any partially received APDU before it issues the RT-P-ABORT indication primitive.

The RT-U-ABORT service allows the RTSE-user to abort the application association. Either user can abort this non-confirmed service.

The RT-CLOSE service is used by the RTSE-user to request the release of the application-association. The requestor can only evoke this service if it has possession of the turn.

RTSE Primitives

The reliable transfer service uses the conventional OSI request, indication, response, and confirm primitives because it is a confirmed service. The majority of the parameters in the RT-OPEN primitives are passed to ACSE or the presentation layer (see Table 10-4). Four parameters are used by RTSE (see Table 10-5). As before, we confine our discussion to the parameters within the subject service element. The reader can refer to the ACSE and presentation layer discussions for an explanation of the other parameters.

The Dialogue-mode parameter identifies the type of application-association as either monologue or two-way alternate. The Initial-turn parameter designates which RTSE-user is to have the initial turn, the association-initiator or the association-responder. The Application-protocol parameter is used only with the X.410 1984 mode and identifies the application protocol that governs the application association. The User-data parameter contains any necessary data for establishing the association. It is not actual user data if it is used with the 1984 mode, but provides information on the result of the RT-OPEN primitive (failure or accepted, and some reasons).

The data transfer service is supported by the request, indication, and confirm primitives (see Figure 10-6). The confirm primitive is an acknowledgment by the accepting RTSE that it has or has not received an APDU within the established tranfer time. This tranfer time value is carried in the parameter of the RT-TRANSFER request primitive. A Result parameter is used by the receiving RTSE-user to convey the outcome of the attempted APDU transfer.

The RT-TURN-PLEASE and RT-TURN-GIVE primitives are non-confirmed and allow the RTSE-user to request or relinquish the turn with its peer. The turn is used for two functions:

- Used by either RTSE-user to transfer APDUs
- Requested by association-initiating RTSE-user to release the application association

A Priority parameter is used with the RT-TURN-PLEASE primitives to define the priority associated with the action. The turn can only be relinquished

TABLE 10-4.   RT-OPEN Parameters Passed to Other Layers

Parameter Name	Note	Req	Ind	Resp	Conf
Mode		A	A		
Application Context Name	2	A	A	A	A
Calling AP Title	2	A	A		
Calling AP Invocation-identifier	2	A	A		
Calling AE Qualifier	2	A	A		
Calling AE Invocation-identifier	2	A	A		
Called AP Title	2	A	A		
Called AP Invocation-identifier	2	A	A		
Called AE Qualifier	2	A	A		
Called AE Invocation-identifier	2	A	A		
Responding AP Title	2			A	A
Responding AP Invocation-identifier	2			A	A
Responding AE Qualifier	2			A	A
Responding AE Invocation-identifier	2			A	A
Result				A	A
Result Source					A
Diagnostic				A	A
Calling Presentation Address		P	P		
Called Presentation Address		P	P		
Responding Presentation Address				P	P
Presentation Context Definition List	2	P	P		
Presentation Context Definition Result List	2		P	P	P
Default Presentation Context Name	2	P	P		
Default Presentation Context Result	2		P	P	P

TABLE 10-5.   RT-OPEN Parameters Used by RTSE

Parameter Name	Note	Req	Ind	Resp	Conf
Dialogue-mode		M	M(=)		
Initial-turn		M	M(=)		
Application-protocol	3	U	C(=)		
User-data	1	U	C(=)	U	C(=)

Notes:
1. Restricted use of parameters in X.410–1984 mode (see following clauses).
2. Parameter absent in X.410–1984 mode.
3. Parameter only present in X.410–1984 mode.
U User option
M Mandatory
C Conditional
A Defined in ACSE specifications
P Defined in Presentation layer specifications

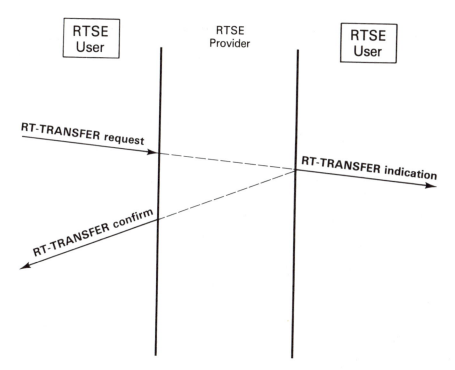

FIGURE 10-6. RTSE Transfer Primitives

if the RTSE has it and is not awaiting a confirmation of the transfer of data units (awaiting an RT-TRANSFER confirm primitive).

The RT-P-ABORT primitive is used by the RTSE-provider to notify the RTSE-users that it cannot maintain the association. The RT-U-ABORT is issued by the RTSE-user to abort the application association.

The RT-CLOSE primitives are used to release the application association. Since the close is a confirmed service, it uses request, indication, response, and confirm. The association initiator can request the release if it has the turn and is not awaiting a data transfer confirm primitive (the RT-TRANSFER confirm). These primitives support the Reason field, which is defined in the ACSE specifications.

RTSE Application Protocol Data Units

The RTSE application protocol data units (APDUs) are defined by abstract syntax notation one (ASN.1), and several examples of the notation for the data units are provided below. The first example shows the ASN.1 definitions for the RTSE APDUs.

```
RTSE-apdus :: = CHOICE{
                    rtorq-apdu  [16] IMPLICIT  RTORQapdu,
                    rtoac-apdu  [17] IMPLICIT  RTOACapdu,
```

```
rtorj-apdu      [18] IMPLICIT   RTORJapdu,
rttp-apdu                       RTTPapdu,
rttr-apdu                       RTTRapdu,
rtab-apdu       [22] IMPLICIT   RTABapdu}
```

The next example shows the ASN.1 definition for a RT-OPEN-REQUEST (RTORQ) APDU. The value set is from 0 to 4. The default values of the check-point, window, and dialogue mode values are given.

```
RTORQapdu :: =      SET {
checkpointSize      [0] IMPLICIT INTEGER DEFAULT 1,
windowSize          [1] IMPLICIT INTEGER DEFAULT 3,
dialogueMode        [2] IMPLICIT INTEGER {monologue(0),twa(1)}
                        DEFAULT monologue,
connectionDATARQ    [3] ConnectionData,
applicationProtocol [4] IMPLICIT INTEGER OPTIONAL --solely
                        in X.410- 1984 mode--}
```

The next example shows the ASN.1 for the RT-TURN-PLEASE (RTTP) APDU. Its only contents is the priority value. It is instructive to note that RTSE does not use a protocol data unit for a TURN-GIVE service because the primitive for this service is actually passed down to the session layer, which is responsible for relaying the value in its data unit to the other session layer and (through primitives) to the other RTSE.

```
RTTPapdu :: = --priority--     INTEGER
```

The last example is the RT-TRANSFER request (RTTR) APDU. This unit is placed into a P-DATA request primitive and relayed down to the presentation layer. Prior to issuing this primitive, the RTSE first issues a P-ACTIVITY-START request primitive. It then sends the data, and next issues a P-MINOR-SYNCHRONIZE request token. In this manner, the RTSE makes use of services at the lower layers to provide for confirmed services. The section on RTSE examples show how these operations are performed.

```
RTTRapdu :: =   OCTET STRING
```

Relationship of RTSE to Other Entities and Layers

Relationship of RTSE to Other ASEs and the Presentation Layer. The OSI Model is quite flexible in how the RTSE is used. Figure 10-4 shows some possibilities. RTSE invokes the services of the ACSE, and it may communicate directly with the presentation layer. In turn, several elements can consider the RTSE as a service provider. For example, a specific applications service element (SASE), such as electronic mail or a file transfer, can invoke the services

Architecture of the Application Layer

of RTSE. Additionally, the remote operations service element (ROSE) can use the services of RTSE (ROSE is discussed next).

Notwithstanding the RTSE services require access to the ACSE A-ASSOCI-ATE, A-RELEASE, A-ABORT, and A-P ABORT services. We have just learned that the RTSE is tasked with seven services. However, these services actually utilize the services of ACSE or the presentation layer. The relationship is as follows:

- RT-OPEN uses the ACSE A-ASSOCIATE service.
- RT-CLOSE uses the ACSE A-ASSOCIATE service.
- RT-TRANSFER uses the P-ACTIVITY-START, P-DATA, AND P-MINOR-SYNCHRONIZE services.
- RT-TURN-PLEASE uses the P-TOKEN-PLEASE service.
- RT-TURN-GIVE uses the P-CONTROL-GIVE service.
- RT-P-ABORT uses the ACSE A-ABORT service.
- RT-U-ABORT uses the ACSE A-ABORT service.

The RTSE services require access to the following presentation layer services:

P-ACTIVITY-START	P-DATA
P-MINOR-SYNCHRONIZE	P-ACTIVITY-END
P-ACTIVITY-INTERRUPT	P-ACTIVITY-DISCARD
P-U-EXCEPTION-REPORT	P-ACTIVITY-RESUME
P-P-EXCEPTION-REPORT	P-TOKEN-PLEASE
P-CONTROL-GIVE	

The RTSE relies on the ACSE to have access to the following presentation layer services: P-CONNECT, P-RELEASE, P-U-ABORT, P-P-ABORT.

Mapping to the ACSE Services. Table 10-6 shows the relationship of the RTSE and ACSE services, as well as the protocol data units.

Mapping to the Presentation Services. Table 10-7 shows the relationship of the RTSE and presentation services, as well as the protocol data units.

RTSE Protocol Machines and State Tables

RTSE operations are based on protocol machines and state tables. Several of the state tables are examined in the next section. The RTSE protocol machines are:

- *Reliable-transfer-protocol-machine:* The protocol for RTSE.
- *Requesting-reliable-transfer-protocol-machine:* The machine whose user is the requestor of an RTSE service.

- *Accepting-reliable-transfer-protocol-machine:* The machine whose user is the acceptor for an RTSE service.
- *Sending-reliable-transfer-protocol-machine:* The machine whose RTSE user is the sender.
- *Receiving-reliable-transfer-protocol-machine:* The machine whose RTSE user is the receiver.

TABLE 10-6. RTSE/ACSE Mapping Functions

RTSE Service	APDU	ACSE Service
RT-OPEN request/indication	RTORQ	A-ASSOCIATE request/indication
RT-OPEN response/confirm	RTOAC	A-ASSOCIATE response/confirm
RT-OPEN response/confirm	RTORJ	A-ASSOCIATE response/confirm
RT-CLOSE request/indication	—	A-RELEASE request/indication
RT-CLOSE response/confirm	—	A-RELEASE response/confirm
association-abort	RTAB	A-ABORT request/indication
association-provider-abort	—	A-P-ABORT indication
RT-P-ABORT indication	RTAB	A-ABORT request/indication
RT-U-ABORT request/indication	RTAB	A-ABORT request/indication

TABLE 10-7. Presentation Mapping Functions

RTSE Service	APDU	Presentation Service
RT-TRANSFER request	—	P-ACTIVITY-START request/indication
	RTTR	P-DATA request/indication
	—	P-MINOR-SYNCHRONIZE request/indication/response/confirm
RT-TRANSFER indication/confirm	—	P-ACTIVITY-END request/indication/response/confirm
RT-TURN-PLEASE request/indication	RTTP	P-TOKEN-PLEASE request/indication
RT-TURN-GIVE request/indication	—	P-CONTROL-GIVE request/indication
user-exception-report	—	P-U-EXCEPTION-REPORT request/indication
provider-exception-report	—	P-P-EXCEPTION-REPORT indication
transfer-interrupt	—	P-ACTIVITY-INTERRUPT request/indication/response/confirm
transfer-discard	—	P-ACTIVITY-DISCARD request/indication/response/confirm
transfer-resumption	—	P-ACTIVITY-RESUME request/indication

Architecture of the Application Layer

- *Association-initiating-reliable-transfer-protocol-machine:* The machine whose RTSE user is the association initiator.
- *Association-responding-reliable-transfer-protocol-machine:* The machine whose RTSE user is the association responder.

An Example of RTSE Operations

This section provides an example of RTSE operations. The example is chosen to show the principal functions involved in the establishment of an application association. Figure 10-7 and Table 10-8 should be used to follow this example.

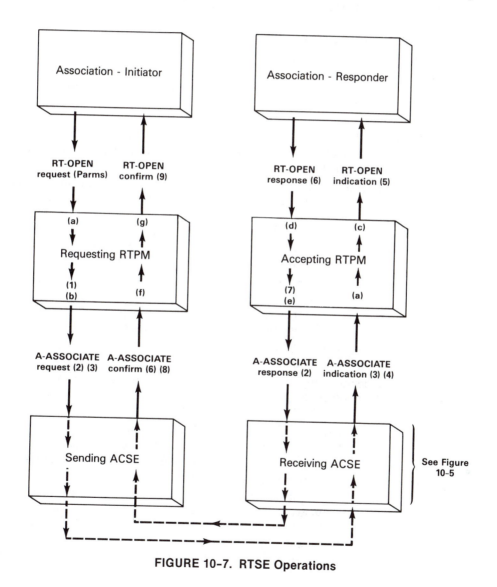

FIGURE 10-7. RTSE Operations

TABLE 10-8. Example of RTSE Operations

Actions and Explanations:

1. Form RTORQ APDU from parameters in the RT-OPEN request primitive.

2. Primitive carries parameters to next service provider (ACSE). Initial turn is assigned to association initiator.

3. Primitive carries RTORQ APDU in user data parameter.

4. Carries parameters to next service user (RTSE).

5. Parameters in the primitive are derived from RTORQ APDU and A-ASSOCIATE indication primitive.

6. Result parameter in primitive specifies if acceptor has accepted or rejected the association.

7. Form an RTOAC APDU using the parameters from the RT-OPEN response primitive.

8. The RTOAC APDU is in the user data parameter in the primitive.

9. Carries parameters derived from the RTOAC APDU and the A-ASSOCIATE confirm primitive.

Explanation of States:

a. Only accepted if in State 0 (STA 0): idle and unassociated and RTPM can support requested application association.

b. Association-initiating RTPM = TRUE; after sending primitive and protocol data unit, enter STA 1: awaiting RTOAC, RTORJ, or an A-ASSOCIATE confirm primitive.

c. Association-initiating RTPM = FALSE; after sending primitive and protocol data unit, enter STA 2: awaiting RT-OPEN response (with a confirmed or not confirmed signal).

d. Only accepted if in STA 2 and receiving an RT-OPEN response. Also, turn is assigned to RTPM.

e. After sending primitive and protocol data unit, enter STA 22: associated; RTPM is association-responding and receiving RTPM.

f. Only accepted if in STA 1 and receives an RTOAC protocol data unit (or RTORJ, or the abort PDUs).

g. After sending primitive, enter STA 11: associated; RTPM is associating-initiating and sending RTPM.

Figure 10-7 illustrates how RTSE supports a service user and also how it interacts with the ACSE in establishing an application association.

The operations begin when the RTPM receives and RT-OPEN request primitive from the association initiator. The RTPM can only accept this request if it is in state 0 (idle and unassociated) and the RTPM can support the association.

The RTPM constructs an RTORQ APDU from the parameters of this primitive. We assume for this example that this RTPM passes in its primitive to ASCE that it is to have the initial turn. It then issues an A-ASSOCIATE request primitive to ACSE in order for ACSE to negotiate the association. The RTORQ protocol data unit is carried in the user data parameter of the A-ASSOCIATE primitive. After sending this primitive, the requesting RTPM enters into state 1 (awaiting an RTOAC or RTORJ unit).

The ACSE relays the RTORQ through its layer to the lower layers of OSI. As discussed in the section of ACSE, it will at this time set up an application association.

The receiving RTPM receives the RTORQ data unit through an A-ASSO-CIATE indication primitive from ACSE. It accepts this primitive only if it is in state 1. The RTPM examines the fields in the RTORQ data unit to determine if the unit is acceptable. If it is not acceptable, an association is not established.

If the RTORQ is acceptable to the receiving RTPM, it issues an RT-OPEN indication primitive to its service user (the association-responder). The parameters in this primitive are derived from the fields in the RTORQ protocol data unit and the parameters in the A-ASSOCIATE indication primitive. After the accepting RTPM sends this primitive to the user acceptor it enters into state 2 (awaiting a response primitive from the user).

We assume the accepting RTPM receives an RT-OPEN response primitive from its upper layer service user acceptor. Since it is in state 2, it will not accept any other type of primitive. This primitive contains the Result parameter, which signifies whether the receiving user has rejected or accepted the association. The RTPM then forms an RTOAC protocol data unit using the parameters in the RT-OPEN response primitive parameters. It sends an A-ASSOCIATE response primitive to ACSE with the RTOAC protocol data unit carried in the data parameter. It then enters into state 22 (associated; this RTPM is the association-responding and receiving RTPM). This state means that this RTPM cannot transfer data until it is given the turn.

The ACSE receives the RTOAC protocol data unit and relays the unit down to the lower OSI layers.

The requesting RTPM receives an A-ASSOCIATE confirm primitive. Since it is in state 1, it only accepts an RTOAC or RTORJ, protocol data units.

Assuming the association is accepted, the A-ASSOCIATE confirm primitive Result parameter signifies acceptance and the User Data parameter contains the RTOAC APDU. The originating RTPM then issues to the service requestor an RT-OPEN confirm primitive which contains parameters derived from the RTOAC ADPU and the RT-OPEN confirm primitive. The requesting RTPM now enters into state 11: associated; this RTPM is the association-initiating and sending RTPM. The association is established and the RTPM can begin data transfer.

During this process, the RTORQ data unit has been used to negotiate the checkpoint size, window size, and dialogue-mode.

REMOTE OPERATIONS SERVICE ELEMENT (ROSE)

Up to this point in our discussion of the application layer architecture, we have not examined any services to support interactive communications between two distributed entities, yet some of the operations in this type of environment are common to many applications.

Most applications designers develop interactive applications based on two operations: (a) a transaction from an originator to the recipient which requests that an operation be performed, and (b) a transaction from the recipient to the originator that describes the result of the requested operation. A third option is usually included to provide an error report about problems resulting from the transactions and to allow the transaction to be aborted, if necessary.

As a point of emphasis, the originator (or invoker) can invoke operations in another system (the performer). Since the performer system may be different from the one in which the invoker resides, the interactive transaction may involve remote operations; hence the name remote operations service element (ROSE).

The CCITT and the ISO have published the Remote Operations Service Element (ROSE). These standards define the procedures for supporting distributed, interactive applications processing. The two specifications are technically aligned with each other. The remote operations specification was published in 1984 with the X.400 MHS recommendations (X.410). It was recognized applicable for general use and was published in the 1988 Blue Books as ASEs.

The ISO and CCITT publish the following standards and recommendations for ROSE:

- Service Definitions: ISO 9072-1; CCITT X.219
- Protocol Specifications: ISO 9072-2; CCITT X.229

ROSE does not have any transfer capabilities. It uses other ASEs for this operation. Additionally, ROSE is not a confirmed service. Some applications need confirmation of a transaction submittal and some do not. In any event, ROSE can achieve almost the same result by requiring the performer to report the outcome of the operation. If this capability is not sufficient, ROSE can invoke the services of RTSE to obtain reliable transfer of its data units. However, this might be unduly burdensome for ROSE implementations that require the performer to report the outcome of the operation.

Most of the parameters in the ROSE protocol data units are transparent to ROSE and are used by the ROSE service users to manage their dialogue. Consequently, ROSE is not concerned about the nature of the user application. It simply provides a mechanism to (a) invoke a user-defined action at an AE, and (b) receive information about the results of the action.

ROSE bears many similarities to some of SNA's services. Table 10-9 summarizes these features.

ROSE permits two modes of operation. The synchronous mode requires the performer to reply to the invoker before the invoker can invoke another operation, which is a common method to control interactive, transaction-based systems. The asynchronous mode allows the invoker to continue invoking operations without requiring a reply from the performer.

TABLE 10-9. Classification of ROSE Operations

Result of Operation	Expected Reporting from Performer
Success or Failure	If successful, return result. If a failure, return an error reply
Failure Only	If successful, no reply. If a failure, return an error reply
Success Only	If successful, return result. If a failure, no reply
Success or Failure	In either case, no reply

The reporting requirements (Table 10-9) are combined with the mode definitions to define five classes of operations. These operations are summarized in Table 10-10.

ROSE also provides for the grouping of operations together in the event that the performer notifies the invoker that it must also perform some operation(s). This function is called *linked operations*. Figure 10-8 illustrates the concept of linked operations. The invoker of an operation invokes a parent operation which is executed by the performer (i.e., the performer of a parent operation). This AE can invoke one or more child operations, which are performed by the invoker [i.e., the performer of child operation(s)].

ROSE also uses four macros, which are defined in ASN.1. (The reader should obtain ISO 9072-1 and read Annex B. It contains useful tutorial information on the use of the ROSE macros.) The four macros are:

- BIND: Allows the specification of the types of user data values to be exchanged in the establishment of the application association.
- UNBIND: Allows the specification of the types of user data values to be exchanged in the release of the application association.
- OPERATION: The type notation in this macro allows the specification of an operation and user data to be exchanged for a request and a positive reply. This macro can specify a list of linked child operations if the operation is a parent operation.
- ERROR: The type notation in this macro allows the specification of an operation and user data to be exchanged in a negative reply.

TABLE 10-10. ROSE Operation Classes

Class Number	Definition
1	Synchronous: Report success (result) or failure (error)
2	Asynchronous: Report success (result) or failure (error)
3	Asynchronous: Report failure (error) only
4	Asynchronous: Report success (result) only
5	Asynchronous: Report nothing

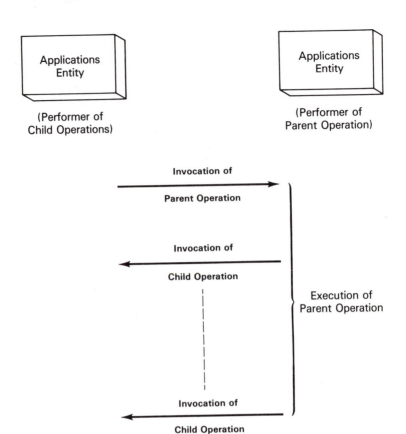

FIGURE 10-8. Linked Operations

A brief explanation of the ROSE services follows; more detail is provided in subsequent sections. As we shall see, ROSE makes use of ACSE and, optionally, the direct use of the presentation layer and RTSE.

- RO-INVOKE
- RO-RESULT
- RO-ERROR
- RO-REJECT-U
- RO-REJECT-P

The RO-INVOKE service allows the invoker AE to request that an operation be performed by a performer AE. This service begins when the ROSE receives a request from the ROSE user (the invoker) to be performed by the other ROSE user (the performer). This service is a non-confirmed service.

The RO-RESULT service is also a non-confirmed service. It is used by a ROSE user to reply to a previous RO-INVOKE to notify of the completion of a successful operation.

The RO-ERROR service is a non-confirmed service to reply to a previous RO-INVOKE. Its purpose is to notify of an unsuccessful operation.

The RO-REJECT-U service is a non-confirmed service which rejects an RO-INVOKE service. It is also used to reject a RO-RESULT and a RO-ERROR, if necessary.

Finally, the RO-REJECT-P service is used by the ROSE provider to inform the ROSE user about a problem.

ROSE Primitives

Table 10-11 lists the ROSE primitives and their associated parameters. Table 10-12 provides a brief description of the functions of the parameters.

TABLE 10–11. The ROSE Primitives

Parameter Name	Request	Indication
RO-INVOKE Primitive		
Operation-value	M	M(=)
Operation-class	U	
Argument	U	C(=)
Invoke-ID	M	M(-)
Linked-ID	U	C(=)
Priority	U	
RO-RESULT Primitive		
Operation-value	U	C(=)
Result	U	C(=)
Invoke-ID	M	M(=)
Priority	U	
RO -ERROR Primitive		
Error-value	M	M(=)
Error-parameter	U	C(=)
Invoke-ID	M	M(=)
Priority	U	
RO-REJECT-U Primitive		
Reject-reason	M	M(=)
Invoke-ID	M	M(=)
Priority	U	
RO-REJECT-P		
Invoke-ID		O
Returned-parameters		O
Reject-reason		O

TABLE 10-12.   The Functions of the ROSE Primitive Parameters

Parameter Name	Function of Parameter
Invoke-ID	Identifies the RO-INVOKE service and correlates the request with corresponding replies
Linked-ID	Identifies a child operation and specifies the invocation of a linked parent operation.
Operation-value	Identifies the operation to be performed. The value is supplied by the requestor and must be agreed upon by the acceptor.
Operation-class	Defines a synchronous or asynchronous operation and the type of expected reply.
Argument	The argument of the invoked operation.
Result	The result of an invoked and successful operation.
Error-value	Identifies the error that occurred during the operation.
Error-parameter	Provides additional information about the error.
Priority	Defines the priority of the corresponding APDU.
Reject-reason	Identifies the reason for a rejection.
Returned-parameters	Contains the parameters of the primitive if a corresponding APDU cannot be transferred by the ROSE provider.

ROSE Protocol Data Units

As with the analysis of the other protocols in this chapter, this section lists several of the ROSE protocol data units. The following data units are defined:

rOSE APPLICATION-SERVICE-ELEMENT :: = {joint-iso-ccitt remote-operations(4) aseID (3)}

ROSE apdus :: = CHOICE {
    roiv-apdu [1] IMPLICIT ROIVapdu
    rors-apdu [2] IMPLICIT RORSapdu
    roer-apdu [3] IMPLICIT ROERapdu
    rorj-apdu [4] IMPLICIT RORJapdu

APDU types

ROIVapdus :: = SEQUENCE {
    invokeID InvokeIDType,
    linked-ID [0] IMPLICIT InvokeIDType OPTIONAL,
    operation-value OPERATION,
    argument ANY DEFINED BY operation-value OPTIONAL}
    --ANY is filled by the single ASN.1 data type following the key

Architecture of the Application Layer

```
                        --word ARGUMENT in the type definition of a particular
                        --operation.
  InvokeIDType :: = INTEGER
  RORSapdu   :: =   SEQUENCE {
                        invokeID InvokeIDType,
                        SEQUENCE {  operation-value OPERATION,
                                    result ANY DEFINED BY operation-value
                                    --ANY is filled by the single ASN.1 data
                                        type
                                    --following the key word RESULT in the
                                        type
                                    --definition of a particular operation.
                            } OPTIONAL }
  ROERapdu :: =  SEQUENCE {
                        invokeID InvokeIDType,
                        error-value ERROR,
                        parameter ANY DEFINED BY error-value OPTIONAL}
                        --ANY is filled by the single ASN.1 data type following the
                            key
                        --word PARAMETER in the type definition of a particular
                        --operation.
  RORJapdu :: =  SEQUENCE {
                        invokeID CHOICE {InvokeIDType,NULL},
                        problem CHOICE {
                        [1] IMPLICIT GeneralProblem,
                        [2] IMPLICIT InvokeProblem,
                        [3] IMPLICIT ReturnResultProblem,
                        [4] IMPLICIT ReturnErrorProblem}}
  GeneralProblem :: =  INTEGER {        --ROSE-provider detected
                        unrecognizedAPDU (0),
                        mistypedAPDU (1),
                        badly StructuredAPDU(2)}
  InvokeProblem :: =  INTEGER {        --ROSE-user detected
                        duplicateInvocation (0),
                        unrecognizedOperation (1),
                        mistypedArgument(2)
                        resourceLimitation(3)
                        initiatorReleasing(4)
                        unrecognizedLinkedID(5)
```

                           linkedResponseUnexpected(6)
                     unexpectedChildOperation(7)}
ReturnResultProblem :: = INTEGER {   --ROSE-provider detected
                     unrecognizedInvocation (0),
                     resultResponseUnexpected(1)
                     mistypedResult (2)}
ReturnErrorProblem :: = INTEGER {   --ROSE-provider detected
                     unrecognizedInvocation (0),
                     errorResponseUnexpected(1)
                     unrecognizedError(2),
                     unexpectedError(3),
                     mistypedParameter (4)}

END   —of ROSE Protocol specification

Relationship of ACSE to Other Entities and Layers

Mapping to the RTSE Services.   The relationship of the ROSE and RTSE services and protocol data units are listed in Table 10-13.

Mapping to the Presentation Services.   The relationship of the ROSE and presentation services and protocol data units are listed in Table 10-14.

TABLE 10-13.   RTSE Mapping Overview

ROSE Service	APDU	RTSE Service
RO-INVOKE request/indication	ROIV	RT-TRANSFER request/indication/confirm
RO-RESULT request/indication	RORS	RT-TRANSFER request/indication/confirm
RO-ERROR request/indication	ROER	RT-TRANSFER request/indication/confirm
RO-REJECT-U request/indication	RORJ	RT-TRANSFER request/indication/confirm
RO-REJECT-P indication	RORJ	RT-TRANSFER request/indication/confirm
Managing the turn	—	RT-TURN-PLEASE request/indication
	—	RT-TURN-GIVE request/indication

TABLE 10–14   Presentation-Service Mapping Overview

ROSE Service	APDU	Presentation Service
RO-INVOKE request/indication	ROIV	P-DATA request/indication
RO-RESULT request/indication	RORS	P-DATA request/indication
RO-ERROR request/indication	ROER	P-DATA request/indication
RO-REJECT-U request/indication	RORJ	P-DATA request/indication
RO-REJECT-P indication	RORJ	P-DATA request/indication

ROSE Protocol Machines and State Tables

Like the ACSE and RTSE standards, ROSE operates with protocol machines and state tables. Examples of state tables are provided in the next section. The following protocol machines are used:

- Remote-operation-protocol-machine (ROPM): The protocol machine for the ROSE.

- Requesting-remote-operation-protocol-machine: The machine whose user is the requestor of the ROSE service.

- Accepting-remote-operation-protocol-machine: The machine whose user is the acceptor for the ROSE service.

An Example of ROSE Operations

Our example of ROSE operations is the invocation of an operation by a ROSE user and the return of the result by the performer. Figures 10-9 and 10-10 and Tables 10-15 and 10-16 should be examined as we proceed through this example.

TABLE 10–15.   ROSE Operations

Actions and Explanations
1.   Form ROIV APDU from parameters in the RO-INVOKE request primitive
2.   Receives ROIV APDU from the indication primitive
3.   If ROIC APDU acceptable, issue RO-INVOKE indication primitive to acceptor (performer).

Note: Use of RTSE provides a confirmed service of the transfer. Use of the presentation layer directly does not provide a confirmed service.

Explanation of States
a)   Only accepted if in STA02: associated.
b)   Remain in STA02 after transferring an RT-TRANSFER request primitive (if RTSE is used) or a P-DATA request primitive (if RTSE is not used and the presentation layer is used).
c)   Only accepted if in STA02.

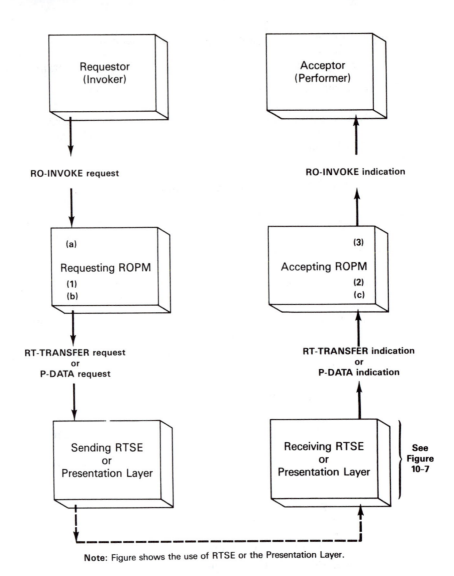

Note: Figure shows the use of RTSE or the Presentation Layer.

FIGURE 10-9. ROSE Operations: Invocation of an Operation

First the ROSE protocol machine must be in state 2 (STA02). This means the machine is associated; that is, the underlying ACSE has formed an association between the users. The operations for this association were described earlier (see Figure 10-5). Given that the machine is in this state, it can accept an RO-INVOKE request primitive for the requestor or an ROIV APDU as user data in a transfer indication primitive. The requesting ROPM receives the RO-INVOKE request primitive from its user. It then forms the ROIV APDU and issues an RT-TRANSFER request primitive to RTSE or a P-DATA request primitive directly to the presentation layer.

Architecture of the Application Layer

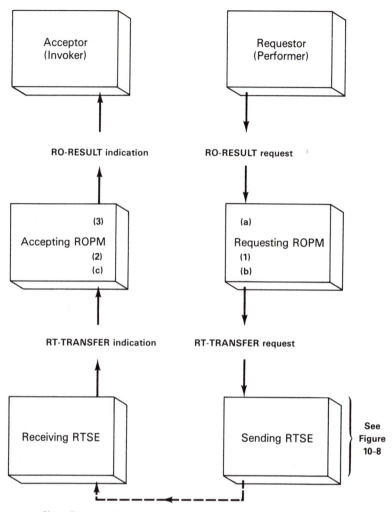

Note: Presentation layer did not participate in this operation.

FIGURE 10-10. ROSE Operations: Returning the Result

Upon the issuance of this primitive, the requesting Remote Operation Protocol Machine (ROPM) waits for an indication primitive from the RTSE or the presentation layer directly. It may accept any other primitive from the requestor. It remains in STA02.

The accepting ROPM must be in STA02. It receives the ROIV APDU from the transfer indication primitive or P-DATA indication. Assuming the parameters in the field are acceptable, it then issues an RO-INVOKE indication primitive to the acceptor. It then waits for any primitive from the acceptor or for another transfer indication primitive from the transfer service provider. It remains in STA02.

TABLE 10-16. ROSE Operations

Actions and Explanations

1. Form RORS APDU from parameters in RO-RESULT request primitive.

2. Receives RORS APDU on the RT-TRANSFER indication primitive

3. If RORS APDU is acceptable, issue an RO-RESULT indication primitive to the invoker.

Explanation of States

a) Only accepted if in STA02.

b) Remain in STA02 after transferring the RT-TRANSFER request primitive to RTSE.

c) Only accepted if in STA02.

This completes the actions shown in Figure 10-9. Be aware that the performer is not required to return a result, because the invoked service is nonconfirmed. Indeed, if RTSE is not used, ROSE provides no guarantee that the performer of the operation will return any information about the results. RTSE can be invoked to ensure that the performer sends a data unit back to the invoker.

However, in Figure 10-10 the performer does return the results and also uses the RTSE (and not the presentation layer) to obtain a confirmed service. Please note the roles of the two RPOM service users have been reversed—the requestor is now the acceptor and the acceptor is now the requestor. Notwithstanding these role changes, the terms invoker and performer remain the same.

The performer performs the operation and sends an RO-RESULT request primitive to the ROPM. The ROPM then forms an RORS APDU and issues a transfer request primitive. The RORS APDU is the user data in the primitive. The "remote" ROPM remains in STA02.

The RORS APDU is transferred to the originally requesting ROPM through a transfer indication primitive. Assuming the fields in the data unit are acceptable, it issues an RO-RESULT indication primitive to the user that initially invoked the service.

We are reminded once again that ROSE does not participate in the actual operation, nor is it aware of the nature of the results of the operation, be it successful or unsuccessful. It merely provides a mechanism for the two users to exchange the transactions.

COMMITMENT, CONCURRENCY, AND RECOVERY

The commitment, concurrency, and recovery (CCR) specifications describe the actions for managing activity between more than one application, perhaps across multiple sites. Most of the functions in CCR support the transfer and updating of elements (records, fields) in data bases.

Architecture of the Application Layer

Consistency, Concurrency, and Atomic Actions

A key concept of CCR is the provision for *consistent* states for all applications and/or data involved in the activity. A consistent state means that the affected systems are accurate and correct and any duplicate copies contain the same values.

In order to attain consistent states, CCR must be able to effect *concurrency control* and achieve *atomic actions*. Thus, we come full circle to Chapter 1 and our discussion of the design principles of the OSI Model. (If you wish to refresh your memory; see the section titled "Design Principles of Layered Systems" in Chapter 1.) Concurrency control is implemented by CCR through atomic action principles to ensure the affected system/datum does not have external changes made to it during an established state, and that all needed resources are committed to the full and complete execution of the state. It is irrelevant what the state is—it could be a data base update, multiple file transfers, the downloading of object code to packet switches, etc.

Another key concept is that CCR assumes an upper level protocol is available to assume the role of a master site (superior) to the other sites (subordinates). It further assumes that, even though the systems may be distributed, a "centralized" superior is controlling the activity between the applications and/or data bases.

An example of the complexities and problems of data transfer, access, and update is provided in Figure 10-11. Users A and B simultaneously access and update item XYZ in the data base. In the absence of control mechanisms, the data base reflects only the one update; the other update is lost. This happens when both users retrieve the data item, change it (add or subtract from the value), and write their revised value back into the data base.

Lockouts and the Deadly Embrace

The most common solution to this problem is preventing sites A and B from simultaneous executions on the same data. Through the use of lockouts, for example, site B would not be allowed to execute until site A had completed its transaction.

Lockouts work reasonably well with a centralized data base. However, in a distributed environment, the sites may possibly lock each other out and prevent either transaction from completing its task. Mutual lockout, often called

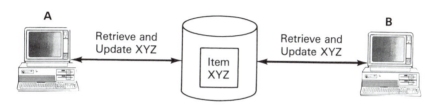

A   B

Retrieve and Update XYZ   Item XYZ   Retrieve and Update XYZ

FIGURE 10-11. File Access Problems

deadly embrace, is shown in Figure 10-12. Users A and B wish to update base items Y and Z, respectively; consequently, user A locks data Y from user B and user B locks data Z from user A. To complete their transactions, both users need data from the other locked data bases. Hence, neither can execute further, and so the two sites are locked in a deadly embrace. Clearly, the deadly embrace is an unacceptable situation and the system must be able to detect, analyze, and resolve the problem. We address this problem shortly.

Update and Retrieval Overhead. The use of locks is a widely accepted method for achieving consistency. When properly implemented with serialized scheduling, locks provide a very valuable method for maintaining data base integrity. However, consistency of the distributed data does not come without cost. For example in Figure 10-13, site C issues a transaction to update two replicated data bases at sites A and B. The following communications messages must be exchanged over the network between site C and the two other sites:

Event 1:   Site C sends lock request messages to A and B.

Event 2:   Sites A and B send lock grant messages to C (if the request is acceptable.

Event 3:   Site A transmits the update transaction.

Event 4:   The receiving sites update the data bases and transmit to C the acknowledgment of an update completion.

Event 5:   Site C receives the acknowledgment and transmits messages to release the lock.

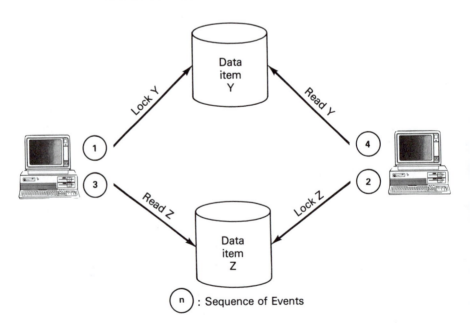

n : Sequence of Events

FIGURE 10–12. Mutual Lockout

Architecture of the Application Layer

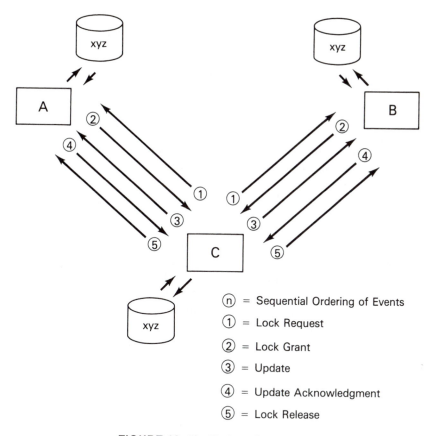

(n) = Sequential Ordering of Events

(1) = Lock Request

(2) = Lock Grant

(3) = Update

(4) = Update Acknowledgment

(5) = Lock Release

FIGURE 10-13. Update Overhead

A typical locking algorithm requires $5(n-1)$ intersite messages to manage an update transaction among n distributed sites. This could be considered an extreme example. The messages in events 1 and 3 can be piggybacked onto each other. The update portion of the message would only be used after an established time had elapsed and site C had not been sent a revoking message indicating one of the sites had sent site C a lock denial. However, the $5(n-1)$ algorithm is simpler and more reliable.

This overhead is the tip of the iceberg; each of the messages requires a number of lower-layer protocol data units to ensure that the data base messages are properly received. The number of these control units varies, so let us assume the value of D. Consequently, the locking algorithm is actually D $\times$ $5(n-1)$, where D is the number of overhead messages needed to manage one user message flow. In the example in Figure 10-13, assuming a communications overhead factor of 2, the calculation reveals that 20 messages are transported through the system to accomplish one update at two sites: $20 = 2 \times 5(3-1)$. Finally, the example did not calculate the additional costs of environments that have heterogeneous topologies and/or data systems. Protocol conversions and data structure translators consume additional overhead. It takes little imagination to recognize that the proper placement of files in a system is a very important task.

Retrieval overhead presents problems also, especially in a partitioned data base. A data retrieval request may require the "rounding up" of the needed data at several data bases in the network since the data have been partitioned into subsets and assigned to different locations. The data link control protocol conversion, data structure translation, data base software execution, operating systems efficiency, and machine processing power are important considerations in the decisions of how to partition the data bases.

Failure and Recovery. The efforts to achieve resiliency in a distributed system are quite different from those in a conventional centralized environment. The centralized approach assumes the availability of much information about a problem or failure. The operating system can suspend the execution of the problem program and store and query registers and control blocks, during which time the problem component does not change.

In a distributed system, the time delay in gathering data for analysis may be significant; in some cases, the data may be outdated upon receipt by the component tasked with the analysis and resolution. The problem may not be suspended as in a centralized system, since some distributed systems have horizontal topologies and autonomous or near autonomous components.

Referring again to Figure 10-13, one can gain an appreciation of the situation. Let us assume the update executed successfully at site B, but site C experienced problems due to a hardware or software failure. The update must be reversed in the site B copy. All items must be restored, transactions eventually reapplied, back-up tapes made, and log files restored to the preupdate image.

These operations are called *rollback* and *recovery.* The rollback is used for site B to delete the task. The recovery is used for site C to restore the system back to its original state.

A rollback must be implemented with great care. For example, if other transactions from other applications have been received to be applied to the data base, these transactions must be examined to determine if they were dependent on the suspended transaction. It takes little imagination to gain an appreciation of session layer control protocols.

Of course, in our simple example, one has the option of maintaining the site B update, continuing subsequent updates, and bringing the site C data up to date at a later time. This is hardly a choice if the data bases must be consistent in a real-time mode. Moreover, the affected nodes cannot independently make these decisions; all must be aware of each other if the data bases are to be properly synchronized.

A key question must be answered: Does the organization need timely data at the expense of consistency? Stated another way, must all copies be concurrent with each other? Practically speaking, certain classes of data (such as historical data) may be allowed to exhibit weak consistency: data are not kept concurrent. On the other hand, other classes of data (real-time data, for example) may need strong consistency. The designers must examine the user requirements very carefully. The benefits of strong consistency must be weighed against the increased costs of additional complexity. Notwithstanding these somewhat philosophical pronouncements, the CCR standard addresses the issues of concurrency, consistency, rollback, and recovery with the concept called the two-phase commitment.

The Two-Phase Commitment

The simple lockouts just described can be enhanced considerably by the concept of a two-phase commitment. We describe the idea with an example, and then examine the ISO Commitment, Concurrency, and Recovery (CCR) protocol.

System Architecture. The network data base system is organized around the transaction manager or module (TM) and the data manager or module (DM). Each site has a computer running the TM and DM software (see Figure 10 -14). The TM supervises transactions and all network actions to satisfy the user's transaction request. The DM manages the data bases and the DBMS. The architecture functions through four operations at the transaction/TM interface:

1. BEGIN: TM sets up work space for the user transaction (T). It provides temporary buffers for data moving into and out of the data bases.
2. READ(X): TM looks for a copy of data X in T's work space. It returns it

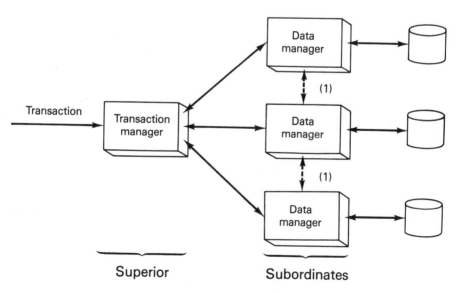

Superior   Subordinates

(1) Dialogues for Recovery from Transaction Manager Failure.

FIGURE 10-14. Superior/Subordinate Relationship

to T. If the data are not in the work space, it issues a dm-read(x) command to one of the network DMs, which accesses the data and returns them to T's work space.

3. WRITE(X): TM looks for a copy of X in T's work space. If found, it updates the "old" copy with the current value of X. If the data are not in the work space, a copy of the current value is placed into it.

   Notice that no changes have yet been made to the data bases. That is, no dm-write(x) commands have been issued by the TM to the DMs. The system uses a two-phase commitment procedure to assure (1) restart/recovery integrity, (2) adherence to atomic commitment, and (3) resiliency across nodes.

   Restart/recovery: The DBMS can restart a transaction at any time before a dm-write(x) is executed.

   Atomic commitment: Two-phase commitment keeps all nodes' data base actions related to one transaction isolated from each other.

   Resiliency: Failure of a component during a Write does not lock up or bring down other components in the network.

4. END: For the first phase of the two-phase commitment, TM issues a preWrite(x) to each DM in the network. The DM copies X from T's work space onto some form of secure storage. At this point, the DM must have isolated the affected data and be committed to the action and a rollback, if necessary. After all DMs have executed the preWrite, the second phase of the commitment begins by the TM issuing a dm-write(x) to the DMs. The DM then updates the data base from T's secure storage and informs the TM of the success of the operation.

The prewrite commands specify all DMs that are involved in the two-phase commitment. Consequently, if a TM fails during the second phase, the DMs time-out and check with other DMs to determine if a dm-write(x) had been received. If so, all other DMs use it as if it were issued by the TM. In the event of a DBMS failure during the Write, secure storage is used to recover data. If a DM operation fails, the TM so informs the DMs, which initiate a rollback and recovery.

ISO 8649 and 8650 CCR

The Commitment, Concurrency, and Recovery (CCR) specifications (ISO 8649 and ISO 8650) operate in a manner similar to the previous example. CCR also uses a two-phase commitment operation:

Phase 1: Superior determines which subordinates are to be involved in the activity and informs each subordinate of actions. Subordinate agrees or refuses to perform the actions.

Phase 2: Superior orders the commitment or releases the resources to their beginning state.

Architecture of the Application Layer

CCR contains the concept of atomic action trees (see Figure 10-15). With this approach, a subordinate can also assume the role of a superior to another subordinate, and each branch of the tree is an application association. CCR operates its atomic actions on the basis of a Boolean AND. All subordinates must agree in order for the atomic action to take place. If one or more refuses, the action is not committed and a rollback occurs.

If all subordinates commit, phase 2 is executed. During this phase, if any problems occur, a recovery process must be initiated. Be aware that the recovery operations are not defined in CCR but are application-specific.

CCR Primitives

CCR uses several primitives to invoke, process, and terminate an atomic action. These primitives are explained in Table 10-17. Please note the use of the presentation layer primitives.

The parameters in several of these primitives contain values that are essential to their proper execution:

- C-BEGIN: An atomic action identifier parameter unambiguously identifies the superior's name and the specific atomic action. A branch identifier identifies the superior for the branch in the atomic action tree. It also includes a branch name. An additional parameter is an atomic action timer. It is optional and is used by the superior as a time-out mechanism of the beginning of a rollback.

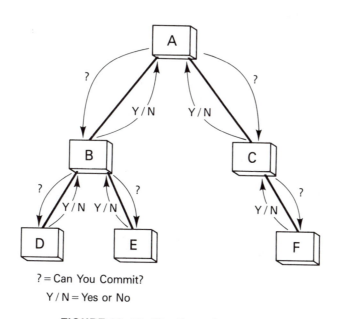

? = Can You Commit?

Y / N = Yes or No

FIGURE 10–15. The Commitment Tree

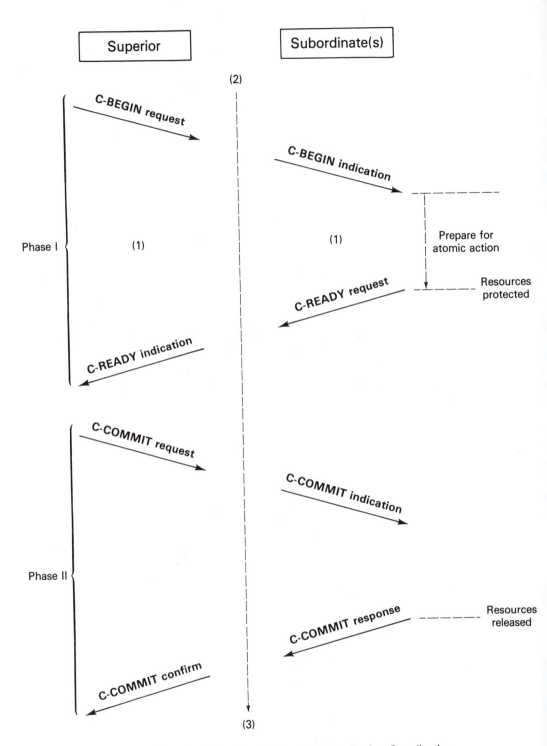

Note (1): Other Exchanges May be Made for Further Coordination.
Notes (2)-(3): Superior Responsible for Restart or Rollback.

FIGURE 10-16. Normal Commitment Procedure

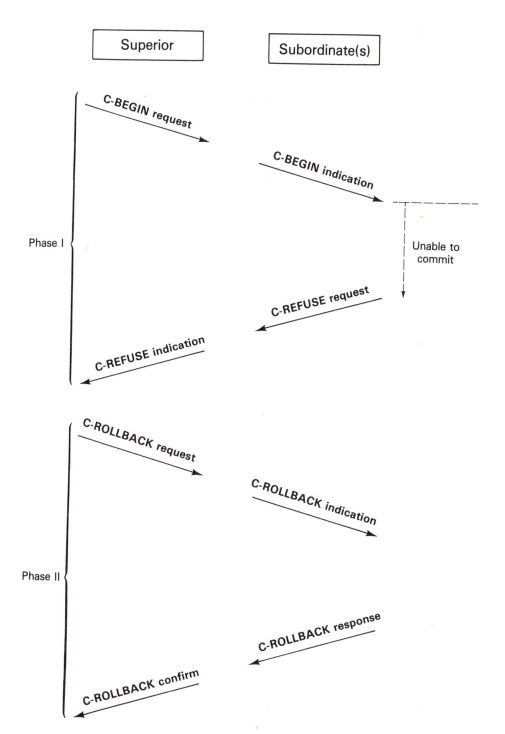

FIGURE 10–17. Atomic Action Refusal

TABLE 10-17. CCR Primitives

Primitive Name	Function
C-BEGIN	Issued by initiator to begin atomic action. Not confirmed. Maps into a P-SYNC-MAJOR primitive.
C-READY	Responder issues when ready to commit to the action, *and* to roll back, if necessary. Maps to a P-TYPED-DATA. Confirm not required.
C-COMMIT	Issued by initiator to order the commitment. Maps to a P-SYNC-MAJOR. Confirm required.
C-PREPARE	Issued by initiator (optional) and issued by superior to determine if subordinate is prepared to commit. Maps to P-TYPED-DATA. Confirm not required.
C-REFUSE	Issued by responder up to a C-READY. It is a refusal to commit and maps to a P-RESYNCHRONIZE (ABANDON). Confirm not required.
C-ROLLBACK	Issued by initiator to revert back and restore the initial state before the commit. Maps to P-RESYNCHRONIZE (ABANDON). Confirm required.
C-RESTART	Issued by either initiator or responder to initiate recovery procedures. Maps to P-RESYNCHRONIZE (RESTART). Confirm required.

- C-RESTART: These primitives also contain the atomic action identifier and the branch identifier. In addition, they contain the resumption point parameter in the request and indication primitives. This parameter is used to indicate the following: (a) ACTION: restart at the beginning; (b) COMMIT: restart at the last commitment; (c) ROLLBACK: roll back to the synchronization point. The resumption point parameter takes on the following values in the response and confirm primitives: (a) DONE: rollback or commitment is done; (b) ACTION: action is to be restarted; (c) REFUSE: the commitment is refused by the subordinate and the superior must issue a rollback; (d) RETRY-LATER: a subordinate cannot execute a restart, and request a later attempt.

A normal sequence of CCR operations is shown in Figure 10-16. In contrast, Figure 10-17 illustrates a situation in which the subordinate refuses to undertake the atomic action.

SUMMARY AND CONCLUSIONS

The entities within the application layer provide common services to end-user applications. With recent OSI publications, these entities are designated as application service elements (ASEs). The most common application layer service elements are ACSE, ROSE, RTSE, and CCR. The ASEs are now being developed by manufacturers for purchase as off-the-shelf software. This approach allows a user to acquire the modules and configure them in accordance with the standard or the user's preference.

CHAPTER 11

The Application Layer Application Service Elements (ASEs)

INTRODUCTION

Our objectives for this chapter are to examine the following major application layer recommendations and standards:

Message Handling Systems (MHS, CCITT X.400–X.420)

The Virtual Terminal (VT, ISO 9040 and 9041)

File Transfer, Access, and Management (FTAM, ISO 8571)

Job Transfer and Manipulation (JTM, ISO 8831 and 8832)

As we learned in Chapter 10, these standards are classified as application service elements (ASEs) because they provide services to applications. We also learned that ASEs may invoke the services of each other, the association control service element (ACSE), the commitment, concurrency, and recovery (CCR) service element, and other ASEs.

Be aware that you must know the terms and concepts introduced in Chapter 10 in order to understand the subject matter in this chapter.

MESSAGE HANDLING SYSTEMS (MHS)

Before we enter into an examination of the prevalent OSI application layer ASEs, it should prove useful to introduce the concept of electronic mail. Electronic mail is so named because it uses telecommunications facilities to deliver correspondence. It is considered an application layer service.

Electronic mail is used extensively throughout the data communications industry. The technology offers faster delivery than conventional mail-courier

413

service, and, as several studies indicate, costs are now beginning to favor electronic document deliveries over the postal service.

Figure 11-1 depicts the major features of an OSI electronic mail system, more accurately referred to as a message handling system (MHS). These terms are used in the CCITT X.400 MHS recommendations.

The *user agent* (UA) is responsible for interfacing directly with the end user. Since it is an applications process, MHS does not define how it interacts with the end user or how it performs solitary actions. In the "real world" it prepares, submits, and receives messages for the user. It also provides text editing and presentation services for the end user. It provides for other activities, such as user-friendly interaction (as examples, selective viewing, using ikons and menus). It supports security, priority provision, delivery notification, and the distribution of subsets of documents. The user agent is the familiar electronic mailbox.

UAs are grouped into classes by MHS based on the types of messages they can process. These UAs are then called cooperating UAs.

The *message transfer agent* (MTA) provides the routing and relaying of electronic mail. This function is responsible primarily for the store-and-forward path, channel security, and the actual message routing through the communi-

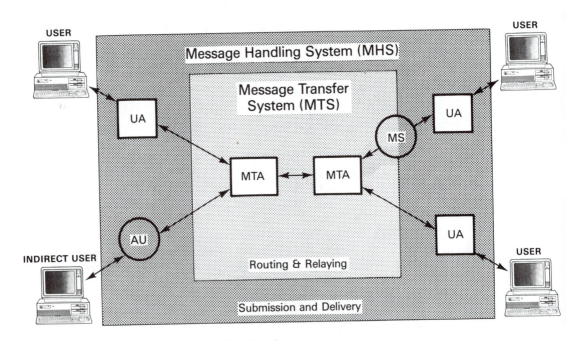

UA = User Agent
MTA = Message Transfer Agent
MS = Message Store
AU = Access Units

FIGURE 11-1. The MHS Model

The Application Layer Application Service Elements (ASEs)

cations media. Upon receiving a message from a user agent, the MTA checks it for syntax problems. If the message passes the check, the message is either delivered to another local UA or forwarded to the next MTA.

A collection of MTAs is called the *message transfer system* (MTS). These functions usually are specialized to a particular vendor's product, but recent efforts have pointed the way to more standardized systems.

It is important to understand that the MTS neither examines nor modifies the information part of the message, except for conversion of the *encoded information type* (ASCII code, Group 3 FAX, etc.). Another important point is that MHS considers the MTS to be application independent.

The *message store* (MS) provides for the storage of messages and their submission and retrieval. The MS complements the UA for machines such as personal computers and terminals that are not continuously available. The job of MS is to provide storage that is continuously available.

Finally, the *access units* (AUs) support connections to other types of communications systems, such as Telematic services, postal services, etc.

MHS uses the terms *content* to describe the information of the message. It is analogous to a letter. The term *envelope* describes control information used to effect the delivery of the content. It is analogous to the envelope we use for postal service, except an MHS envelope contains information the MTA needs to invoke many service elements that the postal service does not perform.

MHS also supports the use of *distribution lists* (DLs). A DL is similar to a distribution list in a typical office. For example, an MHS message originator may provide MHS the name of the DL. It is the task of MHS to "expand" the list to the recipient names and distribute a copy of the message to each recipient user.

We shall have more to say about these MHS functional entities as we delve into the details of MHS.

The reader who wishes only an overview of the major MHS functions can turn directly to the section titled "MHS Service Elements." The reader who needs to understand the architecture of this complex and rich protocol should read on.

THE STRUCTURE OF X.400 MHS

The CCITT publishes a series of recommendations, titled Message Handling Systems (MHS), in the X.400 documents. The term X.400 is used in this chapter as a general descriptor of recommendations X.400–X.420, unless otherwise noted. Due to the length and breadth of MHS, we must confine ourselves to an overview of its major features.

During our analysis of the X.400 specifications, it will be helpful to the reader to try to relate the MHS services to the mail and message services (manual and automated) currently available in his or her own workplace.

The MHS recommendations provide message services with two principal features for end users (originators and recipients of the messages). The *message transfer* (MT) service supports application-independent systems. It is responsible for the "envelope" of the letter. The MTS is the means by which the UAs exchange messages. The *interpersonal messaging* (IPM) service supports communications with existing CCITT, Telex, and telematic services, and defines specific user interfaces with MHS. It is responsible for the contents within the envelope. It uses the capabilities of the MT service for sending and receiving messages. MHS considers the IPM service to be a standardized application.

MHS uses the term *functional objects* to describe the components of the system. For example, the message handling system, users and message distribution lists (DLs) are classified as primary functional objects. Message transfer systems (MTSs), user agents (UAs), message stores (MSs), and access units (AUs) are classified as secondary functional units.

MHS Messages, Probes, and Reports

The MHS and MTS convey information of three types: *messages, probes,* and *reports*. The structure of the MHS messages consists of (a) an envelope which carries the information needed to transfer the message; and (b) the content, which is the information the originating user agent (UA) wishes delivered to one or more UAs (see Figure 11-2). The contents consist of a heading and a body, which are collectively called the Interpersonal Message (IP).

One piece of information carried by the envelope is the type of the content, which is an ASN.1 Object Identifier or Integer. This information denotes the syntax and semantics of the content. It is used by the MTS to assess the message's deliverability of users.

A probe is an information object that contains only an envelope. It is delivered to the MTAs serving the end users. It is used to determine if the message can be delivered, because it elicits the same behavior from the receiving MTS as would a submitted message. This handy feature is like saying, "I am considering sending you correspondence. These are its characteristics. Will you accept it?" In this way, a lengthy message or a message requiring substantial processing is less likely to be rejected by the receiver.

The report is a status indicator. It is used by the MTS to relate the progress or outcome of a message's or probe's transmission to one or more potential users.

MHS places rules on which functional objects are the ultimate sources or ultimate destination of messages, probes, and reports. These rules are listed in Table 11-1.

The MHS Specifications—An Overview

Since X.400 is an involved and detailed specification, an overview of each recommendation is provided in this section. A comparison with the ISO MHS publications is provided in Table 11-2.

X.400 describes the basic MHS model in accordance with the Open Systems Interconnection (OSI) Reference Model. X.400 describes in very general

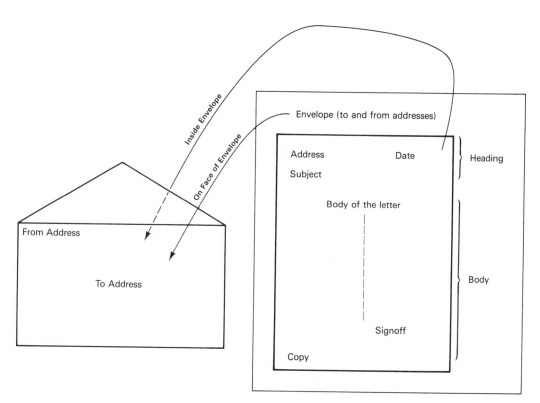

FIGURE 11-2. An Interpersonal (IP) Message

terms how an originator interacts with the user agent (UA) system to prepare, edit, and receive messages. It describes how the user agent interacts with the message transfer (MT) network. X.400 describes the interaction between the user agent entity (UA) and the message transfer entity (MT), and also describes naming and addressing conventions. This document provides a very valuable summary of the all-important MHS *elements of service,* and we pay considerable attention to this aspect of MHS in a later section.

X.402 describes the overall achitecture of MHS, and provides examples of

TABLE 11-1. Conveyable Information Objects

Information Object	Functional Object				
	USER	UA	MS	MTA	AU
Message	S/D	—	—	—	—
Probe	S	—	—	D	—
Report	D	—	—	S	—

S = Ultimate Source   D = Ultimate Destination

TABLE 11-2. Structure of MHS

Name of Recommendation/Standard	CCITT	ISO
MHS: System Service and Overview	X.400	10021-1
MHS: Overall Architecture	X.402	10021-2
MHS: Conformance Testing	X.403	
MHS: Abstract Service Definition	X.407	10021-3
MHS: Encoded Information Type Conversion Rules	X.408	
MHS: MTS Abstract Service Definition and Procedures	X.411	10021-4
MHS: MS Abstract Service Definitions	X.413	10021-5
MHS: Protocol Specifications	X.419	10021-6
MHS: Interpersonal Messaging System	X.420	10021-7

possible physical configurations. This specification contains some very useful definitions and rules for naming and addressing. The interested reader will find it a good reference point for studying X.400.

X.403 provides directions on conformance testing. It is a very detailed and lengthy document which defines conformance requirements, testing methodology, test structures, timers, protocol data units, and so forth.

X.407 specifies conventions used in a distributed information processing task. It describes these tasks in an abstract manner.

X.408 provides recommendations for code and format conversion; for example, conversion between International Alphabet #5 (ASCII Code) and the S.61 Teletex character set.

X.411 describes the message-transfer layer (MTL) service. This recommendation describes how the MTS user transfers messages with the MTS by defining the service definitions and the abstract syntaxes.

X.413 contains the provisions for the message store (MS). It describes how MS acts as an intermediary between the UA and the MTS.

X.419 defines the procedures for accessing the MTS and the MS, and for the message exchanges between MTAs. It describes the application contexts with three MHS protocols, known as P1, P3, and P7.

X.420 describes the interpersonal messaging service (IPM). This service defines the semantics and syntax involved in the receiving and sending of interpersonal traffic. In addition, it recommends the operations for the transfer of the protocol data units through the system.

OSI Realization of MHS

MHS uses the principles of the OSI Reference Model. The entities and protocols reside in the application layer of the Model. From the context of the OSI Model, MHS appears as depicted in Figure 11-3. As we learned earlier, the application entity (AE) consists of the user element (UE) and the supporting application service elements (ASEs). The message-handling ASEs can perform two types of service. The symmetric service means a UE both supplies and con-

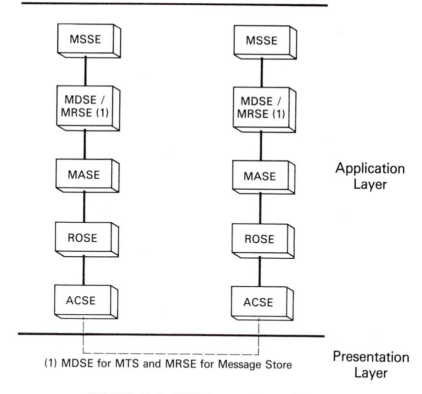

FIGURE 11-3. MHS Access Protocol Model

sumes a service; the asymmetric service means the UE either consumes or supplies a service, but does not do both.

Access to MTS or MS is provided by a number of application service elements (ASEs), as shown in Figure 11-3.

- *Message Submission Service Element* (MSSE): Supports the services of the submission functions.
- *Message Delivery Service Element* (MDSE): Supports the services of the delivery functions.
- *Message Retrieval Service Element* (MRSE): Supports the services of the retrieval functions for MS.
- *Message Administration Service Element* (MASE): Supports the services of administrative functions among UAs, MSs, and MTAs, and controls subsequent interactions by the means of the ASEs listed directly above.

These ASEs also can be supported by three other ASEs (described in Chapter 10):

- Remote Operations Service Element (ROSE)
- Reliable Transfer Service Element (RTSE)
- Association Control Service Element (ACSE)

A combination of these message-handling and supporting ASEs defines the application context of an application association. Remember from Chapter 10 that an application context specifies how the association is to be established and which ASEs are used. Every application context is identified by an ASN.1 Object Identifier, and the user that initiates an association provides the responder with this name through the ACSE. The application context also uses ASN.1 Object Identifiers to identify the application protocol data units (APDUs).

Table 11-3 is a list of the MHS message handling ASEs and their associated functional objects.

Use of ROSE, RTSE, ACSE, and Other Layer Services

Application Layer Services. MHS is designed to use a variety of combinations of underlying application layer services, which were examined in Chapter 10. Figure 10-4(a) in Chapter 10 depicts the permissible combinations.

MHS uses ROSE for the request/reply operations. The remote operations of the MTS access protocol (P3) and the MS Access protocol (P7) are ROSE Class 2 operations. The ASEs are the users of the following ROSE services:

RO-INVOKE	RO-RESULT
RO-ERROR	RO-REJECT-U
RO-REJECT-P	

If the RTSE is used in the application context, the MTS and MS are the sole users of the RT-OPEN and RT-CLOSE services of the RTSE. The ROSE is the sole user of the following RTSE services:

RT-TRANSFER	RT-TURN-PLEASE
RT-TURN-GIVE	RT-P-ABORT
RT-U-ABORT	

TABLE 11-3. Message Handling ASEs

ASE	Form	Functional Objects			
		UA	MS	MTA	AU
MTSE	SY	—	—	C/S	—
MSSE	ASY	C	C/S	S	—
MDSE	ASY	C	C	S	—
MRSE	ASY	C	S	—	—
MASE	ASY	C	C/S	S	—

SY = Symmetric   C = Consumer
ASY = Asymmetric   S = Supplier

The RTSE may or may not be used in the application context. If RTSE is not used, the MTS and MS are the sole users of the A-ASSOCIATE and A-RELEASE services of the ACSE in normal mode. The ROSE is the user of the ACSE A-ABORT and A-P-ABORT services.

If RTSE is used in the application context, the RTSE is the sole user of these ACSE services: A-ASSOCIATE, A-RELEASE, A-ABORT, A-P-ABORT.

The use of the normal mode of the RTSE also implies the use of the normal modes of the ACSE and the presentation layer.

Presentation Layer Services. At the presentation layer the following rules apply. The ACSE is the sole user of the P-CONNECT, P-RELEASE, P-U-ABORT, and P-P-ABORT services. If the RTSE is not included in the application context, the ROSE is the sole user of the presentation layer P-DATA service. If the RTSE is included in the application context, the RTSE is the sole user of the following presentation layer services:

P-ACTIVITY-START	P-DATA
P-MINOR-SYNCHRONIZE	P-ACTIVITY-END
P-ACTIVITY-INTERRUPT	P-ACTIVITY-DISCARD
P-U-EXCEPTION-REPORT	P-ACTIVITY-RESUME
P-P-EXCEPTION-REPORT	P-TOKEN-PLEASE
P-CONTROL-GIVE	

Session Layer Services. If the RTSE is used in the application context, these session-level functional units are used by the presentation layer: Kernel, Half-duplex, Exceptions, Minor-synchronize, and Activity-management. If the RTSE is not used, the presentation layer uses the session-level Kernel and Duplex functional units.

Transport Layer Services. The use of transport class 0 is required. Expedited service is not allowed. Other classes are optional.

Lower Layer Services. MHS does not concern itself with the protocols in the lower three layers of the OSI Model. The MHS message can be transported through X.25 networks, ISDNs, telephone connections, and other types of lower layer systems.

MHS Management Domains

A collection of at least one MTA and zero or more UAs that is administered by an organization is called a management domain (MD). The management domain is the primary building block of the MHS. An MD controlled by an administration (for example, a Postal, Telephone and Telegraph Agency, or PTT) is designated as an administration management domain (ADMD), and one managed by any other organization is called a private management domain (PRMD).

The basic purpose of the MHS recommendations is to enable the implementation of a global MHS. The concept is illustrated in Figure 11-4(a). The ADMDs play the central role in the global MHS. They connect to each other to form the backbone for the global MHS. They are responsible for the originator/recipient names (O/R names), discussed in the next section. The PRMDs are attached to the ADMDs, and as such play a peripheral role in the MHS. Figure

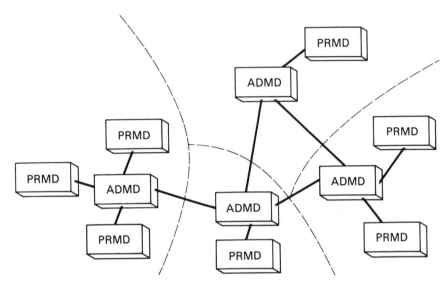

ADMD: Administration Management Domain
PRMD: Private Management Domain

(a) Management Domains

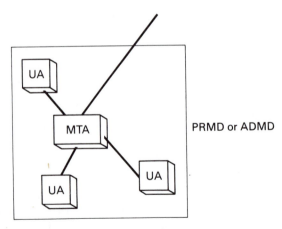

PRMD or ADMD

(b) Inside the Domain

FIGURE 11-4. X.400 MHS Domains

The Application Layer Application Service Elements (ASEs)

11-4(b) is drawn to re-emphasize that the MTAs and UAs reside within the AD-MDs and PRMDs.

Naming, Addressing, and Routing in MHS

Key to the management of the global MHS are the conventions for naming and addressing. Every user or distribution list (DL) must have an unambiguous *name*. MHS uses two kinds of names. A primitive name identifies a unique and specific entity such as an employee number or a social security number. A descriptive name denotes one user of the MHS, such as a job title. A descriptive name could identify different entities (in this example, people) as they move through a job. On the other hand, the primitive name is specific to the entity (a person). It may have global uniqueness (e.g., a social security number) or it may not have global uniqueness (e.g., an employee number). A name is permitted to have attributes which further identify an end user (entity) by including more detailed parameters.

The MHS *address* specifies the information needed for a message delivery. It can identify the locations of the MHS entities. Typically, a name is looked up in a directory to find the corresponding address, but MHS does allow an O/R name to be a directory name, an O/R address, or both, so as to give the user considerable flexibility in this important area.

MHS addresses consist of *attributes:* An attribute describes a user or a DL, and it may also locate the user DL within the MHS. An organization has many choices for an attribute list. Generally speaking, the attributes fall under four broad categories (see Table 11-4). Specifically speaking, X.402 defines the standard attributes that comprise an address (see Table 11-5).

The management domain (MD) is responsible for ensuring that each UA has at least one name, and it must allow users to construct any attributes that are needed by other MDs.

Security Features in MHS

As the reader might expect, a message system should provide security for the users' traffic. MHS supports a variety of security service elements. Many of

TABLE 11-4. Typical Examples of Originator/Recipient (O/R) Names

Personal Attributes	Surname, Initials, First Name, Qualifier (II, Jr.)
Geographical Attributes	Street name and number, Town, County, Region, State, Country
Organizational Attributes	Name, Unit(s) within organization, Position or role within organization
Architectural Attributes	X.121 address, Unique UA identifier, Administration management domain, Private management domain

TABLE 11–5. Standard Attributes

Attribute Type	Attribute Description
Administration-domain-name	ADMD relative to a country name
Common-name	Identification such as an organization or job title
Country-name	Country identifier with X.121 or ISO 3166
Extension-O/R-address-components	Additional identifier within postal address (organizational unit)
Extension physical-delivery-address-components	Additional identifier within postal address (room and floor numbers)
Local-postal-attributes	Identifies locus of distribution (geographical area)
Network address	X.121, E.163, E.164, PSAP address
Numeric-user-identifier	Identifies user relative to the ADMD
Organization-name	Identifies an organization
Organizational-unit-names	Identifies units of an organization (e.g., division)
Physical-delivery-service-name	Identifies physical delivery relative to the ADMD
Personal name	A person's name
Physical-delivery-country-name	Country in which user takes delivery
Physical-delivery-office-number	Distinguishes among several post offices
Physical-delivery-organization-name	A postal patron's organization
Physical-delivery-personal-name	A postal patron
Post-office-box-address	Number of post office box
Postal-code	A geographical area postal code
Poste-restante-address	Identifies code given to post office collection of messages for user
Private-domain-name	Identifies a PRMD
Street-address	Identifies a street address
Terminal-identifier	Identifier of a terminal
Terminal-type	Type of terminal (Telex, FAX, etc.)
Unformatted-postal-address	Postal address in free form
Unique-postal-name	Identifies a unique postal name (a plaza, hamlet, etc.)

these services rely on the use of encryption/decryption techniques and a separate directory that is very secure. MHS does not define the actual encryption/decryption and directory operations, but relies on the use of other OSI services. On a general level, the following security services are available:

- Authentication of the originator of the message
- Authentication of the originator of a non-delivery notice
- Authentication that the message was delivered, that its contents were not altered, and that all recipients received a copy
- Proof that message was not altered
- Measures to prevent the examination of the message
- Authentication of correct message sequencing
- Inability of a recipient to claim the message was not received
- Inability of sender to claim the message was sent, when it was not submitted to MHS (No longer can we say, "The check is in the mail!")

Table 11-6 lists the specific security service elements for MHS. The reader can refer to the section titled "MHS Service Elements" for more information on these services (or to the original source, X.400/ISO 10021-1).

MHS Protocols

Figure 11-5 provides a functional diagram of the MHS protocols. They are designated with the letter P and a number. P2 is the interpersonal messaging pro-

TABLE 11-6. Security Elements of Service

Service Elements	Sending MTS User	MTS	Receiving MTS User
Message Origin Authentication	P	U	U
Report Origin Authentication	U	P	—
Probe Origin Authentication	P	U	—
Proof of Delivery	U	—	P
Proof of Submission	U	P	—
Secure Access Management	P	U	P
Content Integrity	P	—	U
Content Confidentiality	P	—	U
Message Flow Confidentiality	P	—	—
Message Sequence Integrity	P	—	U
Non-repudiation of Origin	P	—	U
Non-repudiation of Submission	U	P	—
Non-repudiation of Delivery	U	—	P
Message Security Labeling	P	U	U

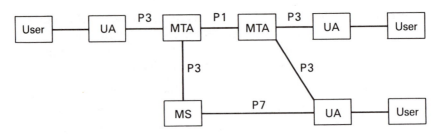

FIGURE 11-5. MHS Protocols

tocol (IPM). It defines the operations to manage the message transfer between the users. It is concerned with the header and body of the message (see Figure 11-2). We will examine the IPM services shortly.

MTA to UA.   As discussed earlier, the message transfer agent (MTA) provides the user agents (UAs) the means to transmit and receive messages. As the reader might expect, the services are invoked by a number of primitives that flow between the UA and the MTA. These primitives are used to support the MHS service elements (described later).

On a general level, the following operations are used to establish standard interfaces and procedures between the user agent and the message transfer agent:

1. Establishment and release of connection between the UA and the MT
2. Modification of parameters at the MT by the UA
3. Control by the UA of the message types and lengths
4. Submission of a message by UA and the assignment of a unique number and time to each message
5. Determination by MT if message can be delivered
6. Delivery by MT of a message to a UA
7. Non-delivery notification by MT to a UA
8. Delivery notification by MT to UA
9. Cancellation by UA of an MT submitted message

To accomplish these services the MTS uses the following operations between a user agent entity (UAE) and the MTA, referred to as the MTS Access Protocol (P3):

- *MTS Bind and Unbind:* These services allow an MTS-user to establish and disestablish an association with the MTS, and vice versa. The bind establishes the application-context, the security-context, and the credentials for the association.
- *Submission Port:* These operations permit the MTS-user to submit a message or a probe to the MTS. They also allow the user to cancel a previously

The Application Layer Application Service Elements (ASEs)

submitted deferred-delivery message. Additionally, these services allow the MTS to limit the operations of the MTS-user due to excess traffic, etc. These services are provided by the MSSE.

- *Delivery Port*: These operations allow the MTS to deliver a message to the MTS-user and to define how the MTS acknowledges to the user the outcome of a prior message or probe submission. They also allow the MTS-user to limit the operations of the delivering MTS. These services are provided by the MDSE.

- *Administration Port*: The administration port allows the MTS-user to change parameters held by the MTS. It also allows the MTS or the MTS-user to change their credentials. These services are provided by the MASE.

The abstract syntax definition for the ports are defined in X.411 as:

submission PORT
CONSUMER INVOKES {MessageSubmission, ProbeSubmission, CancelDeferredDelivery}
SUPPLIER INVOKES {SubmissionControl}
      :: = id-pt-submission
delivery PORT
CONSUMER INVOKES {DeliveryControl}
SUPPLIER INVOKES {MessageDelivery, ReportDelivery}
      :: = id-pt-delivery
administration PORT
CONSUMER INVOKES {ChangeCredentials, Register}
SUPPLIER INVOKES {ChangeCredentials}
      :: = id-pt-administration

MTA to/from MTA. It may happen that messages are transferred between MTAs without the intervening user agents. X.411 defines these operations also. They are quite similar to the operations described in the previous paragraphs, except the dialogue occurs between two MTAs. They consist of (a) MTA bind and MTA unbind operations and (b) transfer port operations. These operations are defined with the P1 protocol.

Message Store. The message store (MS) service was added to the 1988 Blue Book. It is called the MS Access Protocol and designated as P7. It consists of the following operations:

- *MS Bind and MS Unbind*: These services bind the indirect submission, retrieval, and administration ports of the MS-user and the MS-supplier (the message store).
- *Message Submission Service*: These operations are quite similar to the sub-

mission port operations of the MTS (just discussed) because they use the MSSE.

- *Message Retrieval Service:* These operations use the MRSE. A number of services are provided: (a) a summary of the stored entries, (b) the stored entries, (c) selected information from a specific entry, (d) deletion of selected entries, (f) administrative matters, such as the registration or credentials and security labels with the MS.

- *Message Administration Service:* The administration port allows the MS-user to change parameters held by the MS. It also allows the MS or the MS-user to change their credentials. These services are provided by the MASE.

The MHS Primitives

The reader should analyze the MTL primitives (see Table 11-7) with the notion that their purpose is to establish a standard procedure for interactions between the user agent (UA) and the message transfer agent (MTA), regardless of the specific vendor architecture. Of course, we emphasize once again that this is the principal idea of the OSI Model.

To initiate a session with an MTAE, a UAE issues a LOGON.Request primitive. This primitive contains the name of the O/R user that wishes access to the MTAE. It also contains a password for the UAE. The MTAE returns the LOGON.Confirmation primitive. It indicates if the logon request was successful. If successful, it also indicates the number of messages awaiting the UAE (if any) and their priorities. If the logon request fails, this primitive provides the reason for the rejection.

TABLE 11-7.   X.411 Message Transfer Layer Primitives

Issued by UAE	Issued by MTAE
LOGON.Request	LOGON.Configuration
LOGON.Response	LOGON.Indication
LOGOFF.Request	LOGOFF.Confirmation
REGISTER.Request	REGISTER.Confirmation
CONTROL.Request	CONTROL.Confirmation
CONTROL.Response	CONTROL.Indication
SUBMIT.Request	SUBMIT.Confirmation
PROBE.Request	PROBE.Confirmation
	DELIVER.Indication
	NOTIFY.Indication
CANCEL.Request	CANCEL.Confirmation
CHANGE-PASSWORD-Request	CHANGE-PASSWORD.Confirmation
	CHANGE-PASSWORD.Indication

The Application Layer Application Service Elements (ASEs)

The MTL can also initiate a session (usually, as a result of receiving messages from a remote UAE) by transferring a LOGON.Indication primitive to the local UAE. The primitive contains three parameters: (1) the name of the MTAE sending the primitive; (2) the number of messages awaiting delivery to the UAE; and (3) the password of the MTAE. The receiving UAE responds with the LOGON.Response primitive. It indicates if the logon is successful, and if not, the reason for its rejection (busy, faulty password, etc.).

The LOGOFF primitives are used to terminate a session between the UAE and the MTAE. The UAE issues the LOGOFF.Request and the MTAE returns the LOGOFF.Confirmation. They have no parameters associated with them.

The REGISTER.Request primitive is used by the UAE to change the values of its parameters that are maintained by the MTAE. The five parameters for this primitive convey the following information: (a) the types of messages the UAE can accept; (b) the length of the longest message the UAE can accept; (c) the default values for the parameters that can be established by the CONTROL.Request primitive; (d) the address of the UAE if it is needed; and (e) the O/R name of the UAE if it is needed. The MTAE returns the REGISTER.Confirmation primitive to indicate the success or failure of the REGISTER.Request.

The CONTROL.Request primitive is used by the UAE to change the restrictions currently in force with the MTL (what messages the MTL can send to the UAE). It only affects messages that are subject to the register parameters. This primitive is also used to direct the MTAE to hold messages for delivery. The CONTROL.Request primitive contains five parameters that perform the following functions: (a) the encoded information types (i.e., ASCII/IA5 code, Telex code, etc.) that can be sent by the MTAE to the UAE; (b) the length of the longest message the UAE will accept; (c) the priority of the least urgent message the UAE will accept; (d) an indication if the UAE will accept messages; and (e) an indication if the UAE will accept notifications. The MTAE returns the CONTROL.Confirmation primitive to indicate if the CONTROL.Request was accepted or rejected. It also indicates if messages and notifications are waiting as a result of the CONTROL.Request.

The CONTROL.Indication is used by the MTAE to identify what messages it will accept from the UAE. It contains four parameters that perform the following functions: (a) the length of the longest message that the MTAE will accept; (b) the priority of the least urgent message that the MTAE will accept; (c) indication if the MTAE will accept a probe from the UAE (discussed later); (d) indication if the MTAE will accept messages from the UAE. The UAE, in turn, sends back the CONTROL.Response primitive. It has only one parameter to indicate if it is holding messages or probes due to the CONTROL.Indication primitive.

MHS uses three primitives to actually transfer messages between the UAEs and the MTAEs:

- SUBMIT.Request
- SUBMIT.Confirmation
- DELIVER.Indication

The SUBMIT.Request is used by the UAE to send a message to the MTAE. The MTAE returns a SUBMIT.Confirmation primitive and forwards the message into the system. At the recipient node, the MTAE delivers the message to its UAE with the DELIVER.Indication. Several of the parameters of the SUBMIT.Request and DELIVER.Indication primitives are similar (see Table 11-8). These parameters are listed side by side to give you an idea of which of the parameters are finally mapped to the remote user agent entity, but be aware some convey different information to the remote UAE.

The reader should study the entries and footnotes in Table 11-8 to gain an

TABLE 11-8.   MHS Message Transfer Primitives and Parameters

SUBMIT.Request Primitive Parameters A	DELIVER.Indication Primitive Parameters B	Notes
Originator-O/R-Name	Originator-O/R-Name	
Recipient-O/R-Name	This-recipient-O/R-Name	
	Other-recipient-O/R-Names	
Content	Content	1
Content-type	Content-type	
Encoded-information-types	Original-encoded-information-types	2
	Converted-encoded-information-types	
Deferred-delivery-time	Delivery time	3
NDN-suppress		4
Priority	Priority	
Conversion-prohibited	Conversion-prohibited	5
Explicit-conversion		
Delivery-notice		6
Disclose-recipients		
Alternate-recipient-allowed	Intended-recipient-O/R-name	7
Content-return		8
UA-content-id		
	Submission-time	9
	Delivered-event-id	10

NOTES:
1. End-user information.
2. The type(s) of information sent and, if converted, the original encoded information type(s).
3. Earliest date/time permitted for delivery and the date/time delivered at recipient.
4. Suppress non-delivery notification.
5. Indicates a conversion to another type code is to be prohibited.
6. Requests notification of message delivery.
7. Submitter allows an alternate recipient and receiver is notified of intended recipient.
8. Return message contents if it is not delivered.
9. Time the message was submitted for delivery.
10. The DELIVER.Indication event identifier.

The Application Layer Application Service Elements (ASEs)

understanding of the data and actual control signals passed between the UA and MT.

The SUBMIT.Confirmation primitive contains five parameters that perform the following functions: (a) an indication of the success of the SUBMIT.Request; (b) the time the MTAE accepted the request; (c) an identifier of the SUBMIT.Request; (d) the reason for the rejection (if it occurred); and (e) an identifier for the message contents that were generated by the UAE (UA-content-id).

The PROBE.Request primitive is used by the UAE to inquire if a SUBMIT.Request primitive (with the same parameters) would be a successful delivery. The primitive contains nine parameters that convey the following information (a) recipient; (b) originator O/R names; (c) the content type; (d) the encoded information type(s) of the possible message to be transmitted; (e) indication of a conversion prohibition; (f) alternate recipient is allowed; (g) estimated length of probed message; (h) the UA-content-id; and (i) explicit-conversion. The MTAE sends back a PROBE.Confirmation primitive to inform the UAE of the success or failure of its probe.

It can be seen that the PROBE primitives do not convey the data, but conveys the estimated length of the message, along with other identifiers. This concept aids in decreasing the unsuccessful submission of messages, which of course, is a wasteful exercise.

The NOTIFY.Indication primitive is used to inform the UAE whether or not a message was delivered. The primitive contains eleven parameters that convey the following information: (a) indication of delivery or non-delivery; (b) identification of the primitive that evoked this primitive; (c) identification of the original recipients related to the notification; (d) reason for non-delivery (if delivery was not performed); (e) time of delivery; (f) type of converted information type(s), if conversion occurred; (g) O/R name of original recipient; (h) possible additional information; (i) the content of the returned message, if it was returned; (j) identification of UAE (private or owned by administration); and (k) the UA-content-id.

The CANCEL.Request primitive is used by the UAE to request that a delivery to a recipient UAE be canceled. The UAE is notified by the MTAE of the cancellation attempt with the CANCEL.Confirmation primitive, which indicates the success or failure of the request.

Finally, the three CHANGE-PASSWORD primitives are used to change a UAE's logon password or to indicate whether the request was successful. The primitives contain: (a) the current value; (b) the new value; and (c) indication, if it was changed successfully.

MHS Service Elements

Several references have been made to service elements. They represent the "heart" of the MHS recommendations because they define the features and functions of the system. Since the service elements are quite important to MHS, it is appropriate to examine them in some detail. The full list of the service elements is provided in Table 11-9, and a short paragraph describing each service element follows. Table 11-9 specifies if the service element is part of the 1984 or 1988 CCITT release.

MHS Service Elements Descriptions

We now examine each of the MHS service elements. In examining these elements, you will most likely recognize the richness of functions inherent in the MHS. At the same time, it is recognized that this section may be a bit tedious, because each service element is described, and there are many elements, as evidenced in Table 11-9. Therefore, you may wish to scan through this section and read only the descriptions of the service elements that are of interest for your application.

To facilitate comparison of the entries in this section to the list of service elements in Table 11-9, most of the service elements are in alphabetical order, unless they are described with other complementary service elements.

The *access management* service element provides the support for the UA and MTA to communicate with each other through the identification and validation of names and addresses. This service element allows the UA to use its O/R name for access security. The MTS passwords used for this service element are different from any of those used by the UA itself to authenticate the end user. If the MHS user wishes a more secure form of access, the secure access management service element can be used.

The *additional physical rendition* allows the originating MHS user to request the kind of physical rendition that is to be done on the message. Physical rendition is the transformation of the electronic message to a physical message, such as the type of paper, the kind of printing, stipulation for color rendition, etc. This service is performed by the physical delivery access unit (PDAU). Use of this service element requires bilateral agreement.

The *alternate recipient allowed* service element allows the originating UA to specify the delivery to an alternate recipient. The destination management domain (MD) uses the user attributes to select the recipient UA.

The *alternate recipient assignment* service element gives the UA the capability to have certain messages delivered to it even when there is not an exact match in the attributes or descriptive names of the UA. In this situation, the UA is specified in specific attributes and also in other attributes for which any value would be acceptable. This is useful when a message is sent which contains the proper domain name and perhaps company name, but the person's name in the message does not match. This means the UA still would have the message delivered to it. The message will not be rejected, but manual procedures could be implemented to handle the notification to the person or to locate the individual. Typically, certain attributes must match (such as company name), while other attributes need not match (such as a person's name).

The *authorizing users indication* service element allows the originator to identify the names of one or more persons who have authorized the sending of the message. The actual purpose of this service element is to give the receivers

TABLE 11-9. MHS Service Elements

Service Element	MT	IPM	PD	MS
Access Management	84	—	—	—
Additional Physical Rendition	—	—	88	—
Alternate Recipient Allowed	84	—	—	—
Alternate Recipient Assignment	84	—	—	—
Authorizing Users Indication	—	84	—	—
Auto-forwarded Indication	—	84	—	—
Basic Physical Rendition	—	—	88	—
Blind Copy Recipient Indication	—	84	—	—
Body Part Encryption Indication	—	84	—	—
Content Confidentiality	88	—	—	—
Content Integrity	88	—	—	—
Content Type Indication	84	—	—	—
Conversion Prohibition (CH)	84	—	—	—
CH in Case of Information Loss	88	—	—	—
Conversion Indication	84	—	—	—
Counter Collection	—	—	88	—
Counter Collection With Advice	—	—	88	—
Cross-referencing Indication	—	84	—	—
Deferred Delivery	84	—	—	—
Deferred Delivery Cancellation	84	—	—	—
Delivery Notification	84	—	—	—
Delivery Time Stamp Indication	84	—	—	—
Delivery Via Bureaufax Service	—	—	88	—
Designation of Recipient by Directory Name	88	—	—	—
Disclosure of Other Recipients	84	—	—	—
DL Expansion History Indication	88	—	—	—
DL Expansion Prohibited	88	—	—	—
Express Mail Service (EMS)	—	—	88	—
Expiry Date Indication	—	84	—	—
Explicit Conversion	84	—	—	—
Forwarded IP-message indication	—	84	—	—
Grade of Delivery Selection	84	—	—	—
Hold for Delivery	84	—	—	—
Implicit Conversion	84	—	—	—
Importance Indication	—	84	—	—
Incomplete Copy Indication	—	88	—	—
IP-message Identification	—	84	—	—
Language identification	—	88	—	—
Latest Delivery Designation	88	—	—	—
Message Flow Confidentiality	88	—	—	—
Message Identification	84	—	—	—
Message Origin Authentication	88	—	—	—
Message Security Labeling	88	—	—	—
Message Sequence Integrity	88	—	—	—
Multi-destination Delivery	84	—	—	—
Multi-part Body	—	84	—	—

(continued)

TABLE 11-9.   MHS Service Elements (continued)

Service Element	MT	IPM	PD	MS
Non-delivery Notification	84	—	—	—
Non-receipt Notification Request Indication	—	84	—	—
Non-repudiation of Delivery	88	—	—	—
Non-repudiation of Origin	88	—	—	—
Non-repudiation of Submission	88	—	—	—
Obsoleting Indication	—	84	—	—
Ordinary Mail	—	—	88	—
Original Encoded Information Type Indication	84	—	—	—
Originator Indication	—	84	—	—
Originator Requested Alternate Recipient	88	—	—	—
Physical Delivery Notification by MHS	—	—	88	—
Physical Delivery Notification by PDS	—	—	88	—
Physical Forwarding Allowed	—	—	88	—
Physical Forwarding Prohibited	—	—	88	—
Prevention of Non-delivery Notification	84	—	—	—
Primary and Copy Recipients Indication	—	84	—	—
Probe	84	—	—	·
Probe Origin Authentication	88	—	—	—
Proof of Delivery	88	—	—	—
Proof of Submission	88	—	—	—
Receipt Notification Request Indication	—	84	—	—
Redirection Disallowed by Originator	88	—	—	—
Redirection of Incoming Messages	88	—	—	—
Registered Mail	—	—	88	—
Registered Mail to Addressee in Person	—	—	88	—
Reply Request Indication	—	84	—	—
Replying IP-message Indication	—	84	—	—
Report Origin Authentication	88	—	—	—
Request for Forwarding Address	—	—	88	—
Requested Delivery Method	88	—	—	—
Restricted Delivery	88	—	—	—
Return of Content	84	—	—	—
Secure Access Management	88	—	—	—
Sensitivity Indication	—	84	—	—
Special Delivery	—	—	88	—
Stored Message Alert	—	—	—	88
Stored Message Auto-forward	—	—	—	88
Stored Message Deletion	—	—	—	88
Stored Message Fetching	—	—	—	88
Stored Message Listing	—	—	—	88
Stored Message Summary	—	—	—	88
Subject Indication	—	84	—	—
Submission Time Stamp Indication	84	—	—	—
Typed Body	—	84	—	—
Undeliverable Mail with Return of Message	—	—	88	—
Use of Distribution List	88	—	—	—
User/UA Capabilities Registration	88	—	—	—

The Application Layer Application Service Elements (ASEs)

the identification of the people who are authorized to send the traffic, in contrast to the person who sent it. The latter person is the originator, the former is the authorizer.

The *auto-forwarded indication* service element is used to determine whether an incoming IP-message contains a message that has been auto-forwarded. The auto-forwarded IP-message may be accompanied by the information that was intended with its original delivery, such as code conversion indications and time stamps.

The *basic physical rendition* service element allows the physical delivery access unit (PDAU) to provide the conversion of the MHS message to actual physical copy, with specified physical characteristics such as the color of paper, etc.

The *blind copy recipient* indication service element allows the originator of the message to provide the O/R names of additional recipients of the traffic. These names are not disclosed to any of the other recipients. Distribution lists (DLs) can also be blind copy recipients.

The *body part encryption* indication service element is used by the originator to inform the receiver that the body part (or a portion thereof) in the IP-message has been encrypted. In turn, it can then be used by the recipient to determine which part of the message must be decrypted. The service element does not perform any encryption or decryption.

The *content confidentiality* service element is used by the originator of the message to prevent the disclosure of the message to unauthorized recipients. This service element is used on a per-message basis and can use asymmetric or symmetric encryption.

The *content integrity* service element is used by the originator to give the recipient the means to ensure that the contents of the message have not been modified. The service element is used on a per-message basis and can use asymmetric or symmetric encryption.

The *content type indication* service element supports an originating UA's indication of the content type (syntax and semantics) for each message. The recipient UA may have one or more content types delivered to it. The content type identification specifies the particular type.

The *conversion prohibition* service element is used by the originating UA to instruct the MTS that the message is not to have any implicit encoded information type conversion performed on it (for example, IA5 code to group 3 FAX).

Four other service elements in this category provide complementary services. The *implicit conversion* service element instructs the MTS to perform conversion for a period of time. It is so named because the UAs are not required explicitly to request the service. When the conversion is performed and the delivery made, the recipient is informed of the original and current encoded information types.

In contrast to the implicit conversion service element, the *explicit conversion* service element is used by the originating UA to instruct the MTS to perform specific conversion services. When using this service element, the receiving UA is informed of the original code types as well as the newly encoded types of the message.

The *conversion prohibition in case of information loss* service element is used by the originating UA to direct the MTS not to perform code conversion if it might possibly result in the loss of information. This service element could be used if, for example, the characteristics of the recipient's I/O device are not known.

The *conversion indication* service element is used by the MTS to inform a recipient UA that the MTS performed code conversion on a delivered message. The service element allows the recipient UA to be informed of the resulting code types.

The *counter collection* service element is used by the originator to instruct the physical delivery system (PDS, like a postal service) to hold the physical message for pick-up by the recipient.

The *counter collection with advice* service element allows the originator to inform the PDS to hold the message and to inform the recipient that the message is available for collection. The originator provides the identification (telephone number, etc.) of the recipient.

The *cross-referencing indication* service element is used to identify associated IP messages. This is useful to allow the IPM UA to retrieve copies of the referenced messages.

The *deferred delivery* service element is used by the originating UA to inform the MTS that the message is to be delivered by a specified date and time. The MTS attempts to deliver the traffic as close to this time as possible. It does not deliver the traffic before the deferred delivery time and date stamp. The originator's management domain (MD) may place a limit on the parameters in the service element.

The *deferred delivery cancellation* service element is used by the originating UA to inform the MTS that it is to cancel a message which was previously submitted. The cancellation may or may not take effect. For example, if the message already has been forwarded within the MTS, it will not be canceled.

The *delivery notification* service element is used for an end-to-end acknowledgment. This allows the originating UA to request that it be informed when the message has been delivered successfully to the recipient UA or the access unit. This service element also stipulates the time and date of the actual delivery. The service element does not mean that the recipient UA has acted on the message or even has examined it. It only states that the delivery did occur. It is similar in concept to receiving a receipt of a delivery of a letter through the postal service—it merely means that the recipient has signed for the letter, not that the recipient has read the letter. The originator may also request this service element on a multi-destination message, on a per-recipient basis.

The *delivery time stamp indication* service element is used by the MTS to inform the recipient UA of the time and date the MTS delivered the message. If the message is delivered to a PDAU, this service element indicates the time and date the PDAU has taken responsibility for the message.

The *delivery via Bureaufax Service* service element is used by the originator to direct the PDAU and the PDS to use the Bureaufax Service for the delivery of the message.

The *designation of recipient by directory name* allows the originating UA to use a directory name instead of the recipient's O/R address.

The *disclosure of other recipients* service element allows the originating UA to require the MTS to disclose the O/R names of all the other recipients after they have received a copy of a multi-recipient message. The recipients' names are originally supplied by the originating UA, and the MTS then informs the UA when each recipient receives the message.

The *distribution list (DL) expansion history indication* service element gives the recipient information about the DLs used to effect the message delivery.

The *DL expansion prohibited* service element is used if the originator does not wish a recipient to refer to a distribution list. If so, then no DL expansion can occur and a non-delivery notification is returned to the originating UA.

The *express mail service (EMS)* service element is used by the originator to direct the PDS to deliver the physical message through an express mail service.

The *expiry date indication* service element is used by the originator to indicate to the recipient the date and time that the IP-message will no longer be valid. However, MHS does not specify what happens in the event the expiration time and date are exceeded.

The *forwarded IP-message indication* service element is used to forward the IP-message as the body of the IP-message. In a multi-part body, the forwarded parts can be included along with the message body parts of other types of traffic. The message indicates that the body part contains a forwarded IP-message.

The *grade of delivery selection* service element allows the sending UA to request the MTS to transfer the message on an urgent or non-urgent basis rather than a normal basis. The recipient of the message also receives notice about the grade of delivery. The service element does not stipulate the specific times for the grade of delivery selection.

The *hold for delivery* service element is quite similar to the postal department's practice of holding mail for individuals. This allows the UA to request the MTS to hold its traffic for delivery as well as any returning notifications. The UA can use this service element to inform the MTS when it is unavailable and when it is again ready to accept traffic, although MHS stipulates that the criteria for requesting this service element are restricted to the following: (a) encoded information type, (b) content type, (c) maximum content length, and (d) priority.

The hold for delivery service element is a temporary storage facility only. It should not be confused with the MHS message store service. The message store is intended to provide storage for an extended period of time.

The *implicit conversion* service element is discussed in context with the conversion prohibition service element.

The *importance indication* service element is used to establish a priority for the IP-message. MHS defines three levels of priority: low, normal, and high. While this service element is used to indicate how important the traffic is, it is not related to the delivery selection service provided by the MTS itself. MHS does not specify how to handle this service element. This service element is not related to the grade of delivery service element, discussed later.

The *incomplete copy* indication is used by the originator to indicate problems with the IP-message. It indicates that one or more body parts or heading fields are missing.

The *IP-message identification* service element is used by the IPM UAs to convey an identifier in each IP-message.

The *language indication* service element allows the originating UA to indicate which languages are in the IP-message.

The *latest delivery designation* service element is used by the originating UA to stipulate the latest time the message can be delivered. If the MTS cannot meet this time, the message is canceled and not delivered. If a message is destined for several recipients, a time expiration will affect only those recipients who have not yet received the message.

The *message flow confidentiality* service element is used by the originator to prevent an interpretation of the message contents by observing the message flow. The 1988 MHS release does not fully support this service element.

The *message identification* service element is used by the MTS to give the UA the unique identification for each message or probe sent to or from the MTS. The UAs and MTs use these values also to identify previously submitted traffic of other service elements, such as confirmation and non-delivery notification.

The *message origin authentication* service element provides MTA information on the authentication of the origin of the message to message recipients(s) and any MTA. This service can be provided on a per-message or per-recipient basis and uses encryption techniques.

The message security labeling service element is used by the originator to identify the sensitivity of the message through the use of a security label. The label is used to determine how to handle the message. MHS does not define the handling procedures.

The *message sequence integrity* service element allows the recipient to confirm that messages have arrived from the originator in the proper order.

The *multi-destination delivery* service element is used by the originating UA to stipulate that a message is to be submitted to more than one receiving UA. The specification does not place a limit on the number of UAs that can receive the message, nor does it place rules on simultaneous delivery.

The *multi-part body* service element is used by the originator to send to the recipient an IP-message which is in several parts. Each part contains the nature, attributes, and type of the message.

The *non-delivery notification* service element is used by the MTS to inform an originating O/R if a message was not delivered to the receiving UA. The reason for the non-delivery is indicated as part of the service element. This service element supports multi-destination messages and distribution list expansions.

The *non-receipt notification request indication* service element is used by the originator to request it be notified if an IP message is not delivered. This can be requested on an end-recipient basis for a multi-destination message. The receiving Interpersonal message (IPM) UA must return a non-receipt if the message was forwarded to another recipient, if the recipient did not subscribe to the service, or if the message was discarded before the reception actually occurred. The non-receipt notification must contain the identification of the IP message involved in the non-delivery, as well as reasons for the non-delivery.

The *non-repudiation of delivery* service element gives the message originator absolute proof that the message was delivered to the recipient. It eliminates the possibility that the recipient can claim the message never arrived. The service element is provided using asymmetric encryption techniques.

The *non-repudiation of origin* service element allows the recipient of a message to have absolute proof of the origin of the message. It prevents the originator from denying to be the originator. It also prevents the originator from revoking the message. The service element is provided using asymmetric encoding techniques.

The *non-repudiation of submission* service element is similar to the non-repudiation of delivery, except it pertains to the MTS. In other words, it prevents the MTS from denying that the message was delivered to it.

The *obsoleting indication* service element is used by the originator to indicate that one (or more) IP-messages previously sent is (are) no longer valid. The IP-message identifying this situation supersedes the previous IP-message(s). This MHS service is a useful tool for purging old and/or obsolete messages from a file.

The *ordinary mail* service element allows the physical delivery system (PDS) to deliver the letter produced by the MHS through the postal service.

The *original encoded information type indication* service element is used by the sending UA to identify the code type of the message submitted to the MTS. When the message is delivered to the recipient UA, it gives this UA the information about the information code.

The *originator indication* service element is used to identify the originator of the traffic. It is the responsibility of the MTS to provide the proper O/R address or directory name to the receiver. MHS states that the originator can be identified to the MTS in a "user-friendly" way.

The *originator requested alternate recipient* service element allows the originating UA to designate one alternate recipient for each intended recipient. If the delivery cannot be made to the intended recipient, the message is passed to the alternate. The alternate may be a distribution list (DL). MHS considers the delivery of the message to the alternate recipient to be the same as a delivery to the intended recipient in the matters of delivery and non-delivery notifications.

The *physical delivery notification by MHS* service element is used by the originator to request that MHS notify the originator of the successful or unsuccessful delivery of the physical message. The physical delivery service (PDS) does not provide a physical record of this notification.

The *physical delivery notification by PDS* is similar to the above service element, except the PDS provides the notification and a physical record for the originator.

The *physical forwarding allowed* service element is used by the PDS to send a physical message to a forwarding address, and the recipient has made this address known to the PDS.

The *physical forwarding prohibited* service element allows the originator to prevent a message from being forwarded to a forwarding address.

The *prevention of non-delivery notification* service element is used by the sending UA to inform the MTS not to return a non-delivery notification if the message is not delivered. This situation is not unusual in electronic mail when non-priority bulletins are sent to various recipients. The service can be requested on a per-recipient basis for a multi-destination message.

The *primary and copy recipients indication* service element is used by the originator to provide the names of the users and distribution lists (DLs) who are the primary recipients of the IP message as well as the identification of the individuals and DLs who are copy recipients only. This is the counterpart to the "to" and "cc" identifiers of a typical letter.

The *probe* service element is used by the sending UA to determine if a message can be delivered before it actually is sent. The MTS is responsible for providing the submission information by generating either non-delivery or delivery notifications. The useful aspect of the probe service element relates to the possibility that different codes, different message sizes, or even different content types might not be deliverable. In such a case, the originating UA might alter some of its size, content types, and codes as a result of the probe. If the probe is based on a DL, it only indicates that the originator has the right to submit the DL; it does not ensure successful delivery.

The *probe origin authentication* service element is used to authenticate the origin of the probe. This service uses the asymmetric encryption technique.

The *proof of delivery* service element is used to authenticate the identity of the recipients and the content of the delivered message. In a sense, it is similar to the practice of message echo used in some lower layer protocols. The service uses symmetric or asymmetric encryption techniques.

The *proof of submission* service element is used by the originator as an assurance by the MTS that the message was submitted for delivery to the recipient.

The *receipt notification request indication* service element is used by the originator to request that it be notified of the receipt of the IP-message. The receipt notification must include the identifier of the message to which the notification is applicable, the time of destination receipt, the O/R name of the recipient, and an indication if any code conversion was performed.

The *redirection disallowed by originator* service element is used to override the redirection of incoming messages service element. In this situation, the message will not be redirected, even though the recipient has so requested.

The *redirection of incoming messages* service element is used by a UA to request the MTS to redirect messages to another UA or a DL. The service can be established for a specified period of time, or it can be revoked at any time.

The *registered mail* service element is used by the originator to direct the PDS to handle the physical message as registered mail.

The *registered mail to addressee in person* service element is used by the

The Application Layer Application Service Elements (ASEs)

originator to direct the PDS to handle the message as registered mail and deliver it only to the addressee.

The *reply request indication* service element is used by the originator to request that the receiver send an IP-message and reply to the original message. This service element also allows the originator to specify the date on which to send the reply and the O/R names of those who should receive the reply. The recipient is responsible for deciding whether or not to reply to the traffic.

The *replying IP-Message Indication* service element is used to indicate that the IP-message is sent in reply to another IP-message. The reply may be sent only to the originator or to other users who received copies of the message. It also can be sent to a DL.

The *report origin authentication* service element is used by the message or probe originator to authenticate the origin of a report on the delivery or non-delivery of a message or probe. The service uses the asymmetric encryption technique.

The *request for forwarding address* service element is used by the origina-tor to direct the PDS to give the originator the forwarding address for the mes-sage recipient, if the recipient has provided one to the PDS. This service can be used in conjunction with the physical forwarding allowed and prohibited service elements.

The *requested delivery method* service element is used to request a method of preference for the message delivery. For example, an access unit (UA) or physical delivery access unit (PDAU) can be designated.

The *restricted delivery* service element is used by the recipient UA to in-form the MTS that it cannot accept messages from designated UAs or DLs. These entities become unauthorized originators.

The *return of content* service element is used by the sending UA to request that the content of its message be returned in the event of non-delivery. The return will not occur if the system has encoded the message into a different code.

The *secure access management* service element is an MHS security feature. It allows the establishment of associations between MTS users, MTSs, or MTAs and supports the associations through strong credentials. The concept of cre-dentials is discussed in the X.500 Directory material in Chapter 12.

The *sensitivity indication* service element is used by the originator to pro-vide guidelines about the security of the IP-message. This service element indi-cates whether the recipient should have to identify itself before it receives the traffic; whether the IP-message can be printed on a shared device; and whether the IP-message can be auto-forwarded. The service specifies three levels of sen-sitivity: (a) personal: the IP-message is sent to an individual recipient, not based on the role of the individual in the organization; (b) private: the IP message contains information to be used only by the recipient and no one else; and (c) company confidential: the IP message contains information that should be used only according to company procedures.

The *special delivery* service element is used by the originator to direct the PDS to send the physical message through the postal service's special delivery service.

The *stored message alert* service element allows a user to specify to its message store (MS) a set of criteria that are used to cause the MS to send an alert to the user. The alert is sent to the user through the user's UA.

The *stored message auto-forward* service element requests the MS to forward certain messages automatically. The MHS user registers with the MS the criteria to be used to determine whether or not the message is to be forwarded. The messages that meet a set of criteria are forwarded to one or more users or a DL.

The *stored message deletion* service element is used by the recipient UA to delete messages from the MS queues. Messages cannot be deleted until they have been listed to the UA.

The *stored message fetching* service element is used by the recipient UA to retrieve a message or a portion of a message. The fetching is based on a set of criteria obtained from the use of the stored message listing service element.

The *stored message listing* service element is used by the MS to provide the recipient UA with a list of messages at the MS and the attributes of the messages. The UA can limit the number of messages listed to it.

The *stored message summary* service element is used by the UA to request that the MS provide a count of the number of messages stored at the MS. The count is based on selection criteria (attributes) chosen by the UA.

The *subject indication* service element is used by the originator to indicate to the receiver the subject matter of the IP-message.

The *submission time stamp indication* service element is used by the MTS to inform the sending UA of the date and time the message was submitted to the MTS.

The *typed body* service element defines the attributes of the body of the IP-message. For example, it may describe the type code (IA5) or indicate whether it is a facsimile or a teletext document. These descriptions are carried in the message along with the body.

The *undeliverable mail with return of physical message* service element is used by the physical delivery service (PDS) if it cannot deliver the physical message. The message is returned to the originator with a reason for the non-delivery.

The *use of distribution list* service element allows the originating UA to use a DL in place of a number of individual recipients. These recipients can be users or DLs.

The *user/UA capabilities registration* service element allows the UA to inform its MTA of the nature of the messages it wishes to have delivered to it. Delivery restrictions can be based on (a) content type of message; (b) length of message; (c) encoded information type of message.

Basic and Optional MHS Services

The use of all the available service elements in a system usually is unnecessary. Most users do not need all the services, and a full-feature implementation requires the writing of a considerable amount of code. Like several of the other layers and entities of OSI, the MHS is divided into "required" and optional services. This approach permits a developer to implement a subset of MHS. The required services are called *basic* (or base) services. Table 11-10 lists the basic services. The other service elements are optional.

The 1984 and 1988 Recommendations

The 1988 MHS Recommendations are quite different from the 1984 Recommendations. The changes were made to make them easier to understand, align them to the OSI Model, and increase the services to the user. This section should help the reader to understand the relationships between the two sets of documents. In the following list, each 1984 MHS Recommendation is "tracked" to the 1988 release.

- 1984 X.400: Refer to 1988 X.400 and F.400
- 1984 X.401: Refer to 1988 X.400 and F.400
- 1984 X.408: Refer to 1988 X.408

TABLE 11-10. MHS Basic (Base) Elements of Service

Service Element	MT	MH/PD	MS	IPM
Access Management	X	—	—	X
Basic Physical Rendition	—	X	—	—
Content Type Indication	X	—	—	X
Conversion Indication	X	—	—	X
Delivery Time Stamp Indication	X	—	—	X
IP-message Identification	—	—	—	X
Message Identification	—	—	—	X
Non-delivery Notification	X	—	—	X
Ordinary Mail	—	X	—	—
Original Encoded Information Type Indication	X	—	—	X
Physical Forwarding Allowed	—	X	—	—
Stored Message Deletion	—	—	X	—
Stored Message Fetching	—	—	X	—
Stored Message Listing	—	—	X	—
Stored Message Summary	—	—	X	—
Submission Time Stamp Indication	X	—	—	X
Typed Body	—	—	—	X
Undeliverable Mail with Return of Message	—	X	—	—
User/UA Capabilities Registration	X	—	—	X

- 1984 X.411: Refer to 1988 X.411 and X.419
- 1984 X.420: Refer to 1988 X.420
- 1984 X.409: Refer to 1988 X.208 and X.209
- 1984 X.410: Refer to 1988 X.218, X.219, X.228, and X.229
- 1988 X.403: New
- 1988 X.407: New
- 1988 X.413: New

THE VIRTUAL TERMINAL (VT)

Even though you may not realize it, when you communicate in your home or office with an application through a communications network, you probably use at least a rudimentary form of the virtual terminal (VT) concept. The idea of the virtual terminal is to define the "behavior" of terminal from the standpoint of its operating characteristics and network sessions. Ideally, the definition procedure is flexible enough to allow the terminal user to (a) readily change the behavior of the terminal, and (b) provide a means for a terminal or a user application to access a variety of other terminals and applications.

The latter feature is especially difficult to provide, because most vendors' terminals use different upper-level protocols. While it is true that some terminals use the same codes for some functions, such as carriage return, escape, cursor movement, etc., it remains that most vendors use their own approaches. The situation is made even more complex because the vendors also use different approaches to keyboard commands and screen control programs. IBM solves the problem by placing all terminals onto a host machine and using the same (or nearly the same) terminal protocols. However, this approach becomes unwieldy in large, distributed systems that must support a heterogeneous terminal environment.

The central concept of the virtual terminal is to isolate the terminals and applications from each other. In this manner, different terminals can access different applications running on different systems. The VT achieves this worthy goal by one VT entity (a) simulating a real terminal and (b) negotiating the terminal's operating characteristics with another VT entity. It becomes the task of the VTs to resolve potential differences and incompatibilities between the terminal and the application.

If you find yourself muttering that the VT concept is really nothing new and the industry has been using terminal simulation for many years, you are absolutely correct. As with most of the OSI standards, those for VT services are not intended to blaze new technological trails but simply to establish a standard way of connecting heterogeneous systems.

Terminal Modeling

In this section, we examine two approaches for obtaining VT services (and concentrate on the latter):

The Application Layer Application Service Elements (ASEs)

- *Parameter Model:* Use of codes and parameters to describe the terminal.
- *Object Model:* Use of abstract objects to model the terminal characteristics and functions.

The parameter model is explained with the CCITT X.3, X.28, and X.29 protocols, which are not covered in detail here because they are not OSI protocols. The object model is explained with ISO 9040 and ISO 9041.

The Parameter Model. When X.25-based packet networks came into existence in the 1970s, it was recognized that many terminals in operation were (and are) asynchronous, scroll-mode devices. A scroll-mode terminal has limited capabilities. It is so named because each received character is placed on the screen and as new lines are created on the screen, the old lines are scrolled upward and off the screen.

Even though these terminals are quite simple, they may still differ in how they accept and interpret control characters such as line feed, horizontal tab, and so on. Obviously, an interface was needed to interconnect these terminals with each other. (Keep in mind that they were communicating through packet networks.) Consequently, standards were developed to provide protocol conversion and packet assembly/disassembly (PAD) functions for the asynchronous terminal. After the initial 1976 draft of the X.25 standard, the standards committees followed up in 1977 with recommendations for three specifications to support X.25 with asynchronous terminal interfaces: X.3, X.28, and X.29.

The PAD is actually a parameter-driven virtual terminal (VT). It provides protocol conversion for a user device (DTE) to a public or private network, and a complementary protocol conversion at the receiving end of the network. In so doing, it allows different types of terminals to communicate with each other. The goal is to provide a transparent service to user terminals through the network. While X.3 and its companion standards X.28 and X.29 address only asynchronous devices (which constitute many of the devices in operation today), many vendors offer other PAD services to support link-level protocols such as BSC and SDLC, and higher layer functions as well.

The asynchronous-oriented PAD performs the following functions:

- assembly of characters into packets
- disassembly of user data field at other end
- handling virtual call setup, clearing, resetting, and interrupt
- generation of service signals from PAD to user terminal
- mechanism for forwarding packets (full packet or timer expires)
- editing PAD commands
- automatic detection of data rate, code, parity and operational characteristics of user terminal.

X.3. The 1984 version of X.3 stipulates a set of 22 parameters the PAD uses to identify and control each terminal communicating with it. When a connection to a PAD from the DTE is established, the PAD parameters are used to determine how the PAD communicates with the user DTE. The parameters define certain attributes of the user terminal as well as several services that are provided by the PAD. The user also has options of altering the parameters after the logon to the PAD device is complete. Each of the 22 parameters consists of a reference number and parameter values. These parameters and references are explained in more detail in almost any book dealing with data communications.

The Object Model. The object model developed by the ISO uses abstract data objects to model common functions and characteristics found in terminals. The idea is that the terminals' functions can be described in an abstract notation in order to facilitate the interworking of terminals and applications processes.

The basic idea of an object model virtual terminal is as follows. Each terminal is described by a data structure (or object) and a profile. A profile may be part of the data structure. A profile is a set of parameters which define the characteristics of the terminal. The data structure not only describes the terminal's profile, but defines the specific terminal operation. The object model differs from the parameter model in that the object model terminal (or a device acting as its agent) is considered to be much more intelligent, perhaps able to assume different profiles.

The terms associated with virtual terminals need to be explained before we can study the ISO standards. First, examine Figure 11-6. A terminal is to communicate with an application residing in a host computer. Either entity can begin the communications process by informing the other with some preliminary handshaking signals. Then the entities can begin a negotiation process to determine what terminal capabilities can be supported. The terminal and host computer operate through their respective VTs where local mapping occurs. The mapping entails selecting and using the characteristics and capabilities acceptable to the terminal and the application.

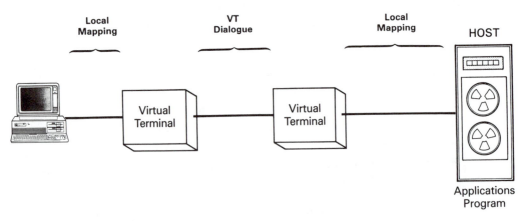

FIGURE 11-6. Virtual Terminal Dialogue and Mapping

TABLE 11–11. Typical VT Parameters That Can Be Changed (not all-inclusive)

Character sets allowed	Screen refresh and erase attributes
Hardcopy output	Scrolling attributes
Dimensions of output (1, 2, 3)	Sound features
Minimum line length of display	Foreground and background color
Minimum page length of display	Downline loading of forms, screens, etc.
Color characteristics of display	Updating each entity's shared VT work areas
Meaning of control characters	Attention and interrupt handling
Font assignment and capability	Local echo control

Table 11-11 contains a list of common capabilities that could be negotiated. The negotiation process changes control tables in each of the VT entities (see Figure 11-7). These control tables determine how the contents of the terminal memory will be mapped onto the display screen. However, since there is more memory than can be placed onto a screen at one time, the VT process entails using the control tables to determine how to map the *conceptual memory/display* contents onto the real display of the screen.

The mapping process is achieved with the *device object,* as seen in Figure 11-8. A device object exists for each real device used at the terminal (screen, keyboard, printer, plotter, scanner, etc.). Another term used to describe the conceptual display is the *display object.* Under the VT concept, a display object is mapped by the device object into a real display.

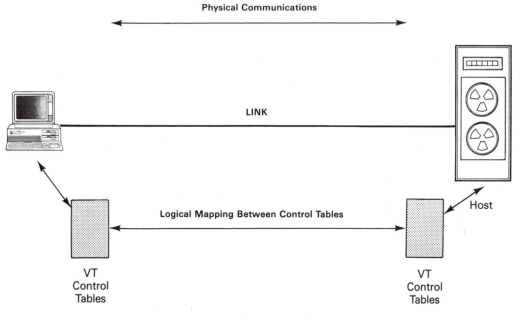

Physical Communications

LINK

Logical Mapping Between Control Tables

Host

VT
Control
Tables

VT
Control
Tables

FIGURE 11–7. Control Mapping Tables

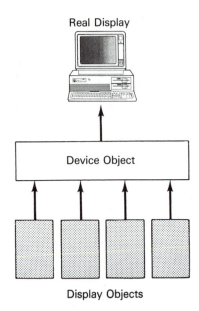

Real Display

Device Object

Display Objects

FIGURE 11-8. Virtual Terminal Objects

The VT standards also use a *control object* to define the physical aspects of the devices, such as bells, buzzers, lights, mouse movements, and other activities not related to the manipulation of text.

After the negotiation is completed, the two entities should be able to communicate with the same set of VT services.

ISO 9040 and ISO 9041

These two specifications describe a basic class virtual terminal service and protocol, respectively. They describe how the entities establish and negotiate a VT association to obtain service profiles, transfer data, control access to the entities' control tables, and release the association.

Virtual terminal users communicate with each other through a *conceptual communication area* (CCA). The CCA is illustrated in Figure 11-9. This area contains the control objects and device objects described in the previous section. The CCA is shared by the VT users and information is exchanged by either VT user updating its contents and through the service provider making it available to the other VT user.

The control and device objects collectively comprise the profile of a virtual terminal environment (VTE). As we learned earlier, the third object type is called a display object, which describes the actual VT display images.

The display object is a one-, two-, or three-dimensional array of elements. The dimensions are called X, Y, and Z, and each is capable of handling one "character-box" graphic element. This element (a) is empty: nothing assigned

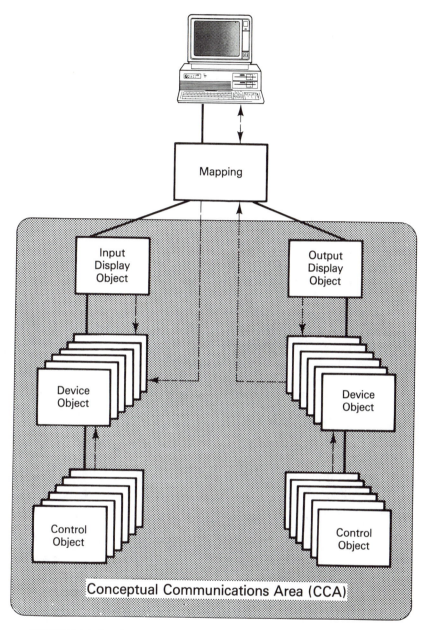

FIGURE 11-9. The VT Conceptual Communications Area (CCA)

to it; (b) contains a primary attribute: a value that selects a specific graphic element; (c) contains a secondary attribute: a value which selects attributes for the display object, such as color, intensity, blinking, font, etc. ISO 646 and ISO 2022 could be used to define a graphic element. ISO 646 defines a 7-bit coded character set and ISO 2022 defines a 7-bit and 8-bit set.

Each array element is addressed by a display pointer and each element is completely independent of other elements.

It is quite important that the display objects and control objects in the conceptual communications area be updated in a manner that does not disrupt the ongoing terminal displays. One obvious problem arises if both VT entities attempt to update the shared area at the same time. The approach taken by the ISO is through the use of S-mode or A-mode operations.

These terms mean the following:

- Synchronous mode (S-mode): Two-way simultaneous access
- Asynchronous mode (A-Mode): Two-way alternate access

The S-mode and A-mode terminals operate on the basis of access rights. An access right is the permission to perform some kind of operation. The VT Basic Class uses one access right called the WAVAR (Write Access Variable). It is reassigned between the users during the session. The access rights also may be established by a pair of access rights that are not reassigned during the session. The WACI (Write Access Connection Initiation) is always owned by the initiating VT user and the WACA (Write Access Connection Acceptor) is always owned by the user that receives the request for a VT association, that is, the association acceptor. S-mode uses WAVAR and A-mode uses WACI and WACA.

The S-mode and A-mode cannot be changed during an association. They use the session layer two-way simultaneous and two-way alternate services, respectively, and these session layer services cannot be renegotiated during an association.

Virtual Terminal Service Sequences and Phases.   The VT standard is organized around service sequences and phases. The service provider is required to pass through these phases under strict rules defined by the use of specific service definitions. The phases are:

- *Idle:* No VT-association exists.
- *Data Handling:* Information is being exchanged between VT-users.
- *Negotiation Active:* Interaction negotiation services are being used to create a new VTE.
- *Negotiation Quiescent:* Neither data transfer nor negotiation is taking place.

Virtual Terminal Service Definitions.   As the reader might expect, VT services are defined with service definitions and primitives. The service primitives are listed in Table 11-12 with a brief description of their functions. Be aware that the table does not show the possible variations of the request, indication, response, and confirm operations. The services summarized in Table 11-12 are explained in more detail in the next section.

TABLE 11-12. **The VT Service Definition Primitives and Phases**

Service	IDLE	DATA HANDLING	NEGOTIATION ACTIVE	NEGOTIATION QUIESCENT
VT-ASSOCIATE	A	N	N	N
VT-RELEASE	N	A	N	A
VT-U-ABORT	N	A	A	A
VT-P-ABORT	N	A	A	A
VT-DELIVER	N	A	N	N
VT-ACK-RECEIPT	N	A	N	N
VT-GIVE-TOKENS	N	A	A	A
VT-REQUEST-TOKENS	N	A	A	A
VT-DATA	N	A	N	N
VT-START-NEG	N	A	N	A
VT-END-NEG	N	N	A	N
VT-NEG-INVITE	N	N	A	N
VT-NEG-OFFER	N	N	A	N
VT-NEG-ACCEPT	N	N	A	N
VT-NEG-REJECT	N	N	A	N
VT-BREAK	N	A	N	N
VT-SWITCH-PROFILE	N	A	N	A

A = Available   N = Not Available

Virtual Terminal Functional Units. Like the vast majority of OSI standards, the VT protocol is designed to present a number of options to the user. As we have discussed in previous parts of this book, these options serve as a convenient means to model a standard's architecture. At the broadest level, the VT services are divided into functional units. The functional units are further classified by facilities within the functional units. Lastly, the facilities are classified by the services provided. Figure 11-10 depicts the relationships of the functional units, facilities, and services.

The *kernel* functional unit is not an optional capability; it is considered the most basic set of services to be established between two VT users. The facilities of the functional unit are shown in Figure 11-10.

As the name suggests, the *switch profile negotiation* is used to switch the profile between the association of the two VT users. The operation entails one user proposing a VT profile by providing VT argument values in the proposal. The protocol allows the service provider and the receiving VT user to return an agreed-upon set of profile values, but only if they are within the range offered by the initial service initiator. This is quite similar to the other OSI protocols in which negotiation begins with the initiator and can then be changed first by the service provider and next by the receiving service user.

The *multiple interaction negotiation* functional unit is used to negotiate a

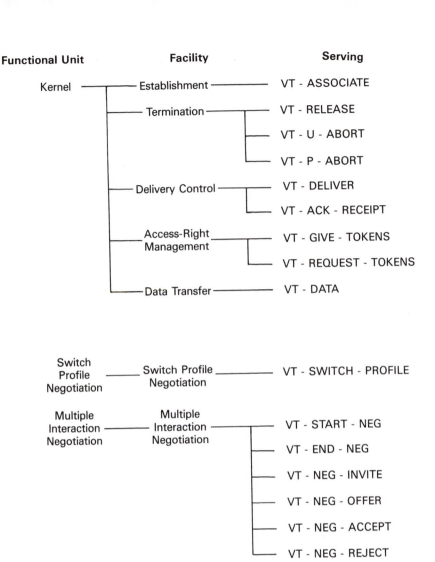

Functional Unit	Facility	Serving

Kernel — Establishment ——————— VT - ASSOCIATE

— Termination ——— VT - RELEASE
— VT - U - ABORT
— VT - P - ABORT

— Delivery Control ——— VT - DELIVER
— VT - ACK - RECEIPT

— Access-Right Management ——— VT - GIVE - TOKENS
— VT - REQUEST - TOKENS

— Data Transfer ——————— VT - DATA

Switch Profile Negotiation — Switch Profile Negotiation ——————— VT - SWITCH - PROFILE

Multiple Interaction Negotiation — Multiple Interaction Negotiation ——— VT - START - NEG
— VT - END - NEG
— VT - NEG - INVITE
— VT - NEG - OFFER
— VT - NEG - ACCEPT
— VT - NEG - REJECT

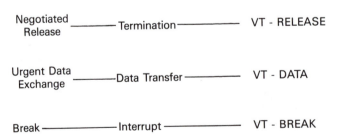

Negotiated Release ——— Termination ——————— VT - RELEASE

Urgent Data Exchange ——— Data Transfer ——————— VT - DATA

Break ——————— Interrupt ——————— VT - BREAK

FIGURE 11-10. The Virtual Terminal Architecture

The Application Layer Application Service Elements (ASEs)

set of VTE parameter values which allow one VTE to ask another VTE to actually propose values for the VTE parameters. These values are proposed and they may or may not be accepted by the inviting VTE user. It can be seen that the multiple interaction negotiation functional unit differs from the switch profile negotiation functional unit in that the inviting VTE user provides the invitation for the responding VTE user to provide its own parameters.

The *negotiated release* functional unit allows the VTE user to reject a request from its peer VTE user to release the VTE association. However, a release cannot be rejected unless the negotiated release functional unit has been established.

The *urgent data* functional unit allows the VT user to send a small amount of data to the peer VTE user, usually bypassing exchanges of lessor priority. The VT standards do not stipulate how the urgent data are to be handled.

The *break* functional unit is used to support the destructive interrupt facility, which is described in the next section.

VT Facilities. In this section we take a brief look at the VT facilities. The *establishment* facility has one service associated with it, called VT-ASSOCIATE service. Its purpose is to establish a VT association between two VT users. It also may be used to refuse the establishment of the association. It is a confirmed service utilizing the request, indication, response, and confirm primitives listed in Table 11-12.

The establishment facility requires that a number of parameters be used in the primitives to establish the association. For example, one of these optional parameters would include the VT-WAVAR owner, would be used as a parameter for an optional offering, and would be applicable only if the value of the service parameter of the VT mode is the S-mode. The parameters used with this facility and service are:

- *Called/Calling Application Entity Title:* Titles of the applications entities with which the VT association is to be established.
- *Responding Application Entity Title:* Title of the application entity responding to the association request.
- *VT-Class:* Established the virtual terminal class (presently "basic") for the association.
- *VT-Functional Units:* Defines the functional units to be used with the association (see previous section).
- *VT-Mode:* Defines the mode to be used with the association and is taken from the set (S-mode and A-mode).
- *VT-WAVAR-Owner:* If S-mode is used, this parameter allows the VT users to negotiate the initial ownership of the WAVAR access right.
- *VTE-Profile Name:* Forms the parameters for the initial VTE for the VT association. The name is used to choose a list of parameters to negotiate. If a parameter is not present, the service provider can use a default VTE

profile. ISO 9040, Annex A describes the default profiles for both A-mode and S-mode operations.

- *VTE-Profile-Arg-Offer-List:* This parameter is used if the VTE Profile Name is a parameterized list. It contains one or more VTE profile values. The parameter contains the offer values for the VT association.
- *VTE-Profile-Arg-Value-List:* The values in this parameter contain the accept values for the VTE profile.
- *VT-Result:* Indicates the results of the VT service as (a) failure, (b) success-with-warning, (c) success.
- *VT-User-Failure-Reason:* States the reason for the user rejecting the VT association.
- *VT-Provider-Failure-Reason:* States the reason that the VT service provider rejected the VT association.

The *termination* facility consists of three services: VT-RELEASE, VT-U-ABORT, and VT-P-ABORT, along with the supporting primitives listed in Table 11-12. As might be expected, the VT-RELEASE is used to request an orderly termination of the VT association. The two abort services do not allow an orderly release of the association, but force an unconditional termination of the VT association from either the user or the service provider.

The *delivery control* facility consists of the VT-DELIVER and VT-ACK RECEIPT services. The purpose of these two services is to designate delivery points in a stream of updates to objects and to request acknowledgment of their receipt. The VT-DELIVER service provides this function. In turn, the VT-ACK RECEIPT service acknowledges the delivery point identified by the receipt of the data unit.

The *access write management* facility consists of two services: VT-GIVE-TOKENS and VT-REQUEST-TOKENS. These services are used to pass all defined service tokens (the WAVAR access-right) to the peer virtual terminal protocol machine (VTPM). Of course, the VT-REQUEST-TOKENS service is used to request possession of the WAVAR access-right. This facility is only valid in the S-mode and is initiated by the current owner of the access-right.

The *data transfer* facility consists of the VT-DATA service and the VT-DATA (urgent) service. These services are used to convey updates to control or display objects in the following manner: (a) updating objects for which the priority parameter has a high value, (b) in the A-mode, indicating if echoing may take place after the processing of the data item, and (c) conveying updates to control objects for which the priority parameter has the value urgent.

The *switch profile negotiation* facility consists of one service element, the VT-SWITCH-PROFILE service. The purpose of this service is to negotiate a switch from a named VTE profile to new full-VTE profile. This service also indicates the failure or success of the attempted negotiation. The parameters (previously explained) used with this facility are:

- VTE-Profile-Name
- VTE-Profile-Arg-Offer-List

The Application Layer Application Service Elements (ASEs)

- VTE-Profile-Arg-Value-List
- VTE-Result
- VT-User-Failure-Reason
- VT-Provider-Failure-Reason

The *multiple interaction negotiation* facility consists of six services: (a) VT-START-NEG, (b) VT-END-NEG, (c) VT-NEG-INVITE, (d) VT-NEG-OFFER, (e) VT-NEG-ACCEPT, and (f) VT-NEG-REJECT. These services perform the following functions:

- Request the synchronized termination of a multiple interaction negotiation.
- Provide a transition to the data handling phase.
- Respond to a request to terminate a negotiation.
- Select values for the VTE parameters specified in a previous VT-NEG-OFFER protocol element.
- Reject VTE parameters contained in previous negotiations whose values are unacceptable.
- Pass a list of VTE parameters once the multiple interaction negotiation has been agreed upon.
- Request the establishment of a negotiation active phase.
- Indicate the success or failure of the attempt to establish a negotiation active phase.

The *termination* facility consists of the VT-RELEASE (adding negotiated release) service.

Finally, the *interrupt* facility consists of the VT-BREAK service. This service requests and acknowledges a destructive priority interrupt to be indicated and acknowledged to/from the remote VT user with regard to the remote VTPM.

FILE TRANSFER ACCESS AND MANAGEMENT (FTAM)

The efficient management of data, data bases, and files (usually called data management or data administration) presents major challenges to companies and organizations. While this fascinating subject is beyond the scope of this chapter, the transfer, access, and management of files between two communicating applications and/or data systems is certainly a communications process. Consequently, this section of the book examines the subject from the standpoint of file transfer, with emphasis on the ISO file transfer, access, and management (FTAM) specifications.

From the inception of the commercial computer, files and data bases have been transferred between machines. Moreover, since data were (and are) considered a valuable resource in an organization, many companies implemented file management schemes to govern who had access to the data, how the data was read and written (changed), and the procedures for transfer of the files to other users and files. Usually, procedures were established to determine how to read, change, delete, and append both local or remote files. The ISO has recognized the need to standardize these important operations to ease the task of transferring data between different systems. The FTAM standards are the result of the ISO efforts.

The FTAM Documents

The FTAM specification is divided into five parts:

8571/1	Introduction to the FTAM concepts; discusses file transfer problems.
8571/2	Explains the terms, concepts and vocabulary used in FTAM (file name, contents, access codes).
8571/3	Describes interface required between the two entities that participate in the file transfer process.
8571/4	Defines the specific rules for the activities in part 3.
8571/5	Describes the conformance statement.

The Virtual Filestore Concept

Although data usage often varies among different applications, a common model for all data files and data bases can provide a common foundation for file transfer, access, and management among diverse applications. This model is called the *virtual filestore*. It is an abstract model that describes the file's characteristics, structure, and attributes. Its objective is to reduce the amount of detail needed to communicate with a file located in a remote part of the network.

The basic idea of virtual filestore is to provide a mapping of file definitions to/from actual files, which are called real filestores (see Figure 11-11). The filestore definitions form a schema (or set) of the file; subset descriptions of files form subschemas (or subsets). (The concepts of schemas and subschemas are very well known and understood in the data base management industry. The terms sets and subsets are used with virtual filestore.)

The set provides a mapping of the data from an actual file to a modeled virtual filestore. It shows the names of the file attributes and establishes the relationships of the data elements in the file. It provides the overall view of the file. OSI FTAM describes only the characteristics of the virtual filestore and not the characteristics of the actual file. This approach permits different files of varying complexity and formats to be interworked with each other because a mapping function is provided between the real systems.

Typically, organizations have hundreds of subsets, and individual users

The Application Layer Application Service Elements (ASEs)

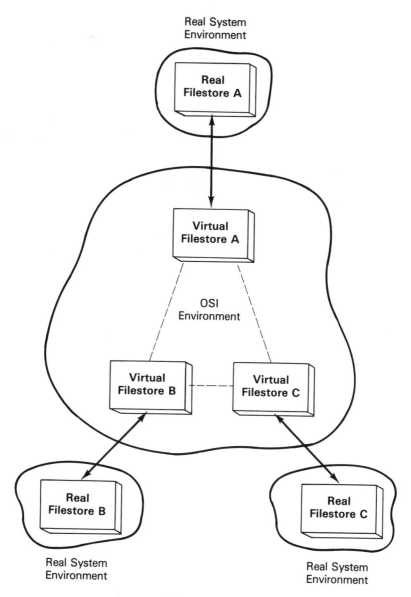

Real System
Environment

**Real
Filestore A**

**Virtual
Filestore A**

OSI
Environment

**Virtual
Filestore B**

**Virtual
Filestore C**

**Real
Filestore B**

**Real
Filestore C**

Real System
Environment

Real System
Environment

FIGURE 11-11. Virtual Filestore

often have multiple subsets to satisfy different kinds of retrieval and update requirements. This presents a challenging problem for the data base and network designers: They must provide for a physical design that satisfies all user "views" at all nodes in the network. The emerging ISO standards provide methods to join different subsets between systems at the presentation layer and additional procedures to manage file service dialogue at the session layer.

File Access Data Units (FADUs)

The FTAM model is a hierarchical structure resembling a tree (see Figure 11-12). The tree can have a single root and a number of nodes below the root. Each node is identified and can have a data type associated with it. In virtual filestore, the conventional notion of a "data record" is called a data unit (DU), and a node may or may not have a data unit associated with it. The DUs are related to each other through a hierarchical structure called file access data units (FADUs). Operations on a file are performed on an FADU through FADU identifiers (or names). The FADU is identified as a typed data unit at the presentation layer. The DU is considered to be the smallest amount that can be accessed.

Preorder Tree Traversal. The FTAM can take several forms for purposes of accessing a file or a portion of a file. For example, a file can be accessed starting from the root and traversing down through the nodes in a set order. As another example, FADUs can be accessed by "next," "last," "previous," and "beginning" signals.

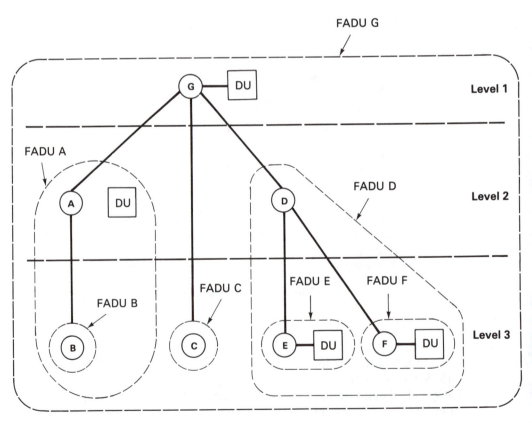

FIGURE 11-12. File Access Structure

The Application Layer Application Service Elements (ASEs)

The preorder tree traversal is a method to describe the structure of the tree by defining the ordering of the nodes in the following manner:

- Enter the tree through the top node.
- Go through the nodes from the top, going down and to the left.
- Go to the right in the tree when no paths remain by going down.
- Go up in tree if the search cannot go down.

For example, the preorder tree traversal for the tree in Figure 11-12 is: G, A, B, C, D, E, F.

FTAM Access Contexts. A file user often does not need access to all the data in a file. The detail needed depends upon the user's access requirements. Consequently, FTAM provides the access context which allows the user to describe the logical view of the data needed for the access. FTAM supports the following access contexts:

- Access only the DUs within an addressed FADU but do not provide any FADU information.
- Access only the DU that is associated with the root of the FADU, again without providing any FADU information.
- Access all DUs in an FADU level but do not provide any FADU information.
- Access all DUs in an FADU and provide all FADU description information.
- Access the FADU description information but do not provide any DU information.

Attributes

FTAM also is organized around the concept of the attribute, which describes the properties of a file. Presently, four groups of attributes are defined:

Kernel group: Properties common to all files.

Storage group: Properties of files that are stored.

Security group: Properties for access control.

Private group: Properties beyond FTAM scope.

The kernel group consists of the file name, a description of the file structure (sequential, hierarchical), access restrictions (deletion, reads, etc.), location of the file user, and the identification of the application entities involved in the FTAM communications process.

The storage group describes several properties of a file. The properties are either (a) information about the ongoing characteristics of the file, or (b) information about the latest operations on the file. The following properties are included in the storage group:

- Date and time of last read, change, or attribute change.
- Identification of creator, last reader, last modifier, or last attribute modifier.
- File size and availability.
- Identification of party to be charged for file storage and file access activities.
- Description of any locks on the file.
- Identification of initiating FTAM user.

The security group includes attributes on access permission criteria, encryption procedures, and legal qualifications (trademarks, copyrights, etc.).

The private group is not defined by the FTAM standard. It is used for files beyond the virtual filestore attributes.

FTAM File Service Regimes

Yet another way to view FTAM is through the concept of file service regimes. A file service is performed through a series of steps which build up a set of file contexts. The steps may include:

- The initiator and responder handshaking with each other to establish their identities.
- Identification of the file to be accessed.
- Establishing the file attributes.
- Providing for any file management actions.
- Locating the units in the file to be accessed.
- Operating on the units in the file.

The file service regimes define how FTAM primitives are used for the file activity. A regime is a period in which a common state is valid for the service users. Regimes provide the protocol for file selection, file opens/closes, data transfer, and recovery operations. Figure 11-13 shows the relationships of the regimes and primitives. (The primitives are explained shortly.) Four types of file service regimes are defined:

- *Application association regime*: exists during the lifetime of application association of two file service users.
- *File selection regime*: exists during the time in which a particular file is associated with the application association.
- *File open regime*: exists during a particular set of presentation contexts, concurrency controls, and commitment controls in operation for data transfer (these concepts are explained shortly).

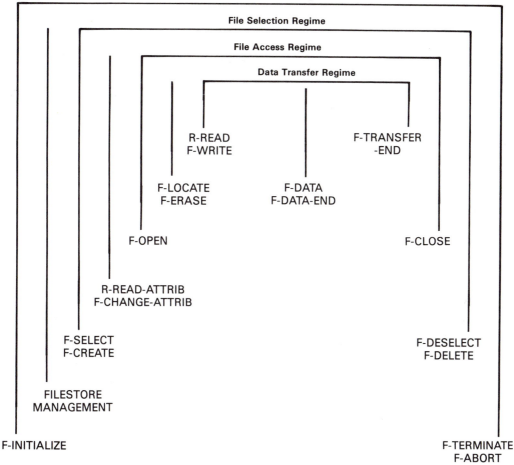

Application Connection Regime

File Selection Regime

File Access Regime

Data Transfer Regime

R-READ
F-WRITE

F-TRANSFER
-END

F-LOCATE
F-ERASE

F-DATA
F-DATA-END

F-OPEN

F-CLOSE

R-READ-ATTRIB
F-CHANGE-ATTRIB

F-SELECT
F-CREATE

F-DESELECT
F-DELETE

FILESTORE
MANAGEMENT

F-INITIALIZE

F-TERMINATE
F-ABORT

FIGURE 11–13. FTAM Regime

- *Data transfer regime:* exists when a particular access context and direction of transfer are in force.

The dialogue proceeds through a series of protocol exchanges, such as the reading of a file access data unit. Specific times in which these exchanges occur are called phases. During a phase, FTAM imposes strict rules on state transitions and the use of primitives and state diagrams. The phases are sequential; they cannot be nested.

Virtual Filestore Actions

Virtual filestore defines two types of "actions" on files. The first encompasses actions to the contents of a file such as locating and reaching a file. This type also describes the protocol for inserting, replacing, extending, and erasing an FADU within virtual filestores.

The second type defines actions on a complete file. For example, procedures describe the creation of a file, as well as its deletion. In addition, the read, open, close, and select attributes of the file also are defined within this action type.

Architecture of FTAM

As we have done in describing other application layer standards in this chapter, FTAM can also be understood by examining some of the very basic operations it supports. These services are classified as functional units and service classes and serve as a convenient (if arbitrary from the writer's viewpoint) means to explain the architecture of FTAM.

Functional units. Functional units describe the specific services of FTAM. The idea is quite valuable because FTAM allows the functional units to be negotiated when an FTAM regime is initialized. Consequently, FTAM entities do not have to implement all the features of the FTAM standard (to do so might be prohibitively costly). In essence, the negotiation of functional units allows freedom but reduces unneeded options and variety. The FTAM functional units are listed in Table 11-13. (Note: an initiator is a user that requests an FTAM regime establishment and a responder is a user that accepts an establishment.)

Service Classes. Service classes are yet another way to tailor the FTAM service. A service class is defined by the functional units it contains. Presently, five service classes are defined (see Table 11-14).

File Service Primitives

As the reader might expect, the FTAM services are managed with primitives to invoke specific file services. These primitives and their associated parameters are summarized in Table 11-15, and the functions of the primitives and the parameters are described below.

Descriptions of Primitives. A brief description follows on each primitive. The F-INITIALIZE primitive allows the service user to enter the FTAM regime. It is issued by the service initiator to begin operations. The parameters for this primitive are used to create a new regime and cannot be used on an existing regime. As is evident from Table 11-15, a number of parameters are passed with these primitives to establish the regime.

An FTAM regime is terminated with the F-TERMINATE primitives. The F-TERMINATE primitive is issued only by the initiator when no actions are in progress.

The F-U-ABORT and F-P-ABORT are used to achieve abrupt termination

TABLE 11-13. FTAM Functional Units

Kernel (U1)	Provides basic FTAM services, such as establishment, release of sessions and file selection regimes.
Read (U2)	Establishes open regime and transfers data from responder to initiator.
Write (U3)	Establishes open regime and transfers data from initiator to responder.
File Access (U4)	Allows an FADU to be located and manipulated.
Limited File Management (U5)	Allows the creation and deletion of files and the interrogation of file attributes.
Enhanced File Management (U6)	Provides limited file management and the modification of attributes.
Grouping (U7)	Groups more than one regime into one exchange by combining more than one primitive into a procedure.
Locking (U8)	Supports the use of concurrency locks on an FADU.
Recovery (U9)	Allows an initiator to recreate an open regime that was destroyed.
Restart (U10)	Supports the interruption of a data transfer for a later restart based on a negotiated restart point.

of an FTAM regime by the user and provider, respectively. Both sets of primitives result in the file activity being abandoned, which can cause the loss of data and the loss of management information, such as charges.

The F-SELECT and F-CREATE primitives result in the service users entering into a selected regime by selecting an existing file or creating a new one. As suggested in Table 11-15, several actions are determined, such as concurrency control, account identification, etc. Conversely, the F-DESELECT primitive re-

TABLE 11-14. FTAM Service Classes

File transfer	Mandatory: U1, U7, U2 and/or U3 Optional: U5, U6, U9, U10
File access	Mandatory: U1, U2, U3, U4 Optional: U5, U6, U7, U8, U9, U10
File management	Mandatory: U1, U5, U7 Optional: U6
File transfer and management	Mandatory: U1, U2 and/or U3, U5, U7 Optional: U6, U9, U10
Unconstrained	Mandatory: U1 Optional: U2 through U10

TABLE 11-15. File Service Primitives

Primitive	Parameters
F-INITIALIZE	State result, Action result, Called application title, Calling application title, Responding application title, Called presentation address, Calling presentation address, Responding presentation address, Presentation context management, Application context name, Service class, Functional units, Attribute groups, Shared ASE information, FTAM QOS, Communication QOS, Contents type list, Initiator identity, Account, Filestore password, Diagnostic, Checkpoint window
F-TERMINATE	Shared ASE information, Charging
F-U-ABORT	Action Result, Diagnostic
F-P-ABORT	Action Result, Diagnostic
F-SELECT	State result, Action result, Attributes, Requested access, Access passwords, Concurrency control, Shared ASE information, Account, Diagnostic
F-DESELECT	Action Result, Charging, Shared ASE information, Diagnostic
F-CREATE	State Result, Action Result, Override, Initial attributes, Create password, Requested access, Access passwords, Concurrency control, Shared ASE information, Account, Diagnostic
F-DELETE	Action Result, Shared ASE information, Charging, Diagnostic
F-READ-ATTRIB	Action Result, Attribute names, Attributes, Diagnostic
F-CHANGE-ATTRIB	Action Result, Attributes, Diagnostic
F-OPEN	State result, Action result, Processing mode, Contents type, Concurrency control, Shared ASE information, Enable FADU locking, Diagnostic, Activity Identifier, Recovery mode
F-CLOSE	Action Result, Shared ASE information, Diagnostic
F-BEGIN-GROUP	Threshold
F-END-GROUP	—
F-RECOVER	State result, Action result, Activity identifier, Bulk transfer number, Requested access, access passwords, Contents type, Recovery point, Diagnostic
F-LOCATE	Action result, FADU identity, FADU lock, Diagnostic
F-ERASE	Action result, FADU identity, Diagnostic

The Application Layer Application Service Elements (ASEs)

leases the binding between the file and the file select regime, and the F-DELETE primitive releases an existing file selection regime in such a manner that it is not available for reselection.

The F-READ-ATTRIB and F-CHANGE-ATTRIB primitives allow the file attributes of a selected file to be read and changed, respectively. If a change is made, the filestore provider notes the date and time of the last attribute change and the identity of the last attribute modifier.

The F-OPEN and F-CLOSE primitives open and close a file regime, respectively. The open services establishes presentation contexts, processing mode, and concurrency control for the data transfer activity.

The F-BEGIN-GROUP is used to establish the beginning of a set of grouped requests (a number of primitives within a group). These requests are treated as a group. The F-END-GROUP ends the grouping operation that was initiated with the F-BEGIN-GROUP.

The F-RECOVER primitive initiates recovery operations on an open regime after some type of failure has occurred. It uses information, known collectively as a docket, that is stored by the initiator and the responder to recreate the open regime.

The F-LOCATE and F-ERASE primitives specify the identity of a FADU for accessing and erasing, respectively.

Descriptions of Primitive Parameters. A brief description of each of the parameters follows. After a review of this section, it should be obvious to the reader that FTAM is quite rich in functions and gives its users many options to tailor their file transfer and management operations.

State Result: This parameter is used to determine the success or failure of FTAM actions that involve state changes in the protocol machine. It is returned in a response or confirm primitive and is coded as failure if the services do not change to the required state as established by a preceding request or confirm primitive. It is not used in primitives that do not cause a state change.

Action Result: The action result parameter is used in conjunction with the diagnostic parameter and contains a summary of the diagnostic codes. The parameter also is used to map the result of an action from the internal file service (IFS, not seen by the FTAM user) to the external file service (EFS, seen by the FTAM user).

Called/Calling Application Title: The called application title is an application entity title value used to identify the filestore. The calling application title identifies the initiating FTAM entity.

Responding Application Title: This parameter is returned by the responder. It is used to assist in the re-establishment of a failed association.

Called/Calling Presentation Address: These two parameters identify the called and calling PSAPs, respectively.

Responding Presentation Address: This parameter is a PSAP address and is used to re-establish a failed association.

Presentation context management: This parameter allows the initiator of the filestore action to indicate if the presentation context management functional unit (in the presentation service) is to be used during open and recovery operations.

Application Context Name: This parameter identifies the application association.

Functional Units: This parameter is used to negotiate the use of the functional units to be used during the association. The kernel functional unit is not negotiated. The request and indication primitives carry the functional units that can be supported by the initiator and the response and confirm primitives carry the functional units that will be used during the association.

Shared ASE Information: This parameter allows the FTAM primitives to share information from other ASEs. The application context establishes how this is accomplished. Annex C of ISO 8571-3 provides an example of shared ASE information with the combined use of FTAM and CCR.

FTAM QOS: This parameter is used to provide information about the user's susceptibility to error. Based on the value in this parameter, the service provider adds the restart and/or recovery functional unit parameter(s) as a result of interpreting the originator's FTAM QOS value.

The parameter can contain the following information:

- No error recovery, not susceptible to errors.
- Susceptible to errors which damage the data transfer regime.
- Susceptible to errors which damage the open or data transfer regime.
- Susceptible to errors which damage the select, open, or data transfer regimes, or errors which cause the loss of the application association.

Contents Type List: This parameter carries information to allow the negotiation of the presentation contexts at the time the FTAM regime is established. It is required in the transfer, access, and transfer and management classes if the presentation context management functional unit is not being negotiated. The initiator starts the negotiation by presenting a list of document type names or abstract syntax names, from which a list of required abstract syntaxes is constructed. This is used in the ACSE A-ASSOCIATE primitive in the presentation context definition list. The values in the parameter may be reduced by either the service provider or the responder.

Charging: This parameter provides information on the costs to an account at the end of a regime. It is available only if the account parameter is available at the beginning of the regime.

Attributes: This parameter conveys the file attribute names and values that are associated with the file. The parameter in the F-INITIALIZE sets up the attributes for the duration of the FTAM regime.

Initial Attributes: This parameter has the same form as the attributes parameter. FTAM permits two classes of attributes: file and activity. Each file is defined by a set of attribute values. Each FTAM activity takes place within an FTAM regime and is described by one or more activity attribute values.

Diagnostic: This parameter contains many codes to indicate the success or failure of an operation and the reason for the success or failure. It amplifies the information in the action result parameter.

Service class: This parameter defines the file service classes: (1) file transfer, (2) file management, (3) file access, (4) file transfer and management, (5) unconstrained. Recall that the FTAM service classes are categorized based on the functional units.

Attribute groups: This parameter is used to negotiate optional file attribute groups for the association.

Communication QOS: FTAM provides various quality of service features (QOS). This parameter is used to identify and negotiate them. It may be reduced by the service provider and/or the responder. The QOS features are defined in ISO 8649.

Initiator identity: This parameter identifies the calling user. It is used to set the current initiator identity activity attribute.

Account: The account that is charged for this association is identified in this parameter. It is used to set the current account activity attribute.

Filestore password: This parameter identifies and authenticates the initiator to the responder. If it is not acceptable to the responder, it may be refused with appropriate primitives.

Checkpoint window: This parameter indicates the number of checkpoints which may remain unacknowledged. It is conditional upon the recovery and restart functional units.

Access passwords: This parameter pertains to the actions associated with the access control parameter and is available only if the security attribute group has been negotiated.

Concurrency control: This parameter allows the file users to define a file select or file open regime in relation to other activities on the same file. It is used in conjunction with the requested access parameter and contains the same elements.

Account: This identifies the account to which the costs are charged. It relates to the regime which is being established for the activity.

Override: This parameter allows the user to select a file, if it already exists, or to delete a file and create a new one.

Processing mode: This parameter is used to indicate a subset of actions to be performed as a result of access control and bulk data transfer requests.

Activity identifier: This parameter defines a unique identifier for the file activity that is to be performed within the open regime if the recovery functional unit has been negotiated. A different activity identifier is assigned to each activity of a pair of initiating and responding entities. It is used to reestablish the data transfer regime after an error has occurred.

Recovery mode: This parameter identifies the error recovery facilities that are to be used for recovery during the current open regime. For example, the parameter can specify no recovery is to be performed or that recovery is to be done at any active checkpoint and at start of file.

Create Password: This parameter is used to ensure that the service user has the right to create files. It is carried in the F-CREATE parameters.

Requested Access: Following the operation of the F-CREATE operations and the storing of the initial attribute values, this parameter allows the user to choose the specific access control actions to be performed on the file. This parameter allows the user to choose a subset for this selection. This can be used for F-CREATE, F-SELECT, and F-RECOVER primitives. This parameter is used in conjunction with the concurrency control parameter to determine how more than one user accesses a file. The basis for the access control are: read, insert, replace, extend, erase, read attribute, change attribute, and delete file actions, and whether the action is required.

Access Passwords: This parameter is used to verify that a user is authorized to a specific access (i.e., a specific operation) to a file. It is used only if the security group attribute has been negotiated.

Concurrency Control: This parameter is used to control multiple activities on one file. For example, it is quite important in a shared file environment to have a means to prevent a user from accessing a part of the file while that same part is being changed by another user. It is used to determine which access locks are required for: read, insert, replace, extend, erase, read attribute, change attribute, and delete file.

Concurrency control supports the following locks:

- None required: User will not perform the action but others are allowed to do so.
- Shared: All users may perform the action.
- Exclusive: User may perform the action and others may not.
- None: No user is allowed to perform the action.

Attribute Names: Using the F-READ-ATTRIB primitives, this parameter specifies which file attributes in the filestore definition are to be read.

Contents Type: For the open operations, this parameter identifies the document type name or an abstract syntax with a constraint set name. An open will occur in the following circumstances:

- For the abstract syntax and constraint set name: if a match is made to the pair in the contents type file attribute.
- For the document type name: if the name is identical to the document type name in the contents type file attribute or if certain other criteria are met.

Threshold: This parameter specifies the number of primitives within a group to be analyzed without errors before any group can succeed.

Recovery point: This parameter identifies a checkpoint at which recovery is to take place. It also can specify that recovery is to begin at the start or end of the file.

FADU Identity: This parameter provides the identity of the FADU with which the data access is associated.

Enable FADU Locking: This parameter allows locks to be performed on an FADU instead of the entire file. The parameter is only available if the concurrency control parameter is present and the storage attribute group has been negotiated. It is used with the F-OPEN primitives.

FADU Lock: This parameter is used with the F-LOCATE primitives. It sets individual locks to indicate: (a) none required, (b) shared, (c) exclusive, (d) none (see the concurrency control parameter for a description of these terms).

Activity identifier: This parameter is used to provide an unambiguous identifier for re-establishing the data transfer regime after errors. It is available only within the internal file service and only if the recovery functional unit was negotiated with the F-INITIALIZE primitives.

Bulk Transfer Number: This parameter is a number (beginning with 1 in the open regime) that identifies which data transfer is to be recovered. But the recovery is made using the recovery point parameter. This number is in reference to the bulk data transfer procedure.

Requested Access: This parameter defines the actions to be performed on a file that is being selected or recovered. The permitted actions are: read, insert, replace, extend, erase, read attribute, change attribute, and delete file.

Example of FTAM Operations

Figure 11-14 is an example from ISO 8571-1 Annex A of an FTAM operation entailing a remote file access and transfer. The operations begin with the initiator issuing the F-INITIALIZE request primitive to enter the FTAM regime. This process establishes the functional units and service classes to be used for the association. All titles and names are identified with this primitive. As the figure indicates, the responder returns an F-INITIALIZE primitive with its own set of parameters, perhaps to negotiate the initiator down to a lower level.

Assuming the F-INITIALIZE operations succeed, the file selection regime is entered with the F-SELECT primitives. At this time the requested access parameter is used to stipulate the types of actions that are to be performed on the file (read, write, etc.). The concurrency control information is set up at this time and the passwords are examined to determine the initiator's rights to the file access.

If all goes well, the next regime to be entered is the open regime with the F-OPEN primitives. At this time the initiator is allowed to establish specific actions to be performed on the file by coding values in the processing mode, concurrency control, and contents type parameters.

Data transfer operations begin with the F-READ and F-DATA primitives. The initiator indicates the cessation of the data transfer with the F-TRANSFER-END primitives.

Finally, the regimes are "exited" one at a time with the F-CLOSE, F-DESELECT, and F-TERMINATE primitives.

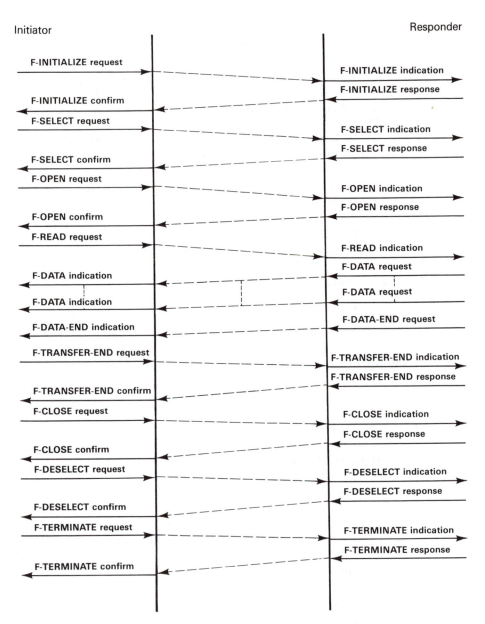

Source: ISO 8571-1

FIGURE 11-14. FTAM Operations

The Application Layer Application Service Elements (ASEs)

JOB TRANSFER AND MANIPULATION (JTM)

In a typical data processing environment, users and programmers submit "jobs" to the computer. These jobs are tasks for the computer to perform such as data retrieval, file updates, etc. In the past, most jobs were submitted by coding punched cards with job control language (JCL) statements. Today, many jobs are submitted through a terminal by the execution of JCL statements previously stored on disk. The statements (generally called a cataloged procedure) are used to invoke the desired tasks.

JCL directs the actions of the computer by identifying the programs and data files that are to participate in the "job." The JCL also directs the disposition of the programs, files, and job output, such as reports and listings.

The purpose of the Job Transfer and Manipulation (JTM) standard (ISO 8831 and ISO 8832) is to allow jobs submitted on any open system to run on any other open system. It must be emphasized the JTM does not address the standardization of job control languages. Indeed, it requires the user to specify the system where work is to be done. Furthermore, the user must know about the JCL, facilities, and functions where the work is to be done. So the idea of JTM is: (a) to specify the jobs to be executed on a system; (b) to control the movement of job-related data between systems; and (c) to monitor and manage the progress of the activity.

JTM can support the traditional "batch" jobs and it can support other types of jobs such as transaction processing, remote job entry (RJE), and distributed data base access.

JTM Concepts and Terms

The JTM services are provided by the JTM application service elements (ASEs), the ACSE, and the CCR protocols. As shown in Figure 11-15, these combined services make up the JTM service provider. The JTM standard describes how the service provider interacts with the JTM users to support the JTM opera-

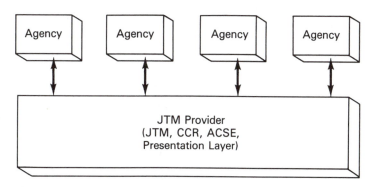

FIGURE 11-15. Job Transfer and Manipulation (JTM) Functional View

tions. The JTM users are represented by *agencies*. These agencies and the service provider pass *work specifications* between them to define how the work is to be done. The work specification contains *documents* each of which forms a unit of interaction between the agency and the service provider. JTM specifies with *transfer control records* how to manage the movement of the documents around systems. The type of document is of no concern to JTM—it could be a program or a cataloged procedure of JCL.

JTM also provides for reporting and monitoring services, which are organized around an *OSI job monitor*. Reports are sent to the job monitor that describe the status of an OSI job.

Four types of agencies are described in the standard:

- *Initiation:* An agency that causes a work specification to be created.
- *Source:* An agency that is a member of any part of an open system. It is capable of providing documents for the work specification at the direction of the service provider.
- *Sink:* An agency (also a part of an open system) which receives documents passed by the service provider.
- *Execution:* An agency which acts initially as a sink and later as a source as a result of processing earlier documents.

The JTM work specification might specify further work in other open systems. For example, a list of JCL statements might invoke the execution of another set of JCL statements in another computer. The total work created by the initial work specification is called an *OSI job*. The specification of further work is called a *proforma*. The creation of a new work specification from a proforma is called *spawning*.

Figure 11-16 shows an example of how spawning proformas can occur. The initiation agency creates the initial work specification (work specification A) containing one to *n* documents and a proforma (proforma 1). This proforma is used by an execution agency to create a new work specification (work specification B). The execution agency also executes part of the OSI job (an OSI subjob). The work defined by work specification B is performed by a sink agency as another OSI subjob.

JTM Service Primitives

Service primitives are used to invoke JTM procedures between the end users and the presentation layer. This section provides an explanation of the primitives and their associated parameters. Table 11-16 was extracted from ISO 8831 and should be examined while studying this section.

Four sets of primitives are used by an initiation agency to create a new work specification:

1. J-INITIATE-WORK: Used to create a work specification for a document movement.

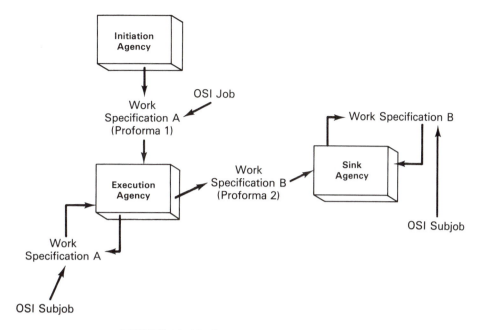

FIGURE 11-16. Spawning and Proformas

2. J-INITIATE-WORK-MAN: Used to create a work specification from existing work specifications.

3. J-INITIATE-TCR-MAN: Used to create a work specification for the manipulation of transfer control records.

4. J-INITIATE-REPORT-MAN: Used to create a work specification for the manipulation of reports received from an OSI job monitor.

Three groups of primitives are used by the JTM to move documents to and from agencies. These primitives are used as a result of the J-INITIATE primitives:

1. J-DISPOSE: Used to pass a document to a sink or execution agency.

2. J-GIVE: Used to request a document from a source or execution agency.

3. J-ENQUIRE: Used to obtain from a source or execution agency a list of document names.

The sink or execution agency can issue three types of primitives to control certain aspects of an ongoing job:

1. J-SPAWN: Used by the execution agency to indicate that a spawning from a proforma is to occur.

2. J-MESSAGE: Used by the execution agency to request the JTM service provider to generate a USER-MESSAGE report work specification.

TABLE 11–16. JTM Primitives

Primitive	Request	Indication	Response	Confirm
J-INITIATE-WORK				
document movement spec	X			
OSI job local reference				X
J-INITIATE-WORK-MAN				
work manipulation spec	X			
OSI job local reference				X
J-INITIATE-TCR-MAN				
transfer manipulation spec	X			
OSI job local reference				X
J-INITIATE-REPORT-MAN				
report manipulation spec	X			
OSI job local reference				X
J-DISPOSE				
provider activity id		X		
user authority		X		
user account		X		
agency parameter/filestore name		X		
document se reference		X		
additional authorizations		X		
errors		X		
document and document type		X		
agency activity id			X	
J-GIVE				
user authority		X		
user account		X		
agency parameter/filestore name		X		
document source reference		X		
additional authorizations		X		
document type		X		
document group		X		
document type and document group			X	
J-ENQUIRE				
user authority		X		
user account		X		
agency parameter		X		
document source skeleton		X		
additional authorizations		X		
document type		X		
document selector		X		
document group		X		
list of name lists			X	

The Application Layer Application Service Elements (ASEs)

TABLE 11–16.   (Continued)

Primitive	Request	Indication	Response	Confirm
J-SPAWN				
provider activity id	X			
proforma name	X			
J-MESSAGE				
provider activity id	X			
message	X			
J-END-SIGNAL				
provider activity id	X			
J-STATUS				
agency activity id		X		
status message			X	
J-HOLD				
agency activity id		X		
J-RELEASE				
agency activity id		X		
J-KILL				
agency activity id		X		
J-STOP				
agency activity id		X		

3. J-END-SIGNAL: Used by a sink or execution agency to indicate the end of an activity.

The JTM service provider uses five types of primitives to control an activity with a sink or execution agency:

1. J-STATUS: Used to obtain status information about an activity.
2. J-HOLD: Used to place a hold on the execution of an activity.
3. J-RELEASE: Used to cancel a hold.
4. J-KILL: Used to terminate an activity with no provision for any documents.
5. J-STOP: Used to terminate an activity with a provision for documents.

Functions of the Primitive Parameters.   Several of the primitives' parameters are called *action parameters*. The entries in Table 11-16 titled (a) document movement specification, (b) work manipulation specification, (c) transfer manipulation specification, (d) report manipulation specification are the action parameters. These parameters are used to define actions specific to the types of primitives in which they are used. Specific documents, modification of work specifications, controlling transfer of work, and controlling reporting management functions are set up in the action parameters.

Most of the other parameters are used to authenticate and identify the service users and the documents used in the OSI job. We briefly describe them in the remainder of this section.

The *OSI job local reference* is inserted by the JTM service provider to unambiguously identify the job. It is placed in the J-INITIATE confirm primitives.

The *provider activity id* is not standardized. It may be used locally to identify the activity for future actions such as J-MESSAGE, etc.

The JTM service provider uses the *user authority* and *user account* parameters to validate operations for the J-DISPOSE, J-GIVE, and J-ENQUIRE services.

The *agency parameter/filestore name* and the *document se reference* are additional identifiers for the operations. The documents themselves are identified and defined with the primitive parameters beginning with the word *document*.

As might be expected, errors are exchanged through the *errors* parameter.

Use of Other OSI Services

JTM makes use of the presentation layer, the ACSE, and CCR in the following manner:

- Presentation layer: JTM uses P-DATA request to transfer data and control information to lower layers and its peer JTM entity. JTM also receives data and control information from the lower layers and its peer entity with the P-DATA indication.
- ACSE: JTM uses all the request, indication, response, and confirm primitives of A-ASSOCIATE, A-ABORT, and A-RELEASE.
- CCR: JTM uses all the CCR request, indication, response, and confirm primitives.

Example of a JTM Operation

Figure 11-17 shows an example of a JTM operation. Four JTM service providers, labeled A, B, C, and D, are involved in this OSI job. The sequence of events in the operation are labeled with the numbers 1 through 12 and follow this process flow:

1. The initiating agency creates the work specification with the J-INITITATE-WORK request to JTM service provider A.
2. Service provider A analyzes the request and returns a confirm to the initiation agency. At this time, the JTM uses the OSI job local reference to unambiguously identify the job.
3. Service provider A sends the work specification to service provider B. Remember that a JTM interaction is performed through CCR and the presentation layer. Therefore, the transfer of the work specification to B is achieved through CCR and the presentation primitives and protocol data units.

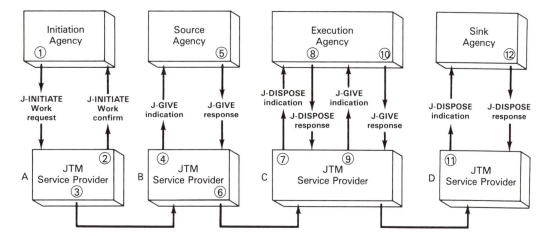

(n) : Sequence of Events

FIGURE 11-17. Example of a JTM Process

4. Service provider B request a document from a source agency with the J-GIVE indication.

5. The source agency responds with the J-GIVE response.

6. Service provider B forwards the work to service provider C.

7, 8, 9, 10. The document is meant to be disposed. However, the execution agency participates in a spawning operation and the work specification is moved to JTM service provider D.

11, 12. At this time the sink agency and service provider effect the necessary operations to dispose of the work specification.

SUMMARY AND CONCLUSIONS

The application service elements (ASEs) directly supporting the user application are beginning to emerge in the industry. Like their lower sublayer counterparts in the application layer (for example, ACSE, ROSE, and RTSE), these ASEs are considered to be commonly used modules which are intended to become community code. The most prominent ASEs are the X.400 Message Handling Systems Recommendation published by CCITT and the File Transfer Access and Management (FTAM) standard published by the ISO. These standards are part of the MAP, TOP, GOSIP, and COSAC protocol suites.

CHAPTER 12

Information Systems Management in the OSI Environment

INTRODUCTION

An OSI-based information system and network is of little long-term use if it cannot be managed properly. One can imagine the difficulty of trying to interconnect and communicate among different computers, switches, PBXs, etc., if the conventions for managing the use of alarms, performance indicators, traffic statistics, logs, accounting statistics, and so on, are different.

In recognition of this fact, the ISO has been working on several OSI management standards for a number of years. Some of the documents have completed the draft proposal (DP) stage; others have completed the draft international stage (DIS); most are slated for final approval as an international standard (IS) during the years of 1989–1991.

A large number of suppliers and vendors have participated in the development of the OSI management standards since 1979. Companies such as IBM, AT&T, DEC, and British Telecom have all made major contributions to the standards discussed in this chapter. In addition, over 15 countries have provided input into these specifications.

This section of the book provides an overview of the OSI management standards that are published by the ISO. Be aware that these standards are subject to change as they wind their way through the approval process. Notwithstanding, all specifications that are examined here are completed working documents, and most are completed DPs. Also be aware that some of the explanations in this chapter are somewhat terse because the specific document is incomplete.

This chapter concentrates on two aspects of OSI management: the OSI management standards and directory management. The former is highlighted

479

with the ISO standards and the latter is highlighted with the CCITT X.500 Directory Recommendations. Our goal in this chapter is to provide an overview of the terms and concepts within these subjects in order to enable the reader to delve into the specifications for more detailed information.

OSI MANAGEMENT SERVICES

ISO 7498 describes the principal services provided by OSI management:

- Identification and authentication (if needed) of the intended communication partners through names, addresses, encryption, etc.
- Determination of whether the intended partners are available, whether they have the authority to communicate, and whether they have the resources to support the communications process.
- Agreement on the cost allocations for the process and the privacy procedures to be used during the process.
- Agreement on an acceptable quality of service (QOS) for the communications process.
- Agreement on the type of dialogue to be used during the process and the method of synchronizing the exchange of data.
- Agreement on a transfer syntax.
- Determination of procedures and responsibilities for error recovery and data integrity.

Key Terms and Concepts

OSI management is constrained to the services and functions that are used to supervise and control the interconnection activities of data processing and data communications resources. OSI management is not concerned with resources that do not interconnect.

As depicted in Figure 12-1, the resources that are supervised and controlled are called *managed objects*. A managed object can be anything deemed important by the organization that is using the OSI management standards. As examples, hardware such as switches, work stations, memory-resident queues, and multiplexers can be identified as managed objects. Software, such as queuing programs, routing algorithms, and buffer management routines can also be treated as managed objects.

These objects have certain properties that distinguish them. These properties are called *attributes*. The purpose of an attribute is to describe the operational characteristics, current state, and conditions of operation of the managed objects.

Managed objects are managed by a *management process*. A management process is an application process. Management processes are categorized as either a *managing process* or an *agent process*. A management process is defined

Information Systems Management in the OSI Environment

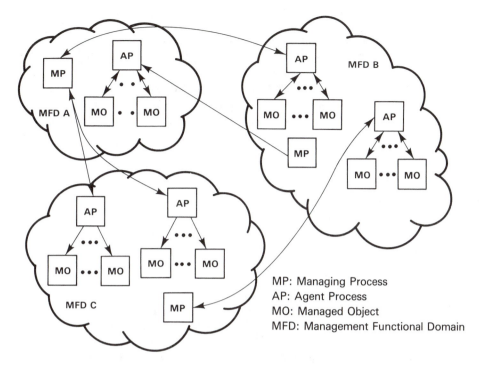

MP: Managing Process
AP: Agent Process
MO: Managed Object
MFD: Management Functional Domain

FIGURE 12–1. The OSI Management Relationships

as part of an application process that is responsible for management activities (a broad definition, to be sure). An agent process performs the management functions on the managed objects at the request of the managing process.

OSI management uses a *management information base* (MIB) to control the communications in the OSI environment. The MIB is a composite of management information about the open system. The MIB is used by the system management entities in the application layer to communicate with each other and the (N)-layer management entities. An (N)-layer may be given some of the OSI management functions.

An application entity is involved in OSI management. It is called the *systems management application entity* (SMAE). It is responsible for implementing the system-wide (OSI system) management activities.

Practically all management systems for communications networks support the transfer of different types of information exchange about a managed object. OSI management classifies this information as:

- *Data:* This type of exchange embodies the acquisition of information by an initiator to a responder. It could be information on the status of a communication link, such as: (a) link inoperable, (b) link in standby mode, (c) link in operation.

- *Control:* This type of exchange between two users of the OSI management services changes the attributes or status of a managed object. For example, control information could change a communications link from standby to active.
- *Events:* This type of exchange is used to notify a user of an event happening. Typically, it is accompanied with the time the event occurred and the time it is being reported. For example, an event exchange could notify the user that a link was changed from standby to active and the time this event occurred.

The non-OSI resources are called a *local systems environment* and are outside the OSI standards.

STRUCTURE OF OSI MANAGEMENT

The OSI management standards do not entail the management of the end-user application processes. They are concerned with the management of the elements in OSI used for establishing, monitoring, and controlling communications between OSI entities. Within this context, the OSI management architecture is based on three forms of operation: (a) systems management; (b) (N)-layer management; and (c) (N)-layer operation. See Figure 12-2 for a visual depiction of these concepts.

Systems management is used to manage an entire OSI system. It provides mechanisms to manage multiple OSI layers, and is accomplished through application layer protocols. (The use of application layer protocols is an attractive aspect of system management, because it is anticipated that many of the operations dealing with OSI management will include applications invloved in context negotiation between end systems. Systems management is effected through the systems management application entity (SMAE).

The (N)-layer management structure is used to manage communication activities within one OSI layer, although it can manage multiple instances of communication. This management activity communicates about activities within the layer and the layers below it. It does not replicate functions from the layers above it. The (N)-layer management is effected through the layer management entity (LME).

The (N)-layer operation manages a single instance of communication within one layer (for example, the establishment of a network logical channel reset with the X.25 Reset packet). The (N)-layer operations are effected through the layer entity (LE).

The OSI management information base (MIB) is an open repository used by systems management, (N)-layer management, and (N)-layer operation. In this manner, information can be shared between the layers and systems management.

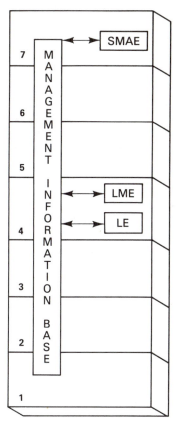

SMAE: Systems Management Application Entity (SMAE)
LME: Layer Management Entity
LE: Layer Entity

FIGURE 12-2. OSI Management Structure

OSI Management Functional Areas (Facilities)

Presently, five OSI management functional areas (also called facilities by some people) have been defined by the ISO. These functional areas will likely not become finalized ISs until 1991 and 1992, but they are stable enough to warrant a general examination. They are:

- Fault Management
- Accounting Management
- Configuration and Name Management
- Performance Management
- Security Management

Fault Management. Fault management is used to detect, isolate and repair problems. It encompasses activities such as tracing faults through the open system, carrying out diagnostics, and acting upon the detection of errors in order to correct the faults. It is also concerned with the use of error logs.

Accounting Management. This facility is needed in any type of shared resource environment. It allows usage, charges, and costs to be identified in the OSI environment. It allows users and managers to place limits on usage and to negotiate additional resources. These latter features are quite important in environments where the users have contractural relationships with service providers.

Configuration and Name Management. This facility is used to identify and control managed objects for the purpose of initializing, operating, and closing down the managed objects, and for the purpose of reconfiguring the open system. Is is also used to associate names with managed objects and to set up parameters for open systems. It collects data about the operations in the open system in order for users to be able to recognize a change in the state of the system.

Security Management. This facility is concerned with protecting OSI management and the managed objects. It provides authentication procedures, maintains access control routines, supports the management of keys for enciphering code, maintains authorization facilities, and manages security logs.

Performance Management. This facility is more complete than the other facilities. As suggested in the title, it supports the gathering of statistical data and applies the data to various analysis routines to measure the performance of the open system.

The Systems Management Application Entity (SMAE)

The OSI management model is consistent with the application layer architecture discussed in Chapter 10. It consists of the systems management application element (SMAE), the association control service element (ACSE), and other service entities. One configuration is shown in Figure 12-3. Other configurations are permissible. We will introduce the service elements in this section and then examine them in more detail in subsequent sections.

The systems management application service element (SMASE) creates and uses the protocol data units transferred between the management processes of the two machines. These data units are called management application data units (MAPDUs). For convenience, the services provided by the SMASE are categorized as functional units, and they identify the type of management information that is to be exchanged between the management processes. The SMASE may use the communications services of application ser-

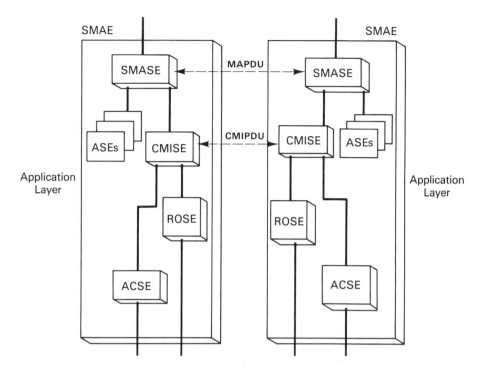

FIGURE 12-3. OSI Management in the Application Layer

vices elements such as FTAM or the common management information service element (CMISE).

In accordance with OSI conventions, two management applications in two open systems exchange management information after they have established an application context. As we learned in Chapter 10, the application context uses a name that identifies the service elements needed to support the association. ISO 10040 states that the application context for OSI management associations implies the use of ACSE, ROSE, CMISE, and SMASE.

Common Management Information Service Element (CMISE) and Common Management Information Protocol (CMIP)

The CMISE defines an application service element (ASE) which may be used for OSI systems management. Like other OSI service definitions, it describes the primitives and their associated parameters that constitute the service.

The CMIP specifies the creation and use of common management information protocol data units (CMIPDUs), which are exchanged between the peer CMISEs in the two machines. As depicted in Figure 12-3, the use of CMISE implies the use of ROSE and ACSE.

The CMISE is organized around three major types of services (described in a later section):

- Management association
- Management notification
- Management operation

OVERVIEW OF THE OSI MANAGEMENT STANDARDS

The OSI management standards are listed in Table 12-1. As can be seen from this table, the OSI management standards consist of a variety of separate specifications. Please be aware that several of the document numbers and names

TABLE 12-1. The ISO OSI Management Standards (subject to change)

	OSI Management Framework and Overview
7498-4	OSI Basic Reference Model Part 4: Management Framework
10040	OSI Systems Management Overview

	Association Management, Service Elements, and Protocols
N740	Association Management
9595	Common Management Information Service (CMIS)
9596	Common Management Information Protocol (CMIP)

	Management Function
10164-1	OSI Systems Management: Object Management Function
10164-2	OSI Systems Management: State Management Function
10164-3	OSI Systems Management: Relationship Management Function
10164-4	OSI Systems Management: Error Reporting and Information Retrieval Function
10164-5	OSI Systems Management: Management Service Control Function
2686	Configuration Management
3310	Software Distribution Management
3312	Fault Management
3313	Performance Management
3338	Security and Audit Management
3314	Accounting Management
3309	Log Control Management
117	Object Schema Management

	Structure of Management Information Models (SMI)
3324	Management Information Model
3301	Definition of Support Objects
3302	Definition of Management Attributes
3437	Definition of Management Objects

will change when they become fixed standards. We briefly examine each of these in this section.

OSI Management Framework and Overview

The ISO documents 7498-4 and 10040 provide general overviews of the OSI management standards. They establish the overall structure for the OSI management operations.

7498-4 Management Framework. The foundation OSI management document is 7498-4. It provides the concepts and definitions for OSI management. It also introduces the five major functional components of OSI management: accounting, security, configuration, fault, and performance. In addition, it explains the concept of individual layer management and the concepts of managed objects. As an appendix (which is not considered part of the standard) it describes the OSI management structure, which is depicted in Figure 12-2 of this chapter.

10040 Management Overview. Another foundation document is 10040. This standard identifies the underlying OSI services used by the management entities. It describes the concepts of distributed systems management, introducing the agent and management processes (see Figure 12-1). ISO 10040 also establishes the structure for the applications layer interactions among the ASEs (see Figure 12-3).

ISO 10040 defines the concepts of functional and administrative management domains, which are similar to the administrative domains found in X.400. Real systems are organized into sets to: (a) meet certain requirement functions such as fault management, accounting management, etc;(b) assign the roles of the agent and manager; and (c) establish some kind of control over the process.

These sets are called *management functional domains* (MFDs). The management functional domains are under the control of a *administrative management domain* (ADM), which is responsible for the transfer of the control of resources between the management functional domains. To illustrate these ideas, refer back to Figure 12-1. MFDs A, B, and C could be under the control of one or more ADMs.

Association Management, Service Elements, and Protocols

These standards are considered to be some of the more important parts of OSI management because they describe the service definitions (primitives) and the protocol data units for the management operations.

740 Association Management. Document 740 defines the negotiation of the functional units within an application context between management processes. It defines the relationship of the OSI management ASEs to the ACSE. It describes the requirement for the cooperation of the management processes in making known their capabilities during an association establishment. It describes the M-INITIALIZE service for the establishment of an association with a peer CMISE service user.

9595 *Common Management Information Service (CMIS).* The common management service elements (CMISs) are defined in document 9595. As the title suggests, it identifies the service elements (primitives) used in common management and their arguments (parameters). As discussed in the introductory part of this chapter, CMISE is organized around three types of services.

The *management association services* consist of:

- M-INITIALIZE: This service is used to establish an association with a peer CMISE service user. In so doing, it must use the underlying ACSE (see Figure 12-3). It passes the necessary control information to establish the association.
- M-TERMINATE: This service is used to obtain a normal termination of the association between the CMISE service users.
- M-ABORT: The service user can obtain an abrupt release of the association with the use of this service.

The *management notification services* consist of:

- M-EVENT-REPORT: This service is used to report an event to a service user. The event is not defined by the standard but can be any event about a managed object that the CMISE user chooses to report. The service provides the time of the occurrence of the event as well as the current time.

The *management operation services* consist of:

- M-GET: This service is used by a CMISE user to retrieve information from its peer user. The service uses information about the managed object to obtain and return a set of attribute identifiers and values of the managed object or a selection of managed objects.
- M-CANCEL-GET: Invoked by the CMISE user to request a peer to cancel a previously requested M-GET service.
- M-SET: A CMISE user can use this service to request the modification of attribute values (the properties) of a managed object.
- M-ACTION: This service is used by the user to request another user to perform some type of action on a management object.
- M-CREATE: This service is used to create a representation of an instance of a new managed object, along with its associated management information values.
- M-DELETE: This service performs the reverse operation of the M-CREATE. It deletes a representation of a management object.

Information Systems Management in the OSI Environment

9596 Common Management Information Protocol (CMIP). The ISO 9595 establishes the protocol specification for CMIP. CMIP supports the services listed in Table 12-2. These services were explained in the previous section. Notice that some of the services are confirmed, nonconfirmed, or have an option of using either confirmed or nonconfirmed operation. These services allow two OSI management service users to set up actions to be performed on managed objects, to change attributes of the objects, and to report the status of the managed objects.

Like the other OSI protocols, CMIP must follow rules on the composition and exchange of protocol data units (PDUs). All the CMIP PDUs are defined by ASN.1. The operations are defined in ISO 9072-1 (ROSE) with the OPERATION and ERROR external macros described in Chapter 10. Due to its dependence on ROSE, CMIP does not contain state tables, event lists, predicates and action tables.

Use of Underlaying Services and Layers. The following CMIP service elements M-INITIALIZE, M-TERMINATE, and M-ABORT must use the ACSE. The remainder of the service elements must use ROSE. In turn, ROSE uses the P-DATA service of the presentation layer. The ROSE services invoked from CMIP are RO-INVOKE, RO-RESULT, and RO-REJECT.

Example of CMIP Operations. Figure 12-4 depicts one of the principal operations of the CMIP—event reporting. The operation between the two CMIP machines (CMIPMs), the CMISE service users, and the underlying ROSE follow these steps:

1. The CMIPM receives an M-EVENT-REPORT request primitive from a CMISE service user. The parameters in the primitive contain values which (a) identify this operation from others supported by the CMISE, (b) provide information about the managed object, (c) describe the type of event being reported, (d) include a time stamp specifying the time of the generation of the event and (e) provide information about the event.

TABLE 12-2. CMIP Services

Service	Type of Confirmation
M-INITIALIZE	Confirmed
M-TERMINATE	Confirmed
M-ABORT	Nonconfirmed
M-EVENT-ACTION	Confirmed/nonconfirmed
M-GET	Confirmed
M-SET	Confirmed/nonconfirmed
M-ACTION	Confirmed/nonconfirmed
M-CREATE	Confirmed
M-DELETE	Confirmed

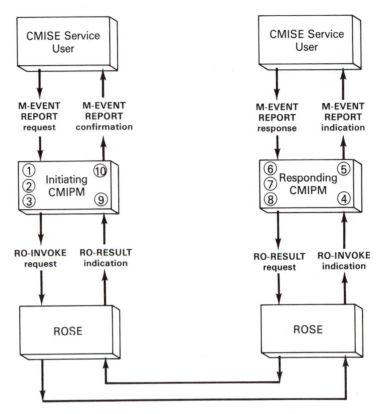

FIGURE 12-4. CMIP Reporting Operation

2. The CMIPM examines the primitive and constructs an m-Event-Report APDU.

3. It then sends this APDU to the ROSE through the RO-INVOKE request primitive. ROSE sends this unit to the presentation layer through the P-DATA primitive.

4. The receiving CMIPM receives the APDU through the ROSE RO-INVOKE indication primitive.

5. If the data unit is acceptable, it issues an M-EVENT-REPORT indication primitive to the receiving CMISE service user. The peer service user now has received the necessary information to direct it as to how to report on a managed object.

6. The CMISE service user sends an M-EVENT-REPORT response primitive to its CMIPM. This primitive contains values which: (a) identify this operation from others supported by the CMISE, (b) provide information about the managed object, (c) describe the type of event being reported, (d) include a time stamp specifying the time of the generation of this response, and (e) indicate the result of the event report. If this primitive is a failure

response, an error parameter is included to describe the nature of the error.

7. The CMIPM uses these parameters to construct an ADPU.

8. It sends the ADPU to ROSE through an RO-RESULT request primitive.

9. The initiating CMIPM receives the ADPU through the RO-RESULT indication primitive.

10. If the APDU is acceptable (well-formed), it issues an M-EVENT-REPORT confirmation primitive to the CMISE user. This primitive contains the information created by the other CMISE user in event 6. The reporting procedure is complete.

Management Functions

The management function standards are fairly terse descriptions of several important OSI management functions. It is anticipated that their approval as an international standard will occur in late 1991.

10164-1 Object Management. DP10164-1 lays the foundations for the other standards. It defines managed objects as well as the creation and configuration of managed objects. It defines the rules for the creation, deletion, renaming, and listing of managed objects. It also defines how to delete and make attribute changes to objects.

10164-2 State Management.   This standard identifies the state model for the managed objects. The OSI management standards permit two major state classifications: administrative and operational. Within the operational state an object can be defined as busy, active, enabled, or disabled; within the administrative state, the object may be shutting down, unlocked, or locked. These states are defined as follows:

- *Disabled:* A managed object is inoperable because it is defective or some other object on which it depends is not available.
- *Enabled:* A managed object is operable and available for use but not in use.
- *Active:* A managed object is operable, in use, and available for additional use.
- *Busy:* A managed object is operable and in use, but not available for additional use.
- *Locked:* A managed object is prohibited from use.
- *Shutting Down:* A managed object is permitted for use by existing users, but additional users are prohibited from its use.
- *Unlocked:* A managed object is permitted to be used but is dependent on the operational state.

The standard includes a number of useful and easy-to-read state diagrams to explain how the objects are to be locked, enabled, and so on.

10164-3 Relationship Management. This specification defines the relationships of the managed objects. The standard establishes the following relationships:

- *Direct:* Some portion of information associated with one managed object expressly identifies the other managed object.
- *Indirect:* A relationship is deduced between two managed objects by the concatenation of two or more direct relationships. See Figure 12-5 for a comparison of direct and indirect relationships.
- *Symmetric:* Interaction rules between two managed objects are the same. For example, an interaction rule could stipulate the right to change an attribute of an object.
- *Asymmetric:* Interaction rules between two managed objects are different.

In addition to these definitions, relationship management defines the service aspects of the management relationships with the CREATE, GET, and SET services.

10164-4 Error Reporting and Information Retrieval. This document defines and identifies the five basic categories of errors which comprise the 10164-1 kernel functional unit. Each error type is accompanied by probable cause parameters. This information is shown in Table 12-3.

The error types are further classified by five levels of severity: (a) indeterminate, (b) critical, (c) major, (d) minor, and (e) warning.

This standard uses the underlying CMIS and its M-EVENT-REPORT service to carry these parameters.

10164-5 Management Service Control. This standard establishes the components to support remote event reporting and local event processing. The standard is formed around the concept of a set of *discriminators.*

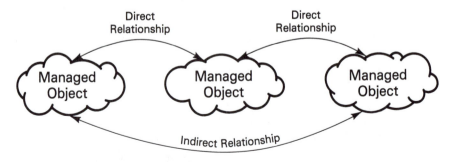

FIGURE 12-5. Managed Object Relationships

Information Systems Management in the OSI Environment

TABLE 12-3. Error Types and Probable Causes

Type of Error	Probable Causes
Communications type:	Loss of signal Framing error Transmission error Call establishment error
Quality of service type:	Response time excessive Queue size exceeded Bandwidth reduced Retransmission rate excessive
Processing type:	Storage capacity problem Version mismatch Corrupt data CPU cycles limit exceeded Out of memory
Equipment type:	Power problem Timing problem Trunk card problem Line card problem Processor problem Terminal problem External interface device problem Dataset problem Multiplexer problem
Environmental type:	Smoke detection Enclosure door open High/low ambient temperature High/low humidity Intrusion detection

As an example, the event forwarding discriminator is responsible for filtering events based on a number of selection criteria and deciding if the event is to be reported. In so doing, the discriminator uses a discriminator construct which establishes the thresholds and other criteria which must be satisfied for the event to be forwarded. These criteria can include the parameters in Table 12-3. This standard needs considerably more work before it is complete.

2686 Configuration Management. It is recognized that a communications system, by its very nature, must support a dynamic environment. Changes within the system occur constantly. Switches, multiplexers, and modems operate at various levels of operability and performance and their relationships with each other vary. For example, a packet switch may be removed as a node in the network due to a hardware or software failure. If the problem is transient, it may be necessary only to logically remove the switch by routing traffic around the node. In such a case, a part of the network would be reconfigured to handle this problem.

The ISO configuration management document establishes facilities to manage logical or physical configurations in an OSI environment. It is responsible for the following services:

- The identification of any managed object and the management of the assignment of names to the object.
- The definition of any new managed object.
- The setting of the initial values for the attributes of objects.
- The management of the relationships of managed objects.
- The changing of the operational characteristics of managed objects and reporting on any changes in the state of the objects.
- The deletion of managed objects.

The ISO configuration management specification relies on several other ISO management standards for the definition of its functions. For example, the concepts of locked states, actives states, etc., in 10164-2 are integral to this standard.

ISO configuration management is organized around five facilities:

- *Object Configuration:* Manages the addition, deletion, enrolling, de-enrolling, and naming of instances of managed objects. The term enroll refers to how one CMISE service user announces to another that an instance of a managed object has arrived at the announcer's MIB.
- *State Management:* Manages the examination, setting, and notification of changes the management state of managed objects.
- *Attribute Management:* Manages the examination, setting, and notification of changes the general attributes of managed objects.
- *Relationship Management:* Manages the examination, setting and notification of changes in the relationships of managed objects.
- *Software Distribution:* Manages the distribution of software and the notification of version changes, as well as the triggering of boot procedures within a managed object.

3310 *Software Distribution Management.* The software distribution standard describes and defines the attributes relating to the management of distributed software. The following attributes are defined: version identification of the software, data and time software is installed, installation instructions, patch list, checksum, and appendices. It also identifies the following service requirements: delivery, installation, reversion, inquiry, removal, and validation. At this time, it is not clear how this standard will be used with the software distribution facility in the configuration management standard.

3312 Fault Management. A considerable amount of work remains to be done on this OSI service. At this point, fault management is defined to include (a) the maintenance of error logs, (b) performing actions upon error detections, (c) performing diagnostic tests, (d) tracing faults, (e) correcting faults.

3313 Performance Management. The performance management document defines the performance management requirements and criteria. It also defines a number of parameters relating to workload, throughput, resource waiting time, response time, propagation delay, availability, and any QOS changes. The performance activity defined in 3313 is modeled as a monitoring and tuning protocol, in that it continuously monitors OSI resources to (a) measure system performance, (b) adjust measurement criteria, and (c) determine if performance is satisfactory.

3338 Security and Audit Management. The security and audit management standard establishes the requirements for security audit trails including alarm deliver, selection analysis, event detection, and recording these operations. In addition, it defines the nature of services to control audit trail logs and alarm distribution.

3314 Accounting Management. The accounting management standard identifies and defines the accounting management requirements for OSI. It also provides an accounting operations model. In addition, it provides guidance on the use of units of charge, accounting logs, records (such as duration of calls), service provided, charge rate, source, and destination ID.

3309 Log Control Management. The log control management standard identifies the following logging services: initiate, terminate, suspend, resume, modify attributes, and retrieve. It describes the attributes for the log itself, such as a discriminator, construct, create, begin and end time, maximum and current log size, log full action, and capacity alarm threshold.

117 Object Schema Management. This specification describes the requirement for the managed object scheme negotiation, which is used during the association of the distribution manager and its agent processes.

Structure of Management Information Models (SMI)

The SMI part of OSI management is divided into four parts. These parts are described in the following documents.

3324 Management Information Model. SMI part 1 identifies the attributes of the managed objects that can be manipulated. It also identifies the operations of object attributes, such as get, set, derive, add, and remove, and the operations that may apply to the object itself: read, delete, and action.

10165-2 *Definition of Support Objects.* This specification identifies common object classes used by OSI management. At the present time, it only defines the object class for discriminators: event, report, and service access.

10165-3 *Definition of Management Attributes.* Document 10165-3 defines management attributes and, as the title suggests, it specifies the attributes used by management: state change, error cause state, configuration state, object class DN, counters log, definitions, severity, trend indication, etc.

3437 *Definition of Managed Objects.* Finally, this specification provides guidelines for the specification of the managed objects. It also provides a template for defining the managed objects with respect to naming and class relationships.

USING DIRECTORIES FOR OSI MANAGEMENT

Directories have been in use in computer installations for over a decade. Some organizations have used them for simple operations such as storing source code for software programs. Others have built data directories to store the names and attributes of the organization's data elements. Some forward-thinking companies now use directories to show the relationships of data elements to data bases, files, and programs. The directory is used to check all key automated systems for accuracy and duplication, and permits an organization to assess the impact of system changes to all the automated resources. The directory has become a vital component in an organization's management of its automated resources.

Typically, each organization and vendor has developed a unique and proprietary approach to the design and implementation of directories, which greatly complicates the management of resources that are stored in different machines and data bases. In the spirit of OSI, the purpose of the Directory is to provide a set of standards to govern the use of directories/dictionaries.

The ISO management standards discussed in the first part of this chapter cite the use of the OSI Directory in their operations. For example, configuration management uses the OSI Directory services to register names, deregister names, and retrieve addressing information that is associated with a name. Without question, directories will play a key role in OSI management.

THE OSI DIRECTORY (X.500 AND ISO 9594)

The X.500 Recommendations and the ISO 9594 Standards describe the operations of the Directory. It is designed to support and facilitate the communication of information between systems about *objects* such as data, applications, hardware, people, files, distribution lists, and practically anything else that the organization deems worthy of tracking for management purposes. The Direc-

TABLE 12–4. Specifications for Directories

CCITT	ISO	Name of Specification
X.500	9594-1	The Directory—Overview of Concepts, Models, and Services
X.501	9594-2	The Directory Models
X.509	9594-8	The Directory—Authentication Framework
X.511	9594-3	The Directory—Abstract Service Definition
X.518	9594-4	The Directory—Procedures of Distributed Operation
X.519	9594-5	The Directory—Protocol Specifications
X.520	9594-6	The Directory—Selected Attribute Types
X.521	9594-7	The Directory—Selected Object Classes

tory is intended to allow the communication of this information between different systems, which can include OSI applications, OSI layer entities, OSI management entities, and communications networks.

The CCITT and ISO Directory specifications encompass eight recommendations, collectively known as X.500 or ISO 9594. Table 12-4 shows the designators for the CCITT and ISO Directory. For purposes of continuity, this section examines the CCITT Recommendations, generally called the X.500 Directory.

Key Terms and Concepts

Our first task is to come to grips with several key terms, concepts, and definitions used by the X.500 specifications (see Figure 12-6). The information held in the Directory is known as the *Directory Information Base* (DIB). It is accessed by the Directory user through the *Directory User Agent* (DUA), which is considered to be an applications process. The DUA is so named because it acts as an agent to the end user vis-à-vis the DIB.

Figure 12-7 shows that the entries in the DIB are arranged in a tree structure called the *Directory Information Tree* (DIT). The vertices in the tree represent the *entries* in the DIB. These entries make up a collection of information about one *object,* such as a person, a data element, a piece of hardware, a program, and so on. The object entry is the primary collection of information in

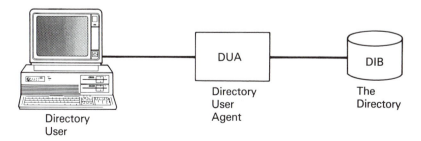

FIGURE 12–6. Directory Access

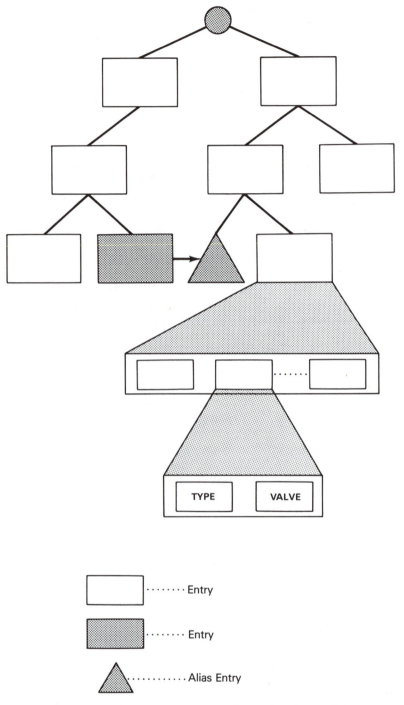

FIGURE 12-7. The Directory Information Tree (DIT)

the DIT. An object belongs to at least one object class and objects that share certain characteristics can form a collective object class. It is important to note once again that the entries in the Directory contain information about a single object.

The *alias* is also permitted. It points to an object entry and permits the use of alternative names for an object entry.

Each entry consists of *attributes,* and each attribute is made up of a *type* and one or more *values.* The attribute is the information about an object and appears in the entry of DIT. The attribute type specifies the syntax and the data type of the value. It is defined as:

```
Attribute     :: =
    SEQUENCE{
        type            AttributeType
        values          SET OF AttributeValue
        —at least one value is required}
```

Each entry has a relative distinguished name (RDN). The RDN consists of a set of attribute value assertions concerning the distinguished values of the entry. The set must contain only one stipulation about each value in the entry.

Each entry must also have a *distinguished name.* The term means the name is unique and unambiguous in identifying the entry. The distinguished name is made up from the name of its superior entry (the above entry in the tree) and some other meaningful identifier.

X.500 uses the term schema in a different context than other data base systems. A schema is a set of rules to ensure the DIB maintains its logical structure during modifications. It prevents inconsistencies in the DIB such as incorrect subordinate entries' class, attribute values, etc.

X.500 ensures that the Directory can be distributed across a wide geographical area. To support this environment, the Directory System Agent (DSA) provides access to the DIB form the DUAs or other DSAs. Figure 12-8 shows the relationship of the distributed Directory. A DUA is permitted to interact with a single or multiple DSAs. In turn, to satisfy a request the DSAs may internetwork with other DSAs through referrals.

The DUAs and DSAs communications are governed by two protocols:

- *Directory Access Protocol* (DAP): Specifies actions between DUA and DSA.
- *Directory System Protocol* (DSP): Specifies actions between DSAs.

The Directory is administered by the *Directory Management Domain* (DMD), which consists of a set of one or more DSAs and zero or more DUAs. The DMD may be a country, a PTT, a network, or anything designated to manage the DIB.

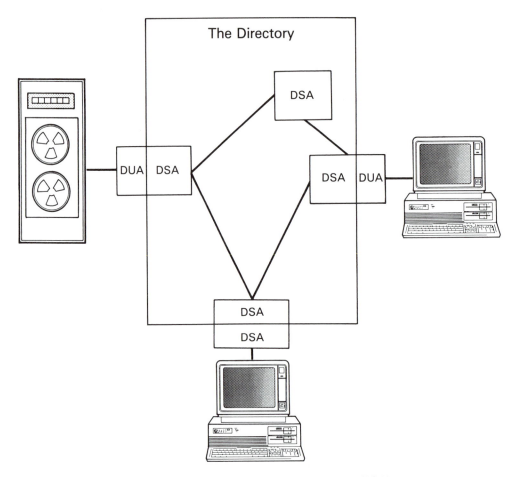

FIGURE 12–8. Directory System Agent (DSA)

The Directory Abstract Service Definitions (X.511)

A considerable portion of the Directory is devoted to abstract service definitions. X.511 is devoted exclusively to the ASN.1 notations and describes the operations between the Directory and a DUA. This section uses one ASN.1 example (a read) to explain some of the operations of the Directory.

The operations (actions) between the Directory and the DUA are called ports. Three ports are defined:

- *Read port:* Supports reading information from a DIB. The DIB consumer can invoke (a) Read; (b) Compare; (c) Abandon.
- *Search port:* Allows an extensive examination of the DIB. The DIB consumer can invoke (a) List; (b) Compare.
- *Modify port:* Allows the DIB entries to be modified through (a) adding an

entry; (b) removing an entry; (c) modifying an entry; (d) modifying a relative distinguished name (RDN).

Read Operation

Our example is the read operation. A read extracts information from the DIB or verifies a distinguished name. It takes the following ASN.1 form:

```
Read            :: = ABSTRACT-OPERATION
    ARGUMENT        ReadArgument
    RESULT          ReadResult
    ERRORS{AttributeError, NameError, ServiceError, Referral, Aban-
            doned, SecurityError}
ReadArgument            :: = OPTIONALLY-SIGNED SET {
    object          [0]  Name,
    selection       [1]
    EntryInformationSelection
                                        Default {},
        COMPONENTS OF CommonArguments}
ReadResult  :: =            OPTIONALLY-SIGNED SET {
    entry           [0] EntryInformation,
        COMPONENTS OF CommonResults }
```

The error entries are described in another section of this chapter. The other parameters for this operation are described in the following paragraphs.

The object argument identifies the object entry that is to be accessed for the requested information. The selection entry is a key search beyond the object argument in that it further refines the search to define the requested information from the entry. This entry specifies the set of attributes and, optionally, information about the selected attribute that will be returned. The common arguments are used to define: (a) what controls are to be used during the operation (chaining, use of alias, etc.); (b) what security parameters are to be used (certification required, etc.); and (c) what role the DSA is to play in the operation.

AUTHENTICATION PROCEDURES FOR DIRECTORY
ACCESS (X.509)

It is reasonable to expect an information repository as important as an information resource directory to have security features to prevent unauthorized access. The Directory includes these types of support features in X.509. Presently, two types of authentication are defined. *Simple* authentication uses a simple password authentication scheme, and *strong* authentication uses public key cryptographic techniques. The user may choose between simple and strong authentication, depending upon the need for secure services.

Simple Authentication

Simple authentication is supported only within a simple directory domain and is restricted to use between one DUA and one DSA or two DSAs. The procedure for simple authentication is shown in Figure 12-9. User A sends to user B its distinguished name and password (step 1). This information is then forwarded to the Directory and the password is checked against an appropriate password in the Directory (step 2). The Directory then informs B that A's credentials are valid or invalid (step 3). Finally, B informs A about the results of the Directory authentication operation (step 4).

Other procedures are also supported. For example, it is possible for B to check the distinguished name and password. Another approach is to use a random number or a time stamp with the distinguished name and password to enhance the validation procedure.

Strong Authentication

The CCITT has adapted the public key crypto system (PKCS) for the Directory's strong authentication operations. The public key concepts were developed in the early 1980s and are now widely used throughout the industry. A brief tutorial follows on the public key concept.

The use of public keys has been in existence for some time now. The advantage that public keys have over private keys is the ease of their administration and the ease of changing their values. The concept of public keys is illustrated in Figure 12-10. As noted, user A has in its possession the public key for B and the private key for A. In turn, user B has in its possession the private key for B and the public key for A. It is essential that both A's and B's private and public keys be derived from the same function.

As shown in the figure, A can use B's public key to encrypt the data to be transmitted to B. In turn, B uses its private key (which is available to no other user) to decipher the traffic. The reverse process occurs by user B using A's public key for encryption, transmitting the data to A, which then applies its private key for decrypting the traffic back to clear text.

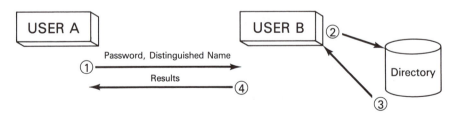

FIGURE 12-9. Digital Signatures

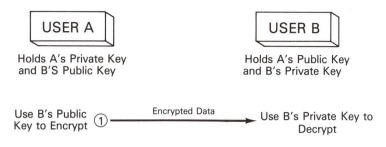

FIGURE 12-10. Public Keys

Digital Signatures. The previous example shows the use of the public key for enciphering data and a complementary private key used for deciphering the data. This process can be reversed to provide a very powerful authentication procedure, known as a *digital signature*. A digital signature operation is illustrated in Figure 12-11. User A employs its private key to encipher a digital signature (say a password or some other form of identification). This is transmitted to user B, which has possession of user A's public key. Any user that has possession of the public key can decipher the data, but only A can perform the complementary encryption because it alone has the private key.

User A first informs user B that it is indeed A. Next, it sends the encrypted traffic and B uses A's public key to decipher the protocol data unit. If user A stated it was someone else, it would not have the proper private key to create the digital signature. In this manner, a user can be authenticated and the source of the information can be verified.

Although not all systems employ authentication and digital signatures, the OSI Model and the X500 directory employ digital signatures for authentication. X.509 requires that both the secret key and the public key be used for encryption and decryption in the following manner:

- Public key used to encipher, secret key used to decipher
- Secret key used to encipher, public key used to decipher

A specific encryption/decryption algorithm is not defined by the Directory. As long as the users involved in the authentication process use the same system and each possesses a distinguished name, the Directory will support the authentication process.

FIGURE 12-11. Digital Signatures

The Directory Error-Reporting Procedures

The Directory provides a number of error-reporting procedures. It is quite important that they be implemented as part of the ongoing operations because they provide important diagnostic and troubleshooting services.

The Directory ceases to perform operations once an error has occurred and has been detected. It is possible that more than one error may be detected, in which case the error is reported in accordance with a logical precedence list. In the following list, error reporting for a higher entry has precedence over the next lower entry. A discussion of each type of error follows.

> NameError
>
> UpdateError
>
> AttributeError
>
> SecurityError
>
> ServiceError

The next list of errors do not use any reporting precedences:

> AbandonFailed
>
> Abandoned
>
> Referral

The NameError is used to report any error dealing with a name. This operation is invoked if any one of six conditions are detected:

1. A name supplied in an argument to access the Directory does not match the name of any object in the Directory.
2. An alias problem has been encountered (i.e., the alias has no object).
3. An attribute type is not defined.
4. An attribute type and an accompanying attribute value are not compatible.
5. An invalid list operation has been encountered.
6. An alias problem has been encountered (i.e., the alias is not allowed).

The UpdateError is used to report any error relating to the operations of add, modify, or delete. This operation is invoked if any one of seven conditions are reported:

1. An attempted modification or addition to the Directory is not in consonance with the rules of the DIT.
2. An attempted update is not consistent with the definition provided by the object class.
3. An attempted operation is not permitted (permitted only on leaf entries).

4. An attempted operation would adversely affect the relative distinguished name (RDN).
5. An attempted operation would create a redundant alias.
6. An attempted operation would affect multiple DSAs (not allowed).
7. An object class attribute cannot be modified.

An AttributeError is used to report a problem related to an attribute. The operation identifies the attribute type and the value that caused the problem. Five conditions are reported:

1. The named entry does not have one of the attributes specified in the argument.
2. An attribute value in the argument does not conform to the syntax of the attribute type.
3. An argument has an undefined attribute type.
4. A matching rule was used that is not defined for the attribute type.
5. An attribute value violates an attribute definition.

The SecurityError is used to report an error relating a security problem. Six conditions are reported:

1. The requestor's credentials are insufficient with the required protection.
2. The requestor does not have the proper access rights.
3. The requestor's credentials are invalid.
4. The requestor's signature is invalid.
5. The argument is not signed.
6. An invalid service is used in the DSA operations.

The ServiceError is used to report a problem about a service provision. The following problems are reported:

1. The Directory is not available.
2. The Directory is too busy to provide a requested service.
3. A chain operation is required to provide the service, but a chaining prohibited option is in effect.
4. The service is denied because it would consume excessive resources.

MHS USE OF THE DIRECTORY

The X.400 message handling system recommendations suggest the Directory be used with MHS in the following areas:

- *Naming*: Use the directory as a look-up for user-friendly names instead of computer-oriented names.

- *Distribution Lists:* Store distribution lists in the Directory.
- *UA Capabilities:* Store the capability profile of the recipient UA.
- *Authentication:* Use the Directory to authenticate the MHS users.

OSI NETWORK MANAGEMENT USE OF THE DIRECTORY

It is certain that the OSI Network Management standards will make extensive use of the X.500 Directory services. Indeed, many of the key concepts of OSI Network Management (such as attributes, objects, the MIB, etc.) were derived from the X.500 Directory.

MIGRATION TO THE OSI STANDARDS

The discussion in this book on the OSI Model is of little use if an organization does not have an implementation strategy and transition plan for OSI. The organizations that have begun to address this issue vary in their approach, but some common approaches are being taken that can provide guidance for the development of a plan.

Mixed and Pure OSI Stacks

Most organizations currently have a "grab bag" of protocols in their stack of layers. As examples, the IBM user typically has the SNA "protocol stack," and the Department of Defense (DOD) user has the DOD stack. Some organizations have migrated to a *mixed* stack, with protocols in the layers from more than one vendor and/or the OSI suite. Other organizations have a *pure* stack, using homogeneous and compatible protocols throughout the layers. As an example, the use of DECnet would be a pure stack, because Digital Equipment Corp., even though it has X.25 and Ethernet in the stack, has designed the interfaces to complement each other. Another example of a pure stack is the DOD suite of protocols.

In the simplest terms, the problem of transition to OSI is how to move (a) from a vendor's pure stack to the OSI stack, or (b) from a mixed stack to the OSI stack.

The mixed protocol stack approach (wherein the organization migrates to the use of both OSI and non-OSI protocols) has the advantage of providing a faster migration to the use of OSI services, in that it allows the OSI layers to be brought into the system on a piecemeal basis. However, it has the substantial disadvantage of increased complexity in interfacing of the different types of protocols between and among the stacks. Realistically, it is quite difficult to implement the full OSI stack in one fell swoop, so you may be faced with a mixed stack for a long period of time.

Most companies, organizations, and standards groups recognize that it is impossible to migrate immediately from a vendor-specific or mixed stack to a pure OSI stack. Invariably, the movement to OSI will require what are known in the industry as *transition aids*. Essentially, these transition aids act as protocol convertors between the different layers in the stacks.

Moreover, it is recognized that a movement to OSI requires an extended period where different protocols exist and may even inter-operate with each other. This coexistence is usually planned to be provided for an extended period of time because of cost considerations as a result of the migration.

Several standards groups, private companies, and government agencies are well into their planning and implementation stages for OSI. Due to the complexity and cost of this transition, some of the organizations have adapted several levels for achieving OSI functionality. As an example, the Department of Defense has specified three levels of OSI implementation and functionality: limited, OSI equivalent, and advanced.

Limited OSI Capability. With this approach, the users in an organization may specify and use OSI protocols in addition to or in place of the protocols that are attached to their networks. However, the full OSI model is not implemented. Rather, the most important protocols are acquired or developed, such as X.400 and FTAM.

In most organizations, this immediate use of OSI also entails the use of X.25. It may also entail the use of standard NSAP address formats. As just mentioned, other products which allow the immediate use of OSI deal with the X.400 Message Handling System and the NIST phase one implementor agreements for FTAM.

Equivalent OSI Capabilities. The second stage of implementation involves a more advanced implementation of OSI. For example, the DOD has established the next phase as phase two of the NIST FTAM functions as well as the Virtual Terminal protocols based on the ISO standards.

Advanced OSI Capabilities. The last stage provides advanced OSI capabilities. This entails the implementation of many of the 1988 Blue Book specifications. The 1988 X.400 recommendation is substantially different from the 1984 recommendation, so the final stage would bring the 1988 X.400 recommendation into the DOD protocol suite.

In addition, the ISO X.500 directory services will be part of the advanced phase. The OSI management protocols will also be included here (although they are still in various stages of development). It is also anticipated that the international standards for security services will be brought into the last stage.

What Must Be Accomplished with the Transition

As we have discussed, a mixed protocol suite is, at best, a mixed blessing. This section examines the major issues that must be addressed if an organization is to (a) stay with a mixed suite or (b) migrate to the OSI suite, with an interim mixed suite. Two major areas must be addressed in a plan:

- Interfaces between the adjacent layers and layer entities in the same computer
- Interfaces between the peer layers and layer entities in different computers

The first issue entails the development of interlayer interfaces during the transition period. As an example, consider an organization that is using TCP at the transport layer, and is planning to implement the ISO 8473 (connectionless network protocol [CLNP]) to replace IP at the network layer.

A very obvious challenge is to solve how to interface TCP with 8473. The first problem is that TCP uses different primitives (I/O or subroutine calls) than does 8473. The parameters in the primitives are quite different, both in the functions they invoke and in their number. Consequently, a transition plan must include provisions to handle two issues:

- An intermediate module that rests between the two protocols that "maps" the primitives as they are passed between the two layers.
- If primitive functions do not map directly between the two layers, the transition aid must either generate a comparable function call, or provide the function that is required as a result of the parameter in the call.

The first issue is not an easy one to resolve, because some of the primitive parameters between the two layers simply are meaningless. For example, the IP *precedence* parameter has no meaning to 8473. Therefore, it may be necessary for the mixed suite to be modified during the transition period, possibly deleting or even adding support functions. Whatever is done, the process is not simple.

The second issue, the interfaces between the peer layers in different machines, is just as challenging. First, consider that practically all vendors' layers are not comparable to the OSI layers. For example, SNA's network layer performs many functions different from any of the OSI network layer protocols, such as X.25, X.75, and ISO 8473. So the transition plan must include how to provide these functions without rewriting currently existing software. It may require the "patching" of some of the entities in the layers in order to accommodate the functions. Without question, the preferable approach is to implement the specific OSI layer entity in both machines at the same time.

It is quite possible that two different protocol entities may provide functions which are similar to each other. For example, SNA and OSI provide for the fragmentation and reassembly of protocol data units. In such a case, the patching may be simplified (assuming they are in comparable layers!). However, even if the functions are similar, it is quite likely that they use different headers (protocol control information, PCI).

These headers usually differ in both their content and format. Therefore,

Information Systems Management in the OSI Environment

the transition aid must be able to map the differing formats between the layers. Again, this is not a trivial task, especially if the two computers are using different protocols and/or different versions of the same protocol.

Moreover, the fields in the headers are used to invoke functions between the peer layers. Consequently, if the fields between the entities are different, some means must be available to delete or add the functions that use the incompatible fields.

Without question, the migration to OSI is not an easy one. Nonetheless, the problem dictates a solution, or at least an attempt at a solution. The next section provides some possibilities for the reader to consider.

Inventory the Organization's Information Resources and Plan the Changes

The migration to OSI is certainly a technical problem, but it is also a very big management problem. One approach to any large conversion effort (which has stood the test of time) can be summarized with the following points:

- A migration plan is meaningless until a fairly accurate assessment of the impact of the migration upon the organization is known.
- This impact can only be known after it is determined which automated systems (applications software, systems software, data base software, communications software, data bases, files, hardware) must be changed, or replaced. . . . and what must be added.
- The migration plan must also take into account any possible personnel and facility changes.
- An assessment must be made of the effect of the migration on the organization's mission.
- Once these four bases of knowledge are known, the organization can then begin an evaluation of the time and money required to achieve the migration. From this evaluation, the organization can make trade-off decisions, develop the plan, and begin staffing accordingly for the effort.

Status of Conformance Testing Activities

Ideally, an organization will ensure a product conforms to the OSI specification before it acquires it. In reality, most organizations are not equipped mentally or technically to meet this idealistic goal. Notwithstanding, some means must exist to test the product. As discussed in Chapter 2, several organizations in the United States, Europe, and Japan are now in operation that are tasked with the important job of conformance testing: that is, testing if the product performs in accordance with the international standard.

As the layers of OSI become more widely used, conformance testing will become quite common; presently, it is still somewhat limited. In this section, we will take a look at some of the more significant activities in the conformance testing arena.

The reader should be aware that a protocol that is "certified" by a testing organization does not mean it will operate with another seemingly "like" protocol. Conformance testing means that the product has been implemented in accordance with the standard, and that it processes the relevant protocol data units (PDUs) as stated in the standard. This means it operates satisfactorily with a testing machine.

Due to differences in other aspects in the implementation of a product (timers, retries, etc.), the two products may still not "interoperate." Consequently, some organizations also provide tests between two real systems to determine if they can communicate. This type of test is called *interoperability* testing.

It should also be stressed that some tests consist of a paper evaluation wherein the vendor's implementation conformance statement, as stated on a piece of paper, is evaluated against the standard. This approach works well enough if its limits are recognized, but the next step should be to test the product against the standard.

This type of testing evaluates how the product performs in accepting, using, and creating the relevant protocol data units. That is to say, the tests typically do not analyze the internal operations of the product. Therefore, the tests can reveal when something goes wrong, but they do not reveal why the problem occurred.

ISO 9646: OSI Conformance Testing Methodology and Framework. The ISO is responsible for publishing standards on conformance testing under ISO 9646. The specification (not yet finished) is divided into five parts:

- *Part 1:* Describes the general concepts and architectures for conformance testing
- *Part 2:* Describes the Protocol Implementation Conformance Statement (PICS). This document is submitted by the manufacturer of the product, and is used to evaluate compliance with the paper evaluation. Part 2 also describes in an abstract way how to structure tests and is used to evaluate compliance with the paper evaluation. Part 2 also describes in an abstract way how to structure tests and how to specify tests through special languages.
- *Part 3:* Describes the relationship between abstract and actual test systems.
- *Part 4:* Defines the output requirements of the tests.
- *Part 5:* Defines the test laboratory operations.

The Corporation for Open Systems (COS). The Corporation for Open Systems in McLean, Virginia, was founded to establish conformance testing and to ensure a product operates in accordance with a standard. It now consists of over 45 vendor organizations and a number of other members. The COS certifies a tested system by placing a certifying mark on the product, something like the Good Housekeeping Seal of Approval.

COS has adapted a realistic and productive approach to its selection of protocols based on the NIST Workshop of Implementors of Open Systems Interconnection agreements. Initially, it focused its attention on two application layer protocols, ISO FTAM and CCITT X.400. These applications were selected because they are the most widely known international standards for this layer. Table 12–5 shows the suite of COS protocols for the FTAM file transfer and the X.400 applications.

The COS approach is to perform the testing or task the vendor with the job. It does not perform interoperability testing. COS has the Online Error Reporting and Tracking System (CERTS) available to the sites that wish to license the procedure. It also has available the Transport Conformance Test System (TCTS), which is a system that analyzes conformance to Transport layer. Class 0 or class 4COS conformance testing runs on SUN workstations.

The Industrial Technology Institute (ITI). The ITI is located in Ann Arbor, Michigan. It is a private testing facility that supports the Network Evaluation and Test Center (NETC), which conducts conformance testing for the MAP (Version 2.1) suite. NETC conducts interoperability testing.

ITI and NETC support the following standards:
FTAM
Directory Services
CASE
Session Layer
Transport Layer
Internet Protocol
Broadband and Carrierband (5 and 10 Mbit/s)
Network Management

TABLE 12–5. COS Protocol Support

Layer	File Transfer	Electronic Mail
Application	ISO 8571/8860	CCITT X.400
Presentation	ISO 8823	ISO 8823 (MHS)
Session	ISO 8327	ISO 8327
Transport	ISO 8073, Class 0,4	ISO 8073, Class 0,4
Network	ISO 8473, CCITT X. 25	ISO 8473, CCITT X.25
Data Link & Physical	Various combinations	ISO 8802/2, 7776, 8802/3, 8802/4, 8802/5

CONCLUSIONS

Like most of the issues in the computer and communications industry, we have no absolute and clear answers for the best approach to the management of standards and the migration to the use of standards. But the progress in the last few years (even months) has been quite noteworthy. These trends will almost certainly continue.

At long last, the foundation is being laid for a cohesive and coherent computer/communications architecture in our society. While the issues in this book have dealt with the technical and managerial aspects of computer/communications protocols, it should be recognized that the progress in this seemingly dry and mundane subject has a great deal to do with the progress of many of the critical facets of our information-based society. And this, if for no other reason, is an impetus to move to computer and communications standards.

APPENDIX A

Summary of ISO OSI Communications Standards

INTRODUCTION

This appendix provides summary information on the ISO OSI standards. The standards in this appendix are described by a number and an abbreviated title. The number in the first column is the ISO number. For purposes of simplicity, the prefixes ISO, DIS, and DP have been omitted. The second column is a brief description of the standard. This description is derived from the standard's title.

Be aware that this list is a summary. The documents are grouped around a numeric identifier, and the titles are a summary of the specific titles of the standard(s). The list does not include all the ISO standards, since this organization publishes standards on other activities such as coding conventions for financial transactions. Also, a single-line entry may denote more than one document. For a detailed title description, contact the ISO. In the United States, Omnicom, Inc., in Vienna, Virginia, has a very useful reader service and can provide these standards.

OSI Model and OSI Management Standards

3310	Software Management
3311	Configuration Management
3312	Facilities Management
3313	Performance Management
3314	Accounting Management
3315	Security Management

7489	OSI Reference Model, including specifications for security, naming and addressing, management, connectionless service
8509	OSI service conventions
9575	OSI routing framework
9594	The Directory used for OSI management
9595	OSI management information service definition
9646	OSI conformance testing
8882	X.25 DTE conformance testing
9834	Procedures for registration authorities
10165	Structure of Management Information (SMI)
10040	System Management Overview
10164	System Management

Physical Layer

2110	The 25 pin connector assignments
2593	The 34 pin connector assignments
4902	The 37 and 9 pin connector assignments
7477	Physical connections using V.24 and X.24 interchange circuits
7480	Start-stop signal transmission quality
8480	DTE/DCE interface backup control
8481	X.24 interchange circuits using DTE provided timing
8482	Twisted-pair multipoint interconnections
8877	Interface for ISDN basic access at the S and T reference points
9067	Fault isolation using test loops
9314	Fiber Distributed Data Interface (FDDI)
9543	Synchronous transmission quality at DTE/DCE interface
9578	Communication connectors used in LANs
10022	OSI physical service definition

Data Link Layer

1745	Basic control mode procedures for data communications systems
2111	Basic control mode procedures for code independent data transfer
2628	Basic control mode procedures, complements version
2629	Basic control mode procedures, conversational information message transfer
3309	HDLC frame structure, and addendum
4335	HDLC elements of procedures

7448	Multilink procedures (MLP)
7776	HDLC-LAPB compatible link control procedures
7809	HDLC-consolidation of classes of procedures; list of standard HDLC protocols that use HDLC procedures
8471	HDLC balanced, link address information
8802	Local area network standards, largely derived from the IEEE 802 standards
8885	HDLC-additional specifications describing use of XID frame, and multilink operations
8886	Data link service definition for OSI
9234	Industrial asynchronous data link procedures

Network Layer

4731	End system to intermediate system, to be used with 8208
8208	X.25 packet level protocol for the DTE
8348	Network service definition, including addressing conventions, connectionless mode, and additional features
8473	Connectionless-mode network service
8648	Internal organization of network layer
8878	Using X.25 to provide OSI connection-oriented network service
8881	Using X.25 in local area networks
8882	X.25 conformance testing
9068	Connectionless network service using ISO 8208
9542	Routing exchange protocol to be used with connectionless-mode network service
9574	Operations of a packet mode DTE connected to an ISDN
9577	Protocol identification in the OSI network layer
10028	Relaying functions of a network layer intermediate system

Transport Layer

8072	Transport service definition, connectionless-mode
8073	Transport service definition, connection oriented
8602	Transport service for connection-mode protocol
10025	Conformance testing for connection-mode transport protocol operating on the connection-oriented network service

Session Layer

8326	Session service definitions
8327	Session layer protocols
9548	Connectionless-mode session service

Presentation Layer

8822	OSI connection-oriented and connectionless presentation services
8823	OSI amendment for PICS proforma
8824	Abstract Syntax Notation One (ASN.1)
8825	Basic encoding rules for ASN.1
9576	OSI connectionless protocol to provide connectionless service

Application Layer

8211	A data descriptive file for information exchange
8571	File transfer, access, and management (FTAM)
8649	OSI common application service elements (ACSE)
8650	OSI protocols for ACSE
8831	OSI job transfer and manipulation (JTM)
8832	Basic protocol class for JTM
9007	Concepts/terminology for the conceptual schema and the information base
9040	Virtual terminal protocol (VT)
9041	Virtual terminal protocol (VT)
9545	OSI Application layer structure
9804	Application service elements for commitment, concurrency, and recovery (CCR)
9805	Protocols for commitment, concurrency, and recovery (CCR)

═══ APPENDIX B

Summary of CCITT OSI Communications Standards

INTRODUCTION

By nature of the CCITT membership (consisting of PTTs, carriers, RPOAs, etc.), its OSI publications are not as extensive as the ISO's. In many cases, the ISO and CCITT standards/recommendations parallel each other. The CCITT OSI-related recommendations are numbered under the X.200 Series. However, the X.300, X.400, X.500, and I Series (ISDN Series) all are considered a complementary part of the X.200 OSI Series.

The CCITT uses a convenient numbering scheme to distinguish between the service definitions and the protocol specifications. The following sections explain the scheme.

Be aware that the titles in this appendix are summaries of the actual CCITT title.

Service Definitions

The reader is reminded that the OSI Model is developed around the concept of *service definitions:* the specification of the services and activities between adjacent layers. The second aspect of the OSI Model is the concept of *protocol specifications:* The descriptions of the activities of the layer and the actions on the PCI (protocol control information). Each layer in the X Series OSI model defines the service definitions between adjacent layers. These are as follows:

X.211   Physical Service Definitions
X.212   Data Link Service Definitions
X.213   Network Layer Service Definitions
X.214   Transport Layer Service Definitions

X.215	Service Layer Service Definitions
X.216	Presentation Layer Service Definitions
X.217	Application Layer Service Definitions (Association Control Definitions)
X.218	Application Layer Service Definitions (Reliable Transfer Service Element Definitions)
X.219	Applications Layer Service Definitions (Remote Operations Service Element Service Definitions)

The X.217, X.218, and X.219 recommendations describe service definitions between service elements within the application layer. This approach was deemed necessary to meet the intent of several of the design principles of OSI (see Chapter 1 for a description of these design principles).

Protocol Specifications

The CCITT protocol specifications do not encompass all the layers, as do the service definitions explained above. One reason for this seeming anomaly is that the OSI model was written and implemented after some of the lower layer protocols were already in place. Consequently, a mapping of the OSI model and the X Series actually begins at the transport layer. Nonetheless, the CCITT provides guidance for the use of the X Series within the OSI framework for all seven layers. This guidance is provided by a very useful and simple set of protocol stacks, which are illustrated in the X.220 document (and analyzed in several parts of the main body of this book). The following list summarizes the major CCITT OSI-related protocol specifications:

X.224	Transport Layer Protocol Specification
X.225	Session Layer Protocol Specification
X.226	Presentation Layer Protocol Specification
X.227	Association Control Protocol Specification
X.228	Reliable Transfer Service Element Protocol Specification
X.229	Remote Operations Protocol Specification

Other CCITT X.200 Recommendations

The other X.200 Series documents are:

X.200	Reference Model for OSI (the CCITT foundation document for the model)
X.220	Use of X.200 services in CCITT applications
X.223	Use of X.25 to support connection-oriented operations (X.213)
X.244	Procedures for the exchange of protocol identification during VC establishment.

Index

AARQ protocol data unit, 373–74
Abandon, 309, 349
Abstract syntax notation one (ASN.1)
  examples of, 337–39
  protocol data units, 351
  rules and conventions, 334–36
  specifications, 331–32
  symbols, 336–37
  types, 332–34
Accepting association control protocol machine, 376
Accepting reliable transfer protocol machine, 386
Access control machine (ACM), 147
Access management service element, 432
Access passwords, 468
Access units, 415
Account, 467
Accounting for traffic, 114–15
Accounting Management, 484, 495
Acknowledge protocol data unit, 261, 262
Acknowledge time parameter, 268–69
Acknowledgment, 23, 151–52
Action result parameter, 465
Action tables, 18–19
Active mode, 286
Active resynchronization, 278
Activity, 296
Activity identifier, 467, 469
Activity rules, 297
Activity service, 310
ADCCP, 108
Additional options parameter, 268
Additional physical rendition service element, 432
Address, 169
Address field, 111, 113
  extension, 123
Addressing conventions, 204, 206
Administration management domain, 487
Administration port, 427
AdvanceNet, 47, 62–63
Agent process, 480
Alias, 499
Alternate mark inversion code (AMI), 95, 96
Alternate recipient allowed service element, 432
Alternate recipient assignment service element, 432
Alternative protocol classes parameter, 268
Alternative protocol parameter, 268
American National Standards Institute (ANSI)
  code, 4
  description of, 39, 45
  transport layer, 246
  X3.66, 108

Amplitude modulation, 99–100
Angle brackets, 336
Application association regime, 460
Application context name, 368, 466
Application entity, 364, 365
Application layer
  application associations, 366, 368
  application context, 366, 368
  architecture, 364
  authentication procedures for directory access (X.509), 501–5
  commitment, concurrency, and recovery protocol, 400–410
  consistency, concurrency, and atomic actions, 401
  deadly embrace, 401–2
  failure and recovery, 404–5
  file access problems, 401
  file transfer access and management, 455–70
  function of, 10
  ISO OSI standards, 516
  job transfer and manipulation, 471–77
  lockouts, 401–2
  presentation layer and, 362, 363
  real open system, 364
  reliable transfer service element, 379–89
  remote operations service element. See Remote operations service element
  services, 420–21
    message handling systems (MHS), 420–21
  session layer and, 362, 363
  sublayers, 365–67
  superior/subordinate relationship, 405
  update and retrieval overhead, 403–4
  virtual terminal, 444–55
Application layer application service elements (ASE), message handling systems, 413–44
Application process, 364
Application-wide type class, 334
Applications, 37
Applications service element (ASE), 364, 365, 420, 477
Architecture
  application layer, 364
  definition of, 3
  file transfer access and management, 462
  GOSIP, 48–49
  OSI, 10–13
  session layer, 320
  vendor specific, 4–5
ARPANET, 54, 285
ASCII, 4
Association, establishment, 376–79
Association control protocol machine (ACPM), 375–76

Association control service element (ACSE), 420
  invocation, 366, 367
  limitations, 369
  mapping, 374–75
  operations, example of, 376–79
  primitives, 370–73
  protocol data units, 373–74
  protocol machines and state tables, 375–76
  relationship with ASE layers, 374–75
  services, 368–70
  standards/recommendations, 368
Association header, 375
Association initiating reliable transfer protocol machine, 387
Association management standards, 487–88
Association protocol control information (APCI), 375
Association release, 379
Association responding reliable transfer protocol machine, 387
Asynchronous mode, 390, 450
  balanced, 111, 120
Asynchronous response mode, 110, 111, 120
Atomic actions, 6–7, 14, 407
AT&T/Bell specifications, 67
Attribute groups, 467
Attribute names, 468
AttributeError, 505
Attributes, 423, 424, 466, 480
Australian National Protocol Support Center (NPSC), 40
Authority Format Identifier (AFI), 170, 171
Authorizing users indication service element, 432, 435
Auto-forwarded indication service element, 435
Automatic request for repeat, 153–55

B channels, 92
Balanced configration, 109, 110
Basic activity subset (BAS), 317, 320, 321
Basic combined subset (BCS), 317, 320, 321
Basic Encoding Rules (ISO 8825), 331, 339–41
Basic physical rendition service element, 435
Basic synchronized subset (BSS), 317, 320, 321
Baudot code, 4
Binary synchronous control, 175
Binding, 6
Biphase code, 95, 96
Bipolar AMI code (alternate mark inversion code), 95, 96–97
Bit string, 342–43